Mongolia

the Bradt Travel Guide

Jane Blunden

www.bradtguides.com

Bradt Travel Guides Ltd, UK
The Globe Pequot Press Inc, USA

edition
3

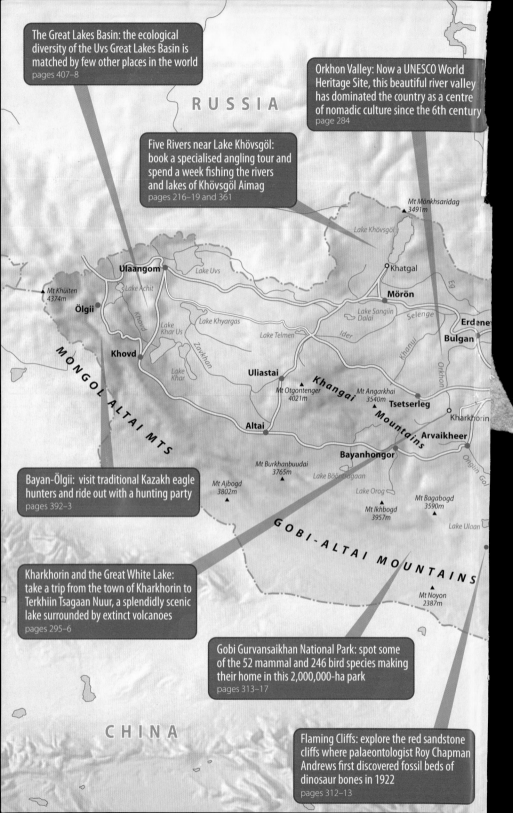

The Great Lakes Basin: the ecological diversity of the Uvs Great Lakes Basin is matched by few other places in the world
pages 407–8

Orkhon Valley: Now a UNESCO World Heritage Site, this beautiful river valley has dominated the country as a centre of nomadic culture since the 6th century
page 284

Five Rivers near Lake Khövsgöl: book a specialised angling tour and spend a week fishing the rivers and lakes of Khövsgöl Aimag
pages 216–19 and 361

Bayan-Ölgii: visit traditional Kazakh eagle hunters and ride out with a hunting party
pages 392–3

Kharkhorin and the Great White Lake: take a trip from the town of Kharkhorin to Terkhiin Tsagaan Nuur, a splendidly scenic lake surrounded by extinct volcanoes
pages 295–6

Gobi Gurvansaikhan National Park: spot some of the 52 mammal and 246 bird species making their home in this 2,000,000-ha park
pages 313–17

Flaming Cliffs: explore the red sandstone cliffs where palaeontologist Roy Chapman Andrews first discovered fossil beds of dinosaur bones in 1922
pages 312–13

RUSSIA

CHINA

MONGOL ALTAI MTS

KHANGAI Mountains

GOBI-ALTAI MOUNTAINS

Mt Mönkhsaridag 3491m
Lake Khövsgöl
Khatgal
Mörön
Eg
Ulaangom
Lake Uvs
Lake Achit
Lake Sangiin Dalai
Selenge
Erdene
Mt Khüiten 4374m
Ölgii
Khovd
Lake Khar Us
Lake Khyargas
Lake Telmen
Ider
Bulgan
Khovd
Zavkhan
Lake Khar
Uliastai
Mt Otgontenger 4021m
Mt Angarkhai 3540m
Tsetserleg
Khamar
Orkhon
Kharkhorin
Altai
Arvaikheer
Mt Burkhanbuudai 3765m
Bayanhongor
Lake Böörtsagaan
Onghin Gol
Mt Ajbogd 3802m
Lake Orog
Mt Bagabogd 3590m
Mt Ikhbogd 3957m
Lake Ulaan
Mt Noyon 2387m

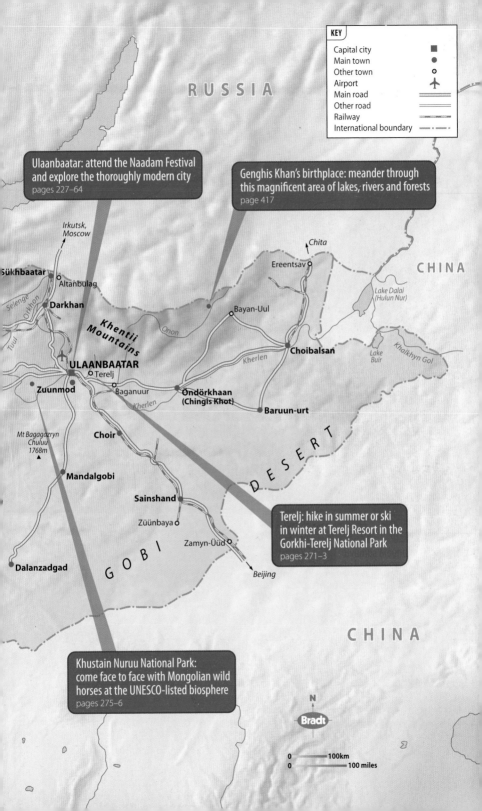

Ulaanbaatar: attend the Naadam Festival and explore the thoroughly modern city
pages 227–64

Genghis Khan's birthplace: meander through this magnificent area of lakes, rivers and forests
page 417

RUSSIA

CHINA

Irkutsk, Moscow

Chita

Ereentsav

Lake Dalai (Hulun Nur)

Sükhbaatar

Altanbulag

Selenge

Orkhon

Darkhan

Tuul

Khentii Mountains

Bayan-Uul

Onon

Choibalsan

Lake Buir

Khalkhyn Gol

Kherlen

ULAANBAATAR

Terelj

Zuunmod

Baganuur

Öndörkhaan (Chingis Khot)

Kherlen

Baruun-urt

Mt Bagagazryn Chuluu 1768m

Choir

D E S E R T

Mandalgobi

Sainshand

Züünbaya

Zamyn-Üüd

G O B I

Beijing

Terelj: hike in summer or ski in winter at Terelj Resort in the Gorkhi-Terelj National Park
pages 271–3

Dalanzadgad

CHINA

Khustain Nuruu National Park: come face to face with Mongolian wild horses at the UNESCO-listed biosphere
pages 275–6

N

Bradt

0   100km
0   100 miles

KEY

Capital city
Main town
Other town
Airport
Main road
Other road
Railway
International boundary

Mongolia
Don't
miss...

Enjoy traditional Mongolian music
The two-stringed horse-head fiddle is an ancient instrument thought by some to be the father of all European bowed string instruments
(SS) page 108

Landscapes and wildlife
Mongolia is home to six different vegetation zones, each of which supports its own distinctive flora and fauna
(MP/S) pages 121–35

Mongolian nomadic lifestyle

Nomadic lifestyle over the centuries has principally depended on this classic, collapsible, round tent – the *ger*
(PJ) pages 80–2

Ulaanbaatar

The 20th-century Zaisan Memorial is situated on a hill with stunning views over the city
(c/S) page 260

Ride a horse or camel

Horse riding is a popular option for exploring the beauty of the Mongolian landscape, such as here at Khövsgöl
(G) pages 210–12

Mongolia in colour

above   The Choijin Lama Museum in Ulaanbaatar hosts a wonderful collection of religious relics, including *tsam* masks and costumes (JS/AWL) pages 255–6

below   Young monks blow into conch shells to call the lamas to prayer at the Lavrin Temple, Erdene Zuu Monastery (AP/AWL) pages 286–9

above   Previously a Winter Palace for the eighth Öndör Gegeen,
          the Bogd Khan Green Palace is now a museum and exhibits
          everything from fine art to stuffed animals
          (JS/AWL) page 255

right   A woman in traditional dress at the National Costume Parade
          during Naadam (G)

below right Erdene Zuu monastery in the Orkhon Valley was one of only
          a handful that survived the destruction of religious buildings
          that took place in the 1930s (JS/AWL) pages 286–8

below left   The 40m-tall Genghis Khan statue was built in Tsonjin Boldog
          facing northeast, the direction of the Great Khan's birthplace
          (OTMT) page 279

How did it all happen? George (my then husband) and I wrote the first Bradt guide – about hiking in Peru and Bolivia – on an Amazon river barge, and typed it up on a borrowed typewriter. We had no money for the next two books so George went to work for a printer and was paid in books rather than money.

Forty years on, Bradt publishes over 200 titles that sell all over the world. I still suffer from Imposter Syndrome – how did it all happen? I hadn't even worked in an office before! Well, I've been extraordinarily lucky with the people around me. George provided the belief to get us started (and the mother to run our US office). Then, in 1977, I recruited a helper, Janet Mears, who is still working for us. She and the many dedicated staff who followed have been the foundations on which the company is built. But the bricks and mortar have been our authors and readers. Without them there would be no Bradt Travel Guides. Thank you all for making it happen.

Hilary Bradt

AUTHOR

Jane Blunden fell in love with Mongolia on her first visit in 1978. That year, she travelled to China and Mongolia for the *Irish Times* to complete a series of feature articles. Her original quest was to find a Mongolian wild horse for the Kingussie Wildlife Park in Scotland. Instead she found herself confined to asking questions, and travelled nowhere outside Ulaanbaatar. On the way home, by introduction of her Mongolian guide, she met academician Vladimir Sokolov in Moscow, who invited her to join his summer fieldtrip to the Gobi Altai. The results of expedition searches confirmed that Mongolian wild horses were extinct in the wild but survived in zoos in Europe and North America. She continued her quest and over a decade later she was responsible, among others, for helping to return Mongolian wild horses, *takhi,* as they are known in Mongolia, to their homeland – a world conservation success story.

Jane's other interests include film making, restoring old buildings and food – she ran a country auberge in the Dordogne in France. Her film 'Collecting Chinese Paintings' was made in 1986 with her twin sister, Caroline Blunden, historian and Chinese art expert. She worked in London as a journalist and for Pierre Salinger at the American television network ABC. Much of her knowledge of Mongolia can be credited to her mentor, the late Professor Owen Lattimore.

Jane's long-term interest and fascination with Mongolia, its people and wildlife led her to promote the country wherever she can – first and foremost through her guide book – but also through lectures and talks. Jane lives between Kilkenny, in Ireland, and a remote farmhouse in the Cotswolds, in England. As a writer, recently turned painter, her other hobbies include music, travel and walking and talking with friends.

PUBLISHER'S FOREWORD   *Hilary Bradt*

What adventurous traveller hasn't longed to go to Mongolia, the symbol of untouched remoteness? The history and possibilities for exploration continue to fascinate travellers worldwide. Jane Blunden's guide has made Mongolia accessible to everyone, whether travelling on their own, on an organised tour to savour the wilderness or passing through on the Trans-Mongolian Railway. As one visitor said, 'Mongolia is remote and mysterious, the homeland of the greatest conqueror of all time, Genghis Khan, a country of rugged mountains, rolling steppes and the awesome Gobi Desert.' Who wouldn't want to go there and see it for themselves?

Third edition published in 2014
First edition published in 2004

Bradt Travel Guides Ltd, IDC House, The Vale, Chalfont St Peter, Bucks SL9 9RZ, England
www.bradtguides.com

Print edition published in the USA by The Globe Pequot Press Inc,
PO Box 480, Guilford, Connecticut 06437-0480

Text copyright © 2014 Jane Blunden
Maps copyright © 2014 Bradt Travel Guides Ltd (based on sources provided by Jane Blunden and Alan Sanders)
Map on page 313 uses information © Rio Tinto
Photographs copyright © 2014 Individual photographers (see below)
Project manager: Claire Strange
Cover research: Pepi Bluck, Perfect Picture

ISBN: 978 1 84162 416 7
e-ISBN: 978 1 84164 715 1 (e-pub)
e-ISBN: 978 1 84164 615 4 (mobi)

British Library Cataloguing in Publication Data
A catalogue record for this book is available from the British Library

Contributors to this guidebook are listed under *Acknowledgements* (see pages iv–vi).

Photographs AWL Images: Aurora Photos (AP/AWL), Danita Delimont Stock (DDS/AWL), Jane Sweeney (JS/AWL), Nick Ledger (NL/AWL), Paul Harris (PH/AWL); Emma Thomson (ET); Goyo Travel (G); John Kellie (JK); Off the Map Tours (OTMT); Panoramic Journeys (PJ); Peter Adams Photography Ltd (PAP); Shutterstock: Barbara Barbour (BB/S), cesc_assawin (c/S), Maxim Petrichuk (MP/S), Pierre-Jean Durieu (PJD/S); SuperStock (SS)
Front cover Two young monks at Gandan Khiid monastery in Ulaanbaatar (PAP)
Back cover Stone men are thought to commemorate local chieftains, dignitaries and military leaders (PJ); the population of Mongolia has developed from many different nomadic tribes (ET)
Title page Archers at the Naadam Festival in Ulaanbaatar (OTMT); a yak grazes near a *ger* on the steppe (JK); traditional mask at the Deel Festival, Ulaanbaatar (ZM/S)

Maps David McCutcheon FBCart.S

Typeset from the author's disc by Wakewing
Production managed by Jellyfish Print Solutions; printed in India
Digital conversion by the Firsty Group

As a keen supporter of Mongolia over many years it is with pleasure I write a few introductory words for the third edition of Jane Blunden's *Mongolia* guide. I have followed her determined interest in this country and the development of its tourist industry with an enthusiasm that I share. Unfortunately I was unable to attend the launch party of the guide's first edition in 2004, but how I wish I'd been there to see *Mongolia* brought to the heart of the City of London, where the author of this ground-breaking guide celebrated years of travel and research by offering her guests fresh camel's milk in a Mongolian *ger* (tent), along with Guinness and Mongolia's famous *'Chinggis Vodka'* – a drink I recommend.

Education is at the heart of my interest in this country. My first journey was in the 1990s when I led a British trade delegation to Ulaanbaatar. Back then there was a visible lack of resources and infrastructure and no digging in the icy ground. In those days you packed a squash ball in your suitcase to use as a plug in the bath, otherwise all the water ran out – ordinary bath plugs were invariably missing. However in the last decade things have improved vastly. Now you have jolly good hotels and delicious meals at international-style restaurants to recoup after a hard day's work.

What struck me most about travel in Mongolia is the air, the light and the endless distant views. When you arrive at a home, or at a factory, you may be presented with a blue silk scarf. Please do not put it around your neck as I did, not knowing it was intended as a special Buddhist blessing. I quickly learned this from my driver who quietly explained it was sacred, to be treated with great respect. My blue scarf is among my most treasured possessions.

Jane Blunden's guide gives the true flavour of Mongolia – the open grasslands involving traditional nomadic life, the recent transformation of the country by minerals and mining wealth, along with information about the youthful population of Ulaanbaatar and the lives of those in smaller settlements, and, not least, extraordinary rare animals like the Gobi bear and *takhi* (Przewalski's horse), that this country is conserving. No persons travelling to Mongolia should be without this guide. They can find the answers to all their questions through reading it. Enjoy what I know will be a wonderful experience.

Acknowledgements

This guide has been put together from original sources by those who have experienced Mongolia first-hand and those who have read, listened and learned, and been generous enough with their time and effort to contribute to this guide. Inevitably, the writing of any book is a team effort. I am happy with the result of our combined endeavour and the values – generosity, giving and sharing – that the work has been based upon. I acknowledge with respect those who, having put a hand to the plough, did not turn back.

Errors will continue to crop up, despite all our efforts, and I take full responsibility for them. While no guidebook is up-to-the-minute – since information on a country is always new and forever changing – there are some things in this book which will change little over time: the general overview, for instance, which incorporates many different experiences of life in Mongolia. The things that change – hotels, restaurants, addresses and so forth – will need updating in subsequent editions.

I have tried to let people and circumstances speak for themselves. I am in no position to judge what may appeal to you; some details may bore one reader and thrill another. My sincere thanks to all those who have helped me so willingly and to many Mongolian guides, drivers and *ger* camp owners.

In the first edition: particular thanks to Alan Sanders for his valuable linguistic expertise and scholarly support throughout the entire production of the book; also to the late Sir Alan Goodison, to Nicholas Haydon, Alan Copps, Joanna Switalska and Julian Shuckburgh, who contributed, unstintingly, their valuable insights, corrections and advice. My thanks to Dervla Murphy and John Durham for kindly reading the manuscript. Special thanks to Allan Stokes for computer help; Gunjimaa Ganbat, Marie von Karaisl, Susan Ellis and Mary McKenzie, a formidable research team; Maurice Temple Smith and John Clark for editing advice; Mongolian Ambassador Tsedenjavyn Suhbaatar; British Ambassadors John Durham and Kay Coombs and Mongolian desk officers at the Foreign and Commonwealth Office, Sue Curtis, Eric Taylor, Claire Allbless, Naomi Kyriacopoulos and Karen Maddocks; Chuluun Ganbold for his generosity and assistance in Ulaanbaatar and for providing the Mongolian Email Daily News Service; Dr Ian Jeffries (Cardiff University), and Dr Alicia Campi (US–Mongolia Advisory Group) for information on the Mongolian economy; Prof J Bat-Ireedui (National University of Mongolia), the Mongolian National Tourism Centre, Kh Ankhbayar of 'Juulchin', Professor S Shagdar, Catherine and Enkbold Darjaa of Off the Map Tours for valuable information on Mongolia; Dr Liz Chaddick for her drawings of Mongolian flora; Catherine Darjaa and Sarah Fox-Pitt for Mongolian paper cuts, Julian Matthews and his company Discovery Initiatives for his support and information on the Khövsgöl area; Pemmy and the late Clay Frick, Paul and Cecily Pennoyer for financial and personal support; the late Dr Guido Pontecorvo, the late Roland ('Bee') Beamont and Charles Lysaght for wisdom and inspiration during the writing period; the late James Teacher, the late Sydney Watson, John Watson, Bob and Chrystal (Ibsen) Loverd, Lord Moyne and Anthony Athaide for sponsoring my early journeys to Mongolia; Ch Sharavrentsen, my first guide in Mongolia (1978); the late Professor Owen Lattimore for the greatest conversations on Mongolia; the late Dr Gerry Piel for excellent Bombay gin lunches to help me face my publisher; academician Vladimir Sokolov, for inviting me on the Joint Mongol/Soviet Gobi Expedition to look for wild horses in 1979; Dr Richard Teng (acupuncturist) and Bikram Yoga (instructors Ian Clifford and Debbie Corbett) for treatments and exercises to help counteract long hours at my computer.

In the second edition: my thanks to Ambassador Dalrain Davaasambuu, Joey Kaempher, Jen Pennoyer Emerson, Mary van der Westhuizen, Connie Haydon, Sir Theodore and Lady Brinckman, Ian Davis, Catherine Tye, Enkhsanaa Jambalsuren, Munkh Jargal Ayurzana, Zara Fleming, Dr Nancy S Tokola, Ross Tokola, Pauline Shearman, Clare Ed, Vanessa Buxton, John Pirie, Patrick Hopkins, Sarah Georgina Head, Sam Strauss, Amy Boeder, Alan Gates, Nick Fox, Philadelphia Stockwell, Alistair Carr, Barry Jiggens, Josie Hinton, Isabella Pele Hentsch, Sarah and Cici Henson, Theresa Booth, Kerry Dean, Sam Glover, Susan Swingler, Dr Enkhmandakh, Stephen Edwards, William Dodsworth, Kate Greer, Helenita Noble, Clare Burges Watson, Lord Patrick Beresford, Joanna Codrington, Rob Kinder, Faith Trend, Lindsay Perry, Corrie Wingate, Hallie Swanson, Emma Clark, James Tallant, Batbayar GaltBalt, Jargal Jamsranjav, Dr Richard Kock, Tom Morton, Christopher Hinde, Richard Austen, Danielle Bennet, Ollie Steeds, Dr David Sneath, Jennifer, Marchioness of Bute, Aza Ulziitogtokh, Polly Keep, Carroll Dunham, Tom Kelly, D Gankhuyag, Gonzon Jargalsaikhan, Hazel Adamson, Dr Tony Whitten and Finola Sumner.

In the third edition: my sincere thanks to Mary-Lynn Chamberlayne, Sergio de Alvim Caneiro, Victor Chan, John Hare, Allan Stokes, Jane Shortall, Beshlie McKelvie, Barry Jiggens, Andrew Harding, Jennifer Russo, Bill Patterson, Prof James Glazier, Jim Fergussen, Bill Manley, Ed and Charli Whetham, Ian and Elizabeth Clark, Jane Grendon, Marie Lippens, John Collis, Richard Foord and members of the rugby team of Hertford College Oxford. Thanks also to Angar Davaasuren, Enkhtuya Banzragch, Bill Munns, Paul Craven, Karina and James Morteon of Panaromic Journeys, Zanjan Fromer, Tudevee Battulga, Agii Maksam of Kobesh Travel, Faraz Shibli, Will Tindall, Zaya, Enkhsanaa, Bunkhjin Batsumber, Suvd-Erdene Erdenebileg, Munkhjiin Arligden, Eric Wong, Dr Theresia von Wietersheim, Christopher and Enkha Giercke, Dr Nathan Conaboy, Dr Gitanjali Bhattacharya, Dr Gombobaatar Sundev, John Farrington, Dr Kouftubh Sharma, Dr B Chimid-Ochir, Dr Khayankhyarvaa Terbish and Shinebayar Urantsetseg of Great Genghis Expeditions, Catriona Gardiner, Ryan and Amanda van Geest, Yamamoto Ichiro, Christopher Stuart, British Ambassador in Mongolia, FCO Mongolian Desk Officer, Ashley Hilsdon, Mongolian Ambassadors, Bulgaa Altangerel and Tulga Narkuu, and staff of the Mongolian Embassy in London and Baroness Trumpington for writing the foreword to this edition. My very grateful thanks again to Alan Sanders and Joanna Switalska for their advice and for checking the text; for ongoing determination and creative thinking, thanks to the late Frank Horwill (athletics coach), Dr Max Nagel and Fausto Alvim; also to Donald Greig, Dr Adrian Phillips, Rachel Fielding, Claire Strange, Maisie Fitzpatrick and the team at Bradt Travel Guides. Special thanks to Sir Michael and Lady (Betty) Kadoorie, Cannon Gerald Newell and Dr Rachel Newell of Staffa, Christine de Castelbajac and Heinrich Prinz Reuss; Sir Sydney and Lady (Felicia) Kentridge, Yves and Albertine de

Saussure, Robin Kindersley and, lastly and most importantly, my own family and friends (many mentioned above) – especially my sisters, Caroline and Lizzie, and neighbours, Harvey and Allison McGrath, for their friendship and wonderful home cooked meals, great company, with excellent wine and conversation on countless weekends over the writing period. I could not have managed without the support of all those involved.

At the end of his travelling days, when asked, 'Is there anywhere else you wished you had travelled to?' the late Wilfred Thesiger, one of the greatest explorers of our times, replied, 'Mongolia is the place I am always sorry not to have visited.'

LIST OF MAPS

Contents

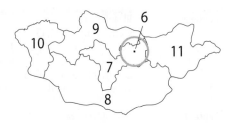

Introduction

There are few places left where there is still a sense of adventure and where you feel you are treading on undiscovered ground. Most of the blank places on world maps have been filled in. But not so Mongolia. My own experiences in Mongolia began when, aged 29, I fought my way around the then impenetrable system, designed to keep Western tourists out, and entered Mongolia by the Eastern Gateway through China – also virtually closed to foreigners in those days. In October 1978, I picked up one of the 4,000 telephones in Beijing and asked for the tourist office in Ulaanbaatar. I spoke to whoever answered my call in rudimentary Mongolian and politely asked for my visa to be sent immediately. The next thing I knew I was on the international Trans-Siberian Railway en route to Ulaanbaatar; the first leg of my journey had begun.

A long love affair followed, as I helped to return the *takhi* – the famous Mongolian wild horses known to the equine world as *Equus przewalskii* – from world zoos to Mongolia. It took time and patience. I might add I was not alone in this effort; there were many hundreds of dedicated individuals who helped to unlock doors, open gates and break down visible and invisible barriers. The country itself had come through the communist period (1921–90), including the Cold War (1947–89), to begin building democracy in 1991. The following year a small band of takhi returned to the freedom of their native land, flown from zoos and semi-reserves in Holland and elsewhere, much to the joy of the Mongolian people still celebrating their newly found political freedom.

My own reaction when I first reached the south Gobi Altai, in autumn 1990, was to fall on my knees in awe at the magnificence of the empty desert at dawn. For a short instant I felt I had arrived, and yet in the next instant I realised there was still a long, long way to go. Wearily, I recognised I had barely scratched the surface. Such travel to a distant country both brings us home and teaches us about ourselves – revealing, perhaps, our true identities and, maybe, our deepest desires and greatest fears.

For a journey to Mongolia you will need stamina and lots of courage. Travels to a far-off place like Mongolia involve personal commitment and purpose, friendship and, not least, a sense of style. In this guide I have asked the question, 'How do we Westerners – tourists and others – approach the frontiers of Mongolian culture and step into a land so vastly different from our own?' The first thing, of course, is to leave all preconceptions aside. You could just turn up with a rucksack and good walking boots, although not everyone wants to travel that way, and helicopters and horses are available, both equally dangerous at times. Mongolia offers amazing opportunities to travel throughout the country since it opened its doors to the Western world in 1990. But there are some constraints – for one thing, Mongolia is a huge country, twice the size of Turkey, four times that of Japan and more than six times the size of Great Britain. Thus some sort of planned approach is essential, especially if you travel independently.

Mongolia is not a country to visit in a hurry (see box, opposite). It is a fabulous wide-open land of extreme climate and extraordinary natural environment. People call it a 'mythical land' or the 'Land of Blue Sky' because of its shimmering, clear air and cloudless skies for most of the year. It is a land of horses and herdsmen and one of the last great undisturbed wilderness areas on earth. Among its 2.9 million people are some of the last truly nomadic pastoralists in the world, and visitors can experience the unique pleasures of staying with nomads and living a lifestyle of centuries ago.

NEW GROUND This guide breaks new ground by including much information on responsible tourism and 'giving something back', which encourages local self-help and volunteer-tourists to participate in local wildlife and cultural projects. Embedded in these plans is the ethos of sustainable development – which means protecting ecosystems, obeying environmental laws and travelling in such a way as helps to build a healthy future for Mongolia. Through tourism (and in other ways) the outside world can help to support Mongolia's nomadic people so that they become part of the modern world while, at the same time, preserving the cultural traditions of their unique lifestyle which has served them so well over the millennia.

THEME, PURPOSE AND LAYOUT The underlying theme of the guide is to trace the development of the Mongolian identity from times past to the present day, taking into account the recent changes and their repercussions, together with the impact of such changes on the culture and the natural environment. At times these changes bring about extraordinary juxtapositions and culture clashes, such as the experience of sitting with herdsmen sipping tea in the timeless steppe to the noisy background of strident TV advertisements. These juxtapositions may surprise (and even dismay) visitors but not the Mongolians, fully aware of their role as an emerging Asian nation.

The first part of the guide aims to equip the traveller with a thorough background to Mongolia. This, I believe, is best absorbed slowly before you begin your travels (or if you run out of time, the same can be done on your return). The guide as a whole is written principally for tourists, but it is also an up-to-date reference book for development-agency staff and for those with business interests.

NOTE FROM THE AUTHOR FOR THE THIRD EDITION The 21st century 'mining boom' has turned around Mongolia's livestock economy into a mining economy, which has highlighted Mongolia on the world map once more. Vast coal reserves along with copper and other minerals are producing new wealth. Buildings and roads and all sorts of new service industries have transformed the capital Ulaanbaatar. Such changes are happening to a lesser degree in towns and settlements in the countryside – but even in the more remote areas where mining is involved, things are changing fast.

I have included several new sections on archaeology, mining, and the Mongolian economy and have updated all sections of the guide with the help of many contributors. What gave me most satisfaction on my recent journey (September 2013) was to revisit Takhiin Tal 35 years on and see Mongolian wild horses roaming freely in a specially protected area of the Great Gobi National Park. My original project completed, I too share this sense of freedom.

Slow-paced travel includes rafting, horseriding, hiking, biking or a leisurely drive with plenty of quality time for resting and sightseeing. Try not to move on constantly. When possible, allow for short driving trips, otherwise you tend to overdo the distances and end up feeling very tired and grumpy. From experience, it is better to say 'no' to most 'wild ideas' than to travel to every *aimag*! In any case, the exercise of riding, rafting or biking is quite tiring – take time to recover and keep away from motor transport!

Mongolia is not a holiday destination where you 'tick off' a number of places – rather it is a place just 'to be'. The main experiences are centred around the traditional way of life, such as herding livestock or visiting nomads in their *gers* while surrounded by vast and beautiful landscapes. You don't have to travel far – just stay where you are and slow down! This opportunity is available everywhere in Mongolia and is not site-specific. Calm, quiet and freedom from fences are the great characteristics this country offers, along with ancient Mongolian culture.

A final word – find yourself a good guide, sit and talk around campfires, and drink in the ageless presence of nomads, listen to their stories and their songs, and think too about the wildlife 'out there' in the night, who may see a small camp fire glow in the distance under a starry sky. That's what made me return to Mongolia, along with my long-held dreams that have eventually turned into reality.

Enjoy your journey!

FEEDBACK REQUEST AND UPDATES WEBSITE

At Bradt Travel Guides we're aware that guidebooks start to go out of date on the day they're published – and that you, our readers, are out there in the field doing research of your own. You'll find out before us when a fine new family-run hotel opens or a favourite restaurant changes hands and goes downhill. So why not write and tell us about your experiences? Contact us on ☏01753 893444 or e info@bradtguides.com. We will forward emails to the author who may post updates on the Bradt website at www.bradtupdates.com/mongolia. Alternatively you can add a review of the book to www.bradtguides.com or Amazon.

HOW TO USE THIS GUIDE

KEYS AND SYMBOLS Maps include alphabetical keys covering the locations of those places to stay, eat or drink that are featured in the book. Note that regional maps may not show all hotels and restaurants in the area: other establishments may be located in towns shown on the map.

PRICES AND CURRENCY During the update of this guide the exchange rate between the US dollar and the Tögrög moved by some 25%: check the current exchange rate prior to visiting Mongolia. Since 2013 the practice of using US dollars for cash payments is in the process of being phased out. Credit card payments are unaffected.

GRIDS AND GRID REFERENCES Several maps use gridlines to allow easy location of sites. Map grid references are listed in square brackets after the name of the place or sight of interest in the text, with page number followed by grid number, eg: [232 D4].

TELEPHONE NUMBERS As this book goes to press, telephone numbers in Mongolia are undergoing changes. Landline numbers are being revised so that they have a two-digit area code with a six-digit number. When calling from a mobile phone, all eight digits should be used, but when calling from a landline within a local area, only the last six digits are required. Note that some area codes are likely to be subject to change.

SEND US YOUR SNAPS!

We'd love to follow your adventures using our Mongolia guide – why not send us your photos and stories via Twitter (@BradtGuides) and Instagram (@bradtguides) using the hashtag #Mongolia. Or you can email your photos to e info@bradtguides.com with the subject line 'Mongolia pics' and we'll tweet and instagram our favourites.

Part One

GENERAL INFORMATION

MONGOLIA AT A GLANCE

Location Between Siberian Russia and China

Area 1,564,116km² – the size of most of western Europe

Relief Mountains to the north, centre and southwest comprise 40% of the land, the remainder is rolling plateau with great expanses of steppe, semi-desert, and desert plains

Highest point Khüiten peak (4,374m) in the Tavan Bogd range in the Altai Mountains

Climate Continental, marked by four seasons, with sharp variations

Average temperatures 20°C in summer and –24°C in winter

Government Parliamentary democracy with a presidential election every four years

Regions 21 *aimags* (provinces) or administrative regions

Population 2.9 million (2013)

Capital Ulaanbaatar (Ulan Bator), formerly known as Urga; abbreviated to UB

Language Mongolian (an Altaic language); Russian and English widely spoken

Religion Predominately Tibetan Buddhism; Christianity; Islam among the Muslim minorities in the west; traces of ancient Shamanism

National anthem *Khairt Mongol Oronoo Manduuliya* ('Let us Make our Beloved Country Flourish')

Public holidays New Year's Day (1 January), Tsagaan Sar (three-day New Year holiday, celebrated late January or early February), International Women's Day (8 March), Mother and Child Day (1 June), Naadam/National Holiday (11–13 July), Genghis Khan Day (November*), Independence Day (29 December) *lunar calendar

Tourist season Mid May to mid September (peak season July–August)

Entry regulations Full valid passport with an entry and exit visa

Health No special vaccination requirements

Air and rail access Via the international airport in Ulaanbaatar, or by rail via China or Russia

Road links Ulaanbaatar to Ulan-Ude in Russia and Erlian (Erenhot) in China

Currency Tögrög (abbreviated to T, Tg or MTG). (June 2014) US$1 = T1,826, £1 = T3,127. See box, page xii.

Hotels Available at reasonable prices in the capital with few hotels outside UB

***Ger* camps** The normal accommodation in the countryside

TV system PAL, SECAM

Weights and measures Metric system

Electricity 220V/50Hz with two-pin sockets (straight-sided)

International telephone code +976

Time Three time zones. The three westernmost provinces of Bayan-Ölgii, Uvs and Khovd are one hour behind the capital; Dornod, Sükhbaatar and Khentii are one hour ahead. The rest of the country follows Ulaanbaatar time: GMT +7 or +8 hours (depending on summer or winter).

1

Background Information

GEOGRAPHY

Mongolia is a fabulous wide-open land of extreme climate and extraordinary natural environment. It's tough at times and even bitterly cold, with surprise snow showers in summer. Travellers might face other climatic challenges, like having to ford rivers in full flood.

Mongolia lies northeast of the Tien Shan Mountains and embraces the great mountain ranges of the Altai, Khentii and Khangai, towering over grasslands and deserts. It is cut off by the Himalayas from the monsoons of oceanic Asia. The land, in sharp contrast to the sky, stretches from horizon to horizon in bands of colour, which, on the whole, mark the major vegetation zones: in the south are the grey-gold, gravelly grounds of the Gobi, merging into green-brown steppe lands or grasslands with barren rocky hills, while further north and west are high mountains, perennially snowcapped, with their lower reaches covered by fir, pine and spruce.

The huge landmass of Mongolia is situated on the plateau at the headwaters of the river systems of Siberia and the Arctic, China and the Pacific, and closed inland desert systems. It has a highly distinct set of geographical features, caused by the area being an ancient dry land (once, over 200 million years ago, an inland sea), with an average elevation of 1,580m. The whole area was lifted by successive geological upheavals and as a result it is deeply eroded mountainous country, with snow-capped mountain ranges, forested slopes, open high-plateau steppe land, rolling into semi-desert Gobi and sandy desert in the extreme south.

The prevailing dry winds blow mostly from the northwest and over millions of years China has been the beneficiary of Mongolia's soil erosion.

The country lies between latitude 42° and 52°N and longitude 87° and 119°E, and extends for 2,392km from west to east and 1,259km from north to south. The total area is 1,564,116km², over six times the land area of the UK and nearly three times that of France. It is the fifth-largest country in Asia.

Mongolia's political borders are with the Russian Federation to the north (3,543km) and with the People's Republic of China to the west, south, and east (4,709km – since 2009). Mongolia is thus a landlocked state, and its nearest access to the sea is at the Chinese port of Tianjin.

TOPOGRAPHY Western Mongolia is dominated by the Mongol Altai Mountains. This major mountain chain is a continuation of the Altai Mountains of Siberia. It extends southeastwards within Mongolia from the Tavan Bogd peaks, at the western junction of the borders of Mongolia, Russia and China. The Mongol Altai is bounded by the Züüngar Basin (in China) to the southwest, and by the low-lying area of the Great Lakes to the northeast. There is marked glaciation in the Tavan

Bogd area, where the Potanin Glacier stretches for 19km. The Gobi dominates southern Mongolia and, although it is known as a desert, strictly speaking it is a semi-desert, which provides grazing for herds of camels, sheep and goats. Rolling steppe covers one-third of the country, where pastoral nomadism has been the way of life for centuries. The grasslands of the eastern plains are home to hundreds of thousands of migrating gazelle. Mongolia's many lakes contain curative minerals and medicinal mud. The numerous hot springs around the country make one wonder if they will become a tourist attraction.

Some 63% of Mongolia's territory is within the permafrost zone, and 30% is sporadically covered by rocks and soils frozen down to a depth of 5m or more. The western half of the country is a region of intensive mountain building and high seismic activity, and small tremors are relatively frequent. There were powerful tremors in 1957 (Gobi-Altai) and 1967 (Mogod), but because of the nomadic lifestyle and the scattered population, damage to buildings or injury to people from earthquakes have been very rare. Dariganga on the country's southeastern border with Chinese Inner Mongolia is a volcanic plateau with the cones of extinct volcanoes.

Geology The geological record shows that Palaeozoic marine flora and fauna developed extensively across the territory of Mongolia. In the Mesozoic the Gobi was covered by lakes, and the warm climate and plentiful vegetation encouraged the development of molluscs and crustaceans. The Mongolian Cretaceous period was rich in dinosaurs, including herbivores like protoceratops and hadrosaurus and predators like velociraptor and oviraptor. The world's first nest of fossilised dinosaur eggs was discovered in the South Gobi by American palaeontologist Roy Chapman Andrews in the 1920s. The Chapman Andrews expeditions were followed by Mongolian, Soviet and Polish ones in the communist period and, since 1990, American teams are again making new discoveries.

Mountain chains (Nuruu) Some two-thirds of Mongolia is covered by mountains. The main ranges are the Altai and the Khangai mountains which run from northwest to south, across the northern central part of the country. These forest and mountain zones are relatively well watered and surrounded by mountain-meadow and flat grassland. From the western mountain chains open steppe stretches to the southeast and merges into semi-desert in the south. The Sayan Mountains mark the boundary between Siberia and Mongolia north of Lake Khövsgöl, while the Khentii range is located north of Ulaanbaatar in the central northeastern part of the country. The southern Gobi contains the famous 'Three Beauties', or Gurvansaikhan Mountains, one valley of which shelters a tiny 'glacier' in its surprising alpine/desert setting. This accumulated frozen snow along the sheltered riverbed of the Yolyn Am Valley canyon survives (most years) throughout the hot summer months.

Mongolia's highest mountain, Khüiten (4,374m), is found in the Tavan Bogd area of the Altai Mountains. Mönkhkhairkhan (4,204m), Mongolia's second-highest mountain, rises on the border of Bayan-Ölgii and Khovd aimags, or provinces. Owing to their isolation, they represent a challenge to the most skilful mountaineers. The Gobi-Altai Mountains are a continuation of the Mongol Altai chain. They extend southeastwards 700km to descend into the Gobi. There are no big glaciers or snowfields. The highest peak, Ikh Bogd, (3,957m), is in Bayankhongor Aimag.

The Khangai Mountains give rise to Mongolia's major rivers which flow in a northerly direction. Spurs extending north and northeast form the watershed between the Arctic Ocean and central Asian basin. Slopes forested by birch and larch drop down from snow-covered crests to fine pastureland. Sheer, rugged peaks include Otgontenger (4,021m), the range's highest summit, in Zavkhan Aimag at the western end, with a glacier and eternal snow. It is a very special sacred mountain, worshipped by many Mongolians – particularly Zavhan Aimag local people.

The third range of importance is the smooth and rounded Khentii range, which stretches 200km from the Mongolian capital to the northern border and forms part of the watershed between the Arctic and Pacific oceans. The highest point is Asralt Khairkhan (2,800m), some 60km north of Ulaanbaatar.

Lakes (Nuur) Water is distributed unevenly in Mongolia, predominately in lakes and rivers to the northwest. The low-lying area between the Mongol Altai and Khangai mountains is often called the 'Depression of the Great Lakes', although it is technically not a depression (ie: below sea level). The area is 600km long and up to 250km wide. At its lowest, northernmost point is Lake Uvs, Mongolia's largest saltwater lake (3,350km²). Lake Uvs is relatively shallow, 20m at its greatest depth; it lies 759m above sea level. The northeastern corner of the lake lies in Russian territory, having been annexed by Ambassador Molotov in 1957. Gobi-type soils and sands fill this low-lying area where smaller lakes and the world's northernmost sand dunes are found.

Lake Khövsgöl, the deepest lake (282m), is the country's largest freshwater resource. Over 90 rivers enter it, and one flows out, the Egiin Gol (475km), a tributary of the river Selenge which flows into Lake Baikal, in Siberia. Baikal is the world's biggest body of fresh water and is linked by the rivers Angara and Yenisey to the Arctic Ocean. Lake Khövsgöl is the second-largest lake in Mongolia (2,760km² and 136km long).

The lowest point in the country is a small lake, Khökh Nuur (560m above sea level), in Dornod (eastern) Aimag, not far from the border with China. Another lake, Buir, measures 615km² and averages 10m in depth on Mongolia's southeastern border with China. Although its commercial fish and water resources are within Mongolia, that does not put a stop to Chinese poaching. All Mongolian lakes freeze in winter.

Rivers (Gol) In the mountainous northwest, large rivers originate and drain into either the Arctic or the Pacific. A continental watershed divides the country and the smaller rivers of the south tend to be lost to the dry ground. There are 3,800 rivers in Mongolia, and were one to add their combined length it would total 67,000km. The largest rivers entering the closed central Asian basin are the river Khovd (593km), running from Tavan Bogd into Khar Nuur, and the river Zavkhan (808km) in western Mongolia, which flows from the Khangai westwards through the desert into Airag Nuur and Khyargas Nuur.

The river Delgermörön (445km) rises in the mountains near Khövsgöl and joins the Selenge (1,024km in total, 615km in Mongolia) to flow via Lake Baikal to the Arctic Ocean. Other tributaries of the Selenge include the Orkhon, which flows near the former capital of Mongolia, Karakorum, and the Tuul, on which Ulaanbaatar stands. The Orkhon (1,124km) rises in the Khangai Mountains and the Tuul (704km) rises in the Khentii range.

The largest rivers reaching the Pacific Ocean are the Onon (298km in Mongolia), rising in the Khentii range and flowing across the border with Russia into the Shilka and the Heilongjiang (Amur) River, and the Kherlen (1,090km), which also rises in the Khentii and drains into Dalai Nuur (Lake Hulun) in China. The Khalkhyn Gol

1

(233km) flows via Lake Buir into Dalai Nuur, which is linked (except in dry years) to the Heilongjiang (Amur) by the river Ergun.

All Mongolia's rivers freeze in winter for five or six months, the ice averaging 1m thick. Rivers in the mountains remain ice-bound until mid May, while those in the plains usually become free of ice a month earlier. Spring floods from mountain snow melt occur in April–May, and rain storms may cause more floods in July and August.

Steppe Steppe (grassland) covers much of the country and predominates in central and eastern areas. The Eastern Plain, averaging 1,100m above sea level, extends for several hundred kilometres. It is gently undulating grassland with hills of 50–100m height.

Deserts and the Gobi Sand and sand dunes occupy about 10% of Mongolia's territory, but much of the Gobi is a plain of scrub and gravel rather than sand, with scattered salt and soda lakes. Summer flash-floods spread widely across the impermeable surface to create raging torrents which cut channels 1m or more deep as the water drains off to find its level and then soaks away. These dried-up channels represent a hazard to cross-country vehicles.

The Trans-Altai Gobi, between the Gobi-Altai and the border with Chinese Xinjiang, is the last-known habitat of the takhi, the Mongolian wild horse or Przewalski horse, which was returned from captive-bred foreign stock (in international zoos, reserves and private collections) after the pure native variety became extinct (see pages 277, 345–6 and 366). Also in this region are *khulan*, or wild asses, and saiga antelope – found only in southwest Mongolia.

Vegetation zones Mongolian scientists divide the country into the following natural zones:

- The high-mountain zone, roughly 4.5% of the whole territory, largely consisting of alpine meadow
- Mountain taiga (4%), particularly the Khövsgöl area and parts of the Khentii Mountains, with dense cedar and cedar-larch forest

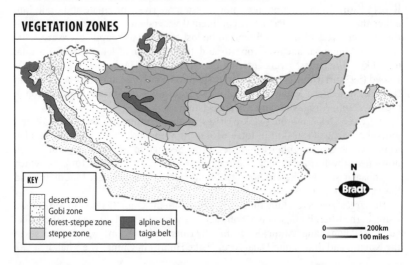

VEGETATION ZONES

KEY

desert zone
Gobi zone
forest-steppe zone   alpine belt
steppe zone   taiga belt

N

Bradt

0 ————— 200km
0 ————— 100 miles

- The mountain forest-steppe zone (23%) including most of the Khangai, Khentii and Mongol Altai mountains, where there is alternation of forest and steppe, the forest growing on the upper parts of the northern slopes, with strips of larch and birch
- Steppe (grassland) occupies some 26% of Mongolia's territory, in particular the plains of eastern Mongolia, with various feather grasses and pea-shrubs (Caragana)
- The transitional desert-steppe zone (21.5%), especially the Gobi-Altai region, with low grasses and semi-shrubs
- Desert accounts for some 10%, especially in the southern border zone, where any vegetation is extremely sparse but includes zag (saxaul or haloxylon) bushes, whose wood the Mongols burn for fuel; the Trans-Altai Gobi oases have poplar trees fed by ground water.

Desertification Recent drought conditions are causing waves of sand to menace desert-dwellers. Pastures that used to exist are now barren land. The grasses have all but disappeared. Rising sands and barren ground are part of a new desert and are the result, scientists say, of severe overgrazing that has destroyed the thin topsoil. A decade of hotter, drier weather means the menace is here to stay, threatening exposed, rural settlements and the nomadic herders' only means of livelihood – their herds of camels, horses, sheep, and goats and hence, in time, their way of life. The significant factor is that once the desertification process gets started it tends to expand very fast.

Nomadic pastoralists have to roam further afield to find edible grass and some are forced to pay for winter fodder, a thing they never had to do during socialist times. Although some winter fodder has been stockpiled around the country it remains a huge logistical process to deliver it to the hardest-hit areas in time, and it is usually not enough. Emergency shipments of grain and relief food supplies were flown in from Russia and elsewhere to help the nomads to cope with *zud* disasters of recent winters. (The expression '*zud*' describes the conditions that prevent livestock from grazing, including drought, deep snow or overcrowding. See page 8.)

CLIMATE

Mongolia has an extreme continental climate: that is, hot summers and very cold winters. The country lies at the heart of continental Asia, far from seas and oceans, in the lee of surrounding high mountains – all factors that contribute to its dry climate. There is a marked decrease in cloudiness from north to south, where average annual sunshine reaches 3,200 hours. As a result, Mongolia is known as the 'Land of Blue Skies'. In winter, the weather is dominated by a stable high-pressure region over northwestern Mongolia; there is little cloud and little snow cover, but intense cold. In spring, warm winds from the south meet cold winds from the Arctic Ocean, and wind and dust storms are typical of this season.

Winds are stronger in the southern regions and violent dust storms whip the ground at speeds that could knock over a *ger*, although these regions are virtually uninhabited. Weather changes can be abrupt and storms can strike with little or no warning.

Precipitation exceeds 500mm a year in the mountains, 200–300mm in the steppe and less than 150mm in the Gobi; 65–75% of annual precipitation falls as rain in the three warm summer months, while autumn is cool and dry. The Khentii and Khövsgöl regions are the wettest parts of Mongolia. Marshes in mountainous areas

Zud literally means 'lack of grazing' but is also translated as 'starvation due to fodder shortage'. *Zud* occurs when there is a thaw followed again by freezing conditions. The grass becomes sheathed in a film of ice and the animals cannot graze and subsequently they die, by the thousand. There is either too much snow for stock to get to the fodder, or not enough snow to serve as a substitute for water. The different types of *zud* are:

- *Gan zud* ('hard zud') The ground is covered with a layer of ice after a warm spell in winter.
- *Khar zud* ('black zud') A lack of snow in a waterless region.
- *Tsagaan zud* ('white zud') Heavy snowfall prevents livestock from grazing.
- *Tuurain zud* ('hoof zud') Pasture is trampled down as a result of overcrowding, predominately a manmade situation. It is considered to be the most catastrophic.

Zud disasters of the winters of 1999/2000, 2000/2001 and 2009/10 will go down in history for claiming around six million head of Mongolian livestock. Of these, 85% were sheep and goats, the remainder being horses, cattle and camels. Long-term loans from the World Bank and other aid organisations helped to restock sheep and goat herds. Since then the Mongolian government has taken pre-emptive measures to ensure better-organised distribution of sufficient fodder to formerly badly hit regions during excessively cold weather – something which was sorely lacking in recent *zud* winters.

are sometimes a barrier to summer travel, and drought is not uncommon elsewhere because of low average soil water levels. High mountains are snow-covered from October to April, but elsewhere snowfall is usually not significant and does not accumulate but melts, evaporates or is dispersed by the wind. The most serious condition for animals is zud (see box, above), which causes massive losses to livestock in severe winter weather.

January is the coldest month of the year, with the average temperature at −35°C in the valleys and −20°C in the Gobi. The lowest recorded temperature was −55°C at Lake Uvs in northwestern Mongolia. July is the warmest month, with the average temperature 15–20°C in the mountains and 20–25°C in the south. A temperature of 40°C has been recorded at Sainshand in the Gobi.

An important consequence of the Mongolian climate, with its hard winters, late spring and early autumn frosts, is the short period of plant growth, which is limited to about 100 days – from late May to the end of August. If you travel in Mongolia during summer time you will have an illusion of richness – knee-deep grass as far as the eye can see and meadows garlanded with millions of wild flowers. But in fact the flora is not as diverse as that of neighbouring China, Siberia or eastern Kazakhstan. In Mongolia, due to the altitude, relief and wind, there is considerable diurnal variation in temperature which may fluctuate by up to 30°C. You may experience blistering hot days and chilly or freezing nights – days that warm up and cool down equally dramatically as the sun rises and sets.

Although the Mongolian winter is the longest season, lasting from about November to March, it is also the sunniest. Throughout the year the skies are blue and the sun shines for over 250 days. There are four distinct seasons, each with its own special attraction. In winter, because of the dry air, there is a crisp atmosphere, even when the sun is out and the daytime temperatures rise; without the damp chill factor even the cold seems less biting. Beware though, when the sun goes down, the temperatures plummet, so you have to wrap up well at night. Spring can be cool, windy, dusty and changeable. Summer is short, hot and sometimes rainy. The warm October days in autumn are the finest, with ideal temperatures, when the lowering sun casts long amber shadows across the craggy boulders that tower above the burned, summer grasslands. Overall, Mongolia is a very dry country, and the almost continuous blue skies help you feel on top of the world. However, bring warm clothes – even in summer. These are, of course, essential in winter when temperatures drop to –30°C.

CLIMATE CHANGE Climate change is associated with unrestrained increases in emissions of greenhouse gases (GHG), particularly carbon dioxide. The United Nations predicts that global average temperatures could rise between 1.4°C and 5.8°C over the next century. This would mean more droughts, the melting of glaciers and the extinction of species. Mongolia, being far removed from industry, might seem unlikely to be much affected by global warming, but this is not the case because change comes to the most marginal lands. The whole of Mongolia's fragile landscape, and herding and agriculture based upon it, is therefore directly involved (see sections on conservation and responsible tourism on pages 149–54 and 154–9). See recommended websites on page 444. For Mongolia weather reports see www.mongolclimate.mn.

SOME ARCHAEOLOGICAL TERMS

PETROGLYPHS Imagery gouged or pecked into the surface of rocks or boulders. Stones or rocks on which multiple images or single images occur showing for example stylised animals, birds and abstract lines.

MOUNDS (KURGAN, KHURIG SUUR) Piles of stones that mark a grave at the time of an individual's death. Mounds may be simple or ringed by standing stones; these stones may be arranged in different positions according to the compass: north–south layouts are understood to be burial mounds of the late Bronze to early Iron Ages.

Kurgan is the Turkic word for a tumulus or mound of earth and stones raised over a grave. These can be of the Bronze Age, Iron Age or later periods – also known as Khirig suur.

STANDING STONES (BABAL OR STONE MEN, TAMGA) Vertical stones of different sizes. They may be carved or uncarved and can take their name from the carved images, ie of deer, becoming **deer stones**. Some of these image stones are from a specific period, ie Turkic Memorials. Unsculpted standing stones are known as 'false images'.

Standing stones are also known as **tamga** (the meaning of tamga is a seal, stamp or brand mark, for example, on stone). Small standing stones believed to be clan signs linked to the Turkic period can be located beside larger standing stones. Inscriptions are usually associated with the Turkic period although some scholars say they pre-date Turkic or Mongol times.

ARCHAEOLOGY

BRONZE AGE TO IRON AGE TIMELINE The Bronze Age in Mongolia dates from the 3rd millennium BC, to around the time of first Chinese Emperor, Qin Shi Huang-Di, (259BC–210BC) who unified China and built the Great Wall to keep the Mongolian steppe horsemen from raiding northern Chinese borderlands. Spanning several centuries, it is a period of huge change. The Bronze Age is characterised by the use of copper and tin to make bronze. Besides constructing the Great Wall, this dynamic age includes some of the greatest 'monuments of time', such as the pyramids of Egypt and Stonehenge in Britain. It was also the time of Moses and The Ten Commandments, Etruscan civilisation in Italy and the beginning of Taoism in China. The golden age of bronze gave way to a harsher, more cruel age of Iron – which, like Bronze, was used in weaponry. The Iron Age began with the Warring States period in China (403BC–221BC). It included the famous Pazyryk culture of the Altai (a continuation of the Mongolian Altai) – where horse-riding nomads of the steppes traded with Persia, India and China. The region of the Altai was most likely the homeland of iron-working Turks who dominated Eurasia in the late first millennium AD.

ARCHAEOLOGY – 'FACE TO FACE WITH ANCIENT MONGOLIA' (PART 1)

Professor James Glazier

Mongolia is full of the traces of ancient man. The leading question for the non-specialist, or tourist, is how to recognise them. One can follow the traces of ancient man through Neolithic stone tools in the Gobi and continue on through the omnipresent Bronze Age (2500BC–700BC), when *khirig suur* (kurgans) or tomb mounds were so common that even today they blend into the landscape. Your 'face to face' journey may involve you in the discovery of the ancient walled enclosures of the Uighurs (6th–7th centuries AD), Khitan (10th–11th centuries AD) and Mongols (12th–14th centuries AD). While impressive, these remains are mute to non-specialists. Far more eloquent are the late-Bronze Age (11th–7th centuries BC) standing stones with incised decorations representing tattoos or embroidery, called deer stones. To those who research or visit these ancient sites they open up the wonders of the ancient world, its people, and cultures.

Deer stones were not grave markers but clan totems and worship sites, sometimes single, sometimes in large groupings, though some are associated with (slightly later) *Khirig Suur* (kurgan) burials. While the exact meaning of deerstones is lost, they are clearly totemic markers with shamanic content, symbolising simultaneously a stylised human form (ancestor or spirit power), the sacred cosmos and the fertilising phallus. The Forest God in the Japanese film *Princess Mononoke* gives a flavour of these overlapping meanings. Mongolian-style deer stones all show highly stylised beaked bird-reindeer (some with bird claws rather than hooves) flying between earth and heaven. Some are drawn in a distinctively economic but expressive style, with open beaks and spiralling horns; a belt, representing the earth and its mountains, also doubles as ears; some have projecting stylised rays, earrings, a line of dots that demarcate both the heavens and the glans of the penis. Others are decorated with chevrons, which may be a shield or a shamanic cloak or a bag. Weapons (sword, bow, quiver, bow case, axe, dagger) are also common, as are round mirrors. A few deer stones show animals, like tigers, horses, and onagers, and while most don't actually represent the face explicitly, a few have sculpted human faces. The slightly later Altaic-style

TYPES OF BRONZE AGE AND IRON AGE MOUNDS Late Bronze Age mounds, piles of rough stones usually connected to burial sites, have been identified and are usually found in rows in north-south alignment. In the Mongolian Altai region there are several types, including *Khirigsuur* – a structure that has a central mound. Mounds are found with Turkic image stones; they may have acted as altar structures and many take the form of a circle. Turkic memorials are usually rectangular in shape and recognisable as burial mounds, sometimes filled with boulders and sided by darker stones. The thinking of these ancient people remains a mystery and although experts have observed certain patterns in the stone monuments, they do not know what the relationship of monuments and their natural features or directionality signify.

TO PARTICIPATE Earthwatch runs a number of archaeological field trips open to beginners in the summer months in Ikh Nart Reserve located in Dornogobi Aimag (province), some 300km southeast of Ulaanbaatar. The reserve is accessible by train or 4x4. Participants identify and document (but do not excavate) significant archaeological and cultural sites, and field trips last from one week to a month.

deer stones of western Mongolia and Kazakhstan are found as far west as Poland. They have more varied designs and may have been erected by a different culture. Most deer stones were erected on south-facing bluffs overlooking rivers, where they would be visible from a distance and in a position to influence the fertility of the valley. Deer stones were once considered rare, but later builders of Square Tombs recognised their sacred power and would drag them several miles to reuse as the walls and covers of their tombs. Recent excavations of Square Tombs have revealed more than 700 deer stones. They dot the northern two-thirds of Mongolia, but be forewarned – they can be hard to find.

LOCATING DEER STONES You can start your exploration with the fine deer stones moved to the National History Museum in the capital, Ulaanbaatar. Arkhangai Aimag, located west of UB on the slopes of the Khangai mountains, has the most easily accessible clusters of deer stones, especially along the Tamir and Khanui rivers (these are also great fishing rivers). To find the 26 Jargalantyn Am deer stones in Khanuii Brigad (at 48°10′25″ N 101°5′29″ E), drive north from the Millennium Highway along the Khanui; this includes the largest deer stone known and (controversially) re-erected. You can find more than 30 fine deer stones in their original locations in Ikhtamir sum (county), a few hours north of the highway along the west bank of the north Tamir (starting at 47°45′37″ N 101°20′34″ E); the Golden Chair cluster of deer stones (depicting equids) is located on top of a mountain at 47°33′1″ N 101°1′55″ E – about an hour south of the highway. Look out for the occasional deer stone-style reindeer carved as a petroglyph.

For more deer stone images and locations visit www.flickr.com/photos/jag_jaf_travel/sets/72157621717719067/. For a good introduction to deer stones, look for Turbat, J. Bayarsaikhan, D. Batsukh and N. Bayarkhuu, *Deerstones of the Jargalantyn Am*, 2011, ISBN 978-99962-845-8-8.

For a rough location map of Arkhangai province and other information go to: www.infomongolia.com/ct/ci/207/70/.

Professor James Glazier

Another way to see ancient Mongols 'face-to-face' is through rock carvings and rock paintings (petroglyphs). While these can date from the Mesolithic (10,000BC) to the introduction of Buddhism (16th century through to the end of the 19th century AD), the majority are late Bronze Age (1200BC–700BC). These late Bronze Age petroglyphs were carved by ancient hunters, often on cliffs where they would wait to scan the landscape below for passing herds. The classical image is of a single ibex (once very common in Mongolia, now almost extinct), but you will find many animal species, including horses, dogs, wolves, reindeer, yaks … and humans engaged in a variety of tasks, including riding, bow hunting, chariot driving and sex. A few rare and unusual emblems include stylised 'astronaut' faces, bear paws and grass-skirted dancers (very early, fourth millennium BC). From more recent eras, you can find clan marks and Buddhist inscriptions. While every aimag has petroglyphs, they are often hard to spot from a distance.

LOCATING PETROGLYPHS To locate petroglyphs, look for south facing, red basalt cliffs and isolated peaks with a large field of view (the basalt cinder cones of extinct volcanos are favourite places). Once you have found one petroglyph, you will usually find others nearby. Key petroglyph clusters include the north Tamir river valley in Arkhangai Aimag, several groups in Khovd Aimag, and the Javkhalant Khairkhan petroglyphs. The great expert on Mongolian petroglyphs is Esther Jacobsen. Look for her books, especially E. Jacobsen-Tepfer and J. E. Meecham, *Archaeology and Landscape in the Mongolian Altai: An Atlas*, ESRI Press, 2010. After millennia of peace, many petroglyph sites are being destroyed by modern graffiti – please don't add your name to the vandalism!

The goal of the project is to establish baseline archaeological inventory data. For bookings and further information go to: www.earthwatch.org/exped/wingard_archaeology.html or www.ikhnart.com/directions.html.

OBJECTS EXCAVATED FROM THE KURGANS The woollen rug found at the Pazyryk burial mound in the Russian Altai represents one of the most ancient rug-weaving techniques in the world. From a later period low furniture (with removable legs) and horse trappings were found decorated with fantastic zoomorphic images. Creatures like deer and elk were carved with precise detail, which showed not only the powers of observation of the artist, but an understanding of the animals themselves. Such ornamental pieces were laid alongside the body of a dead chieftain to accompany him to the 'other world'. They included delicate antelopes with oversized antlers, gargoyle-type griffins with large, bulging eyes and fantastic creatures with sharp teeth or fearsome beaks. Sometimes the heads combined the features of several animals.

Representations of deer, horses, bears and birds were carved in wood, decorated in a unique style and then covered by a thin sheet of beaten gold – fit, one assumes, for that journey to the 'other world'. Examples from the Altai tombs were first excavated in the early 20th century and represent the most important finds of nomadic art, dating from the fifth to the second century BC. Surprisingly, some wool and felt objects also survived. The tombs were situated in the high mountains in cold, dry conditions all the year round. They were covered by large heaps of loose stones, which created a patch of permafrost underneath, and cold air sank into the tomb, freezing everything inside. Thanks to these conditions, the contents of the tombs were preserved for centuries: human remains, clothing, carpets and other artefacts.

The early discoveries were made by Soviet archaeologist M P Griaznov in 1929, and further researched by S I Rudenko in the late 1940s. Among examples of steppe art are the felt swans of Pazyryk, now in the Hermitage Museum in St Petersburg. Recent excavations of burial mounds on the Russian–Mongolian western border were made by N V Polosmak in 1996. Since then archaeologists from European countries (Germany, France, Italy and England to name a few) and the USA have worked in Mongolia. See: Joint Mongolian–Smithsonian Deer Stone Project: www.si.edu/mci/english/research/conservation/deer_stones.html.

HISTORY

CHRONOLOGY
Early history: partial chronology of north China

475–22BC	Warring States period: expansion of the Xiongnu (Huns)
221–207BC	Qin dynasty
206BC–AD5	Western or Former Han dynasty (the Western Han was overthrown in AD5 and restored in AD25 as the Eastern Han
6–24	Xi dynasty
25–220	Eastern or Later Han dynasty; drove Xiongnu back to the Altai Mountains
266–316	Western Jin dynasty
317–420	Eastern Jin dynasty
386–528	Northern Wei dynasty of the Xianbei (Toba)
581–618	Chinese Sui dynasty supports western Turks against eastern Turks
618–907	Tang dynasty controls northern China
744–840	Uighurs, allies of the Tang, displace Turks from Mongolia
840–920	Mongolia controlled by the Yenisey Kirghiz
947–1125	Sinicised Mongol Qidan drive away Kirghiz and establish the Liao dynasty in north China
960–1127	Northern Song dynasty
1034–1227	Xia (Tangut) dynasty
1115–1234	Jin (Jürchen) dynasty

From the birth of Genghis Khan to the end of the 19th century We possess
minimal records of the Mongols during the period of their greatness in the 12th and 13th centuries at the time of the Mongol Empire, despite the Uighur script being introduced in 1204 by Genghis Khan for keeping records. Among the few surviving records is the 13th-century *Secret History of the Mongols*. Their character and habits at the time are only slightly known to us, because, like other nomads, they left little in writing. There is some archaeological evidence of early tribal history, but on the whole Mongolian history cannot be compared with English or European histories. One reason there are so many unfilled gaps is that original sources were compiled by historians of other cultures, so great linguistic skills and cultural understanding are required to piece together the Mongol past from languages that include Mongolian, Persian, Arabic, Chinese, Japanese, Russian, Latin and others.

1

1162	Birth of Temüchin, the future Genghis Khan
1189	Proclaimed Genghis Khan after rallying the Mongol tribes
1206	Proclaimed Great Khan of all Mongolia
1227	Died after defeating the Tanguts
1229	Ögödei Khan (Genghis's third son) proclaimed second Great Khan
1235	Ögödei Khan builds the Mongol capital Karakorum
1236	Invasion of Russia, and establishment by Batu Khan (Genghis's grandson) of the Russian Khanate known as the Golden Horde
1246	Guyuk (Ögödei's son) proclaimed the third Great Khan Visit to Mongolia by the Pope's envoy, John di Plano Carpini
1251	Möngke Khan (son of Genghis Khan's youngest son) proclaimed fourth Great Khan
1260	Möngke's brother Kublai proclaimed fifth Great Khan
1275	Marco Polo at the Mongol's summer capital Shangdu (Cambaluc) – so he claims!
1294	Death of Kublai Khan, followed by several short reigns
1368	Ming dynasty founded in China
1380	Mongol capital destroyed by Ming army
1414	War between the Oriats (western Mongols) and the eastern Mongols
1450	A time of peace between the Mongols and the Ming boosts trade links
1578	Altan Khan of the eastern Mongols converted to Buddhism and gives title 'Dalai Lama' to Tibetan leader
1586	Founding of Erdene Zuu, Mongolia's first Buddhist monastery
1639	Zanabazar proclaimed Öndör Gegeen, leader of Mongol Buddhists
1642	Manchu forces cross the Great Wall
1644	Qing (Manchu) dynasty established in China
1691	Mongols swear allegiance to the Manchu emperor
1728	Russia and Qing China sign the Kyakhta border treaty
1832	First 'tsam' religious dances performed in Ulaanbaatar (at that time called Urga or Khüree)
1838	Founding of Gandan Monastery in the capital
1869	Birth of the eighth Öndör Gegeen

The 20th century

1904	13th Dalai Lama flees to Mongolia from British troops in Lhasa
1911	Declaration of Mongol independence: eighth Öndör Gegeen proclaimed Bogd Khan
1915	Russian–Chinese–Mongolian Treaty awards Mongolia autonomy
1917	Bolshevik Revolution in Russia brings political change
1919	Chinese troops invade Mongolia
1921	Revolutionaries of the Mongolian People's Party (MPP) install 'People's Government' with Soviet help
1924	Former religious and political leader 8th Bogd Khan dies Mongolia proclaimed the Mongolian People's Republic Capital renamed Ulaanbaatar (previously Niislel Khüree) MPP renamed Mongolian People's Revolutionary Party (MPRP)
1937	Choibalsan becomes minister of war; campaign against Buddhism launched
1940	Tsedenbal becomes secretary-general of the MPRP

1946	Mongolia recognised by Republic of China
1961	Mongolia joins the United Nations
1962	Mongolia joins the Council for Mutual Economic Assistance (CMEA, also known as Comecon)
1974	Tsedenbal becomes head of state
	Jambyn Batmönkh becomes prime minister
1984	Tsedenbal removed from post
	Batmönkh becomes MPRP general secretary and head of state
1990	Demonstrations for democracy
	MPRP Politburo resigns; Gombojavyn Ochirbat becomes general secretary
	Punsalmaagiin Ochirbat becomes head of state
1991	Gombojavyn Ochirbat replaced by Dash-Yondon as MPRP leader
	Privatisation vouchers issued
1992	New constitution adopted; Mongolia ceases to be a republic
	Puntsagiin Jasrai appointed prime minister
	Democratic parties unite to form the National Democratic Party
	Last Russian troops leave Mongolia
1993	Country's first presidential elections won by Punsalmaagiin Ochirbat
1996	MPRP loses the election and for first time Mongolia is ruled by a coalition of the Mongolian Social Democratic Party and Mongolian National Democratic Party (MNDP)
1997	Natsagiin Bagabandi elected president

The 21st century

2000	MPRP wins elections, Nambaryn Enkhbayar appointed prime minister
2001	Natsagiin Bagabandi re-elected president
2002	840th anniversary of birth of Genghis Khan celebrated
	Adoption of Land Law and Land Privatisation Law
2003	Visit to Mongolia by Chinese President Hu Jintao
	Mongolian army peacekeepers sent to Iraq and Afghanistan
	Prime Minister Enkhbayar meets President Putin in Moscow
2004	Settlement of Mongolian aid debt to Russia announced
	MPRP–Motherland Democracy election tie, coalition government formed
	Enkhbayar appointed speaker and Tsakhiagiin Elbegdorj prime minister
	President Bagabandi visits the US
2005	Speaker Enkhbayar wins presidential election, surrenders MPRP chairmanship
	Miyeegombyn Enkhbold elected MPRP chairman
	Tsendiin Nyamdorj elected speaker
	Revolutionaries Sükhbaatar and Choibalsan cremated, mausoleum demolished
	US President George W Bush visits Mongolia
2006	840th anniversary of Genghis Khan's foundation of the Mongolian state
	Coalition government collapses, Enkhbold appointed prime minister

2006	Elbegdorj elected chairman of the Democratic Party
	Official opening of Genghis Khan memorial on site of the former mausoleum
	President Enkhbayar meets President Putin in Moscow
2007	Helicopter crash kills 14 firefighters and crew, national mourning
	Speaker Nyamdorj dismissed for violating the Constitution
	MPRP Congress changes its leadership when MP Mr Sanjaagiin Bayar elected party chairman (24 October); earlier it had been resolved that chairman and prime minister would be the same person
2008	President Enkhbayar declares state of emergency after post-election rioting
	Mineral boom begins
2009	Former prime minister Tsakhiagiin Elbegdorj wins presidential election
2010	Extreme winter cold causes heavy losses of livestock
2011	Coal deposits are developed in the Gobi desert
2012	Parliamentary elections. Democratic Party wins a majority and forms a coalition with the MPRP
	Former president Nambaryn Enkhbayar is sentenced to four years in jail for corruption
2013	President Elbegdorj of Democratic Party re-elected in presidential elections.

PRE-MONGOL HISTORY: THE STEPPES THROUGH THE AGES The life of the Mongolian nomad has remained virtually unchanged for centuries. Like contemporary nomads, the early inhabitants of the central Asian steppes were tent-dwellers moving from pasture to pasture with their herds of horses, camels, sheep and goats.

The Scythians Between 750BC and 700BC, according to Greek historians, the Scythians, who were also known as the Saka (an Indo-Iranian nation), lived as nomads on the steppes of southern Russia, moving into Turkestan and the Tien Shan (a mountain range in northeast China). They are famous for their decorative animal-style art in gold and bronze. The Scythians invaded the Caucasus and were allies of the Assyrians. Darius launched a campaign against them around 514BC, but the Scythian nomads joined forces with Finno-Ugrian tribes from northeast Russia and the Persians were unable to conquer them.

The Sarmatians Around 179BC, another nomadic nation related to the Scythians, known as the Sarmatians and from the Aral Sea area, crossed the Volga and pushed the Scythians southwards. The motifs of their animal art were similar and were developed by the Siberian craftsmen of the upper Yenisey and Sayan foothills, who made bronze daggers and other iron tools and weapons from around 200BC.

The Huns The eastern steppes were dominated by the nomadic people known to the Chinese from the 3rd century BC as Xiongnu – the Huns. Archaeological discoveries indicate that Hun territory covered a vast area from Lake Baikal to Chita in the north, the whole of present-day Mongolia, and as far south as the Yellow River and Ordos in China (which was then a much smaller state than it is today). The various kingdoms of northern China organised defences against the marauding nomads, developing their cavalry and building fortifications. These were linked together to form the first stage of the Great Wall of China by the first emperor of the Qin dynasty (221–207BC). Our knowledge of this early period comes from Chinese annals, whose authors naturally gave Chinese names to the various ruling dynasties, although they were not all Chinese. Their descriptions of the physical appearance and dress of the Xiongnu, and their titles and military organisation, suggest that they were similar to the later Turks and Mongols.

Under their ruler, the *shanyü*, the Huns devastated what is now north China, besieging the Han dynasty capital of Taiyuan and driving the Yüehchih (Tokharians) westwards out of Gansu, a region in north China. Divisions among the Huns and their eventual defeat by Han China put an end to this threat. China was then able to gain control of Turfan and the Silk Road through what is today called Xinjiang. The northern Huns in the Orkhon Valley were subjugated around AD155 by Mongol Xienbei tribes. The southern Huns established a dynasty called the Northern Han, proclaimed in AD308 by Hun chief Liu Yuan at Taiyuan; they captured the Chinese Han dynasty capital Loyang. This was a period of great instability, with much of northern China overrun by nomadic tribes.

Their leaders' feuding led to the Huns' decline, division and eventual dispersal. The western Huns reached the Carpathians and Hungary in the 5th century AD. In AD441, Attila crossed the Danube but, in AD451, his advance across France was halted by the Roman and Visigoth armies at Troyes. Attila's empire disintegrated after his death in AD453.

The Jujuan In the 4th century, northern China was dominated by the Northern Wei dynasty of the Toba Turks, who fought with the Mongolian Jujuan (Juan-Juan) tribes for control. The Jujuan forced the Xiongnu to the northwest, their ruler Shelün assuming the title 'khagan' (khan) in AD402. His capital was in what is now Arkhangai Province in central Mongolia. His state was eventually weakened by division, and the Jujuan Khanate was absorbed by the Altai Turks.

The Turks Known to the Mongols as T'u-chüeh, or Tujue, the Turks formed an alliance in AD546 under their chief, Bumin (T'u-men), with the now-Sinicised Toba to defeat the Jujuan. The Turkic Khanate under Bumin established its capital in the Orkhon Valley – often called the cradle of Mongolian civilisation. Known as the Orkhon Turks, they were excellent craftsmen in iron and stone, besides being herdsmen, hunters and warriors. Monuments to their leaders are inscribed in Turkish runic script on stelae, standing stone slabs that still survive today in the Mongolian countryside. In AD553, Bumin's son became khan of the Eastern Khanate (Mongolia), while his brother received the Western Khanate (Djungaria and Issyk Kul). After 50 years of rule by Tang dynasty China, the Turks re-established their khanate, but violent revolt and infighting broke out among the tribes, which led to the destruction of the Turkic Khanate in AD745 and the supremacy of their former Uighur subjects.

The Uighurs The Uighur Khanate which followed reached its peak under Moyunchur Khan (AD745–59). The Uighurs made their capital at Khar Balgas on the Orkhon River (see page 296). They were primarily Shamanists but religions such as Buddhism, Manichaeism and Nestorian Christianity were permitted. They adopted the Sogdian script (derived from Aramaic), a script that the Mongols later utilised for their language. Attacked by the Kirghiz from the north, the Uighur Khanate declined in AD840. The Kirghiz themselves were threatened and eventually driven away by the Qidan (Khitan), a tribe related to the Mongols.

The Qidan At its greatest strength the Qidan state (AD947–1125) controlled central Mongolia and much of northeastern China and established a hereditary monarchy known as the Liao. The Qidan had their own literature in a script based on Chinese characters. It was a settled period when the arts and sciences flourished, but in 1125, under the combined attacks of Song dynasty China and the Jin state of the Jürchen, the Qidan state collapsed.

THE MONGOL EMPIRE TO MANCHU CONTROL

The Mongols The Jürchen, a Tungusic people, fought several unsuccessful battles against the Borjigin Mongols, a clan that emerged in central Mongolia in the 12th century. In 1161, however, the Jin defeated them by joining forces with the Tatars, their former enemies, who lived on the river Kherlen. Yesügei, a descendant of the Mongol Qabul Khan had a son, born in 1162, whom he named Temüchin, after a Tatar captive. This child was later to become the greatest of all Mongolians, known to the world as Genghis Khan. Temüchin's father was murdered by the Tatars and he, his mother and brothers were forced to scavenge on the steppe for their survival. To nourish her children, Lady Ho'elun, their mother, used a pointed juniper stick to dig up wild leeks, onions, and garlic which they ate with freshwater fish. It was a hard struggle for the family to survive and during his youth Temüchin learned the value of building strong friendships. As a young man he made alliances and rallied tribal leaders. Charismatic and with a strong personality he had natural qualities of leadership and from obscurity he shot to the rank of a world leader. In 1189, the Mongol tribes proclaimed him Genghis Khan of the Mongols. In 1198 and 1202 he twice defeated the Tatars, and after the submission of the Naiman, the Mongol tribes were eventually united. In 1206, Genghis Khan was proclaimed the Great Khan of all Mongolia. He then began a series of campaigns against neighbouring states – the Tangut (1207), the Uighurs of Turfan (1209), the Jin (1215), the Qidan (1218), and Samarkand (1221) – and died in 1227, having finally destroyed the Tangut. Genghis Khan achieved his vision of forging a Mongol world empire, a legacy which he passed to his sons and grandsons, who further enlarged it to form different khanates extending from Mongolia and China: the Golden Horde in Russia, the Chaghatai Khanate in central Asia and the Ilkhanate in Persia.

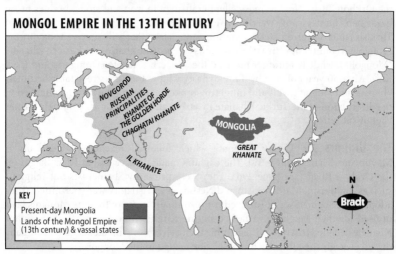

MONGOL EMPIRE IN THE 13TH CENTURY

NOVGOROD
RUSSIAN PRINCIPALITIES
KHANATE OF THE GOLDEN HORDE
CHAGHATAI KHANATE
IL KHANATE
MONGOLIA
GREAT KHANATE

N

Bradt

KEY
Present-day Mongolia
Lands of the Mongol Empire
(13th century) & vassal states

THE ELDEST SON?

Jochi, Genghis Khan's eldest son, died just before his father, thereby resolving any dispute about his right to the succession – he may have been conceived while his mother Börte, Genghis Khan's first wife, was briefly a captive of the Merkits. Shortly after their marriage, Börte was abducted by the khan of the neighbouring Merik tribe. Her warrior husband rode to her rescue during a night raid, and when Börte recognised Temüchin's call, she struggled from her captors and the two escaped in the darkness of night. Although Genghis Khan had many wives, Börte, who was a year older, remained his favourite. Their marriage was arranged by his father when they were children of just nine and ten years old. Ogodei, Genghis Khan's third son (and favourite) was nominated Khan in 1219 before the death of his eldest brother Jochi (1227), whose paternity was questionable and who later on may have fallen out with Genghis Khan.

Genghis Khan's successors Genghis Khan's third son Ögödei was proclaimed the second Great Khan (1229–41). His forces stormed into Europe to Poland and Hungary and were poised to attack Vienna in 1241 when Ogödei Khan died and the Mongols turned and rode back home; the succession then passed to Ögödei's son Güyük (1246–48). Jochi's son Batu was enraged by this decision to bypass the eldest son Jochi's line, and with his support Möngke, son of Genghis Khan's youngest son Tolui, was proclaimed the fourth Great Khan (1251–58). The Mongol forces continued their rampage through China and western Asia to deal a deathblow to the Abbasid Caliphate, taking Baghdad in 1258. Möngke's brother Kublai succeeded in 1260, but was challenged by another brother, Arigbökh. In 1264, Kublai's victory over Arigbökh confirmed him as the fifth Great Khan. Kublai moved the Mongol capital to Beijing and proclaimed his Yuan dynasty in 1271.

Batu Khan had invaded the weak Russian principalities in 1236 and Kiev fell to the Mongols in 1240. From 1243 Batu's khanate became known as the 'Golden Horde'. Batu died in 1255, but Mongol rule over the Russians continued – the 'Tatar yoke' as they called it. The Russian princes were required to offer submission and pay tribute to the Great Khan. In 1380, the year the old Mongol capital at Karakorum was destroyed by Chinese Ming dynasty troops, the Golden Horde suffered a heavy defeat at the hands of Grand Duke Dmitrii Donskoi at the Battle of Kulikovo. However, the 'Tatar yoke' was not cast off until 1480, when Grand Duke Ivan III forced the Golden Horde out of Russian territory.

By the end of the 13th century the Mongol Empire was the largest land empire in history, stretching at its greatest extent from central Europe to China and Korea, and from Russia to Iran and Vietnam. The Mongols learned naval warfare on the Yangtze River and attempted to invade Japan in 1274 and again in 1281, but storms sank Kublai's fleet. In 1293, there was an unsuccessful attack on the island of Java in Indonesia, where the tropical climate proved to be the Mongols' undoing. However, during the reign of Kublai Khan, Genghis's grandson, there were periods of peace and prosperity in the territory of present-day Mongolia and mainland China, when the arts and culture flourished. After Kublai, the Yuan dynasty in China was weakened by internal struggles and the Mongol Empire in China faded and declined. In 1368, a peasant uprising spawned the Chinese Ming dynasty which replaced the Mongol Yuan dynasty. The power of the Mongol Empire declined as suddenly as it began, and most of the Mongols returned to the steppes.

The Manchus As the Mongol Empire broke up into its component parts under the new dynasties inaugurated by Genghis Khan's successors, there was a long period of civil war in Mongolia itself, as Mongol chiefs fought for control of the tribes. The Oirat, or western Mongols, became a new power, threatening the Khalkha Mongols of central Mongolia. To the northeast, a great expansionist power was on the move – the Manchus. In 1624, the Manchus advanced from what is now northeast China into the border area of southern Mongolia and subjugated the Gorlos and Khorchin tribes. In 1636, the Manchus proclaimed their Qing dynasty, and in 1644 they took Beijing as the Ming emperor committed suicide. In 1673, the Khalkha came under renewed Oirat attack and sought refuge beyond the Great Wall. In 1691, the Khalkha princes joined the southern Mongol chieftains in swearing allegiance to the Qing emperor, Kang Xi, at Dolonnor.

Lamaism Kublai Khan had established a special relationship of patron and priest with the Tibetan Phagspa Lama, but in 1578, Altan Khan of the Tümet, a southern Mongol tribe, recognised the Tibetan religious leader, the Abbot of Sera monastery, as the 'Dalai Lama' (Sonam Gyatso). It was his Gelugpa, or 'yellow hat', school that was promoted under Qing rule. The influence and power of Tibetan Buddhism (Lamaism) was greatly enhanced, with the building of many monasteries and temples and the translation from Sanskrit and Tibetan, and later the xylographic printing, of many Buddhist works. Mongolia meanwhile had produced its own Buddhist leader, Zanabazar, the son of a Khalkha prince. He was proclaimed the incarnation of the Tibetan Javzandamba Khutukhtu in 1639 and accorded the title Öndör Gegeen, or 'High Enlightened One'. Ranking third in the Lamaist hierarchy after the Dalai Lamas and Panchen Lamas, the Mongolian Khutukhtus were the Mongols' spiritual leaders. The eighth Javzandamba Khutukhtu, who was also head of state (Bogd Khan) from 1911, died in 1924.

The Russians Russian expansion into Siberia (with the founding of Tobolsk in 1587 and Irkutsk in 1661) led eventually to a series of clashes with the Manchus. Qing troops destroyed the Russian fort at Albazin in the Amur (Heilongjiang) Valley in 1685. Manchu and Russian envoys met at Nerchinsk in 1689 to negotiate and sign a treaty partitioning the disputed territory east of the Argun (Ergun) River. In 1728, representatives concluded the Treaty of Kyakhta, which determined the border between Imperial Russia and Qing China from the Argun to Shabin Dabaga, a mountain pass on the northern border with the Krasnoyarsk region. Russia thereby acknowledged Manchu control of the whole of Mongolia, including Uriankhai (Tuva).

At the start of the 19th century, both the British and Russian empires were embroiled in an ever-increasing rivalry for power and influence in the area, known as 'The Great Game', whereby Imperial Russia pushed across central Asia towards British India. New knowledge was urgently required of the great wildernesses in between, so far uncharted and unexplained. The journeys of Colonel Nikolai Przewalski to western China and Tibet date from this period. In 1904, the British Younghusband expedition to Lhasa forced the 13th Dalai Lama to flee Tibet and take refuge in Urga (Ulaanbaatar) with the Javzandamba Khutukhtu. Completion of the Trans-Siberian Railway in 1905 coincided with Russia's increased interest in Mongolia at a time when Qing power was in decline.

SELECTED HISTORY This section is based on the life and times of Genghis Khan, and the great Mongol Empire which he and his family created and which dominated the known world from 1206 to 1368.

Genghis Khan: 'World Conqueror', 'Emperor of All Men', 'Scourge of God' or 'Savage Genius'. Whatever the title used, most people have heard of him. Admired as the unifier of the Mongols and founder of the Mongol Empire, Genghis Khan has always had a special place in the hearts of all Mongols. In the last decade a fast-growing personality cult has restored him to centre stage, where he is now a national obsession. To Mongols, he represents the unshakeable symbol of a glorious past.

At birth, following an ancient custom, he was named Temüchin, after one of his father's defeated enemies. The virtue, strength and courage of the enemy was supposed to pass to the newborn baby. His early years were dogged by family difficulties and great hardship; he murdered his half-brother in a teenage dispute, yet grew up to unite the disparate Mongol tribes, who proclaimed him Khan of all the Mongols. He married Börte, an early arranged marriage, and had several other wives.

The only substantial Mongol work about Genghis Khan and the early Mongol Empire is recorded in the partly legendary *The Secret History of the Mongols*. The 'Conqueror of the Steppe' was no simple, savage warrior. On his way to victory, Temüchin was not totally blinded by either greed or lust, and although subjugation came first, policy followed. He organised the nomad world; he then used engineers from defeated armies to build mangonels and siege works against the citadels of civilisation. All his moves were politically calculated. Until his death in 1227, Genghis Khan strongly believed he conquered with the authority of the Ruler of Heaven. By 1280, the Mongol Empire established by Genghis, his sons and grandsons stretched from the Yellow Sea to the Mediterranean. As a military genius, Genghis Khan stands above Alexander the Great, Hannibal, Caesar, Attila and Napoleon.

It is difficult to separate Genghis Khan the statesman and lawgiver from Genghis Khan the warrior. Had it not been for his incredible ability to cross the boundaries of his native steppe and to conquer and claim for himself and his country the world's largest land empire, he might have lived as an unknown local chieftain. The genius of Genghis Khan lay in his military leadership, his knowledge of men and his organisational ability. He was a charismatic personality, astute, intelligent and cunning. No-one around him challenged his authority and his orders were carried out immediately. Genghis was also a reformer and he had a profound effect on the morality of the Mongol people. His laws and disciplines gave the Mongol tribes an identity, which they are proud of to this day. Outside Mongolia, however, in contradiction to his countrymen's hero worship, Genghis Khan is regarded as one of the world's arch villains.

Genghis Khan died in August 1227, during a campaign against the Tanguts. The popular belief is that his body was taken back to his birthplace in Khentii Aimag, northeast of Ulaanbaatar. Huge mystery also surrounds his burial: herds of horses were said to have galloped over the ground; trees were planted and guards posted until the trees grew; accounts say that the Mongol guards who completed the burial were killed to the last man. At Delüün Boldog, in Khentii Province, a monument was built in 1962 to mark the 800th anniversary of his birth.

Genghis Khan and the Mongol Empire Mongol history really begins with Genghis Khan. Most reliable reports prior to the 12th century were written down by others, since the Mongols remained illiterate until then. *The Secret History of the Mongols* (usually abbreviated to *The Secret History*), the first Mongol account of their world, is a curious mixture of myth and reality. It describes the life of Genghis Khan and his unification of the Mongol tribes and begins with the following verse:

> There was a blue wolf which was born
> Having [his] destiny from heaven above,
> His spouse was a fallow doe.

In the legend, the offspring of the wolf and the fallow doe (or of two people with these names) represents the birth of the Mongol nation. *The Secret History* contains many passages of fine poetry that recall the Scandinavian sagas and paints a picture of the young hero Temüchin, who as acclaimed Genghis Khan in 1189, unified the disparate tribes into a formidable army. The account of his epic rise to power describes numerous alliances and betrayals.

Genghis Khan – the law giver Genghis gave instructions that his laws (*yasa*) should be written down. In 1204 he gave orders for the keeping of written records by Uighur scribes. His powerful intelligence more than compensated for his lack of literacy. When the princes assembled to discuss affairs of state, they produced the *yasa* and lived by the rule of law. The *yasa* prescribed the death penalty for desertion,

MONGOLIAN STATECRAFT   *Dr David Sneath*

When his nobles raised Chinggis* (Genghis) Khan as their sovereign in the Year of the Tiger, in 1206, they can be said to have formally established the Mongol state – well before many of the states of Europe. Mongolia's past, in particular the vast empire established by the medieval Chinggisid khans, has made it one of the most influential nations in history. In the so-called 'old world' it was perhaps the first world empire – Pax Mongolica spanned the Eurasian continent, bringing Europe and east Asia into direct contact for the first time.

This was a multi-cultural and religiously plural, tolerant empire and we owe this tolerance not to some barbaric simplicity but to the sophistication and skill of the empire's rulers. Yet despite this unparalleled position in world history, the understanding of Mongolia today is poor and littered with misrepresentations. Many people imagine the place as a timeless wilderness, populated by barbaric tribes.

A tradition of 800 years of state is a venerable enough heritage for any nation (it is rather more than most of the countries of Europe, for example). But the Mongol state was itself the heir of a much older series of political traditions – part of a rich history of political development – sophisticated and very old. These systems of governance were steppe traditions – originated, elaborated and adapted on the grasslands of what has become Mongolia.

Members of the great noble houses of the steppes were at various times patrons of religion and the arts, sophisticated political operators and gifted military leaders. The first European accounts of the 13th-century Mongol state were those written by monks such as John di Plano Carpini and William of Rubruck. When they met Mongol aristocrats they described them as 'dux'. Early translators however translated this as 'duke' and so in the earliest English accounts we read of the friars theft, adultery and false testimony, and lesser punishments for taboos like urinating in rivers, or polluting running water by returning water used for washing to the river. Beheading was the usual form of execution, although, because it was decreed that noble blood should not be spilled, nobles were strangled with bowstrings, had their backs broken or were rolled in carpets and trampled by horses.

The Mongol army Genghis Khan learned the value of a personal following, which included his keenest generals (or his 'four hounds', as they were known) – Jebe, Jelme and his brother Sübatai, and Kublai of the Barulas clan. They formed the core of his conquering army in the early period. Genghis structured the way in which his soldiers led their lives. From the age of 14, men were expected to join the army. Warriors' wives and children followed behind the troops with herds of sheep and horses, including several re-mounts per man. Warrior units were organised in multiples of ten, an *arban* (10) being a unit of ten men; ten *arban* made up a *jagun* (100), that is, a unit of 100 men; ten *jagun* formed a *minggan* (1,000 men); and ten *minggan* formed a *tümen* (10,000 men). Speedy communication by mounted couriers was later developed (see below).

Training was based on the hunt, a favourite Mongol sport, with the quarry representing the enemy. Various manoeuvres were practised, such as 'ringing' or driving the hunted animals in an arc. Mongol hunters/warriors were experts in signalling to each other using banners, whistling arrows and drums. Every battle was carefully planned and prepared with the help of spies. The soldiers learned the importance of discipline and co-ordination and became the finest army of their time.

meeting various Mongol dukes. But in the age of colonialism these translations changed. Where the term 'dux' was used for European nobles it was translated as 'duke', but where it was applied to a Mongol it was translated as 'chief'.

Another much-remarked-on feature of the Chinggisid state was its decimal system of dual military and civil administration, but in fact these administrative forms stretch back to the Xiongnu Empire of the 3rd century BC, and it was from this tradition of state that the Mongol Empire of Chinggis Khan sprang.

Mongol emperors, like Chinggis Khan, ruled by Heavenly Mandate – similar to, but distinct from, the Chinese tradition of the emperor as 'Son of Heaven'. This was particularly important when Mongols ruled Chinese subjects – as in the Yuan period. By the 17th century much of the Chinggisid nobility were autonomous and ended up swearing fealty to the Manchu Qing dynasty. This was a result of ideological and political change rather than a simple reckoning of kinship links.

Collective sovereignty, by which authority was vested in the entire royal house, is another recurrent theme in the political traditions of Mongolia that dates at least from the early Turkic empires through to the Qing period.

This sophisticated tradition of state – developed over not just 800 years but more than 2,000 years – contains elements of ancient statecraft as part of a dynamic and innovative historical process of development, quite as rich and complex as those of better-known political traditions.

We celebrate this long history with the words *Mongol Uls Mandtugai!* (Long live Mongolia!)

* the spelling Chinggis comes from the Mongolian traditional vertical script.

GENGHIS KHAN'S GENETIC LEGACY

There is an astounding statistic that one in 200 men alive on the planet today is related to Genghis Khan. This was discovered by Oxford University scientists Dr Tatiana Zergal and Dr Chris Tyler-Smith. Over a period of ten years they collected blood from 16 populations that live in and around the Mongol Empire. The analysis of DNA studies of the Y chromosome, used to establish human lineage, shows a genetic signature which passes from father to son. The blood of none of the people outside the Mongol Empire carries this particular genetic signature, except the Hazara people of Afghanistan and Pakistan, former Mongol soldiers who claimed to be descended from Genghis Khan. The genetic chromosome signature belongs to the Mongol ruling house, Dr Tyler-Smith believes. The Mongol khans had access to large numbers of women in the lands they conquered and ruled for two centuries. The evidence is incomplete because the tomb of Genghis Khan has never been found, although it is believed that one-fifth of present-day Mongolian men carry the khan's genes and it is possible that they shared a common ancestor – the Great Khan himself.

All of this is remarkable considering the lowly origins of the Mongol people – obscure nomadic tribes from Asia's remotest uplands. The key to their dominion over those they conquered was the horse. Since its domestication during the 2nd millennium BC, the horse's speed and stamina was exploited by the Mongol nomads. Their principal weapon was the compound bow, made from willow wood and bound by a mixture of silk and resin. They developed the first stirrups on the northern steppe, which allowed warriors to turn in the saddle and shoot arrows back at their pursuing enemies while galloping ahead at full pace, a military tactic known as the 'Parthian shot' used by the ancient Parthians (250BC–AD230). These skills contributed to the emergence of their military might.

Genghis Khan had left his generals to complete this task as his military dream 'to rule the world' led him west, where Samarkand and Bukhara, the great cities of Islam, were destroyed in 1221. Meanwhile, his military commanders defeated the Russian–Kipchak alliance in the Don Valley and the Volga Bulgars were dispersed. From Mongolia Genghis attacked and destroyed the neighbouring Tangut (Xixia) capital in 1227, the year he died.

The mounted couriers The mounted courier service, known as *yam*, was key to the maintenance of the Mongol Empire and dispatch riders on horseback travelled enormous distances at breakneck speed to deliver messages, protected by Genghis Khan's *yasa* (laws). Military units were responsible for the protection of the service and caravan traders also benefited from it. Trade flourished along the protected routes within such a framework of discipline and security. At each post, horses were saddled and waiting for the khan's couriers and news could be relayed at terrific speed, with the riders putting the service ahead of their own lives. Passes called *gerege* (Mongolian), *paiza* (Turkish), were issued to official users of the system but finally traders were obliged to pay for using the *yam* posts.

The Mongol dynasty following the death of Genghis Khan
The 'golden family' Genghis's four sons – Jochi, Chaghatai, Ögödei and Tolui, by his first wife Börte – formed the Mongol Khanate dynastic inheritance. Ögödei

was chosen to succeed as the Great Khan and his brother Tolui promised their ageing father to support him, as *The Secret History* states:

I shall be at his side
His faithful companion,
Reminding him of things he has forgotten,
Waking him when he has slept his fill.

By nominating his third son Ögödei, Genghis Khan broke with tradition. Ögödei was proclaimed the second Great Khan in 1229. This caused acute rivalry and led to fighting among members of the 'golden family' – family tensions not explained in *The Secret History*. The Mongol Empire continued to grow in the third generation, but Genghis Khan's sons and grandsons fought among themselves and lost sight of the 'big idea' of one empire under one ruler, preferring to build their own personal empires on the territories they had conquered, and adopting the customs and religions of their new subjects. Nonetheless the achievements were enormous: Genghis Khan and his successors created the largest land empire the world has ever known.

Mongols attack Europe During Ögödei's reign, Mongol troops invaded their eastern neighbour Korea while at the same time mounted warriors rode west. The horsemen from the east made Europe's knights look like laggards when they swept across the northern steppe towards Europe from central Asia's frozen heights. First they subjugated southern Siberia and then moved on to ravage Transcaucasia and destroy the Kievan army on the Kalka River (1223); and later, one of Genghis Khan's grandsons, Batu, took Moscow (from the southwest by crossing the river Volga) in 1237. Ögödei's son Godan staged the invasion of Tibet but was converted to Buddhism by Sakya Pandita, whose pupil Phagspa later became Kublai Khan's teacher. In 1241, Mongol troops defeated the Polish and other armies at Legnica (Liegnitz). As proof of their victory the Mongols were reported to have collected nine sacks full of right ears from the bodies of the slain. A famous account of the capture of Kraków is commemorated to this day by a trumpet call known as Hejnal (see box, page 26), which sounded the approach of the enemy. After the Battle of Kraków, another Mongol army raided Hungary, resulting in a great slaughter of the Magyar princes under Bela IV beside the river Tisza. Hungarians described the invaders as 'dog-faced Tatars'. Europeans had no knowledge of the lands beyond the Ural Mountains until the marauding Mongol hordes arrived, leaving a trail of destruction in their wake. Had it not been for the death of Ogödei Khan in 1241, European history might have taken a very different course, because the Mongol forces turned and rode home to elect his successor.

The Golden Horde: conquest and colonisation However, the Mongols remained in Russia and set up camp between the Don and the Volga rivers, where they created the 'Golden Horde', named, it is thought, after the colour of the first khan's tent. The Mongols destroyed the Volga Bulgars and changed the political frontiers of Asia and Europe for several centuries. The Mongol Empire transformed the character of the many regions they conquered and opened up the East to the West and vice versa.

The Mongols were able to defeat the disunited and jealous Russian princes one by one. Furthermore, the princes of Rus were obliged to pay heavy tributes to the khan; they were put through rituals they considered humiliating, such as being obliged to

Hejnal derives from the Hungarian word for the dawn and by extension for reveille. The word passed into the Polish language (the 'l' at the end of 'Hejnal' is pronounced 'w') and became one of the most noted trumpet calls in the history of Europe, from the time when it first sounded the alarm of the Mongol invasion of Poland in 1241 (see page 19). As the story goes, the trumpet call rang out from the tower of the ancient church of St Mary's in Kraków, which overlooks the city square. It was normally sounded every hour, day and night, and repeated four times to the north, south, east and west, and consisted of a simple melody. Today the melody is always stopped short in the final cadence. It commemorates the trumpeter who, while raising the alarm, was shot through the throat by a Mongol arrow; nevertheless, his call allowed the citizens of Kraków to flee the city. The survivors endowed a trumpeter to continue this call in perpetuity, and this tradition has been maintained for some 700 years! The melody has been adopted as the signature tune of Polish radio. It is a living memory of the irruption of the Mongol hordes into the heart of Europe.

walk between blazing bonfires for purification and made to prostrate themselves before the khan. Marco Polo's father described the Russian province of the khans as a region of darkness, where tall, fair-haired, Christian men of a light complexion pay tribute to the kings of the western Tatars. He also noted it was an exceedingly cold region. It took the Russian princes several centuries to unite against the Mongols.

FROM THE MONGOL EMPIRE TO THE 20TH CENTURY There is a gap in Mongol history between the colonising of the great land empire of the Mongol khans, from its establishment in the late 12th century until its general collapse in the mid 14th century (although the Golden Horde survived in Russia into the 15th century), and the early 20th-century revolution. The curious reader wonders what happened between then and now. The answer is the Mongols retired to their upland homeland and continued to herd as nomads in the manner of their forebears, which a small nomadic population do to this day. Against this background were inter-tribal conflicts, and during this period Buddhism spread throughout Mongolia.

The Mongol Empire imploded after the collapse of the Yuan dynasty (1368) and the Ming dynasty was established in China. Many of the scholar-bureaucrats who found favour during Yuan (Mongol) rule suffered under Ming rulers. Thousands of people were put to death, and once high-ranking officials became clerks. Meanwhile the famous Chinese civil service examination system got into its stride. Members of the Mongol royal family were kept in the capital, Beijing, and indoctrinated. In 1374, a member of the Mongol royal family was sent back to Mongolia in the hope that he would succeed as khan and eventually bring the whole of Mongolia under Chinese suzerainty. This did not happen.

After 1368, Mongolia was in a state of disorder for many years, so it was natural that some lesser nobles looked to the south to secure a better deal for themselves. The Chinese did their best to encourage this and tried to Sinicise them, as their authority surged further north. The Mongol princes waged guerilla warfare along the Chinese–Mongol border. The 15th and 16th centuries were dominated by internal struggles to decide between the various claimants to the Mongol throne, although few of these struggles lasted for very long. The 17th century was marked by the rise of Manchu and Russian power in Asia, culminating in the absorption of Mongolia into the Manchu Qing Empire (1644–1912). From 1644, for the next 200 years, Buddhism spread among the Mongols. The early 20th century saw Mongolia's unsuccessful bid for its independence and its absorption into the Soviet Empire and, at this period, Mongolia's modern history begins.

The modern period

Autonomous 'Outer' Mongolia The Mongols and Tibetans believed that the Manchus ruled Mongolia and Tibet not as Chinese provinces, but under separate treaties. When the Manchu throne fell, Mongolia, Tibet and China were automatically separated. As the Qing dynasty collapsed in 1911, 'Outer' (Khalkha) Mongolia proclaimed its independence. The 'Living Buddha', head of Buddhism in Mongolia, was acknowledged as head of state with the title Bogd Khan and enthroned on 16 December 1911. One of the first acts of the Bogd Khan was to

'OUTER' AND 'INNER' MONGOLIA

Not all Mongols live in Mongolia proper – or Outer Mongolia, as it is historically referred to – nor are they the majority of Mongols. Most Mongolians live in Inner Mongolia and Xinjiang Autonomous Region of China, bordering the area south of the Gobi Desert along the eastern Silk Route.

The terms Inner Mongolia and Outer Mongolia were used by the Manchu Qing rulers. Inner Mongolia (Övör Mongol or 'Front/Breast' Mongolia) is part of China and largely settled by Chinese people, who outnumber Mongols by 14 to 1. Outer Mongolia (Ar Mongol or 'Back' Mongolia) – the Mongolia of this guide – is an independent country in the process of building democracy, formerly a socialist country for 70 years, and during that time closely linked to the Soviet Union.

Internal conflict and tribal disunity continued to blight Mongolian unity from the 16th century until the modern period. Chinese annals are full of accounts of 'barbarian raids' from the north (Outer Mongolia) on the people living around the Great Wall, which extended in an east–west direction across northern China. Below it was the famous Silk Road, where Turkic-speaking oasis people traded silks and spices from the East to the Mediterranean Sea. This international highway dating back to the first century expanded and was at its height in the 14th, 15th and 16th centuries. The ascendancy of the western (Oirat) and southern Mongols passed to the Ordos Mongols, located in the great loop of the Yellow River, under Altan Khan (1543–83). From them the supremacy passed to the southern tribes living near the Great Wall. At this period Manchu power from China flooded north and their rule encompassed the Mongol tribes. By 1644, the Chinese Qing or Manchu dynasty was established, with profound effects on the fate of the Mongol tribes. Over the next century the northern Mongols of Outer Mongolia were added to their empire. Fighting between the Mongol tribes persisted and the western and southern Mongols revolted against the Manchus in the 1750s. The rebellion was quelled and the Mongol tribes again were dispersed and redistributed. Chinese colonisation encroached on the pasturelands of Inner Mongolia and this uneasy situation was compounded by economic distress and its territory was abolished and replaced by several provinces with Chinese names in the interwar years. Inner Mongolia was declared an Autonomous Region of China (in 1947) while Outer Mongolia became a separate state (in 1911).

Marco Polo (c1254–1324) is widely assumed to have been the first 'foreigner' to reach the Mongol heartlands, to converse with Kublai Khan and to travel throughout China on the khan's orders. Though the original manuscript no longer exists, several early 15th-century copies of *Description of the World*, said to have been written by Marco Polo and the romance-writer Rustichello of Pisa, survive. The first versions of the text were written in medieval French but it was soon translated into most of the major European languages and many dialects. The fact that it first circulated in manuscript has led to problems, for errors crept in as copies were made, and manuscript versions varied quite widely before the first printed versions appeared later in the 15th century.

A prologue which survives in some manuscripts describes how Marco Polo's father and uncle, traders who normally travelled between Venice, Constantinople and the Black Sea, were driven eastwards by Mongol wars and found themselves at the court of Kublai Khan. When they left, they promised to return with holy oil from Jerusalem, and travelled back overland, bringing young Marco with them. Legend has it that he was chosen by Kublai to travel all over southern China and report back on the area that was still being conquered by the Mongols. This he did for 20 years before returning by sea, with his father and uncle, to Venice.

There are several interesting aspects to the Polo legend. The first is that, despite his self-proclaimed closeness to Kublai and his 20 years' service, there is no mention of him in any of the innumerable Chinese annals, nor in Mongol sources. Some have also questioned the fact that he makes no mention of the Great Wall, tea-drinking, foot-binding or the use of chopsticks, but perhaps even more problematic are the passages where he describes the impossible. For example, he claimed to have ended the Mongols' five-year siege of Xiangyang by constructing mangonels to fling stones into the Chinese city; however, Xiangyang fell in 1273, a

order the confiscation of the Manchu emperor's livestock, which was shared out among the Mongol nobility and high lamas. During this turbulent period, the Republic of China was proclaimed in 1912.

An agreement with Russia in November 1912 seemed to accord Russian recognition to Mongolia's independence, but Russia promised only to help protect its autonomy. China remained in charge of foreign relations. Autonomous (Outer) Mongolia had appealed to all Mongols to join together in one independent Mongol state, but China retained its hold on Inner Mongolia, and Mongolia's 'independence' proved short-lived, as Chinese troops occupied the capital of Autonomous Mongolia, Urga (Niislel Khüree), in 1919. The 20th century saw Mongolia free itself from two centuries of Manchu rule, but there was an unsuccessful struggle for independence, a brief occupation by China, followed by a national revolution that succeeded with the support of the Soviets.

Mongolia's revolution A group of Mongolian nationalist revolutionaries took shelter in Siberia in 1920 and were helped by the Soviet authorities to rebel against the Chinese occupation forces in Mongolia. The Mongolian People's Party was set up at a meeting of 26 revolutionaries. They adopted what are called the 'Ten Aspirations', promising to resolve matters of external and internal policy in the long-term interests of the nation, but warned of harsh measures to eliminate things which were backward or did not benefit 'the people'.

year before the Polos could possibly have entered China. He 'describes' Japan and Russia, but no experts think he went to either place. Some have suggested that Marco Polo's *Description of the World* may be a secondhand compilation, based perhaps on Near Eastern sources, in which context it is worth noting that most of the nouns and proper names are Persian or Turkish in origin and not Mongol or Chinese as might be expected.

The Polos' reputation as the first Westerners in Mongolia is also a myth. The first eyewitness account of Mongolia was made in 1246 by Friar John di Plano Carpini, a disciple of St Francis of Assisi, and much detail of the cosmopolitan community in Karakorum, which included a Parisian silversmith (captured by the Mongols in Belgrade in 1254), a Greek doctor and a man called Basil, son of an Englishman and nephew of a Norman bishop, was given by Friar William of Rubruck, a papal envoy who reached the city in 1254.

Arguments over the veracity of Marco Polo's account have raged for over 300 years; the fact remains, however, that the *Description of the World*, attributed to him, contained a wealth of information about Mongolia and the Far East in the 15th century. The fact that the manuscript was widely copied and translated, and that printed versions in all the major European languages have been produced from the 15th century up until the present day, testifies to European interest in Mongolia and China throughout the centuries.

If you wish to read further on this subject, you might try one or more of the following:

Franke, Herbert *China Under Mongol Rule* Aldershot, 1994
Wood, Frances *Did Marco Polo Go To China?* Westview Press, USA, 1998
Yule, Colonel Sir Henry *The Travels of Marco Polo* London, 1920; New York, 1993

In February 1921, Urga was captured by a force of Tsarist Siberian Cossacks and Mongol mercenaries under the command of a Baltic baron, Roman von Ungern-Sternberg, later known as the 'Mad Baron' (see box, page 30). The Mongolian Bogd Khan, the political and religious leader, who had been taken hostage by the Chinese, was released by von Ungern-Sternberg, who set up a new government. But in July that year, the baron's forces were overcome by the Soviet Russian Red Army and Mongolian revolutionaries (headed by Damdiny Sükhbaatar), who installed a 'people's government'.

The revolutionaries, encouraged by the Soviets, adopted a communist, rather than nationalist, approach and there was a limited monarchy until the Bogd Khan's death in May 1924, after which new incarnations and 'Living Buddhas' were forbidden. Mongolia's ties with Soviet Russia were strengthened and the Mongolian People's Party was renamed the Mongolian People's Revolutionary Party (MPRP).

At the end of 1924, a national assembly, or Great Khural, approved the country's first constitution and a second chamber of 30 members, the Little Khural, was elected. It then elected a five-man Presidium and chose the government. The Mongolian People's Republic (MPR) was proclaimed and the capital renamed Ulaanbaatar ('Red Hero'). The Great Khural resolved that Soviet Russia was Mongolia's 'only friend and ally' and that, 'in alliance with the Soviet working class', the MPR would 'bypass capitalism and enter socialism'.

THE MAD BARON

Freiherr Roman von Ungern-Sternberg came from the landed nobility of the Baltic German barons whose ancestors had served the tsars. He was commissioned at the age of 24, in 1908, in the Transbaikal Cossacks. With his liking for adventure and hard riding, he much preferred this to life in one of the fashionable guards' regiments. The following year, the collapse of the Manchu dynasty in China and the proclamation of Sun Yat-sen's republic led to events which were to change von Ungern-Sternberg's life.

He is described as red-haired, with a sabre scar to his head. This scar was inflicted after an officers' brawl resulted in a duel, and apparently gave him spells of madness from time to time. He would wear a fur hat, a short Chinese jacket of cherry-red silk, blue cavalry breeches, and high Mongol boots, with a bunch of twinkling charms hanging from a bright yellow cord fastened around his waist.

In 1914, he won the Order of St George while serving on the German front during World War I. In 1916, he was sent to the Persian border, and in 1917, at 33, he was promoted to major-general. In 1917–18, during the civil war that broke out after the Russian Revolution, he joined Kolchak's 'white' army in Siberia, but with them he was driven back eastwards by Trotsky's new Red Army. Learning that the Reds had killed his wife and child, von Ungern-Sternberg vowed to kill anyone who looked remotely like a Bolshevik. (Although he is rumoured also to have married a Chinese princess.)

The baron assembled a force of Russian Cossacks and moved south into Mongolia. He believed himself destined to create a vast Asiatic empire like that of Genghis Khan, or that he was the reincarnation of the Mongol god of war. At any rate, he won a reputation for appalling atrocities. On 31 October 1920, his force attacked Urga (Ulaanbaatar), but was repulsed by the larger and better-armed Chinese garrison, and had to withdraw. Trying again six days later, the baron's men nearly forced the Chinese out, but the attack failed again.

This reverse encouraged the Chinese to seize and imprison the Living Buddha (Bogd Khan) to the fury of the Mongols, with the result that many of them joined the baron's force. The baron invited the Chinese to surrender and join his army before he launched the attack. Instead they called for reinforcements from Peking (Beijing). He planned to make the Chinese believe he had more men that he really did by lighting fires on the hills above Urga. One of his men accidentally let off a rocket, and the Chinese retaliated with all they had. The baron advanced, inflicting heavy losses and destroyed the Chinese quarter.

The people of Urga saw the baron as their liberator and the 'Living Buddha' bestowed the title of khan on him. In spite of this, he continued his atrocities. Meanwhile, the Mongolian leader Sükhbaatar and his followers set up their revolutionary base at Kyakhta on the Russian frontier with Mongolia. The baron left Urga to attack the Reds as they advanced, but he was beaten off; Sükhbaatar and his revolutionaries captured Urga on 6 July 1921. After several more engagements, the baron was captured by the Reds in northern Mongolia, when he was betrayed by his Mongol escort. He was executed by the Bolsheviks in Novosibirsk on 15 September 1921, although a German source says he was shot three days later in Irkutsk.

The aristocracy and religious leaders still held most of the country's wealth. A swing in the MPRP leadership from moderate 'rightists' to extreme 'leftists' set in motion the confiscation of feudal property, forced collectivisation of stock breeding, the expulsion of Chinese traders and the imposition of a Soviet trade monopoly in Mongolia. The MPRP ordered seizure of religious property, expelled the lamas from the monasteries and imprisoned or killed their leaders in purges that all but destroyed Buddhism. Herdsmen, urged to join the government-run collectives, took fright and slaughtered their livestock and, by 1932, terror and food shortages brought the people to the brink of civil war, prevented only by Soviet intervention. This halted political and economic extremism for a while, but purges of party and government officials continued, taking the lives of prime ministers Genden and Amar, who were both arrested and executed in the USSR. Supreme power was then concentrated in the hands of the prime minister, Marshal Choibalsan – later known as 'Mongolia's Stalin'.

These events coincided with the establishment of Japanese control in neighbouring Manchuria and the threat of further expansion. In 1939, Manchukuo (Manchurian) forces with Japanese military support invaded Mongolia across the eastern border at the Khalkhyn Gol (see box, page 32). Some historians consider that Japan's defeat at Khalkhyn Gol persuaded its leaders to give up plans for the invasion of the USSR in favour of the invasion of southeast Asia, again changing the course of history.

Mongolia's Great Khural met to draw up basic policy, revise the constitution and elect the Little Khural, where power was concentrated in the hands of a small group of leaders who ran the country for long periods free from the need to explain their actions.

Meanwhile, at the Yalta Conference in early 1945, Churchill, Roosevelt and Stalin agreed terms for the Soviet declaration of war on Japan. These included Western recognition of the status quo in Mongolia (ie: quasi-independence under Soviet control). In October 1945, the United Nations held a plebiscite in Mongolia, organised by the Mongolian authorities to satisfy China, in which there was an overwhelming vote for independence. In January 1946, China accepted this and finally recognised the MPR. Ironically it took Mongolia 16 years to join the United Nations. In 1949, on the founding of the People's Republic of China (PRC), Mongolia transferred its recognition to the People's Republic. Marshal Choibalsan died in 1952 and Stalin died in 1953. After Choibalsan's death Mongolia was ruled by Tsedenbal, the MPRP secretary general (first secretary) from 1940 to 1954 and 1959 to 1984, and concurrently prime minister (1952–74) and president (1974–84) of Mongolia.

DAMDINY SÜKHBAATAR

Damdiny Sükhbaatar was a young, gallant people's warrior of the 1921 revolution. Born in 1893, he came from a poor family; he had great ability as a military leader and in 1921 was appointed commander in chief of the Mongolian People's Revolutionary Army. A brave fighter and an inspirational leader, Sükhbaatar became 'Hero of the Revolution', but died two years later (1923) in mysterious circumstances at the age of 30. He set the course of the Mongol revolution towards loyalty to the Russian alliance. In his honour Urga, the capital, was renamed Ulaanbaatar (meaning 'Red Hero'). However. Sükhbaatar's monument still stands there and is a focal meeting point in the city.

THE BATTLE OF KHALKHYN GOL (NOMONHAN)

John Colvin

The Battle of Khalkhyn Gol (Nomonhan), fought in 1939 on the Manchurian–Mongol border, ended Japanese ambitions to control Siberia. Japan's real objectives, it would seem, were to create a buffer state between the port of Vladivostok and Lake Baikal and to integrate the Siberian economy with Japan's. It is one of the most important battles of modern history, taking place only weeks before the outbreak of World War II. The Japanese desire to enlarge their territory by conquering Russia was an appalling dream, if the voices of the Japanese casualties (20,000 men) of the Battle of Khalkhyn Gol could be heard. The shattering defeat of the numerically superior Imperial Kwantung Japanese Army by Russian/Mongol forces marked the end of Japan's search for raw materials and their hopes of expansion in the north. Russia and Japan signed a non-aggression pact. Instead of 'planting the flag in the Urals and watering their horses on the Volga', the outcome of this little-known but decisive battle meant that, from 1940, the Japanese army concentrated its expansion plans on nations to the south. Thus Burma, Malaya, Singapore, Indochina, the East Indies and the Philippines were invaded and the flags of colonial powers like the British and Dutch were lowered. The Mongols have always regarded their geopolitical position as central to Soviet requirements and this battle proved it. Had they sided against the Russians, history would have been dramatically different. All this Japanese history prefers to forget and nowadays refers only to the Battle of Khalkhyn Gol as a border incident. The victory for the Russians allowed them to move their Far Eastern forces west, and to inflict defeat upon Germany.

For further details of this extraordinary battle, see John Colvin *Nomonhan* Quartet Books, 1999.

Building socialism In 1940, Mongolia had predominately a nomadic livestock-raising economy, but in the post-war years herding was collectivised, arable farming was expanded and mining and light industry developed considerably. The Trans-Mongolian Railway linking the USSR and PRC was put into operation in 1955. The Mongolian coat of arms, showing the heads of the 'five animals' and mounted herdsman, was redesigned to show a cog-wheel and wheatsheaf, symbols of industry, agriculture and progress. The goal was to transform Mongolia into an 'industrial-agricultural' nation. By the mid 1950s, collectivisation began to work. Although Mongolia was nominally an independent socialist state, the country depended heavily on financial help from the Soviet Union, and Soviet influence in many ways modernised the country. However, the socialist dream was ultimately to evaporate.

International status Mongolia became a member of the United Nations in 1961; a member of Comecon – the Council for Mutual Economic Assistance (CMEA) in 1962; opened diplomatic relations with the United Kingdom in 1963; and agreed a new Mutual Assistance Treaty with the USSR in 1966. Mongolia's relationship with China, which had been restored after the proclamation of the PRC, went into sharp decline during the Chinese Cultural Revolution and the Sino-Soviet ideological and territorial dispute. Tsedenbal developed a close friendship with Brezhnev, the Soviet Party general secretary and president (1964–82), and Soviet influence in Mongolia grew enormously. Mongolians benefited from this relationship in terms of the standard of living, even if the price was continued political obedience to the Kremlin.

The end of the Cold War, together with the disintegration of the Soviet Union, has fundamentally changed Mongolia's geopolitical environment. Mongolia is now a nuclear-free country with a foreign policy based on political realism, non-alignment and the pursuit of the national interest, at the same time keeping and developing good neighbourly relations.

The 1970s and 1980s Milestones of the 1970s and 1980s were diplomatic relations with Japan in 1972; new confrontations with China over territory and the role of Chinese residents; the first visit to Mongolia by the Dalai Lama in 1979; the completion of the 'Erdenet' copper mine and the first space flight by a Mongolian in 1981; and Tsedenbal's unexpected dismissal from office on grounds of ill health in 1984. In the 1980s the Soviet leader Mikhail Gorbachev's plans for *perestroika* and *glasnost* sounded the end of socialism. Most Mongols were ignorant of the new realities of the Western world. Tsedenbal's successor, President Batmönkh, sensed the need for change but could not deliver. The Berlin Wall collapsed.

The 1990s Mongolia set up legal and constitutional institutions to become a democracy in a peaceful process which brought Mongols into contact with the modern world. The 1990s may be called the 'decade of change' in Mongolia.

The 21st century In July 2008 riots erupted in the capital leaving hundreds injured and five dead. The riots sparked when the opposition accused the governing party of rigging the elections. It was boom times in Ulaanbaatar and the country was beginning to tap into its enormous mineral wealth. This preceded the election of Prime Minister Enkhbayar the following year. He was succeeded by Batbold prior to the disastrous winter of 2010 when millions of valuable livestock died due to frost and cold. In 2011 new mining business deals resulted in a combined

'THE DECADE OF CHANGE': A TRANSITION PERIOD, 1990–2000

Huge changes happened in Mongolia during the 1990s – the transition period after Mongolia's decision to become a democracy and the fall of the Soviet Empire. For most of the 20th century, under the domination of Soviet Russia, Mongolia was virtually closed to Westerners. The year 1990 was the turning point in its modern history, when the country sought political independence, political and economic reform and an independent foreign policy. Two years later a new democratic constitution was adopted. In June 1992, voters in remote areas rode or drove to polling stations throughout the land to return brimming ballot boxes in a turnout of 85%.

During the decade of change, social security systems fell to pieces, unable to keep pace with the rapid political changes that reduced many people to unemployment and poverty in the towns, while natural catastrophes, such as the severe summer droughts and freezing winters of recent years, caused great livestock losses that have brought severe hardship to the rural population. New measures to cope more satisfactorily with the distribution of fodder in times of need have now been authorised by the Mongolian government, and this should help alleviate some of the stress which the herders have had to shoulder over extra severe winters.

ownership of the rich Oyu Tolgoi copper mine located in the south Gobi, with 34% of the mine owned by the Mongolian state – the main shareholder continued to be Rio Tinto. Coal deposits were developed in South Gobi with Japanese funding – but are now 100% owned by SouthGobi Resources – a Mongolian company.

Parliamentary elections in 2012 delivered a majority for the Democratic Party, which went on to form a coalition 'reform government' with the Mongolian People's Revolutionary Party. Former president Enkhbayar received a four-year jail sentence for corruption, which led to the Mongolian People's Revolutionary Party threatening to leave the coalition. That year the ninth Bogd Khan died. Changes in society such as housing development resulted due to the mining boom, with many new domestic and commercial buildings transforming the capital. The presidential elections held in 2013 returned President Elbegdorj to office in June that year, which kept the Democratic Party in power.

The demands of a different age are producing sweeping changes throughout the country, although the concern of many Mongolians is to keep their cultural and herding traditions alive as roads begin to cut into, and destroy, the grasslands. Vast as these grasslands are, the development will change the lives of the few who live there.

THE PROVINCES (AIMAGS)

The territory of Mongolia is currently divided into 21 provinces (*aimags*) and the capital territory (Ulaanbaatar City). Each province is further divided into rural districts (*sum*), usually around 15 to 20. In this guide the provinces are grouped into five regions: central, southern, northern, western and eastern. Some national parks and protected areas cross provincial boundaries, and are noted in more than one province. A map of these areas can be found on the opposite page. The major parks are covered more fully under the relevant aimags.

The guide concentrates on the most-visited provinces relating to Mongolia's 'Circuit'. The classical routes which make up the 'Golden Circuit' take you to the Orkhon Valley via the central provinces of Töv, Övörkhangai and Arkhangai, to Lake Khövsgöl in Khövsgöl Province, and to the South Gobi, Ömnögobi Aimag – usually via Ulaanbaatar, where road and flight connections are more easily managed.

POLITICS

The tenth anniversary of Mongolia's democratic reform was marked on 10 December 2000. Ten years previously democracy in Mongolia grew from a meeting of the Mongolian Democratic Union. This turned into a demonstration of thousands of people in Ulaanbaatar on a square now known as Liberty Square. In the second decade of the 21st century democracy is still new and fragile but on the whole political reforms have succeeded and Mongolia has been transformed into a free market capitalist system.

20TH-CENTURY BACKGROUND In 1911 Mongolia declared its independence but Russia and China allowed it autonomy only. China sent in troops in an attempt to reassert its rule following the Russian Revolution of 1917, but was defeated by units of Red Russians and revolutionary Mongol troops in 1921. A short-lived restoration of the traditional feudal Buddhist monarchy was followed in 1924 by the declaration of a People's Republic under the Mongolian People's Revolutionary Party (MPRP).

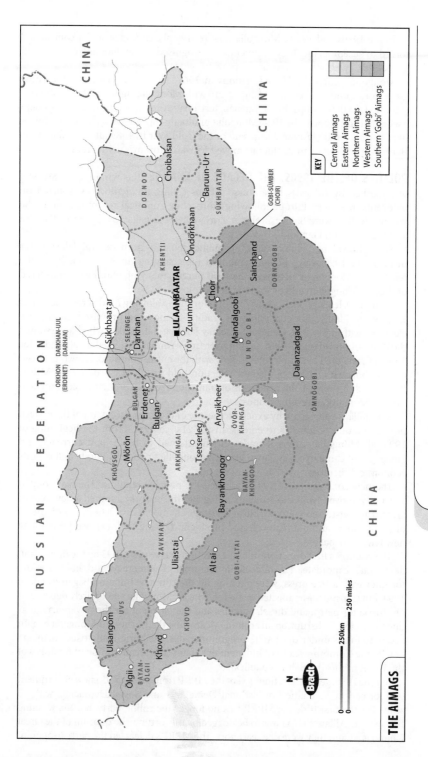

THE AIMAGS

KEY

Central Aimags
Eastern Aimags
Northern Aimags
Western Aimags
Southern 'Gobi' Aimags

CHINA

CHINA

CHINA

RUSSIAN FEDERATION

Choibalsan

DORNOD

Baruun-Urt

SÜKHBAATAR

KHENTII

Öndörkhaan

GOBI-SÜMBER (CHOIR)

Sainshand

DORNOGOBI

Choir

Sükhbaatar

DARKHAN-UUL (DARHAN)

SELENGE

Darkhan

■ULAANBAATAR

Zuunmod

TÖV

Mandalgobi

DUNDGOBI

ORKHON (ERDENET)

Erdenet

BULGAN

Bulgan

Dalanzadgad

ÖMNÖGOBI

KHÖVSGÖL

Mörön

ARKHANGAI

Tsetserleg

Arvaikheer

ÖVÖR-KHANGAY

Bayankhongor

BAYAN-KHONGOR

ZAVKHAN

Uliastai

GOBI-ALTAI

Altai

KHOVD

Ulaangom

UVS

Khovd

BAYAN-ÖLGII

Ölgii

N

Bradt

0   250km
0   250 miles

Background Information   POLITICS

1

35

In the 1920s and 1930s, Mongolia was steadily placed under Soviet control and forced to accept its ideology. China finally recognised Mongolian independence in 1946, after a plebiscite in favour the previous year. Mongolia joined the United Nations in 1961. As Soviet relations with China grew worse, under a new friendship treaty with Mongolia signed in 1966, Moscow stationed 75,000 troops in Mongolian territory. After the removal of President Tsedenbal from power in 1984 Mongolia gradually moved towards its own forms of *perestroika* and *glasnost*. At the end of the Cold War in 1989 after the fall of the Berlin Wall, Mongolian democrats moved forwards towards democracy.

POLITICS OF THE 1990S: THE DECADE OF CHANGE
The winter of 1989/1990 was marked by (illegal) student associations calling for democracy, spurred on by events in eastern Europe following Gorbachev's political reforms. Among the young idealists were Sanjaasürengiin Zorig (see box, page 38), Erdeniin Bat-Üül and Davaadorjiin Ganbold.

The removal of Stalin's statue by public demand from central Ulaanbaatar in February 1990 was a potent symbol of the changing times, especially for the relatives of Mongolian victims of the 1930 purges, many of whom were murdered or died in Mongolian and Siberian prison camps.

Mongolia's leaders, seeing the wind of reform was blowing hard across the Soviet Empire, decided to adopt a policy of gradual change and promised multi-party elections within months. General Secretary Jambyn Batmönkh, who had assumed the office of president in 1984 (taking over from Yumjaagiyn Tsedenbal, leader for 30 years), resigned in March 1990 – along with the entire politburo. He was replaced by Gombojavyn Ochirbat. A general election held in July was won by the MPRP. By the end of the year the principles of transition from a command economy to a market economy were agreed upon.

Mongolia is considered by experts to be one of the most successful of the eastern post-communist countries to emerge in the 21st century. From the beginning of 1991, all Mongolia's external trade settlements had to be in hard currency and Soviet credit came to a halt. Japan granted Mongolia financial aid to help it over its economic difficulties.

The new constitution of 1992 abolished the people's republic. The five-pointed star was removed from the Mongolian flag and the country adopted a new coat of arms. The constitution also established a single chamber Great Khural (parliament) of 76 members and a directly elected president. During the next two years many new laws were passed.

The country's first direct presidential election was won in 1993 by the opposition democrat's candidate, Punsalmaagiin Ochirbat. Democracy and liberalisation, together with a free press, were opening up the country. Inflation began to fall in 1994, but transport was affected by fuel shortages. Mongolia was entirely dependent on Russia for petrol and diesel. Supplies and the payment for them were irregular due to economic disruption all around. Meanwhile the EU helped Mongolia to gain access to funds under the TACIS programme, designed originally to aid members of CIS, the Commonwealth of Independent States (the former union of republics of the USSR minus the Baltic republics).

In June 1996, general elections swept the MPRP from power and a new government was formed by a coalition of National Democrats and Social Democrats with 50 seats. For the first time the MPRP was no longer the ruling party, but the winning Democratic Alliance (DA) was to be dogged by misfortune: the quorum of the Great Khural is 51 and they were one seat short. The MPRP's defeat led the party to appoint a younger, more dynamic, general secretary, Nambaryn Enkhbayar, and the second presidential election in 1997 was won by the MPRP candidate, Natsagiin Bagabandi.

POLITICS IN THE 21ST CENTURY In 2000, the MPRP won the election with an overwhelming majority. However within four years the political situation changed dramatically. The fourth parliamentary elections were held on 27 June 2004. The MPRP was widely expected to win, but the unofficial results showed that both the MPRP and Motherland Democracy Coalition (MDC) had won 36 seats each. The Republican Party won a single seat and three independents with close ties to the Coalition won the remaining three seats.

Talks between the MPRP and the MDC led to an agreement to form a 'grand coalition' government of national unity. Tsakhiagiin Elbegdorj was appointed prime minister and Nambaryn Enkhbayar was elected chairman of the Great Khural (speaker). The new government was approved by parliament and sworn in on 28 September 2004. However, on 11 January 2006, ten ministers of the MPRP, who formed a majority in the cabinet (ten of 18), resigned in protest at the country's domestic political course. This ended the coalition government of the MPRP, Democratic Party and other smaller parties (the MDC).

Tsakhiagiin Elbegdorj (Democratic Party) stepped down as prime minister. The MPRP subsequently gained agreement from other small political parties to form a new coalition government, with Miyegombo Enkhbold as prime minister. Until early November 2007, he led the 'national solidarity' government with three different political parties including the MPRP, the Motherland Party and the National New Party. In June 2006, the MPRP won a by-election giving it a majority of one seat in parliament. In October 2007 Enkhbold lost the chairmanship of the MPRP to Sanjaagiin Bayar, who took over as prime minister in September. On 1 July 2008, riots occurred in the capital following demonstrations accusing the government of rigging the Great Khural elections; the HQ of the MPRP was set on fire, and President Enkhbayar declared martial law for a short period. Bayar proposed a joint government with the DP leader and Elbegdorj won the presidential elections in May 2009. Sükhbaataryn Batbold, who in 2008 had won a seat in the Great Khural and was appointed Minister of External Relations, replaced Bayar as Prime Minister in October 2009 and in April 2010 was elected chairman of the MPRP.

In November 2010 the MPRP Congress confirmed Batbold's chairmanship and resolved to revert to the party's previous name – the Mongolian People's Party (1921–25). Members who opposed this move, including the former president and prime minister Nambaryn Enkhbayar, left the MPP taking with them the name MPRP, which they managed to register officially in January 2011, despite opposition from the MPP. In January 2012 DP chairman Altankhuyag broke up the

1

ONGOL ULSYN IKH KHURAL (MONGOLIAN GENERAL ASSEMBLY)

The government, elected for four years, comprises the prime minister and cabinet members. The prime minister is nominated by the president in consultation with the majority party and voted into office by the Ikh Khural, which then discusses individually each of the ministerial candidates proposed by the prime minister and votes on the appointments. Political parties with seats in the Ikh Khural may nominate presidential candidates. The president is elected for a four-year term and can be re-elected once.

SANJAASÜRENGIIN ZORIG

In 1998, at the age of 36, Sanjaasürengiin Zorig was murdered in his home by persons unknown and never found. He was the nation's father of democracy, and was referred to as 'Mr Democracy'. Born in 1962, he graduated from Moscow State University and became a lecturer at the Mongolian State University. He abandoned Marxism/Leninism to found the Mongolian Democratic Association in December 1989 and later founded the Mongolian Republican Party in 1991. The Mongolian Democratic Association and other parties merged in October 1992 to form the Mongolian National Democratic Party. Zorig was a member of the Great Khural from 1990; he was appointed Minister of Infrastructure and Development in May 1998 and was expected by some to become Mongolia's next prime minister after Elbegdorj lost a vote of confidence in July. Zorig's death was a sad loss to the country's political life. A statue to commemorate him stands beside the Democratic Party youth organisation building, opposite the Central Post Office in Ulaanbaatar. His sister Oyuun founded a new political party, the Citizens Will (*Irgenii Zorig*), to commemorate him, and became its chairman.

'joint government' with the MPP in preparation for the June elections to the Great Khural. These were won by the Democratic Party, which, however, was obliged to form a coalition with 'Justice' (The MPRP and Mongolian National Democratic Party) and the newly amalgamated Citizens Will-Green Party led by Sanjaaurengiin Oyunn, who was appointed Minister of Environment and Green Development in the new government.

In April 2012 MPRP Chairman Nambaryn Enkhbayar (who had served as Mongolian president, speaker and prime minister) was arrested and detained for two months during investigation for failing to respond to summons. He was released pending trial, but was refused registration as a candidate in the Great Khural election. In August he was tried and found guilty of corrupt property deals and sentenced to six years imprisonment, reduced on appeal to four.

Parliamentary elections were held in June 2012. The DP led by Altankhuyag agreed to form a coalition government with populist fringe parties, because they were eight short of an overall majority.

The presidential election of 2013 saw the incumbent President Tsakhiajiin Elbegdorj re-elected. Elbegdorj's main challenger was B Bat-Erdene (MPP), a former champion wrestler, and the third candidate, Natsag Udval (MPRP), was Mongolia's first woman presidential contestant and current health minister.

The discovery of Mongolia's mineral wealth and its development since 2008 has given the country's economy a huge boost. However the market system has yet to make inroads on poverty and unemployment levels. The pace of reform, although slow, is improving dramatically. In 20 years' time Mongolia will be a totally different country in terms of its infrastructure – with improved and new roads, and sections of new railways strengthening the existing fragile transport system and creating closer links between the capital and the aimags.

SOCIAL DEVELOPMENT AND CHANGE

The Mongols have either to modernise their society... or perish

Owen Lattimore, American Mongol scholar (1900–89)

The 21st century opened with the usual concerns about corruption, poverty, unemployment, crime, alcoholism, domestic violence, street children, health, education and other pressing issues. Communication with the outside world has greatly improved in recent years, due, in part, to the global internet explosion which provides broader access to world markets and is a source of information for everyone everywhere, including Mongolia. Mobile phone use has changed the lives of so many people worldwide. On the ground there is also greater mobility abroad for government officials and businessmen and women. Another encouraging factor is the government's co-operation with NGOs to carry out a range of social programmes. Regarding social issues, the government intends to triple the minimum wage and double the salaries of civil servants, and reduce the tax burden on businesses by 30%. From 2003 to 2006 the average GDP was 8.7%; in 2007 it grew at 9.9%, slowing slightly to around 9% in 2008 and 2009. Between 2009 and 2013 the GDP shot up to between 12% and 17% and steadied around 14% in 2013.

The political swings and roundabouts of rapidly changing governance in the 1990s showed how the transition from a command-style economy to a market-orientated one placed additional pressure on the rural economy, leading to economic difficulties and widespread poverty. People moved away from the cities to the countryside in the early 1990s when, with the political upheavals and the collapse of the formerly subsidised state-owned industries, they could no longer find jobs. This situation appears to have been reversed at the start of the 21st century, due to the severe winters of 2000/01 and 2009/10, and people are heading back to the settlements and towns. Alongside the population drift there were major human-development concerns, such as food security and the improvement of women's health, childcare and education.

A middle ground has developed, whereby some women of herding families, living near towns, have set up a shop or a restaurant which they supply from their own produce. This is a welcome change as women are coming into their own in business. However, it is a situation which also means that many less-educated Mongolian men are being left behind (especially in the countryside because they work with livestock). Both in the city and in the countryside, educated women are beginning to advance in the modern world and although schools are co-educational, women have been quicker to pick up on the more subtle modernising values of the entrepreneurial world in which they are now placed.

CHANGE AND THE PEOPLE Recently Mongolian women have organised themselves into a new women's movement called the Liberal Women's Brain Pool (LWBP), also referred to as the Liberal Women's Intellectual Foundation. It is a women's movement which arose like a phoenix from the ashes of the communist period. From the 1990s, independent citizens' groups began to take charge and become instruments of change with more success than many government initiatives.

The LWBP was established in 1992 and has branches throughout the country. A high percentage of Mongolia's graduates are women. The underlying reason seems to be that women were usually housebound and, although they were often looking after young children, many of them also had more opportunity to study than men, who did office or manual work in the towns and outdoor work like herding in the countryside. Despite this, men predominately govern the country and are involved in most of the decision making. The 2012 parliamentary elections which planned a new 20% quota for women in parliament resulted in nine women gaining seats.

MILLENNIUM CHALLENGE AGREEMENT WITH MONGOLIA

Dr Nancy S Tokola

The US Congress passed the Millennium Challenge Act of 2003 in order 'to provide United States assistance for global development through the Millennium Challenge Corporation' – the MCC, which was formally established in January 2004. The mission of the MCC is 'to reduce global poverty through the promotion of sustainable economic growth'.

The four key principles of the MCC are as follows:

* Reducing poverty through economic growth (investments in transportation, water and industrial infrastructure, agriculture, education, private sector development, and capacity building)
* Good policies matter (governing justly, investing in citizens, encouraging economic freedoms, and fighting corruption)
* Operate as partners (identifying the barriers to development, identifying the responsibilities of each partner, and ensuring civil society participation)
* Focus on results (programmes with clear objectives, benchmarks to measure progress, procedures to ensure fiscal accountability, plans for effective monitoring, and plans for objective evaluation)

The MCC assesses the eligibility of developing nation-states for assistance according to per-capita income ceilings of the International Development Association, as defined by the International Bank for Reconstruction and Development. The two categories of eligibility are: Low Income Country and Lower Middle Income Country. On 6 May 2004, the MCC named Mongolia as an eligible Low Income Country, and Mongolia began the long process of developing its MCC programme proposal.

Finally, on 22 October 2007, the president of Mongolia signed the MCC Compact in Washington, DC. The approximately US$285 million of MCC funding is allocated as follows: Rail Project (US$188.38 million); Property Rights Project (US$23.06 million); Vocational Education Project (US$25.51 million); Health Project (US$17.03 million, focusing on reduction of non-communicable diseases and injuries especially in the labour force); administration costs (US$26.3 million); and monitoring and evaluation costs (US$4.7 million). Mongolia has a population of approximately 2.6 million people, and the MCC will directly reach 1.5 million beneficiaries through the property rights, vocational education, and health projects. On-going reports on progress, development and changes, may be found on the website below.

SOURCES

www.mcc.gov
www.mcc.gov/press/releases/2007/release-091207-boarddecisions.php
www.mcc.gov/countries/mongolia/index.php

The feminisation of society is a hotly debated issue among the student population and in the Mongolian press. While the numbers of women who do well at university continues to rise, male student numbers have fallen dramatically. In 2000, the Faculty of Journalism enrolled 1,150 students of which 900 were girls, while medical students are over 80% female and this trend has continued. For the first time, a female candidate, Natsag Udval, was nominated by her party (MPRP) in the presidential elections of 2013.

One imagines Mongolian men to be the warrior type, bold and fierce and macho. This is true, but some men have suffered an identity crisis, finding themselves out of work due to migration to towns from the countryside and other changes and, as a consequence, lost their self-esteem. Some have turned to alcohol and gambling (although they also drank plenty in the former socialist days).

The transition to a market economy was very abrupt and did not give people enough time to adjust. In general, Mongolian women have more experience in dealing with the family's financial affairs, leaving the men feeling inadequate. As one woman said, 'Men are sitting on our shoulders. I wouldn't mind if they would sit steady and not kick so much.' In the 21st century it is everyone for himself/herself.

PROBLEMS WITH HEALTH AND EDUCATION SYSTEMS Twenty years ago literacy was not a problem in Mongolia – nearly everyone aged eight to 80 could read and write. However, new figures show a drop in literacy. Again, the transfer from a command to a free-market economy has meant that often children skip school because their parents need their labour; other reasons are that they are either too far away or cannot afford the costs of books and courses. UNICEF education programmes are helping to remedy this, as well as a World Bank supported project

EDUCATION – TRAINING AND EMPLOYMENT

Big business in Mongolia has committed to helping to provide training and support for students – particularly those involved in engineering and in the mining industry. Rio Tinto, the majority shareholder of the Oyu Tolgoi copper project, located in the south Gobi, is not only a source of economic growth, bringing infrastructure development, but the company is also providing training, education and jobs. In 2013 they employed around 3,500 people, plus a construction workforce of more than 14,000. More recent cut backs and delays in operations at Oyu Tolgoi in 2013 and in 2014 led to some significant job losses.

To meet the demand of skilled workers, Rio Tinto has invested in local communities through a variety of initiatives. They include scholarships, contributions and internships. Education and training will enable the company to meet its commitment to 90% Mongolian employment in the future.

Other sponsorship includes training for medical doctors to live and work in remote parts of Gobi; sponsorship of English-language instruction in Dalanzadgad and Rio Tinto-provided university scholarships to more than 45 high-potential students through the Zorig Foundation. These scholarships provide support to promising young students as they pursue university degrees at local Mongolian universities.

Oyu Tolgoi has committed US$126 million to further education in Mongolia long term. It is the single biggest financial input to education in the country, improving vocational training centres in a number of towns as well as training teachers and providing scholarships nationally and internationally.

Often, trainees go on to work in other businesses in the community or the region, and in some cases, they start their own businesses.

1

(2006) to bring books to primary schools in rural Mongolia (*www.worldbank.org/ en/news/feature/2013/09/19/building-mongolia-future-with-books*).

Health services, which practically disappeared when the Russians walked out, are in need of improvement. Before 1921 there was no modern medicine and Mongolians relied on traditional healers, but during the communist/socialist period (1921–90) the improvements in health and education were remarkable and included the rural population. Then, during the transition to democracy, people were rushed into new situations, often with little training and few skills to cope.

STUDENT LIFE IN THE COLD WAR DAYS (IN THE LATE 1970S)

Jeremy Halford

I arrived in Ulaanbaatar on a mid-winter's day in the middle of the Cold War to study Mongol history. But my steepest learning curve, I soon found, lay in how to deal with the elements. I learnt that –40°C is the point where degrees centigrade equal degrees fahrenheit. However, it was ten degrees colder than even that; if you took alcohol with you to warm you on forays into the countryside, you had about 90 seconds to drink it once poured, before it froze over. Shortly before, a Western ambassador who shall remain nameless had sought to remove the ice from his embassy's car park by spraying steaming hot water on it – within two minutes he had created a perfectly smooth ice-skating rink which kept his vehicles grounded for two months!

The People's Republic of All Peaceable Mongols, as it was then known, formed the strategic fence between Beijing and Siberia. But the Mongols did not have the luxury of sitting on it and had fallen firmly within the Soviet camp. Theirs was the first state to which the adjective 'satellite' has been applied by foreign commentators. In Ulaanbaatar, in scenes which would have been familiar to anyone who had seen colonialism in action, Russians had their own housing blocks, their own stores (replete with goods Mongols could only dream of) and their own buses. Non-Russians were not admitted.

Outside the Academy of Sciences, where I was to work, stood one of the few remaining statues of Stalin in the world. It set the political tone of the state. The Communist Party ruled and was seen to rule. Its flagship newspaper, *Unen* (meaning 'truth', as does the Russian word *pravda*), brooked no dissent and few foreign journalists received visas, so alternative views did not receive an airing. My Mongol-language teacher at the university once made an engaging attempt to justify this rigidity: 'Imagine that the only people from your country that foreigners had heard of were Attila the Hun and Genghis Khan. Wouldn't you be cautious about what image you let be projected?'

To return from the academy to the student hostel that was my home involved traversing the huge expanse of Sükhbaatar Square. To do so after midnight could be enervating. The only sounds were your footsteps and the barking of packs of wild dogs or wolves which could be heard and sometimes glimpsed through the ice fog, circling lone pedestrians as they hurried on their way. An additional hazard was that these animals had become such a menace that the police had been armed with rifles and offered a bounty for each one shot. Sometimes pot-shots from the corners of the square punctuated the night air. Fortunately, standards of Mongol marksmanship had not suffered in the transition from bows to carbines.

Sadly, in the city, contact between Mongols and Western foreigners was restricted from the Mongol side as a matter of policy. Those that there were were

The Beehive Project This was initiated by the Government of Mongolia to promote the return of overseas educated Mongolians. Over 200,000 students train abroad. The appeal, directly from the prime minister, in 2012, was for students, especially those studying medicine and engineering, to return home.

Ten years have seen many changes and huge improvements at management level. The main health services are still state-run, even if there are a few private doctors and hospitals, but there is still a long way to go to develop Mongolia's health and education services and, in general, its infrastructure.

often monitored and many that might have been were no doubt nipped in the bud by the understandable reluctance of Mongols to draw unwanted attention upon themselves from the authorities. So the handful of Westerners mingled with other nationalities in a cosmopolitan melting pot: it was not unknown for parties to include ten people speaking variously in seven or eight languages. On special occasions, a visit to one of the two discos in the main hotels might take place. But woe betide those who did not take their own tapes as the discos usually only had one each of their own. Little did Boney M know that they had made it to the top of the unofficial Mongol charts. 'Ra-Ra-Rasputin' never sounded so good.

Getting food was a major concern unless you were as avid a meat eater as the Mongols. Even if you were, you could still have problems. Meat was specified by the name of the beast and a quality grade between one and three (the latter the lowest grade). Horse Grade 3, I soon discovered, was so tough that my Western teeth couldn't even rip pieces off the hunk provided with a view to trying extended chewing later on. At weekends you could visit an unofficial market to the north of the city, where members of the city's small Chinese community sold home-grown vegetables. Every few months, deliveries occurred of exotica such as Vietnamese pineapples and we feasted for weeks afterwards. On one occasion, I was invited to the opening of Mongolia's first supermarket. Along with the worthies, I marvelled at the long aisles stacked with cans of food. Only when I walked all the way round did I discover that they were only selling three different products in the whole shop.

As winter passed into summer, a three-week trip by truck was offered and seized upon by those wishing to see something of the steppe and Gobi. Many memorable evenings ensued under the felt roofing of Mongol *gers* as we drank the evenings away, experimented with fermented goat's milk and listened to the haunting melodies of '*khöömii*' two-tone singing. Even the presence of official minders could not keep the warmth and hospitality of the Mongol herders from breaking through. A message to the wise traveller, however: in a country with virtually no roads, take thick-soled (preferably parachuting) boots. One of my fellow travellers was thrown fully out of the back of the truck when we hit a particularly big bump. He sailed through the air and landed upright and looking very bemused in the middle of the road about 20ft behind us.

All too soon it was over. I returned to Britain, a small-scale Rip van Winkle who had heard nothing of the outside world for six months. My ignorance soon showed. A passing acquaintance on the bus back from the airport asked if I had seen *Saturday Night Fever*, then all the rage. 'What's *Saturday Night Fever*?' I asked.

She looked appalled: 'Where have you been? In Outer Mongolia?'

'Ah,' I replied.

VULNERABILITY OF CHILDREN IN MONGOLIA

Dr Nancy S Tokola

Childhood is the most vulnerable part of life, and children growing up in poverty-entrenched environments are especially at risk. Vulnerable children need protection by the adults and institutions in their societies. The Year 2000 United Nations Millennium Declaration emphasises 'Protecting the Vulnerable' by respecting international humanitarian law and international human rights law.

Child protection issues in Mongolia include: child labourers (working as herders or in mines, markets, and waste disposal sites); children with disabilities; children without carers (neglected, abandoned, orphaned, and street children); children exploited through juvenile sex work; trafficked children; children as victims of crime (domestic and non-domestic violence); and children as perpetrators of crime (leading to incarceration in detention centres and prisons).

According to the United Nations Children's Fund (UNICEF), there are two classifications of street children. 'Children **in** the street' are out of school while interacting on the street during the day for socialising or for procuring resources, but then these vulnerable children return to their parental homes during the night – bringing home expected money from begging, working, or stealing. 'Children **of** the street' live on the street 24 hours per day seven days per week and may have no contact with any family members. According to the Christina Noble Foundation this situation has greatly improved since 2010 and there are far fewer street children in UB. The Child Address Identification Centre (CAIC) in Ulaanbaatar operates under the juvenile division of the General Police Department, under the Ministry of Justice. The police social workers register new street children who are not yet experienced enough to escape police round-up operations. Mongolia has care centres (eight state-operated and 24 internationally operated), which help children who are not under the supervision of a parent, other relative, or guardian.

The government of Mongolia is committed to promoting child rights through its Law on the Protection of Children's Rights. Furthermore, the government is committed to reducing child vulnerability through its National Programme of Action for the Development and Protection of Children, which is aligned with the United Nations initiative called A World Fit for Children through the contextualised initiative A Mongolia Fit for Children. The Millennium Development Goals (MDGs) have a deadline in 2015. What happens next? Please follow the global debate known as 'post-2015' debate. www.unicef.org.uk

SOURCES

UNICEF *The Millennium Development Goals: They Are About Children* New York, 2003

Government of Mongolia *First National Summit on Child Issues, The Mongolian National Programme of Action on the Development and Protection of Children* Ulaanbaatar, 2004

www.gmfc.org (Global Movement for Children (GMC))

www.unicef.org/specialsession/wffc/ (World Fit for Children (WFFC))

Both the health and education services were severely hit by the budgetary restrictions of recent years, with cuts of 24% and 53% respectively in real terms since 1990. There has been a decline in the number of clinics, primary schools and kindergartens, a cutback of staff, and a shortage of teachers and basic teaching materials. However, infant mortality has decreased since 1990.

A particular source of concern in the countryside is a lack of safe drinking water, as well-water in Mongolia contains a high concentration of mineral salts and basic sanitation. The average life expectancy is 68 years (in 2011). Regarding nutrition, while protein levels remain high there is a lack of vitamins and minerals – especially vitamin D, and iron deficiency is high among mothers and children. Throughout the country, berries have traditionally provided a much-needed source of vitamin C.

CHRISTINA NOBLE CHILDREN'S FOUNDATION (CNCF) IN MONGOLIA

CNCF provides education to children in the Boys and Girls' Prison who have been imprisoned mainly because of poverty-related crimes. A sponsorship programme seeks to prevent children ending up on the streets by providing financial assistance to destitute families, enabling a child to remain living at home and in full-time education. A US$24 monthly contribution can change the life of a child and provide them with security to complete their education and therefore bring them a step nearer to breaking the cycle of poverty. The healthcare programme provides life-saving medical assistance and treatment to children and their siblings on the sponsorship programme.

There was a serious issue with children living in manholes and underground up until about 2010. At the height of the problem in 2006 there were an estimated 1300 street children in UB. The government, in partnership with international organisations and NGO's, have made great efforts over the last several years to address this problem and the efforts have been extremely successful to the point that CNCF had to cease its mobile night-clinic project as there were so few street children left. Over the last three years the manhole covers have been welded shut. In Ulaanbaatar it is now very rare to see a street child or any children begging. There are a number of state run shelters that are not overcrowded as reunification with the family is the government's key priority. In 2009, when Ivanhoe Mines and the Mongolian government signed the stability agreement, a lot of foreign direct investment began pouring into Mongolia and the government finally had the funding to address a lot of the social and infrastructure issues. Due to this influx of cash, the government began providing every Mongolian child a small stipend each month. This also helped get the children off the streets and back with relatives or friends.

Mongolia has now become far more accessible to travellers, and more and more young people are visiting. In recent years CNCF has been one of the official charities of the Mongol Rally; the rally starts in Hyde Park, London and finishes in Ulaanbaatar, and as well as being a huge adventure, the participants raise funds for many deserving charities including CNCF with projects in Mongolia. CNCF Mongolia has received many visitors from the rally teams and welcomes visits to its *Ger* Village.

CNCF *PO Box 2150, Ulaanbaatar 2112 13;* \ *+976 11 315611;* e *mongolia@ cncf. org; UK office: 11–15 Lillie Rd, West Brompton, London SW6 1TX;* \ *020 7381 8550;* e *uk@cncf.org; www.cncf.org*

THE WORLD BANK AND THE ENVIRONMENT IN MONGOLIA

Dr Tony Whitten

The World Bank (*www.worldbank.mn*) pursues an integrated and holistic approach to poverty reduction, which seeks to prevent environmental degradation.

Over the last ten years in Mongolia the World Bank has been strengthening government and civil society efforts to improve the environment as a core part of its agenda. This is translating into preventing pollution, conserving biodiversity, co-ordinating activities of different donors and galvanising new ways to support awareness to preserve Mongolia's treasures. Through a large number of grants it has supported improved urban stoves and a new air pollution management project, local-language field guides to plants, mammals and birds, a major research project on permafrost melt and biodiversity loss around Lake Khövsgöl (*www.hovsgolecology.org*), work with Buddhist communities on environmental management (*www. buddhistecology.org*), facilitating a co-ordinating web database on all donor-funded environment projects in Mongolia (*www.domo.mn*), support for barbless-hook fishing of the huge *taimen* salmon to encourage responsible sport fishing (*www.taimen.org*), support for consultations prior to the passing of the new toxic chemicals and protected areas laws, innovative work uncovering the extent of the illegal wildlife and timber trades, a natural resources strategy for the Gobi region, an assessment of the threats facing the rare Asiatic ass (search 'khulan' and 'World Bank' on YouTube), and a new project on forest landscapes and their conservation.

There has also been a very successful US$1 million small-grants programme arranged through the Open Society Forum (OSF) (*www.forum. mn*) and the Ministry of Environment and Green Development. This aims to enhance national and local environmental performance, to strengthen public environmental awareness and to develop strategic environmental plans at a local level. More than 400 applications were received from NGOs, private companies and research teams. From these, 62 proposals were selected. Small grants for the environment have also been provided through its Development Marketplace.

Although nutrition has improved in the city, it is still a problem in rural areas where it undermines health.

POVERTY ALLEVIATION Government poverty programmes have suffered from financial constraints facing the country in general. At the turn of the 21st century, people living below the poverty line constituted almost a third of Mongolia's population, over half of them in urban areas. Street children have appeared and begging is now commonplace – it is worth being wary of pickpockets, both children and adults, in public places such as markets, buses and shops.

CHARITIES AND AID ORGANISATIONS

Ulaanbaatar Rotary Club The Rotary Club of Ulaanbaatar is the first Rotary Club founded in Mongolia. Sponsored by the Rotary Club of Shatin, Hong Kong, it was admitted into Rotary International in 1995. In 2000 it was renamed Hong Kong, Macau & Mongolia. The Rotary Club of Ulaanbaatar is English speaking & has 34 members including a number of foreign members – citizens of

USA, UK, Germany, India, Japan, Israel & Australia. It meets every Wed 12.30–14.00 at Wine House, Bayangol Hotel. In the past the club has awarded educational grants to music students, helped street children & raised funds for emergency relief work during the national *zud* disasters of recent winters. Contact: www.ubrotary.org.

Rotaract Club of Ulaanbaatar Founded in1999 under the guidance of the Rotary Club (see page 46), it is the first of its kind in Mongolia, with 30 members aged 18–30. Members are young people who are working & studying in different fields & want to contribute to the international community. The club meets

VSO – BASIC HEALTHCARE IN MONGOLIA

Josie Hinton

I arrived in Ulaanbaatar where the temperature was −30°C; the snow-topped mountains on the horizon formed a staggering backdrop to the flat landscape before me; the tall chimney tops puffed dark grey smoke into the clear blue sky; it was a landscape of contrasts. Three days later we travelled north for seven hours on a Russian sleeper train, to Sükhbaatar, a northern town, where the air was much warmer. The town was bleak and dusty, dogs wandered around in packs of three or four, young children played freely in the central square. The wooden houses, shops and towering concrete blocks of flats were painted either blue or yellow.

I lived in an apartment, near the town centre, with a family of three and Daria, my Mongolian 'counterpart'. The family spoke little English; this was a challenge, but a good way of getting an insight into Mongolian culture. Although initially language posed a barrier to the development of close relationships, taking part in family life meant that a 'family bond' soon started to form. I learnt to cook traditional Mongolian soup and how to cope with an antique, non-automatic washing machine! We exchanged family pictures and shared in each other's national traditions; I learnt how they celebrated Naadam, a traditional Mongolian sporting festival, which involves archery, riding and wrestling, and at Easter I bought them all Easter eggs.

Daria and I worked three days a week in the general hospital. Together we created health presentations and workshops on a number of themes particularly relevant to the concerns of the community, for example dental health, stomach problems and healthy living. Initially my contribution seemed unclear, as carrying out these presentations clearly required verbal communication. However we soon devised ways in which I could get involved, for instance during the dental health workshops, my job would be to demonstrate the step-by-step guide on how to brush your teeth correctly using a huge model mouth and a toothbrush; we made the workshops as creative as possible, and found fun ways in which children and adults could learn about basic health issues.

An important part of VSO's exchange programmes is the Global Citizenship Framework, designed to guide our learning about global issues: sustainability, poverty and inequality. This allowed us to examine the influence that communism has had, and continues to have, on the mentality of most of the Mongolian people I met. They are struggling to come to terms with democracy and the freedom it gives them to reflect on their past, to use their own initiative and to make choices in their own lives.

Mongolia is steeped in its own traditions and has a very strong identity. Going to a country with such a turbulent political past, but where its people remain so united, was a unique experience.

Wed 19.00–20.30. Contact: e raclub.mn@gmail.com. See www.racub.webs.com.

The English Speaking Union Dartmouth Hse, 37 Charles St, London W1J 5ED; ✆ 020 7529 1550; www.esu.org, & **ESU Mongolia** Heinii Chimeg-language Link Co Ltd, PO Box 501, Ulaanbaatar 46a; e info@esum.mn; www.esum.mn. The English Speaking Union creates global understanding through English. It is a membership organisation & educational charity. Today the ESU is represented in 47 countries in the 5 continents. It states that it is proud that Mongolia is part of the ESU family, & is consequently building bridges between cultures & geographies.

Save the Children Fund 17 Grove Lane, London SE5 8RD; ✆ 020 7703 5400; www.savethechildren.org.uk & www.savethechildrenmongolia.mn (a more interesting site!). Save the Children Fund (SCF), a non-government organisation supported by charitable donations, & the UK's leading international children's charity, has been involved in helping social work programmes operate in Mongolia since 1994. SCF has developed sustainable & appropriate models of training to make positive changes in the lives of vulnerable children & their communities. Training-needs assessment was completed in 1996 & by mid 1997 programmes were put into practice. These included working with children & families & with street children. Welfare centres & children's camps have been successfully established. SCF supports Mongolia's National Poverty Alleviation Programme (NPAP) & provided funds for a Targeted Assistance Fund (TAF), designed to provide aid to the poorest families in the community & their children. SCF works in close collaboration with the British Embassy, which it assists with the British Small Grants Scheme. The latest schemes include one to reduce the number of pupils dropping out of school, & another to integrate disabled children into ordinary kindergartens.

SMALL PROJECTS INVOLVING SOCIAL DEVELOPMENT

International aid agencies and overseas organisations have initiated many small projects in agriculture, environment, engineering, childcare, health, education and other fields. Without going into too much detail, here are some examples of typical projects:

SHUTTLE VET PROJECT In a nation with 14 head of livestock for every person, vets play a key role. One organisation, in partnership with the Mongolian Private Herders Association, developed a new model of providing veterinary care for animal health in response to the breakdown of state-provided animal-health services. The project provides practical information and training. The VetNet Project is an expansion of the Shuttle Vet Project, where the focus is on research and development of a vaccine against brucellosis, a very important public health problem in Mongolia. This programme continues strongly as VetNet is an NGO. See: www.cvmcanada.org/mongolia.html.

BLIND SCHOOL The Mongolian Association for the Blind has identified that one of the challenges facing blind people living in Ulaanbaatar are the kerbs and pavements. Paving stones are broken, there are holes in the road and the kerbs are ill defined. These problems have greatly improved in recent times. In the provinces there are some 8,000 people who are blind or partially sighted. However there is only one school for the blind in Mongolia. The Danish Association for the Blind sponsored a Massey teacher to train six young people in orientation mobility.

***GER* KINDERGARTEN PROJECT** This project has met a variety of needs of disadvantaged children and their families living in the *ger* compounds around

Voluntary Service Overseas (VSO) 317
Putney Bridge Rd, London SW15 2PN; ✆ 020
8780 7500; e enquiry@vso.org.uk; www.vso.org.
uk. VSO's programme in Mongolia aims to equip
disadvantaged Mongolians with the necessary
skills to manage the transition to democracy & a
free-market economy. It targets specific regions
where people need help. The organisation is aware
of the importance of the responsible use of natural
resources & volunteers are placed in education &
training which focuses on the environment. English-
language teaching is needed & VSO teachers work in
schools & colleges around the country. Fire-fighting
is a programme which illustrates the sort of job
VSO does (see page 157). The organisation has
volunteer members in Mongolia, in the areas of
education, health, business & social development,
& the environment. It costs VSO £25 per month to
support each volunteer in his or her work overseas.
To make a donation, call the credit-card hotline on
020 8780 7234.

**GIZ – Deutsche Gesellschaft fuer
Internationale Zusammenarbeit GmbH**
Sky Centre 14, PO Box 1264, Ulaanbaatar 21;
e gtznaturecon@magnicnet.mn; or the Mongolian
Ministry of Nature & Environment, Hydromat Bldg,
Room 119, Khudaldaany Gudamj 5, Ulaanbaatar
210646; ✆ +976 11 329323;. Literally translated as
the German Association for Technical Co-operation,
GIZ/GTZ helps to monitor work in the national
parks of Mongolia. Environmental projects include
Integrated Urban Development, Climate Change
& Biodiversity; Promotion of Renewable Energy
Resources & Energy Efficiency in the Networked
Energy supply. Also projects in legal & financial
areas.
United States Peace Corps Peace Corps
Mongolia; ✆ +976 11 311518/311580; www.
peacecorps.gov. The US Peace Corps is the largest
volunteer organisation in the world & operates in
Mongolia, where its goals are to provide technical
assistance, & programmes which allow US citizens

Ulaanbaatar. The project employs a holistic philosophy and includes education,
social care, nutrition, healthcare and a community approach to problem-solving.
See photos: http://travellingartist.wordpress.com/2012/10/22/kindergartens-in-
the-middle-of-nowhere/.

GOAT PROJECT Goats are kept mostly for cashmere production. Little attention
has been given to goat milk production. However, in the suburbs of UB, families
keep goats for milk purposes; the goat is known as the poor people's cow. There
are big problems with overgrazing as the number of goats is too great for the
amount of pasture. The aim of the project is to develop better dairy goat products
to help poor families have better nutrition and to generate income. The project
is carried out in co-operation with the Agricultural University of Ulaanbaatar. By
using cross-breeding with artificial insemination treatment, it is hoped that the
new goats will produce better milk yields.

AGRICULTURAL DEVELOPMENT IN THE GOBI-ALTAI Traditional agriculture consists of
herding animals and selling unprocessed skins, wool and meat, while new
development projects focus on arable farming, livestock/dairy management and
the setting up of small-scale family businesses. Cheese-making and other food–
processing techniques are being developed and women are being encouraged to
produce knitted items, handcrafted jewellery and other small souvenirs for sale
to tourists.

ARTISALTAI This women's group makes very high quality jewellery – you may buy
this jewellery at the Mary & Martha shop in Ulaanbaatar, or go to: www.artisaltai.
org/uk/.

1

to learn about Mongolia. Since 1991, Peace Corps volunteers have taught English, helped with environmental work & organised computer projects.

GAP-YEAR TRAVEL Those who wish to become involved in charitable projects in Mongolia during a gap year should contact Voluntary Service Overseas (see box, page 47). For eco-volunteering contact Earthwatch Institute (*www.earthwatch. org/europe*), the Steppe Forward Programme (*www.steppeforward.com*, see box, pages 122–3), or The National University of Mongolia for summer schools (see page 445).

SUMMER SCHOOLS For those who literally want to 'dig into' Mongolian culture, the Faculty of Social Sciences and other departments of the National University of Mongolia offer summer field school courses in anthropology and archaeology. Three weeks are spent in the countryside studying the culture of the nomads, visiting cultural events and historic sites. For more information, contact Dr D Tumen, Department of Anthropology and Archaeology (✎ +976 11 311671; e timen@num.edu.mn).

LANGUAGE COURSES Language courses are also on offer: a four-week course aims to introduce foreign students to special issues on Mongolian history, culture, modern socio-economic development, politics and foreign affairs. In their free time students are involved in visiting Mongolian families, cooking meals, and taking trips to the countryside – available as part of the National University of Mongolia's International Summer Programme. For more information, contact Ms T Otgontugs (✎ +976 11 320159; e rel@num.edu.mn).

ECONOMY

The three mainstays of the Mongolian economy are mining (the most important sector), agri-industry and tourism. Mongolia remains a mix of the modern and the ancient. While it is a youthful country, it was very difficult for everyone, Mongolians and foreigners alike, to keep pace with the changes in Mongolia's economy following the transition period of the 1990s into the mineral boom times of the 21st century.

Now that minerals have taken over the economy, the capital investment from overseas is growing annually. But, as foreign investment increases, donor aid declines. Foreign investment fell in 2013.

The Mongolian people have previous experience of weathering the toughest storms, so despite some economic difficulties, the general impression is that 21st century Mongolia is thriving. With modern equipment, printing and publishing are forging ahead, while the previously neglected service industries have developed enormously, including new hotels, restaurants and supermarkets, industrial developments, commercial and domestic property, and roads and railways – although the railways are yet to be constructed.

MINING Undeniably the new economic prosperity today in Mongolia is due to mining. But are Mongolian herders happy with this development? Some, it appears, are not too pleased with the changes it inevitably brings in terms of disruption to the landscape and herding practices in mining localities. However, not all woes the country faces are the fault of mines and miners. Environmental stewardship projects run by the Mongolian government, the World Bank and others are raising awareness of the country's pristine environment. Mongolians continue to take charge of this themselves, although the litter and pollution that come with modern commercial life is creating problems. Care of the land as one Mongolian executive said is this:

> We need to think about ways to preserve Mongolian traditions, while at the same time developing mining …
> Such values are connected with the idea of a pristine environment, if we don't resolve the issue now, many aspects of our culture will disappear.

The rewards of environmental stewardship will benefit Mongolia in the long term. In this period of rapid economic growth hard questions are being asked about issues beyond mining. For example, there is the serious matter of desertification, overgrazing, and soil erosion due to climate change that immediately affects people and landscapes, especially life on the margins of deserts, like the Gobi. But it is not all bad news; the younger generation in Mongolia is benefiting from the new mineral development through training courses and new opportunities that will boost the economy as a whole (see box, pages 52–3). Brown coal is producing huge revenues for Mongolia. As a result, there will be more new wind farms, roads and rail links. The mining boom and growth for the country is the start of what may make Mongolia a region of new prosperity in the Asia Pacific area.

Neighbouring China has a huge appetite for Mongolia's mineral wealth – enough coal to power all China's needs for decades to come – so extensive are Mongolia's brown coal deposits. Copper is in big demand too in the building of China's mega cities, and Mongolia is close at hand to satisfy demand.

Copper prices plunged in 2009 and in Mongolia economic growth collapsed due to the mining slow-down before righting itself in the following two years. Now that production at Oyu Tolgoi copper mine in the Gobi has begun (see box, pages 312–13), forecasts are that mineral revenues are expected to rise sixfold by 2020 as the mining sector expands. In this development Mongolia is modelling itself on several other countries, notably Chile, a world-top producer of copper, which is showing Mongolia the way ahead. It set up two wealth funds – a pension fund and an economic and social stability fund – to help the government steer its way

1

through contingency liabilities and future shocks in the market, as well as providing structural balance and the ability to offer important returns in cash and kind (new infrastructure, education and social welfare) to its citizens.

> In the past we had no money. Now, we are seeing capital come into the country, and the challenge is to manage that capital. *Chuluuny Ganhuyag*

Copper The mining industry has taken off with international companies like Rio Tinto's involvement and co-ownership with the government of Mongolia in the copper mine at Oyu Tolgoi. Rio Tinto's copper joint venture with Russia in the northern city of Erdenet has increased its copper concentrate output. See box, page 54.

Coal All the big power stations burn lignite (soft coal), which adds to the serious urban air pollution caused largely by the urban poor who burn the poorer-quality coal on inefficient stoves, especially in winter. However the massive coal deposits now being mined at Tavan Tolgoi in the Gobi are putting Mongolia on the map as one of the chief power providers for neighbouring China. Currently the coal is being trucked out to China for use there, and for shipping abroad. Japan also has a huge holding in Tavan Tolgoi. New cross-border rail links are being negotiated by the Mongolian government both to Chinese and Russian sea ports.

Gold and other minerals The mountains of Mongolia, especially the Khangai and Khentii ranges, are treasure-troves of untapped gems and mineral resources. Gold is mined in Ömnögobi Aimag and in the river valleys of northern Mongolia. Past gold taxes have rendered some mines unprofitable but this industry has seen a

MONGOLIAN ECONOMY *Angar Davaasüren*

Mongolia operated as a Soviet-style centrally planned economy until the establishment of a new coalition government in 1990. Since 1990, Mongolia has transitioned into a market-oriented economy, with the private sector constituting 75.2% of the nation's GDP in 2011. Over the past two decades, Mongolia has transformed itself from a socialist country with a planned economy into a vibrant multi-party democracy with one of the world's fastest growing economies. From 2007 to 2011, Mongolia's real GDP grew at a compound annual growth rate of 7.7%. In 2011, Mongolia's economic real growth rate was 17.5%.

A number of significant projects have been undertaken in recent years to develop Mongolia's mineral resources. The Oyu Tolgoi mine is believed to be one of the world's largest copper-gold reserves under development. Other major projects are in the coal sector. According to the World Bank, the Tavan Tolgoi formation is believed to be one of the world's largest coal deposits under development, with an estimated 7.4 billion tonnes of coking and thermal coal resources. The total production of Tavan Tolgoi Project is expected to be 40–50 million tonnes of coking coal annually from 2017.

One of the key objectives of the Mongolian government is the further development of the country's abundant resources to transform its mining industry from the extraction and export of unprocessed commodities to the domestic production of value-added products. The construction of the Sainshand Industrial Park, where facilities to process raw materials and new huge increase in production in recent years. Fluorspar, an industrial mineral, is an important export too. Iron ore is mined in Darkhan Aimag.

Oil Although exploratory extraction of oil has been restarted by Western companies in Dornogobi Aimag and the Tamtsag Basin in eastern Mongolia (Dornod Aimag), where it was first found by Soviet geologists, output from the wells is low. It is stored in barrels and trucked across the border into China, where it is piped to a refinery. Mongolia has an estimated six billion barrels of oil reserves. No natural gas deposits have been found in Mongolia so far. A giant pipeline across Mongolia from Kovykta in Siberia to China may or may not be built. There are ongoing debates about this.

Detrimental effects of mining While mining is having a positive affect on the Mongolian economy and will increasingly help the general population, it is also creating problems. Pollution of waterways, illegal mining and incomplete cleaning up have all caused environmental damage, as will proposed transport networks. Prior to new roads being built trucks are also creating damage as new routes cut across fragile semi-desert land and grasslands. In addition, a social/cultural problem has developed as trained workers brought in from China become isolated or keep to themselves, living in housing or *ger* camps on their own, without mixing with the local population. There are also ongoing debates for rail and road transport to deal with the minerals for export.

AGRI-INDUSTRY Animal husbandry is the traditional mainstay of Mongolia's economy. The herd remains vital. In 1975, the national herd stood at 24 million, and according to expert opinion a population of 27 million head of stock is sustainable.

railway lines are being built, is expected to accelerate progress in this effort. The Mongolian government is implementing a plan to construct 5,600km of new railway lines which will connect major mining areas to export markets of Russia and China. The government is also in the process of building a 990km north/south trans-Mongolian highway with the objective of promoting the development of cross-border trade between China, Russia, and Mongolia.

According to the *Doing Business 2013* report published by the World Bank and International Finance Corporation, Mongolia has a friendly and attractive business environment for foreign investment. Out of 185 countries, Mongolia is ranked 22nd in terms of how easy it is to register property, 25th for investor protection and 39th in terms of how easy it is to start a business.

Mongolia has recently passed a series of measures and policies targeted at ensuring macroeconomic and fiscal stability in order to sustain its long-term growth. These measures include a Fiscal Stability Law and a Budget Law to ensure that the resource-wealthy country is able to sustain the pace of its economic development and meet its objectives of improving the living standards of its citizens and reducing poverty. Measures relating to foreign investment and social and economic development include the Law on Regulation of Foreign Investment in sectors of strategic importance, which requires foreign investors in strategic sectors (mining, banking and finance, telecommunication) to obtain government or parliamentary approvals in certain cases.

COPPER IN MONGOLIA

RIO TINTO Copper has played an important role in human civilisation for thousands of years. In today's technological world, copper is an essential mineral that is found in nearly every aspect of our lives and, in many respects, makes modern life possible. This dynamic metal is easily shaped, moulded, rolled into sheets, and drawn into thin wire. It doesn't rust, blends easily with other metals to form useful alloys, and is an excellent conductor of electricity and heat. It is found in everything from kitchen utensils, coins and artwork, to electrical, plumbing and roofing materials. Copper is an essential component of 'green' technologies, from electric vehicles to solar energy.

Today, more than 15 million tonnes of copper are mined each year. During the mining and refinement process, crushed copper ore is finely ground, then concentrated, smelted and refined, or it is plated directly on to metal sheets. At each stage, the copper content increases as impurities are removed. Some of these impurities may include gold, silver or molybdenum, which can be sold as by-products. Eventually, refined copper of 99.99% purity is produced.

Mongolia is a potentially important source of copper. The region is rich in minerals and home to the Oyu Tolgoi mine (see pages 312–13). As populations grow richer, especially in India and neighbouring China, it is expected there will be ongoing increases in consumption of copper. With these mining operations in place, Mongolia is now set to be the leading producer of this much-needed and sought-after element in the developing Asian world. Copper can contribute to national development priorities, such as increasing employment, providing skills training and scholarships, export growth, environmental conservation and infrastructure development. With copper's popularity on an upward trajectory for the foreseeable future, Mongolia is in place to be an international key player for this key commodity.

However, overgrazing is widespread and is posing new difficulties for the herders. In the past decade herd size has dramatically increased in Mongolia to around 38 million – far above the proposed land-carrying capacity.

Traditionally, Mongolian herders kept their wealth on the hoof. One reason for the increased numbers of livestock is that the previous barter system with the Soviets for meat in exchange for petrol, oil and machinery has closed down. Since 2000, meat exports have not risen or expanded into new markets, and the knock-on effect of *zud* disasters meant herds actually shrank, nomads moved to towns and an increased price of meat has caused local inflation.

However, opportunities abound for renovating and creating animal by-product processing plants and introducing Mongolia's totally naturally grown meat, skins, and casings to the world markets. Mongolia is the world's second-largest producer of cashmere after China. Yet net earnings from the export of all cashmere products have barely grown since 1992 because of the collapse of market prices and the failure of Mongolia to attract investment in higher value-added processing plants. The Mongolian government is now doing something about it and in 2013 a new cashmere processing plant was opened in Erdenet. However, Chinese itinerant pedlars still roam the southern Gobi provinces and buy directly from the nomads as they did in the 19th century, so the government is losing considerable taxable revenue because of extensive cross-border smuggling.

The herding economy was hit with a series of *zud* environmental disasters – see page 7. The importance of the herding sector to Mongolia's rural economy and society makes it impossible to ignore the great risks to the herders imposed by *zud*. It is estimated that more than two million livestock died each bad winter, leaving many of the smaller herders facing ruin. International relief has helped Mongolia, and problems such as overgrazing and poor productivity of herds are now being studied. Measures have been put in place such as an index-based Livestock Insurance Project that is receiving US$10 million in additional financing from the World Bank and the governments of Korea and Switzerland. The government realises that sustainability of the rural areas, where almost half the population lives, depends on modernising the livestock sector and encouraging the growth of food processing and improving land management.

In one area agricultural crop production is improving: the growing and marketing of vegetables is increasing from year to year. In the summer Ulaanbaatar's vegetable markets supply root and green vegetables, tomatoes, and lettuce. In this respect the diet of townspeople is becoming distinctly different from that of their country cousins.

Mongolia has never had large-scale private land ownership. Land in Mongolia is under state ownership, although, in the past, the Bogd Gegeen (see page 96) owned estates and serfs. In modern times, nomads graze land widely without ownership, being primarily concerned about land usage and migratory rotation rights. This explains why Mongolia has been slow to create a land ownership law for crop (1.5% of territory) and steppe (90%) land. Novel solutions such as long-term land leasing are being debated by the parliament to solve land tenure disputes

Traditional processing industries, manufacturing foodstuffs, leather goods and woollen textiles have had a difficult transition from state to private ownership.

Cashmere The story of cashmere is market economy with a vengeance. In recent years new factories, especially in China, have sprung up because of a boom in overseas and domestic demands since 1992. The best cashmere comes from goats living in cold, mountainous areas, with specific climatic conditions, so output cannot be easily increased, but what has happened in the Gobi is a cause for grave concern. Intensification of animal grazing, especially goats, has threatened the fragile ecosystem and a combination of necessity, greed and demand has despoiled the traditional animal-production ratios. Under socialism a series of quotas kept strict guard on production but free enterprise is now showing that freedom to produce what sells is accompanied by new responsibilities. In addition, global warming and desertification in the Gobi area have added to the dilemma.

The world cashmere output is between 15,000 and 20,000 tonnes a year. China is the premier source, Mongolia is the world's second largest, producing around 6,700 tonnes, followed in far lesser quantities by Iran, Turkey and other countries. The combined effect of Chinese competition and free-market capitalism has left Mongolia's cashmere industry in disarray. As mentioned, the world's finest cashmere comes from Mongolia and it is unmixed with lower-quality produce. Unfortunately, a world cashmere glut, on top of a booming cashmere industry in Inner Mongolia, has not given Mongolia much economic benefit.

The cashmere goat originated in the Himalayan region of Kashmir. Cashmere, or *nooluur* in Mongolian, comes from one of the many different types of goats that produce wool, meat and milk. Each cashmere goat produces on average 141g, or 5oz, of cashmere each year; this amounts to just a quarter of a jumper! Unlike sheep, which are sheared, cashmere is combed from the goat each spring. Cashmere is the

1

rich, downy undercoat, the inner layer that keeps the goat warm. Good cashmere is both warm and lightweight. It is the queen of animal products – delicate and beautiful – and it is also referred to as 'golden fleece'.

'De-hairing' is a complex process of separating the goat's coarse 'guard-hair' from the soft undercoat of cashmere. Buying cashmere can be as tricky as purchasing a diamond. It is precious and fashionable mainly because it is not available in abundance. The higher the altitude the finer the raw material the goat will produce. Over time it will become evident whether one has chosen a high-quality cardigan or not. Poor-quality items have a greater tendency to 'pill' – a deterioration whereby tiny balls of lint form on the surface of the garment. A tightly woven garment made up of single ply, or twisted strand, of the finest cashmere outranks a two-ply item of inferior-grade cashmere. Again, the proof is in the touch.

Good cashmere fibres are between 13 and 16.5 microns thick – the finer the fibre, the warmer the garment. Chinese manufacturers blend short and long fibres while, in general terms, Mongolian cashmere has longer fibres than cashmere produced in China. Much of Mongolia's exports of raw cashmere and wool pass into China through official crossing points on the southern border but there are concerns about illegal trade in cross-border smuggling. Western consumers and buyers are beginning to discriminate and recognise the higher quality of its fibres and particularly of its white cashmere.

Cashmere bonds Cashmere provides a vital income for herders. However, there has been instability in the industry following bonds raised in 2011 to support this important sector of Mongolia's economy. Herders and traders are trying to fix prices for raw 'greasy' cashmere by holding on to their stock. Chinese buyers dominate the markets and most of the revenue – around US$180 million annually – comes from selling raw cashmere to China. This revenue could be trebled if Mongolia produced more cashmere products. It is a volatile industry given that the harsh weather can also decimate the only source of the product: cashmere goats.

TOURISM

Man's joy is in wide open empty spaces.

Mongol saying

The third major economic sector for Mongolia is tourism. There was little reliable data on tourism before 1998 and although the country has many attractions connected with its ancient culture to interest foreign visitors, the government has been slow to initiate a national effort to promote tourism. In 2000, there were 33,232 tourists, and there has been considerable improvement in the industry since then with 450,000 visitors in 2012. The Mongolian airline MIAT, Russia's Aeroflot, and Japanese, Korean, Chinese and Turkish airlines serve Ulaanbaatar (see pages 170–1). There are an increasing number of top hotels in the country and *ger* camps have increased dramatically in the provinces. Manufacturing and handicrafts are small and local in character but they form an important part of an industry that is growing on account of tourism. Woollen and leather products, furs, wooden toys and sculptures, traditional clothing, watercolours and jewellery are increasingly needed as gift items for the tourist trade. The food and drinks industry is included in this growth. The raw product is available – the whole country is a natural paradise – but there is a strong need for improvement in basic services and in the area of waste disposal, particularly in the countryside. This does not only demand financial resources but the will to re-train and re-think. Tourism is a fragile and fluctuating industry, vulnerable to change, often without warning, therefore it is as unpredictable as the weather or the stock market, but reliant on both. Tourism is a naturally interdependent industry and its roots go deeply into the rural economy. Mongolia, like other nations, is learning to balance these interests with some difficulty.

> Of all the commercial sectors in Mongolia, the tourism industry is the weakest, the most inarticulate and the most fragmented. We have to stand together.
> *Mr Nergui, Juulchin World Tours Corporation*

The focus of Mongolia's tourism is nature and the environment, the nomadic way of life and places linked with Genghis Khan. It is now possible to visit this 'last place on earth'. In the final decade of the 20th century Mongolia opened its doors to the world and with air travel and the advantages of the internet, Mongolia is, virtually, a step away. For centuries Genghis Khan and the Mongol Empire have held a fascination for the Western reader and many people have dreamed of going there.

The country is of enormous size and magnificent proportions – with sights to fill the imagination for a lifetime. It is a land that invites exploration and when you get there you will see for yourself the undisturbed beauty and freshness of its wilderness areas – a vast land sparsely inhabited by some of the last nomadic people on earth. Mongolia's herdsmen are still living the life of semi-nomadic pastoralists, just as their forefathers did for centuries, unchanged by the passage of time. But this may not last, since television brings the latest world news and along with it the intrusion of modern civilisation.

The future of tourism Ecotourism involves tourists with wildlife conservation work and environmental programmes – as volunteers or clients. People have a choice to participate in wildlife projects or simply to book into specially designed eco-*gers*, often sited in a national park visitor zone, which help the local community financially and otherwise. Ecotourism comes in many different shades (dark to lighter green) depending on how intensely eco-conscious you are.

Cultural tourism involves participants in restoration work on temple buildings and craft-based projects and businesses. A growing number of volunteer tourists choose to spend their holidays in Mongolia this way. Cultural tourism is a two-way stream, whereby the host country signposts people to major sites of cultural heritage and offers traditional entertainment which attracts tourists, for example, to travel to Mongolia for a festival like Naadam. It invites them to participate not only as audiences, but to become involved and to help develop local projects (all very hands on!).

Adventure Tourism involves both individuals and groups who decide to travel on expeditions and specialised tours, which involve horseriding, biking, climbing or whatever their particular interest happens to be. Mongolia offers world-class adventure tours. See *Tour operators* (pages 165–7 and 237–9). See also *Responsible tourism*, pages 154–9.

TRADE AND TRANSPORT Mongolia's 1,000km railway line from the Russian border to the Chinese border passes through Ulaanbaatar and several other towns. It is of great economic importance, since it handles most of Mongolia's export and import goods and it is a transit route for goods traded between Russia and China. Moreover, the main line and its various branch lines carry significant quantities of internal freight, especially coal, although currently coal is exported mostly across the country in trucks. When international agreement is reached on the choice between broad- and standard-gauge railway tracks, new railways will be built. Mongolia and Russia use broad gauge (1,520mm) while China uses standard gauge (1,435mm).

The red lines marked on many maps of Mongolia suggest that there is an established network of main roads, but only about 1,500km of Mongolian roads have a hard surface, and most of those are in or between the main towns. Some roads may have 'improved' (levelled-gravel) surfaces, but most are simply sets of wheel ruts across the countryside. Driving anywhere outside the towns takes a long time and is often rough and uncomfortable. New paved roads connecting all aimag centres to the capital are planned. An east–west road is under construction from Choibalsan in the east to Uliastai in the west (with improved gravel roads connecting the major road to the far western provinces). Mongolian roads are difficult to maintain and very bumpy.

IMPORTS AND EXPORTS Mongolia's mineral exports of copper, gold and coal go chiefly to neighbouring China where there is ongoing demand to fuel and fund its new mega cities. Former chief textile exports (including cashmere knitwear and woollen goods) and traditional hide exports make up the total.

Mongolian imports include medicines, machinery, paper and newsprint, and consumer goods like television sets, refrigerators, cars, tobacco and cigarettes, beer and soft drinks. Petrol, diesel and aviation fuel are imported from Russia.

MONGOLIAN BUSINESS OPPORTUNITIES   *Enkhsanaa*

Mongolia offers an attractive risk return environment among emerging markets. Key factors include the small population size that allows for easy access to key local figures and the country's 'third neighbour' policy that encourages an increasingly friendly political and economic environment.

In recent years Mongolia has attracted huge attention due to its mineral resources and this situation will be the major economic driver for some time to come. The GDP has grown between 12% and 17% in the last three years and so far most foreign investment has focused on a few mining projects in the south of the country. As a result, the services in the mining supply chain, along with other industries, are playing catch up. As a young Mongolian working for an investment bank based in Mongolia, I find that most small and medium companies are in need of investment to cope with the rate of expansion. Many interesting opportunities can be found in the mining supply chain, such as transportation business and real estate development; agricultural projects are becoming a key growth industry along with new financial services.

Mongolia's mineral deposits include the world-leading copper mines at Oyu Tolgoi and Tavan Tolgoi. However, a number of other projects are under way in the outlying aimags that are directing the business focus away from the capital. To date large to middle-size companies are mostly involved with mining and mining supply chain businesses based in Ulaanbaatar.

An interesting example of business development is in the South Gobi – Tavan Tolgoi has developed from being a sleepy little town of 3,000 people into a mineral boom town within a few years thanks to the creation of the Tavan Tolgoi mine. More than 17,000 people have recently moved to live and work there from nearby towns and even from as far afield as the provinces of northern Mongolia. The town now boasts modern apartment blocks connected by paved roads on

FINANCE, AID AND INVESTMENT Mongolia joined the IMF (International Monetary Fund) and the World Bank in 1991. It also became a country of operation of the European Bank of Reconstruction and Development in 2006, the main activity of which is to support private-sector development. It is a member of the Asian Development Bank and receives aid from the EU's Technical Assistance Programme. During the period 1991–2000, foreign countries and international organisations pledged US$2.6 billion of assistance, including loans, technical assistance and grants. Much of this money has been spent on the country's new infrastructure – on banking and financial restructuring, energy and communications, municipal and other services. From then to now the Mongolian government has concentrated its efforts on developing the social infrastructure and agriculture, which is in need of help.

Inflation In recent years the rate of inflation rose to nearly 18% in 2012 and is forecast at 12% in 2014.

BUSINESS

At the beginning of the 21st century, both small- and large-scale business opportunities abound in Mongolia. The country offers favourable opportunities for foreign investors, extensive untapped natural resources and a strategic location between the large markets of Russia and China. Following the mineral boom in

which heavy duty trucks and the ubiquitous Toyota Land Cruisers drive to and from Ulaanbaatar. There is also a new air strip.

As businesses boom there is increasing migration from rural areas to urban areas. This opens an opportunity for service, construction and retail industries to flourish. According to JICA (Japanese International Cooperation Agency), Ulaanbaatar needs to build around 17,000 units of apartment accommodation every year to keep up with the scale of the new industries. So far construction companies have only been able to build half that number.

As for the retail sector, the majority of Mongolians still buy cheap Chinese imported products, but increasingly the young and wealthier middle-class Mongolians are becoming brand driven. This can be witnessed by the many luxury shops recently opened in the centre of Ulaanbaatar.

As people move into towns a new strain has been placed on the traditional food supplies, mainly meat. In the past people would always have a relative or someone in the countryside who would supply them with meat. But now more than 90% of meat sales are done through a middle man, resulting in rapid meat price increases. In the last two years meat prices have been one of the main drivers of inflation.

All in all Mongolian businesses are becoming more diverse and interesting. The growth of business 'know how' and entrepreneurial activity is becoming more valued and appreciated in Mongolia. Bear in mind that most Mongolian businesses are on the small side by comparison with those in Europe but the potential to do business in Mongolia is great and it may also be extremely rewarding.

About the author: Mr Enkhsanaa is a young Mongolian businessman who lived in London and spent the last 10 years working in Mongolia, most recently for CPS International. In July 2012, his company started an advisory and investment fund for business that focuses on non-mining opportunities in Mongolia.

Pauline Shearman

The first sponsored British Trade Mission to Mongolia took place in 1987, organised by the London Chamber of Commerce and the Chamber of Commerce of the Mongolian People's Republic. Owing to the trade mission support system at that time there was a rather generous travel grant available which meant it was never difficult to find intrepid businesspeople who secretly always wanted to visit 'Outer Mongolia'. Flying by Aeroflot was in those days one of the most arduous elements of the whole experience; they never issued tickets until the day before departure and the mission organiser had to collect them in person.

The first intrepid trade mission arrived in Moscow by late afternoon with a few hours to kill before onward travel to UB (in later years that time was spent in the Irish bar at Sheremetyevo). By some miracle all luggage stayed with us. We arrived at 07.00 in Ulaanbaatar, having flown through the night for nine hours. The magical part of the experience, even for travel-hardened businessfolk, was to look out of the window over Mongolia and see absolutely nothing but the undulating landscape below; no roads, no cities, only the very occasional tiny white dot – a *ger*.

Back then, the airport in UB was very small indeed. We were met on the tarmac by the British Ambassador and taken straight to the first briefing session, followed by a stop at the hotel to check in, a full day of meetings and an evening at the ballet – the entire first British Trade Mission was fast asleep by the finale (although polite enough not to snore!) On subsequent visits we were allowed to rest the first morning which improved our staying power no end. The programme usually consisted of formal meetings with every relevant ministry. All enterprises were still state-owned and central planning still in operation. Access to the countryside was restricted (for Western visitors) but some were lucky enough to visit agricultural

2008 foreign investment poured into the country and Mongolia's future as a key player is assured in the North Asia Pacific region as a provider of copper and coal in large quantities. This will mean increased wealth and power for the country and development on a grand scale for years to come.

The Business Council of Mongolia (BMC) was founded in 2007 and details can be found online: www.bcmongolia.org. Its mission is to work for increased trade and investment, to work for the reform of laws and to represent the public views and interest of investors in Mongolia's economy.

More than 1,000 companies from 70 countries have active investments in Mongolia, which encourages further investment. The GNP growth is forecast to be 12% in 2014. The transition to a market economy would appear to have been achieved despite many setbacks, including a lack of skilled people such as doctors and technicians, but new education and training programmes are being set up.

BANKING AND INSURANCE Before 1924, Mongolia had no banks or currency of its own (foreign silver coins or silver ingots were used for payments). Commodities were bartered, so that, for example, livestock was exchanged for tea. The new socialist government transformed this chaotic monetary situation. In 1925, the tögrög became the official national currency. Only in 1933 did enterprises start to keep accounts and use banks – detailed paperwork was not the strong point of a previously nomadic and religious general population. The first bank, the Mongol centres and see animal husbandry at work. A visit to the Gobi cashmere plant was always included and there we found beautiful low-cost cashmere sweaters to bring home, as well as camel-hair fabrics and blankets.

Receptions were held by the Mongolian Chamber and the chairman, Mr Dorj, a tall and venerable-looking man, was surprised to find that the London Chamber representative was a diminutive lady of around 30. He was an eminent ethnographer and took us to the countryside to explain the symbolism of everything in the *ger,* Mongolian etiquette and local customs. This made a deep impression on the delegation. It contrasted to the rather Soviet-style protocol of the business side.

The London Chamber Mission to Mongolia became an annual fixture with a core group of devotees. As things changed so the business meetings became less formal and communication became easier (in the early days telex was the principal means of long-distance communication). Back then, the streets of UB were completely devoid of traffic – today they are filled with cars and businesspeople talking on mobile phones, which are, of course, ideal in a country where landlines are totally impractical.

From our small commercial beginnings when Mongolia was completely isolated from the rest of the world, international investment in the country has increased dramatically with multi-national mining companies set to invest billions of dollars in Mongolia's minerals and mining sector. The resurrection of the Silk Route as a major transport corridor for the US$100 billion-plus trade between Europe and Asia is now becoming a real possibility. Perhaps the historic disadvantages of being sandwiched between Russia and China are about to become advantages thanks to the commercial opportunities on both sides.

Bank, was government controlled. It handled all international trade and operated locally through its 400 branches around the country. In the late 1980s, the State Bank granted short-term credits to co-operatives and state enterprises and long-term credits to the country's industrial sector. It worked closely with the Ministry of Finance, which also controlled a national insurance and welfare system. All this changed with the new institutions of democracy when people had to take charge of their own lives and begin to operate private businesses.

There are now a number of major private banks in Ulaanbaatar, including the Golomt Bank of Mongolia (*Commercial St 6, Ulaanbaatar 36; call centre* \ *11 310639/323844; www.golomtbank.com*). Golomt Bank provides a 24-hour branch service, credit cards, personal current accounts, telephone banking, internet banking, Premier banking, Western Union money transfer service, 'Golden Ear' Yuan card service, Floating Interest Rate Deposit, and Certificates of Deposit.

For banks in Ulaanbaatar see page 252.

LAW Mongolia has passed an array of administrative, regulatory, and fiscal laws to improve the attractiveness of its business climate. A new fiscal stability law commits the government to using long-term copper and coal prices as a basis for mining revenues with specified ceilings on government expenditure, with a proportion of the funds being invested outside Mongolia; it includes the proviso that the public debt does not exceed 40% of GDP. An integrated budget law was passed in 2011, and a social welfare law in 2012, which lays the foundation for a cost-effective welfare system in Mongolia to protect the poor. Time will tell if the framework set down is working as it should. It is a huge challenge in the long-term for Mongolia. But the mineral wealth which is such a blessing to the country may provide the necessary resources, as all Mongolians hope, for a lasting prosperity.

TAX MEASURES Both corporate and individual taxes were reduced in 2006. Since then appropriate amendments have been made to investment and mining laws and regulations under pressure from the public. The effectiveness of the new taxation systems required by the market economy has been reduced by delays in payment of business tax by large enterprises and firms and the avoidance of personal income tax. However, there was little consultation with the public and business and this led to frequent amendments to fix errors.

The maximum tax for companies is now 25%, the minimum is 10%; tour operators pay corporate tax. The personal income tax rate for individuals is now established at the single flat rate of 10%. VAT has been reduced from 15% to 10%.

To capture a higher share of the revenue accruing to copper- and gold-mining companies from high export prices, there is a 68% tax rate applied to copper revenue from prices exceeding US$2,600 per tonne. The windfall tax applies only to the export of copper concentrate, not to the export of copper cathodes and further processed coppers. For gold, the tax is 68% of the difference between the London gold price and the base price set at US$500 per ounce.

In addition, the new mining law enacted in 2006 provides for royalties ranging from 2.5% for energy, coal and common mineral resources to 5% for sales of copper, gold and other products.

DEVELOPMENTS Plans include the division of Mongolia into five development zones: western, Khangai, central, eastern and Ulaanbaatar, and the construction of a new millennium road, a 2,400km east–west highway. In Ulaanbaatar several new top hotels are in the process of construction, such as The Hyatt, and others. Assistance for businesspeople interested in new developments is available from the **Mongolian National Chamber of Commerce** (*MNCCI Building, Mathatma Gandhi St, Ulaanbaatar 170111;* \ *11 327176/312501/312371;* e *chamber@ mongolchamber.mn; www.mongolchamber.mn).*

In the UK, the Mongolian British Chamber of Commerce is reached via www. mongolialondonbusinessforum.co.uk.

The **Netherlands-Mongolia Trust Fund for Environmental Reform (NEMO)** was established in April 2005 with the objective of strengthening and advancing the environment and natural resources agenda in Mongolia. Administered by the World Bank and the Mongolian government, NEMO was run on a budget of US$6 million. Building on the success of NEMO 1, a four-year, second-phase, NEMO 2 was initiated in 2007 and ended in December 2011.

Activities included providing support for an air-quality development programme; strengthening the performance of provincial environmental departments; translating modern literature; implementing recommendations of the Silent Steppe report by supporting forest ungulate and marmot surveys; and expanding biodiversity monitoring through camera traps carried out by **Steppe Forward** (see box, pages 122–3). Additional surveys were on damaged and restored mining lands and on rare birds, such as the threatened saker falcon in the Galba Gobi. Grants were given to map forestry in northern Mongolia, and for programmes implemented by German universities and institutes along with GTZ (see page 49).

MILLENNIUM DEVELOPMENT GOALS OF MONGOLIA

Dr Nancy Tokola

Through a three-part process in the year 2000 – the Millennium Declaration, the Millennium Agenda, and the Millennium Development Goals (MDGs) – the United Nations acknowledged global needs and set the date of 2015 for achieving targets, measured by indicators of progress.

The **Millennium Declaration** was drafted, adopted, and signed by 189 nation-states, including Mongolia, during the 55th session of the United Nations General Assembly in September 2000, known as the United Nations Millennium Summit. It included values and principles of freedom, solidarity, tolerance, respect for nature, and shared responsibility.

The **Millennium Agenda** is 'a collective commitment of the international community, united by shared values and the dream of a better future for all' through upholding the rights of all people 'to be free from want and fear, free to sustain their lives on this planet, and free from poverty'.

Following the Millennium Declaration and the Millennium Agenda, the United Nations established the eight global **Millennium Development Goals (MDGs)** as being 'visionary and pragmatic, galvanising change at the country level'. In October 2004, the government of Mongolia reinforced its commitment to achieving these global MDGs, in the specific context of the needs of the Mongolian nation-state and of the Mongolian population, especially by establishing a ninth MDG.

1 Eradicate extreme poverty and hunger
2 Achieve universal primary education
3 Promote gender equality and empower women
4 Reduce child mortality
5 Improve maternal health
6 Combat HIV/AIDS, malaria and other diseases
7 Ensure environmental sustainability
8 Develop a good partnership for development
9 (Mongolian MDG) Strengthen human rights and foster democratic governance

SOURCES

Government of Mongolia *Millennium Development Goals: National Report on the Status of Implementation in Mongolia* Ulaanbaatar, www.un.org/millenniumgoals

CHALLENGES FACING MONGOLIA Twenty-first-century Mongolia is adapting as people juggle between 'old' and 'new' systems, and experience the impact of the world's mineral giants pursuing business on their doorstep. On the one hand nomads may not understand share certificates and wonder if they have a future in the modern world. On the other hand there are choices to be made to balance regional budgets while keeping a firm grip on the economy and ensuring the local community 'voice' is taken seriously. Rap is one way of getting this message across and young activist singers are making their voices heard both in UB, around the country and publicised abroad on social networks.

2

People

There are more animals than men, so they still have the world as God made it, and the men are the noble synthesis of Genghis Khan, the warrior, and the Dalai Lama, the gentle religious leader.

Zahava Hanan, Canadian writer and poet

Mongolia is a land of horses and herdsmen and one of the last great, undisturbed wilderness areas on earth. Among its 2.9 million people are some of the last truly nomadic pastoralists in the world – but how long they will survive is questionable. About one-third of the scant population is concentrated in the capital, Ulaanbaatar, whereas the dwindling population of nomads, herdsmen with their millions of head of livestock, are spread throughout the country. The people are well matched to the land they inhabit, they are tough, resilient, stoical by dint of necessity, but genuinely fun-loving, easy going and kind.

Since earliest times, tribes have moved across the great central Asian plains and mountain ranges that cover present-day Mongolia, but little is known of the ethnic origins of the proto-Mongol people. The mystery lies tangled in the fact that we are dealing with a fluid and changeable nomadic society. The division between Inner and Outer Mongolia (the latter being the area covered by this guide and Outer Mongolia being a historical concept only, no longer the country name) was effected by the Qing dynasty Manchus of China (1644–1912), who conquered southern (Inner) Mongolia before northern (Outer) Mongolia. This has resulted in differences between the two areas.

On the whole, within the city, the nomadic culture of the countryside mixes easily with the modern urban culture of Ulaanbaatar and the two often combine without fuss. This is best seen in Ulaanbaatar, where a Mongol teenager wearing a silk tunic, fur hat and long leather boots might jump off his horse (which is quickly ridden away by a friend since, according to recent law, animals are not allowed in the town centre), contact his mother by mobile phone to say he will be home late, and then spend the evening with his girlfriend, either shopping in a modern supermarket, or dancing in one of the city's new bars or discos.

Mongolia is connected to the fashion houses of the world through its marketing of cashmere. In Ulaanbaatar it is not surprising to see the latest Asian or European up-to-the-minute designs in clothing and trendy footwear. Young city Mongols are very style-conscious; chart music in UB discos is as modern as it is in London or Tokyo. Internet café culture is well established and the capital can boast many new restaurants serving international cuisine.

What is clear is that the life of the Mongolian nomad is changing fast. On the steppes, there are more satellite phones than people and even more numerous trucks that have taken the place of horse-riding couriers, who in the days of the Mongol

Empire covered vast distances at a gallop, bringing news to and from outlying regions. As more modern machinery enters a Mongolia that is beginning to abandon its ancient disciplines, one wonders what it will do to the countryside and its people. The slow and fast tracks of the ancient as well as the modern world have their individual and separate consequences. The nomad is slowed down by lack of machinery and his workload increased, whereas machines only present more problems in isolated places when it comes to replacing broken parts. Extreme concerns are that although Mongolia is open to the world of trade and tourism, the natural environmental and traditional livelihood of the nomads is likely to suffer, unless financial assistance for rural development, with stricter laws on planning, and other controls are put in place. This is particularly the case following the hard winters that in recent years have brought about overwhelming livestock losses alongside other socio-economic difficulties. Should this situation last, it could threaten the original identity of all Mongolians, particularly the truly pastoral nomads who embody Mongolia's cultural heritage. The thought that they might face extinction is an irony because it was their heritage, with its openness and toughness, which helped to make the successful switch from a command economy to a market-orientated one.

MONGOLIAN NATIONAL GROUPS

The Mongols constitute one of the principal ethnographic divisions of Oriental, or Asian, peoples. Over time the once great corridor of migration across the northern grasslands between Hungary in the west, and Manchuria in the east, became blocked by manmade divisions in the name of civilisation. The origin of the Mongols themselves is from the Tungus people (the modern Evenki of southeast Mongolia) from Siberia and Manchuria, and in the west from the Huns (Xiongnu) and the Turks that lived in Mongolia and north China and moved westwards.

Although the population of Mongolia was 2.9 million in 2013, it has consisted of many different nomadic tribes from ancient times until the present day. On the surface, visitors may only notice that in the countryside some tribal minorities wear slightly different dress, but there are differences between minorities, especially Oirat (western) Mongols, and the Khalkha majority who predominate. Generally, the further west of Ulaanbaatar you go, the more different the people are, until you reach the Uriankhai and Kazakh minorities. Population figures are given for the various national groups described below. These figures and percentages are based on 2010 census figures.

KHALKHA MONGOLS The Khalkha (Halh) Mongols number just over 2 million and account for some 81.5% of the total population. They live all over Mongolia and their language (Khalkha) is the state language.

The 56,573 Bayat, mostly now inhabiting the far western Uvs Aimag, but who may have come originally from the Selenge Valley in central Mongolia, and the 27,412 Dariganga, who live in Dariganga district of Sükhbaatar Aimag in southeastern Mongolia, also speak dialects of Khalkha.

NORTHERN MONGOLS The 45,085 Buryat people that inhabit the northern border areas of Dornod, Khentii, Selenge and Khövsgöl aimags are related to the Buryats of the Buryat Republic and adjacent regions of the Russian Federation. Mongolia's Buryats arrived from Russia in the 20th century, mostly as political refugees from tsarism or communism. Their northern Mongol dialect has its own strong literary tradition in the Buryat Republic.

Some 2,500 Barga belong to a tribe related to the Buryat; they live in Dornod Aimag on the border with China. There are over 70,000 Barga living in Hulun Buir league of Inner Mongolia Autonomous Region in China, where their territory was once also called Barga.

SOUTHERN MONGOLS Small groups of Mongols like the Chakhar (Qahar) and Kharachin live near the border with China in the south and are related to tribes of the same name in Inner Mongolia Autonomous Region, where they are much more numerous.

ALTAI MONGOLS The 26,654 Altai Uriankhai Mongols inhabit upland areas of Khovd and Bayan-Ölgii aimags.

OIRAT MONGOLS The Oirats of western Mongolia are descendants of the tribes of the Jungarian Khanate who survived slaughter by the army of the Manchu Qing dynasty in the 18th century. The 72,403 Derbet found in Uvs and Bayan-Ölgii aimags in far western Mongolia constitute the largest Oirat tribe. The 28,450 Zakhchin, another Oirat tribe, live in Khovd Aimag, southwestern Mongolia. Other minorities are the 14,176 Torgut concentrated in Bulgan district of Khovd Aimag and on the border with China's Xinjiang region. The Ööld or Eleuth live in Khovd and Bayan-Ölgii aimags, and the Mingat live in Myangad district of Khovd Aimag.

MONGOLIA'S TURKS Mongolia's 101,526 Kazakh form the largest minority nation and live mostly in western Mongolia's Bayan-Ölgii and Khovd aimags, with concentrations in industrial towns elsewhere. There have been several migrations, including the arrival of Kazakhs from Xinjiang in the 1880s, and in recent years the departure of Kazakhs from Bayan-Ölgii in large numbers to work in Kazakhstan. The Kazakhs are herdsmen who hunt with eagles and live in *ger* similar to Mongolian *ger*. The crops grown by settled communities include melons. The Kazakhs are traditionally Sunnis, and mosques that were destroyed during Mongolia's anti-religious campaigns have been rebuilt.

The 9,000 Khoton who live in the far western Uvs Aimag speak Oirat (western Mongol) dialect, while the 21,558 Darkhad who live in northern Mongolia's Khövsgöl Aimag are also Mongolised Turks but speak Khalkha.

OTHER NATIONALITIES There are many Russian and Chinese traders and other visitors and their numbers are hard to verify. Among the tribes of very limited numbers are the Khamnigan, an Evenki people, who are members of a Tungusic tribe in Khentii and Dornod aimags, and most of whom speak Buryat, the language of neighbouring southern Siberian Buryats. There are also some 282 Tsaatan, the reindeer people who live near Lake Khövsgöl.

Mongolians outside Mongolia Not all Mongols live in Mongolia proper, nor are they the majority of Mongols. Most numerous are the Mongolians who live in Inner Mongolia and Xinjiang Autonomous Regions of China, south of the Gobi Desert, above and along the Silk Road.

The *Hazara* of Afghanistan There are three types of Mongols living in Afghanistan, collectively known as Hazara or Hasarajar. These tribal people, living in the high mountainous central plateau of Afghanistan, are said to be the descendants of Genghis Khan's grandsons, whose armies crossed through this country, in bands of 1,000 horsemen, known as *hazara*. The Mongols withdrew leaving a remnant trapped in this inhospitable terrain, where they have remained ever since. The Hazara resemble Mongols and are distinguished from other Afghans by their facial features – high cheekbones, broad, flat faces and almond eyes. They are also a nomadic people. The western Hazara in Afghanistan are Sunni and they speak Dari (an Afghan/Persian language). The eastern Hazara who live in Iran are Shi'i (Shi'ite) and their language contains a sprinkling of old Turkic and Mongol words. Fascinating recent genetic studies show that the Hazara people are indeed related to Genghis Khan and carry evidence of this in their genes.

MONGOL CHARACTERISTICS

Nomadic people are perceived to be self-assured and proud; they are survivors in an extremely difficult climate and harsh land. At times one wonders whether they can be the descendants of the highly trained mounted warriors of the 12th- and 13th-century Mongol khans, with their discipline and obedience. History has shown that the Mongol warriors were indeed wild and bloodthirsty, murderous and rough, but it must be remembered that the early historic Mongol character has changed radically with the passage of time under the influence of Buddhism and Soviet 'nannying'.

There is an apparent split in the Mongol personality. On the one hand they are vivacious, open and carefree, with a tendency to live for the moment, yet on the other they are prudent, cautious and disciplined. Perhaps this is a direct result of their extreme climate and inhospitable environment – the same environment that nurtures in them a great sense of hospitality and giving.

The lack of a permanent home, the portability of possessions, the fact that wealth is calculated in the numbers of livestock, and a reckless sense of self-sufficiency surrounds the Mongol nomads and cultivates in them endurance, hardiness, hospitality and a spirit of freedom. Each person of the household, isolated in his tented home, is both dependent on the others and in turn his own master.

Waiting for an auspicious moment is a distinctive Mongol characteristic and, in general, is part of Mongolian lifestyle. Tourists need to understand this at the start of their holiday. In many cases auspicious signs and omens help Mongols

MONGOLIAN PROVERBS

He who has read the book of proverbs requires no effort to speak well.

While your father is alive, get to know people.

A man with acquaintances is the size of the steppe.

When the ibex antlers reach the sky, the camel's tail touches the ground (ie: don't try to reach for the moon)

The greatest treasure is knowledge.

Material wealth is of least importance.

If a man fails seven times, he succeeds on the eighth.

Respect for one's elders is deeply rooted in the Mongol character. According to tradition, the man of the family was highly respected. Wives addressed their husbands by their names with the addition of the word *'ta'*, which signified respect. The head of the family always sat at the north end of the *ger*. This 'place of honour' (also for important guests) is called the *khoimor* in Mongolian. His hat and belt were treated with special care and placed on a chest near the altar. He was first to be offered tea and food in a separate bowl. He never performed household chores.

His job was to entertain guests and to make all the important decisions – when to move camp, where to move and which pastures to select. Some more traditional rules forbade family members from carrying out business deals such as buying and selling animals without his permission. All important matters needed his approval and it was his duty before his death to ensure his authority continued by nominating his successor.

This might suggest a male-dominated world among the nomads, which in many ways is true. Nevertheless, Mongolian women, unlike other Asian women, have always played an important role and shared many responsibilities besides household duties. Although the old family traditions still survive, things have changed dramatically in the past decade. Mongolian women have taken on the role of breadwinners and since they have had more time to study they have ended up better educated than the menfolk, who have stuck to herding and the outdoors. Mongol women are beginning to take future leadership roles, for example the current Minister of Health Mrs Natsagiin Udval was nominated as presidential candidate by her party, the MPRP. In politics, for example, women are amply qualified but some still lack experience.

reach a decision and can lead to baffling delays, which leaves the visitor distraught, especially when little or no explanation is given. Perhaps it is that some Mongols prefer to think back on their glorious past than to move forward with the anxieties and expense of modern technology. One could say it is how Mongolians choose to conduct themselves in a charming, relaxed and flexible way. Mongolian time-keeping is slack. So take a break, switch to holiday mode, wind down and try not to get upset. Mongolians are enormously laid back.

Mongolians do not like to say a direct 'no'; they would rather remain quiet or change the subject … and naturally, of course, there are unavoidable delays. Mongolians also hate to 'lose face'. They often choose to ignore difficult behaviour such as drunkenness, a personal embarrassment or a public showdown.

Something worth mentioning is the Mongol temper, infrequently displayed because for the most part it lies dormant, placated by centuries of Buddhism perhaps. It appears that the cruelty of 'the armies of Genghis Khan' has been transformed and mellowed into human tolerance and kindness. Perhaps this is the result of being subjugated for so many generations (as well, of course, as the influence of Buddhism), so that no unkind thoughts, no shouting, no killing and so on are the principles that, by and large, govern the lives of the majority today.

Good humour must be the essential Mongolian characteristic that goes hand in hand with hospitality and entertainment. Mongolians are not just good to foreigners, they are extremely good natured to each other. Respect for older people

People **MONGOL CHARACTERISTICS**

2

is common practice and strict forms of etiquette are observed, especially in the countryside. Hours are spent chatting with friends. Most Mongols enjoy a good joke and have a great sense of humour. Conversation is a national pastime in towns, whereas country folk may be shy and are more likely to smile and say little.

Although Mongolian nomads survived in a predominately 'barter society', once money was introduced in the 1920s, they used it. One shudders to see green dollar signs appear in the eyes of Mongolia's youth and even in the eyes of remote tribes like the Tsaatan or 'reindeer people', around Lake Khövsgöl, when the tourists arrive. But such are the opportunities of the 21st century and this generation must take them or they will not survive.

DRESS

MONGOLIAN *DEEL* The *deel*, the colourful national dress, is worn by men and women. It is an elegant three-quarter-length gown that buttons at the right shoulder to a high round-necked collar. That worn in winter is made of cotton lined with sheepskin, and in summer of silk with traditional patterns and designs, in shining bright colours – red, orange, blue and green. The winter colours are darker – deep purple and dark blue. A colourful sash of a contrasting colour is worn. The sleeves are so long that they cover the hands so Mongols never need wear gloves. Heads are covered by exotic fur hats and scarves.

In towns, people dress for work in conventional European clothing, and in the capital it is not surprising to see pinstriped suits for gentlemen and chic, well-tailored couture suits for ladies, although the usual scruffy duffel coat and beret or bobble hat are more commonplace. However, everyone has a best deel for special occasions. In the countryside the deel is the practical everyday working garment and may be quite dirty and shabby from wear and tear. A deel has multi-purpose uses, acting as a blanket at night, as a mini tent when getting dressed or undressed, and as a private canopy when there is no cover (for miles!) and you need to relieve yourself with a little dignity.

MONGOLIAN BOOTS Mongolian knee-length boots, *gutal*, have exotic upturned toes and are made of brightly coloured leather, stencilled and incised with patterns.

COLOUR AND SYMBOLIC MEANING

The symbolic meaning of colours plays an important role in Mongolian life. Three colours – red, black and white – are associated with an early culture pre-dating the introduction of Lamaism. White signifies truth, honesty and kindness. Black is representative of misfortune and disaster, and is associated with poverty or loneliness. Red is the colour of joy. Mongols also love the colour blue, which symbolises eternity and loyalty. They even called themselves the 'blue people' in the past. Gold or yellow are respected colours and the word for gold, *altan*, was often added to descriptions of the steppe. Primary colours are mainly used when painting buildings. Red is the special colour for nearly all household utensils and furniture. The dyeing of fabrics or felt was not known in Mongolia, except by the Kazakh people in the far west. Most brocade, silk and other material was purchased from Chinese itinerant merchants. Mongolians attach specific colours to the points of the compass – black for north and red for south. Dairy foods are called 'white foods'.

Clare Ed

The weather is a major influence on modern Mongolian fashion. However, some women can't live without their stilettos even during the icy months and so have perfected the ice-slide: they do not take their foot off the ground and shuffle around on the ice and make it look effortless, aka 'The Stiletto Shuffle' – Western catwalk models eat your hearts out!

The traditional Mongolian dress is the *deel* (pronounced 'dell'). This is a distinctive loosely fitted silk coat which has an ornate fastening comprising several buttons, often of silver or stone. Men and women both wear the *deel* which originates from being a multi-purpose jacket that would serve as a blanket during the winter or for women to cover up. Mongolians enjoy bright and distinctive clothing and decoration for their homes, which perhaps compensates for their cold and harsh winters and nomadic lifestyles. Shorter-length *deels* made out of woollen materials are worn on a day-to-day basis, particularly in the countryside today.

During the winter people wear fur and a lot of it – hats, coats, linings for boots, etc. Whatever your view on fur one needs to remember that this has always been the way humans have kept warm over the centuries. If you are tempted to buy something like a hat it is worth paying extra for a high-quality product which has been properly treated otherwise it will start to smell. I sat next to someone on the plane on the way home who had a corduroy coat with a fur lining and the smell was oppressive and foul.

Inspired by a holiday in Mongolia and a chance meeting with a group of inspirational Mongolians, I started my company, Gifted Label. The aim is to mix ancient skills and techniques with my modern designs and to enable our customers to learn the history and story of the people who make our products. Gifted Label supports the idea that good suppliers and manufacturers lead to good products and we do whatever we can to ensure the wellbeing of the people with whom we do business.

The leather is also stained in different colours and decorated by scoring the surface or stamping with a hot iron. Nowadays, *gutal* are almost exclusively the footwear of wrestlers. They are worn with thick felt socks embroidered round the top. Today country people don long Russian leather boots, or felt boots that are both comfortable and warm in winter (but not waterproof).

MONGOLIAN HATS The unusual spiked hats worn by Mongol men in the past have sadly gone out of fashion for everyday use, but may still be seen in museums or stage productions. Fur hats, or padded hats with ear-flaps, are worn in winter, and in summer trilby hats are popular with the men while the women wear shawls or scarves. However, traditional Mongolian hats, especially those for men, are used mainly during wrestling competitions to honour the winner. They are uniquely designed and sculpted, complete with their raised top knots and cause a real stir when worn in the West.

TRADITIONAL COSTUME In former times, Mongol women wore traditional silver and coral jewellery – rings, necklaces, earrings and pins. Head and hair decorations (for married women) divided the hair into extraordinary-looking 'wings' on each

People DRESS

2

side of the head. The hair was clipped back with silver pins, plaited and passed through two silver tubes that dropped to the waist on both sides. Mongolian men still carry embroidered pouches for their drinking bowls and tobacco, which are tucked into their sashes, along with a modern cigarette lighter instead of the ancient flint and steel! Examples of all these items may be seen at the National Museum of Mongolian History in Ulaanbaatar, see page 258.

GREETINGS

Mongolia has a unique tradition of greetings that are used primarily in the countryside; some are understood only by Mongols, as there are many puns and hidden meanings. For example, to greet someone by asking 'Are you wintering well?' has the connotation of asking if they are happy and well. The word 'peace' means 'good wishes' and is part of many Mongolian greetings. It is a good thing as a visitor to memorise a Mongolian greeting as it will create an immediate bond with the people you meet. See page 437.

When saying goodbye to guests, the Mongolian tradition is to wish them a happy journey and then to invite them to visit again and again. The response is to say 'Stay well!' If you offend in some way, Mongolians are fairly relaxed because they believe that where there is ignorance, there should be no embarrassment.

TRADITIONAL PIPE SMOKING From ancient times, the pipe and tobacco pouch have been the sign of peace and manhood. Smoking tobacco originated with indigenous tribes in the Americas. History credits no single person with its introduction to Asia but by 1575 it was traded there and then moved to the rest of the world during the next 50 years. Smoking has a specific symbolic meaning. When nomads meet on the steppe, they light a pipe. This in itself is a form of greeting, showing mutual respect. Smoking ceremonies have rituals. Before entering a *ger*, a herdsman would leave his whip outside and arrange his clothes. Inside, he would greet his host, enquire about the health of the elders, and listen intently to the replies. When all were seated, and silent, then was the moment to light a pipe.

A man's smoking set consists of a pipe, a cleaning stick, flints, a pouch and a fastener with a cord for tying it to the nomad's belt. By tradition, the pipe is carried at the top of the right boot, and the pouch (with its effects) is tied to the left side of the belt. Pipes vary in design from province to province. They are usually made from willow wood and many are ornately carved and inlaid with semi-precious materials. The mouthpiece might be crafted from silver, copper, amber or wood.

SNUFF When men greet one another, snuff bottles (with the lid slightly opened) are passed around in the upturned palm of the right hand. The recipient takes a pinch of snuff with a tiny spoon-like scoop which is attached to the lid, and places it on the back of his hand before inhaling it, or he may hold the bottle to his nose and pass it on. Snuff bottles are traditional items and, after his horse, one of the most valued possessions of a Mongolian man. Snuff bottles are carved from semi-precious stones or wood and also made of porcelain. These valuables are carried in carefully embroidered pouches and indicate the wealth and status of their owners. The demand for unusual and costly snuff bottles was an indirect, but important, sign of the wellbeing of the rural population.

CUSTOMS AND CEREMONIES

SITTING CUSTOMS There are several traditions on how to sit in a Mongolian *ger*. These apply to different age groups and to different types of people (but not to foreigners, who are not obliged to sit in any special way). For example, it is considered offensive for teenagers to sit cross-legged in the lotus position, since lamas usually sit this way. The following are some of the customs that apply:

- **Sitting on bent legs** For young women.
- **Sitting with legs extended** Natural for children.
- **Squatting** The position of a herdsman.
- **Sitting with knees crossed** Considered a sign of disrespect.
- **Sitting in a position with fingers of the hand spread out** Expresses profound sadness.

The following customs are mostly observed by Mongolians. Tourists need not be inhibited or overwhelmed by any such rules, as visitors are always made to feel most welcome. Mongolians are naturally superstitious. Their traditions dictate ritual behaviour that is part of their folk culture and religious practices.

Do
- keep your hat on when entering a *ger*, but lift it as a sign of greeting
- sit immediately – or the host may feel uneasy
- talk about where you come from and show photographs of home if you have any with you
- shake a person's hand if you accidentally tread on or kick his or her foot
- dip the ring finger in the vodka and flick it in the air as a blessing, when offered vodka
- receive food, a gift or anything similar from a Mongolian with both hands or with the right hand supported at the wrist or elbow by the left hand
- take at least a sip or nibble of the delicacies offered – hold the cup to your mouth if you don't want to drink
- ensure that your sleeves are rolled down
- move inside the *ger* in a clockwise direction
- have a song ready to sing
- give gifts on departure, not on arrival – and place gifts on a table, not on the floor, as a sign of respect.

Do not
- step on the threshold of the *ger* – since this insults the owner
- trip on the threshold – happiness is driven away; if you trip, return and place a piece of fuel on the fire
- enter the *ger* with a sigh – this is considered disrespectful
- cross the path of an elderly person – this shows a lack of respect

- step over a hat – this insults the owner
- step over a lasso – it brings bad luck
- take food from the plate with your left hand
- touch the rim of the cup with your fingers – that is a bad omen
- throw away tea leaves – they are otherwise used in animal feed
- sit in the back of the *ger* without being invited
- turn your back to the altar or sit in front of it
- whistle in a *ger* – it brings bad luck.

CUSTOMS RELATING TO FIRE
Do not
- stamp out a fire with your feet – fire is sacred
- step on fire ashes – otherwise the spirit of the dead enters the ashes
- bring fire to people in another *ger* – unless closely related
- use an axe near a fire – it threatens the god of the fire
- lie with your feet pointing towards the fire – it drives out the household gods
- put anything into the fire.

OVOO **(MOUNTAIN/ROCK SHRINE) CEREMONY** *Ovoos* are cairn-like piles of rocks, branches and other natural materials. They belong to ancient Mongolian beliefs and folk religion and are considered by Mongols to be sacred places where people come to pay their respects to the spirits of nature. Ovoo ceremonies take place traditionally at the end of winter and are mainly private occasions, not easily intruded upon. Local people gather on certain dates to leave offerings of money, milk, cheese and curds by the stones. Monks who attend chant prayers to the mountain gods (each mountain has its own), asking the spirit of the mountain to bless the region, to grant good weather and to increase the livestock herds. Those present – usually men only – walk around the ovoo three times. This is a regular ritual, especially when going on journeys, to ensure safety en route. The driver will stop by an ovoo, and he and the passengers will silently walk around the stones. Where and when the ovoo tradition originated is unknown but it is so important that the presidents of Mongolia have institutionalised regular mountain cairn worship at the country's most important mountains.

MILK-SPRINKLING CEREMONY Milk sprinkling is done to honour the gods of fertility and protection. To perform a traditional 'finger-dipping' ritual, the middle and ring fingers are dipped in milk, or vodka, and a few drops flicked in the air. A small amount of milk poured over an object is a method of asking for a blessing. It is performed to wish 'bon voyage' to travellers when milk is sprinkled on the horse's head and rump and in the direction the traveller is taking, while everyone present prays or, as the Mongols say, thinks good thoughts.

FELT-MAKING CEREMONY Country people make felt at the end of summer. They usually celebrate the occasion with a party or ceremony. The order is as follows: a date is announced, family members gather and some of their neighbours join them. First tea is served and then food before the work begins. Wool is cleaned and pounded with short sticks to loosen and fluff up the fibres. At this stage it is laid out evenly in layers on a piece of start-up felt or 'mother roll' and moistened with water. Layer upon layer is added to the 'mother roll', which is finally bound by leather straps and attached to a camel or a horse who pulls it for several kilometres, allowing it to roll along the ground. Milk or *airag* is ceremoniously sprinkled on top to ensure the felt turns out well. Riders keep the roll turning for 15–20km until the wet fibres bind into a thick mat. When unrolled and thoroughly dried the result is a blanket of felt, which is ready to wrap around the *ger*.

HAIR-CUTTING CEREMONY Traditional hair-cutting ceremonies take place when a child reaches four years old. This is a big family affair and cause for celebration with food, drink and music. There are also times for cutting animal hair and auspicious days are set for catching foals and trimming horses' manes.

OUR MONGOLIAN WEDDING   *Karen Skjott*

Erik and Karen Skjott, a young Danish couple, decided to marry in Mongolia in 1992. After months of planning and preparation they boarded the Trans-Siberian Express in Moscow and headed for Ulaanbaatar. This is their story:

We decided to go by train to ensure that our spirits travelled with us all the way, which the Mongolians said was a good idea. The ceremony was co-ordinated with the help of friends at the University of Mongolia. My husband-to-be, Erik, kept everything a secret so it was with some suspense that I arrived for the fitting of my wedding dress – a beautiful silk *deel*. I knew that much, but nothing else about the arrangements, which turned out to be the best surprise of my life.

The ceremony was extremely serious and everyone who took part wanted it to be both meaningful and typically Buddhist. We met with our lama in the afternoon of the first day and were immediately given a bowl of *airag*, fermented horse's milk, which I learned to like. The lama said the Tibetan calendar confirmed that the best date for us would be 2 September, the sign of the snake, at a certain time of day which corresponded to the signs of the sheep and the horse. We found no reason not to accept. Incense was offered and rituals symbolising fertility and prosperity were performed at the altar along with prayers said by the lama.

Next we found ourselves 60 miles outside UB, sitting in a Mongolian family *ger* – for the occasion we were both adopted by different Mongolian families – where we were welcomed by more bowls of *airag* and the traditional exchange of snuff. The next two days took us through a labyrinth of traditions and rituals. An English-speaking professor from the University of Mongolia acted as our translator.

At the very beginning Erik had to set up our own *ger* where we would spend our wedding night. All the male members of 'his family' helped. The women did not participate and my task was to help them milk the horses which turned out to be quite a challenge, and later to find and capture a fat-tailed sheep for the wedding breakfast. My Mongolian father, a famous Mongolian folk singer, slaughtered the animal, which is not a procedure to be seen by squeamish people. That evening young and old gathered to celebrate the first day of our wedding. Erik was not allowed to drink vodka as he was not yet a married man.

The wedding itself passed like a dream. We spent the whole day at the Buddhist temple where dancing and other celebrations took place, following a solemn ceremony. The fun part came when Erik had to raid 'my family' *ger* at night and carry me off on horseback to our new home. I shall never forget the surprise and delight of being married in Mongolia!

People   **CUSTOMS AND CEREMONIES**

2

WEDDING CEREMONY During the communist period, traditional Buddhist weddings were stopped. Instead couples married Western style – in white dresses and dark suits, at the 'Wedding Palace' in Ulaanbaatar. After the recent political changes, statues of Buddha reappeared. Small braziers (*tulga*) are lit to represent the eternal bond between the bride and groom as 'two flames becoming one'. Monasteries have become involved again in the marriage ceremony, which is nowadays blessed by a local lama.

Although young Mongols are getting married later than they used to, marriage remains an important tradition in the countryside, where weddings take place in the family home. A new *ger* is usually provided for the young couple. The groom's relatives visit the bride's family to request her hand on an auspicious day, and are often refused several times in a show of feigned but respectful denial. Eventually, when the bride's parents agree, she receives presents and both sides settle the marriage date. The mother gives her daughter a present of some milk before she leaves the parental home. In the groom's family prayers are said and then the wedding party begins. After a few days the wife's relatives visit the young couple to see if they have settled down and the celebrations begin again. Note: cohabitation has become common, and when couples decide to marry their children usually attend the ceremony.

The traditional Mongolian calendar, like the Chinese and Tibetan calendars, is based on 12 years named after 12 animals. The years are divided alternately into male and female, or hard and soft, years. It was traditionally important, in the case of marriage, that a bride and bridegroom were compatible according to the various animal signs. For instance, the bridegroom born in the year of the mouse would be unwise to choose a wife born in the year of the tiger in case he lost his authority as head of the household. Animal names are linked to the five elements – wood, fire, earth, iron and water – which match an auspicious colour system of blue, red, yellow, white and black.

For herding and other customs specific to Mongolian nomads, see below.

'ON THE MOVE': THE WORLD OF THE MONGOLIAN NOMAD

Most Mongolians now live in urban centres and visit relatives in the country. Of Mongolia's 2.9 million people only 35% live as nomads or semi-nomads away from towns and they are almost totally dependent on animal herding for their livelihood. But of the total population fewer than 15% are fully nomadic, that is to say, constantly on the move. However, at heart, every Mongolian is a nomad.

Several conditions define Mongol life and culture. The principal one is that the people are pastoral nomads and, therefore, unable to possess many precious things, except the absolute essentials. In fact, they live and travel with little heavy baggage and few personal belongings. So from the earliest times they tended to ornament objects of daily use, such as knives and saddles, and to carve and decorate the posts and doors of their tented homes – the *ger* – along with small items of furniture like stools and tables, which traditionally were, and still are, painted an orange/red colour.

Mongolian national identity is grounded in their nomadic culture. Animal husbandry and herding are part of the country's agri-industry, but at the same time they are an integral and important part of Mongolian heritage. Over the centuries Mongolian nomads have not always been free to roam where they pleased. In other words, there were strings attached: ancient tribal loyalties and family ties and other limiting factors, like walls (eg: the Great Wall of China) and boundaries imposed by history and politics. During the 17th and 18th centuries Mongol herders were subjects of local khans, under the thumb of the Manchu (Chinese Qing dynasty) authorities, when their freedoms and mobility were further restricted and transhumance practices – seasonal migration to pasture animals – were curtailed. Old herding patterns were broken. They were again fragmented in the 20th century by communist ideology and agricultural reforms.

STATE FARMS AND COLLECTIVES State farms, which came and went in the 20th century, were state-run enterprises that had paid employees. Mongolia's state farms, like those in the USSR, mainly grew wheat and other crops, but had some livestock. Collectives, on the other hand, which owned most of the livestock, were a type of co-operative (*negdel*), run by a committee of members, in which herders had shares and payments were usually in kind. After several false starts, collectivisation was completed in 1957 as part of the socialist restructuring and development of agriculture. At first they were resisted and herders preferred to kill their stock rather than give them to the state, but gradually they were drawn into the system.

Collectivised herders, state farm workers and other citizens were permitted to keep some animals of their own. Model farms were on display and workers were rewarded by being given medals for excellent performances or high productivity. The collectives were disbanded in the early 1990s.

AGE-OLD TRADITIONS MEET MODERN REALITIES For centuries Mongolian nomads have eked out an existence on the desolate, isolated central Asian steppes, but, whatever the circumstances, they have lived in their own smaller world, happy to mix among themselves and free, to a greater or lesser extent, to do what they wanted. The nomads have fought hard to retain this measure of freedom. But now, having thrown out a command economy and the restrictions it imposed, they are about to be reined in once more by the harsh reality of their lack of finance, which is required for modernisation and a market economy. As the late Professor Owen Lattimore, foremost authority on Mongolia in the 20th century, once remarked, 'the poor nomad is the pure nomad.' But who wants to be kept poor and pure these days? Not Mongolian nomads.

The nomadic population is not only under threat from economic hardship, but also under pressure from urbanisation and climate change.

THE DAY-TO-DAY LIFE OF NOMADS To see nomads moving camp is an age-old sight: a dismantled *ger* and other possessions are loaded aboard homemade carts when they move from exhausted pastures to new grazing. Depending on the time of year and the size of its herds, a family may have to 'move house' every two months or so. Until the 21st century, relatively small populations and open grassland made such mobility possible without undue competition. But there are recent changes: the newly introduced market economy, larger herd sizes, mining and other new developments together with concerns that land may at some time in the future be privatised, are altering the known traditional patterns of nomadic life. New patterns are beginning to emerge, migrant workers of foreign nationalities stay for a season, work and move on depending on contracts not on grass or water. Mongolian nomads on the other hand are finding it more lucrative to quit herding for legal or illegal mining; they sell their animals or ask a friend to manage them, and move into houses, demanding a huge change in lifestyle. These totally new patterns are very different to the traditional herding lifestyle and *ger*-style living that has gone on in the past in an unbroken chain for generations.

The greatest change in recent years to the herders' lives is political, although their basic living conditions and herding routines continue to develop with the use of more machinery, like motorbikes and solar panels, to help them gain a foothold in the modern world. Under socialism, nomads were salaried and collectives provided veterinary care and winter fodder in times of shortage. Today this is not the case and the nomads must fend for themselves.

Agriculture is not large scale in Mongolia. Potato and cereal crops are grown in the northern and western regions, where you see cultivated areas of barley and wheat. Long-distance food distribution is extremely difficult. The centralised delivery

AGE-OLD MONGOL HERDING SYSTEMS AND LIFESTYLE

The following account of the herding systems and the lifestyle of Mongolian herders was related to the author by the late Professor Owen Lattimore, American Mongol scholar:

The Chinese describe nomads as people who follow grass and water, implying that any type of grass and water would be suitable, which is not the case. Nomads practise a system of interlocking rotation of pasture and animals geared to the changing seasons, and they herd more than one kind of animal. Each animal type grazes differently on the same kind of pasture and some do better than others on different pastures.

Altitude, temperature and rain have a great deal to do with the conditions under which nomads live and pasture their animals. In the semi-arid steppe, grasses which contain salt and soda deposits are good for the animals, whereas in the Gobi, low bush-type foliage provides fodder for camels only and is unsuitable for other animals. Sheep dislike burrs or grass heads but horses can graze this type of pasture, eating the top of the grass, whereas cows graze the foliage lower down the stem and sheep crop plants closest to the ground. Therefore, you can follow horses or cows with sheep but not the other way around.

A diversity of animals is the nomads' 'insurance policy'. Sheep and goats are their main 'money-earning' flocks, supplying all the basic needs: food (mutton), clothing (wool), housing material (felt), fuel (dung) and milk and cheese. The yearly cycle involves bringing livestock through the severest winters. Horses survive best as they can uncover the grass through snow by using their hooves, whereas cattle and sheep must be kept at lower levels or where the wind blows snow into drifts exposing pasture. In the past, cattle were kept in corrals with covered sheds and let out to graze every few days. Special breeds of Mongolian sheep have adapted to various pastures from high cold pasture to low and sandy grazing grounds.

From time immemorial nomads have shared herding responsibilities with neighbours. One family will take the camel herds and keep them watered, while others will see that the sheep and goats are well pastured. In fact travellers seeing animals waiting by a well looking thirsty will often water them using hand-hauled buckets of water, which they spill into long, wooden troughs. Such traditions may continue to dominate in the countryside because people and their livestock must rely on each other to survive. In the past as now, pastoral nomads and their livestock have survived and will continue to do so, not by rules, but by good practices – if they can pass them on to the next generation.

HERDING RULES AND CUSTOMS

- Treat nature with respect
- Do not stay too long in one place
- Recognise the quality of pasture and find suitable pasture for your herds
- Follow restrictions on killing or frightening animals
- Do not shout at your horse – it is man's best friend
- Choose your campsite wisely according to the season
- Do not cut flowers or spoil plants needlessly
- Do not kill animals for pleasure
- Take care of the environment and it will take care of you.

There are different rules regarding the herding of cattle, horses and other animals:

- It was forbidden for a Mongol herder to ride on a saddled animal into pasturing cattle in case it disturbed the cattle who would then lose condition
- Superstition did not allow Mongol herdsmen to count cattle by pointing with a finger in case it resulted in the decline of numbers
- Mongols do not put a sweating horse on a hitching post on an overcast day. This common-sense rule is meant to avoid the horse getting cold, should it rain
- Mongols do not bridle a horse that is hobbled. This avoids difficulties in catching an animal and shows mutual respect and trust between man and animal
- Mongols always mount a horse from the left (near) side.

system no longer exists. Nomads live on meat and dairy products from their own herds, supplemented with game and other wild foodstuffs. They sell or barter wool, sheepskins and meat to obtain manufactured materials and other necessities.

Obtaining and transporting food is easier than it was in the past, when it took a camel ride to stock up on provisions – if there were any. These days a trip by truck or a hitchhike to the local shop, which is fairly well stocked, can easily be achieved on a weekly basis. The biggest problem is having an income in cash for purchases.

In the past, pack animals, like yaks, usually transported the household goods. More recently, however, there has been increasing reliance on motorised transport. However, when it breaks down, Mongol herders have to return to animal transport and the age-old method of cutting hay by hand, which slows them down and increases their workload.

Herding Transhumance is a long-standing practice of herding livestock in accordance with the seasons. Herding families move with their cattle, sheep or horses to higher ground when the first fresh grass appears – a lifestyle that occurs in many areas of the world. In Mongolia, the journeys to fresh 'spring' pastures are across country (covering long treks) as well as shorter journeys up and down the mountain valleys. Some herding families make all their seasonal moves in one area, generally moving from the lower ground where they winter to high spring and summer pastures as they do in the Swiss Alps. Others undertake much longer treks. Herding households around Lake Khövsgöl, in the north, use the lakeshore

People   'ON THE MOVE': THE WORLD OF THE MONGOLIAN NOMAD

2

pastures to winter their cattle, because the snow is sometimes deeper in the valleys, and when spring arrives they migrate to higher ground and remain there until the weather turns cold again.

Agronomists say that eco-efficiency is the key to sustainable development. In simple terms this means continuing to follow age-old practices that have been carefully tried and tested over generations. Mongolian herders are now seeking the advice of their elders on how to deal with the *zud* disaster of recent winters and with herding ecology.

The *ger* – the nomad's tent The *ger* (pronounced 'gair') is the focus of the herdsman's world and its circular shape is repeated for him in a concentric outside world. Nomadic lifestyle over the centuries has principally depended on this classic, collapsible, round tent. The *ger's* durability, lightness and low cost are all points of tremendous advantage to the nomad.

The *ger* is more than a tent, it is a 'home', since Mongols live in their *ger* throughout the year and tend to prefer them to other forms of housing. The Russian name for *ger* is *yurta*, from which we get the word 'yurt'. The *ger* is a unique model of engineering – an ingenious prefabricated home. The design of this compact tent is ideally suited to nomadic lifestyle. It combines coolness in summer and warmth in winter. Made mostly of wood and other locally available materials, it can be quickly assembled or taken to pieces, and is easily transported from place to place on camelback or, more often than not these days, by truck.

Construction details The lower portion of the *ger* consists of sections of trellis-like wall made of willow wood, incorporating the door within its circular framework. The upper part consists of two long upright poles supporting a central wooden roof ring, or 'window', on to which numerous thinner poles are placed, like the fan of an umbrella. Depending on the size of the *ger,* roof poles can number up to 108 (a sacred Buddhist number). Each one fits on to the lattice walls, fixed by straps of raw hide, usually made from camel skin. The roof ring (*toono*) is the most complex component of the *ger's* structure. Apart from holding the poles in place and acting as a smoke vent or window, it is also a natural sundial. The slant of the early-morning rays indicate times for milking and pasturing animals. If the light shines to the back of the *ger*, it is usually after midday and 'too late' to set out on a long journey. During bad weather, the single roof ring 'window' is covered with a piece of felt, or hide, called an *örkh*.

The whole frame is covered with felt made from sheep's wool by a special treatment consisting of pulverising, damping and rolling the fleece fibres into long widths of material. Felt pieces are unrolled and wrapped around the outside wall and placed across the top of the *ger*, leaving the roof ring open for the stove's chimney, light and air. Sheets of canvas for waterproofing cover the *ger* and are tied around the outer wall by three rows of rope, usually made from horse hair. In winter, extra felt is added for insulation so there is no need to fear the severity of sub-zero temperatures. In summer, the wall felt can be rolled up from ground level to let in the breeze. The *ger* is usually pitched directly on the ground, and the floor area is covered by carpets, unless the *ger* is intended to stay in place for some time, in which case a wooden floor is laid. Ts Balkhaajav, a Mongolian writer, observed that, 'From the air the *ger's* dome-shaped structure looks like natural pearls scattered on green silk.'

Interior life The stove sits in the centre and furniture is simple. There is an unusual sequence in assembling the *ger*. Large items like beds, cupboards and storage chests

A GER

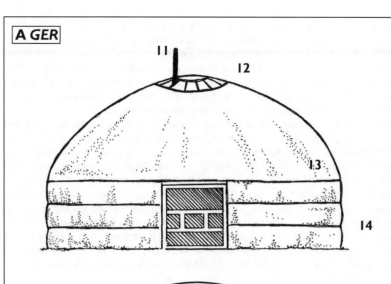

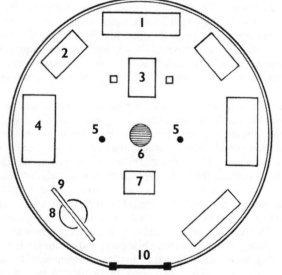

KEY

1	cupboard	8	koumiss bag
2	chests	9	shelves
3	low table and stools	10	door
4	beds	11	stove pipe
5	roof posts	12	roof rings
6	stove	13	canvas cover
7	fuel box	14	horsehair ties

are placed out in the open air, looking like a surreal stage without walls, and the structure is assembled around them, because such items are too big to fit in through the door – which, by tradition, always faces south.

Inside the *ger* everything has its specific place according to ancient custom. The north section is the place of honour, where guests may be invited to sit. The family shrine is placed on a cupboard or chest against the wall on the north side of the *ger*. Usually it proudly contains a picture of the Dalai Lama and a small statue of Buddha lit by oil lamps. Alongside these treasured possessions are family photographs and letters and photographs received from visitors. Beds are nestled close to the east and west sides and stacked with colourful cushions, packed full of blankets and neatly folded bedclothes for the night. Everything is kept tidy. Work equipment is stored on the man's side, the west-side front of the *ger*, where he normally puts his saddle and tack on a stand. Nearby, a calfskin sack is slung especially for fermenting mare's milk, *airag*. A long-handled ladle extends through the neck which is turned by family members as they pass by, to help the fermentation process. Other items like saws and axes are stored by tucking them into the trelliswork. On the woman's side, the east-side front of the *ger*, there are usually open shelves for jugs, pans and bowls with space beneath for milk churns and a cupboard for other cooking and eating utensils.

At dawn, the woman of the house rises first to light the stove. She sprinkles a little incense on the flames, which gives a lovely aromatic smell. The fuel box is usually placed next to the stove on the door side. Fuel may be wood or even coal briquettes if the *ger* is situated in one of the big-fenced *ger* encampments in towns. In the countryside, animal dung (which is odourless and burns like coke) is used. It dries out naturally in the low humidity and is collected in a special basket.

Exterior life The area surrounding the *ger* has to be kept clean and tidy, so the rubbish tip and latrine pit are some distance away. Some families have a second *ger* that is used for storage. The outer ring is where the horses are tied and domestic work is done, and outside that is a much larger area where sheep and goats are tended by the woman or older children. The man's herding area is bigger still, and as the concentric world of the herder expands he may take his cattle and horses to pastures and water many kilometres away, only to return home at nightfall.

Herdsmen and their families live between 12 and 20 miles, or sometimes further, from their nearest neighbours. As members of herding co-operatives during most of the 20th century, nomadic families were visited regularly by co-operative officials to enquire if their quotas were being met and to check out their political duties (eg: voting in elections). Now that they live independently the arrival of an unexpected visitor is something of an event. In the past, Mongol herdsmen were always hospitable to casual visitors, and offered food and drink and even a bed for the night and it was unheard of for travellers to steal from rural families; changing times, however, have made them more cautious. They are curious and sharp-sighted, and quickly aware of the dust of an approaching jeep.

Food and drink Mongolian women and girls usually do the milking, while the men and boys look after the animals and ensure that the herds have enough fodder and water. You will see lines of horses tethered to a long rope pegged to the ground, or suspended in the air like a washing line, between two posts. The animals are tied to this line by ropes attached to their rough, leather halters. During the summer months, weathered boots and tack are repaired or replaced; hides are tanned in a salt and whey solution to fashion into strips of leather, while horse hair is cut and twisted into ropes. Bags are cut and stitched from cow hide to hold *airag* (mare's milk), herders' favourite drink. On the whole, Mongol herders are closely bonded to their animals – particularly their horses. They are experts in the treatment and handling of their livestock.

Over the years, Mongolian nomads have developed a number of unique dairy products, which include different types of yoghurt, cottage cheese, dried curds and *airag* (and *koumiss*, a fermented alcoholic drink made from milk). To make *airag*, fresh mare's milk is poured into large, wooden churns or hide containers that are traditionally slung on the trelliswork or stand to the left side of the *ger* door. A long-handled ladle protrudes from the churn or sack, which churns the milky contents 1,000 times or more – pummelled to aid fermentation by everyone coming in or going out about their daily business. The choicest *airag* is made in autumn after the animals have eaten their fill of summer grasses. It has a tangy fizzy taste. It may be further distilled to produce a more intoxicating drink called *shimiin airag*. During the cold winter months, cow's milk is also distilled to produce *shimiin arkhi* – best consumed when warm and fresh. When and how to consume milk products was bound by strictly observed rules among nomads, who only used dairy products from mid spring to mid autumn, a habit which has almost died out. Some milk is boiled in large pans to make *tarag* (a sour drink). During the summer months, cheese is squeezed between rocks to remove the moisture and dried to form protein-rich nuggets, which are preserved to last during the long winter months.

Meat, usually mutton, is eaten in the cold season and is dried during summer. Mongolian nomads slaughter their sheep by blocking the main heart artery by hand, through a neat cut in the animal's chest. This is done as quickly as possible to avoid causing the animal pain or suffering. Because Mongolians hate to waste any animal products they use a sheep's stomach for storing butter. After slaughtering a sheep, the blood is collected in a bowl and added to mincemeat, along with some fresh herbs, onions and salt, and used to make sausages by stuffing this mixture into the sheep's intestines. The result is delicious when barbecued. Nomads also collect and store animal dung for fuel for cooking, which saves cutting down brush wood, like saxaul, in the Gobi.

VISITING NOMADS

Happy is he whom guests frequent. Joyful is he at whose door guests' horses are always tethered.

Mongolian proverb

Few places in the world provide an opportunity to experience a lifestyle that has changed so little over hundreds of years. Times are changing and with them the lifestyle of nomads – but the old customs are deeply respected and certainly kept going, although for how long more one wonders. Mongolian cultural traditions are so different that it is possible you might unknowingly offend your hosts in some small way, so it is probably best to observe quietly what goes on around you when you enter a family *ger* for the first time. Mongolians are very warm and friendly and soon make you feel one of the family. The most humbling thing is when your Mongolian hosts (sometimes an elderly couple) insist on giving you their bed and then proceed to sleep on the floor beside you. This is not considered at all unusual – it is never too much trouble to prepare food and to share with you whatever they have.

Most nomadic families have not been exposed to the full blast of Western lifestyle, except via the television. Modern conveniences, which we so often take

2

for granted, like electricity and running water have not yet reached the majority of nomads, who live a simple life of natural survival, miles from most services. They slaughter animals for their food; draw water from wells and carry or truck river water home in buckets – in winter bringing home large blocks of ice from the frozen rivers to melt down for drinks and other purposes. But modern ways of living will eventually reach even the remotest corners of the country.

Tourists need to be conscious that although it is the custom to show hospitality to guests, there is work to be done. The lifestyle appears to be easy and attractive during the summer days, but it is quite the opposite for most of the year. Try to help out in any way you can and be aware not to overstay your welcome. It is a balance which you must weigh up for yourself, since visits mean a great deal to isolated nomads and often they will press you to stay on.

The unwritten law of hospitality

The hard conditions of Mongolian life have given them a tradition of friendliness and there is an unwritten law of hospitality that has evolved from experience over centuries. Traditionally, complete strangers could enter a *ger* without knocking. There was an understanding in the countryside that should a traveller come to an unoccupied *ger*, the door would not be locked, travellers could enter, brew tea and eat there, before continuing on their way. Herdsmen shared their food and drink freely and usually provided travellers with a small bundle of provisions for the onward journey. A word of caution, though: however friendly the nomads may be, watch out for their dogs – they can bite. If you approach an unknown *ger*, it is advisable to shout '*nokhoi khor!*' – 'hold the dog!' Shout loudly in any language (the dogs seem to understand) and they will get out of the way! They will certainly sense it if you hesitate and are afraid of them; the main thing is not to catch their fleas, so don't even try to pat them and always carry a stick!

Between nomads there is no payment because they know they will also ask for hospitality many times during the year, perhaps when beaten off track by bad weather, or just broken down on the road, which often happens, judging from the number of truck and jeep carcasses one sees dotted along the Mongolian country tracks. Local *gers* automatically provide an emergency 'rescue service' which has worked well over time, like the bush telegraph.

Payment to nomads

The situation is changing with regard to receiving day visits from foreign tourists. Some form of payment is usually pre-arranged by tour companies. If not, perhaps you might consider other ways to compensate the nomads for their help and hospitality. One of the best ways is to buy their merchandise or souvenirs, if they produce any, or offer to pay for the musical entertainment, if they will accept. Bring a few small presents to give away, such as non-spicy packet foods or simple household items, or books and pens for children.

First-time visit to a Mongolian family *ger*

Visitors usually sit around the stove on small stools at a low table, where various dried cheeses and fried pastries are available. First the host offers tea, to which the hostess adds butter, salt and sometimes roasted millet for taste, before adding milk. Vodka, or local drinks *airag* (fermented mare's milk) or *shimiin arkhi* (cow's-milk vodka) may also be offered. In summer, the nomads tend to eat less meat and more 'white food' – the dairy produce of their own animals. In winter, especially during family celebrations, dried-milk products are arranged in spectacular tiers on a large dish and offered to guests.

Meals mostly consist of mutton (with surprise delicacies such as goat meat or marmot). The table is spread with great care and bowls of steaming stew are handed round to each guest by the host, who holds the bowl with both hands when he offers food in a traditional Mongolian manner to each person in turn, starting with the eldest or most important person. To show his or her appreciation, the guest receives the bowl, likewise, with both hands, or by taking it with the right hand supported at the elbow by the left. Silence means that one accepts the dish with thanks. Another way to honour the guest is to offer him or her a special portion of meat. The best piece of mutton is considered to be the massive rump, which is usually placed in the centre of the dish. The host cuts a slice and offers it first to the guests, then everyone begins to eat. Mongolians are always delighted if visitors enjoy their food.

After the meal Mongolians have a tendency to burst into song – even the most timid-looking nomad is persuaded to sing. A small cup of vodka is passed around and if it stops in front of you then it is your turn to sing, so come prepared. Nomads enjoy this sort of entertainment. Sitting in a *ger* in the middle of nowhere, singing or just listening is a magical experience.

Most tour operators offer special programmes and visits to nomads can be easily arranged. During the day guests may accompany their hosts on the steppe, riding out to water their herds of camels and horses. You may experience some of their routine tasks closer to home, where the women and girls milk the goats and horses while the men go herding, or even help them to move camp and set up a *ger*. Then you can really appreciate and understand their natural lifestyle and lack of possessions.

Washing facilities at family *gers* Away from Ulaanbaatar conditions are very basic. In the remote Gobi-Altai, for example, there is usually no running water and washing is done by dampening a cloth and giving your face and hands a wipe. A simple water can with an open top and a small tap attached to the base is sometimes found, hung on the left front wall by the door. A stand with a tin washbasin allows adequate provision for washing and doing teeth (rinse outside). If the *ger* is newly sited on summer pasture, it may have no pit latrine; if this is the case just walk away from the residence to urinate. If the *ger* is semi-nomadic or pitched in a settlement or compound, there are usually pit latrines in a shed to the side of the *ger*. Your host will point the way. It is wise to bring a flashlight with you at night.

FUTURE CONCERNS
21st-century nomads Mongolian nomads will have to adapt or die. They are the remnants of a disappearing culture that has survived for millennia, mostly in harsh, isolated conditions. For generations their lifestyle survived on a knife edge, protected by their isolation. But with improved transport and an influx of modern technology, things are changing almost too fast for Mongolia's remaining nomads. Their age-old traditional lifestyle is being buffeted by serious 'winds of change' that bring them into contact with petrochemicals and polythene, iPads, mobile phones and other gadgets – all part of global technology growth. The changes that modern life bring certainly impact the nomads' traditional skills, such as repairing wooden lattice with raw hide, stitching and making ropes from camel hair and wool, and travelling by horse and camel. Riding out to herd animals is done nowadays on motorbike – similar to in the Australian outback. Trips to town happen more regularly, processed food replaces mutton stews, and fizzy drinks may soon replace salty-milky-tea or *airag* (mares' milk). But some traditions die hard because Mongolians everywhere love their mutton stews and milk products!

However, despite the old ways dying and handicrafts and horses being replaced by modern machinery, the actual population of nomads has fallen – difficult to say by how many – as the city-dwelling population increases.

Herding life is tough and winters have been even tougher than normal in the last decade. That places nomads in the 21st century on the margins of existence, surrounded by a vast unpopulated territory. Their lives and the lives of their animals are further threatened by climate change – droughts are regularly affecting areas that once fed and watered herds. Hit by hard winters in recent years, nomads have drifted to the outskirts of cities or settlements, their herds diminished if not wiped out entirely by *zud* (see page 7). Mongolia's severe continental climate has always challenged the survival of these resilient people and they need all the skills of millennia to come through winters of incredible cold, through violent dust storms in spring, and through summers of low rainfall, especially in the south when temperatures soar to 40°C in a Gobi heatwave. Yet, Mongolia's nomads have coped with all that; and they have survived far-reaching political change during most of the 20th century under a one-party communist state, when their herds became collectivised. Again they adapted to these changes. But the speed of 21st-century change is challenging their adaptability to the extremes, although it may actually make their lives easier in some ways with solar power generators and motorbikes. However, many nomads have moved of necessity into settlements in provincial towns and many more have gravitated to the capital, where they have become semi-settled – neither one thing nor the other – caught in no-man's land. Ulaanbaatar and indeed other towns in Mongolia are surrounded by *ger* encampments, some regulated, others haphazard. People arrive with their *ger* and put a fence round the land they claim, hoping later to build a shack that may be converted into a semi-permanent building.

Most land ownership in Mongolia is held in common – so that each citizen has a share in the ownership today of the great mineral wealth that is currently being explored and developed. In theory this will make all Mongolians rich, but the wealth has yet to be properly managed and distributed. Since the mining boom in 2008 trust funds have been set up by the government and there is a pay out of shares or cash. Mining brings with it both social and environmental change with river courses altered and land claimed for development. All that glisters is not gold because, for nomads, besides their families, their animals, shelter and some money in their pockets, there is an even more precious commodity – and that is water.

Survival – a fragile balance

The Mongolian climate is so extreme that winter storms, droughts and desertification all threaten the nomads' existence, affecting their livelihood. Summer drought and stunted forage have resulted in animals not gaining sufficient weight to withstand the ferocity of the super-cold winters of late. Nomadic pastoralists have had to roam further afield to find edible grass for their animals and some have been forced to buy winter fodder where available. Emergency shipments of grain and food supplies have been supplied by Russia and other countries, to help the nomads cope with the fodder shortages, due also to a preceding drought in the winter of 1999 – the worst conditions in living memory. The following winters, 2000 and 2001, were almost as bad. But the cycle of recurring bad winters seems to be happening more frequently – as was the case in 2009/10. However, despite the effects of severe winters and summer heat in the Gobi areas, in other parts of the country grain production has been rising.

Drought is causing problems, especially in the Gobi where surface water is so scarce. In steppe areas, pastures that used to exist are now arid and useless because the grasses have all but disappeared. Desertification is a gradual process when the grass is uprooted leaving the soil bare and prone to erosion. A decade of hotter drier weather means that this situation will not go away and directly threatens the herders' only means of livelihood – their herds of camels, horses, sheep and goats – and over time will erode their way of life. The trouble is that once the desertification process starts it tends to expand very quickly.

Mongol nomads have a deep respect for nature, based on an extensive knowledge of pasture, plants and vegetation. They have managed their natural resources very economically and effectively over hundreds of years to meet the requirements of their livestock under difficult and extreme climatic conditions. But there is a precarious balance between respecting the ecosystem and the new demands placed upon it by human activity. Unfortunately, scrap metal, old tyres, bottles and plastic bags and other rubbish are dumped along the main routes of travel.

Large-scale overgrazing is presenting the rural economy with a new problem: it is not just the number of animals that is important but the ratio of one type of animal to another. Many ancient herding rules have been broken by the 'gold rush' to farm cashmere with the result that in Ömnögobi Aimag, for example, the herds of goats outnumber the sheep herds in many cases. Experts currently calculate 1.4ha per animal is needed, ideally, to avoid this problem. At present less is available.

Although the herding community was badly hit and the country as a whole suffered greatly from recent severe winters, the *zud* disaster has highlighted the urgent problems of overgrazing and animal ratios are now being scientifically studied. The government has realised that sustainability in rural areas, where almost half the population lives, depends on modernising the livestock sector, encouraging the growth of food processing, improving land management, improving breeds and yields and building more winter shelters.

It is thought that the transition from a strict quota system (under socialism) to a free-market economy (from 1990) prompted herders to increase the numbers of their livestock far beyond the capacity of the fragile steppe land. This was particularly true of the sharp growth in goats as the cashmere industry took off. Also the rural population rose slightly and became better off as a result of the increased stock holdings, while unemployment hit settled communities. The trend had been of a population shift back to the land but it is now the reverse as nomads crowd back into the towns.

MONGOLIANS AND THEIR DOMESTIC ANIMALS

Tavan hoshuu mal in Mongolian means 'five kinds of animals'. The word *hoshuu* translates as 'muzzle'. It is interesting to note that Mongolians divide their animals into warm-muzzled and cold-muzzled types: horses and sheep are warm muzzled, while cows, camels and goats are cold muzzled. Mongolia's herding economy depends on the horse, cattle, Bactrian camel, sheep and goat. These provide the herdsmen with food and drink, transport, and raw materials, such as felt to cover their *ger*, leather for harnesses, boots and household items, and wool and cashmere for sale.

MONGOLIAN HORSES Once seen as notable proof of a nomad's status and success, Mongol horses are really pony size – around 14 hands high. For generations, these tough little horses have provided the herder with transport and entertainment, such as racing. The range-bred horse has great strength and stamina and can withstand all types of weather without additional feeding as it can kick back the snow and ice in winter to uncover the grass beneath. Coat colours vary from deep brown to dapple grey. The famous Mongolian wild horse (*Equus przewalskii*), the *takhi*, an unridable ancestral horse type, survived in Mongolia only up to the 1960s when it became extinct in the wild. A number of *takhi* were returned to Mongolia in the 1990s by European and American breeders, see page 130. The *takhi* are now breeding naturally in several release sites in Mongolia including Khustain Nuruu National Park, see page 277, near Ulaanbaatar, where they can be visited.

The cult of the Mongol horse
Man and the horse have been intimately linked through the ages. The cult of the horse has grown from ancient times and it was even stronger than the cult of the Great Khan himself. Horses were status symbols belonging to princes and warriors. As the contents of steppe tombs have revealed in different regions across the Eurasian steppe, horses have been worshipped – and also sacrificed, so that chieftains can ride into the next world – for thousands of years. Bones, bridles and bits tell the story of their supreme value to the nomads.

Mongolian nomads and their horses are inseparable. In fact, one without the other is unthinkable. In terms of identity, the Mongol horse symbolises the free spirit and independence of all Mongols. It is relevant in many ways to nomadic culture and to the steppe economy. Not only is the horse the chief means of transport on which the nomads have most relied over centuries, but it is also a comrade and friend. Much of a nomad's enjoyment in life is derived from his horse, as Mongolian folk songs testify.

Small, muscular and swift, the Mongol pony provided the ideal mount for the many tasks a soldier had to perform in battle. They could wheel around quickly and their size meant the nomad/warrior could dismount easily and jump back quickly on to his horse. Mongolians have so many ways to identify a horse (the language is rich in horse descriptions) that they have no need to give them individual names. One way to describe a good horse is to say his eyes are full of fire. Genghis Khan himself was described as having fire in his eyes – recorded in *The Secret History of the Mongols*. In many respects his success was due to the lifestyle of the nomads and above all to the stocky, range-bred Mongol pony which gave his army the mobility it needed.

The horse and the pace of life
Riding, I soon found, wasn't much fun.

Beatrice Buxtrode, 19th-century traveller

The herder's pace of life is governed by the speed of a horse. The Mongolian horse has eight different paces, one of which is ambling. Some Mongol ponies will automatically break into this pace over long distances as it is much more comfortable for the rider. The range horses give a thoroughly uncomfortable ride. The solution is to do what the Mongolian herdsmen do, and rise at the trot and stay standing in the stirrups, balancing with the legs and letting the ankle, knee and thigh joints take the strain. That is all very well if you have cast-iron leg muscles, but if you haven't, as travellers have discovered, it is agony. On other occasions the herdsman's technique is to allow his body to relax, and here *airag* or vodka serves its purpose, helping him to sit (or slump) in the saddle, relaxing every limb.

Riding equipment
Saddles Saddles are decorative as well as functional. Often the more ornate saddles belonged to women and were a part of their dowry. Decorative saddles

are prized possessions in central Asia both as items of daily use and as examples of material wealth. The pommel, or front part of the saddle, is high and the back part curves. The seat is made of wood and hard and uncomfortable. Felt or fleece padding enables the rider to sit astride with more comfort. Although it is customary for Westerners to rise to the trot on every second stride, Mongol horsemen usually stand in their stirrups avoiding the bumpy, seated position. On expedition or riding tours there is no need to bring a Western riding saddle as a Russian or leather Mongol riding saddle is adequate.

Ironwork and the bit According to the 13th-century Persian historian Rashid-ad-Din, the Mongol tribes of 2,000 years ago were so fierce that they destroyed one another until just four couples remained. They settled in a remote valley and began a new nation. These pioneers discovered how to forge iron by making a huge bellows from the skins of bulls and horses that they used to smelt iron ore at high temperatures by burning surface coal and wood. The trade of the blacksmith thus began. Iron bits, found in Altai tombs, date back to the 5th century BC.

CATTLE (INCLUDING YAK) Concentrated in the central and northern provinces and raised for meat and milk, cattle graze close to nomadic settlements and often take themselves to pasture and return in the evening with little attention from the herder. Yaks and *haynags* (cow/yak cross) account for a fifth of the country's cattle. Yaks (Tibetan oxen) number 500,000. They are shaggy beasts but agile and well adapted to high mountain pastures, because their long, thick hairy coats can withstand the cold. Yak hair is collected by plucking after the winter is over. They are used to transport *gers* in the northern regions. Yak milk is particularly rich and makes delicious yoghurt. Clotted cream (*öröm*) is partially dried to turn into soft round cakes – a high-cholesterol treat!

SHEEP Sheep are raised for wool and meat. Mutton is the staple food of Mongolia and sheep's milk is made into cheese and curds, which are dried in summer for winter use. Selection and cross breeding have developed different varieties of sheep in different regions: in the east the black-headed fat-tailed sheep predominate; the Orkhon Valley sheep are known for their semi-fine fleece; and the long large-tailed sheep have coarse but very white wool. *Argali* (*Ovis ammon*), the rare Mongolian wild sheep variety, are also known as 'blue sheep' or 'Marco Polo sheep'. They are found in the Gobi-Altai Mountains and hunted by trophy hunters.

GOATS Famous for their hair (cashmere), not for their meat, goats are herded with sheep and are concentrated in the central and southwestern provinces. Cashmere is the rich, downy undercoat, the inner layer that keeps the goats warm. In spring, cashmere is combed (not sheared, like wool from sheep) from the goats' underbelly and back. The fibres of Mongolian cashmere are top quality, long and very fine. Mongolia accounts for about 30% of the world's raw cashmere exports.

BACTRIAN CAMELS The two-humped variety, and used for riding and as draught animals, Bactrian camels can carry up to 200kg. Their meat is not usually eaten, but their milk is made into curds and cheese. Camels are concentrated in southern and western provinces. Some people comb out, others shear, the hair in June. Camel wool (for blankets and other garments) provides a good source of income for the herders. In recent times the camel population has been in gradual decline, and there is grave concern among conservationists about the plight of the wild camels (*khavtgai*) found in the Gobi regions, because they are becoming dangerously few in number – the world population numbers fewer than 1,000 animals.

Camel milk and riding habits The two-humped Bactrian camel, unlike the one-humped dromedary, can survive exceedingly cold temperatures. Newly born camels (*botgo*) arrive at the end of the long, hard winter when there is hope of fresh grazing in March or April. Yearlings (*torom*) are tied to a rope on the ground while their mothers are milked. Milking is a special skill and females have to be coaxed by whistles and songs to let down milk. Camel's milk tastes slightly tangy and rather salty. It is not everyone's favourite drink.

Bactrian camels live to be 14 or 15 years old and can be ridden from the age of five or six. A camel saddle is made without any wood and fits snugly between the two humps. The camel's gait is unlike a horse's but one soon gets used to its sway and horseriders will easily adapt. The camel saddle is more comfortable than the traditional horses' saddle, with its thick under-saddle carpet and thicker top-saddle carpet.

The foot area of the camel stirrup is almost round in shape and made of a much heavier metal than a Western riding stirrup. The camel drops to its knees to enable you to mount. This may not always be easy, depending on the temperament of your camel – and they are temperamental creatures. Camel halters are made from rope attached to a peg in the nose. Reining is 'cowboy-style' neck reining – rein to the right to go right, rein to the left to go left. Stopping is more difficult for beginners and the word 'whoa!' (which is the same in Mongolian) is accompanied by a tug on the rein. If for any reason your camel bolts, take a good hold, hang on and relax as it will eventually run out of steam.

LANGUAGE

When the Mongol Empire collapsed, the majority of Mongols returned to their beloved uplands. They settled back to their usual herding occupations and fought among themselves – forgetting about military conquests. Despite such isolation, the Mongol language was greatly enriched by its international past.

Mongolian (Mongol) is an Altaic language, related to the Turkish spoken in modern Turkey and other Turkic languages of central Asia like Kazakh and Tuvan.

HOW THE MIGHTY CAMEL LOST HIS ANTLERS

The following is a folk tale explaining how the camel came to lose its antlers:

One day the camel went down to the spring for a drink. There he met a deer, which had been looking longingly at his magnificent set of antlers. Finally the deer plucked up courage and asked if he could borrow the camel's antlers for just one day. The camel, being a generous beast, said, 'Yes, of course you may borrow my fine antlers.' The following day he went to the spring to retrieve his precious headgear, but there was no sign of the deer. To this day the camel will raise his head when drinking and look out across the country in search of the deer and his missing antlers.

Mongolians describe the camel's trait as being one who is over generous to his own cost.

It is the language of the majority Khalkha Mongols. Together with its various dialects, it is spoken by some six million people in Mongolia, Russia and China. There are four main dialects:

- **Oirat** Spoken in the western regions
- **Buryat** Spoken on the northern borders near Lake Baikal
- **Khalkha** The main dialect of Mongolia
- **Inner Mongolian dialects** Found among people living near Mongolia's southern borders; corresponding to the dialects of similar adjacent tribes in Inner Mongolia.

The Mongol–Turkic vocabulary of the ancient nomads has expanded over the centuries to embrace Tibetan and Sanskrit expressions from Buddhism, Chinese and Manchu words introduced during the rule of the Qing dynasty, Russian technical and political terms from the period of Soviet influence, and, during the 1990s, English words that are part of the international language of commerce, science and computers.

TRANSCRIPTION, SPELLING AND PRONUNCIATION Mongolian has many sounds that are unfamiliar and difficult for English speakers. It is not an easy language to learn and its transcription is complex. Mongol words consist of stems to which suffixes may be attached consecutively (ie: agglutinated). Altaic languages feature vowel harmony which means that 'back' and 'front' vowels (produced at the back and the front of the mouth) do not mix together in the same word, so the vowels of the suffixes harmonise with those of the stems.

New Mongolian spelling doubles its vowels to indicate a stressed vowel length. Thus 'Ulan Bator' becomes 'Ulaanbaatar'. The choice of *h* or *kh* in transliteration is a difficult one, as there is currently no standard transcription system for translators to follow. The letter *x* in Cyrillic is rendered as either *h* or *kh*; I have opted in this guide for the most used system of *kh*, which sounds like the *ch* in 'loch', as pronounced with a raspy Scottish accent. The use of *i* and *y* also varies. The endings *g* or *k*, and to a lesser extent *d* and *t*, are practically impossible to distinguish by ear. There is little consistency and until very recently practically no guidance for the beginner wishing to study Mongolian. Words run together. Often the first syllables are the accented ones, while the rest of the word tails off in a 'shwoosh' of descending tones. There is no agreement about the spelling of Mongol names in foreign languages – some books use one system, and some another.

In this guide the most common Mongolian words like *khan* and *aimag* are not printed in italics, but other Mongolian words like *airag* (vodka), *deel* (Mongol tunic/dress), *ger* (yurt) and *ovoo* (cairn) are printed in italics. For further information, see pages 436–40.

SCRIPT Mongol was put into writing 800 years ago on the orders of Genghis Khan, according to *The Secret History of the Mongols*. Mongolia has used a number of scripts throughout its history but the most used has been the Uighur Mongolian script. The Mongol script is based on the Uighur alphabet, derived in turn from Sogdian. Uighur and Sogdian were both written horizontally and vertically, but Mongolian script is written in vertical columns from left to right. Its letters vary slightly in shape depending on whether they are at the beginning, the middle or the end of a word, as in Arabic. Over the centuries some new letters were introduced into the Mongol script, initially to reduce ambiguity, and later in order to incorporate certain Tibetan and Russian words. Attempts to reintroduce the Uighur Mongolian script widely in recent years have failed because it had been abandoned in favour of modified Russian Cyrillic – children were not taught to write it, books were not printed in the 'old' Mongolian writing, and during the 20th century only grandfathers and grandmothers kept it alive. Schools and other institutions thought it would prove too disruptive to re-introduce, and there was also a shortage of suitable typesetting equipment. Most people tended to prefer a modified Cyrillic for everyday use.

Khalkha Mongolian is written in the Cyrillic alphabet with two extra letters. Following a political decision in the 1940s to abandon the experimental Romanisation of Mongol and minority languages in the USSR, this modified Cyrillic alphabet was brought into general use in Mongolia in 1946. It is much closer to modern spoken Mongolian than the classical language of the Mongol script, whose use was discouraged.

RELIGION

Mongolian herders have a reverence for the land, although many will tell you they don't know why they feel this way.

Anonymous

Shamanism and folk religion have ancient roots. But as the Mongol Empire expanded, the Mongols came into contact with Nestorian Christianity, Buddhism and Islam. Each established some influence at the Mongol court. Genghis Khan seems to have been interested in Tibetan Buddhism and Christianity, although this bred rivalry among the shamans. It is said that Genghis Khan was interested in all religions and in none. He drew his power from the Eternal Blue Heaven – like the Chinese emperor, the Son of Heaven. Mongolia was converted to Tibetan-style Buddhism twice, first by the example of Kublai Khan, Genghis Khan's grandson, who adopted it as the state religion in the 13th century, and again in the 16th century, when Altan Khan took Buddhist vows and created the title Dalai Lama for the Tibetan leader.

At the end of the 20th century there were some 136 registered monasteries, temples, mosques and churches in Mongolia. About 120 of these were active Buddhist monasteries and temples with some 5,000 lamas (monks) holding regular religious services. The numbers are imprecise because there are many small Buddhist temples in the Mongolian countryside that are opened only for festivals. Others are *ger süm*, or felt 'temple-tents', for religious services at the sites of monasteries and temples destroyed in the anti-religious campaigns of the 1930s. A national survey of monasteries was undertaken in 2007 by the Arts Council of Mongolia. At the time of writing there were more than 1,200 monasteries (including ruined sites) on record. To follow their progress, visit www.mongoliantemples.net.

The communists persecuted all religions, and both monks and shamans were killed in their thousands during political purges. Since 1990, there has been freedom to practise religion. Buddhism, the main belief, has experienced a strong resurgence. While it would be true to say that Mongolians respect, even revere, religious rituals and practices, communist ideology shattered their beliefs. Some say that in the past Lamaism burdened the ordinary people with an impossible degree of servitude, but when the ideals of communism were abandoned, a vacuum was created for both spiritual and political 'belief'.

Mongolians in the 21st century are reviving their grandparents' religious beliefs and many are open to the acceptance of other faiths. Christianity is an alternative

OVOOS – SACRED STONES

These cairns of stones and rocks occur on mountain passes and at crossroads. They are sacred, ceremonial places. Most people are unaware of why they walk around an *ovoo* and will admit to not knowing why with a shrug of their shoulders. They do it to make sure the truck doesn't break down or that things go well on a journey. According to an ancient rite it is proper to walk around the *ovoo* three times in a clockwise direction. *Ovoo* ceremonies led by a lama are meant to banish demons and plagues, stop wolves from attacking flocks, and thieves and brigands from attacking travellers. Another explanation is that in the days of Genghis Khan, each warrior accompanying him on a campaign had to place a stone on a pile. On return, each warrior removed a stone and the number left on the pile indicated the number killed in action.

religion and appeals to some young people, who are keen to trust more and learn new values following the collapse of socialism. Shamanism has also been revived and is of interest for cultural reasons.

SHAMANISM This religion, the oldest religion practised in Mongolia, centres on beliefs and rituals associated with a shaman, a man or woman regarded as having access to the 'spirit world'. Mongolian shamans enter an ecstatic trance state in which the shaman is empowered to engage with the spirits in order to protect and heal members of the community, to guide souls and cure illnesses. Shamanism is found in many primitive cultures like those of the Siberian Tungus, from whose language the word 'shaman' (*samán*) derives. Under Genghis Khan's rule, the 'Eternal Blue Heaven' was idolised as the source of his power. A shaman at his court named Kököchü was appointed Teb Tenggeri ('great heaven'), and would select favourable days for moving camp, getting married, declaring war, or choosing a successor. He tried to stir up trouble between Genghis Khan and his brother Qasar, and had his back broken as a punishment by order of the khan. Shamanism is a faith without books. All teaching and instruction has been given orally, passed from shaman to shaman over the centuries, and its traditions learned by heart.

Shamanism went underground and almost died out during the former socialist period. Becoming a shaman involves the gift of divination, such as psychic power, and further involves initiation rites. The shaman's dress also has symbolic significance; in some cases it is decorated with gleaming plates, bells and strips of cloth, all attached to the costume. The shaman might wear a headdress to resemble a bird, with the tail of a pheasant and the body costume of a fish. Drums are used to help the shaman enter a trance-like state, as chanting begins and the shaman 'transcends' into another world while the body dances, swirls or totters with jerky movements. The shaman sometimes tells those present about the experience to help cure the sick, or just collapses with exhaustion on the floor. People are very secretive about the whole subject.

FOLK RELIGION Folk religion is concerned with individuals and families and, like Shamanism, has ancient roots and traditions. It is based upon superstitious beliefs and involves the worship of sky, fire and ancestors. Incense is burned and blessings chanted. In contrast to Shamanism, these prayers were written down. A fire-worship ceremony has recently been introduced as part of the president's New Year duties. Many of the ancient rituals and ceremonies, such as the *ovoo* ceremonies (see box, page 93), are steeped in a mixture of folk and other religions. The 'white old man' appears in many folk prayers. He is portrayed dressed in white, leaning on a stick and has a long white beard. His title is 'lord of the earth and the waters'. Mythological figures include Geser Khan, son of Hurmast Khan, ruler of the heavens. Equestrian deities bestow good fortune on hunting and protect flocks and herds, allowing the 'windhorse flag' to fly, which guards domestic stock from predators such as wolves. Mounted deities are said to have military prowess. Several Mongolian presidents have participated in another renewed custom, worship of sacred mountains.

BUDDHISM Buddhism is a world religion with a historical founder, Prince Siddhartha Gautama. He is thought to have lived between 563BC and 483BC. Buddhism, like Hinduism, teaches that reincarnation (a cycle of death and rebirth) is based on *karma* (acts or deeds). When Buddha became 'enlightened', he achieved a blissful state known as *nirvana*. In so doing he eliminated the causes and cycle of rebirth. The Buddhist doctrine contains 'Four Noble Truths' and the 'Noble Eightfold Path'. The Four Noble Truths state the following:

- To exist is to suffer
- Suffering is caused by attachment
- Suffering ceases once attachment ceases
- There is a 'way' to end suffering.

The Noble Eightfold Path involves:

- Right speech
- Right livelihood
- Right action
- Right effort
- Right mindfulness
- Right concentration
- Right opinion
- Right intention.

The aim is to achieve wisdom beyond mere faith and instruction. Subsequent stages, called 'attainments', bring awareness and joy and finally there is a cessation of perception and feeling. A monk's duties are his spiritual exercises and the instruction of novices and lay people. Esoteric Buddhism (Vajrayana) was practised in Mongolia. It shortens this process, but for this you need a teacher or 'guru'. Tantric Buddhism is symbolised by the union of male compassion with female insight – often depicted in art form by an embrace, known in Tibetan as *yab-yum*. The 16th century saw the massive conversion of Mongols to Tantric Buddhism, as practised in Tibet.

THE DALAI LAMA VISITS MONGOLIAN BUDDHISTS

His Holiness the 15th Dalai Lama first visited Mongolia in 1979. His fairly frequent visits are always a source of inspiration and a cause for celebration among Mongolia's Buddhists. Across the open steppe, conch shells and long horns announce his arrival as he flies in. During his visit in 1997 he spoke to an audience of thousands, urging the people to drink less vodka and suggesting they stick to mare's milk (which is less intoxicating). He appealed for help for street children. Throughout his visit people hung on his every word. The Dalai Lama always draws enormous, enthusiastic crowds. Because of sensitivities about the Chinese control of Tibet, the Mongolian government cannot host the Dalai Lama, who visits as a private individual.

Even more anomalous was the position of the Tibetan lama, recognised by the Dalai Lama to be the ninth Bogd Gegeen, leader of Mongolian Buddhism. He lived at the Dalai Lama's headquarters in Dharamsala and visited Mongolia for the first time in the summer of 1999. He was taken to Erdene Zuu and enthroned, but the Mongolian government was nervous because of a contemporary visit by the Chinese president. But the Dalai Lama again visited in August 2006 when Mongolians came from all over the country to hear him speak. As His Holiness said on this visit, 'We need to focus on modern, current education, but not forget our traditional ways of life.' In November 2011, the Dalai Lama made another visit to Mongolia on his way home from Japan. He held public teachings in the Sports Palace in Ulaanbaatar. His visit was associated with the enthronement of the 9th Bogd Javzandamamba Khutagh. His incarnation was identified as a small child, born in Tibet, who fled to India to join the Dalai Lama. He was enthroned in 2011 as the 9th Bogd Gegeen, having been granted Mongolian citizenship the previous year. To support Buddhism in Mongolia, visit www.tibet-foundation.com.

History of Mongolian Buddhism Kublai Khan appointed a Tibetan lama, Phagspa Lama, to be the spiritual leader of his Yuan dynasty. Phagspa Lama interpreted Mahayana Buddhism so as to make Kublai Khan a Buddhist 'universal king' – an important agreement giving Kublai the temporal power and Phagspa the religious power. This form of Tibetan Buddhism combined the scholarly Sakyapa doctrine with tantric mysticism and ritual; it is called 'Red Hat' Lamaism, originating in southern Tibet, named after the hats worn by its followers. When the Yuan dynasty fell in 1368 most Mongols reverted to Shamanism. In 1578, Altan Khan of the Tumet Mongols had a meeting in Qinghai with Tibet's religious leader, the Gelugpa Abbot of Sera monastery in Lahsa. In a similar arrangement to that between Kublai and Phagspa, Altan gave the abbot the title Dalai Lama, 'dalai' means 'ocean' or 'all-encompassing' in Mongolian and 'lama' means 'spiritual master' in Tibetan. The majority school of Buddhism in Mongolia today is the Gelugpa 'Yellow Hat' sect, named after the yellow hats worn by the monks. In 1639 Zanabazar, the young son of the Mongolian Tüsheet Khan, was recognised as the incarnation of a Tibetan spiritual leader and enthroned as Bogd Gegeen (holy enlightened one). Zanabazar, also known as the Javzandamba Khutagt, was proclaimed the spiritual leader of Mongolian Buddhists and became a highly skilled sculptor of Buddhist art. He and subsequent incarnations occupied third place in the Gelugpa hierarchy, after the Dalai Lama and the Panchen Lama.

Buddhism was adopted as the official religion in Mongolia and the first Buddhist centre was developed at the monastery of Erdene Zuu in the Orkhon Valley. Tibetan lamas came to Mongolia to organise the systematic translation of religious literature into Mongolian, and this in turn encouraged the growth of literacy among Mongols (who were sent to Tibet to learn Tibetan and religious practices) and the flourishing of Mongol and Tibetan culture. Altan Khan banned ancient rites of sacrifice at funerals but, while opposing Shamanism, the new religion absorbed some Shamanist rituals, in particular the mountain-top *ovoo* ceremonies (see box, page 93).

In 1639, the Tüsheet Khan, who claimed descent from Genghis Khan, proclaimed his five-year-old son Zanabazar as the highest incarnate lama in Mongolia, and bestowed on him the title Öndör Gegeen. After his monastic studies in Tibet, Zanabazar was recognised by the Dalai Lama and became the head of Mongolian Buddhism. In the course of his long life, Zanabazar did much to cultivate Buddhism in Mongolia, establishing monasteries and temples. He devised a new alphabet and was also a great artist and sculptor (see page 113). He is also credited with the founding of the Mongolian capital of Urga, which was nomadic.

The Bogd Khan ('Holy Khan') Mongolia has had a succession of nine High Lamas, or Öndör Gegeens, who rank after the Dalai Lamas and Panchen Lamas. The eighth Öndör Gegeen had a marathon-length name, not often referred to for obvious reasons: Javzandamba Agvaanluvsanchoijindanzanvaanchigbalsambuu. He was born in Tibet in 1869, enthroned in Urga in 1874, and made the Mongolian head of state in 1911, when the Manchu rule over Mongolia finally collapsed. As head of the Church and state he became the 'Holy Khan' or Bogd Khan, monarch of a theocracy.

The Bogd Khan was briefly held prisoner at Manzshir Monastery by the Chinese. After the victory of the nationalist revolution in Mongolia in July 1921, the Bogd Khan remained head of state, although over the next few years his powers were greatly restricted. The Bogd Khan died in May 1924, and the then increasingly communist ruling party in Mongolia decreed that the search for his incarnation was forbidden. In 1927, all new incarnations were banned. His Russian-style two-storey winter palace has become a museum.

Buddhism under communism The Buddhist Church in Mongolia remained very powerful and wealthy in the 1920s. It controlled monasteries and temples with large estates and thousands of lamas and monastery serfs. As the young communists consolidated their political position and promoted their reforms, the aristocracy and high lamas (the 'black and yellow feudalists') became their chief targets. Following the enactment of a law to limit the powers of religion, in 1926 an uprising of lamas in eastern Mongolia was suppressed. In 1929/30 the country's political rulers set about expropriating feudal property, and in March 1930 there were new uprisings by lamas from western Mongolia. Further counter-revolutions were fiercely suppressed.

In 1935, a new law was published requiring lamas to leave their monasteries and go to work in society, by which the political leaders meant get proper jobs. As the political purges gained momentum, monasteries were closed by the army and subsequently looted, and precious paintings and religious sculptures were destroyed. Lamas were forced to work on the land, to join the army and even to marry, all of which were contrary to their beliefs. To resist meant to be shot, and many were.

Nearly all the many monasteries and temples were destroyed. The capital's Gandantegchinlen Monastery (known as 'Gandan' for short) was closed for many years but somehow survived, to become a showpiece for religious freedom, with a few practising lamas. Folk religion and Shamanism were practised in secret. Otherwise the country was devoid of religious activity.

Buddhism today In the summer of 1990 everything changed. Russian advisors withdrew from Mongolia and the country was freed from the anti-religious sentiment of communism. Monks, under the guise of ordinary citizens, returned to practise their faith openly. Family shrines were unveiled and monasteries began to accept new young monks for training. Mongolian abbots are committed to preserving and promoting the teachings of Buddhism in Mongolia. Prior to this there had been some concessional changes, like the visits of the Dalai Lama and the opening of monastery schools in the 1980s. Following the Buddhist religious renaissance of 1990, there have been numerous changes, including people of all ages requesting prayers or a blessing, the opening of monasteries – mostly *ger*-temples and converted wooden buildings since the rebuilding of permanent monasteries takes time and money; the return of monks to monasteries to teach and learn; hidden treasures silently reappearing in monasteries and temples; small communities of elderly monks emerging from hiding; and women setting up religious communities to become nuns. Despite this, however, perhaps only around 50% of Mongols are Buddhist believers, the rest seeing Lamaism as part of Mongol heritage.

The four main monasteries outside Ulaanbaatar are located in the cardinal directions: Baldan Bereeven to the east, Manzshir Monastery to the south, Erdene Zuu to the west, and Amarbayasgalant Monastery to the north. Erdene Zuu Monastery (the oldest, built in 1585) in Arkhangai Aimag and Amarbayasgalant Monastery (founded in 1722 as a resting place for Zanabazar) near Darkhan, have been returned to the Buddhist authorities for religious use, although they are better known as museums and architectural monuments. Baldan Bereeven Monastery (built in the 1770s) and Manzshir Monastery (built in 1733), near Zuunmod on the far side of the Bogd Uul, near Ulaanbaatar, are slowly being restored, as are many of the provincial monasteries. Further information on all these appears in the relevant sections of *Part Two* of the guide.

At Amarbayasgalant, the magnificent walled monastery, lively young monks in training rely on four elderly abbots, the only survivors of 300 monks who once trained together and practised there. To them it is essential that the teachings are passed on. Charles Bell, a British diplomat and friend of the 13th Dalai Lama, noted that in Lhasa some of the most learned monks came from Mongolia. The sadness is that so much of this learning has disappeared. Manzshir Monastery was destroyed in the purges of the 1930s, and while craftsmen are busy at work repairing the temple buildings, the sound of chanting monks resonates once again within the monastery confines. Seemingly the people of Mongolia want Buddhism revived as a living religion.

However, some Mongolian lamas do not want to reconstruct monasteries on original sites that today have become abandoned. They are not interested in 'preservation' in the usual sense of the word, but rather in the preservation of a community, known as a *sangha* (body of monks), which becomes part of the lay community. The yearning for what has disappeared is enormous and the grief is still being borne by the few who remember.

The income of monasteries comes from Mongolian Buddhists in the form of offerings and donations, including those from overseas Buddhist organisations. Small donations go a very long way in helping to publish books and to meet other modest needs.

After many years of repression, the collective memory of great religious occasions is dim and people are more than curious to learn about religion. For example, the Kalachakra ('wheel of time') initiation is a mysterious ritual believed to have a profound effect on the area where it takes place. However, the modern threats to Mongolian Buddhism no longer come from the authoritarian leaders but from the pressures of modern life and the insecurity and instability of a society caught up in the whirlwind of changing times. Perhaps the most important enemy is time itself as the now ancient lamas take on the new generation's educational needs.

ISLAM Islam is an Arabic word meaning 'submission'. Muslims submit to Allah – God. The word of God was revealed to the Prophet Muhammad (born in 570AD) and written down in the sacred book the Koran (Qur'an). The Koran contains some material from the Jewish and Christian traditions. Islam is a very simple religion with a five-fold path (see below) and consists of belief in the oneness of God. Mecca is the city where the Prophet Muhammad died in 632AD and is a place of pilgrimage for all Muslims. The religion of Islam has neither a clergy nor a liturgy and early Islam did not require a holy place in which to worship. Wherever a Muslim is found there is '*masjid*' (literally a place where one can prostrate to worship God), from which we get the Westernised word 'mosque'. The mosque is the place where prayers are led by an *imam*. It also has an educational role, and teachings there range from advanced theology to the teaching of children.

The 'five pillars of Islam' are:

- **Profession of the faith** There is no God but Allah and Muhammad is Allah's messenger.
- **Prayer** The act of worship is performed five times a day. Muslims face the direction of Mecca and bow in a special series of movements.
- **Alms giving** An offering known as a '*zakat*', or poor tax, is given annually by all pious Muslims.
- **Fasting** Muslims fast from before sunrise until sunset every day for one month a year. This period is known as Ramadan. People do not eat, drink or smoke during the daylight hours at that time, although the elderly, the sick, children, and travellers are exempt.

- **Pilgrimage to Mecca (the *hajj*)** Should be undertaken at least once in a lifetime by those who can afford it. Pilgrims walk seven times around a building called the Kaaba. There are great ceremonies and feasts and animals – goats, sheep or camels – are sacrificed.

Islamic law is called the Sharia, in which religious rules, duties and punishments are specified.

History of Islam in Mongolia
The religious life of Mongolia's Sunni Muslim community, being a small national minority, proceeds largely out of the public eye. It is uncertain how many Kazakhs and other Muslims suffered at the time of the anti-religious campaigns of the 1930s, when their mosques were destroyed. It is known that there were several mosques in what is now called Bayan-Ölgii Aimag, where most of Mongolia's Kazakhs live, two more in the neighbouring Khovd Aimag and at least one in the suburbs of Ulaanbaatar. Kazakh Muslims are increasingly influenced by contacts with the outside Muslim world.

During the period of industrialisation, many Kazakhs gave up pastoral life in western Mongolia to work in the new factories and mines of the central region. Since 1990, some mosques have been rebuilt (not the one in Ulaanbaatar) and Muslim rites and customs are now practised again to some extent. Mongolia's Kazakhs may make the *hajj*. It is less clear whether there are now *madrasas*, or teaching establishments, as well as mullahs. In the 1990s perhaps 100,000 of Mongolia's Kazakhs emigrated to Kazakhstan and as a result the numbers of Muslims in Mongolia decreased. Religion may be freely practised in Mongolia but as with Buddhism, the number of people preserving national customs but no longer practising the religion of their parents and grandparents is quite large.

CHRISTIANITY
Christians believe there is one God, who created the Universe, and that in this one God there are three persons, known as the Holy Trinity: God the Father, his Son (Jesus Christ) and the Holy Spirit. Those who believe become Christians by being baptised – that is, they receive the Holy Spirit and become children of God. Jesus entered history by taking on human flesh and being born of a virgin, Mary. He was fully human but retained his divine nature. Jesus taught, 'Love the Lord your God with all your heart, with all your soul and with all your mind.' This is the greatest and most important commandment. The second commandment is like it: 'Love your neighbour as you love yourself.' He taught the truth in love and lived it out and was crucified for it. He took on himself all the sin of the world, and died and rose from the dead and ascended into heaven that we might all be saved. He came to teach us how to love that we might live in love with him in heaven. Christians remember Jesus' last supper with his disciples, on the eve of his crucifixion, by celebrating the Eucharist, in which prayers are said and bread and wine are consecrated and changed into the body, blood, soul and divinity of Jesus (while retaining the properties of bread and wine) and distributed to those present.

History of Christianity in Mongolia
The Mongols have had various encounters with Christianity over the centuries. Christianity was first brought to central Asia in 635AD by Alopen, an ambassador of the eastern Church. Little happened in Mongolia until the time of the Great Khans, when papal envoys shuttled between Rome and Mongol Asia, usually with political as well as religious agendas. Kublai Khan was sympathetic to Christianity (possibly because his mother, Lady Soyo, was

a Christian). He asked Rome to send 100 Christian men skilled in its religion – an invitation that was not answered for many centuries.

However, during the reign of Kublai Khan, two Nestorian Christian monks from central Asia, Rabban Sauma and his young Mongol disciple called Mark, set out on a pilgrimage to Jerusalem, travelling west along the Silk Road. They carried Kublai's *paiza* or passport of 'free travel' – an engraved gold or silver plate, which hung around their necks. Mark was ordained at Seleucia, near Baghdad, and subsequently became head of the Nestorian Asian Church.

Between the 7th and the 12th centuries, Nestorian Christianity was established in most trading towns along the Silk Road and influenced at least four pre-Mongol tribes. In the 13th century missionary explorers such as William of Rubruck and the Franciscan Giovanni da Pian del Carpine travelled to the heart of Asia but did not stay long to evangelise. Mongol script is thought to have originated from the Syriac script via eastern Christians who travelled there carrying their bibles in Syriac. Later 16th-century Jesuit missionaries arriving in Mongolia from China were Matteo Ricci and Giovanni da Montecorvino.

From the 17th to the 19th centuries, when the Silk Road was no longer travelled, cultural and religious life collapsed. In the latter part of the 19th century, Protestant missionaries focused mainly on Inner Mongolia. James Gilmore, a Scottish missionary, arrived in Mongolia in 1870, teaching himself the language in three months and translating sections of the Bible into Mongolian. Later on Mildred Caple and Francesca French wrote of their missionary journeys in the 1930s in their book *The Gobi Desert*. The first significant translation of the whole Bible (Old and New Testaments) was completed in the 1840s in Buryatia (north of the border with Mongolia) and this Mongol-script version was revised and translated into Cyrillic script in the 20th century. The whole Bible was translated again into Mongolian in 2000, with revisions in 2008. A revised version of the New Testament was printed in 2011.

Christianity today The Christian Church is newly arrived and recently established in Mongolia. In 1991, there were few Christians, although by 2010 there were now thought to be around 60,000. Christianity appeals to the younger generation because it is new and something quite different from the old beliefs. Young Mongolians who recently received theological training are now the leaders of their local churches.

As previously mentioned people are free to worship or not to worship; 'the state respects its religion and religion honours its state' according to the constitution of 1992. The state may not carry out religious activity, the temples and monasteries may not carry out political activity. The Law on State–Church Relations (1993) sought to restrict the dissemination of religions other than Buddhism, Islam and Shamanism, but it was amended after challenges by human rights campaigners as being unconstitutional.

By the 21st century there were over 70 Christian congregations in the country, mainly in Ulaanbaatar. Christian mission agencies joined together to form Joint Community Services International (JCS) (*PO Box 189, Ulaanbaatar 210351;* e *journeywithus@jcsintl.org; www.jcsintl.org*). JCS helps Mongolian people to run projects that include agricultural development, teaching English as a foreign language, and other relief work.

The Russian Orthodox Church was established in Mongolia in the early 20th century but it did not survive the revolutionary period of the 1920s. Holy Trinity Church, which stood in Ulaanbaatar, was closed in 1928 and later demolished. The

Russian Orthodox community has taken its name again and is led by Father Anatolii Fesechko; he takes care of the long-term Russian resident community, of about 1,000 members throughout the country. The Holy Trinity Church community is to be found at 55 Jukovyn Gudamj, Ulaanbaatar, where the building's restoration was completed in 2009.

The Roman Catholic mission in Ulaanbaatar is headed by Bishop Fr Wens Padilla. Archbishop Emil Paul Tscherrig is in charge of Mongolia and South Korea. The Vatican maintains a diplomatic mission in Beijing. Outreach work includes helping street children and the poor. The Verbist Care Centre (*Bayangol District, Ulaanbaatar;* ✆ *11 369295;* e *cicmgibs@magicnet.mn; www.geocities.com*) in Ulaanbaatar is under the direction of Father Gilbert Sales and Sister Lucille Munchi who provide healthcare and education for over 120 children.

FOLLOW BRADT

For the latest news, special offers and competitions, subscribe to the Bradt newsletter via the website www.bradtguides.com and follow Bradt on:

- ▉ www.facebook.com/BradtTravelGuides
- ▶ @BradtGuides
- ▣ @bradtguides
- ℗ pinterest.com/bradtguides

3

Culture

If you drink the water from a place, then also follow the customs of that place.

Mongolian saying

Culture is born of history, language and ideas, and many other invisible strands that make up and characterise a distinct group of people like the Mongols. As the French writer Edgar Morin said, 'Culture is made up of the totality of knowledge, skills, rules, standards, prohibitions, strategies, beliefs, ideas, values, and myths passed from generation to generation and reproduced in each individual, which control the existence of the society and maintain psychological and social complexity'. The Mongolian national identity and culture is best seen in practice in the life and traditions surrounding the *ger*, the nomad's home, and to a lesser extent in urban life through social customs and business practices. It is clearly present in religious celebrations, national festivals, sport, music, theatre and film. Deeply rooted in the natural environment, Mongolian culture has been moulded under the harshest of climates; the identity of these ancient tribal peoples has survived for hundreds of years within traditional nomadic practices. This is reinforced in a statement, attributed to Genghis Khan, that when the Mongol people lose contact with their nomadic lifestyle, they will lose their true identity.

During their greatest period of expansion at the time of the Mongol Empire in the 13th century, the mobility of the equestrian culture of the Mongols brought them into contact with other cultures and allowed them to absorb many different ideas and influences. Diverse cultures, like those of Persia and countries further afield, reached central Asia along the trade routes of the Silk Road, which, at that time, stretched from the Sea of Japan in the east to the shores of the Mediterranean Sea in the west. Silk, spices and ideas travelled overland from east to west and vice versa; and to some extent on a north/south axis. Buddhism, for example, was introduced to Mongolia from Tibet and India. The Mongols, however, did not bring home many comforts from the civilised countries they conquered; nor, it seems, were they particularly interested in doing so.

Although the Mongols conquered vast territories from the saddle, it was impossible to rule these lands from the back of a horse. Instead Kublai Khan moved the Mongol capital from Karakorum in the heartland of the Mongolian steppes, to Beijing, in northeast China, from where he and his successors ruled the Mongol Empire during the Yuan dynasty (1271–1368), absorbing Chinese civilisation, although some say it is the other way around. In recent times, Mongolia has absorbed political and cultural influences from both of its big neighbours and has been ruled and further influenced by them with many consequences. Some 270 years of Manchu rule under the Chinese Qing dynasty (1644–1911) was followed by a revolutionary period in the 1920s and then 70 years of socialist reform under a party communist in all but name that was backed by the Soviet Union. Some simple examples of dress and eating customs makes clear the ways in which these countries have left their distinctive marks. For example, the everyday use of the knife and fork over chopsticks is typically Russian, whereas the *deel*, the traditional Mongolian gown, has similarities to the Chinese tunic. The northern Mongols, who

TRAVEL IN STYLE

Antoni and Caroline Daszewski

Travelling in Mongolia means travelling in style and putting the clock back at least 100 years. The size of our entourage for just the two of us was amazing: we travelled by jeep accompanied by our interpreter and our trek leader, who also happened to be a lecturer at the Mongolian State University in Ulaanbaatar, while the cook and assistant cook joined us travelling in an ex-Russian army cook truck. At camp, besides our sleeping tent, we enjoyed the luxury of a dining tent, complete with a super-efficient, wood-burning (or yak-dung) stove, pine chairs and tables, but ironically it was the loo tent that regularly boasted some of the best views in the world. The food was unfailingly excellent and really fresh, as our truck driver proved to be an ardent and successful fisherman, so many meals consisted of delicious and unusual Mongolian freshwater fish; meat was sometimes bought from local families, who also provided wonderful homemade yoghurt. Every dietary whim was catered for and the only problem seemed to be the super-abundance of food. Each meal became a party, often accompanied by beautiful folk songs sung by our Mongolian staff. On one such evening we were camped on the beach at Khoton Lake, in Bayan-Ölgii Aimag: after dinner an enormous bonfire was lit and we taught the home team how to dance the tango in the snow, by the light of the flames. In contrast, another night, we dined by candlelight – a romantic twosome – in great style, under the star-encrusted Gobi sky.

Riding in Mongolia is to discover another dimension to life. Three Mongol horsemen and ourselves left the vehicles, having made a rendezvous to meet them ten days later. We unpacked the handmade Western saddles, which had come with us from the city so that we could ride in comfort, and watched, amazed, as the horsemen expertly loaded the pack ponies with all the gear, including a more compact dining tent, as well as the smaller travelling stove, complete with collapsible chimney. We set out and were quite free to ride at whatever pace we felt like. Mongolian horses are small and wonderfully behaved, so sometimes we would amble along beside the horsemen, entranced by their singing and at others we galloped like the wind over the vast, empty, endless steppe. Another day the two of us accompanied the 12-camel caravan of a family on the move; we splashed through rivers, and at one point had to gallop after them through the brilliant autumn woods when we had loitered too long enjoying the scenery. We don't believe there is anywhere else in the world which offers such a style of travel – and travel in such style.

Antoni and Caroline's tailormade six-week itinerary was planned by email over a six-month period with a Mongolian travel agent, Great Genghis Expeditions (www.greatgenghis.com). Excluding international fares, but including everything else (internal flights, hotels, food, staff, transport), it cost around £3,000 each.

were not absorbed by the Chinese (unlike the Mongols of Inner Mongolia), have put aside most things Chinese. The irony is that Mongol culture and folklore today – lineages, family history, folk stories and so on – are in some places remembered in Inner Mongolia more than in Mongolia proper, which was subject to sweeping reforms that destroyed much of the local culture.

The Mongols are resourceful and resilient. During the Soviet period new opportunities were opened up to them through education in European history and culture. Despite some financial difficulties of the present and purges and revolutions of the past, Mongolians believe that their cultural heritage is to be cherished and kept alive. The isolation of Mongolia during the 20th century – geopolitically, culturally and in other ways – is over. The future looks less culturally isolated for Mongolia's nomadic population as it becomes linked to the towns and settlements via new roads and mobile phones, which bring all Mongolians in line with the realities of global survival.

ARCHITECTURE

Nomadic architecture is not carved in stone for posterity, but best represented in the transient materials of wood and cloth, in the form of the circular tent, or *ger*, the main Mongolian home. (For further details of the construction of the *ger*, see pages 80–1.) Ancient tribes pitched camp in enclosures or *khürees* for protection. The custom to line up the *gers* in order of social importance, with the top people in the westernmost *ger*, was reported by Friar William of Rubruck, who described Möngke Khan's camp in the mid 13th century.

The description and architecture of temple and monastery buildings is dealt with in *Part Two* of the guide. It is significant that early Mongolian building styles used no nails in the construction of the buildings. Before the monasteries (16th century) there weren't cities or towns and villages throughout the country, other than a few scattered ruins of feudal warfare and disunity which lasted for a long period of time. Contemporary city architecture includes the Ardyn Bank building in Ulaanbaatar, listed as one of the best 1,000 buildings in the world. It is better known as the Blue Glass or Blue Sabre building, designed by the Mongolian architect G Batsükh.

LITERATURE AND LEGEND

Oral traditions have remained at the root of Mongolian culture and are among the most precious of their arts. Songs and legends travelled widely with the nomads, transmitted by bards, and thus preserved through the centuries. As an unlettered people the nomads left no written accounts, and a Gobi-like void existed concerning written work until the 13th century. Genghis Khan's wish to introduce writing among the Mongols shows he was aware of its value in civilisation.

The earliest form of nomadic literature begins with *The Secret History of the Mongols,* often abbreviated to *The Secret History.* The exact title and origin of this important document is uncertain. Several authors of translations suggest that the title may be taken from the first line of the text. Professor Urgunge Onon takes as the title of his translation *Chinggis Khan, the Golden History of the Mongols.* It is known to the Mongols as the *Tobchian* (transcribed from old script, or *tobch, tovchoo,* meaning 'summary') or *History;* other names include *The Life of Genghis Khan, The Real Record of Chinggis Khan* and *The Secret History of the Yuan Dynasty.* The explanation of the 'secret' is that it was kept by the Chinese as a dynastic record and not available to the public – therefore 'secret'. A copy of the text only came to light at the end of the 19th century. The big issue is that it was written in Mongolian transliterated into Chinese characters, which no one (except scholars) could read. No complete Mongolian script version has been found. Since then, scholars have been working on this uniquely important early manuscript, the only near-contemporary account of the life of Genghis Khan and the accomplishments of his son Ögödei Khan (see box on *Secret History*, opposite page). Another early account is the *Altan Tobchi*, or *Golden Chronicle*, supposedly written in the early 17th century. The third Mongolian classic is a work called *Erdeniin Tobchi*, or *The Precious Chronicle*. All three combine legend and history.

The earliest family histories preserved by herdsmen date back to the 18th century. More recent family records were lost or destroyed in the political purges of the 20th century, along with numerous Buddhist manuscripts. These manuscripts comprised single, long-leafed, unbound sheets, kept between similar-sized wooden boards or decorated tablets and then wrapped in silk, cotton or leather for protection. European-style bound books appeared in Mongolia shortly before the revolution of 1921.

Descriptions of the Mongols during the reign of Genghis Khan's grandson, Kublai, are exotic and tinged with a dream-like quality. Some lines have lodged in the minds and imagination of the English-speaking (Western) world through the Samuel Taylor Coleridge poem *Kubla Khan* (first published in 1816, inspired by reading Marco Polo and smoking opium). It conjures up evocative images. Coleridge may not have described the scene correctly, but he alludes to the extravagant nature of Kublai's court at his summer capital Shangdu (Kaiping), near Duolon.

> In Xanadu did Kubla Khan
> A stately pleasure-dome decree:
> Where Alph, the sacred river, ran
> Through caverns measureless to man
> Down to a sunless sea.
> So thrice five miles of fertile ground
> With walls and towers were girded round
> And there were gardens bright with sinuous rills
> Where blossomed many an incense bearing tree;
> And here were forests ancient as the hills,
> Enfolding sunny spots of greenery.

Besides Buddhist religious literature, the 16th century onwards provides many poems, plays and stories written as teaching material. By the end of the 20th century, although the state had suppressed religious teaching ruthlessly, the country achieved 95% literacy, in part due to educational reforms under socialism but at the expense of much oral tradition. *Ülgeriin Dalai* (*The Sea of Parables*) is a collection of short stories, or fables. These stories are commonly told by the older generation in order to teach children good behaviour and better manners. Other popular tales are of Geser Khan, a mythical character of Tibetan origin and Jangar Khan, a legendary hero of the Oirat Mongols.

One popular fable from *The Sea of Parables* is that of the frog and the geese:

> A long time ago, there lived two geese and a frog by a small, isolated mountain lake in the Gobi-Altai Mountains. As time went by the water in the lake began to disappear, causing grave concern. The two geese decided to move elsewhere but the frog, knowing he would be left behind, beseeched his friends, 'Be merciful please and take me to a place where there is water.' The geese replied, 'Tell us how to transport

you and we shall do so.' The frog then produced a small stick and explained, 'I shall grasp the middle of the stick in my mouth if you two would kindly hold the ends in your beaks and fly off with me.' When the two geese flew through the air as instructed by the frog, people looking up exclaimed, 'How wise and skilful these geese are to carry the little frog with them.' This was repeated over and over again, until, at length, the frog could stand it no longer and as he opened his mouth to say 'It was my idea!', he let go of the stick and fell to his death. The moral of the story is that people must overcome the temptation to take vain pride in themselves without allowing credit to be given to others.

Artistic expression is best captured in the legend of the horse-head fiddle or *morin khuur*, a traditional two-string musical instrument which traces its origin back to the time of Hunnu tribes (otherwise known as Xiongnu or Huns), who inhabited the present territory of Mongolia, circa 400BC. The instrument is an integral part of Mongolian culture. There are many folk stories on the origin of the *morin khuur* – here is one:

Once upon a time, a horseman rode through the night sky and spotted the tent of a beautiful herdswoman. He stayed with her for one night and at dawn he rode away. The second night he returned to the woman's delight, but at dawn again he disappeared. After several nights the woman determined to keep the horseman by her side. While he slept she crept out to untie his horse and noticed that the animal had little wings above its hooves. In a drastic moment she cut off the horse's wings. When her lover left the following morning his mount fell to the earth and died. Despairing over the loss of his horse the man grieved night and day. To soothe his sorrow he carved the horse's head from a piece of wood and transformed it into a two-string instrument, using the bone and hide of the dead horse.

SECRET HISTORY OF THE MONGOLS

The Secret History of the Mongols, a fusion of history, folklore and poetry, is a unique document in central Asian literature as it is the earliest surviving Mongolian source about the life of Genghis Khan and his son Ögödei Khan. Scholars believe it was written in the 13th century – the presumed date is sometime during the 1240s after the death of Ögödei Khan in 1241. Its author (or authors) remains unknown. The history has an epic quality similar to the Scandinavian sagas – without the ships.

The early part of *The Secret History* deals with the origins of the Mongol nation, said to descend from the union of a wolf and a doe. The story then enters the real world to provide a historic account of Genghis Khan's childhood and his rise to power and describes the accomplishments of his son Ögödei. It portrays the lifestyle, thoughts and beliefs of the 13th century and ends with the instructions given by Ögödei Khan after his accession in 1228 following the death of Genghis Khan.

The earliest known version is in Mongolian. No complete Mongolian script version has been found, but a copy was transcribed phonetically into Chinese characters. It demanded something of a code-breaking effort to decipher. It was first translated by a Russian Orthodox priest at the end of the 19th century. Translations by eminent scholars include those of Igor de Rachewiltz, Francis Woodham Cleaves, Urgunge Onon and a modern adaptation by Paul Kahn.

CONTEMPORARY LITERATURE Modern Mongolian literature was born in the revolutionary period of the 1920s and until then the Oriental trend dominated. Oriental and Western literature developed alongside one another and Mongolian readers gradually became familiar with the world classics. Much of the poetry of the 'national poet' Dashdorjiin Natsagdorj (1906–37) is known by heart by the older generation. His lyrics are distinguished by a chiselled rhythm of perfect harmony, and the content is about the beauties of the Mongolian countryside. A verse from his poem *My Homeland* is quoted below:

> Mongolia's name resounds through all the world.
> My love for her lies deep within my heart.
> Her tongue, her ways, will hold me till I die –
> Eternal home, my Motherland, Mongolia!

Natsagdorj was also a brilliant prose and short-story writer; among his stories are *The Winged Dun Horse* and *Tears of a Lama*. His only opera, *Three Sad Hills*, is about the 1921 revolution. He was perhaps unequalled, in the sense that after World War II the politicians idealised him as *the* Mongolian revolutionary writer. Another founder of Mongolia's new literature was the poet and writer S Buyannemekh, along with Ts Damdinsüren who wrote about nature, man, revolution and society. Damdinsüren is most famous for developing the Mongolian Cyrillac alphabet and forming the rules of orthography. Much-loved 20th-century Mongolian writers like B Rinchen did their best to preserve what they could of the traditional Mongolian culture in the new age of 'socialist internationalism' (in which the Soviet lead was followed and in many ways traditional art suffered). Rinchen had several brushes with the authorities over his use of old-fashioned times and ideas.

Contemporary Mongolian poets include G Mend-Oyoo and Bavuudorj Tsogdorj, whose works have been translated into English by Simon Wickham-Smith and Lynn Coffin. Simon Wickham-Smith has also translated short fiction from Mongolia: *Stories from the Steppes* was published by the Mongolian Academy of Culture and Poetry in 2012 (e *mendooyo@gmail.com*).

By 1950, many Mongolians had exchanged the nomadic life for sedentary, urban living. Students began to travel to the former Soviet Union for further education and became familiar with both Asian and European art and literature. Since 1990, many young people are being educated in colleges and universities in Europe, America and elsewhere. One can be certain, however, that whether at home or abroad, the nomadic life and its ancient folklore and culture are the inspiration for the expression of their creativity.

MUSIC

There is nothing Mongolians love more than music and the urge to burst into song happens spontaneously. Hour upon hour when travelling across country a Mongol *arat* (herder) will hum or sing and, when happy, he will gallop at full speed in top voice. Singers and musicians are greatly valued in Mongol communities. Nowadays every country town has a pop group, but the Mongols, like the Irish, on the whole prefer traditional music, which is usually played at weddings and other family festivals, when the local horse-head-fiddle players (*morin khuur*) and benediction singers (*yöröölch*) are called in.

The Mongol khans of the 13th century all kept large troupes of dancers and musicians at their courts, accompanied by *morin khuur* and drums. The Western traveller, Friar John di Plano Carpini, mentions 'saddle songs' of the Mongol warriors, and both Marco Polo and Friar William of Rubruck noted the strange musical instruments they saw at the court of the khans.

The horse-head fiddle is an ancient two-stringed instrument and is thought by some musicologists to be the father of European bowed string instruments. *Morin khuur* was very much a part of everyday life of nomads, who worship the fiddle. It is still a custom to keep the instrument in the most sacred part of the home, at the back by the household altar. There was a time when every man could play the *morin khuur*. Its music drifted across the steppes and shepherds would listen to it at the end of the day to forget their weariness. In the early 1940s, the Music College in Ulaanbaatar trained professional musicians to master the *morin khuur*. The famous *Melody of Mongolia*, composed by Jantsannorov, was performed by 108 players at the National Festival of Morin Khuur in Ulaanbaatar in 1989. The National Morin Khuur Ensemble, founded in 1992, has toured internationally and has released a number of CDs. Now you may find video recordings of the most famous (and also unknown singers and musicians) on YouTube, as well as *Morin Khuur* and *khöömii* (overtone singers) and their ensembles.

Other instruments include the *yatga* or zither, which looks like the Chinese *guqin*, a seven-stringed plucked instrument. Strings are made from silk, horse hair or goose gut and the instrument is played either holding it upright or placing it flat on a table or on the player's knees. The *khuuchir*, a bowed string instrument, uses a small round soundboard covered with sheep or snake's skin, while its long neck is made from copper or wood. Another bowed string instrument is the *shudraga*, a three-stringed instrument. Similar instruments were noted in 14th-century Persian literature from where it spread from Persia into China and Japan. Other instruments include the *yoochin*, a dulcimer and cymbals, which produce a light, clashing sound, commonly heard in much Asian music and in many countries from Asia to the Baltic. The flute or *limbe* accompanies the other instruments. It is often played by lone herders to while away the time and its haunting notes may be heard drifting across the grasslands.

To understand the rhythms and haunting melodies of Mongolian music listen to its transformation into Mongolian rap.

MONGOLIAN BLING

Mongolian Bling is a fresh take on the power of contemporary hip-hop culture – struggling to come to terms with Mongolia's recent political transformation has given the country's youth a voice. The modern beats and rhymes of the street are breaking through and forging a new identity told through the passion of young rappers, combined with the wisdom of traditional musicians.

There is a thriving musical scene in Ulaanbaatar. But not everybody is happy as Mongolia develops so rapidly. Bayarmagnai – one of Mongolia's last Epic Singers (songs of good harvests and happiness, usually sung in the heart of winter) – struggles to keep the art form he loves alive. And the ancient tradition of 'throat singing' is being overtaken by this new western hip-hop beat. 'It has to happen,' one singer said, 'it's good, provided traditional music keeps its voice, too.'

Mongolian Bling is the new hip-hop revolution. It's political, powerful and part of the reforms that are sweeping the country this decade.

Culture MUSIC

3

Throat singing (*khöömii*) involves changing the shape of the mouth and creating overtones in the throat, chest or abdomen to imitate the sounds of nature – bird and animal noises as well as the sounds of storms and rivers. *Khöömii* is a truly unusual Mongolian vocal technique where one singer produces two voices simultaneously. The sound of the two voices, steely bass combined with a whistle-like tone, produces an overtone that can only be described as otherworldly, although the predominant bass tone sounds more like the hum of a poorly maintained refrigerator than a human voice.

Khöömii is produced by making a drone and an overtone, simultaneously. The technique is not difficult to learn. Say the letter *i* and reinforce your breath on the *i* sound. Then pronounce two vowels *e* and *ou* by modifying your mouth cavity and you will find you can change the pitch. To achieve the whole range you move your tongue backwards and forwards with surprising musical results. One famous Mongolian overtone singer can produce this effect without the drone by using his open mouth only, which defies all explanation. This kind of throat singing is popular in Tuva, too, and perhaps thought in the West to have originated there. The unique sound of *khöömii* has given Mongol singers a worldwide musical identity. As the sound is produced mainly in the throat, and because of the muscular strength it demands, is mainly the preserve of male singers whose voice range spans five octaves.

The Mongols have always had several singing styles, the most important being *tuuli*, or 'epic songs' – the tales of heroes and great warriors. *Tuuli* performances can be spread over several days. The length of the songs vary – stages of travel can be marked out by songs which take a long time, although this is also a genre, known as 'long songs' (*urtyn duu*). The themes are largely pastoral and celebrate the way of life and magnificence of the steppes, mountains and rivers, lakes and deserts. Great Mongol singers are known to have amazing vocal range and a voice quality that billows and gusts like the wind across the wide-open plains. 'Short songs' (*bogino duu*) are sung at informal occasions (but may be quite long!), with improvised or satirical texts. The tempo of a song depends on the occasion and the mood of the singer. Galloping tunes and songs in praise of horses are well-known favourites. There is a traditional practice of soothing domestic animals with music, especially to induce them to nurse abandoned lambs and young camels. Specific repetitive encouragements of no specific meaning are said to different animals – '*toig, toig*' to lambs, for example, and '*khöös khöös*' to young camels!

DANCE

FOLK DANCING Folk dancing originated in ancient times in connection with the rituals of daily life and nature. Simple circular dances evolved imitating the way birds flew and the way in which animals were trapped by a circle of hunters. A form of this type of dance is accompanied by a tune on the horse-head fiddle. The dancer uses the fluid movements of her arms and upper body to sway to the music. Wrestlers also move in this style between bouts with their arms held high, imitating the flight of the Garuda bird, to celebrate victory over an opponent.

TSAM DANCE In the past, religious festivals included temple dances called *tsam* dances, in which lamas wearing elaborate costumes and brightly painted papier-mâché masks acted the roles of various Buddhist gods – the red-faced Begze and the blue-faced Makhakala, each with three eyes and a tiara of skulls. Garuda, king of the birds, was originally a Hindu deity, but he took on a Buddhist role, first in Tibet and then in Mongolia, becoming a leading character in *tsam* dance dramas. *Tsagaan Övgön*, or the 'white old man', is also an important legendary figure. The masks are works of art, and are displayed in Mongolian temples and museums.

Tsam dance is being revived after an interruption of more than 60 years. The training of many young people has been a success and leading craftsmen have created new costumes and masks for this special ritual dance, which nowadays serves tourism rather than religion.

ART

There are several distinct periods in Mongolian art, which stretches from prehistoric ancient rock art of Palaeolithic and Neolithic times to present-day sculpture and painting. See also the *Archaeology* section (pages 10–13).

- Bronze Age art (4th–2nd century BC) consists of depictions of deer, wolves and horses and other items of hidden treasures in gold and wood, found in the frozen tombs of the Altai area and preserved by permafrost.
- The Huns are believed to have traded with the Roman, Egyptian and Arab worlds, as artefacts and coins from those parts have been found in Hun graves.
- Steppe art of the Turkic/Uighur empires (3rd century AD) produced standing stones and burial monuments built at different periods up to the 11th century inscribed with Turkic runes.
- A gradual blending of foreign influences took place following the establishment of the great Mongol Empire in the 13th century.
- Traders from the territory north of the Silk Road made direct contact with Chinese and Persian traders on this route which flourished between the 13th and 16th centuries.
- The emergence of Buddhism as a religious power in Mongolia in the 16th century brought Mongolia in contact with Tibetan and Indian cultures.
- The monk Zanabazar (b1635) was recognised to be an important incarnation of a Tibetan scholar and proclaimed the leader of Mongolian Buddhists. As an artist, he created many fine sculptures in bronze.
- 20th-century Soviet Russia transformed Mongol art and architecture along the lines of 'socialist realism', as it did the lifestyle of the religious and herding populations. Political reforms closed monasteries and many monks became artisans and took to sedentary, urban living, while arats (herders) were collectivised.
- In the 21st century, contemporary Mongol artists are experimenting with new art forms and are free to travel and attend international art colleges and to exhibit and sell their work worldwide.

PREHISTORIC PETROGLYPHS AND ROCK ART Mongolia's heritage begins with Stone Age rock carvings, showing animal life. The impact of these animalistic drawings on bare rock remains as strong and fresh today as the day they were created. It is as if the artist froze where he stood, to observe and capture the spirit

Zara Fleming

Buddhism has had an enormous impact on the culture of the Mongols in many spheres of life. Theatre, dance, music, painting and other artistic skills were developed in the monasteries. *Thangkas* (sacred scroll paintings) are portable icons painted on a sized cotton or silk cloth and framed in a brocade mount; when not in use they can be rolled up and stored. These can also be created in embroidery or appliqué. Sculptures are made of metal, clay or wood, with the preferred medium being bronze. These may be hand-hammered, but are usually cast in clay moulds by the lost wax method and frequently gilded. Both *thangkas* and sculptures depict Buddhist deities, historical figures and religious teachers.

The tradition of Buddhist art entered Mongolia, firstly through Mongol interaction with other cultures on the Silk Road, secondly with the introduction of Tibetan Buddhism as the state religion during Kublai Khan's reign and thirdly during its establishment in the 16th century. Religious art is highly venerated and serves as a focus of faith and as a visual aid for meditation. It adorned the monasteries of Mongolia, together with ritual Buddhist implements and the masks worn in *tsam* dances. Many temples and thousands of Buddhist artefacts were destroyed during the communist purges of the 1930s, but fortunately much artwork was hidden away for safekeeping. Today this art is seen in the newly opened monasteries and museums of Mongolia, and there is a current revival in the tradition of the sacred art of Buddhism. Unfortunately many fine religious sculptures are displayed in insecure premises. There is a big business in selling and smuggling stolen artefacts.

The most outstanding Buddhist treasures are housed in the collections of the Bogd Khan Green (or Winter) Palace, the Choijin Lama Temple, the Zanabazar Museum of Fine Arts and in the temples of Erdene Zuu. Examples of *thangkas* from the Bogd Khan Green Palace include the magnificent 19th-century *Ganesha* painted in the Da Khüree style. *Ganesha* is a Hindu deity absorbed into the Mahayana Buddhist pantheon, represented here as the auspicious god of wealth. The skilful rendering of the deity, set against a backdrop of rolling hills with the five animals of Mongolia (camel, horse, yak, sheep and goat) depicted in the landscape is a Mongolian masterpiece. Likewise is the complex painting of the *Meditations of the Bogd Gegeen*, which illustrates important happenings in the spiritual and political history of Mongolian Buddhism.

The Museum of Fine Arts has an impressive *thangka* depicting *Begtse*, the protective deity of Mongolia. This is a superb example of Mongolian art, painted by Gendendamba (1865–1935), an artist known for his fluid brushstroke and harmonious composition. Another outstanding artist represented in the museum is Jügder, who paints in a palette of subtle light colours, as seen in his *thangka* of the long life deity *Usnīsaviiavā*. The museum also houses a collection of masterful appliqués, including one of the protector *Dorje Dordan*, made under the supervision of the artist Perenlei. Intricate pieces of silk and brocade are stitched together to depict the powerful protector. The appliqué is further ornamented with tiny coral beads; this addition of gems is not found in Tibetan or Bhutanese appliqués and appears to be a purely Mongolian tradition.

of the animals he sighted. Pre-Hun culture may be glimpsed through the artefacts of the Bronze Age tribal chieftains whose *kurgans*, or burial mounds, have been excavated. Megaliths and monuments to dead chieftains stand silently on the steppe, as a reminder of the past.

The arts and crafts of Mongolia developed over the centuries from the early 'animal-style' bronzes of the so-called 'Karasuk style' of the 2nd millennium BC. It is named after the town of Karasuk on the river Yenisey in Siberia, across the northwest border of Mongolia.

EARLY ART OF THE STEPPES The culture of the central Asian steppes expresses itself vividly in the lifestyle of the nomads who produced 'animal-style art', particularly in the region of the Altai Mountains where gold and silver were mined. Early sites associated with nomadic tribes date back to the 7th century BC, but unfortunately many of the big *kurgans* have been plundered. Archaeological discoveries shed light on the nomads of the time, whose material culture reflected their lifestyle. Where deep burials quickly filled up with snow and ice and froze solid, human remains, clothing, carpets and leather goods were preserved.

TRADITIONAL MONGOL ZURAG PAINTING The country's most striking art form is the unique traditional Mongol *zurag* painting, a type of story-telling art without words that may be described as a developed form of naive painting. Mongol *zurag* portrays everyday country life with images of people, horses and *gers*, combined with folk motifs and legends. Fine line drawings were coloured with natural mineral pigments, such as red ochre and charcoal, until lacquer paints became available in Mongolia.

ZANABAZAR

Zanabazar (1635–1723), a direct descendant of Genghis Khan, was a remarkable man, both as a monk and as an artist. At the age of 15 he travelled to Tibet, where he was recognised by the Fifth Dalai Lama as the incarnation of the great Jonangpa lama Taranatha (1575–1634). He became the religious ruler of Mongolia, the first to hold the title of Öndör Gegeen ('High Enlightened One'). During his long life he greatly influenced religious, social and political affairs and contributed to the country's development in the arts. He was a scholar, an architect, a costume designer, a linguist, and an artist, but above all he was known for his outstanding gilt bronze sculptures.

Museums in the capital, Ulaanbaatar, and at Erdene Zuu Monastery in Övörkhangai Province, have some fine examples of his work. Zanabazar's deities are cast in a single piece connected by fine soldering to their pedestals; a technique unknown in other Lamaistic countries at this time. Inspired by both Pala and Nepalese art, his sculptures depict elegant figures of harmonious proportions that convey the very essence of enlightenment. His representation of the female Bodhisattva of compassion, *White Tara*, in the Fine Arts Museum, shows a profoundly human expression of beauty, while his sculptures of the *Five Transcendent Buddhas* possess a remarkable and divine serenity. Zanabazar was guided by his desire to save all sentient beings from wrath, ignorance, lust, contempt and ill will; and it is said that he entered the very soul of the Mongol people and expressed it in his art.

The best-known master of Mongol *zurag*, Marzan 'Joker' Sharav, painted in the early 20th century. His ethnographic works on monumental backgrounds gave an insight into Mongolian nomadic culture. Sharav's *Day in the Life of Mongolia* depicts dozens of small scenes with men herding livestock, hunting, making felt, putting up a *ger* and slaughtering animals, while women and girls milk animals and prepare food. In the different scenes, people are living and dying, engaged in archery and wrestling, attending religious ceremonies, fighting and making love.

CONTEMPORARY ART Modern Mongolian painting is colourful, interesting, and represented in a variety of styles. It can be seen in a number of modern galleries in Ulaanbaatar (see pages 251–2).

One of the first exhibitions that travelled to the USA, in 2000, included the works of the artists Tsültemin Enkhjin, Mönkhoriin Erdenebayar and Batbayaryn Gansükh. Subject matter usually includes nomadic life, the landscape of the windswept steppes, animals and abstract themes. Works are in oil on canvas and in watercolour on paper. Many country museums sell watercolour paintings, which make excellent presents. Choindongiin Khürelbaatar, chairman of the Union of Mongolian Artists, himself an artist, exhibited in London on many occasions. In the USA his works were exhibited along with calligraphy by Batbayaryn Dovan. In London, the English Speaking Union has exhibited the calligraphic works of Davaakhüügiin Sükhbaatar.

MONGOLIAN ART

Mongolian art is vibrantly alive. It is inevitably influenced by the country's long and turbulent history. Artists draw from nature and a kaleidoscope of colour, movement and space, elements that Mongolia enjoys in abundance – endless blue skies, galloping horses across the steppes and the vast open spaces feature strongly. As one viewer put it: 'Today I was looking at a painting by a lama – it shows nomadic people herding animals, with deer and antelope running around, mountains and rivers … It conveys the peaceful soul of the Mongol landscape that should continue as an element of our destiny. So we need to think about ways to preserve Mongolian traditions, while at the same time developing mining … Such values are connected with the idea of a pristine environment'.

Baatar, a contemporary artist, follows the ancient Mongol *zurag* tradition, using a visual vocabulary of ancient Mongolian references, such as interlocking triangles, which refer to married women. Her colours are bright and clear although her perspective is quite flat. Stylised clouds hang in the sky. Baatar's works are highly sought after in Germany, France and Japan.

The internationally acclaimed British sculptor Richard Long drew inspiration from his visit to the Gobi, and produced works in sand and stone called *Gobi Desert Circles*. Circles, he claims, are timeless, understandable and easy to make. These works were photographed and then left to disintegrate naturally in the desert. Long's idea was to pioneer new ways of thinking about art and environment, while Mongolian sculptor Gankhuag exhibited his *Mirage of a Dream*, an abstract work in copper, in New York City.

Union of Mongolian Artists Chinggis Av 1, Ulaanbaatar 20A; 11 327474, 325849; www.uma.mn

ARTS AND CRAFTS

With the introduction of Buddhism in the 16th century, arts and crafts absorbed elements of Indian, Tibetan and Nepalese art. This is reflected in the Buddhist ritual vessels, incense burners and musical instruments for wind and percussion. Objects of everyday life, dress design and jewellery illustrate the development of crafts, such as leatherwork, appliqué and embroidery.

Through the ages, Mongolian women have occupied themselves with artistic needlework, skills that they may now convert into entrepreneurial activities for the gift industry, as tourism develops. In the past, special garments were decorated with small river gems, corals and turquoise, stitched with fine gold thread by women. The same is done today using modern designs. The complex embroidery and appliqué of coloured leather for saddles, harnesses and leather boots was traditionally achieved by the stronger masculine hand.

The Mongolian *ger* was richly ornamented in times past and decorated both inside and out. A song by an unknown writer describes the ornamentation:

Sculpted on the upper beams are
Peacocks and pheasants,
With outstretched necks.
Hewn on lower beams by doors are
Kites and tumblers,
Swooping in the clouds.
The *ger* is a rich and happy abode,
On firm birch props,
Clustered with animals.

FOLK ART Folk art contains many deeply symbolic meanings hidden in the designs that may decorate the door of the *ger* or other household utensils. Many of these swirling or geometric designs symbolise prosperity and protection; over time they have been combined and intertwined to express feelings of reverence for the beauty of nature. The most popular motif is the 'endless knot', one of the eight sacred symbols of Lamaist iconography. Others include linked circles known as the 'bracelet of the khan'. Mongols are people whose minds are tuned through centuries of Buddhist tradition to seek an inner meaning in abstract forms. So Mongolian decorative art is mostly abstract and manages to create in itself another language.

EMBROIDERY, APPLIQUÉ WORK AND CARVING Embroidery in colourful Chinese silk threads is still widely practised. Its chief purpose is to decorate the much-prized tobacco pouches. One technique employs a series of coloured threads, intricately knotted, with the help of wooden cross pieces. Among the most intricate of modern Mongolian craftsmanship are the chess sets of delicately carved pieces. Besides wood, carvers use amber and bone. In the past, camel bones were boiled to become snow white and then used in craft and jewellery making. Drinking bowls were hollowed from birch-tree roots and rimmed with beaten silver. Hide and wood have been the main materials in the herders' homes. Once used for weaponry and food cauldrons, iron is still used to make the central iron stove. The making of musical instruments is considered an art and the carving, joinery and carpentry work that goes into them is of the highest quality. A special paste called *zümber* is made from crushed porcelain, birch sugar and glue. It is used to create an embossment – a

It is only in recent times that craftsmen have become settled. During the last 200–300 years it was normal for journeymen or itinerant craftsmen to travel the country much as they did in medieval times in Europe. In the 1930s, the closure of the monasteries, which had fostered arts and crafts, created a flood of Mongolian artisans, who had to find other occupations.

Herdsmen practising semi-skilled crafts like woodwork did not make a living from craftwork. Children were trained in a form of apprenticeship with a master craftsman. No money changed hands but the pupil was expected in turn to offer training. The smith was regarded with great superstition and, like a shaman, was respected for his knowledge of the supernatural. The practice of metalwork had certain rituals attached to it. The supernatural world was revered by the nomads, who consulted the deities before moving camp, branding horses, casting an ornament and so forth. The spirits represented by inanimate and natural objects were all-powerful and certain simple rituals, such as flicking milk in the air before drinking or burning juniper twigs in the fire before branding, ensured they were respected.

The manner in which the craftsman worked was meaningful in Mongolia. The calm and concentrated way that Mongol craftsmen and craftswomen worked was associated with the belief that creating is a religious act.

technique known as *tesso duro* in Europe, and probably introduced from Italy by the Dominican monks who visited the court of Genghis Khan.

BANNERS AND FLAG-MAKING These crafts continue to employ appliqué skills, although the manufacture of the rich silks and brocades that lined the *gers* of the khans has become a memory of the past. There has been, however, a recent revival in modern tent-making, including interior and exterior decoration.

SOCIALIST REALISM Under communism, 'socialist realism' was adopted in literature and art, which became filled with communist leaders and labour heroes adopting striking poses against 'politically correct' backgrounds and slogans. The genre is best seen in municipal sculpture created by artists during the 20th century, such as S Choimbol's equine monument of the revolutionary hero Sükhbaatar sitting astride a giant horse in Genghis Khan Square in Ulaanbaatar. The Stalin statue in central Ulaanbaatar was taken down by public demand in 1990 and the statue of Lenin by the Ulaanbaatar Hotel was dismantled in 2012.

In the 20th century the Mongols have managed to preserve some traditional art forms while acquiring new ones from Russian and other European sources, like opera, ballet, theatre and circus. The numerous 'houses of culture' and libraries set up in the socialist period no longer receive much government money to operate, and the arts in Mongolia must fundraise in order to survive. Mongolian artists – musicians, actors and painters – now travel the world.

MONGOLIA ON FILM

A BRIEF HISTORY The first Mongolian films were made privately in the capital Urga (modern Ulaanbaatar) in the early 20th century for Prince Sain Noyon Khan Shirindambyn Namnansüren and the Javzandamba. After the socialist revolution, the

Mongolian People's Revolutionary Party decided in 1925 to use film as an instrument of mass education. From 1926 onwards, Soviet films were shown to the Mongolian people. The first permanent cinema – called 'Ard' (ард, *people*) – opened in the capital in 1934. Eventually every aimag centre had a cinema, and every small unit or *negdel* had a mobile cinema. In the 1990s, many cinemas, fixed and mobile alike, were closed down due to political change and lack of funds.

The first Mongolian-directed film was the black-and-white short feature *Norjmaa's Destiny* (*Norjmaagiin Zam*) by Temet Natsagdorj in 1938. From then on, Mongolian film production focused around heroic revolutionary propaganda and ancient popular legends, often under Russian direction, with movies like *Sükhbaatar* (1942) and *Tsogt Taij* (1945). The studios of Mongol Kino also produced documentaries and current news reports.

In the 1950s and 1960s the focus moved to working-class heroes, reflected in films such as *New Year* (*Shine Jil*, 1954) by Tseveeny Zandraa. The first colour film shown was *The Golden Yurt* (*Altan Örgöö*, 1969), based on a Mongolian folk tale. The 1970s and 80s brought further changes in that fictional stories turned to everyday life in *The Clear Tamir* (*Tungalag Tamir*, 1970) by Ravjagiin Dorjpalam, based on a novel by Chadraabalyn Lodoidamba and including some of the greatest Mongolian stars of the time. It would be wonderful if these films could be shown again. The grape vine says that Café Amsterdam in Ulaanbaatar has winter evenings showing 'golden oldies'.

MODERN FILM On the introduction of the market economy in the 1990s, young Mongolian film makers had the opportunity to seek funding and film partners internationally. The film *Genghis Khan* was the first Mongolian-Japanese co-production. *State of Dogs* (*Nokhoi Oron*, 1998) was written and directed collaboratively by the Belgian Peter Brosens and the Mongolian Dorjkhandyn Turmunkh. *Movement of Sand* (*Elsnii Nuudel*) was a successful film produced for the domestic market in 2007.

Close to Eden or *Urga* by Nikita Mikhalkov, shot around 1990–91, is extremely entertaining and funny, full of reality and charm. The story is about a Russian truck driver who breaks down on the steppes miles from anywhere and encounters a nomadic family that befriends him. It portrays the life of modern day Mongolian herdsmen where bicycles replace horses, TV pictures substitute for natural landscapes and mines begin to replace majestic grasslands. The film was shot in Inner Mongolia.

The Weeping Camel by Byambyn Davaa and Luigi Falorni, shot in 2002–03, is an enchanting story of a baby camel's rejection by his mother. Four generations of a Mongol Gobi family move into action to ensure the little camel's survival. As a last resort, two of the children ride off to find a local musician. The film's sweeping vistas and magical photography capture the very essence of the Gobi herders' lives and the association and sympathy they extend to their animals.

The Cave of the Yellow Dog (by the same directors as *The Weeping Camel*) tells the story of abandoned dogs which go wild and breed with wolves. The Mongolia dog symbolises the social changes Mongolia experienced at that time. The animals are immensely important to Mongolians, whose tradition holds that people are reincarnated from the canine. As people move to the city, dogs are losing their once-vital role as shepherds.

ON DVD *On the Edge of the Desert* (part 1 by Brian Moser; 1975) is the first TV film produced by a Western team in Mongolia.

The City on the Steppe (part 2 by Brian Moser; 1975) is a portrait of Ulaanbaatar and its inhabitants, then back with the herders during Tsagaan Sar, the Mongolian New year celebration. For further details, contact admin@therai.org.uk.

In the Wild – Mongolian Horseman with Julia Roberts is a film by Nigel Cole following actress Julia Roberts as she visits a Mongolian nomadic family to discover why the horse has been such an important player in their lives. Available through www.bbcshop.co.uk.

Long Way Round follows stars Ewan McGregor and Charley Boorman on a 20,000-mile motorbike journey around the world, travelling through Europe to Mongolia and onward. Available through www.easyCinema.com.

ON DVD *3 Steppes to Heaven* is a film produced by Corrie Wingate, which shows how in summer 2000 a group of young Brits set out on an unforgettable journey across Central Mongolia raising funds for 'Guide Dogs for the Blind'. Riding over 200km, the team visited monasteries, camped out and just had fun with new-found Mongolian friends – an amateur spectacular. Contact corriespond@hotmail.com.

Where's Mongolia? is a short film by David Carlyle, showing a feast of highlights from 'Fighting Dinos' of the Gobi, wildlife, fashion and horses (including the *takhi* or Mongolian wild horses) to festivals, sporting events and dancing. It covers a lot of ground in 50 minutes. Contact monsoc@indiana.edu.

4

Natural History and Conservation

NATURAL HISTORY

I'm not saying mining shouldn't happen – when you mine the earth you must then
restore the soil by planting trees. The minerals are like the liver, kidney and heart of
Mother Nature, without these "organs" the environment will die. Imagine nature as
a human, how can a person survive without vital organs? If you respect and worship
nature … She will quickly restore herself!

Mother Tara – Gobi nomad

The real problem is not to preserve the species, it is to preserve a living animal and
plant community.

William Conway, conservationist

What impressed me were the different sizes of the plant species as we moved from the
taiga (forests) to the steppe (grasslands). I saw orange sedum, which I'd never seen
before. I was really excited and wanted to know more about it all.

Visitor to Mongolia

People travel to Mongolia to discover another world. They see the wonders of nature
and find themselves overwhelmed by examples of its rare animal life and unusual
plant species. Fly-fishing and wild flower walks are hugely enjoyable. Remember to
bring a rod and a plant identification book and prepare to be amazed. This chapter
aims to stress the extent to which natural history and conservation are closely
interconnected.

Part of the country's allure lies in its wildness and undisturbed natural beauty.
The play of light and shade upon this wild landscape has a magnetic charm that
pulls the traveller back. Mongolia's geological assets, the bedrock of the country,
are as varied as they are beautiful. Fragments of life millennia ago are found in
fossil and skeletal remains – particularly dinosaurs, for which Mongolia is famous.
Gems and rich mineral deposits are another legacy of prehistoric times found
underground. Geologically, Mongolia comes under the Ural-Mongolian fold belt
and flying over Mongolia on a clear day is the best way to see the land formation.
You will see numerous mountain folds descending south in smooth, curved arcs.

Large tracts of Mongolia, around 12% of its territory, have been turned into
national parks with the aim to place approximately one third of the land under
protection in the future. Mongolia is a huge country and its national parks are a
wonderful help in safeguarding the countryside, habitats and millions of species.
In fact Genghis Khan, the great 13th-century ruler of the Mongol Empire, certainly
visited and appreciated one of the world's earliest nature reserves in the territory

of Bogdkhan Uul, near the capital, Ulaanbaatar. Although officially set up in 1778, Mongolians nonetheless credit the Great Khan himself with the idea. Bogdkhan Uul, my favourite park in Mongolia, protects six kinds of the world's cranes, the symbol of longevity, including the Demoiselle crane. This park leads the way in cross-border conservation in an international agreement between China, Mongolia and Russia to protect the whole area, part of eastern Mongolia's Daurian Steppe.

Mongolia's ecosystems are of global importance because of their diversity, size and continuity. The climate, topography and natural formations divide the country into six zones which comprise desert, Gobi and steppe (grassland) zones, and forest, alpine, and taiga (northern mountain/forest) zones. Mongolia is part of the central Asian plateau. It is a land of contrast and great biodiversity, teeming with rare and exotic species.

The fauna and flora of Mongolia are as distinctive as the vegetation zones they occupy. This is due mainly to the country's unique location between the Siberian taiga and the desert steppe. Mongolia has over 4,000 plant species, 136 species of mammals, 436 species of birds, 75 fish species and more than 15,000 insect species. Conifer forests cover around 11.5% of the territory, some 18 million hectares of land. These forests, principally of Siberian larch, form the southern edge of the vast taiga zone, the largest continuous forest system on earth. Less numerous deciduous species, like aspen, white birch and black poplar, populate the forest-steppe zone. The forests are home to most wild animals and birds, which live undisturbed, since most of the area is uninhabited and inaccessible to human settlement. The rivers are home to fish which grow unusually large like the *taimen* species, belonging to the salmon family. It is no fisherman's tale that they can measure over 6ft in length. Numerous insect and tiny rodent species abound. They need specialist classification because of their multiple variations.

A study of *The Mongolian Red List of Fishes*, carried out by the Zoological Society of London, Mongolian universities and others, shows that 48 of the 64 native Mongolian fish species are on the IUCN (The World Conservation Union)

BIODIVERSITY – WHAT TO LOOK OUT FOR   *John Farringdon*

Mongolia is the world's least densely populated nation and is situated at the junction of the Siberian forest, Central Asian steppe, and Gobi Desert biogeographic regions. Combined with its extensive alpine zones, Mongolia has a remarkable diversity of habitats and large fauna. From moose, roe deer, and brown bears in the northern forests, to the primordial takhi, gazelle, and marmots of the steppe to the wild Bactrian camel, Asiatic wild ass, and Gobi bear of the southern desert, and the alpine-dwelling ibex, argali, and phantom-like snow leopard, anywhere you visit in Mongolia there will be charismatic wildlife for visitors to search for. Those arriving by train from Beijing will awaken on the southern steppe, where the attentive should see Mongolian gazelle along the train line and, in summer, the Demoiselle crane. Bogd Uul Mountain near Ulaanbaatar provides opportunities to see roe deer or wolf, while at nearby Khustai Nuruu it can be difficult to avoid seeing red deer or takhi. Argali and ibex can be viewed in nearly any of Mongolia's western ranges, from Omnogov's Gurvan Saikhan National Park to the western Altai Range and eastward to the Kordol Sairdag Range near Lake Khovsgol. And where argali and ibex graze, the rarely-seen snow leopard will probably be nearby.

endangered Red List; some, like the Amur sturgeon, are listed as data deficient, while other species are known to be threatened or critically endangered. Species such as grayling and taimen may be recreationally fished under licence. In 2013, the Netherlands-Mongolia trust fund for environmental reform (NEMO) also produced a report on fishes and other rare species as part of ongoing research.

Lagoons, lakes and rivers, streams, marshes, oases and other wetlands in each of the six zones support their own distinctive flora and fauna. Wetlands provide crucial habitat for the waterfowl and water-frequenting birds that form the majority of Mongolia's migratory bird species. For keen ornithologists, the reed marshes surrounding the lakes of the western Great Lakes basin and the floodplains of larger rivers provide excellent bird watching possibilities, and, in the far west, in rivers you can spot beaver (*Castor fiber*), muskrat (*Ondatra zibethica*) and otter (*Lutra lutra*).

Several excellent books on Mongolian mammals and a new guide called *The Birds of Mongolia* were published in 2010. Also *A Guide to the Amphibians and Reptiles of Mongolia* by Professor Terbish et al was published in 2013. See *Further information*, pages 443–5.

WILDLIFE HABITATS OF MONGOLIA'S DIFFERENT VEGETATION ZONES

Taiga/forest zone Mongolia's taiga zone is part of the vast forested region of southern Siberia. It is found in the Khentii Mountains near Lake Khövsgöl, and on the north and east slopes of the Khangai Mountains. These Mongolian coniferous taiga forests comprise mainly Siberian larch (70%) and, at higher elevations, Siberian pine, mosses and lichens are abundant. The taiga forests of Mongolia cover around 5% of the country and these areas remain largely undisturbed. In the forests mosses and lichens are abundant and wildlife includes musk deer, moose, reindeer, sable and brown squirrel. Among the bird species found in the taiga forests are cuckoos and great grey owls. These wilderness zones are a reminder of the once numerous primeval forests of Europe – which survive today in isolated pockets in the Carpathian Mountains, in Transylvania, and in a few other parts of central Europe.

Mountain forest-steppe zone The mountain forest-steppe zone is found on the lower slopes of the Khentii and Khangai mountain ranges, in the Mongolian Altai Mountains, in the Orkhon and Selenge river basins, and in the mountains in eastern Mongolia. Steppe species dominate the mountain forest-steppe of the Altai whereas taiga species tend to dominate the northern ranges of the Khangai and Khentii. There is a high degree of biological diversity and wide river valleys separate the territory of the mountain/steppe zone which covers about 25% of Mongolia. Mixed coniferous forest is found on cooler, moister northern slopes, while steppe vegetation predominates on other slopes. Species include elk, wolf, roe deer and Eurasian badger, while the birdlife of the forest/steppe regions includes Daurian partridge, black kites and great bustards. Wild boar and marmot are hunted for the pot (their meat tastes delicious when steamed in earth ovens or roasted on open fires). Herbs and wild grasses add to the natural profusion of meadow flowers (see box, page 138).

Steppe zone Extensive grasslands, or steppe, make up the heart of Mongolia both geographically and economically. The entire far eastern part of the country falls into this area, extending west below the Khangai range to the Great Lakes basin of Uvs Aimag. This sea of grass covers rolling, undulating land for as far as

4

the eye can see, encompassing 20% of Mongolia's territory. It provides the most important grazing lands for Mongolian livestock herds. Some of the southeastern steppe is largely uninhabited and underdeveloped, where hundreds of thousands of migrating gazelles live undisturbed. Distinctive flora and fauna include: various steppe grasses; gazelles and small rodents such as voles and pika; rare species of cranes and birds of prey. Flocks of migratory birds make the eastern plains their feeding grounds for a season and, in the same region, thousands of free-roaming white-tailed gazelle reside, migrating south into China when winter comes.

Desert steppe (semi-desert) Desert steppe occupies 20% of Mongolian territory between the grasslands and the deserts. It includes the Great Lakes basin and most of the lands between the Altai and the Khangai ranges, as well as the eastern Gobi. Low-lying salt plains predominate and rainfall is sparse (100–125mm per annum), and winds and dust storms ravage the countryside; but despite these harsh conditions many pastoral nomads find a livelihood with their herds of camels, sheep and goats in these semi-desert regions. Desert grasses and shrubs provide grazing including feather grasses and various types of pea shrub. The wild

STEPPE FORWARD   *Nathan Conaboy*

Steppe Forward is a joint project between the National University of Mongolia (NUM) and The Zoological Society of London (ZSL), which is supported by the Mongolian Ministry of Environment and Green Development. Steppe Forward was established in 2003; it empowers Mongolians to create conservation programmes by providing them with the necessary tools to design and monitor their own conservation initiatives, assess wildlife populations and manage ecological studies.

Currently the main problems affecting Mongolia's natural environment include degradation associated with rapid economic development, lack of financial resources for national parks, minimal knowledge of species distributions and poor ecological research through lack of training. Steppe Forward addresses these problems by providing high standards of training and practical conservation projects, to strengthen the core skills of Mongolians working in ecology and conservation.

This is achieved through a number of different initiatives. Each summer, NUM students attend a three-week-long ecology field course. The course has been held in the mountains of northern Mongolia, on grassland steppe and in the Small Gobi Strictly Protected Area. During the course, students are trained in ecological census techniques, conservation project design and data analysis. These courses have recently become accredited by NUM, and are designed to teach subjects and skills that the students would not otherwise be taught in the classroom, but are essential for working in conservation biology.

Steppe Forward also runs the Wildlife Picture Index (WPI) for monitoring biodiversity trends in and outside of Mongolia's protected areas. This approach involves remote cameras being set up throughout the countryside. When an animal walks by, the shutter is triggered automatically. The cameras allow sites to be monitored around the clock and elusive species such as the brown bear, lynx and wolf can be observed. The project has been running since 2009 and during this time more than 500,000 photographs have been gathered and scores of rangers trained in camera trapping and other survey techniques. As a direct animals that survive here, like the wild camel and the saiga antelope, are some of the rarest in the world. Hundreds of interesting rodents, lizards and snakes inhabit the stony dry ground, and other species like the long-eared hedgehog and a variety of different types of pika (small rodents) live in these regions of sparse vegetation. Kozlov's pygmy jerboa is found in the Trans-Altai Gobi, along with the thick-tailed pygmy jerboa which is also found in the semi-deserts of the southwest.

Gobi Once an ancient inland sea, the Gobi occupies much of southern Mongolia and northeastern China. It is a place that attracts many fossil collectors. The landscape is rugged and inhospitable, with little vegetation, but it varies enormously, from mountain massifs with barren rocky outcrops to the flat plains where you find poplar-fringed oases and sand dunes. It is the habitat of threatened species, such as wild camel, Gobi bear, known in Mongolian as *mazaalai*, and *khulan* or wild ass. The Dzungarian Gobi, in the west, presents a unique combination of animal and plant life. The extreme climate averages less than 100mm rainfall annually. Temperatures fluctuate from 40°C in summer to –40°C in winter. During the spring and autumn strong winds of speeds up to 140km/h scour the land.

result of this work protected areas have increased in size and Steppe Forward has held a number of training workshops for rangers and park staff. The organisation has also run a number of community projects where nomadic herders in the Gobi Desert have been trained in sustainable resource use and conservation; it plans to develop further conservation initiatives with the nomadic herders of the Gobi Desert.

The Red List project, which is supported by Steppe Forward, assesses the conservation status of Mongolian mammals, fish, reptiles and amphibians. Two conservation assessments and conservation action plans have been published from this work for Mongolian mammals and fish. Steppe Forward is also involved in the ZSL 'Evolutionary Distinct Globally Endangered' (EDGE) programme. This aims to identify the status of poorly known and possibly extinct EDGE species, develop and implement conservation programmes for those not currently protected, and support local scientists in research and conservation efforts. In Mongolia this programme specifically concerns the Bactrian camel, long-eared jerboa and the saiga antelope.

Steppe Forward also produces a number of educational and scientific materials on ecology and conservation. A field guide on Mongolian mammals was published in 2010 and a similar publication on Mongolian birds is soon to be published. Furthermore, Steppe Forward is responsible for establishing *The Mongolian Journal of Biological Sciences*, an official ISSN journal of the Faculty of Biology at the National University of Mongolia. It is published bi-annually and includes papers, short articles and reviews on ecology, behaviour, systematics, evolution, conservation and general biology.

For more information, contact Nathan Conaboy (e *nathan.conaboy@zsl.org*) or Dr Gitanjali Bhattacharya (e *gitanjali.bhattacharya@zsl.org*), Batbayar GaltBalt (e *batbr19@yahoo.com*), or James Tallant (e *james_tallant@ hotmail.com*), or see the Steppe Forward website www.steppeforward.com. Alternatively visit www.zsl.org/mongolia, follow them on twitter @steppeforward and Facebook at www.facebook.com/steppe.forward.

4

FAUNA Mongolia is rich in fauna and is home to some of the world's rarest wildlife. The more exotic rare species include the snow leopard (*Uncia uncia*), the Gobi bear (*Ursus arctos*) and the wild ancestors of three of mankind's most important domesticated animals – the wild camel (*Camelus bactrianus ferus*), the Asiatic wild ass (*Equus hemionus luteus*) and Przewalski's horse (*Equus przewalskii*). Many international wildlife conservation projects are helping Mongolian organisations to safeguard these rare wild animals. Nine species of bird and 38 plant species are on the verge of extinction and there are mounting concerns about the fate of the Gobi bear, the wild camel and the saiga antelope (*Saiga tartarica mongolica*), among other large mammals.

Threatened species Below are some of the most threatened of Mongolia's rare species, together with details of the conservation measures that are aimed at helping to preserve them. The *Mongolian Red List of Mammals* is part of The Zoological Society of London's Regional Red List Series and is available to download from http://library.zsl.org. This collaborative work involved many experts from different institutes and organisations – such as the National University of Mongolia (NUM), the Mongolia Academy of Sciences (MAS), the World Bank, the World Conservation Union (IUCN) and the Steppe Forward Programme (SFP) among others, and is the authoritative work on critically endangered mammals. The *Mongolian Red List of Fishes* has also been published along with the *Summary Conservation Action Plans for Mongolian Fishes* – for details see www.zsl.org.

Snow leopard **(Uncia uncia)** *Irves* in Mongolian (sometimes spelled 'irbis'). Snow leopards are among the most beautiful of the great cats. They are so well camouflaged that the big black rosettes of their tawny spotted coats, which resemble rocks and shade, make them almost impossible to see in their mountain habitat. Males weigh up to 54kg and females slightly less. They breed in winter, giving birth in late spring to between one and four cubs (usually two). They are solitary creatures, except during breeding or cub-rearing times.

Worldwide, the range of the snow leopard is restricted to the Himalayan ranges and the high mountains of central Asia, which include the Mongolian Altai range. Snow leopards are extremely elusive creatures. When they are spotted, it is usually in areas of steep, broken, rocky slopes at elevations up to 5,500m. The world population is estimated, perhaps optimistically, at 7,000, although 4,000 is more likely.

The snow leopard is listed in the IUCN *Red Data Book* and the *Mongolian Red List of Mammals* (2007) as global and regional status: endangered. The Convention on International Trade in Endangered Species of Fauna and Flora (CITES) prohibits its trade, and hunting these animals is considered illegal by conservationists, although a ban is difficult to enforce in Mongolia. These shy felines are distributed over a wide area of western Mongolia, in Kharkhiraa Uul in the Altai, and Khankhökhii Nuruu in the Khangai mountain ranges, as well as in some isolated mountainous sections of the Trans-Altai Gobi. Their total range in Mongolia is some 100,000km². The Mongolian population estimates vary from 800 to 1,500 animals. Highest densities are thought to be in the South Gobi, Central Trans-Altai Gobi, and northern Altai. Remnant populations occur in the Khangai and possibly in Khövsgöl Aimag, although no leopards have been sighted in Khövsgöl Aimag since the 1960s.

Competition with domestic stock and poaching are causes for their declining numbers, which is a similar case for their principal wild prey, ibex and *argali*. Because their wild prey has also declined, in some areas the leopards are becoming increasingly dependent on domestic livestock kills, which leads to more and more human/leopard conflicts.

Despite being protected, hunting of the spotted *irves* in Mongolia remains legal. Legislation adopted by the government, in December 2001, taxes the snow leopard at T100,000 per head when hunted for 'cultural or scientific purposes'. However it is not listed among the animals that foreigners can hunt. Since the leopards often kill domestic horses, yaks and camels, which roam freely in areas where they hunt for their survival, the economic impact to herders can be substantial. New educational ways of working together with herders is helping to offset this problem by providing finance from craft-based industry.

Snow leopards exhibit extremely patchy distribution which, in time, will reduce genetic interchange, making them even more vulnerable. In Mongolia this is already happening to the isolated populations in the Khangai, Great Gobi, South Gobi and other sites. The potential for further fragmentation of the snow leopard's habitats is increased as herding in remoter areas intensifies.

Conservation measures Since the early 1990s, research efforts to preserve the snow leopard have been carried out by the Mongolian government, the Mongolian Association for Conservation of Nature and Environment (MACNE) and foreign scientists. A long-term study using satellite-radio collars on snow leopards in the Gobi Altai has led to many interesting discoveries, including information about their home ranges, which may be as great as $1,000km^2$ – more than 20 times the size of reported home ranges elsewhere. Snow leopards in Mongolia were found to be capable of crossing up to 56km of open desert to reach a neighbouring mountain habitat. Clearly, leopards in Mongolia are on the ecological fringe of their range and must travel farther to gain food.

Given the obvious need to involve and include Mongolia's semi-nomad herders in conservation measures, a unique community-based programme called Irbis Enterprises seeks to foster tolerance and appreciation of the cat among herders who live in the leopard's habitats. Herders agree not to kill either leopards or their prey and to abide by grazing regulations in protected areas. In exchange, Irbis Enterprises provides much-needed access to local and foreign markets for herder-made handicrafts such as felts, mats and goods knitted from camel wool and raw cashmere.

In 2006 Panthera was founded, an organisation devoted exclusively to the conservation of wild cats and their ecosystems – with internationally known experts such as Dr Tom McCarthy, its director, and Dr George Schaller, its vice-president. To learn more about snow-leopard conservation or to participate in active research studies in Mongolia, visit: www.irbis-enterprises.com; www.panthera.org; and The Zoological Society of London at *www.zsl.org*.

The Snow Leopard Conservation Foundation (SLCF), founded in 2007 and based in Ulaanbaatar, is an NGO that supports Snow Leopard Enterprises (SLE) to create projects like quality, local craft production to link herders to international markets and provide another income source for them. A livestock insurance programme has also been initiated. See www.snowleopard.org.

The World Wildlife Fund works with The Land of Snow Project to secure key areas of snow leopard habitat in Mongolia. To protect endangered snow leopards, WWF-Mongolia works with herders in the western Altai-Sayan region, educating them about snow leopard and prey species ecology, strategies for reducing loss of livestock to these cats, and directly involving herders in snow leopard research. As an incentive, WWF also helps herders living in snow leopard habitat to develop alternative sources of income, such as ecotourism and home handicraft enterprises.

4

Through these efforts WWF is helping to secure the long-term future of these majestic cats. To adopt a snow leopard go to: www.worldwildlife.org.

In 2012–13 a Japanese film crew made a series of seasonal documentaries, showing rare shots of a snow leopard mother and her three cubs, in situ, on a mountainside south of Khovd. The series captivated over 4 million Japanese viewers. Such well-produced nature films raise critical awareness and much-needed funds at the same time. The author visited the site in 2013 to meet the crew but didn't see a snow leopard – let's hope the film is shown worldwide.

Gobi bear (Ursus arctos) *Mazaalai* in Mongolian. The first exciting reports of an unknown bear living in an isolated haunt, deep in the Gobi Desert, were recorded in 1900 by V Ladygin, who found bear tracks and diggings near several oases. The first confirmed sightings did not come until 1943. The range of the Gobi bear is currently thought to be restricted to Sector A of the Great Gobi Strictly Protected Area (GGSPA), encompassing 15,000–16,000km². Areas of bear activity centre on the Atas Bogd, Shar Khulst and Tsagaan Bogd mountains. Little investigation of this secretive species has been conducted and information suggests that as few as 40 animals remain, although some people put the figure at 25. Living in such a harsh desert environment, which has been subject to climate change in recent years, it is feared that the bears' continued existence is precarious. The Gobi bear is listed in the IUCN *Red Data Book* as endangered and in the *Mongolian Red List of Mammals* (2007) as global and regional status: critically endangered. No hunting is allowed.

Worldwide, the distribution of the brown bear includes Europe, Asia, and North America. However, the Gobi bear, or *mazaalai*, is unique among brown bears in its use of a barren desert habitat. In contrast to other brown bears, Gobi bears are relatively small. Adults weigh between 100kg and 120kg. The Gobi bear has a light-brown coat, with darker colouring on its head, belly and legs. Light stripes, or a collar of colour, are often discernible around its neck. DNA studies based on hairs taken from empty bear beds, or found on trees against which the animals rub, will help biologists to establish how closely Gobi bears are related to other brown bears – for example, to the far-away Tibetan brown bear, and other brown bears from the nearby Altai Mountains or the neighbouring Tien Shan range in China. It is important to determine the uniqueness of the Gobi bear in order to set appropriate conservation programmes for the animals.

Although humans pose few threats because the Gobi bear's range falls almost entirely within the core area of the GGSPA, where human activity is highly restricted, the bears are being affected by recent climate change – drought and the general drying up of oases and more limited food resources.

Conservation measures Currently management includes leaving supplemental food near key oases each spring when the bears emerge from their winter dens. Additional conservation measures include moving bears between activity centres to improve the genetic interchange. To determine if such measures are needed, recent studies have used non-invasive techniques (genetic fingerprinting using shed hairs) to study the bears. At least 15 individuals are now 'known' and natural movement between oases is being studied with the help of GPS and satellite collars. Checking the drinking water in the area for contaminants is also a key conservation measure. Education, training and the involvement of local residents is critical to this unique brown bear's survival. The Mongolian Ministry of Environment and Green Development (MEGD) designated 2013 as the Year of Protecting Gobi Bear.

Work on Gobi bears and other threatened animals of the Great Gobi has been sponsored by the David Shepherd Conservation Foundation, UK (*www.dscf.demon.co.uk*) and the Wildlife Conservation Society, USA (*www.wcs.org*); see also the Zoological Society of London website (*www.zsl.org*). To follow Gobi bear conservation initiatives go to: beringiasouth.org/Mongolian-Gobi-Bear and www.vitalground.org.

Wild Bactrian camel **(Camelus bactrianus ferus)** *Khavtgai* in Mongolian. Despite the occurrence of domestic Bactrian camels across much of central Asia, the continued survival of their wild forebears was not revealed to science until the late 1870s, when the explorer Przewalski visited the Lop Nor region of China and reported their existence. Hunted for its meat and exceedingly shy of human contact, the wild camel's range has been dramatically reduced since its discovery. The world's remaining wild Bactrian camels, under 1,000 in total, struggle to survive today as a fragmented, remnant population with perhaps 400 occurring in Sector A of the GGSPA in southwestern Mongolia. The Gobi National Park 'A' was established in 1976 to reflect the then-known range of the wild camel. It encompasses 44,190km² and is the largest protected area in Mongolia. By Mongolian law, all human activity, except research, is precluded in the core areas and only limited uses, such as national border patrols, are allowed elsewhere in the reserve. The wild camel is listed in the IUCN *Red Data Book* as endangered and in the *Mongolian Red List of Mammals* (2007) as global status: critically endangered; regional status: endangered. No hunting is allowed. See box, page 346.

Although well protected legally in Mongolia, camels are threatened by illegal hunters. Poaching is rare but it does occur. Detection of illegal activity in the reserve is difficult because the reserve is one of the largest in the world, but has a staff of fewer than ten rangers, few of whom have vehicles (so they rely on their own camels for transport).

Concerns are that domestic camels are allowed to graze in close proximity to the wild camels' range and there is probably some crossbreeding with unknown effects on the wild gene pool. One of the most serious concerns today is the lack of young in the herd. Recent studies have not been able to determine if this is due to poor reproduction or poor survival of calves. Wolves are the natural predators of camels and may be responsible for the loss of young, contributing to their population decline.

Conservation measures A semi-captive herd of wild camels is held near the GGSPA headquarters in Bayantooroi, Gobi-Altai Aimag. In 2004, the Wild Camel Protection Foundation established the Hunter Hall Captive Breeding Centre at Zakhyn Us with 12 wild camels – the only site of its type in the world. In 2010 the population numbered 25. The Zoological Society of London (ZSL) is advising on plans to release the captive wild camels back to the Gobi.

Some of the most important work on the conservation of wild camels has been done by UK explorer and writer, John Hare, who has written widely on the subject. His latest book, *The Mysteries of the Gobi* (2009), tells of his journeys in the Mongolian and Chinese Gobi to find the wild camels and to explain how this species struggles to survive in a harsh and cruel landscape, most threatened at the end of the day by man's illegal mining activities. John Hare founded The Wild Camel Protection Foundation (WCPF) – see his websites: www.johnhare.org.uk and www.wildcamels.com.

Follow news of two-humped camel races, held in other parts of Mongolia to raise funds for WCPF!

4

Work on wild camels and other animals of the Great Gobi has also been sponsored by the David Shepherd Conservation Foundation, UK (*www.dscf.demon.co.uk*), the Wildlife Conservation Society, USA (*www.wcs.org*) and the Zoological Society of London (ZSL) (*www.zsl.org*).

Gazelle During the migration seasons over a million gazelles cross the eastern Mongolian grasslands, unhampered by fences, to both China and Russia. At this time, herds of up to 50,000 gazelle or antelope can be seen. They migrate south to China when the weather gets colder and move north in the hot season. New conservation measures are now in effect to protect them – not only the animals but the land they move across. Although they are an important source of food illegal hunting needs to be monitored. The goal is to protect both the wild creatures and their ecosystems. Two types of Mongolian gazelles are described below: the white-tailed gazelle and the black-tailed gazelle.

White-tailed gazelle (*Procapra gutturosa*) *Tsagaan zeer* in Mongolian. The herds of white-tailed gazelles on Mongolia's eastern plains are one of Asia's great wildlife spectacles. The eastern grasslands themselves are unique and represent one of the few remaining steppe regions where undisturbed animal migration is possible in large groups of between 30,000 and 50,000 animals, although as many as 4.75 million may have occurred in Mongolia as recently as the 1920s. A 2002 nationwide population assessment estimates there are between 800,000 and 900,000 individuals. Mongolian gazelles were once widespread in the central and Khentii provinces, where they are now rarely found because of hunting, although small groups have been found in the Tuul River valley and in areas of the northern Altai. There are around 3,000 white-tailed gazelles in the Gobi Gurvansaikhan National Park in the South Gobi region that are isolated from the eastern herds and do not migrate with them.

The white-tailed gazelle is also known by three other names: Mongolian gazelle or *tsagaan zeer* in Mongolian, *dzeren* in Russian, and Persian gazelle. The gazelles graze on different varieties of grasses, such as allium, artemisa, stipa and festuca. In the hot and hostile conditions of the semi-desert, surface pools provide drinking water after heavy summer rains.

Unfortunately the migratory herds have an uncertain future because of proposed plans for large-scale development of their habitat, which could eventually threaten their steppe-land paradise. Oil drilling and mining ventures are opening up the area by introducing improved roads and pipelines, along with future plans to build a railway. The poorly understood, yet wide-ranging, movements of the gazelles make it impossible to contain them in reserves. This means that sustainable development must be balanced with land management and wildlife conservation to ensure the preservation of the gazelles' migratory patterns across the vast eastern steppe, without impeding its natural development. The gazelles themselves constitute an important natural economic resource. Hunters shoot a certain number of gazelles each year for commercial purposes. The gazelle hunt, which has taken place annually for over 60 years, took around 50,000 head, averaging 726 tonnes of meat per year from 1951 to 1961. In recent years, the numbers have fluctuated from 10,000 to 40,000, taken during the short shooting season from mid November to December. The meat is sold abroad.

Conservation measures Wildlife conservation and management programmes are actively helping to preserve the entire ecosystem, with participation by a number of organisations, among them the Wildlife Conservation Society (WCS) and the United Nations Environmental Programme (UNEP), who have established an Eastern Steppe Biodiversity Project (ESBP). Conservation projects include helping in the training and education of local hunters. Foreign experts are working alongside the hunters in an integrated programme with local companies to ensure that veterinary care and international standards of meat processing are met. Mongolian veterinarians are trained to monitor the gazelles, since domestic animals and wild gazelles co-exist. Health and safety checks are done to help to prevent the spread of any potentially serious diseases, like foot and mouth. It was scientifically proven in 2013 that the wild gazelles are not the drivers of foot and mouth disease and that it is caused most likely by domestic stock. ESBP has also established a project to monitor a number of radio-collared gazelle calves, tracking them over 10,000km^2 of the eastern plains. Further research concentrates on their spring and autumn migration patterns, the distribution and size of the herds and their population dynamics within a larger study area of 75,000km^2. For information on the impact of large-scale road projects, follow the conservation of gazelles on the Eastern Steppe via the Wildlife Conservation Society's website (*www.wcs.org/saving wildlife/hoofed mammals/mongolian-gazelle.asp*x).

Black-tailed gazelle (*Gazella subgutturosa*) *Khar süült zeer* in Mongolian. Black-tailed gazelles are not as numerous as the white-tailed (Mongolian) gazelles, and are found in the South Gobi area where they number around 1,800 head. They form mixed herds with Mongolian gazelles but never with other livestock. In summer the herds are seen in unisex groups of between two and ten animals. In winter they form larger herds of 200–300 animals for protection against wolves. Fawns are born in late June and the young may be left to sleep on the ground where they are perfectly camouflaged by their russet-brown coats, while their mothers feed on saxaul, a desert shrub, and search for water. Black-tailed gazelles were hunted for their meat and horns, but, since the species is becoming endangered, hunting is now restricted. Their most important predator (besides man) is the wolf. Illegal hunting for meat and sport is the primary threat.

Conservation measures Environmental protection is similar to that for the white-tailed gazelle. Hunting of these gazelles is restricted.

Saiga antelope (**Saiga tatarica mongolica**) *Bökhön* in Mongolian. There is mounting concern for the safety of the Mongolian antelope. This species numbered three million in the 1940s, but since then herds have plummeted in number. These snub-nosed antelopes are now confined to one small area of western Mongolia. Although they had declined to under 1,000 individuals in 2003, they recovered slightly by 2005, but the most recent population figures estimate that number to have decreased due to extreme winters and the fact that the saiga are illegally hunted for their horns. However, conservation education is obviously working in the Gobi Altai region where numbers have increased. They are a sub-species and differ from the saiga antelope of Russia and neighbouring Kazakhstan. In the *Mongolian Red List of Mammals* (2007) they are listed as global status: critically endangered; regional status: endangered.

Conservation measures There is an attempt to re-establish a second population of Mongolian saiga, which would require the hand-rearing of young antelopes. See the Zoological Society of London website (*www.zsl.org*), and the World Wildlife

Fund for Nature website (*www.panda.org*). A very active group called *The Saiga Conservation Alliance* – supported by International Institutions like WWF – have an award winning newsletter that may be downloaded in a number of different languages: go to www.saiga-conservation.com

Przewalski's horse (Equus przewalskii) *Takhi* in Mongolian. Przewalski's horse is the only wild horse to survive in modern times. They were once common throughout Mongolia and neighbouring territories, but in time, because of the effects of hunting and the competition of domestic stock at waterholes, they became extinct in the wild in the late 1960s. The species was returned to Mongolia from

MONGOLIAN WILD HORSES RETURN TO MONGOLIA

In 1992 12 *takhi* were transported from European zoos to Takhiin Tal, a remote site in western Mongolia, bordering Great Gobi National Park (Area B). This rare horse species became extinct in the wild in the late 1960s. In 1993, 16 *takhi* reached the Khustain Nuruu reserve area (now a national park) sponsored by a Dutch foundation in co-operation with the Mongolian Association for the Conservation of Nature and the Environment (MACNE).

It took over 90 years of breeding, planning, patience and diplomacy for this to happen. The wild horses were first discovered by the explorer Colonel Nikolai Przewalski, an officer in the Russian Imperial Army, on one of his journeys through central Asia in 1878 and made known to Western science. The capture and transportation of wild horses to the zoo parks of Europe and America is an adventure story in itself, instigated by the Duke of Bedford, of Woburn Abbey in England, and Baron Edward von Falz-Fein, of Askania Nova, in the Ukraine. But of the 54 Przewalski's horses taken into captivity in 1900, only a few produced foals. The world population descends from 12 of these animals and another wild horse caught at a later period and shipped to the Ukraine.

For almost a century the wild horses survived in international zoo parks and private collections, while in Mongolia their numbers declined. The last recorded sightings were in 1968, in the Takhiin Tal area of the southwest Gobi-Altai, after which it became evident that the *takhi* had become extinct in the wild. Little knowledge of the *takhi* reached the West during the Cold War period and the area of Takhiin Tal was impossible for Westerners to visit. The Species Survival Commission (SSC), a branch of the World Wildlife Fund for Nature (WWF), helped to raise awareness of the wild horses' plight and zoo breeders took serious steps to initiate stallion exchanges between America and Europe to increase the gene pool and prevent inbreeding. Interest groups were established, like the Foundation for the Preservation and Protection of the Przewalski's Horse, who provided semi-reserves and organised breeding groups which helped to pave the way for future introductions of wild horses to Mongolia.

While breeding plans got under way, zoologists and other experts made site surveys and funds were raised by the general public, with some government help, to return the wild horses to Mongolia. The Przewalski stud book records are kept at Prague Zoo, one of the oldest pedigree studbooks in the zoo world. *Takhi* are extremely popular in the minds of Mongolian people, who equated their newfound political freedom of the 1990s with the return of this last-known wild horse species, in 1992.

world zoos and reserves to three sites (Takhiin Tal, Khustain Nuruu and Khömiin Tal). The wild horses interbreed easily with domestic horses; therefore, the two populations must be kept separate. They may be distinguished from domestics by their appearance and also, scientifically, by a difference in their chromosome numbers: 66 chromosomes for the Przewalski and 64 for the domestic. Wild horses are stocky creatures with mealy mouths, zebroid stripes on the hocks and a dorsal stripe that runs along the backbone from the shoulder to the tail. They have thick hairy tails, short brushy manes and dun-coloured coats, which turn a lighter colour, especially on the underbelly, during spring and summer when they lose their shaggy winter coats. This heavy-boned ancient horse type survive the extreme winter conditions of the Eurasian steppe by scraping the icy ground with their front hooves in winter to reveal the scant vegetation beneath. Foals are born in spring and usually have a light yellow coat that darkens with age.

Conservation measures These include a continued captive management programme and breeding control based on genetic knowledge. Breeders had an initial objective to return Przewalski's horses to their natural habitat in Mongolia, which has happened, and additionally to set up a long-term sustainable population of *takhi* in free-ranging conditions. The first objective was achieved in 1992 when 21 wild horses were transported from Western zoos and reserves to release sites at Khustain Nuruu (16) and Takhiin Tal (five). The ultimate goal at the Khustain Nuruu site is to see up to 500 free-ranging Przewalski's horses in the park. This is a secure wild habitat where sufficient numbers of wild horses should ensure their continued survival. Another release site has opened for the *takhi* at Khömiin Tal in western Mongolia (Zavkhan Aimag) near Khar Us Nuur National Park, which borders Zavkhan and Khovd aimags. Numbers have grown from 12 animals (2004) to 37 (2013). Besides the Mongolian groups and the captive population in European and American zoos, Mongolian wild horses are found in Canada (in Alberta), France (Cévènnes National Park), Holland (semi-reserves of the Dutch Foundation), the Ukraine (at Askania Nova) and on the Hungarian steppes (Hortobagy Puszta National Park). The most recently reported release site is in Gansu Province in northwest China where 21 wild horses were introduced to the National Nature Reserve in Dunhuang, to join a trial group of seven animals released in 2010. The world herd (including those in captivity in zoos worldwide and those in release sites) numbers over 3,000 Przewalskis (2013). There are around 350 wild horses in Mongolia; however, severe winters can have a very negative effect on small population herd numbers. A once near-extinct species in the 1970s, the wild horses have made a terrific comeback; it is a notable conservation success story. The success of the reintroduction projects of *takhi* to Mongolia is demonstrated by is changes of status in IUCN's Red List – from 'extinct in the wild' in 1996, to 'critically endangered' in 2008, to the less critical status of 'endangered' in 2011.

For further information, see the Zoological Society of London website (*www. zsl.org*) and other specific *takhi* websites *(www.takh.org (Khömiin Tal), www. savethewildhorse.org (Takhiin Tal) and www.treemail.nl/takhi (Khustain Nuruu))*.

Mongolian wild ass (**Equus hemionus luteus**) *Khulan* in Mongolian. The total population of the Asiatic wild ass is estimated at around 10,000, surviving in the southern semi-desert regions. They possess many horse-like features and their vocalisations sound like something between the neigh of a horse and the bray of an ass. The sub-species of Asian wild ass include the *khulan*, the *onager*, the *kiang* and the Indian wild ass. The largest animals of this group are the *kiang*, found in the highlands of Tibet and Qinghai Province, in China. The greatest number of *khulan* occur in the Gobi, mostly in the area of the Great Gobi National Park. The *khulan* are considered globally threatened. Locally they are classified as rare animals and protected under Mongolian law. Large herds live in 'Gobi B' Strictly Protected Area of the national park in southern Mongolia–China border region of Gobi Altai and Khovd aimags.

Recently, the population in the southern Gobi has been disturbed and its territory radically divided and 'cut into' by new mining activities, roads and numerous trucks that transport coal and other materials across its former grazing habitat. Studies are being conducted to minimise this and to help protect the *khulan* by conservationists working alongside mining authorities, such as Fauna and Flora International. *Khulan* now regularly occupy areas near the southeastern boundaries of the Gobi Gurvansaikhan National Park, with the highest population density south of the Zöölön Mountains. When cold weather comes they form winter herds of more than 1,000 animals. In summer, these groups break down into smaller grazing units. Large groups have a higher breeding success because their foals are better protected against wolves. The *khulan* prefer to graze on the desert steppe grasses since the alpine meadows are inaccessible to them and they rarely graze the mountain steppe. The *khulan* seem to be able to sense water below the surface and will dig in riverbeds to reach it; therefore, they can take advantage of pastures not accessible to domestic herds. Some waterholes are known by the local herdsmen as 'khulan waters'. Wild *khulan* wait their turn at waterholes and seepages frequented by domestic animals but, unfortunately, they are considered pests by the locals and are hunted or scared away.

Conservation measures Hunting is banned for foreigners, although because of its practice in the recent past, *khulan* are very timid and flee at the slightest sound of danger. They can be observed only from a considerable distance. For *khulan* conservation information go to: Flora and Fauna International (*www.fauna-flora. org*). For specific Gobi *Khulan* conservation initiatives, see the Association Goviin *Khulan* website: www.goviin-khulan.com, founded by Ann-Camille Souris.

Other species
***Manchurian red deer* (Cervus elaphus)** *Bor göröös* in Mongolian. Manchurian red deer live in the Mongolian Gobi-Altai Mountains, which range across nearly two-thirds of the country. A large species with a reddish-brown summer coat, which becomes thick brown-grey in winter, some of the time they live among the inhospitable craggy peaks, along with snow leopard and ibex, where the harsh climate keeps man at bay, but are usually found on the lower reaches where they scrape their antlers on trees, leaving behind distinctive traces. They are browsing animals but also live on nuts and fruit. Wolves are their principal predators, although hunters also kill them for meat and their antlers are used in traditional medicines.

***Ibex* (Capra sibirica)** *Yangir* in Mongolian. Ibex occur in the mountainous regions of Mongolia and according to a recent survey there are approximately 19,000 Asiatic ibex in the Gobi Gurvansaikhan National Park. In general, ibex congregate during the breeding season in autumn and they gather in herds during the winter when up to 70 animals at a time can be observed. The best time for observations is the rutting season, starting late September or early October before the herds disperse in spring. Females give birth in June. Ibex share their pasture with domestic goats and other species, which they follow on to the lower slopes in winter. As the number of domesticated goats has grown over the last few years, the wild species must move to higher altitudes for summer grazing. Natural enemies of the ibex are the snow leopard and wolf. Herders hunt ibex, especially at the beginning of winter, but their meat is not as popular as the meat of wild sheep. Listed in the *Mongolian Red List of Mammals* (2007) as local status: near threatened. Dominant threats are illegal and unsustainable hunting for meat and skins which are traded, and as trophies which are exported by foreign hunters. Recent harsh winters at the turn of the 21st century also impacted the population sizes. See the Zoological Society of London website (*www.zsl.org*).

Mongolian wild sheep (Ovis ammon) *Argali* in Mongolian. There are 12 *argali* species in the world. A male Altai *argali* weighs 200kg and can move at a speed of 60km/h. *Argali* occur throughout the mountainous areas of Mongolia. They can be observed most frequently in the Gobi Gurvansaikhan National Park where some 3,000 *argali* live, one of the most densely populated areas for this species in the country. The total population in Mongolia is estimated at 12,000– 15,000 head. The *argali* graze in the mornings and evenings, and prefer to spend the day in the shade of rocks. Often they graze together with domestic animals such as goats, sheep, horses and camels when they come down from the hills to graze in the surrounding steppe areas. They join up in herds at the beginning of the breeding season at the end of September. Their worst natural enemy is the wolf, which attacks them on the lower ground, especially in winter. Local people hunt them frequently, mainly in autumn and winter. (Foreigners are allowed to hunt them at a price but the numbers are strictly limited.) Listed in the *Mongolian Red List of Mammals* (2007) as global status: vulnerable; local status: endangered. Trophy hunters can purchase licenses – a percentage of the fee is designated for conservation efforts. The principal threat is illegal or unsustainable hunting, particularly for their remarkable curved horns.

Marmot (Marmota siberica) *Tarvaga* in Mongolian. Two of the world's 14 species of marmot inhabit the Mongolian countryside: black Altai marmot and yellow steppe marmot. The more numerous is the steppe marmot or Siberian marmot. The marmot weighs up to 8kg; it has a flat, robust body and short limbs, a straw-yellow furry coat and small rounded ears. The fur on its head is dark brown to black. Its strong tiny claws dig the hard earth, as it hibernates underground during the long Mongolian winters. It has two lairs: one for winter and another shallower lair for summer. Since it never digs in sand its lairs are on higher ground in clay and gravel soils, which also provide good grazing. They are social animals and enjoy living in colonies. Mating takes place in the open when the males are seen to fight over the females, who later give birth to a single litter of up to six young per year. A *möndöl* is a marmot cub. When frightened, marmots warn each other by a series of loud shrieks, whereupon they all dart back to their holes. They can harbour a flea species known as *Oropsylia silantevi*, which carries bubonic plague.

The steppe wolf (Canis lupus) *Chono* in Mongolian. The steppe wolf is a sub-species of the grey wolf, which is found in central Asia. The wolf is a particularly important animal in Mongolian life, since it is both revered and feared. The word wolf used to be taboo. In *The Secret History* it is said that the Mongol people derived from the union of a doe and a wolf (or people with these names),

4

but they are also a threat and have become man's enemies because wolf packs attack the herders' sheep and other animals. Overall the numbers in Mongolia are decreasing, but in some pockets of the northwest their density is high. The national wolf hunts of the recent past, held bi-annually, no longer take place, but individuals continue to hunt. The tradition for the hunters was to spread out in a large circle, climbing to the higher ground and then begin to shout in order to drive the wolves from their hiding places. In this way the hunt would comb through an area and when the wolves appeared, wild chases on horseback hunted them down, until the exhausted animals were lassoed and "laid out" (a Mongolian euphemism for killed). Wolves usually live and hunt in packs in a known territory. However, lone wolves that move on without territories are called trekking wolves. Increasing numbers of these solitary creatures do more damage than the better-integrated packs, which hunt more efficiently. In winter wolf packs feed mainly on red deer and to a lesser extent on wild boar, roe deer and smaller animals such as steppe marmot, hares and rodents. Cubs are born in May and June, and since the wolves hunt far from home, they communicate to one another by howling, especially at night, which the young cubs imitate. This orientates them and defines the different packs and their territories. The steppe wolf is listed in the *Mongolian Red List of Mammals* (2007) as regional status: endangered. See the Zoological Society of London website (*www.zsl.org*).

Mongolian birdlife Mongolia lies on the migratory routes of a large variety of geese, duck and cranes. There are some 487 bird species in Mongolia of which 30 are game-bird species; they include capercaillie and grouse. Some species produce edible eggs, but Mongolians tend not to make much use of them. Swans and other

MONGOLIA'S BIRDLIFE   *Dr Gombobaatar Sundev*

Mongolia is one of the important countries for conserving, watching and photographing birds. Fascinating bird species include: the Mongolian finch, Mongolian accentor, Mongolian or Henderson's ground-jay; the Mongolian lark, snowcock, Siberian rubythroat, spotted caperciallie, white-naped crane, azure tit, Pallas's fish eagle and swan goose, to name a few species of different natural zones.

One of main reasons Mongolia's rich avifauna is so renowned is because this large landmass is situated at the junction of three main migratory bird flyways of the world. Mongolia is the ideal country for watching and getting to know its birdlife, alongside local Mongolians, who will guide you to bird-watching areas. The unique situation for birds migrating to and from Mongolia gives visitors the opportunity to see these highlighted species. It also enables Mongolian ornithologists and visiting experts to run conservation projects on various bird species migrating to and from areas of Mongolia and Siberia, in autumn and in spring – some returning with beautiful breeding plumage from wintering ground in east Asia to breeding grounds in Mongolia. Today there is national support to help protect bird species in the countryside. Mongolian people, especially nomads, do not hunt and disturb threatened bird species, particularly globally threatened species like the Asian dowitcher, white-naped crane, relicat gull, and swan goose.

Travel to Mongolia will give you a chance to see the harmony of nomadic lifestyle and bird-life protection throughout the country. I recommend a new travel company called Mongolica (*www.mongolica.org*) that focuses on professional rare birds are identified and protected, among them the golden pheasant and snow partridge. Larger birds of prey like eagles can be seen throughout the country, and several species of buzzard are protected. Owls are also protected because they prey on the millions of small rodents that swarm over the pastures and ruin them.

HUNTING Every year the Ministry of Environment and Green Development release quotas and licences on certain numbers of animals and birds that can be hunted by foreign tourists. Tourists keen on hunting have an opportunity to hunt deer, game birds and *argali* (wild sheep). The cost to trophy hunters to go on a properly arranged *argali*-hunting trip will be around US$50,000. A percentage of the licence cost goes by law towards conservation measures. The government and tour companies benefit directly from hunting and fishing. A suggestion is to develop lodges for high paying hunting tourists, and to have fixed concessions strictly regulated for those who pay to hunt, and who would also like to benefit conservation and put money into wildlife parks.

A re-think here is needed. Most tourists coming to Mongolia, like Africa, want to photograph wild animals. Mongolia has much to learn from African 'safari' tourism, its style and development' and from historic hunting regulations for visitors, which have been well thought through and developed over time, to conserve and protect hunting areas and wildlife.

In general, hunting is widespread and one Mongolian family in four owns a gun. It is seen as a natural right and some local people don't understand why hunting should be forbidden inside the national parks and protected areas. They feel threatened (in some instances justifiably) because a no-hunting policy prevents them from hunting wolves that attack their flocks of sheep and goats, but gradually

bird-watching holidays and wildlife-photography tours. These tours will bring you to Khustai National Park (near Ulaanbaatar) where you will see breeding species such as Amur falcon, steppe eagle, cinereous vulture, saker falcon and Mongolian larks; to Ugii lake (Arkhangai Aimag) where you will enjoy 'meeting' the globally threatened swan goose, Pallas's fish eagle, and the ground nesting small snowfinch; to the Gobi (in the south), where there is another possibility to enjoy your holidays with Mongolian birds, such as Mongolian finch, Asian desert warbler, Mongolian ground-jay and saxaul sparrows.

Bird education, conservation and scientific work are open to anyone who would like to join in the activities of the Mongolian Ornithological Society (*www.mos.mn*), a national NGO that has been running bird conservation and scientific fieldwork in the country since 1999. The organisation also runs education programmes for National Bird Watchers' Day and other events. The Mongolian government announced its collaboration with the Ornithological Society and experts of the National University of Mongolia in October 2012. For further information: e info@mos.mn; mongolianbirds@mail.com. See also page 443 for bird books and guides.

The MOS database identifies and lists birds, and reports on news and current events. Bird books to look out for (in English) include *A Photographic Guide to the Birds of Mongolia*, published by Admon Printing Company (2009), ISBN 978-9996200-040-3; and *A Field Guide to the Birds of Mongolia* by A & C Black, published (2010) by Christopher Helm Publishers, UK – available in paperback.

4

people are beginning to understand that conservation laws make long-term sense, although some poaching continues. Wild sheep are hunted because of their tasty meat and big horns, and snow leopards because they are regarded as a threat to the livestock. Nowadays this is less likely to happen owing to the great efforts of national park staff and conservation education.

Hunting traditions One ancient Mongolian custom states that it is forbidden to hunt black-tailed gazelles in autumn when the ground is frost-covered. Hunting was also forbidden if the winter was very severe. Mongolians were careful not to touch an animal den and would not let a human shadow fall on a bird's nest. In 1640, the fine for destroying a nest was a two-year-old cow. It was an unwritten rule not to shoot at close range. No Mongolian hunter ever uses the word 'kill'; instead, he 'lays out' an animal – a bit of an euphemism!

Hunting marmot It is common to see one or two hunters with ancient rifles slung over their shoulders, riding in search of marmots. Marmots are easily mesmerised. An old hunting trick is to distract them by waving a dried yak's tail on a stick in the air. This trick surprises the marmot and makes him sit bolt upright to watch what is going on. He becomes a stationary target, which makes the shot easier. The idea is to make a clean shot in the head so as not to damage the skin. Hunters take some 150,000 marmot skins per annum.

Mongolians are uneasy about offering marmot meat to foreign tourists as it sometimes makes people ill. Some marmots may carry fleas, and therefore bubonic plague, which is the most likely reason for their caution.

Sport fishing The Great Lakes region of western Mongolia offer tourists some shooting and fishing opportunities, strictly under licence. Fishing licences vary from US$50–100, depending on the fish. Sturgeon longer than 1m cost T20,000 and under 1m T15,000; *taimen* cost T10,000 (see pages 216–19.) Please note that the above costs are subject to change. The *Mongolian Red List of Fishes* (2007) is the authoritative work on the status of native Mongolian fish species. Of the 64 native fish species, 48 are classified into the following categories: critically endangered, endangered, vulnerable, near-threatened, and least concern. There is also a data-deficient category. Siberian sturgeon, for example, is critically endangered in northern rivers such as the Selenge which flows north into Lake Baikal in Russia. The dominant threat to the famous *taimen* is overfishing and habitat degradation. Conservation measures require improved communication between rangers in different areas to track the movement of poachers, to promote catch-and-release among all anglers (both foreign and Mongolian), and publish catch-and-release guidelines.

TO COOK A MARMOT

Heat some large, round stones on the fire. While they are heating, scoop out the marmot's innards through the throat cavity, using your hands. Place the hot stones inside the carcass, tie the neck and roast on an open low fire, or steam in an earth oven until done (usually after two hours or so). The meat, although fatty, is very tender and delicious and falls away from the bone when well done. The remains are made into soup and the 'cooking stones' make excellent comforters and, like a hot water bottle, help to relieve aches and pains.

FLORA Mongolian flora has remained undisturbed for centuries, in areas of pristine vegetation, often the last of its kind in the world. The Mongolian steppe is unsurpassed as an open pastureland and various types of grasses thrive on different ground and landscape conditions – from mountain to meadow steppe. There are many different types of steppe – generally named after the geographical terrain or a predominant plant species – just as there are many different types of Gobi. Formations and colonies of plants live in harmony with the soil and climate, where the only danger apart from the severe climate is from natural forest fires or desertification. But things may change, and the dangers grow as roads develop and tourism opens up the country. Certain plants like peonies thrive in shady or cool places (see box, page 138), while others, like saxifrage, can live on dry slopes exposed to the parching wind and powerful sun. Mongolia's diverse and distinctive vegetation includes an important part of Asia's plant life. Over 150 Mongolian plants are listed as endemic species; 133 plants are considered very rare and are registered in the *Red Book* of Mongolia.

Owing to Mongolia's severe continental climate and its altitude, the flora of Mongolia is not as rich as that of neighbouring southern Siberia. Where the plateau descends into southern Siberia, summer temperatures become warmer. In northern Mongolia, another point of interest which you might observe is that trees grow well on the flanks of the northern-facing mountain slopes because moisture brought by the wind from the northern ocean falls as rain on that side of the mountains.

Effect of altitude Vertically, a simple climb from the valley to the snow line reveals some distinctly different vegetation, which in terms of sheer variety is effectively equivalent to a cross-country (horizontal) journey of 1,000km or more.

In the northern and central mountains, beyond the tree line, you will find alpine turf with clumps of flowers – often tiny, bright cushions of startling pink heads and multi-coloured lichens that tinge the rocks many different shades of green, yellow and deep orange. The Mongolian timber line is found at around 2,400m. There is no universal pattern, but it is interesting to note the differences in tree-line vegetation in Mongolia compared with other countries. More than 90% of high-mountain species are adapted to a short growth period. Look out for saxifrages, rock jasmines and gentians. The flat expanses of the Mongolian steppe – averaging 1,580m – are at the altitude of a high mountain village in the Swiss Alps, and you will have no trouble recognising familiar alpine plant species. The forests bordering on meadows are places where Martigan lilies and wild clematis are found, while orchids, like the delicate pink-slipper variety, appear close to the ground. Lowland fens and meadows are the ideal habitat for delphiniums, primulas, anemones and different kinds of grasses. Meadow flowers are profuse: large white gentians and hardy species of edelweiss give the impression that Mongolian soil is richer than it is.

Herbs and grasses thrive on the thinner soil of the steppe land. Pastureland covers 1.22 million km², of which 20,000km² were used for hay, but since the dissolution of the state collectives fodder production has declined.

Certain plants are known to have curative properties, and many wild flowers are used in folk remedies. If you have an interest in wild flowers it is advisable to take a good plant dictionary with you such as *The Flora of Britain and Northern Europe* or Grubov's *Mongolian Flora* (which is difficult to find). The Institute of Botany and Landscape Ecology at the University of Greifswald in Germany offers a virtual guide to the flora of Mongolia (*http://greif.uni-greifswald.de/floragreif/*). Visitors to the website can use the plant database or add to it as a project partner from their fieldwork.

4

Flora and Fauna International (*www.fauna-flora.org/about/*) has a fund of knowledge and opportunities to share in conservation work across the globe to show just how relevant it is to everyone. Projects in Mongolia include the management of the environment and species in mining areas.

THE RICHNESS OF MONGOLIAN FLORA DURING SUMMER SEASON

Ann Hibbert

The Mongolian spring begins in early February, in the 'white month', when the lambing season starts and milk is flowing again. Spring, as we know it, begins much later when the ice has broken on the rivers. By the middle of April there is still no sign of a single flowering plant, only the brilliant lichens on the rocks to give colour to the landscape. Towards the end of the month the early anemone, a mauve pulsatilla, appears sheltering among rocks quite high in the hills. It is soon followed by yellow and white varieties that grow on the uplands in clearings among the larches.

Gradually the flowers begin to appear. Among the first are wild pansies, bigger than English heartsease and bright yellow. Large violets grow in the woodlands and in the open meadows, single, tiny iris, both yellow and mauve. The earliest flowers seem to prefer the higher ground on the northern slopes, which is where the heaviest precipitation falls and where the trees are thickest. At the beginning of June, climbing a hill, we found a carpet of minute flowers, although in the valleys they were still sparse. We came across alyssum, saxifrage and vetches of all kinds, fennels, minute asters and primulas and in general a wide range of alpine varieties. As the rainy season developed we noted a brilliant crimson lily, whole hillsides of them, whose root is regarded in Mongolia as a sort of wild potato.

As the summer advances, the variety of vegetation becomes overwhelming. In the dryness and cold of Mongolia even the most common plants have extraordinarily deep roots. On open rocky hillsides we found stonecrops and great patches of sweet-smelling wild thyme. In places near streams, where in England there would be buttercups and daisies, crowds of golden globe flowers grow and a kind of white anemone, which we gathered in armfuls. Gentians and edelweiss grow like weeds in the open steppe. Meadows filled with delphiniums and larkspur thrilled me and in the broad open valleys the blue iris stretched like wide, shallow lakes reflecting the sky. There are acres of scabious and yellow mustard and fields of asphodel. In the woods, pink roses grow close together and the pale flowers of the Siberian clematis twining among the silver birch trees have a ghostly look. Blue azaleas are to be found in the cool shade of mountain copses, and lovely waxen Solomon's seal hide in the dark crannies and rocks. Some plants grow to an immense size by English standards – wild rhubarb, whose creamy, feathery blossoms reached above our heads, and thistles that grow so big that a true Scot might turn pale with envy.

As August turns into September, the number of varieties begins to dwindle and our attention turned to collecting mushrooms. Some are exceedingly poisonous, besides smelling very unpleasant when drying. By mid September everything was brown again, and in October the hard frost clamped down once more. It is difficult to convey an adequate idea of the richness of the Mongolian flora during the summer months.

NATIONAL PARKS

Large tracts of Mongolia's territory have been turned into national parks, and the aim is to place 30% of its territory under Nature Protection. Currently over 12% of the territory is designated for special protection. Areas are designated for protection in four different categories:

- **Protected Monuments** To protect historical and cultural monuments and natural formations (both inside and outside national parks and reserve areas)
- **National Reserves** To protect natural features and natural resources
- **National Conservation Parks** To include natural and less-threatened zone areas, some in a position to be developed for tourism
- **Strictly Protected Areas** To protect unique features and areas of cultural and scientific interest

The national parks system is a wonderful way of safeguarding the countryside and habitats of millions of species. Mongolia has led the world in establishing one of the first protected areas, the Bogdkhan Uul Strictly Protected Area beside Ulaanbaatar. Very often hunting reserves were turned into nature reserves, and it is clear from conservation history that hunters were the ones who became the world's leading conservationists. An excellent book, *The Penitent Butchers*, traces this process over 75 years of wildlife conservation. The authors' observation was that besides keeping track of the biodiversity in our world, we need beautiful places in order to face the future with confidence. An international award-winning project to preserve the white naped crane shows how seriously integrated conservation measures are taken in Mongolia.

The first step in preserving wild species and their habitats in general was to set up reserves and national parks. There were few examples that could, in the modern sense, be regarded as wildlife sanctuaries before the mid 19th century. Bogdkhan Uul Strictly Protected Area, established in 1778, ranks as one of the world's earliest reserves. Over the centuries Mongolians have passed laws to patrol and protect special areas. The first environmental laws date from the *Ikh Zasag* (Great Code) which recognised a number of mountains and hunting grounds as specially protected places in the 12th/13th centuries – more than likely set up to protect the Khan's property, and because it was considered sacred.

VISITING NATIONAL PARKS The following rules apply when visiting national parks:

- The fee for visiting national parks is US$2.50, to be paid to a guide or park ranger in Ulaanbaatar if possible, before setting off. If you don't manage to locate a guide or park ranger before embarking on your visit, it is wise to have your entrance fee ready in case you are approached during your visit.
- Keep your entrance receipt in case of spot checks.
- Take all solid waste to a disposal site outside the park.
- Stay on designated routes and travel at reasonable speeds. Do not make new tracks.
- Camp outside core areas (maps to some parks, eg: Gobi Gurvansaikhan National Park in the South Gobi, are provided with your permit) and away from water courses and livestock.
- Report any unorthodox activity to park rangers.

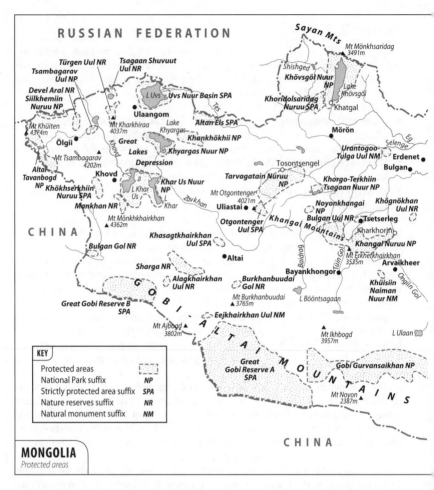

RUSSIAN FEDERATION

Sayan Mts

Türgen Uul NR
Tsambagarav
Uul NP

Tsagaan Shuvuut
Uul NR

Mt Mönkhsaridag
▲ 3491m

Shishged

Devel Aral NR
Siilkhemiin
Nuruu NP

Khövsgöl Nuur
NP

Lake
Khövsgöl

Mt Khüiten
▲ 4374m

L Uvs

Uvs Nuur Basin SPA

Khoridolsaridag
Nuruu SPA

Khatgal

Ölgii

Ulaangom

Mt Kharkhiraa
4037m

Lake
Khyargas

Altan Els SPA

Mörön

Mt Tsambagarav
▲ 4202m

Great
Lakes

Khankhökhii NP

Urantogoo-
Tulga Uul NM

Selenge

Erdenet

Altai
Tavanbogd
NP

Khovd

Khyargas Nuur NP

Depression

Tosontsengel

Bulgan

Khökhserkhiin
Nuruu SPA

Khar Us Nuur
NP

Tarvagatain Nuruu
NP

Khorgo-Terkhiin
Tsagaan Nuur NP

Mankhan NR

L Khar
Us

L
Khar

Zavkhan

Mt Otgontenger
4021m

Uliastai

Noyonkhangai
NP

Khögnökhan
Uul NR

Mt Mönkhkhairkhan
▲ 4362m

Otgontenger
Uul SPA

Khangai Mountains

Bulgan Uul NR

Tsetserleg

Kharkhorin

CHINA

Khasagtkhairkhan
Uul SPA

Khangai Nuruu NP

Bulgan Gol NR

Altai

Bayankhongor

Baidrag

Tüin Gol

Mt Erkhetkhairkhan
3535m

Arvaikheer

Ongiin Gol

Sharga NR

Alagkhairkhan
Uul NR

Burkhanbuudai
Gol NR

Khüisiin
Naiman
Nuur NM

Great Gobi Reserve B
SPA

G
O
B
I
-

A
L
T
A
I

Mt Burkhanbuudai
▲ 3765m

L Bööntsagaan

Eejkhairkhan Uul NM

Mt Ajbogd ▲
3802m

Mt Ikhbogd
▲ 3957m

L Ulaan

KEY	
Protected areas	
National Park suffix	**NP**
Strictly protected area suffix	**SPA**
Nature reserves suffix	**NR**
Natural monument suffix	**NM**

Great
Gobi Reserve A
SPA

M
O
U
N
T
A
I
N
S

Gobi Gurvansaikhan NP

Mt Noyon ▲
2387m

MONGOLIA
Protected areas

CHINA

- Be efficient with your use of water, and where possible avoid using soap. Water in the park is relied upon by local people and livestock, and is very limited. Do not build fires; liquid-fuel or gas stoves should be used.

Stay safe When travelling in national parks and protected areas it is wise to let the rangers' office know your plans when registering for a permit. There is no rescue service in Mongolia. You need to be prepared for emergencies – carry a first aid kit, and if camping independently, choose a camp area near to a local nomad's *ger*. Be well equipped with proper clothing and essential food stocks. Take a good map of the area with you. Local people are very friendly, kind and will help you.

SPECIAL PROTECTED AREAS Establishing protected areas is a means of protecting and preserving Mongolia's rich cultural heritage for future generations, including numerous threatened and endangered animal and plant species, different ecosystems and monuments or sites of cultural importance. It also serves to develop tourism in specifically allocated zones, with eco-*ger* accommodation and special adventure and nature activities, such as climbing or birdwatching, allowed.

RUSSIAN FEDERATION

Mongol Daguur A SPA

Altanbulag
Sükhbaatar
Selenge
Orkhon
Darkhan
Kharaa

Ereentsav
Mongol Daguur B SPA

Onon-Balj Basin B SPA
Ugtam Uul NR
Yakhi Nuur NR
Onon-Balj Basin A SPA

Argun (Ergun He)

Lake Dalai (Hulun Nur)

CHINA

Khentii Mts
Khankhentii Nuruu SPA
Toson Khustai NR
Choibalsan
L Buir
Khalkhyn Gol

Mt Asraltkhairkhan 2800m
Gorkhi-Terelj NP
Kherlen
Tamsag Plain
Nömrög SPA

Khustain Nuruu NP
ULAANBAATAR
Khar Yamaat NR

Baganuur
Nagalkhan Uul NR
Öndörkhaan
Eastern Steppe SPA

Bogdkhan Uul SPA
Zuunmod

Batkhan Uul NR

Baruun-urt

Mt Bagagazryn Chuluu 1768m
Choir
Lkhachinvandad Uul NR

Mandalgobi
Ikh Nart NR
Ganga Nuur NM

DESERT

Sainshand

Zagiin Us NR
Züünbayan
CHINA

Süikhent NM
Zamyn-Üüd

Dalanzadgad

GOBI

Ergeliin Zoo NR

Gobi SPA, Part B

N
Bradt

0 ————— 250km
0 ————— 150 miles

Gobi SPA, Part A

The following information was compiled by Mikkel Wisborg, tourism consultant, from the booklet *Special Protected Areas of Mongolia* (2000), available at bookshops in Mongolia. For further information contact the Protected Areas Bureau, Ministry of the Environment and Green Development (*Baga Toiruu 44, Ulaanbaatar 11; 11 326617; e epa@magicnet.mn*).

Natural monuments of Mongolia
Areas of unique natural formation such as volcanic mountains.

Bulgan Uul (*1,800ha*) This area is situated near Tsetserleg, in Arkhangai Aimag (central Mongolia). A mountain, also called Bulgan Uul, overlooks the town. The area forms part of the watershed between rivers of the internal and Amur river basins and enjoys a special local microclimate (a friend of mine became stuck in a mid-summer snow storm here!) This area is suitable for reintroducing sable antelope.

Urantogoo Tulga Uul (*5,800ha*) Situated in the territory of Bulgan Aimag (northern Mongolia) this area has an inactive volcano with a unique natural

IN QUEST OF THE MONGOLIAN PEONY
Kirsty Fergusson

I must confess to an initial apprehension about the wisdom of committing myself to riding a 200km stretch of the Orkhon Valley on Mongolian ponies, with 18 people I had never met before, in order to raise money for charity, but I also had a dream: to find the elusive Mongolian peony.

However, ten days later, although our little group had been drenched, frozen, burnt, and whipped by winds blowing from Siberia or the Gobi, we were a happy – if rather dirty – crew as we rode the last leg of the journey that had taken us through barren steppe and rushing rivers, high mountain passes and dense forest, towards the great waterfall in a rocky gorge near the source of the Orkhon River. So far, no peonies. On the way we'd been sung to by trained throat singers in the capital, and by boys on their horses in the wilderness. We'd passed herds of yaks and horses and galloped through meadows of sweet thyme and pungent artemisia, dodging marmot burrows and outcrops of volcanic rock. We'd been haunted by vultures and kites, keen-eyed followers of the chuck wagon and mess tent. By luck we had come upon a local horse race, where barefoot children raced their beribboned ponies, whooping and screaming, the length of a ten-mile valley, and witnessed the heroic comedy of a Mongolian wrestling match. We'd been offered *airag* (fermented mare's milk) and salty tea in a nomad family's *ger* and seen poverty matched and outdistanced by resourcefulness and freedom. At night, our horses, hobbled in pairs, grazed freely among the flocks and herds of local families on the open steppe.

So, there we were, on the last day, approaching the Orkhon waterfall. I'd seen drifts of *Iris sibirica* in the damp valleys dotted with purple orchids, mountainsides swathed in tiny alpine flowers humming with bees and other insects, and woods choked with wild roses, veronicas, delphiniums and anemones. It was enough, I'd told myself, as I'd waited to follow the example of our horsemen, who had prayed as they pressed forehead and palms against the trunk of a sacred pine at the mountain-top Buddhist monastery of Tüvkhiin Khiid, the day before. The elusive Mongolian peony would have to live in my imagination for a while yet.

But a brief reconnoitre revealed a steep and rocky path to the foot of the gorge by the waterfall. Wild gooseberries, potentilla and berberis sprang from the rocks: precarious and prickly handholds in the sharp descent. Last down, I could hear the laughter of my companions echoing through the gorge as they made their way through the larches and pines, hunting for a suitable place to bathe in the tumbling, icy river. And suddenly there, under a canopy of wild cherry trees, among a tide of wild roses and strawberries, Himalayan geraniums and thalictrums, clusters of peonies revealed themselves. Huge, established clumps and little self-sown seedlings: the more I looked, the more there were. True, they had finished flowering and only a few faded, dark pink petals still clung to the calcyces, but the fat, shiny seed pods clustered over the elegant, finely toothed leaves like pudgy green fists clutching treasure.

That night, while the horsemen sang, I lay in my tent looking up at the bunches of pods suspended above, drying in the chill, moistureless air. I closed my eyes and saw again the smiling hermit priest of Tüvkhiin Khiid and the sacred pine, and breathed once more the dark aroma of the twisted bark as I pressed my face and hands against it, trying not to ask for too much.

landscape formation. Located 318km from Ulaanbaatar, the volcano is 60km due west of the town of Bulgan. It can be visited on the way to Lake Khövsgöl and can also be reached by train from Erdenet city. There are walking trails and camping.

Khüisiin Naiman Nuur *(eight lakes)* (*11,500ha*) The area is in Övörkhangai Aimag (central Mongolia). Khüisiin Naiman Nuur, with its exceptional configuration, is surrounded by landscape representing the middle part of the Khangai mountain range. These freshwater lakes include the eight lakes known as Khüisiin Naiman Nuur: Shireet, Khaliun, Bugat, Khayaa, Khüis, Shanaa, Döröö and Baga. Riding tours and bird watching are available.

Eejkhairkhan Uul (*22,475ha*) Eejkhairkhan Uul is located in Gobi-Altai Aimag between Tsogt and Altai sums (southwest Mongolia). The rocky strip near Khairkhan Mountain divides the Middle Gobi Mountains on the western side of Eejkhairkhan Mountain. A cave in the region is a major tourist attraction and there are many strange rock formations including a pool called 'The Pots'. The legends of Mother Mountain and the story of the monk Ravdan, who lived there, are told at campfires at night.

Ganga Nuur (*32,860ha*) This lake is located in southeastern Mongolia in Sükhbaatar Aimag close to the border with China, 13km southeast of Darigana. The area surrounding the lake grew as a result of a sand block formed by wind movement. It is a beautiful freshwater lake located between the mountain steppe and Gobi with its own special microclimate. Every year thousands of wild swans may be seen on the lake in autumn from September until late October before they migrate.

Süikhent (*4,830ha*) This area is located in Dornogobi Aimag (southern Mongolia). The site is protected because of its unusual petrified trees rarely found in Mongolia; the petrified trees are 200km southwest of Sainshand town.

Mongolian nature reserves Areas designated to create conditions for protecting, preserving and restoring certain natural features and natural resources.

Batkhan Uul (*58,800ha*) This area is located in Övörkhangai Aimag and Töv Aimag (central Mongolia). Batkhan mountain area is part of the Khangai and Khentii mountain ranges; visitors driving west from Ulaanbaatar often stop here to camp and enjoy the scenery, as the area is conveniently near the main road from Ulaanbaatar to Arvaikheer.

HERBAL CURES FOR AILMENTS

Edelweiss Good for the blood
Potentilla fruticosa (one of the numerous varieties of cinquefoils) Boiled in salt water and used to cure toothache
Yellow poppies Used to help heal wounds
White gentians Collected for lung and chest complaints

'Unknown treatments' for wobbly stomachs or hangovers consist of potent herbal measures, which you should treat with caution – and remember to ask your guide to note down the contents for future reference! See also box, page 188.

Nagalkhan Uul *(3,076ha)* This nature reserve is located in Töv Aimag (central Mongolia). The nature reserve was designated as a reserve to protect the southernmost part of the Khentii mountain range and the surrounding forest-steppe.

Bulgan Gol (river) *(1,840ha)* This reserve is located in Khovd Aimag (northern Mongolia). It was initially designated as a wildlife reserve to protect species such as the beaver, silver-tipped black sable, stone marten and others.

Lkhachinvandad Uul *(58,500ha)* The reserve is located in Sükhbaatar Aimag (southern Mongolia). The purpose of the reserve is to preserve and protect the elk habitat in the mountain steppe.

Ugtam Uul *(46,160ha)* The area is in Dornod Aimag (northeastern Mongolia). It includes two holy mountains, Ugtam and Khairkhan, and the ruins of a Buddhist monastery. It is a particularly beautiful place located in the transition area between forest-steppe and steppe zones.

Sharga-Mankhan *(two areas)* *(390,071ha)* This reserve consists of two parts located in Khovd and Gobi-Altai aimags – the distance between the two is about 200km. It is home to some of the last Mongolian antelope. The reserve is designated to protect the antelope's breeding grounds.

Alagkhairkhan Uul *(36,400ha)* This area is situated in Gobi-Altai Aimag (southwest Mongolia). It is one of the highest mountains of the middle part of the Mongol Altai mountain range, and supports a habitat of rare and very rare plants and wildlife species (*argali*, ibex, snow leopard, and snowcock).

Burkhanbuudai Gol *(52,110ha)* This nature reserve is in the Gobi-Altai Aimag (southwest Mongolia). Many small rivers have their beginning here, and many unique natural rock formations are found. Local people worship a brown stone located at the top of Bogd Mountain that looks like a sheaf of wheat.

Ikh Nart *(43,740ha)* This area is situated in Dornogobi Aimag (southern Mongolia). The northeastern limit of *argali* (wild sheep) habitat, it was designated to extend *argali* territory, and to protect the natural environment. Ikh Nart is a popular reserve with conservation fieldwork and scientific programmes going on there. See page 323.

Zagiin Us *(273,606ha)* Zagiin Us extends into Dundgobi and Ömnögobi aimags (southern Mongolia). The Zagiin Us Valley is composed of saline soil with dry, circular salt marshes and sand dunes. It is a mixed landscape of special ecological interest. It also has areas of saxaul, a bush that grows in the semi-desert; it is the northern limit of the black-tailed gazelle's distribution range and the western extension of the white-tailed gazelle's range.

Ergeliin Zoo *(60,910ha)* This area is situated in Khatanbulag district, Dornogobi Aimag (southern Mongolia) where many famous dinosaur-fossil finds have been discovered. People refer to this region as 'Altan Uul' (Golden Mountain).

Khögnökhan Uul *(46,990ha)* Situated in Bulgan Aimag (northern Mongolia). The reserve represents taiga (forest) and steppe plants in an area that comprises several different natural vegetation and climatic zones.

Toson-Khulstai (*469,928ha*) This area covers parts of the Khentii and Dornod aimags (eastern Mongolia). Toson, Khulstai Nuur and Salbariin valleys are the main habitats of the white-tailed gazelle. It was designated to extend its distribution from the Kherlen River northwards.

Khar Yamaat (*50,594ha*) This area covers parts of Khentii Aimag and parts of Sükhbaatar Aimag (eastern Mongolia). The special formation of Khar Yamaat and Turuu Öndör Mountain is a continuation of the Khankhentii mountain range. Natural vegetation includes pine and aspen groves, berries and medicinal plants rarely found in steppe areas.

Yakhi Lake (*251,388ha*) Yakhi Lake is situated in Dornod Aimag (eastern Mongolia). It is part of the white-tailed gazelle distribution, and is one of the main habitats for migrating birds.

Devel Aral (island) (*10,300ha*) The island is situated in the Usankhooloi and Khovd rivers that feed from Achit Lake located between Bayan-Ölgii and Uvs aimags (northwest Mongolia). This area is home to ring-necked pheasant, wild boar and beaver, which are becoming increasingly rare in Mongolia. It is a main distribution area of sea buckthorn. The area is designated to protect the wild boar and beaver habitats.

Tsagaan Shuvuut Uul and **Türgen Uul** reserves in Uvs Aimag are also marked on the Protected Areas map in this guide.

National parks The 14 national parks listed below are designated for future tourist development but in many cases this has not yet happened. Very few of the areas listed are equipped with tourist facilities, such as offices and entrance gates, information, and on-the-spot services. Among the better-known national parks open to tourists are Gorkhi-Terelj, Lake Khövsgöl, Gobi Gurvansaikhan and Khustain Nuruu. In the remoter areas of western and eastern Mongolia there are no services and visitors must take in everything: transport, tent and food supplies. Be warned, too, that there are no proper roads or route directions; signposting is totally absent. These areas contain natural original conditions that are relatively preserved and which have historical, cultural, scientific, educational and ecological importance.

Khorgo-Terkhiin Tsagaan Nuur (lake) (*77,267ha*) This area is located in Arkhangai Aimag (central Mongolia). It contains spectacular mountain scenery and rock formations created by volcanic eruptions. Accommodation is available locally in tourist *ger* camps.

Khövsgöl Nuur (lake) (*838,070ha*) The lake is situated in Khövsgöl Aimag, which is named after it (northern Mongolia). Known as the 'dark-blue pearl of Mongolia', the lake is one of the largest and most scenic protected areas in the country. Bordering the Sayan Mountains to the north and the Khoridolsaridag range to the west, it is 136km long and 3km wide, and is part of the protected area. Tourist accommodation is available in *ger* camps in the vicinity.

Gobi Gurvansaikhan (*2,171,737ha*) The Gobi Gurvansaikhan is situated in Ömnögobi and Bayankhongor aimags (southern Mongolia). The park protects the main natural characteristics of the Gobi-Altai mountain range. Its landscape includes high mountains, mountain valleys, arid steppe and desert. It is also designated for ecotourism and ecotourists, for example, participate in the park's conservation projects. There are many tourist *ger* camps in the vicinity.

Gorkhi-Terelj (*293,168ha*) The Gorkhi-Terelj National Park is situated in Töv Aimag (central Mongolia). It is one of the most visited national parks in Mongolia because it is so close to Ulaanbaatar. It offers beautiful scenery and the region is well established for tourism with its *ger* camps around the Terelj resort.

Khustain Nuruu (*50,620ha*) This national park is in the Töv Aimag (central Mongolia). It is an example of the steppe landscape of the southwestern part of the Khentii mountain range. It is home to the *takhi* (wild horses), recently reintroduced to Mongolia from European captive-bred zoo stock by a Dutch foundation. There is a good basic *ger* camp in the reserve – around 10km from where you will most likely see a group of wild horses (*see www.treemail.nl/takhi*).

Altai Tavanbogd (*636,161ha*) Situated in Bayan-Ölgii Aimag (western Mongolia). The landscape of this national park represents special characteristics of high mountains, crystal-clear rivers, mountain valleys, and steppe landscape. It is the habitat of *argali*, ibex, elk and other mammals, and bird species like snowcock, eagle and lammergeyer. This area is ideal for mountain sports and tourism, yet to be developed. For the moment, though, the areas is really only suitable for experienced mountaineers, although expedition hiking is possible at lower altitudes.

Khangai Nuruu (*888,455ha*) This national park comprises the central part of the Khangai mountain range, which borders on Arkhangai, Övörhangai and Bayankhongor aimags (in central and southern Mongolia). The area includes high mountains, lakes, forests and meadows. The mountains are of ancient formation producing a variety of landscapes. The rivers flow to either the Pacific or Arctic oceans. Currently undeveloped for tourism, there is a lack of local co-operation and finance, although there is a suggestion that tour companies will start to camp there with eco-tents.

Khar Us Nuur (*850,272ha*) This area is situated in Khovd Aimag (northern Mongolia), located near the Great Lakes basin covering a large area of desert steppe and arid semi-desert with its unique climate and environment: freshwater resources, the Gobi Desert, and steppe valleys alongside the Mongolian Altai Mountains. It is home to rare wildlife and marsh-bird species. Currently undeveloped for tourism. It is an important wetland area noted in for its birdlife by the Ramsar Convention website: www.protectedplanet.net/sites/168269.

Noyonkhangai (*59,088ha*) This mountain area is situated in Arkhangai Aimag (central Mongolia). It is an area of mineral water springs, and rare flora and fauna. It is also an area of age-old traditional worship, as Mongols worship certain mountains. Springs and good camping areas at the base of the mountain attract tourists. Like Khangai Nuruu, this area is under developed. Any entrance fees and payments go directly to the state budget rather than the park administration. However, pasture-related programmes are being set up for local people.

Tarvagatain mountain range (*525,440ha*) This national park is located in both Arkhangai and Zavkhan aimags (central and western Mongolia). The area is the source of the river Selenge, the largest river in Mongolia. The national park comprises areas of historical, cultural and natural heritage. It has great potential to develop its mineral water springs as health spas for tourism, but these areas are not yet developed.

Siilkhemiin Uul *(mountain range)* (*140,080ha in total*) The national park consists of two parts: A and B; both are situated in the Bayan-Ölgii Aimag (western Mongolia). The park is designated to protect the area's resources and the habitat of the mountain sheep (*argali*).

Khankhökhii-Khyargas Lake (*553,350ha*) Situated in Uvs Aimag (western Mongolia). Khankhökhii Nuruu (mountain) is located on the boundary of the Uvs and Khyargas lake basins. The area plays an important role in maintaining the ecological balance by limiting the increase of desert-steppe areas. The area provides a home to numerous endangered migratory bird species. The region is an area of international scientific research, visited by tourists, but there are limited facilities available.

Tsambagarav Mountain (*110,960ha*) This mountain is located between Khovd and Bayan-Ölgii aimags (western Mongolia). The area is of significance for the study of glaciers and is home to the rare snow leopard. It is a regional sacred mountain, accessible from both sides and good for climbing (on expedition). There are Kazakh settlements off the Khovd–Olgii road and some beautiful turquoise mountain lakes to explore with a local guide. There are no tourist facilities.

Onon-Balj Basin (*414,752ha*) This area is situated in both Khentii and Dornod aimags in northeastern Mongolia, and consists of two parts: A and B. The area forms a unique geographical zone of northern taiga forest surrounded by arid-desert steppe valleys. This is a well managed park with a vision and a plan for the future: to protect target species such as the white-naped crane (Grus vipio Pallas) and to open up for responsible tourism. WWF Mongolia supports educational programmes on fire fighting and forestry (*www.econet.mn/local_pa_data/OB-news5.pdf*).

Strictly protected areas These are areas that represent unique features and characteristics of natural zones, preserving the original conditions that are of special scientific and cultural significance.

Khasagtkhairkhan Uul (*27,651ha*) This mountain is located in the Gobi-Altai Aimag (southern Mongolia). It is a forested part of the Mongol Altai mountain range and a homeland for various plant and wildlife species of mountainous steppe and Gobi regions.

Bogdkhan Uul Strictly Protected Area (*41,651ha*) Located at the southern edge of the Mongolian capital (central Mongolia), Bogdkhan Uul is one of the oldest nature reserves in the world (established in 1778) and it is also a UNESCO Biosphere Reserve. The reserve marks the borderline between the forest-steppe and steppe (grassland) regions, as well as the southern limit of larch-forest growth. Visited by tourists; you need a permit to go hiking. There are *ger* camps and hotels nearby at Zuunmod, a day trip from Ulaanbaatar. There are new skiing facilities at Bogd Khan.

Great Gobi (*5,311,730ha*) It consists of two parts: Gobi A and Gobi B. Gobi A is in Gobi-Altai and Bayankhongor aimags; Gobi B is located in Khovd and Gobi-

Altai aimags (in southern Mongolia). It protects a large undisturbed part of the vast Gobi Desert and provides a refuge for very rare species like the wild camels at Zakhiin Us and the wild horses at Takhiin Tal, as well as Gobi bears. In 1991, the United Nations designated the Great Gobi an International Biosphere Reserve, the fourth-largest biosphere reserve in the world, and the largest in Asia (see *www. savethewildhorse.org* and pages 342–4).

Khökhserkhiin Nuruu *(65,920ha)* This crest of the Altai Mountains is situated in Khövd and Bayan-Ölgii aimags (western Mongolia). This area is the main habitat for ibex and *argali* herds. It also helps maintain the original features of the Altai Mountains and the ecological balance of the territory.

Mongol Daguur *(103,016ha)* This protected area is divided into two parts, both in the Dornod Aimag (eastern Mongolia). The larger northern part is contiguous to Russia's Daurski Reserve, and comprises rolling steppe and wetlands, on the southern shore of Lake Torey. The southern part of the protected area encompasses part of the Ulz River and its pristine wetlands, classified as a protected area to conserve the white-necked crane's breeding grounds, and those of other rare crane species.

Eastern steppe *(570,374ha)* This area is located in the Dornod and Sükhbaatar aimags (eastern Mongolia). It represents the only steppe land region where there are no economic activities. The eastern Mongolian steppe is home to 25 species of mammal, dominated by herds of gazelle (over 70% of the white-tailed gazelle population of Mongolia inhabits this area). The protected area is only a small part of the eastern steppe.

Nömrög *(311,205ha)* This area is situated in the Dornod Aimag, and covers the remote and uninhabited far-eastern tip of Mongolia (eastern Mongolia). Ecologically distinct from the rest of Mongolia, this reserve includes the westernmost end of the Hinggan mountain range, which extends into Mongolia from China. One-fifth is forested by small groves of Scots pine, white birch and willow. Manchurian flora and fauna, which occur nowhere else in Mongolia, are found here. Species include Ussurian moose, black-necked oriole, white-breasted rock thrush and the great black water snake.

Otgontenger Uul *(95,510ha)* Situated in Zavkhan Aimag and the highest peak in the Khangai mountain range (central Mongolia). This area represents the biodiversity of the Khangai mountain range and is home to rare and very rare wildlife.

Khankhentii Nuruu *(1,227,074ha)* This mountain range is part of the Khentii Mountains situated in the Töv, Khentii and Selenge aimags (central and northern Mongolia). These mountains have preserved their original features and are located between the Eurasian forest taiga and the central Asian steppe. Three major river systems spring from the protected area: the Tuul, which flows into the Orkhon and then the Selenge, to Russia's Lake Baikal and on to the Arctic Ocean; the Onon and Kherelen rivers flow east to join the Amur, which flows into the Pacific Ocean. The area represents basic characteristics of five different types of taiga landscape. It is the home of Genghis Khan.

Uvs Lake basin *(712,545ha)* The Uvs Lake basin is located in Uvs Aimag (western Mongolia), and named after it. The immediate change of ecological zones in this relatively small area of the Uvs Lake basin is matched by few places in the world, with its perpetual snowfields and permafrost in the Türgen Mountains extending to the sand dunes of Altan Els.

Small Gobi (See *Great Gobi*, opposite, for the total area under protection.) The area represents the main characteristics of the southeastern Gobi region and has preserved most of its original natural features and conditions. It is the main habitat for rare and very rare wildlife, such as *khulan* (wild ass), black-tailed gazelle, *argali* (mountain sheep), and ibex. About 50% of the *khulan* population of Mongolia inhabits this area.

Khoridolsaridag Nuruu (*18,634ha*) This area is situated in the Khövsgöl Aimag (northern Mongolia). Khoridolsaridag is a steep-sided mountain range that combines various landscapes – tundra, taiga, forested steppe and mountains – all at close proximity. Wildlife species such as *argali*, ibex, Siberian moose, snowcock and sable roam these areas.

CONSERVATION

We must work with the grain of Nature ... it is all too easy for us to forget that mankind is a part of Nature and not apart from it.

HRH The Prince of Wales

Modern conservation history began in the 1970s with the Club of Rome meeting in Stockholm (see page 151). Wildlife conservation is an involved and complicated task. People who respect nature will try, in their own way, to do something positive to hand over its resources to the next generation without destruction and damage. In the face of many difficulties, governments are tightening the legal frameworks, and imposing conditions that will continue to allow us to enjoy the world's truly wild places – like Mongolia.

Vehicle tracks in the semi-desert cannot be rubbed out and the impacted damage done to the ecology – increasingly by tourist vehicles – stays for generations. The problem of overgrazing stock on the fragile Gobi environment is easy to see, but very difficult to deal with in human and environmental terms. Likewise, the damage caused by climate change may be irreversible. Some of these issues are beyond our control. We cannot reverse the effects of global warming but we can put a brake on it provided there is the will to do so. We can steer in a direction that helps to solve parts of the problem – for example, by grazing a sensible ratio of sheep to goats and understanding that the Mongolian cashmere industry (presently going through privatisation difficulties) is reliant on the primary resources of the pastures on which the production chain of cashmere is based.

A key element of sustainable development and Agenda 21 (see *Responsible tourism*, pages 154–9) is that the well-intended effort to protect the environment is not just about conservation or even local development, but about people owning these concepts and living them. The Earth Summit in Rio de Janeiro in 1992 made it clear that to develop a sustainable way of life on our planet, we must learn to understand, and if necessary to rethink, the directions in which we are heading. Subsequent world environmental summits must voice this message with more urgency as we enter 'injury time' in terms of environmental resources.

In Mongolia, conservation efforts are focusing on the destruction caused by the use of natural resources for fuel – the deforestation of saxaul in the desert regions, and the loss of timber in the northern mountain areas due to forest fires and the cutting of wood without licence. Other concerns include the destruction of ecosystems through development, overgrazing of pastureland by domestic herds, poaching and illegal hunting of rare Mongolian wildlife, and the unauthorised collection of herbs for medical use.

The Mongolian government is committed to protecting its biodiversity and has passed a number of environmental laws to safeguard its natural resources. It is vitally important that Mongolian wildlife, forests, vegetation, water and air pollution are properly monitored and managed, although the scale of the task is a daunting one.

Mongolia has signed a number of international agreements, including the Convention on International Trade in Endangered Species (CITES) and the international conventions on biological diversity, and participates in a number of other international environmental programmes, including UNESCO's 'Man and the Biosphere' programme. It has several World Heritage Sites: the Uvs Lake basin, the ancient desert of Gobi Gurvansaikhan, and Part A of the Great Gobi Strictly Protected Area (GGSPA).

Vast steppes still cover Mongolia – the largest tracts of undamaged grasslands anywhere in the world. An awareness of the importance of unspoiled landscape is needed in order to preserve this environment for future generations as part of Mongolia's heritage. The grasslands stretch from horizon to horizon, at times, when stirred by the wind, looking like a giant ocean wave of swaying seed heads. The steppe itself reflects a vision of the past: it is both treeless and fenceless. It is also vulnerable to impact, especially human impact, like mining and tourism. Wild and endangered species are among the important attractions of Mongolia to the outside world, which has lost much of its own wildlife heritage. For information on some of the endangered species to be found, and on the conservation measures being taken to protect them, see *Fauna*, pages 124–35.

SUSTAINABLE DEVELOPMENT

Research is easy. Conservation most definitely is not. It cannot be imposed from above. It must ultimately be based on local interests, skills and traditions.

Dr George Schaller, conservation biologist

One of conservation's goals is to build a sustainable society. The word 'sustainability' has been popularised in such a way that people have begun to question its use and meaning. An overall definition of sustainable development translates as 'improving the quality of human life while living within the carrying capacity of supporting systems'. In theory it sounds easy, but it is difficult to put into practice, especially in poorer countries where finance for essential social wellbeing is not available.

Incentives are being offered to investors to create innovative sustainable livelihood projects (identified by the World Bank in Mongolia) to provide longer-term security, especially in depressed rural areas, so that in addition to government support and aid-agency efforts, environmentally integrated private capital will be used for sustainable development. It is an illusion to think that a transfer to sustainable development will happen otherwise.

GLOBAL CONSERVATION NETWORKS

WWF (the World Wildlife Fund for Nature) was set up by a group of eminent people including Sir Julian Huxley (the first director of UNESCO) following an idea by Victor Stolan. Established in the early 1960s, WWF is the largest non-governmental global organisation working for the conservation of nature.

IUCN (the International Union for the Conservation of Nature) is dedicated to pragmatic solutions to conserve species while working with local people; it was set up under several different names from a congress held in Fontainebleau, in France, in 1948.

Ramsar was founded in Iran in1971. It is an organisation that protects wetlands all over the world and promotes the wise use of waterfowl habitats. It is based at IUCN headquarters near Lake Geneva in Switzerland (*www.ramsar.org*).

The Global Nature Fund, founded in 1998 to help protect nature and environments as well as animals, has its headquarters near Lake Constance in Germany (*www.globalnature.org*).

CONSERVATION BIOLOGY Conservation biology is conservation through science, carried out by field biologists, universities and institutes. The American conservation biologist, George Schaller, put it simply: 'The goal is not to tie up neat little packages of data but to spend time revealing the possibilities of new knowledge about a species in order to pass it on to the next generation.' The single most important conservation

FOUNDATIONAL BACKGROUND TO RED/GREEN THINKING

CLUB OF ROME, 1972 At this international meeting, conservationists and other experts examined limits to growth in the light of long-term trends in world population, resource availability, food production and industrialisation. In the same year the United Nations held a conference in Stockholm on the human environment, which led to the establishment of the UN Environmental Programme (*www.clubofrome.org*).

WORLD CONSERVATION STRATEGY (WCS), 1980 The initiatives at the Club of Rome were followed by a programme called the World Conservation Strategy (*http://data.iucn.org/dbtw-wpd/edocs/WCS-004.pdf*). The WCS retained the traditional concept of development with an additional objective: to improve the quality of human life. The WCS's approach concluded that sustainable development was needed that incorporated social and ecological considerations in long- and short-term planning. Thus conservation was linked to development.

BRUNDTLAND COMMISSION, 1987 The WCS was followed by the Brundtland Commission, which redefined development as 'that which seeks to meet the aspirations of the present without compromising the ability to meet those of the future' – similar to the WCS's definition of conservation (*www.un-documents.net/ocf-02.htm*).

These commissions and strategies were followed by the 1992 and 2002 Earth Summits in Rio and Johannesburg and more recently by the Kyoto Protocol. In 2012 the USA became the first major industrialized nation to reach the United Nation's original Kyoto Protocol target for CO2 reductions – without having ever ratified the agreement. The plan was to cut greenhouse gases by 5.2%. Climate change and global warming is of ongoing concern, the first stage of the Protocol was amended in 2012 and the second commitment period from 2013–20 (of 5% reduction and under) appears to be difficult to enforce, and existing policies seem unable to prevent global warming at the industrial level.

4

measure to focus on is the preservation of ecosystems with interlocking habitats, which will give wildlife conservation the opportunity to work.

As Mongolia transfers from one political system to another, the process of conserving such a truly pristine environment, it seems, is becoming more and more complicated.

FUTURE OUTLOOK What begins by being a simple conservation programme often ends by gathering momentum and finally by touching and involving many branches of life. Apart from collecting crucial data and devising conservation strategies, local biologists need training. There is a need to inter-relate and co-operate with a number of different agencies, both government and NGOs, which is not an easy job. Mongolia's Ornithological Society leads the way here.

CONSERVATION MONGOLIAN STYLE

Mongolian people have an honoured and cultural tradition of taking a caring approach towards nature and behaving in accordance with the natural cycles.

Natsagiin Bagabandi (President of Mongolia 1997–2005)

The country's culture is permeated by the traditions of nomadic life, the use of land and nature protection. Nomads in times past had their own rules, norms and values, determined by religion, social practice and land use. They realised that their land was fragile and that disturbing the soil or water sources would be dangerous to the future survival of viable pasture. In order to stress these principles, folk legends and cautionary tales were created to preserve and pass them on and at the same time safeguard the pasturelands for the future. Methods of animal husbandry unchanged for centuries are still in use today, and it is important for the young herders to learn them.

For many Mongolians nature conservation and concern for the environment is part of rediscovering their culture, having experienced limitations within the structures of communism. Mongolians have a long history of nature protection. As long ago as the 1st century AD, the Huns, thought to be the ancestors of the Mongols, respected nature – the blue skies and the towering mountains were sacred. Mongolian Shamanism, derived from worshipping nature, has determined the nomads' behaviour towards nature and set rules for its protection. To Mongolians, the earth is the mother of all things and the sky the father. Hunting was based on elaborate rituals and on the concept that animal spirits gave fertility and prosperity to man, who was responsible for the soil and animal herds.

Genghis Khan adopted one of Asia's first decrees to protect the environment, prohibiting, for example, polluting rivers by urinating in them. Although Mongolians have a deep respect for nature, more recently Soviet communism allowed the Mongols to become careless. Like the Russians, they thought about 'conquering nature', and thereby spoiled it. Look at the massive coal and copper mines and gold mines with the use of poisonous chemicals, and the old car tyres, scrap iron and other unorthodox rubbish in the countryside.

Hundreds of years of nomadic culture has in its own way preserved and conserved the environment and many species of wildlife and vegetation have survived, whereas in other parts of Asia they are dying out or have already disappeared. The worry is that mining and ruthless commercialisation may disturb these ancient practices. National parks are divided into specific zones and tourist activity is limited to particular areas within the protected area boundaries. Visitors are asked to respect these limits. Park maps indicate the zoning.

Fire-fighting: local conservation initiatives The economic and political changes in Mongolia led to a decrease in fire-fighting efforts. The single most important factor was the grounding of the Soviet-backed aerial patrol service. The financial support stopped abruptly and Mongolia could not afford to maintain and operate the needed fleet. Mostly the fire-fighting service parachuted fire-fighters from Antonov An-2 biplanes, but these planes are old and many are unserviceable.

STEPPE AND FOREST FIRES: A HISTORIC OVERVIEW　　*Bill Shaw*

A heavily forested landscape with brown bears and moose roaming through it is not an image that springs to mind when one thinks of Mongolia; but trees it has, and in abundance! About 8% of the land surface is forested (this doesn't sound much, but remember Mongolia is the 14th-largest country in the world). Forests are located in the north of the country and form the southern edge of the vast taiga zone.

The trees are largely coniferous, and most of the area is uninhabited and inaccessible. Unfortunately these rich forests are now being damaged by raging wildfires. Reasonably accurate records of both forest and grassland (steppe) fires exist only from 1981. From 1981 to 1995, an average of 1.74 million hectares of forest and steppe burned annually. In 1996 and 1997 the burning increased dramatically to 10.7 and 12.4 million hectares. In these two years alone more forest was burnt than had been harvested for timber over the previous 65 years. Most fires occurred in the grasslands that lie in the east of the country, but the areas hardest hit by the increases were the forested regions. In 1998 and 1999, the area burnt decreased to three million hectares per year – an area the size of Wales. In 2000, another 5.1 million hectares were reduced to ashes and between March 2012 and December 2013, 115 fires destroyed a territory of nearly 62,000ha, including steppe fires as well as forest fires.

Most (97%) fires are started by careless human activities, such as throwing away a still-burning cigarette end, or not putting out a campfire properly. Only a small number of fires are started by lightning – an additional cause during the summer months. The most recent information on outbreaks of forest fires is reported nowadays by satellite.

Forest fires have an extremely negative effect on the local economy, as millions of dollars of potential timber revenue are destroyed. Many countryside families in the burned areas previously supplemented their low incomes by collecting secondary forest products, such as pine nuts, berries, mushrooms and red-deer antlers (used in Chinese medicine and by European markets for knife handles, buttons and other articles). Ecologically, repeated fires lead to an irreversible transformation of highly diverse forest to grassland through the loss of all the native seed trees. This badly affects the land's water-retention capacity, leading to faster run-off and flooding in some areas and, in others, to the drying up of streams and springs. Studies show that soils newly exposed to direct sunlight (owing to the removal of the tree-cover by fire) are experiencing increases in temperature that are causing the permafrost to melt. Additionally, in these areas the ground becomes saturated and no longer suitable for tree growth. Plans for planting trees as 'green walls' have been evaluated and due to Mongolia's extreme climate, new assessments suggest that natural forestry regeneration has more lasting means than costly tree-planting initiatives.

4

The German Government Development Agency (GTZ) and British VSO volunteers stepped in to focus on a project in the Khankhentii and Gorkhi-Terelj Protected Area – a heavily forested and mountainous region lying northeast of the capital Ulaanbaatar. Cross-border fire-fighting education programmes are part of conservation education in eastern Mongolia's Onon-Balj Basin supported by WWF Mongolia.

INTERNATIONAL CONSERVATION EFFORTS The Mongolian Ministry of Environment and Green Development – the government organisation responsible for developing and implementing conservation policy – has been working together with conservation organisations like the WWF to foster sustainable development around existing protected areas. A 'nature conservation and buffer zone development' was created by GTZ (now GIZ), the German government's technical co-operation programme to improve the management of the national parks in the Gobi and other areas. A Mongolia Biodiversity Project was developed, associated with the United Nations Environment Programme (UNEP) and other environmental programmes supported by the UNDP, Asian Development Bank, World Bank, and the Commission for the Protection of Endangered Species. Mongolian Academy of Sciences (MAS) encourages environmental protection as part of Mongolia's economic development.

RESPONSIBLE TOURISM

The primordial layer may not be open to many of us today, but it is still there in Mongolia.

Zahava Hanan, Canadian writer and poet

NEW THREATS TO WILDLIFE   *John Farringdon*

Despite Mongolia's seemingly boundless grasslands, threats to wildlife abound. Formerly hundreds of thousands of Mongolia gazelle migrated across the steppe each spring from eastern Inner Mongolia to Mongolia's western provinces in Asia's largest ungulate migration. However, construction of the fence-lined Ulaanbaatar–Beijing railroad in the 1950s effectively blocked this migration, restricting large gazelle herds to the eastern half of the country. During the 1990s' economic collapse, gazelle, *argali*, ibex, and other ungulates were widely poached for meat by herders simply trying to survive. Today these same ungulates face severe competition for limited pastures from livestock, populations of which doubled from 20 to 40 million head between 1990 and 2010, also increasing wildlife exposure to common livestock diseases. A major threat to the world's small remaining *takhi* and the wild Bactrian camel populations is cross-breeding with their free-roaming domesticated cousins. Siberian marmot numbers have plummeted over the past two decades as hundreds of thousands of marmot skins are exported annually for the fur trade. Wolves, the traditional enemy of Mongolia's herders, continue to be hunted and poisoned, while retaliatory killing of snow leopards that prey on livestock continues. The habitat of the above-mentioned species is threatened to varying degrees by the rapid development now sweeping Mongolia, which includes widespread mining activities, road and rail construction, and pasture degradation caused by growing cashmere goat herds.

UNEP announced a major partnership with Mongolia in 2013, that year's host country of World Environment Day. It was celebrated on 5 June alongside the country's International Children's Day – a national Mongolian holiday. Mongolia is developing policies on sustainable mining, renewable energy and ecotourism – all three important areas in the current climate – that will help towards environmental awareness and safeguard the country's 'green' future.

Mongolia is one of the first countries in the world to take up UNEP's PAGE Programme (Partnership for Action on the Green Economy), whereby the government commits to ensuring green and sustainable growth. World Environment Day 2013 provided catchy slogans like the Food & Agricultural Organisation's campaign to 'Think. Eat. Save. Reduce your footprint', which targets the amount of wasted food that is binned and not eaten (*www. thinkeatsave.org*).

The World Health Organization (WHO) highlighted the need for cleaner air in the Mongolian capital where car emissions do not meet proper standards and brown coal and wood burners pollute the atmosphere. Sooty pollutants in the *ger* districts of the city damage health and are found to be seven times higher than WHO standards.

World Environment Day celebrates conservation programmes such as saving Mongolian *takhi*, bred now in growing numbers at Khustain Nuruu Reserve near Ulaanbaatar (see page 277).

In Mongolia, responsible tourism seeks to maintain a delicate balance between the modernisation of lifestyle and suppressing change. It claims to 'tread lightly' and will not take the blame for large-scale environmental impact from social and economic development.

A 'green' approach to tourism addresses the growing awareness of the responsibilities that tourism carries. There is a huge expectation of what the industry can do – from identification and data gathering, involving volunteer tourists or ecotourists, to running hotels that are sympathetic to the natural environment in their recycling and staff education programmes.

Around the world there are tour companies and tour operators working together to establish a number of core principles. The hard work has been done and Mongolia is in a fortunate position to put into practice much of this received wisdom so that it will have a positive effect and help to preserve the country's tourist sites, wilderness areas and rare, wild species.

According to the World Tourism Organisation, less than 10% of all tourist dollars make it into the hands of local communities. Part of tourism today is to educate travellers on how they can play a part in responsible tourism. It is vital to modern tourism that some benefits are retained for the local people. By 2020 it is predicted that annual international tourists will reach 1.6 billion. The opportunity is there to shape this industry in an innovative way, yet seldom is it properly used with constructive purpose. The UK's Voluntary Service Overseas (VSO) has launched a worldwide tourist campaign to increase awareness of these problems.

A VSO report confirms that all it requires is a little effort and imagination on the part of every tour operator to provide the advice already offered by some. For example, you might ask:

Natural History and Conservation   RESPONSIBLE TOURISM

4

155

- Can we dispose of our rubbish safely?
- Are the wells (drinking water) safe in this area?
- Do local people own, manage and benefit from tourism?
- What are the threatened species in this area? And why?

BUILDING A SUSTAINABLE SOCIETY One of Mongolia's goals is to build a sustainable society. Sustainable development means ensuring that the economy and society of Mongolia reach their fullest potential within a well-protected environment, without compromising the quality of that environment for the enjoyment of future generations and the wider international community.

The move to sustainable development is a long-term and evolutionary process. Ideally, sustainable agriculture, for example, provides high-quality food from a high-quality, well-managed environment, while securing an acceptable quality of life for the rural community – which in practice is difficult to evaluate and sustain. Mongolian agricultural issues affected by political change in the past 25 years have led to increased livestock production and overgrazing – with significant rises in the number of sheep and goats, especially around towns. This has caused soil erosion in many regions.

Other ongoing issues include waste management, the effects of modern litter and environmental damage from mining activities. Water is an all-important resource. A simple question that tourists often ask is whether or not the drinking water is safe. Since this is not the case everywhere tourists may wish to buy bottled water, or purify their drinking supplies.

Mongolia is very new to any type of eco-auditing (as are most countries) and has few means to measure progress towards sustainability. The question of how to put sustainable development into practice has been surveyed by the United Nations Environmental Programme and a full report may be found on its website (*www. uneptie.org/tourism/new.html*).

RESPONSIBLE ORGANISATIONS

Centre for Environmentally Responsible Travel (CERT) Indaba Hse, 1 Hydeway, Thundersley, Essex SS7 3BE; ☎01268 795772; e certdesk@aol.com. A membership organisation for tour companies based in the UK. Those who sign up commit themselves to an environmental policy.

Greenstop.net ☎+44 1663 744606; e patricia@greenstop.net; www.greenstop. net. Greenstop promotes the use of eco-friendly practices within the tourism industry. The main aim is to set up a co-operative body of genuinely eco-friendly companies and market them to create a demand for environmentally responsible tourism.

Green Globe 21 ☎+61 2 6230 2931; e customer.services@ggasiapascific.com.au; www. greenglobe21.com. Through partnership with Green Globe 21, companies aim to signpost the route to responsible tourism. Green Globe 21 provides information and advice on the ways that operators and companies can improve the environmental quality of their operations. The verification of Green Globe 21's standards is undertaken by an international, independent team of experts.

ECOTOURISM The good thing about this type of tourism is that ecotourists are willing to pay premium rates to visit 'unspoiled' nature, the sort that Mongolia provides in abundance.

When it comes to ecotourism, Westerners have little to teach Mongolian nomads and they on the other hand have a lot to offer us.

Nomadic family *gers* are genuinely eco-friendly. They use natural building materials – felt, wooden trellis and ropes made of horse hair – to construct their homes, and in daily living they use or recycle practically everything. When killing

FIRE-FIGHTER IN MONGOLIA

Bill Shaw

I went out to Mongolia with Voluntary Service Overseas (VSO) for a job placement with the Khankhentii Protected Area, and soon got stuck into working on the prevention side of things.

The key element was to work closely with the local people, so we quickly formed a fire-prevention team, consisting of local schoolteachers and two officers who ran the environmental information centres set up by the German government. The aim was to educate both adults and children on how to behave carefully when in the countryside. The message was communicated in a number of different ways. A fire-prevention curriculum was prepared for schools, which has become a compulsory module, accepted by the Mongolian Ministry of Education. To front the campaign we devised a mascot (along the lines of 'Smoky the Bear' in the USA). A much-loved forest animal, the squirrel, was chosen and named Sonorkhon, which means 'alert' or 'watchful' in Mongolian. Sonorkhon appears in different promotional material and if you ever reach the communities of Batshireet, Erdene Sum, Möngönmorit, Tünkhel or Züünkharaa you will see children wearing a Sonorkhon badge. If not, please ask them where their badge is!

Countryside fire-education excursions taught the children and their parents environmental games, and everyone learned how to build, light and then extinguish a campfire safely. A fire-prevention song was composed and sung, dramas and physical contests were held and poster displays were put up in the information centres, which grew in number. All in all we had a great time and received a wonderful response from the local people. We also achieved our aim in the communities where we were active, as the number of fires began to decrease! Was it the prevention work, or the sterling efforts of the trained fire-fighters, or just luck? Hopefully a mix of the first two.

a sheep for example, every bit is used and the dogs are thrown only the well-picked bones.

However, with the addition of plastic and convenience foods trail walkers are increasingly upset to find discarded rubbish littering campsites and other areas, and walkers are happy to help clear a campsite but often find no bins or safe place to put rubbish where it will be dealt with properly. See John Muir's Young Adventures Club video: www.youtube.com/watch?v=9ZTHyAz3Ges – where young Mongolians and visitors approach this problem together.

Eco-*gers* One of the main goals in developing interest in the environment is to invite visitors to book accommodation in an eco-*ger*. This is the term given to an environmentally friendly place with 'green thinking' and best practices like leaving a clean camp site with careful disposal of rubbish and having respect for nature in so doing. This gives the local people the opportunity to welcome guests and to increase their living standards, as the visitors pay them directly. A small percentage of the booking costs goes to the local national park organisation who helped to establish the eco-*gers*. For example, there are three eco-*gers* located on the Tuul and Bayan rivers in the Gorkhi-Terelj National Park and adjoining Khankhentii Strictly Protected Area, within easy travelling distance from Ulaanbaatar. It is an ideal place to go for the weekend. Horses and ox carts are available for hire, local guides accompany visitors

4

and food provisions may be bought from people in the neighbourhood. An award-winning cultural eco travel agency, GER to GER runs a *ger* network for travellers and is well worth knowing about – see below and page 238.

Conservation work using volunteers or ecotourists
Steppes Travel (see page 165), a UK travel company, supports ecotourism linked to conservation programmes that allow groups accompanied by wildlife experts to enter national parks, like the Great Gobi National Park, an area which otherwise requires special permission. Volunteer tourists are actively involved under the expert guidance of field biologists – helping to gather data on rare wild animals such as the snow leopard, the wild camel and Gobi bear – as part of established conservation programmes. People interested in volunteering may also want to look at Steppe Forward programme (see pages 122–3).

After a day's hard work climbing rocky mountains looking for spoor marks and gathering other data, volunteers soon discover that boiled mutton, sheep intestines and rock-hard cheese-curds never tasted so good! Mongolians are enthusiastic and

SOCIAL TRAVEL ENTREPRENEURS

Tourism can protect culture and help people worldwide to develop themselves and their dreams in a sustainable way that shows respect for people and places – for 'greener lives' in a 'greener world'.

GadAdventure www.gadadventures.com. An online travel agency founded by Bruce Poon Tip that will do your thinking for you & get you out there! It is worth taking a look at this site & getting involved. If you are interested in Bruce's thinking, also visit www.futourism.org.

Planeterra 19 Charlotte St, Suite 200, Toronto, Ontario, Canada M5V 2H5; +416 263 4671; e info@planeterra.org; www.planeterra.org. An organisation that supports social enterprises & small businesses in different parts of the world. Make a donation through your trip (small or big – it all matters and is well spent).

TIES www.ecotourism.org. A non-profit association committed to promoting responsible tourism for the benefit of local people.

GER to GER Arizona Centre, just off Peace Av near Genghis Khan Sq; 11 313336; www.gertoger. org. An innovative Mongolian travel agency & foundation. Its ethos & vision are clearly laid out in G2G's website, such as understanding nomadism & its social cultural frameworks; leaving no-trace travel; travelling from GER to GER using animals & learning the basics of the Mongolian language. It is a website well worth exploring! For further information, see page 238.

happy to welcome researchers into their homes. Part of the repayment for their hospitality is to simply sit and share in conversation and meals.

Cultural conservation and the environment The preservation of culture and artefacts is important to maintain diversity and cultural identity in an ever-shrinking planet. The destruction of cultural heritage and cultural landmarks, and the emergence of tourism as the largest industry in the world, highlight the need to address the possible negative effects of both. An innovative approach is to involve tourist volunteers in helping to save cultural heritage sites currently under threat. Readers will understand why it is illegal to take away 'souvenirs' from archaeological and palaeontological sites.

Tourism has the power to affect cultural change, but there is a tipping point when tourism grows into mass tourism that leads to over consumption and pollution – the balance is there to preserve or destroy.

> Nature and human beings must operate as a whole and integrated system – taking our ancient Mongol wolf-totem as a symbol of endurance, we can forge a new sustainable economy ... and show that nomadic people can, once again, offer something back in terms of environmental responsibility!
>
> *B Gantömör, chairman of Sustainable Tourism Centre*

Natural History and Conservation RESPONSIBLE TOURISM

4

5

Practical Information

WHEN TO VISIT (AND WHY)

The focus of Mongolia's tourism is nature and the environment, the nomadic way of life and places linked with Genghis Khan. In the final decade of the 20th century this 'last place on earth' opened its doors to the world and with air travel and the advantages of the internet Mongolia is, virtually, a step away.

Summer (including the short spring and early autumn) is the main Mongolian tourist season, starting in May and ending in September (sometimes until mid October if the weather holds). However, Mongolia now offers a winter holiday season, which includes some skiing. A Swiss-owned downhill ski resort, *Sky Resort*, is located in the Bogd Khan Uul, some 13km outside Ulaanbaatar: it uses man-made snow, has nine runs with two chair lifts and evening skiing is floodlit from 18.00–22.00. (*www.skiresort.info/ski-resort/ulaanbaatar-resort*). This is a far cry from the original use of overland skis by Kazakh Mongol hunters in the Altai border areas of western Mongolia, as seen in rock paintings. It is notoriously difficult to date petroglyphs, but according to some scientists they could be as early as 8,000 years ago but are more likely dated around 3,000 years ago.

Most people would not choose to visit Mongolia in the depths of winter, but it is an interesting season to travel, bearing in mind that arrangements are equally limited by the weather. Tourists visiting in winter must be prepared to wrap up warmly as the temperatures drop to below –35°C. Central heating is turned up so

MONGOLIA CLIMATE

	Av temp, °C	Humidity, %	Precipitation, mm
January	−26.1	75	1.5
February	−21.7	73	1.9
March	−10.8	66	2.2
April	0.5	50	7.2
May	8.3	47	15.3
June	14.9	56	48.8
July	17.0	65	72.6
August	15.0	65	47.8
September	7.6	64	24.4
October	−1.7	65	6.0
November	−13.7	72	3.7
December	−24.0	75	1.6
Annual average/total	−2.9	64	233.0

high in the major hotels and offices that it reaches tropical temperatures indoors. The solution is to dress in light layers (eg: silk, cotton and wool) and to keep furs, gloves and hats handy when nipping outside. There are so few tourists that you will get wonderful individual attention, especially if your visit coincides with Tsagaan Sar, the New Year festival – held between January and March, depending on the Mongolian moon calendar. Winter journeys need special planning. There is the possibility of skating on frozen rivers or heli-skiing, if you are super adventurous and prepared to fund it. Bring warm clothes and appropriate boots; otherwise, the thick felt boots worn by Mongolians are best and a Mongolian fleece-lined *deel* (the local winter attire) can be purchased on arrival. Several tour companies offer winter travel, especially to the Ice Festival held annually in March on and around Lake Khövsgöl (see *Tour operators*, pages 165–7 and 237–9).

HIGHLIGHTS/SUGGESTED ITINERARIES

The traveller must not count on the distance but on the nature of the ground when trying to estimate his marches.
Douglas Carruthers, British explorer and surveyor in central Asia (1910–11)

At a glance you will find the following activities in the different regions of Mongolia:

- **North** Around Lake Khövsgöl there is riding, fishing, *Tsaatan* (reindeer people – an ethnic minority living in wigwams, but difficult to reach), wildlife of the forest and steppe. For Bronze Age archaeology there are deer stones in the Khövsgöl region.

WHY COME?

Mongolia has an enormous amount to offer visitors, from tumbling waterfalls to the wide-open spaces of the fenceless steppe, not forgetting around 250 days of sunshine a year, while foreign investors may find more allure in Mongolia's mineral wealth – copper, gems, gold and oil. The country's major strengths are its unspoiled countryside, with natural beauty on a colossal scale, immeasurable steppes and unbelievable hospitality, such that the word takes on a new meaning. The generosity and kindness of ordinary Mongolians is overwhelming and *ger* hospitality is legendary. Your eyes might scan the horizon and, sharpening focus, might see nestled together in the dip of a valley, or in some strategic place out of the wind, a tiny collection of *gers* (Mongol tents), set against an awe-inspiring background of mountains and river valleys. It is a land that invites exploration – a vast land of undisturbed beauty and wilderness areas, sparsely inhabited by some of the last nomadic people on earth.

Boundless space, like the ocean, encourages the visitor to relax. Bumped around in the back seat of a Russian jeep on Mongolian roads you have no other choice or, if you ride on horseback or camelback for hours across country, relaxation becomes a matter of survival, otherwise you are liable to do some damage, or, more seriously, if pitched off, break bones. To experience the reality and to fully understand Mongolia's attractions, contradictions and surprises you must travel there and see for yourself. Mongolians are people of the moment, fun-loving as well as hospitable, and their outlook is 'come what may, let tomorrow look after itself'.

- **South** In the Gobi region are places where dinosaur fossils have been found, unusual cliffs and rock formations, temples, *ger* camps, camel rides, cashmere goats and sand dunes.
- **East** In the grasslands are found Genghis Khan's memorial site, gazelles, the ruins of ancient cities, bird watching, camping and riding.
- **West** In Kazakh country are the Kazakh minority people, hunting for foxes and rodents with trained eagles, mountain peaks for climbers, wonderful wild landscape, *argali* sheep and other wildlife.
- **Central** Around Karakorum, ancient capital of the Mongol Empire, are monasteries, good camping sites, rafting, waterfalls, ancient rock art, polo in the Orkhon valley, and the herding lifestyle.

Use the following as a broad indicator of what and how much can be done during visits of varying lengths:

- **A weekend** Visit Ulaanbaatar, with its restaurants, theatres, museums and temples.
- **Five days** Visit one countryside area near UB (eg: Terelj resort, Khentii river valley eco-*gers*, wild horses at Khüstain Nuruu National Park).
- **Ten days–two weeks** Visit countryside areas – fly/drive between provincial centres. Fly to Khovd, capital of Khovd Aimag, meet your horse and saddle up for a riding experience. Hike and climb in the mountains, staying in tented camps or in local herders' *gers*, before returning to UB to explore the capital's museums, restaurants, bars and nightlife.
- **Three weeks** A good length of stay. Allows time to visit the countryside – to 'do' the Naadam Festival and to travel the 'Golden Circuit' (Khövsgöl, the Orkhon Valley and the South Gobi). After arriving and winding down in UB for a night, you could set out by jeep for Lake Khövsgöl, via Amarbayasgalant Monastery. Spend several days camping and exploring the country on horseback. Drive south to Kharkhorin and visit the famous monastery of Erdene Zuu, nearby. If there is time, you might extend your journey to the South Gobi, by flying to Dalanzadgad (from Ulaanbaatar – it's the only way) and visiting its major sites including the Flaming Cliff area, famous for dinosaur fossil finds. On your final return to Ulaanbaatar, allow a day to shop and see the city.
- **Two to three months** Time required to travel the country properly – you can do it in six weeks, but you should be aware of certain shortcomings regarding Mongolian roads (or lack of them) and the availability and quality of transport and communication, especially in more remote areas, as they may have an impact on your plans.

TRANS-MONGOLIAN/TRANS-SIBERIAN RAIL JOURNEY
These rail journeys might include tours of Beijing, Ulaanbaatar and Moscow. The great cities of Beijing and Moscow owe much of their importance to the Mongols. Beijing became the capital of the Mongol Empire during the 14th century under Kublai Khan and his successors. Another of Genghis Khan's grandsons backed local princes, so that Moscow became the centre for Russian rule. A suggested route is to fly to Beijing and return by rail. Spend some days in Beijing visiting the wonders of the 'Forbidden City', home of the Chinese emperors for 500 years. If you have some days to spare, drive to a section of the Great Wall, passing through small towns and villages in Inner Mongolia before reaching the border with Mongolia where you may catch the train to UB. Otherwise take the train from Beijing (the

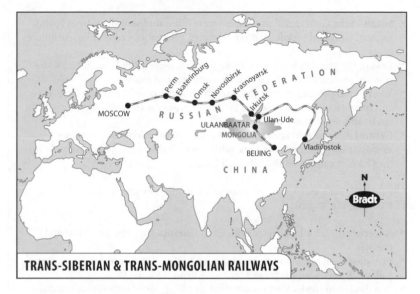

Chinese terminus of the Trans-Siberian/Trans-Mongolian line) to Ulaanbaatar. You will pass other sections of the Great Wall and you will wake to see the Gobi Desert. Later that evening you will have time to go to your hotel and to visit parts of the city, like the Gandan Monastery. Spend a weekend in the Khentii mountains or at the Gorkhi-Terelj National Park, which offers overnight stays with herders' families in traditional Mongolian *gers*, riding and other outdoor activities – fishing or hiking – before continuing the train journey. Then you can settle down with a book, in the comfort of your compartment, or watch the countryside flash past, including Lake Baikal in southern Siberia, until four days later you find yourself in Moscow – another fascinating capital to explore with its onion-domed churches and Kremlin treasures.

Tour operators such as Off the Map Tours, Great Genghis Expeditions and Panoramic Journeys can help to organise the above.

THE 'GOLDEN CIRCUIT' Mongolia's 'Golden Circuit' highlights the most-visited regions of the country: Lake Khövsgöl, the Orkhon Valley and the South Gobi. You may have time to visit one or two of the areas mentioned – all three, if you stay over three weeks. Lake Khövsgöl is the famous blue lake in northern Mongolia bordering Siberia, near many great fishing rivers. It is an area of outstanding natural beauty and offers good accommodation and many activities like riding, hiking and climbing. From Ulaanbaatar you may also travel to the Orkhon Valley, with its forested mountain landscape, waterfalls, spas and temple sites, to visit the site of Karakorum, the ancient capital of the Mongol Empire and the monastery of Erdene Zuu. You may fly (via Ulaanbaatar – the hub of all transport) or drive to Dalanzadgad, the aimag centre of South Gobi, from where you may visit the golden dunes of the Gobi and the dinosaur area of the famous Flaming Cliffs at Bayanzag. From each of the areas mentioned above you will be able to visit national parks, spend time with nomadic families and ride across country camping out, or simply experience a day's riding in and around one of these areas. Mongolia's far western mountains and lakes and the eastern plains offer wonderful tours as well, although they are less visited.

TOUR OPERATORS

UK

Bamboo Travel Director Tim Milner; Spectrum Hse, 9 Bromell's Rd, Clapham Common, London SW4 0BN; ☎020 7720 9285; e info@bambootravel. co.uk; www.bambootravel.co.uk

Far Frontiers Ninestone, South Zeal, Devon EX20 2PZ; ☎01837 840640; e info@farfrontiers.com; www.farfrontiers.com. Escorted journeys & tailor-made travel to lakes & mountains.

Goyo Travel Talbot Lodge, Ardley Rd, Middleton Stoney, Bicester OX25 4AD; ☎01869 866520; e info@goyotravel.com; www.goyotravel.com. Small group and tailor-made tours – experts in the field of Mongolia travel. Founded & run by Goyo & Oliver Reston. See ad in 2nd colour section.

Mountain Kingdoms 20 Long St, Wotton-under-Edge, Glos GL12 7BT; ☎01453 844400; e info@mountainkingdoms.com; www. mountainkingdoms.com. Fully guided small-group treks.

Off the Map Tours UK agent: 20 The Meer, Fleckney, Leicester LE8 8UN; ☎0116 240 2625; e info@ mongolia.co.uk; www.mongolia.co.uk. Head office in Mongolia: Bayanzurkh district, 13th Microdistrict, Bldg 4, No 184, Ulaanbaatar; ☎+976 11 458964. Active adventure tours, cultural experiences; specialists in train travel; mountain-bike tours. Family holidays organised by inspiring family-run company (Catherine & Enkhbold Darjaa), with offices in the UK and Mongolia. See ad, page 160.

Panoramic Journeys Granary Barn, Chapel Rd, Chadlington, Oxon OX7 3NX; ☎01608 676821; e info@panoramicjourneys.com; www. panoramicjourneys.com. UK & Mongolian company specialising in small-group journeys & tailor-made travel. From adventurous expeditions (dog-sledding or on horseback) to cultural journeys in comfort & style. Quality service & expertise. Top UK specialists in Mongolian travel. See ad, page 160.

Regent Holidays 6th Flr, Colston Tower, Colston St, Bristol BS1 4XE; ☎020 7666 1244; e regent@ regentholidays.co.uk; www.regentholidays.co.uk. Pioneers in travel to Mongolia.

Round the World Flights ☎020 7704 5700; www.roundtheworldflights.com. Based in Islington in London; can arrange Trans-Siberian rail tickets.

Steppes Travel The Travel Hse, 51 Castle St, Cirencester, Glos GL7 1QD; ☎0843 636 8243;

USA toll free 1 855 203 7885; e sales@ steppestravel.co.uk; www.steppestravel.co.uk. Cultural, family, walking & riding tours in Khövsgöl, Altai, Gobi & Karakorum.

USA

Boojum Expeditions 14543 Kelly Canyon Rd, Bozeman, MT 59715; ☎+1 800 287 0125; e info@ boojum.com; www.boojumexpeditions.com. Specialist in adventure travel & ecotourism.

Distant Horizons 350 Elm Av, Long Beach, CA 90802; ☎+1 562 983 8828, +1 800 333 1240; e info@distant-horizons.com; www.distant-horizons.com. Cultural tours.

Mongol Caravan PO Box 191, Clifden, NJ 07011 0191; ☎+1 973 594 0655; f +1 209 729 4674. Independent itineraries for travellers to Mongolia; 'The Mighty Mongolia' tour; 'The Naadam Festival' tour, with an optional add-on to the Great Wall of China.

Mongol Global Tour Company Inc 10073 Valley View St #232, Cypress CA 90630; ☎866 225 0577; e tourrequest@ mgtourco.com; www. mongolglobaltours.com. Specialises in Indiana Jones-type adventures; customised tours.

Nomadic Expeditions 1095 Cranbury-South River Rd, Suite 20A Monroe Township, NJ 08831; ☎+1 800 998 6634; e info@nomadicexpeditions.com; www. nomadicexpeditions.com. Adventure & classic tours. See ad, page 302.

AUSTRALIA

Karakorum Expeditions (Australian-run company based in Ulaanbaatar) Gangariin Gurav Bldg, south side of State Circus, Sükhbaatar district, Ulaanbaatar 210638; ☎+976 11 315655; e info@GoMongolia.com; www.GoMongolia.com. Specialist in active adventure travel & ecotourism; Mongolian getaways; cross-border itineraries to Inner Mongolia.

CANADA

Exotic Tours 1117 Ste Catherine, Suite 806 Montreal, Quebec H3B 1H9; ☎+1 514 284 3324; f +1 514 843 5493

FRANCE

Air Sud 25 Bd Sebastopol, 75001 Paris; ☎+33 1 40 41 66 70; f +33 1 40 26 68 44

Terres d'Aventure 6 rue Saint-Victor, 75006 Paris; www.terdav.com
Terre Mongolie 17 rue de la Bucherie, 75005 Paris; ✆+33 1 44 32 12 83; www.terre-mongolie.com

GERMANY

Athena Weltweit Hohe Bleichen 21, 20354 Hamburg; ✆+49 40 351 257; e info@athena-studienreisen.de
Marco Polo Reisen Dettweilerstr 15, 61476 Kronberg/Ts; ✆+49 61 7370 9716; e h-liebelt@marco-polo-reisen.com
Off the Map Tours German agent: Demminerstr 9b, 13059 Berlin; ✆+ 49 30 928 8344; e enchsaichan@aol.com; www.mongolia.co.uk. See under *UK* for tours offered.
Wikinger Reisen Koelnerstr 20, D-58135 Hagen; ✆+49 23 3190 4785; e ovid.jakota@wikinger.de

ITALY

Focus World Services Corso C Colombo 10, 20144 Milano; ✆+39 2 894 02052; e focus.himalaya@virtualia.it

JAPAN

Mongol Juulchin Tours 3/Floor Dai-2 Kawana Building, 14-6, Shibuya 2-Chome, Shibuya-ku, Tokyo 150; ✆+81 3 3486 7351; e info@juulchinworld.mn; www.juulchinworld.mn

NETHERLANDS

Global Train Anne Kooistrahof 15, 1106 WG Amsterdam; ✆+31 20 696 7585; e goldentrains@pi.net
Tseren Tours Run by Dutch/Mongolian couple Ric & Tseren – see local travel agents in Mongolia, page 239.

SPECIALIST TOUR OPERATORS
Mountaineering and adventure
Karakorum Expeditions See page 238 for contact details. 'Five Holy Peaks' of the Tavan Bogd tour; tailor-made climbing tours.
Kazakh Tour Co Social Services building 2nd floor, Main Sq, Bayan-Olgii ; PO Box 111, Olgii, Bayan-Olgii; m +976 994 22006, 994 29696; e dosjan@yahoo.com; www.kazakhtour.com
Kobesh Travel Co m +976 99107676, +976 98167676; e maksum_agii@yahoo.com; www.kobeshtravel.com. Located in Khovd town, Bayan

Olgii – founded & managed by expert guide & local school teacher, Agii Maksum. See ad, page 382.

Biking
For biking tours, consider contacting Tseren Tours (*ww.tserentours.com*) or Off the Map Tours (*www.mongolia.co.uk*). See pages 239 and 165.

Riding (horses/camels)
The fence-free riding experience on the Mongolian steppes, the clear air, altitude and sunshine is a thrilling experience. Added to it is the exuberant company of Mongol horsemen, singing about the beauty of the countryside as they gallop. Riding tours are generally unsupported by vehicles, people camp in tents and live outdoors, visiting nomadic herding families – often eating meals with them. Costs vary according to the number of people in a group. The season begins in June and goes on until late September. More popular tours combine a ride before or after the Naadam Festival in mid July. Approximate cost for an 11-day riding tour is US$2,145 (exc international flights). For further information on horse riding in Mongolia, see pages 210–12.

Equitour Riding Holidays 15 Grangers Pl, Bridge St, Witney, Oxon OX28 4BH, UK; ✆01993 849489; www.equitour.co.uk. Horse tours only. 'Riding with Eagles' & 'The Reindeer Herders of Khövsgöl' tours.
Genco Tour Bureau Bayangol Hotel B-201, 5 Genghis Khan Av, Ulaanbaatar 43; ✆+976 11 328960; e info@ genco-tour.mn; www.genco-tour.mn. Horse- & camel-riding tours.
In the Saddle Reaside, Neen Savage, Cleobury Mortimer, Shropshire DY14 8ES, UK; ✆01299 272997; e rides@inthesaddle.com; www.inthesaddle.com. An excellent company offering riding tours to Mongolia.
Ride World Wide Staddon Farm, North Tawton, Devon EX20 2BX, UK; ✆01837 82544; e info@rideworldwide.com; www.rideworldwide.co.uk. Horse tours only. 'The Khenti Ride', 'Khövsgöl & the Reindeer People Ride' & 'Karakorum Ride' tours.

Ecotourism
To give credit to the tourist industry, most travel companies offering tours in Mongolia are environmentally aware and eco-friendly. The leading experts are listed below:

Boojum Expeditions www.boojum.com. See page 165.

Goyo Travel www.goyotravel.com. See page 165.

Great Genghis Expeditions www.greatgenghisexpeditions.com. See page 238.

Karakorum Expeditions www.gomongolia.com. See page 238.

Kazakh Tour www.kazaktour.com.See page 238.

Kobesh Travel www.kobeshtravel.com. See opposite and ad, page 382.

Nomadic Expeditions www.nomadicjorneys.com. See page 238.

Off the Map Tours www.mongolia.co.uk. See page 165.

Panoramic Journeys www.panoramicjourneys.com. See page 165.

Tseren Tours www.tserentours.com. See page 239.

Wild Earth Journeys www.wildearthjourneys.com. See below.

Fishing

Angling Travel Orchard Hse, Gunton Hall, Hanworth, Norfolk NR11 7HJ; ✆01263 761602

Fish Mongolia/Nomadic Journeys www.fishmongolia.com, www.nomadicjourneys.com. Fish Mongolia was founded by Andy Parkinson the most experienced individual in the game and acquired in 2013 by Jan Wigsen of Nomadic Journeys. See page 238.

Frontiers (US office) PO Box 959, Wexford PA 16090-0959; ✆+1 724 935 1577; e info@frontierstrvl.com; www.frontierstrvl.com

Frontiers London (European office) 18 Albemarle St, London W1S 4HR, UK; ✆020 7493 0798; e info@frontierstrvl.com; www.frontierstrav.com

Nomadic Journeys One Sükhbaatar St, Ulaanbaatar; ✆+976 11 328737, 323978; e infomongolia@nomadicjourneys.com; www.nomadicjourneys.com

Roxton, Bailey Robertson Worldwide 25 High St, Hungerford, Berkshire RG17 ONF, UK; ✆01488 689701; e fishing@roxtons.com; www.roxtons.com

Sweetwater Travel 5082 US Highway 89 South, PO Box 668, Livingston, Montana 59047, USA; ✆+1 406 222 0624; e info@sweetwatertravel.com; www.sweetwatertravel.com. UK contact: ✆0845 603 1552. Irish contact: ✆+353 1890 882 347

Wild Earth Journeys www.wildearthjourneys.com. Fishing days, alongside other activities in a wonderful wilderness retreat location.

Ox-cart adventure tours This unusually slow method of touring allows you to relax completely & unwind as you travel at the pace of an ox cart in the Khentii Mountains around Mount Asraltkhairkhan. For further information contact **Mongol Khaan Travel Company** (e anna@mongolkhaan.mn; www.mongolkhaan.mn).

Winter tours In addition to that below, several UK companies specialise in winter travel, including Panoramic Journeys & Steppes Travel, as well as Juulchin (see page 238) & Great Genghis Expeditions (see page 238).

Off the Map Tours (see page 238). Offers special winter weekend breaks to Gorkhi-Terelj National Park on the edge of the Khentii Mountains, near Ulaanbaatar. A typical weekend would include driving to Terelj & checking into a *ger* camp for 3 days, where you will have great opportunities to sit & chat with local people & taste some delicious Mongolian hot soups & stews. Return to Ulaanbaatar, visit the cashmere factory & the city's temples & museums.

Family holidays Many families would shy away from bringing children of any age to Mongolia but this need not be the case, as proved by Rupert Isaacson in his book *Horse Boy* (2009) – see page 442. He travelled with his seven-year-old son Rowen (who suffers from autism) to Mongolia in a quest to find healing. This book is a must-read for those wanting to bring children on holiday. The friendships they forge with Mongolian children & their animals are extraordinary. One tip: find a good holiday spot in the countryside & stay there – don't move around. There is nothing more tedious for a child or teenager than to spend long hours in a car or jeep travelling, for what to them seems for ever. Generally what they want to do is to learn to ride & make friends. The following websites give valuable information: www.family-travel.co.uk; www.jojomamanbebe.co.uk and www.babygoes2.com; for what to wear: www.youngexplorers.co.uk; and for health: www.netdoctor.co.uk.

TOURIST INFORMATION

⚹ Mongolian National Tourist Centre (MNTC)
Baga Toiruu 55, Central Sports Palace, Ulaanbaatar.
POB 1520 index 211213, Central Post Office
Ulaanbaatar; ☏ 11 318493/311102/318492;
e info@mongoliatourism.gov.mn; www.
mongoliatourism.org. Established in 1999 to
answer questions, provide information & support
the development of Mongolian tourism. MNTC has
an excellent website.

**⚹ Mongolian Tourism Association
(MTA)** Genghis Khan Sq, Bldg of Mongolian
Trade Unions Confederation, 3rd Floor, Room 318,
Ulaanbaatar 11; ☏ 11 323026 m 09980 3632;
e touristmask@magicnet.mn; www.
travelmongolia.org.

RED TAPE

ENTRY AND EXIT REQUIREMENTS A valid passport and entry/exit visa are required prior to travel. Visitors to Mongolia should carry their passports with them at all times.

Visas For information on Mongolian visas go to www.mongoliavisa.com or www. embassyofmongolia.co.uk The first step is to check with the Mongolian Embassy/ Consular Department if you need a Mongolian visa, which depends on your nationality and length of stay. It is highly advisable to obtain your visa in advance from Mongolian embassies or consulates abroad rather than at points of entry, train stations and airports, as this facility, once on offer, has been withdrawn. You will be required to submit your passport, one passport photograph and to complete a visa form. This may be done online, but if not, allow two weeks and be sure to attach your full return address for your passport.

A 30-day tourist visa for UK citizens (at the time of writing) costs £40 (£60 fast track) and takes two to five working days; a double entry and exit visa costs £55 (£75 fast track); a multiple-entry visa costs £70 (£90 fast track); and a transit visa costs £35 (£55 fast track). Check with the embassy for the current cost.

Extending visas If you are going to stay more than 30 days you must extend your visa at the **Mongolia Immigration Agency** within seven working days of your arrival in the country. For more information please visit http://immigration.gov.mn.

If you are a tourist, you will need a passport and official letter from your tour operator/company. If you are an independent traveller, you will need to submit your passport, one photo, and the fee, having completed the application form. If for work, you will need to submit your passport and an official letter from your employer. Forms are in English. Travellers arriving or departing from Mongolia through Russia or China should also be aware of Russian and Chinese visa regulations.

Police registration and de-registration All visitors spending more than 30 days in Mongolia must register with the police department. Those visiting Mongolia for 30 days or less do not need to register. Visitors with a visa for more than 30 days or those who enter without passing through immigration must register within ten days of arrival in Mongolia. A visitor's first registration must be made in Ulaanbaatar at the Office of Immigration, Naturalisation and Foreign Citizens, located near to the airport, next to the new Wrestling Palace. Subsequent registrations can be made at the police departments in aimag (provincial) centres.

Visitors staying over 30 days who travel and stay outside Ulaanbaatar for more than seven days in one place should obtain permission before departing for the countryside. The required letter of permission available from the State Centre for Registration is free of charge. When a visitor stays in the countryside, they must register with the aimag police department on entry and exit from that location. Visitors who intend to visit several countryside locations, for more than seven days each, should obtain a letter of permission that can be used for all the aimags.

Police registrations are valid for as long as the visitor's visa is valid, up to a maximum of one year. The initial charge is T25,000. To de-register, it is important to remember to go to the same office and get a de-registration stamp on your registration paper. If you do not do this you may have to return to Ulaanbaatar from a border point, or an airport, to de-register.

Customs regulations Tourists must complete a customs declaration form on entry, which should be kept until departure. This allows for the free import and re-export of articles intended for personal use for the duration of stay, like cameras and recorders, as well as personal jewellery. You may also have to register the amount of foreign currency you are carrying. Goods to the value of T20,000 are allowed to be exported from Mongolia. Prohibited items include: palaeontological and archaeological finds; uncertified antiques; collections of various plants and their seeds; and raw skins, hides and furs without permission from the appropriate authorities.

Luggage On international flights the luggage allowance is 20kg per passenger. Excess luggage is usually charged at US$1 per kilo, subject to negotiation on the day.

TRAVEL INSURANCE It is advisable to have a comprehensive policy in place and to let your insurance company know that you will be travelling in Mongolia. Make sure you will be covered if you have any health problems. There may be some additional charges.

MONGOLIAN EMBASSIES AND CONSULATES

Belgium 18 Av Besme, 1190 Brussels; 2 344 6974; f 2 344 3215; e brussels.mn.embassy@chello.be

Canada 151 Slater St (Suite 503), Ottawa ON K1P 5H3; 613 569 2623; f 613 569 3919; e consul@mongolembassy.org

China 2 Xiushui Beijie, Jian Guo Men Wai Da Jie, Beijing; 10 6532 1203; f 10 6532 5045; e mail@mongolembassychina.org

Czech Republic Na Marne 5, Prague 6, 16000; +4202 243 11198; f +4202 243 14827; e mongemb@bohem-net.cz

France 5 Av Robert Schumann, 92100 Boulogne-Billancourt, Paris; 1 46 05 23 18; f 1 46 05 30 16; e ambassademongolia@yahoo.fr

Germany Dietzgenstrasse 31, 13156 Berlin; +49 3047 480614; f 30 4748 0616; e mongolbot@aol.com

India 34 Archbishop Makarios Marg, New Delhi 110003; 11 2463 1728; f 11 2463 3240; e mongem@bol.net.in

Japan Pine Crest Mansion, 21-4 Kamiyama-cho, Shibuya-ku, Tokyo 150; 47 469 2088; f 47 469 2216; e embmong@gol.com

Kazakhstan Almaty, ul Musabaeva D1; 3272 551278; f 3272 581727; e info@mongemb.kz

Korea, Republic of Hannam-dong, Yeongsan-gu, Seoul 140-885; e mongol5@kornet.net

Poland ul Rejtana 15 m 16, 00478 Warsaw; 22 849 9391; f 22 848 2063; e mongamb@ikp.atm.com.pl

Russia Borisoglebskii Pereulok 11, Moscow; f 7495 291 4636; e mongolia@online.ru

UK 7 Kensington Court, London W8 5DL; 020 7937 0150; f 020 7937 1117; e office@

5

embassyofmongolia.co.uk; ⊕ 10.00–12.30 Mon–Fri

ⓔ USA 2833 M St NW, Washington, DC 20007; ☎+1 202 333 7117; f +1 202 298 9227; e esyan@ mongolianembassy.mn

For overseas embassies in Mongolia, see page 253.

GETTING THERE AND AWAY

BY AIR The main connection to Mongolia from Europe is via Berlin with MIAT (Mongol Irgenii Agaaryn Teever – Mongolian Airlines). **MIAT** (see below) flies to international destinations such as Moscow, Beijing, Seoul, Irkutsk, Berlin, Huhhot (in Chinese Inner Mongolia) and Osaka. MIAT has branch offices in Korea, China, Taiwan, Japan, Germany, Italy, Holland, France, Russia, Canada and the United States. It no longer flies domestically. **Turkish Airlines** (see opposite page) launched its first flight to Ulaanbaatar (UB) in 2012. You may also fly from most European capitals directly to Beijing in China and change planes (if on another carrier) to **Air China** (www.airchina.co.uk) in Beijing for the two-hour flight to Ulaanbaatar. There are direct flights from Moscow to Ulaanbaatar with **Aeroflot** (*www.aeroflot. com*). Costs vary, depending on when you travel – high or low season. Air fares normally increase by 4% to 5% annually.

Before departure remember the following three things:

- Reconfirm your return flight at least 24 hours prior to your departure.
- Check in two hours before your departure time for international flights.
- International departure tax of around T18,000 (US$12) is payable in local currency.

Buyant-Ukhaa (Chinggis Khaan International) Airport is situated 18km southwest of the capital. Facilities at the airport include a restaurant, a café, bureau de change and several duty-free shops selling souvenirs, spirits and perfumes.

Airlines

✈ **MIAT (Mongolian Airlines)** Head office in Mongolia: Miat Building, 45 Buyant-Ukhaa, Ulaanbaatar 34; ☎+976 11 325633/379935/ 379519; www.miat.com. Reservation & ticket office is newly located east of Genghis Khan Sq (opposite the Puma Imperial Hotel); ☎+976 11 333311. Office at Buyant-Ukhaa Airport: ☎+976 11 379935. Main European branch office, Germany: Chaussee Strasse 84, Berlin 10115; ☎+49 30 2849 8142. Route: Berlin–Moscow. Flight: weekly flight on Sun (winter); twice weekly, Thu, Sun (summer). Cost: £860. Travel time: 12hrs 40mins. To check international flights to & from Mongolia, & for further information, see the website.
✈ **British Airways** 156 Regent St, London W1R 5TA; ☎01914 907901 or 0844 493 0787; www. BA.com. Route: London–Beijing direct (transfer to Air China for Beijing–Ulaanbaatar flight). Flights: 3-times weekly – Mon, Wed, Sat. Cost: London–

Beijing economy return (inc tax), from £700 (winter), £1,015 (summer). Travel time: 10hrs.
✈ **Air China** Main UK office: 41 Grosvenor Gardens, London SW1W 0BP; ☎020 7630 7678; www.air-china.com. Local offices: Room 201, Bayangol Hotel, Ulaanbaatar; Ikh Toiruu, 12 Khoroolol; ☎+976 11 328838. Route: London–Beijing/Beijing–Ulaanbaatar. Flights: from £805 (inc tax) in summer. Because of flight scheduling you may have to stay overnight in Beijing. Travel time: London–Beijing 10hrs; Beijing–Ulaanbaatar just over 2hrs.
✈ **Aeroflot** (Russian airlines) UK Booking Office: 70 Piccadilly, London W1V 9HH; ☎020 7355 2233; www.aeroflot.co.uk. Office in Mongolia: ☎+976 11 320720. IMS (Agents for Aeroflot in London) 9 Mandeville Pl, London W1U 8AU; ☎020 7224 4678; e info@imstravel.co.uk; www.imstravel. co.uk. IMS will make bookings & you can pay by

credit card. Route London–Moscow–Ulaanbaatar (changing planes in Moscow). Flights: once a week on Fri (winter); 3-times weekly – Mon, Wed & Fri (summer). Cost: high season from £950 (inc all taxes) low-season return, £750 (inc all taxes). Travel time: London–Moscow 3hrs, Moscow–Ulaanbaatar 8½hrs.

✈ **Turkish Airlines** Turkish Airlines General Management Building, Ataturk Airport, Yesilkoy

34149, Istanbul, Turkey; ☏+90 212 463 63 63; www.turkishairlines.com. London head office: Lyric House, 149 Hammersmith Road, London W14 0QL; reservation and sales: ☏0844 800 6666, 020 7471 6666; e info-uk@thy.com; ⏰ 09.00–17.30 Mon–Fri. Flights operate 3 days a week from Istanbul via Bishkek to Ub (Mon, Wed, Fri), returning Tue, Thu, Sat. From £650 return inc tax (summer). Book early – full economy is quoted at £1,420.

BY RAIL One of the most exciting railways in the world – the Trans-Siberian Railway – runs from Moscow to Vladivostok. There are several branches on this line – one through Mongolia, another through Manchuria, while the main Siberian line continues to Vladivostok, the eastern terminus on the Pacific coast. The Trans-Mongolian (Ulaanbaatar) Railway is connected to the Trans-Siberian by a branch line from Ulan-Ude, providing a link between the Trans-Siberian and the Chinese railway system.

Proposals to build a trans-Siberian railway were put forward to the Russian government as early as 1857, by an American, Perry Collins, who proposed a steam railway to transit Siberia. His plan was rejected. A similar Russian proposal was also rejected, and so was the English proposal for a tramway driven by horses.

In 1887, work began on the western Siberian railway line, which was opened by the tsar in May 1891. The mid section, started in 1893, was completed in 1899. It took until 1904 to open the eastern sections around Lake Baikal. Finally, the railway line crossed a bridge over the Amur River to reach Vladivostok on the Pacific coast. The Trans-Mongolian Railway from the Russian border to Ulaanbaatar (built by Russian political prisoners) opened in 1949, and was connected from Ulaanbaatar to the Chinese border in 1955. The total distance from Moscow to Ulaanbaatar is 6,304km, and from Moscow to Beijing is 7,865km. The Trans-Mongolian covers 1,000km from the Russian border to the Chinese border, passing through Ulaanbaatar and several other towns. The Trans-Mongolian railway line is of great economic importance to the country, since it handles most of Mongolia's export and import goods. The main line and its various branch lines in Mongolia carry internal freight, especially coal. It is also a transit route for goods traded between Russia and China.

There are three services a week between Beijing and Moscow that run throughout the year on the Trans-Mongolian and Trans-Manchurian routes. It takes six days from Moscow to Beijing (a day from UB to Beijing). Train #3 leaves Beijing weekly at 19.40 on Wednesday and arrives in Moscow at 19.00 on Monday. China Train #4 leaves Moscow weekly at 19.50 on Tuesday and arrives in Beijing at 15.30 on Monday.

Since many student travellers arrive in China, travel up to Mongolia by train and return to China, or travel on to Moscow, it is important to understand the options offered by Trans-Siberian/Trans-Mongolian railways. There are Russian trains Moscow–UB–Beijing and Moscow–UB and return; there are Mongolian trains UB–Moscow and return; and there are Chinese trains Beijing–UB–Moscow and return. The Russian, Chinese and Mongolian rail authorities decide on the annual schedules, so firm bookings may be taken, usually, after May. Although times may change, once you understand the routes, the basic information remains the same with small adjustments, and possibly the inclusion of an additional train, so it is important to check the schedules when planning your travels.

Booking tickets Train tickets are available at eticket.mtz.mn; ☎ +976 21 244450, e railtoursec@mtz.mn; www.mongolianrailtour.mn.

In Ulaanbaatar Railway bookings for international train fares can only be made at the Foreigner's Booking Office (Room 212, 2nd floor) in the International Railway Ticket Office (*for reservations and information:* ☎ *+976 11 944868;* ⏰ *09.00–18.00 Mon–Sat, 10.00–14.00 Sun*), a yellow building beside the railway station in Ulaanbaatar. It is essential to bring your passport if booking international rail tickets yourself. Mongolian tour companies will help you to make reservations for a small commission.

International rail costs Costs depend on the route you plan. A rough indication of costs in US dollars from UB to Moscow is from US$370 to US$540;

OUR BIG PUSH FOR MONGOLIA

Cecilia Henson

Usually, and quite rightly, my mother tends to ignore my travel whims but when I mentioned Mongolia I could see I had struck a chord!

I had the chance to join a trip to Mongolia: two weeks trekking and two weeks helping in an orphanage. BUT I had to raise over £3,500. How so much? An expensive tracking device had to travel with us; a very high insurance policy to ensure that should disaster occur we would be located and airlifted out and home. The price also covered two accompanying professional English guides, ably assisted by locals with their vehicles and ponies.

How to raise such a sum? We were totally flummoxed. At the start of my fundraising, I was still 14, at boarding school, so weekend jobs and babysitting were out during term and the sums were pitiful in any case. I tried old campaigners for advice. The best was 'Get yourself sponsored to do a parachute jump' – not something I fancied but needs must. No! You have to be 16 years old and my 16th birthday was to fall five days after I was meant to have left for Ulaanbaatar!

Resort to mother! As ever, she came up with an extraordinary plan: being wheelchair-bound (following a riding accident), I should push her from Stoke Mandeville hospital in Aylesbury, where she had been looked after, to Great Ormond Street Hospital in London, where I had been looked after. A mere 42 miles! We planned to take two to three days over the trip. My brother said, 'That is far too tame – no-one will bother sponsoring that! Let the rest of the family join in and let's try to do it in a day!' So our humble version of The Big Push was born. Unbelievably it took my mother and me weeks of planning, letter writing and persuasion to organise.

A Sunday at 05.00 saw us set out from Stoke Mandeville in the dark and by 18.00 we were at Great Ormond Street Hospital – wet, tired but victorious. Tragically, at one stage, a freak accident had momentarily tipped my mother out of the wheelchair and when we finished we discovered both her legs were broken but she decided even after four months' bed recovery it had been worth it, as we had not only raised all the money for my trip, but £7,000 a piece for the two hospitals.

I was lucky enough to have an unforgettable trip to Mongolia.

Neil McGowan

Many people are tempted by the chance to take one of the world's most renowned rail journeys on what is usually called the Trans-Siberian Railway. There is no train called the 'Trans-Siberian Express'. All trains which cross this central area of Russia are Trans-Siberian trains, whether their route is between Moscow and Beijing via Mongolia – sometimes called the Trans-Mongolian (although there is no train called that either) – or the non-Mongolian routes from Moscow to Beijing via Manchuria, and Moscow to Vladivostok on the Pacific coast.

From Moscow to Mongolia, there are two potential routes, of which only two are fully practicable. The less practicable one is unromantically named Train #4, informally known as 'The Chinese Train' (because it's the homeward run of a Chinese Railways train which came up to Moscow from Beijing the previous week – staff and rolling-stock are Chinese). It is also called the Trans-Mongolian. You board this train in Moscow for Beijing and intermediate stops are not permitted. So, you must buy a through-ticket to Beijing in order to leave the train at Ulaanbaatar. This train offers the highest level of on-board comfort of any train on the route – better than first class is deluxe class, which is unique to Chinese Railways. The two-berth (one up, one down) compartments have jet-air ventilation, an armchair and share a small WC/washroom with the neighbouring compartment. Byzantine but effective drop-lock systems guarantee your ablutions are not disturbed and ensure inter-compartmental security. Other carriages consist of four-berth compartments, called first and second class according to décor and comfort. Train #4 runs weekly from Moscow to Beijing so if you are going to jump off in Mongolia, then be ready to do so at around 08.00, UB time, five days later.

Train #6, sometimes called the UB Express, runs twice weekly between Moscow and UB. Train #6 has first-class (two-berth) and second-class (four-berth) compartments. This train permits you to devise a multi-stop itinerary *en route* (joining or leaving the train at major stations along the way).

The traveller grapevine says that conditions on the Russian train are very much better than the Mongolian one. This is based on the fact that the Mongolian traders (who bring cheap Mongolian produce to sell in Moscow and return with hard-to-find consumer goods) can buy tickets much more cheaply on their own national railway than on a Russian train. You may find yourself sharing a compartment with several Mongolians, crammed into a small space with their latest purchases – a microwave, car tyres, a hot-water boiler and so on. Another option is to travel with the aim to stop *en route* in Siberia. Please note that you must have a pre-booked itinerary to do this before your Russian visa application will be processed.

Food on board is the same story for all the trains, including Train #4 (mentioned above). By international convention, the restaurant-car franchise on any international train goes to the country across whose territory you are travelling. This means that from Moscow to the Mongolian border, Russian Railways will be your hosts in the dining car, with a cafeteria-style menu at reasonable prices. In the past, caviar and champagne often featured, but they may no longer be on the menu at such fantastically low prices. Nevertheless, it is always a journey of a lifetime!

Nicolas Gardner

It was still daylight when the train reached Erlian on the Chinese–Mongolian border. Another Queen's Messenger and myself had been travelling since 08.00 and memories were fading of the noisy chaos at Beijing railway station. It was more interesting to stay on board to watch the changing of the bogies for the larger-gauge Mongolia track, and so I did. In an enormous shed, the carriages were swiftly separated and jacked up – the old bogies were lifted and new ones inserted in an operation directed by whistle blasts. These formalities complete, the train trundled gently into Mongolia at Zamyn-Üüd and we were met by smart-looking officials in uniforms, with polished knee-boots and high-peaked caps, who put their Chinese counterparts to shame. All passports were taken, and silence fell. Ages later they were returned, each with a neat entry stamp beside the Mongolian visa.

It was well after midnight when my fellow Queen's Messenger and I retired to our berths – soon to be tucked up in clean sheets and warm blankets for the night. Our adjoining compartments had an interconnecting bathroom where we stored our food bag. Past experience had taught us to self-cater rather than to risk the restaurant car. In the morning, hot water for morning tea was supplied by a Chinese attendant – who travels through to Moscow.

At last we entered the Gobi proper. It appeared absolutely huge and empty under a cloudless sky. There were distant hills (difficult to judge how far away they were) and very little vegetation other than a thin covering of dead-looking grass. No roads. Telephone poles and lines followed the railway track. Occasional groups of animals attended by herdsmen flashed by and isolated *gers* were glimpsed, looking to all the world like field mushrooms. I wished I had my binoculars as it was hard to tell if the animals were sheep, cattle or horses. We spotted small birds and, occasionally, larger hawk-like species; a single lorry motored alongside the train at a distance, trailing a plume of dust, until we came to a halt in a sad-looking village of tin-topped dwellings, with plaster peeling off the walls. A number of men wore traditional *deels* (tunics) with belts of brightly coloured cloth, topped by incongruous-looking pork-pie hats. Energetic children looked inquisitively at us. Co-passengers descended to the platform for fresh air (but one of us remained behind to watch the bags). It was cooler here, being early September. Attendants shooed us on board and with a hoot of the horn we were off again. We lunched on corned beef, tinned sardines and excellent bread from the Beijing Hotel, which drew interested looks from passers-by in the corridor.

At last I spotted trees and we entered the grasslands. A herd of camels came into view and horsemen were seen galloping full pelt across the dry, flat steppe carrying long poles with lassos attached to the end, the Mongol method to ring animals. Finally, we saw the outskirts of Ulaanbaatar where modern construction is supplanting older Soviet-style buildings, but traditional *gers* remain in wooden-fenced compounds. After much blowing of the horn, the train halted. Swarms of flat, flushed Mongolian faces greeted us and we spotted the British Land Rovers and smiling embassy officers. The bacon had arrived!

from Ulaanbaatar to Beijing is US$140 (depending on the class). All trains have two classes, luxury or four-bed compartments. The Chinese trains offer an in-between class with softer beds. All classes are comfortable in terms of train travel. Boiling water is available from a large boiler at the end of each carriage for thermos flasks. Although most local travellers bring their own food, there is a restaurant car, which mainly serves Westerners and the better-off Chinese and Mongolian traders.

BY ROAD The two most used borders into Mongolia are on the main road from Russia in the north at Altanbulag near Sükhbaatar and in the south at Zamyn-Üüd in Dornogobi on the Chinese–Mongolian border. However, note the restrictions on driving in China for foreigners. There is a further border open to foreigners in the west near Tsagaannuur in Bayan-Ölgii Aimag, complete with a brand new border post building. From Tashanta in Russia the paved road (M52) reaches the Mongolian border and this road continues to Tsagaannuur and Olgii. There are currently no border crossings for visitor traffic in the east.

Road border crossings are still limited to nationals of the border countries only on any of the other 40 bilateral crossing points into Russia or China – except with permission (for rallies and other) on the main crossings already mentioned – in the west, north and south.

Car rallies There are several car and bike rallies driving through Mongolia. The main ones are the Mongol Rally and the Mongolia Charity Rally.

Mongol Rally (*www.mongolrally.com*) The Mongol Rally is the original driving adventure to Mongolia, a 10,000-mile journey in a car that's more suited for a nip to the shops. Started back in 2004, the annual motor rally has grown to be the largest event of its kind in the world and is run by the award-winning socially responsible company, the Adventurists. Over the years teams have driven everything from Minis and Honda C90s to London Taxis all the way to Mongolia. Usually about 60% make it to the finish line in one piece. The event raises huge amounts of money for excellent charities, each year bringing in around £300,000 and working closely with, for example, the Christina Noble Children's Foundation – see box, page 45, Mercy Corps and other charities. When the cars arrive they are auctioned to raise further funds for the charities involved.

Mongolia Charity Rally (*www.mongoliarally.com*) The Mongolia Charity Rally is the only 100% charitable rally to Mongolia. Organised by the UK-based charity Go Help, the teams set off from start points in the UK and Europe and aim to reach Ulaanbaatar. The teams can take any route they choose and some travel as far south as Iran, or as far north as the Arctic Circle and Moscow. The challenge is not about speed but about adventure. Teams can take any vehicle they wish, ranging from a motorbike to a double-decker bus. All of the vehicles that complete the journey are donated to Mongolian charities or auctioned with the proceeds going to the charities. Teams taking part also raise money for a range of charities in Mongolia and in their home countries.

Full details including reports from teams on previous trips are available on the website. The Mongolia Charity Rally is just one of many charity rallies on the community website www.charityrallies.org. Tips: I drove a total of 15,434km over 41 days and used 1,446l of diesel. There's a map of our route and more information on our website, www.mongolresponse.co.uk.

IS IT POSSIBLE TO CROSS THE BORDERS INTO MONGOLIA WITH A CAR? It is quite possible to drive yourself to Mongolia if you are going to leave the country again with your vehicle. You need only to turn up at the border. If you intend to leave your vehicle in the country you need to make arrangements before you enter. Import taxes on older vehicles can be very high.

WHICH BORDER TO TAKE? The main borders that are open to foreigners are at Tsagaannuur and Altanbulag, both coming into Mongolia from Russia. The easier road is from Altanbulag to Ulaanbaatar as it is paved all the way – a journey of four–five hours. The northwest road from the Tsagaannuur border to UB takes a minimum of a few days, and normally four–six days. There are a number of routes but the main road west–east is the southern route through the North Gobi regions. The route is unpaved except for short sections within the towns of Khovd, Altai, Bayankhangor and Arvaikheer (where the paved road to UB finally begins). The northern and central routes from the west are extremely tough. On both routes rains can dramatically and quickly affect your ability to cross rivers, and surfaces can vary from sand to hard, smooth ground.

WHAT DO I NEED TO TAKE WITH ME FOR SUCH A JOURNEY? You will need at least one jerry can for fuel and ensure that you fill up your vehicle whenever you see a petrol station. A shovel and some zip ties are useful. Whatever you prepare for it is almost guaranteed that something else breaks down, but you should try and bring some spare parts specific to your car, and especially those that you don't think the locals can make out of bits of scrap.

WHAT ARE THE HIGH AND LOWS OF DRIVING IN MONGOLIA? The highs of driving in Mongolia are the incredible scenery and the feeling of being in the wilderness. The clear, still air can make distant mountains appear closer than they really are, leaving you wondering if you are driving towards a mirage that you will never reach. It can be incredible fun and the Mongolians you meet will make your journey an unforgettable one. However, it is not for the faint-hearted. Traffic certainly isn't a problem until you reach the capital.

FURTHER INFORMATION For more details, see www.drivetomongolia.org.

BY MOTORBIKE The celebrities Ewan McGregor and Charlie Boorman have put motorbiking on the map – especially in Mongolia – on their epic motorbike ride around the world, described in their book (and film) *Long Way Round*. The Mongolian section of their journey was arranged by Panoramic Journeys (see page 165).

RIDING, HIKING AND BIKING

Horse riding If planning to organise your own riding trip, a thorough knowledge of horses is required. Such a journey should not be embarked upon by riders with little experience of either horses or the country itself unless on an arranged riding tour, or with friends who have riding experience. Mongolia offers the keen rider many different conditions – from desert-steppe to forested, mountain rides. For those with the will to endure a little hardship, the country is a dream come true. Mile upon mile of virgin pastureland and mountain ranges with no boundaries, and often without tracks to follow, open up in front of you.

PEKING TO PARIS RALLY VIA MONGOLIA

Tracey Curtis-Taylor

We participated in the Peking to Paris Rally in a 1941 Chevrolet Coupé. It was exactly 100 years since this was first done by Prince Borghese and Luigi Barzina in an Itala. Our route approximated theirs, taking us across the Gobi from northern China via Sainshand to Ulaanbaatar and from there in a westerly sweep through Kharkhorin, Bayankhongor, Altai, Khovd, and Tsagaannuur up to the Siberian border.

We were travelling anywhere between 200km and 400km a day in old cars which involved long hours of hard driving on some extremely rough roads: boulder-strewn, dry riverbeds and deeply trenched tracks cleaved with gullies and eroded in places to bare rock. We drove hundreds of kilometres over severe corrugations that literally shook us to bits. Many of the cars sustained serious damage with broken suspensions, broken chassis, steering columns, etc. But driving on packed sand and open tracks where we could literally fly through the desert was a fantastic experience. One of the most memorable spectacles was seeing all the lovely old cars – Bentleys, Bugattis, Delages, Rolls-Royces and even a couple of Italas – roaring over the plains sending up plumes of sand that could be seen for miles.

There were 130 cars on the rally so it was quite a cavalcade with all the supporting marshalling, emergency and mechanical crews which accompanied us. We stayed at two *ger* camps and then camped in our own tents the rest of the time. At our first camp we experienced a violent sandstorm which seemed to blow up out of nowhere. Some 30 cars got lost in the desert that night and one of the emergency vehicles was rolled and badly damaged in the rescue operation. GPS was an essential part of the navigation, particularly where there were no roads and no landmarks, so we were literally following an arrow on a compass face for great distances between checkpoints.

The Mongolians were magnificent at helping us with our repairs and whether it was in the middle of the Gobi or in one of *machiny grash* in remote towns at all hours of the night and day, we met with great willingness and resourcefulness. The Mongolian men we encountered were intensely curious about the cars with a veritable passion for tools, a few of which we lost on the way – where they ended up no-one knows. Security was an issue and we had to keep a close eye on our possessions but never at any time felt personally threatened.

The cost to take part in such an event was over £100,000, which included the buying and preparing of a suitable car, the rally entrance fee, shipping the car to Beijing, all accommodation and meals on the way and the big party in Paris at the finale. As a once-in-a-lifetime experience, it was worth every penny and Mongolia was the undisputed highlight of the rally for most of the participants.

The company who organised the rally is The Endurance Rally Association (*St Mary's Road, East Hendred, Oxon OX12 8LF;* 01235 831221; *www.endurorally. com*). Support in Mongolia was provided by Nomads Tour Company (*www. nomadstours.com*).

Practical Information GETTING THERE AND AWAY

5

The challenge for some people is to buy their own ponies and to have the excitement of planning a route. In doing this you will have a closer relationship with the nomads. If you stay in a family *ger*, you will be privileged to absorb their nomadic customs automatically. Others, through lack of time, or out of preference, leave all the planning and arrangements to a tour company. Numerous travel companies offer riding tours in Mongolia and take care of all the basic details. You will usually camp in tents or find *ger* accommodation, but rest assured, nothing is too tame or 'touristy' in Mongolia, so you will also experience the nomadic life. Generally you are so tired that by the end of the day you fall asleep immediately on the hard ground without even thinking.

Cycling/motorbiking Make no mistake, the going is tough in Mongolia. At times you will be riding on pebbles and rough ground for hours – it doesn't let up, especially if you are riding in a dry riverbed over stony ground. Be realistic when estimating the distance you hope to achieve in a day, in training or

SORE BUMS: MOTORBIKING THROUGH MONGOLIA

Simon and Georgie McCarthy

As we like places that are a bit wild and undeveloped, Mongolia was one of the highlights of our 18-month trip on a 1990 BMW R100GS.

So what would a biker need to know about the country?

We found Mongolia beautiful because there's 'lots of nothingness'; the exact reason why an Australian biker we met disliked the country. We minimised the risks and maximised the enjoyment and you'll need to do that too because getting to and around Mongolia is a mammoth effort.

You already know that Mongolia is very remote and surrounded by countries with restrictive visa regulations. We chose to ride through the Central Asian 'Stans' and Russia before entering and leaving Mongolia through the Sükhbaatar border crossing. We needed a number of visas for those 'Stans'. We could have made life easier by travelling through Russia but wanted to experience the varied cultures and to avoid riding through thousands of kilometres of steppe and forests.

Mongolia has only about 1,000km of tarmac (although this is changing as more roads are now paved or under construction) spread across a country the size of Spain, France and Germany, so if you're riding outside UB, you'll be on dirt tracks across vast grasslands. Luckily the grass is short, flat and easy to ride on, so if you don't like the track you're on, you can ride on the grass next to the track. However, if you're there too early the tracks will be slippery mud, and if you're there too late the snows will set in. We were there for a month from late August; the tracks were nice and dry, but it began to snow as we left. We used road tyres on the dry tracks; knobblies would only be needed in the wetter seasons. The tracks will also limit your daily mileage; some days we only managed just 70km. So don't be too ambitious – we did a 2,000km route west of UB in about ten days – otherwise you'll be rushing and that's when you fall off and get hurt.

On health, remember that you're often a long way from a hospital (days in the back of a truck), so ride safely and avoid risks. We had rabies jabs before we left the UK.

Fuel is not a major problem. There's always a small town somewhere nearby where you will find a man with a drum of fuel. You'll be lucky to find fuel better on expedition. It is better to get there, bar accidents or breakdown, than to 'get lost' overnight.

Specialist bike and motorbike tour operators include Off the Map Tours (*www. mongolia.co.uk*) and Tseren Tours (*www. tserentours.com*).

Hiking Mongolia is a paradise for hikers. The area of the Bogdkhan National Park and Terelj, near Ulaanbaatar, provide wonderful short-distance day walks from the capital. To go further afield you will need a guide and transport. National parks around the country offer some of the best hiking routes and, depending on where you want to go, local tour companies, or the national park offices, will suggest or help to make the necessary arrangements. It is safest to hike in twos or threes. Essential gear includes a water bottle, good footwear and camping gear if travelling outside a guided tour. Don't forget to carry good maps, binoculars and some mosquito repellent during the summer season.

For further information on what to pack, see pages 191–6.

than 80-octane, but speed is limited by the nature of the terrain. We fitted a 43-litre tank to our bike, so we didn't feel the need to carry a spare can of fuel, and we always had sufficient fuel for our petrol stove.

Similarly, there is plenty of water around in lakes, rivers and the occasional well. We used an MSR water filter on everything we drank. You'll need to stock up with food in the small towns, but you can get some cooked food at *gers* that show the sign *'Guanz'*. The food can be weird but tastes good when you're hungry. We enjoyed mutton and noodles, butter, tea – think of it as 'soup' rather than a 'nice cuppa', and yak cheese – served as bread with heavenly clotted yak cream. Less tasty were the things made from mare's milk – cheesy vodka, rock-hard cheesy nuggets, and fermented mare's milk.

If your bike breaks down, a friendly local will always help you out. More space-age systems aren't worth the risk which is why we chose a bike with carbs and simple electrics, rather than one with computers and sensors. Welding (*svarka*) takes place in road maintenance depots (the Russian word for welding is *gagnoor*); remember to disconnect your battery during welding! Tyres are a real rarity – bring a spare rear with you. If you have a breakdown, relax, take your time and see what comes along.

Maps are a problem until you get to UB. Before we left London we bought several maps from Stanfords but they turned out to be too large in scale and the routes too approximate. In UB, the Map Shop on Ikh Toiruu (1km west of the main square) provided 1:250,000 maps. Although they were not cheap, they were accurate and, combined with a simple GPS (Garmin 12XL) and more importantly 'sign language with the locals', enabled us to do some pretty fancy routes.

A couple of final thoughts. Learning how to read Russian (Cyrillic) is useful but don't expect the words you read to be Russian – they'll be Mongolian words written using Cyrillic text. And take care not to fall in love with the country too deeply; we loved the place so much that we called our first-born 'Oscar Bataar McCarthy'. He doesn't know it yet, but he's got a long bike ride ahead of him some time in the future!

See website: www.sorebums.net

A useful overland bike site is: www.horizonsunlimited.com

I travelled to Mongolia to participate in Macmillan Cancer Relief's 'Mongolia Cycling Challenge'. My challenge took me, and a group of 30 others, to cycle off-road for 385 gruelling kilometres (about 240 miles) in Mongolia. We started from the edge of the Gobi Desert, continued across the stunning Khangai Mountains, stopping at villages where we visited hot springs, which the Mongolians use for curing ailments. We climbed 2,600m and at the top was an *ovoo* – a pyramid of stones, sticks and silk scarves, a Shamanistic offering to the gods. We then raced on to the ancient city of Karakorum.

We camped under the stars, scaled mountains and free-wheeled faster than the wild horses over the Mongolian steppes. The nomadic people we encountered were inquisitive. We had some fun together: we frequently exchanged our 21-gear mountain bikes for their horses and wooden saddles at our nightly camping grounds. We were invited into the nomads' *gers*, their round felt homes, which are extremely tidy and unlike the interior of our tents. Their diet is basic: in the summer they eat cheese and dairy foods, and in the winter meat. My personal memory will be the vast open spaces, a harsh environment – no shelter from the elements – few trees and nothing for miles. The country is a mixture of Russian industrialism and China's Buddhist lifestyle and temples, which I also found fascinating.

It was the experience of a lifetime, but one incident surprised me: in the market in Karakorum, a little girl just had to touch me – either to feel my Lycra cycling gear, or to see if I was human! I also found out that any amount of training in Richmond Park, in the gym and in spinning (fitness bike) classes over the winter months did not prepare me for the terrain, which was like cycling for miles over the pebbles on Brighton beach! Nor was I prepared for snow in early September.

HEALTH   *Felicity Nicholson*

VACCINATIONS No vaccinations are compulsory for Mongolia but the following are the minimal recommendations – hepatitis A, typhoid, tetanus, diphtheria and polio. Other vaccinations to consider are hepatitis B, rabies and, for those who are travelling and camping in the northern provinces and coming in contact with ticks via animals, tick-borne encephalitis.

Tetanus needs to be boosted ten-yearly and is now conveniently combined with diphtheria and polio in a single vaccine (Revaxis), which lasts for ten years.

Hepatitis A vaccine (Havrix Monodose or Avaxim) comprises two injections given about a year apart. The course costs about £100, but may be available on the NHS, protects for 25 years and can be administered even close to the time of departure. Hepatitis B vaccination should be considered for longer trips (two months or more) or for those working with children or in situations where contact with blood is likely. Three injections are needed for the best protection and can be given over a three-week period if time is short for those aged 16 or over. Longer schedules give more sustained protection and are therefore preferred if time allows.

The newer injectable typhoid vaccines (eg: Typhim Vi) last for three years and are about 75% effective. Oral capsules (Vivotif) are a viable alternative for those aged six and over who are not immunosuppressed. Three capsules are given on alternate days and give a similar level and duration of protection as the injectable typhoid vaccines.

They should be encouraged unless the traveller is leaving within a few days for a trip of a week or less, when the vaccine would not be effective in time.

Meningitis ACWY vaccine may be recommended especially if you are working with children or if you are staying in the capital, Ulaanbaatar. A single dose of vaccine is effective for three years.

Vaccinations for rabies (see page 184) are ideally advised for all travellers as there is unlikely to be all the treatment needed to prevent rabies in Mongolia, if the pre-exposure vaccines have not been taken.

For those travelling in the spring and summer months who want to do forest walking then be aware of tick-borne encephalitis (see pages 184–5). There is a tick-borne encephalitis vaccine available for those aged one and above, which comprises a minimum of two doses given at least two weeks apart.

BCG is no longer routinely given in schools, and would only be recommended if you have not had one previously and are 16 or under and intend to spend at least three months in Mongolia. The vaccine may also be considered for those who are non-immune (tuberculin negative) and are at risk through their occupation and are under 35 years of age. Only people at high risk through health care work would be considered for vaccination if they are 35 or older as the vaccine is not thought to be so effective.

It is wise to go to your doctor or a travel clinic about eight weeks before departure to arrange your immunisations. For further information, see below.

TRAVEL CLINICS AND HEALTH INFORMATION A full list of current travel clinic websites worldwide is available on www.istm.org. For other journey preparation information, consult www.nathnac.org/ds/map_world.aspx (UK) or http://wwwnc.cdc.gov/travel/ (US). Information about various medications may be found on www.netdoctor.co.uk/travel. All advice found online should be used in conjunction with expert advice received prior to or during travel.

PERSONAL FIRST-AID KIT A minimal kit contains:

- Aspirin or paracetamol
- Throat lozenges
- Indigestion tablets (Alkaseltzer)
- A good drying antiseptic, eg: Savlon dry or any equivalent make
- Suncream (or sunblock – factor 30 recommended for bikers)
- Water-purifying tablets
- Insect repellent
- Antibiotics – as advised by doctor
- Hydrocortisone cream for bites or allergic skin problems
- Antifungal cream (eg: Canesten)
- Loperamide, ciprofloxacin or norfloxacin, for severe diarrhoea
- Tinidazole for giardia or amoebic dysentery
- Antibiotic eye drops, for sore, 'gritty' eyes (conjunctivitis)
- A pair of fine-pointed tweezers to remove thorns, splinters
- Tick tweezers
- Scissors
- Alcohol-based hand rub or bar of soap in plastic box
- Plasters, tubigrip support bandages
- Needle and syringe kit
- Condoms

LONG-HAUL FLIGHTS, CLOTS AND DVT   *Dr Felicity Nicholson*

Any prolonged immobility, including travel by land or air, can result in deep-vein thrombosis (DVT) with the risk of embolus to the lungs. Certain factors can increase the risk and these include:

- Previous clot or a close relative with a history
- Being over 40, with increased risk over 80 years old
- Recent major operation or varicose-veins surgery
- Cancer
- Stroke
- Heart disease
- Obesity
- Pregnancy
- Hormone therapy
- Heavy smoking
- Severe varicose veins
- Being very tall (over 6ft/1.8m) or short (under 5ft/1.5m)

A deep-vein thrombosis causes painful swelling and redness of the calf or sometimes the thigh. It is only dangerous if a clot travels to the lungs (pulmonary embolus). Symptoms of a pulmonary embolus (PE) – which commonly start three to ten days after a long flight – include chest pain, shortness of breath, and sometimes coughing up small amounts of blood. Anyone who thinks that they might have a DVT needs to see a doctor immediately.

To **prevent DVT**, try the following: keep mobile before and during the flight; move around every couple of hours; drink plenty of fluids during the flight; avoid taking sleeping pills and excessive tea, coffee and alcohol; and consider wearing flight socks or support stockings (see *www.legshealth.com*). If you think you are at increased risk of a clot, ask your doctor if it is safe to travel.

Pre-packed complete medical kits for travellers save you time and trouble in collecting the necessary components. **Lifesystems** (✆ *020 8881 8283;* e *explore@ nomadtravel.co.uk; www.lifesystems.co.uk*) First Aid Kit for Travellers is excellent; part of the set ensures that travellers carry basic medical/dental single-use items which come into direct contact with the bloodstream and may not be available when they are needed. Knowing your blood group may be helpful, though hospitals would always retest before giving type specific blood.

Alternative health supplies Many people prefer to take some alternative health remedies. Many traditional herbal medicines are well accepted today. Alternative supplies do not replace the conventional medical kit. Talk to your GP before you travel if you are in any doubt about health matters, including alternative supplies. See box *Alternative health supplies*, page 188.

HEALTH HAZARDS There are several health hazards worth mentioning, although they are, on the whole, rare. Avoid drinking raw (unpasteurised) milk, since there is brucellosis in Mongolia. It is safer to drink boiled milk, which is what you are usually offered. There is a small chance that you might come across plague – treat both with great caution. The main risk here is if you are travelling alone in remote rural areas and see a dead animal in your path. If this happens, keep your distance and steer a very wide circle around it. Never approach to see what it is. It could be an animal dying of the plague – which can be caught from marmots in an infected area by inhaling air-borne bacteria, and by flea bites. Mongolia is also considered to be high risk for rabies, so avoid contact with any warm blooded mammal.

Travellers' diarrhoea Travelling in Mongolia carries a fairly high risk of getting a dose of travellers' diarrhoea; perhaps half of all visitors will suffer and the newer you are to exotic travel, the more likely you will be to suffer. By taking precautions against travellers' diarrhoea you will also avoid typhoid, paratyphoid, cholera, hepatitis, dysentery, worms, etc. Travellers' diarrhoea is caused by the transfer of microbes from hand to mouth. You will be safe if your food has been properly cooked and arrives piping hot. The most important prevention strategy is to wash your hands before eating anything. The maxim to remind you what you can safely eat is:

PEEL IT, BOIL IT, COOK IT OR FORGET IT.

This means that fruit you have washed and peeled yourself, and hot foods, should be safe but raw foods, cold cooked foods, salads, fruit salads which have been prepared by others, ice cream and ice are all risky, and foods kept lukewarm in hotel buffets are often dangerous. That said, plenty of travellers and expatriates enjoy fruit and vegetables, so do keep a sense of perspective: food served in a fairly decent hotel in a large town or a place regularly frequented by expatriates is likely to be safe. If you are struck, see box, below, for treatment.

TREATING TRAVELLERS' DIARRHOEA   *Dr Jane Wilson-Howarth*

It is dehydration that makes you feel awful during a bout of diarrhoea and the most important part of treatment is drinking lots of clear fluids. Sachets of oral rehydration salts give the perfect biochemical mix to replace all that is pouring out of your bottom but other recipes taste nicer. Any dilute mixture of sugar and salt in water will do you good: try Coke or orange squash with a three-finger pinch of salt in to each glass (if you are salt-depleted you won't taste the salt). Otherwise make a solution of a four-finger scoop of sugar with a three-finger pinch of salt in a 500ml glass. Or add eight level teaspoons of sugar (18g) and one level teaspoon of salt (3g) to one litre (five cups) of safe water. A squeeze of lemon or orange juice improves the taste and adds potassium, which is also lost in diarrhoea. Drink two large glasses after every bowel action, and more if you are thirsty. These solutions are still absorbed if you are vomiting, but you will need to take sips at a time. If you are not eating you need to drink three litres a day plus whatever is pouring into the toilet. If you feel like eating, take a bland, high carbohydrate diet. Heavy greasy foods will probably give you cramps.

If the diarrhoea is bad, or you are passing blood, or you have a fever, you will probably need antibiotics in addition to fluid replacement. A dose of norfloxacin or ciprofloxacin repeated twice a day until better may be appropriate (if you are planning to take an antibiotic with you, note that both norfloxacin and ciprofloxacin are available only on prescription in the UK). If the diarrhoea is is accompanied by burps, one likely cause is giardia. This is best treated with tinidazole (four x 500mg in one dose, repeated seven days later if symptoms persist).

Brucellosis Mainly a disease of cattle, goats and sheep, and humans catch it through infected milk, cheese or butter. It is prevented by making sure all milk is boiled and avoiding unpasteurised milk products. Symptoms are tiredness and aching joints. It is diagnosed by tests on blood serum.

Rabies Mongolia is considered to be high risk for rabies. The virus can be carried in the saliva of all mammals, though dogs are the most likely culprits. It is passed on to man through a bite, scratch or a lick of an open wound. You must always assume any animal is rabid, even though they can look perfectly healthy, and seek medical help as soon as possible. Meanwhile scrub the wound with soap under a running tap or while pouring water from a jug. Find a reasonably clear-looking source of water (but at this stage the quality of the water is not important), then use some form of antiseptic afterwards. The soap helps stop the rabies virus entering the body and the antiseptic will guard against wound infections, including tetanus.

The post exposure treatment for those who have not had vaccine before travel includes starting a course of rabies vaccine (5 doses over about 28 days) and at the start of treatment having a preformed antibody called Rabies Immunoglobulin (RIG) put into the wound. This is very unlikely to be available anywhere in Mongolia as it is in world-wide short supply. This means that you would have to evacuate to get treatment.

Getting a pre-exposure course of rabies vaccine, which involves three doses of vaccine being given over a minimum of 21 days, means that you no longer need the RIG and would only need a couple of booster shots of vaccine given three days apart if you have an exposure. The modern cell derived rabies vaccines are well tolerated, relatively painless and a pre-exposure course is thought to last at least ten years and probably for life.

Tick-borne encephalitis This disease is spread by bites of infected ticks and is more common during the warmer spring/summer/autumn months (eg: for ramblers, scouts, forestry workers or long-term residents in rural areas). It is a viral infection of the brain, which although it has a low mortality rate (1–2%), around 10–20% of people who contract the disease are left with permanent neurological damage. In 2004, endemic areas were described next to the borders with Russia in the north of the country (the provinces of Selenge and Bulgan), and around the capital Ulaanbaatar.

Tick-borne encephalitis vaccine is now readily available in the UK (Ticovac, Ticovac junior). A primary course consists of two vaccines given a month apart and a third dose given 5–12 months later if there is a continued risk. If time is short then the first two doses can be given as little as two weeks apart.

Other precautions should be taken, whether or not you have been vaccinated. This includes using tick repellents, wearing hats, long-sleeved clothing and trousers tucked into boots. Ticks should ideally be removed as soon as possible as leaving ticks on the body increases the chance of infection. They should be removed with special tick tweezers that can be bought in good travel shops. Failing that, you can use your fingernails by grasping the tick as close to your body as possible and pulling steadily and firmly away at right angles to your skin. The tick will then come away complete as long as you do not jerk or twist. If possible douse the wound with alcohol (any spirit will do) or iodine. Irritants (eg: Olbas oil) or lit cigarettes are to be discouraged since they can cause the ticks to regurgitate and therefore increase the risk of disease. At the end of the day it is best to get a travelling companion to check you for ticks and if you are travelling with small children remember to check their heads, and particularly behind the ears. An area of spreading redness around the bite site, or a rash or fever coming on a few days or more after the bite, should stimulate a trip to the doctor.

Bubonic plague Plague is still around in Mongolia, and causes a few deaths each summer. Outbreaks are reported to the authorities, who immediately quarantine the region. Bubonic plague is a contagious disease carried by fleas. However, these days it is easily curable by antibiotics, if you discover it in time. Towards the end of summer in certain remote areas in Mongolia there may be infection, where travel is banned, while in other places there is none. It is an extremely difficult disease to stamp out since it is carried by rodents, insects and fleas. Such animals, like the marmot, which disappear underground and hibernate in burrows, make its eradication virtually impossible. In the 1960s, the reported incidences of human infection were practically nil, or went unreported, but since 1990 reported outbreaks have increased. Tourists should be aware of the risks, especially lone travellers. If you see a dying marmot, steer away. Do not even approach as this is an air-borne disease (like flu), transmitted within a short radius of an infected animal, and also transmitted by infected fleas. If you encounter any problems or need further advice get in touch with an institute for the prevention of infectious diseases in your home country, or the State Natural Nidus and Contagious Disease Fighting Board in Ulaanbaatar through the Ministry of Environment (*Khudaldaany St 5, Ulaanbaatar;* ✆ *11 326649; www.pmisgov.mn/menon*).

Sexually transmitted diseases Mongolia is not immune from sexually transmitted diseases, including HIV/AIDS. Preventative measures are essential, such as using condoms.

IN MONGOLIA
Advice for travellers Thanks to the climate (although extreme) and its small population, Mongolia is a reasonably healthy place to travel. Some of the most likely hazards in Mongolia are from severe heat or cold. There are several immediate things to watch out for, such as sore throats from the dry atmosphere – bring plenty of throat lozenges – and the possibility of stomach upsets due to a change of diet. One of the best tips is to keep your fingernails very short and wash your hands more often than usual. Countryside cooking in Mongolia usually involves boiling or steaming. Vegetables and fruit are plentiful in the capital but not in the countryside, so you may need to travel with additional fibre in a pill form. Remember to drink plenty of water.

Drinking water In Ulaanbaatar you can drink the tap water; however, as a general rule it is advisable to use chlorine dioxide water-purifying tablets, filter the water using a water filter such as Aquapure or to boil drinking water. In many parts of Mongolia, especially the mountain-forested regions, you will find springs of pure, crystal-clear water. In southern regions of the Gobi the water is often sandy and has a very high mineral content – as a result the local people suffer from stomach and tooth complaints. Wells installed in the Gobi during the socialist years have not been maintained, so water is now scarce and of dubious quality. Mining has caused damage to rivers and drinking water (particularly illegal mining).

Altitude Mongolia is located at altitude – the average is 1,580m above sea level – which affects people differently. Although Ulaanbaatar is only at 1,350m, some people are sensitive to this and will need several days to adjust, which means taking it easy on arrival and not rushing around immediately. This is usually sufficient to adjust. However, it is more likely that travellers will only experience problems over 2,000m. More adventurous trekkers may wish to visit the Khentii Nuruu, a popular and accessible mountain range to the northeast of the capital, where heights of up to 2,800m can be reached. Remember anyone, even the very fit, can suffer from altitude sickness if they try to ascend too fast. But if you have any heart or lung problems you should consult with your doctor to check that it is safe for you to go. Over 3,500m, about 50% of people will experience symptoms of altitude sickness. These may include headaches, nausea, anorexia and difficulty in sleeping. The best approach is to walk slowly and steadily and maintain a good fluid intake (at least three litres of water a day). However, if you do experience symptoms, however trivial they may seem, then you should alert someone (preferably your guide!). If the symptoms persist or you become breathless, lethargic, start to vomit, or suffer from vertigo, you should descend immediately. Even going down 500m is enough to start recovery.

If you are intending to reach heights in excess of 3,500m and a gradual ascent cannot be guaranteed (300m or less per day over 3,000m) then you may wish to use acetazolamide (Diamox). However, this drug should NEVER be used as an excuse to race up the mountain! It should only be taken after consultation with a (travel clinic) doctor and, although it may be beneficial in assisting adaptation to altitude, there may be some side effects. The current dose is 125–250mg twice a day starting three days before reaching 3,500m and continuing to maximum altitude. Most doctors prefer that you try it for two days at least two weeks before travel to see if it suits you.

One advantage of being in a 'higher' country is that there are fewer mosquitoes around and therefore no risk of malaria or Japanese encephalitis.

Medical help If you need to see a doctor while you are in Ulaanbaatar, the **Korean Friendship Hospital** (\ *11 310945;* ⊕ *working hrs 09.00–17.00 Mon–Wed (closed*

AGE-OLD REMEDIES   *Jane Blunden*

CHARCOAL Derives its medical value from its high absorbing capacity for all kinds of material, like toxins, poisons, etc. It is a simple and highly effective treatment. It may also be taken as a remedy for upset stomachs. If you fall and graze yourself badly, make a paste using charcoal and water to put on the wound immediately to help to draw out any harmful matter. Available in capsule or biscuit form (traditional Braggs charcoal biscuits in the UK). A pharmacist can advise regarding powder form.

ECHINACEA One of the most vulnerable times for travellers is at the start of their journey. Echinacea (tinture) is said to reduce infection especially if taken during long distance flights, to ward off colds and sore throats.

GARLIC To cleanse the blood; also thought to keep fleas and insects at bay. Eat one clove of raw garlic a day. Do not chew and to avoid the smell, peel a clove, prick it with a sharp instrument (fork or tip of a knife) and swallow whole with water. Also available in capsule form.

GINGER An effective natural preventative for motion sickness and any type of nausea. Also helpful because of its warming and stimulating effects when suffering from cold injury. Available in root or capsule form.

1hr for lunch), 09.00–12.30 Thu–Sat, closed Sun) is situated on Enkh Taivan (Peace Avenue), not far from the Foreign Ministry. There's a consultation fee (T5,000, roughly US$5) for any laboratory tests, and since few Mongolians can afford the fee, you will be seen quite quickly. Several staff speak English. The new **SOS Medica Mongolia** (*International Clinic, 4a Building, Big Ring Road, 15th Microdistrict; 7th Khoroo, Bayanzurkh district, Ulaanbaatar;* ✆ *11 345526, 11 464325, 11 464326, 11 464327;* m *(24hrs): 997 50967;* e *sosmedicamongolia@ mongolnet.com and admin@ sosmedica.mn*) off Chinggis Avenue (not easy to find) has expatriate staff.

Emergency rescue service In an emergency it is best to ask a Mongolian/English speaker to make the necessary calls to avoid language difficulties. In cases of medical emergency, you would be taken to the appropriate government hospital where a decision on the best action to take (treatment or repatriation) would be made by specialist staff. In the countryside some towns have a functioning hospital or health centre with qualified staff – usually a surgeon, an obstetrician and a paediatrician. However, treatment seems to follow the principle of the more the better and Mongolian health practitioners are particularly fond of injections. Sometimes medical staff are unavailable – so you may have a long wait to see a doctor in the countryside.

Pharmacies In Ulaanbaatar and most larger towns there are pharmacies selling a variety of drugs. Counter assistants may not be qualified to give advice, so ask to speak to a doctor or pharmacist if you need medical help (bring a Mongolian friend or a translator with you in case of language problems). Travel with your own first-aid kit and definitely don't forget to bring an ample supply of any regularly prescribed medicines, because they may not be available in Mongolia. The Altai Pharmacy (✆ *11 360014/361620*) in the Bayangol district, Ulaanbaatar, has Western and Mongol medicine.

INJURIES
Road accidents Car/truck/jeep accidents happen so be aware and try to reduce the risks – even if you have hired a vehicle and driver. Travel during daylight hours and listen to local advice concerning weather. Avoid high-risk situations where there is likely to be danger. When fording rivers, for example, use common sense. Check water levels with wading poles for safety. Be proactive: don't expect your driver to do all the thinking. If travelling at night, it is advisable for a passenger (or guide) to stay awake to help with navigation and to prevent the driver from falling asleep at the wheel.

Fractures For arm fractures, remove the patient's watch and rings. Splints should be applied above and below the joint to give the maximum immobilisation. Never try to mend the fracture.

Heat injury
Sunburn The intensity of UV radiation is increased by high altitudes. Watch out for the reflection of UV rays from snow, which may lead to severe sunburn. Dress to protect the skin and apply sunscreen frequently – not forgetting to apply lipsalve, which is essential for those with lip sores caused by herpes 1 (*Herpes labialis*).

Heat cramps Occur in muscles after exercise has stopped; from loss of fluid through sweat; recent ingestion of alcohol; lack of sleep; inadequate diet; lack of acclimatisation. Relieve symptoms by stretching the cramped muscle. Treat fluid loss and rest in a cool environment. Salt tablets should be avoided.

Heat exhaustion Weakness, fatigue, headache, dizziness, nausea, muscle cramps, confusion and irritability may occur. The cause is from dehydration following inadequate fluid intake especially during exercise in a hot climate. Treatment involves rest in a cool environment. Usually saline solutions are made to 0.9% saline solution because this is the same as body fluids. Instructions for making the correct rehydration fluid should be included with your medical kit; alternatively, it is available in sachet form (eg: Dioralyte).

ALTERNATIVE HEALTH SUPPLIES   *Susie Penny*

Important Please note that alternative remedies are not recommended as a substitute for conventional medicine. Always consult your doctor before making dietary changes or supplementing with any of the herbal nutrient recommendations below.

CITRICIDAL A natural all-in-one protection made from grapefruit seeds. A few drops in drinking water will help prevent infection. If you have diarrhoea, take ten drops in water three times a day. Always dilute when applying to the skin.

LACTOGEST The perfect travelling probiotic. The friendly bacteria in this formula are not sensitive to heat so there is no need for refrigeration. It will fight any foreign, unfriendly bacteria. Taken at meal times, it will boost your intestinal micro-flora and keep tummy upsets at bay. (Although Mongolian *airag* and yoghurt will more likely take care of that, they may also be the cause of it!)

CAT'S CLAW (Peruvian rainforest bark) Packed with phyto-nutrients, it is a great immune booster and helps maintain optimum energy.

SUPERGAR (GARLIC) AND B COMPLEX A natural mosquito repellent, garlic has been used for centuries as a powerful protector against infection. Eat plenty of garlic supplemented with a B-vitamin complex. Starting at least one week before the holiday the combination can act as a skin deterrent to insects like mosquitoes.

MSM CREAM AND ALOE 300 MSM is a natural source of organic sulphur. Using MSM cream before and after sunbathing reduces UV damage and helps relieve sunburn. MSM cream and aloe vera gel can also be used to accelerate wound healing and prevent scarring in the event of any holiday accidents.

VITAMIN C Nature's antihistamine. If you suffer from prickly heat or heat rash then pack some vitamin C. This natural antihistamine helps to calm down the skin's inflammatory response to heat. True Food C is recommended. It is 11 times more powerful as an antioxidant than isolated vitamin C, and sustains vitamin C levels in the blood for well over eight hours.

The above products are available from many health stores. If in doubt, contact The Nutrition Centre (*Burwash Common, East Sussex TN19 7LX;* ✆*01435 882880*).

If your transport breaks down, the general advice is to stay by the vehicle. In Mongolia it is surprising to find how many people turn up in the middle of nowhere. For safety's sake let people know your route and try not to get lost! If caught out in the cold and snow, try to follow the following advice:

- Dig in, if the snow is deep enough
- Build a windbreak
- If there is any, use vegetation such as fir-tree branches to lie on
- Make a fire (always carry a lighter or matches in your pocket)
- Put on the fire anything which will smoke to attract attention and signal for rescue. A properly prepared signal fire can be the difference between life and death
- If you have an insulation (space) blanket, use it during the daylight to reflect light as an emergency signal
- Drink. The body under stress produces more urine, and if you don't replace the fluids the body is in danger of dehydration. As a result, the danger of problems with circulation will increase
- It is important to have a positive mental attitude. Do things to keep the spirits up, such as telling jokes or having sing-songs.

Heat stroke Can occur in young, healthy individuals on a sporting holiday, when unacclimatised. The onset is rapid. Treat by removing the patient to a cool place, taking off as much of their clothing as possible, and fanning and splashing water, if available, on the body. Apply cold packs to the neck, groin and scalp.

Cold injury

Frostbite Is associated with fatigue or accidents due to prolonged exposure to the cold. Signs of frostbite are intense pain at the site – cheeks, chin, ears, nose, hands and feet – followed by a hard whitening of the skin. The best advice is to be frequently checked by travelling companions because frostnip can quickly lead to frostbite. However, if you are travelling alone, check your fingers yourself for sensation by touching the little finger to the thumb, and check all parts of your face. If caught in cold weather with frostbitten feet, it is advisable to continue walking in an attempt to reach safety.

Prevent by keeping dry, dressing sensibly, allowing for ventilation by wearing layers, wearing nothing too tight, covering your head and ears and watching out for each other. Treat frostnip by re-warming (eg: by blowing warm breath into a gloved hand). Do not rub the skin. Treat frostbite by protecting the affected part, and re-warming in water (not above 40°C).

Hypothermia Occurs when the temperature of the body core falls below 35°C. Symptoms are exhaustion, numb skin – particularly the toes and fingers – shivering, slurred speech and muscle cramps. To treat this condition, remove the sufferer to a warm, dry place out of the wind. Insulate the patient's head, because up to 70% of the body's total heat production is lost via the head. Insulation should be provided between the patient's body and the ground. Remove wet clothing and put on layers of dry clothing. Do not rub the patient or put him or her near a fire. Encourage the patient to take liquids (not alcohol) and to eat.

5

Surround the patient with human body heat, or place the patient in a warm tub of water, if available.

SAFETY

WOMEN TRAVELLERS Many women travellers have survived alone in Mongolia without too many problems – they tell the usual funny stories about being chased around a *ger* by a friendly drunk. However, on a more cautionary note, women should be aware of heavy drinking and associated behaviour problems in Mongolia, as elsewhere. There is little to no danger from a cultural and social point of view. Use common sense, and when hitchhiking do not accept a lift if the driver's breath reeks of alcohol. Sometimes in isolated situations you have little choice but to accept the first lift that comes along – that being the case, the consoling thought is that there is very little to hit in the wide expanse of the Mongolian steppe except, in order of seriousness, a large boulder, a deep rut or a dried-up riverbed!

ADVICE IF IN TROUBLE If a foreign visitor is arrested and taken to a police station, the visitor is entitled to make a telephone call. The police must contact the visitor's representative embassy within 24 hours of the arrest.

Lost passport Take extra passport-size photographs with you and a photocopy of the main pages of your passport, and a separate record of all details. An emergency one-way document can be issued by your embassy should there be insufficient time to replace a passport. Report the loss immediately to the local police. Report theft to the Ulaanbaatar Robbery Unit (\ *11 318783*) or Tourist information (\ *70 101011*).

Lost cash Western Union (*Ulaanbaatar office* ✆ *11 450444*) is a quick and efficient way to have cash sent from home.

Lost credit cards and lost mobile phones Inform your bank immediately of lost cards (keep a record of details) and please don't forget that mobile phones are as important to report stolen as soon as possible – especially if you are under contract to a provider (keep a separate record of emergency numbers).

Medical emergencies Documentation – give the hospital photocopies and not the originals of your passport and other travel documents. If possible, take away any notes or X-rays when you are discharged. Keep all receipts.

Personal possessions Don't bring valuables and keep jewellery to a minimum.

WHAT TO TAKE

> Pack courage in your suitcase – live as the local people do, if they have survived – most likely you will too!
>
> *Ella Maillart, Swiss author, traveller and photographer*

Packing advice Mongolia is a country of extremes and what you take will depend on where, and when, you intend to travel, and the way in which you travel – with a backpack, on an expedition, on an organised tour, or on business. However, knowing what to pack is a great help, especially if packing in a hurry. Checklists are provided below for seasonal travel and special activities such as riding tours or expeditions.

There is one word you need to know when packing: reduce. Lay out everything you intend to bring and reduce it. Whatever way you travel basic packing principles are the same. When it is cold, put on layers: cotton, silk and cashmere … it sounds extravagant but it's not, as you will find plenty of cashmere jumpers, jackets and mittens at wonderful prices in Mongolia. In winter, hotels in Ulaanbaatar are overheated, so wear lightweight clothes and bring a down-filled coat. You can always buy leather gloves and a fur hat for outdoors locally. In summer, the lighter you pack the better, remembering a cashmere wrap or a fleece for the cool evenings. Select long jumpers and long jackets that cover your bottom as you may spend more time than you think sitting on the ground! If you are thinking of trekking it is essential to bring a backpack; otherwise travel with lightweight luggage and a daysack. If on expedition, bring steel containers/boxes with locks for main supplies, which can withstand rough conditions and be left in storage with safety.

CLOTHING

For spring, summer and autumn Tracksuit (to relax in), T-shirts, shirts (long- and short-sleeved – linen is the best material in hot or cold weather), cotton polo-neck, cotton slacks, shorts (watch the backs of your legs for sunburn), fleece or cashmere jumper, dress or skirt (women), small scarves (cotton and silk), lightweight jacket and tie (men), cotton and light woollen socks, leather boots (tried and tested), trainers, lightweight shoes or sandals, sunhat (wide-brimmed), large cotton scarf or sarong (acts as towel, neck guard, sleeping wrap), 'long johns' (doubles for nightwear), small towel, lightweight poncho or alternative wet-weather gear (as below), waterproof suit (trousers and jacket).

WAIST POUCH Keep your passport, credit cards, cash and a list of emergency addresses in your waist pouch.

TRAVEL PACK Put in your travel pack: airline tickets, four–six passport-sized photographs and a photocopy of the main pages of your passport, driving licence, insurance documents, travellers' cheques, bank account details, credit-card numbers (and expiry dates), a copy of all the relevant email addresses and telephone numbers, and a copy of medical and optical prescriptions. Leave a second copy at home just in case you lose everything when travelling!

LUGGAGE Tag your bags. The essential thing is to travel light so don't pack too much. The final word in this section is to travel with an unencumbered mind – ie: leave your worries behind!

> Like the winds of the sea are the ways of fate,
> As we voyage along through life:
> 'Tis the set of a soul that decides its goal,
> And not the calm and the strife.
>
> *E W Fox*

For winter You can buy Mongolian felt boots and a fleece-lined *deel* on arrival in addition to the warm clothes you bring. Wear layers of clothing: silk, wool and cotton under fleeces, furs and waterproofs. Bring thermal underwear, cotton shirts, polar jacket and trousers, fleece and fleece trousers, a selection of cotton and woollen socks, leather boots (worn in and comfortable), gaiters (if skiing), ski gloves (with length of tape attached to each glove – pin on to coat to prevent losing), silk or cashmere under gloves, woollen hat with ear flaps, wet-weather gear (waterproof and windproof), good clothes for hotels. Otherwise the same as summer (see above).

ITEMS FOR ALL SEASONS
- First-aid kit (see page 181)
- Money belt or neck pouch (for passport, documents and cash)
- Washbag/personal kit (including some often-needed items such as eyedrops, throat lozenges, moisturising lotion, shampoo, insect repellent, sunblock, lipbalm, nail clippers, toothpicks)
- Day bag (to carry water bottle, water-purification tablets, camera equipment, extra films or accessories for digital camera)
- Water bottle (one-litre size)
- High-protection sunglasses (two pairs)
- Extra prescription glasses (if worn)
- Torch and extra batteries
- Maps, magnifying sheet and map folder; compass, whistle
- Notebook, pencils
- Guidebook, phrasebook
- Swiss army knife or equivalent (with blade, scissors, can opener, screwdriver, corkscrew and file)
- Reliable watch (with alarm)

- Bio-friendly soap, toilet roll, sachet of clothes-washing powder, sealable plastic bags (for wet clothes)
- Identification labels (to attach to items if travelling in a group)
- Mini-sewing kit (scissors, needle and thread, safety pins)
- Ear plugs, eye shades
- Light binoculars
- Snacks (eg: energy bars, energy powder that you add to water, glucose tablets, boiled sweets, chocolate)
- Matches and lighter; candles (in case of power failure)
- Insulation (space) blanket (for warmth and emergency use).

Extras
- Song book (songs or poems you might like to recite)
- Paints and sketch book
- Digital camera
- Inflatable travelling pillow (if camping)
- Mobile phone or satellite phone (mobile phones now work in more remote areas but not always!)
- Universal plug (if you bring a laptop)
- A car cigarette-lighter adaptor lead, useful on expedition for battery recharge, or a recharger.

PRESENTS FOR YOUR MONGOLIAN HOSTS You will, no doubt, be overwhelmed by the hospitality shown to you by Mongolian families. Giving money to show your appreciation can sometimes offend, but gifts are much appreciated. Bring a small bag of various useful and novel items as gifts for people of all ages. The ideal present in rural areas is a portrait photograph of your hosts, standing or sitting formally, wearing their best *deels* in front of their home. It is more effective if taken by a Polaroid camera. The delight on receiving the photograph, the marvelling looks as it develops, and the following peals of laughter definitely make it worth investing in this camera. Polaroid films are highly sensitive to heat and light so wrap them in foil. Watch out for batteries and camera equipment in the cold. Keep cameras well insulated, so the mechanisms do not freeze. Some other gift ideas are frisbees, balloons (children love them), small packs of crayons or felt markers (as a change from standard pens), tapes (folk music from home), postcards, chocolate, dried fruits, boiled sweets, ribbons and pretty clips for the girls' hair, pillow cases with brightly coloured embroidery, threads for the women, cotton handkerchiefs, small penknives or snuff for the men (buy in UB), sea shells. Photos of the Queen (Her Majesty Queen Elizabeth) and the Dalai Lama are popular. Presents of food are appreciated – staples or unusual tins.

TRIPS – AND WHAT TO TAKE
Camping and hiking In addition to the clothes and essential items listed above, bring: backpack (with a waterproof liner – pack light and balance well), sleeping bag (three or four season), three-season mat for sleeping (alternatively use local felt or fleece), tent (sturdy and free-standing: three-person Terra Nova tents are recommended), camp stove and cooking pot, mug, dish, knife, fork and spoon set, tin foil (to protect films and for baking fish), thermal mountain blanket, waterproof cape (fleece lined in winter, lightweight in summer), talcum powder (invaluable to prevent blisters if hiking in summer), first-aid kit (including blister pack; see page 181), one-litre water bottle (metal army-type, or Sigg water bottle),

water-purifying tablets or system, night lights, kit bags for camping equipment and food supplies.

Biking On a biking tour, a follow-up vehicle usually carries all the camping equipment and supplies. Bike specialists will provide bikes, although many experienced bikers choose to bring their own saddles and pedals. The following are the basic essentials: bum bag (waterproof and padded; avoid bum bags with water bottles, as they bounce around and may damage maps), front cycling bag (to attach to bicycle; front bags usually have a plastic front cover for maps), water bottle, tools, wet-weather clothing (trousers and tops), padded cycling gloves (quick-dry material), long cycling trousers, helmet, helmet torch, cotton underwear, panty-liners (ladies), sun screen (high factor 30+ and total block for face), protective sunglasses (with plutonite lenses, for high-velocity impact). Bikers are recommended to pack the following in their first-aid kits: insect repellent, plasters, Vaseline (for saddle sores), arnica cream (for bruises), ibuprofen (for pain relief), heat cream (for backache and sore muscles), anti-fungal cream (for athlete's foot), antibiotics (a broad spectrum type such as amoxycillin; metronidazole is useful for anaerobic infections, including dental and vaginal infections and for acute amoebic dysentery and giardia, dehydration sachets (for diarrhoea), imodium tablets (for diarrhoea; very strong, use only in emergencies), anti-bacterial gel (for washing hands – no water needed), wet wipes (they become your best friend). For further information, see *Cycling/motorbiking*, pages 178–9.

Horse riding Comfortable riding trousers, leather boots with leather or rubber soles (you may find yourself walking so it is vital to have comfortable footwear), low 'chaps' (to prevent chafing inner thighs), poncho (if it's one that rustles, beware when mounting your Mongolian pony – you may not reach the saddle before the animal bolts), plastic bags (for wet clothes), extra mosquito repellent, hard hat, riding gloves, head torch, protective sunglasses (with a strong tie to prevent them flying off when galloping).

Fishing Warm clothing (dress in layers), chest waders (experienced anglers only), windbreaker/fishing jacket, chamois flannel or fleece vests, hiking boots (waterproof), fishing hat with visor, woolly hat, fishing mitts, polarised sunglasses (two pairs), a head net to protect against midges, camera and film (insulated and waterproof-packed), waterproof tackle bag. Pack the rods in tubes, and bring a wading rod, forceps or pliers to remove hooks from fishes' mouths, scales, a ruler and mousetraps!

NEW TRAVEL GISMOS

FOOT WARMERS Insoles which keep your feet warm for up to four hours, slipped between sole and sock. Ask at UK stockists.

ZEISS COMPACT BINOCULARS See www.warehouseexpress.com.

NIGHT WRITER PEN With a built in torch that illuminates the page: see www.magellans.co.uk.

PAINTING KIT Windsor and Newton Cotman Travel Bag containing watercolour paints, brushes, pads and other materials. UK stockists (☎ 020 8424 3253).

BROUGHT FROM HOME
Marmite – for the very British – perks up a fried egg no end!
Tabasco, chilli sauce or mustard – if you find boiled mutton hard to swallow
Good-quality fruit or green tea
Vanilla pods – to take the edge off curdled milk
Good-quality coffee
Vitamin tablets
Mazola with dried fruit and nuts – to supplement bland porridge oats.

TO PICK UP IN MONGOLIA
Porridge oats
Nuts, raisins
Rice
Stock cubes
Instant soup
Noodles – Mongolian spaghetti or packets of Chinese soup noodles
Garlic
Onions
Spices – chillies, bay leaves, small bottle of soy sauce
Black tea – comes in large blocks from China
Instant coffee – individual servings
Sugar and salt
Some tinned fish or meat
Boiled sweets
Chocolate
Supplemented by local meat and dairy products – buy along the way.

EXPEDITION SUPPLIES

Food If you are starting your travels from Ulaanbaatar provisions can be bought from numerous shops and markets (the State Department Store has a very good Western supermarket). The Black Market, also known as Ulaanbaatar Central Market, has everything you need from food to kitchenware, clothes, boots, camping kit, saddles, etc. There are certain items that are best brought from home – the little luxuries that make life kinder

For expedition food supplies you will usually shop in Ulaanbaatar and supplement your provisions in country markets along the way. Mongolia's staple diet (whatever the season) is a rich mixture of meat and dairy products.

Best-buy tents Expedition tents are available at a range of prices from the following retailers and manufacturers: Blacks (*www.blacks.co.uk*), Go Outdoors (*www.gooutdoors.co.uk*), Millets (*www.millets.co.uk*), Recreational Equipment Inc (*www.rei.com*), Robens (*www.robens.de*), Snow and Rock (*www.snowandrock.com*) and Terra Nova (*www.terra-nova.co.uk*). Price and weight are important considerations when choosing a tent, but also think about bulk, ease of pitching and stability in high winds.

MAPS Under the Manchu Empire areas of Mongol tribal pasturelands were recorded as early as 1686. Specific pasturelands were allocated to individual Mongol tribes to prevent territorial disputes and piles of stones marked the frontiers. The

Practical Information   WHAT TO TAKE

5

Western map-making process began in the second half of the 19th century, when explorers like Nikolai Przewalski made original maps and freehand drawings during their explorations in Mongolia.

Maps of Mongolia may be examined at the British Library and at the Royal Geographic Society in London. Stanfords Travel and Book Shop (*12–14 Long Acre, London WC2E 9LP;* ✆ *020 7836 1321; www.stanfords.co.uk*) provides the most up-to-date travel maps of Mongolia. *Travel Map of Mongolia* 1:1,200,000, by International Travel Maps and Books (2000), costs £7.95.

The latest tourist travel maps can be bought in Ulaanbaatar at the major hotels and in bookstores in town. The University Library in Ulaanbaatar contains many early maps.

MONEY AND BUDGETING

During the update of this guide the exchange rate between the US$ and the Tögrög moved by some 25%: currency rates need to be checked by travellers prior to visiting Mongolia. Make sure to change money at banks in Ulaanbaatar as it is impossible to change money in the Mongolian countryside. Pounds sterling are not used locally.

Since 2013 the practice of using US dollars for cash payments is in the process of being phased out. However, in the countryside it is wise to carry both US dollars and Tögrög. Credit card payments are unaffected.

CREDIT CARDS Credit Cards are widely accepted. Larger bills (in most hotels and some restaurant and shops can be paid by credit card, especially in Ulaanbaatar. American Express and Visa are the most-used credit cards, if you need to draw cash. It is advisable to have local currency in your wallet in shops and bazaars; otherwise you can settle your UB hotel bills and most major restaurant bills by credit card. Hotels will change US dollars cash. In the countryside even tourist *ger* camps will not accept travellers' cheques in place of cash. If you arrive in Mongolia at a weekend with travellers' cheques, you may find you have no time to exchange them for cash if setting out for the countryside immediately. So bring cash which your hotel (or a local bank in office hours) will change.

BANKS Branch offices have opened in aimag (provincial) centres. Banks open, in general, 09.30–12.30 and 14.00–15.00 weekdays, and 09.30–11.30 on Saturday. Note that when changing money you should ensure that you give or receive crisp, undamaged dollar notes. Just in case you don't find a bank again, change money at the airport on arrival or in UB before heading off to the aimags. For banks in Ulaanbaatar, see page 252.

TIPPING On tour it is recommended to provide a generous tip (which supplements local wages and is in keeping with general expectations). Some suggestions (for a two- to three-week trip):

- US$60–100 for the cook per group
- US$60–100 per group to each guide, interpreter or Mongolian staff member on the trek
- US$100 per group to each driver, a higher amount to the head driver.

Use your discretion as to how to compensate helpers and trek leaders on a day-to-day basis.

It used to be the case that a barter arrangement was considered to be a fairer way to compensate herders for their kindness and hospitality. Nowadays people expect cash if they have gone to the trouble to provide horses, meals and other facilities that have overheads. This is not spoiling the market or ruining hospitality, it is simply being fair. Tipping in restaurants and hotels is up to the individual: 10% never goes wrong here, and would be fair in other circumstances as well.

BUDGETING The cost of living in Mongolia is lower than in Europe and the USA so your dollars will stretch further. Expect to pay the tourist price for services and transport. So, for example, internal airline tickets will cost about double for foreigners than for Mongolian nationals, and foreigners must pay in US dollars. Standard tourist costs for accommodation, food and drink, entertainment and transport are listed below. Do note, however, that factors such as rising petrol prices mean that such costs are subject to change.

Taxis T500–700 per kilometre.

Airport transfer in Ulaanbaatar (by taxi) T28,500 per vehicle (tourist price).

Hotels in Ulaanbaatar Top hotel US$300 (single), US$500 (twin); good/medium hotel US$95 (single), US$200 (twin); guesthouse/small hotel US$20–30 (single), US$30–45 (twin).

Countryside hotel US$20 (standard single), US$20–50 (twin), US$60 (de luxe).

City restaurant T6,000 (plus tip). You can get a good two-course meal for T30,000 (US$21) in many Ulaanbaatar restaurants, hotel restaurants tend to charge more; credit cards are widely accepted in the city.

Museum entrance T2,000–5,000

Theatre performance Around T14,000

Cinema T3,000 (latest releases); T2,000 (English-speaking video shown on large TV)

Bars in UB Beer prices T3,000–4,000; whisky around T11,300 per glass (10cl); vodka T5,000 per glass

Nightclub/disco entrance Average T11,300 (double in some places)

Food in UB Hamburger T5,000; roast chicken and chips T8,500; pizza T10,000; lasagne T6,500

Countryside canteen From T2,000 per plate, eg: mutton and rice

Buses in UB (flat rate) T600 per ticket; trolley bus T200

Buses (long-distance) T20,000 to Kharkhorin

Internal flights Around US$500 (return) Ulaanbaatar to Khovd; US$350 (return) to Mörön

Train fares Beijing to Ulaanbaatar (single) RMB600 (Chinese currency: renminbi) (US$95) hard-sleeper; RMB800 (US$130) soft-sleeper. From Ulaanbaatar to Beijing (single) around T70,000 hard-sleeper; T95,000 soft-sleeper. The above prices are approximate and subject to change. Experience has shown it has been difficult to date for individuals to buy rail tickets; should a travel company purchase tickets on your behalf, add at least 50% to the above rail prices. For this edition to give a general idea of costs to travellers from the UK in pounds sterling, the train from Moscow to Beijing will be around £470 one way on Train 4 in hard class (four-bed sleeper), up to around £700 for a two-bed sleeper. To stop in Mongolia it increases the cost of the ticket by a small amount. To journey from Irkutsk to UB costs around £150 and from UB to Beijing around £140 (prices quoted in sterling are via an agent). Don't forget to add between £100–200 for visas depending which visas you need. Budget also for one overnight hotel stay at around £40 – in Moscow for example.

Student travellers Students can get around Mongolia (excluding flights) for T43,000 a day making all their own arrangements, sharing transport, eating at local canteens, camping in the countryside and staying in guesthouses and local hotels in UB and provincial centres. Time is an important factor in these calculations. As one student traveller put it, unless you are on an organised tour, allow one month to do any major journey.

Organised tours For those on organised tours, which include accommodation in good hotels/*ger* camps, itineraries, guides, interpreters, transport, meals, sightseeing, horses and so on, prices will vary depending on the size of the group. A typical tour for two people might cost US$250 per person, per day, whereas the same tour for a group of ten people would cost US$110 per day.

Day trips May be budgeted at US$100+ (lower if sharing) per person, per day, to include vehicle, driver and guide. *Ger* **camps**, including food, may be budgeted at US$70 per person, per day (average price is US$45–50). The rate is reduced by the size of a group and the length of the stay. Organised **riding tours** cost around US$2,225 per person for nine days, excluding international flights.

GETTING AROUND

Transport systems in Mongolia failed to develop in the same way as they have developed in the West for the simple reason that the horse and the camel are the most natural and effective means of travel in a land like Mongolia. This has resulted in an almost total lack of road and bridge building. Rivers were more easily forded on horseback and camels and horses could travel faster than any other means of transport in the 19th and early 20th centuries. But, with the arrival of the first American motor vehicles in the 1920s, followed by Soviet cars, jeeps and lorries from the 1930s and increasing numbers of Japanese motorbikes in the 1990s, things are beginning to change and motorised transport is threatening to replace the nomads' four-legged friends.

BY AIR
Domestic flights The name of Mongolian Airlines group officially changed to **Hunnu Airlines** (*Chinggis Av 10-1, Sukhbaatar district, Ulaanbaatar-48;* \ *7000 1111 (reservations); www.hunnuair.com*) in 2013 due to the conflict with name of MIAT. Hunnu Airlines uses Fokker 50 aircraft and their performance is good.

Local airlines In addition there are some private local airlines – **Tas** (✎ *11 379657*) and **Hangard** (✎ *11 311333*) – flying on domestic routes. Note that on internal flights the luggage allowance is restricted to 5–10kg; it varies depending on the number of people on the flight. Two new airlines now operate, catering for internal flights (and some international flights) in Mongolia:

Aero Mongolia (*PO Box 105, Buyant-Ukhaa Airport, Ulaanbaatar 34;* ✎*11 983212/ 330373;* e *management@aeromongolia.mn; www.aeromongolia.mn*) was set up in 2002 by the national carrier MIAT. Flights on its Fokker 50 and 100 aircraft operate to domestic destinations in Mongolia, including: Choibalsan, Mörön, Ölgii, Ulaangom, Oyutolgoi Airport, and Uliastai.

Eznis Airways (*Headquarters: 4F, 8 Zovkhis Bldg, Seoul St, Ulaanbaatar 211213;* ✎*11 313689; at Chinggis Khan International Airport:* ✎*11 283201;* e *feedback@eznis.com: www.eznis.com*) currently operates scheduled and charter flights to 14 destinations, including: Khövsgöl, Ömnögobi, Dornod, Bayankhongor, Uvs, Khovd, Uliatsai (Zavkhan), Tosontsengel, Oyutolgoi and Ölgii.

BY ROAD The red lines marked on many maps of Mongolia suggest that there is an established network of main roads, but few Mongolian roads have a hard surface.That is starting to change – however, most highways or paved roads are in or between the main towns. Otherwise, what you drive on are simply sets of wheel ruts which criss-cross the countryside and following them can be hazardous, particularly after dark. Driving anywhere outside the towns takes a long time and is often rough and uncomfortable.

Most Mongolians leave the city by various modes of transport ranging from bus and train to minivan, shared jeep or taxi. Hitching rides is considered a normal occurrence in Mongolia, especially in the countryside, when often there is no public transport, but expect to pay a nominal sum for your ride. Travelling overland by jeep is the best option to reach the more remote areas, and a network of roads (mainly unpaved) connects the 21 aimags to the capital, and urban areas to smaller centres and remote settlements throughout the country. You may end up travelling with the help of a compass across virgin territory in the most remote regions – following no roads or tracks.

RUSSIAN JEEPS – A WORD OF WARNING *Philadelphia Stockwell*

If you are faint-hearted do check with your tour company if you are going out into the countryside that their vehicles are comparatively modern and have seat belts. Some years ago we found ourselves in a very ancient Russian jeep, which I gather has the benefit of being cheap and easy to fix, but it had no seat belts, which was hairy enough in the constant traffic jams of UB, but over the snow-covered steppe where the roads had vanished and vehicles, such as they were, were all over the shop, it was quite the most frightening journey of my life! The other problem with our particular jeep was that one of the doors, the one beside me, kept flying open. I had to hang on to it for seven hours from UB to Kharkhorin. I could have done with a roll of duct tape to fix it! Although modern 4x4s are now the norm, when thinking back to the older vehicles, they were often pretty reliable and definitely easier to mend on the roadside!

To experience the Mongolian spirit, take a journey by public transport (bus or jeep). You will be jostled and tossed together with your fellow passengers over many kilometres of bone-rattling roads and you'll find yourself clinging on to one another for mutual comfort and survival. It is somewhat disconcerting to see abandoned or broken-down trucks in remote areas. Do not be alarmed; Mongolians are helpful, hospitable and resourceful and will always come to the rescue should your vehicle break down, although you may experience long hours of waiting by the roadside for a spare part to arrive. To cheer yourself up on particularly monotonous sections of the journey, the tedium may be broken by singing traditional 'long songs', which provide great entertainment when everyone joins in. However, it can be unsettling to discover that your driver navigates according to his instinct and you may find that you are heading in the wrong direction, or about to strike a huge pot-hole. Somehow a sixth sense always seems to rescue Mongolian drivers, just in time to avert real disasters. In the summer months the rivers tend to flood and the search for a safe crossing point may divert you dozens of kilometres from your intended itinerary.

Car rental Depending on the car, expect to pay T50,000–150,000 per day for a car and driver; 4x4s are at the expensive end, and some tour companies rent motorcycles at a cost of anything between T50,000 and T100,000. See page 236.

From Ulaanbaatar to other aimags by bus There are two **long-distance bus terminal**s in Ulaanbaatar: buses to the western and southern provinces depart from the Dragon Centre in Songinokhairkhan district, and from Auto station in Bayanzürkh district to the Eastern provinces.

The **western bus station**, known as the Dragon Centre, is located in the western part of Ulaanbaatar city; from the city centre take bus numbers 5, 23, 26, 27, 36 and 41. It takes 30–40 minutes to get there. The **eastern bus station**, known as

Bayanzürkh (Auto station) is located in the eastern suburbs of UB. To get there it takes 30–40 minutes from the city centre by local bus, numbers 27, 32 and 14.

You will require local assistance and a translator to get to grips with the bus system. In the station, discover where and when your bus departs and buy your ticket. Always check the destination sign (name of the terminus) at the front of the bus before departure. When travelling by long-distance bus it is essential to realise that it is not the easiest way to travel, so you need time on your side and plenty of patience.

Timing Long-distance bus journeys are difficult to arrange without the help of a Mongolian-speaking guide. The fare will cost slightly less if booked in advance, rather than on the day, and don't expect the buses to leave according to the time printed on a bus schedule.

TRAVELLING INDEPENDENTLY AS A SMALL GROUP

Marianne Heredge

For four women travelling together, I reckoned that the best way to get about would be to hire a couple of jeeps with drivers. We were all limited to three weeks' annual leave and had been warned about the problems of getting about by public transport in Mongolia. I had heard that the roads were difficult to use without someone with local knowledge, so it would not make sense for us to expect to hire a jeep and drive it ourselves. Emailing the list of travel agents in Ulaanbaatar nearly all of them responded with various ideas. Quite a few had packages that they could offer us, which they also provide to a number of foreign tourist companies. As we didn't want a package, one of the agents (MAT) stood out as seeming more flexible. Working out a circuit from UB to visit some of the places of interest in central Mongolia, we 'discussed', via email, routes and various options. The deal was two jeeps with drivers, an English-speaking guide and a cook for our three-week trip. Self-sufficient and camping most of the time, we used our own tents, as we were advised they would be more reliable. To illustrate this, for most of the trip the cook and guide were very lucky that it did not rain much, as whoever had packed their igloo tent had forgotten the flysheet. When visiting towns, we stayed in a variety of hotels or tourist *gers* for a few days along the way.

It was an excellent way to see the countryside and to meet local people in the towns, villages and tiny nomad settlements. Very conscious of how unspoilt the countryside is and how much we were a novelty as tourists, we were very keen to try to minimise our impact. On leaving our campsites, hopefully no-one would have been able to detect much evidence of our stay. On visiting families in their *gers*, we were very careful to respect their customs and avoid abusing their hospitality.

The roads, if they can be called that, were mainly mud tracks that wriggled into the distance. It never ceased to amaze how our drivers never got lost. In any vehicle other than a jeep, many of the routes would have been inaccessible. Twice, the jeeps briefly took turns to sink in some mud, but after some mysterious adjustments to the wheels, we were off again without any problem. A few times we passed buses stopped by the roadside, with the passengers sitting nearby watching as huddles of men changed tyres or poked around underneath the stricken vehicles.

5

Travel in Mongolia is haphazard and to be played by ear with great patience and understanding if one wants to do ANYTHING out of the ordinary and go to out-of-the-way places, like we did.

MY TIPS

* We stayed at the Puma Hotel in Ulaanbaatar, which was excellent and very central.
* When travelling in the countryside and you need to hire a car, get an owner-driver vehicle, not one driven by a hired driver to whom it does not belong. Breakdowns are sure to occur all along the non-existent tracks and only the owner will know his own car well enough to be able to conjure up repairs.
* Beware of mosquitoes at beautiful campsites near water!
* Rather than hiking miles in flat terrain to go to the loo, do as the local women do and have a voluminous skirt/gown/raincoat to crouch in.
* Russian or Western saddles are usually available but it would be worth taking one's own stirrup leathers and leaving them there; possibly stirrups too. Chaps are also useful.
* Head-torches are essential – then give them as presents along with some extra batteries; self-inflating mattress for camping, etc.
* Tserentours (*www.tserentours.com*) (Rik who is Dutch and his Mongolian wife Tseren were most helpful and patient) made travel arrangements, although the journey and itinerary was self-arranged.

On the day of travel, go to the main bus station, the Dragon Centre (if heading west) or Bayanzürkh (if heading east), to wait for the bus. As a rule, buses (and particularly shared jeeps) leave when full, and not before, although buses do try to run on schedule. It's best to go to the bus station on the day you wish to travel, relax and be prepared to wait ('Mongolian style')!

Bus schedules are given on page 441.

Shared jeeps and minibuses Most tourists prefer to use shared jeeps or minibuses, which leave from the bus station when full. Minibuses are slightly more expensive, but much more comfortable to travel in than long-distance buses and you are guaranteed a seat. They depart in the afternoons and service the aimags surrounding the capital, although they also travel longer distances. The normal rate from Ulaanbaatar to Dalanzadgad in the South Gobi is around T20,000. Rates for Russian jeeps vary around T800 per kilometre. Japanese jeeps are more expensive and cost around T1,500 per kilometre. Long-distance mini-vans and jeeps depart from the eastern and western bus stations.

Trucks Passenger trucks (lorries with seating in the back for passengers) leave UB from the long-distance bus station from the southwest corner. They leave when the truck is full of passengers and not before. Costs vary and are best negotiated with the driver. The standard rate of T250 per kilometre applies and indicates the cost; hitchhikers usually negotiate costs with the truck driver; these amounts vary hugely depending on the journey. In any event, expect to pay a contribution for your hitchhike.

Taxis Taxis are limited to paved roads and well-worn rough tracks. They travel at speed around the city and can be hailed by raising a hand. You will be surprised at how many private cars turn into taxis at the wave of a hand. The fare is worked out at the end of the ride by the car's mileage or kilometre clock. Expect to pay T500 per kilometre in the city, T400–700 for longer trips – negotiate petrol costs and distance with the driver. Tipping is optional. Some taxi drivers are very helpful and will offer to act as your local guide.

BY WATER Lake Khövsgöl and some of Mongolia's northern rivers are navigable during the summer but are rarely used as transport routes. You can hire a fishing boat on Lake Khövsgöl for between US$5–10 an hour.

ACCOMMODATION

When planning your itineraries from base camp it is well to know that there are very few hotels of top/medium standard outside Ulaanbaatar. People rely on *ger* accommodation – which is excellent – or they camp. For hotels in Ulaanbaatar, see pages 240–2. Provincial hotels, although not as frequently used as *ger* camps, are listed in each province in *Part Two* of the guide. A standard cost for camping in Mongolia in *ger* accommodation is around US$20, plus meals (breakfast US$6, lunch US$10, supper US$9) – in total around US$50 per person per day. Near Ulaanbaatar this may increase to around US$120pp for accommodation and meals.

TOURIST *GER* CAMPS In the bigger towns and cities there are some new hotels, and older ones are being upgraded. Note though, many do not have constant water, food and heating. Outside Ulaanbaatar by far the best option is to stay in *ger* camps. These have been set up in the most popular places to cater for travellers, both Mongolian and foreign. Most of the camps run during the summer only; in some camps *gers* are taken down in October until the following spring. This depends on the weather. However, there are *ger* camps near Ulaanbaatar which are open all year round and are used by hikers or cross-country skiers during the winter.

These traditional *gers* have brightly coloured furniture and a wood-burning stove in the centre (if it's cold they provide wood). Each *ger* has two, three or four beds. Most camps have a toilet and shower block nearby with hot water some or all of the time. Nearly all camps have a restaurant (often itself a large *ger*) where they serve Mongolian and European food. Vegetarians have to give the cook plenty of notice or they'll end up with the same as everyone else but minus the meat.

The cost of staying in a *ger* varies around US$45 or US$65 per night and includes three meals. They'll often pack a picnic lunch for you if you ask, which is useful since you may be several hundred miles from the nearest shop. At some places you can make a deal just to pay for the bed (anything from US$10+, a separate *ger* will

5

ACCOMMODATION PRICE RANGES		
Approximate price per person in a standard double room.		
$$$$	Upper range	US$120–200
$$$	Mid range	US$90–120
$$	Budget	US$50–90
$	Guesthouse/hostel/country hotel	Less than US$50

In my view, staying in hotels outside Ulaanbaatar would be inappropriate. However, as hotels of a tourist level barely exist elsewhere, *ger* camps are the only option.

Camps generally comprise around 30 *gers*, a washroom block and a dining *ger* or building. The *ger* construction of a wooden frame covered by felt and an outer layer of canvas is the same as the nomads' version. Most have two beds, though some contain three or more, and there are sometimes a few single *gers*, with just one bed. These are made up with duvets, with freshly laundered linen. Small towels are provided. The brightly painted furnishings include a table, bedside tables and an occasional chair. There are usually a few hooks, a coat hanger or two, and a mirror. Wood-burning stoves are lit by staff upon request, or automatically if the weather is cold. It is advisable not to attempt this oneself in case the ventilation roof flap has not been adjusted. Staff open and close these as appropriate. If rain starts during the night staff will go around the camp closing all roof flaps, which can be a little alarming if one isn't expecting it! For further ventilation a section of the 'skirt' of the *ger* can be hitched up at ground level. Most camps have generators which run from sundown till around 23.00, although there is currently a big push to change to solar energy. The light in one's *ger* will flash several times before the generator goes off, giving you a few seconds to locate your torch. Some *gers* contain an electrical socket to recharge batteries. Staff can supply adaptors, or will recharge batteries behind the scenes. Flasks of hot water are provided either automatically or upon request in the evening, and the water is still hot by the morning. It is therefore worthwhile bringing your own coffee and tea.

cost around US$30) and then you can bring your own food or just choose what you want from the restaurant menu and pay accordingly.

The *gers* are a really enjoyable and authentic form of accommodation; they are also warm in the winter and cool in summer. The main disadvantage is trying to book beforehand, and also you can't be sure of the standard of service until you get there. New *ger* camps are springing up all the time, and unprofitable ones closed down. At the height of the tourist season some camps are full, and at other times there may be no food or staff if they are not expecting you. The best way round this is to book through a local travel company, who would have the most up-to-date information on new camps and non-existent ones. It would be quite irritating to drive for several days on bad roads to reach a particular *ger* camp, only to arrive to find it gone!

The telephone numbers given in *Part Two* of this guide are often not the *ger* camps themselves, but the Ulaanbaatar offices of the companies operating the camps. It's worth saying that the availability of contact telephone numbers is patchy – *ger* camps in the countryside don't generally have telephones on site for public use. People use their own mobile or satellite phones. Sometimes there are several *ger* camps owned by different companies situated in the same area (eg: Moltsog Els).

COUNTRYSIDE HOTELS All the provincial centres provide hotel accommodation (listed in *Part Two*). The hotels are often pretty tatty and you cannot always rely on the services of food and water – often because of matters beyond the hoteliers' control, such as transport, the availability of items, delivery because of weather conditions and so forth. Standard country hotels cost from T20,000–100,000 per person per night.

The washrooms are fairly basic. Water is generally heated with wood or dung fires or solar panels so isn't dependent on the generator. However, it is advisable to check what hours the hot water is available. One can usually scruff around and find some soap, but it is safest to bring your own.

There is little or no choice at meal times, though efforts are made to accommodate special requirements. Food is good, wholesome home cooking. A limited selection of very acceptable wine is available, as are beer and soft drinks. However, they are seldom well chilled as the generator is switched off during the daytime.

Often entertainment is provided in the evenings, for a reasonable fee. The standard is high, and includes the renowned throat singers and the inevitable contortionist. Sometimes the staff will put on a simple show free of charge after dinner, perhaps featuring a horse-head fiddle.

The situation of *ger* camps tends to be convenient for sites of interest. However, the logistics of one's proposed itinerary should be studied carefully before selecting camps. With few but increasing number of paved roads in Mongolia it's advisable to minimise on connecting mileage!

In summary, there are good and not-so-good *ger* camps, but the difference from one to another is not enormous. Some take care of the drivers and guides, some don't. The smarter camps often expect drivers to sleep in their vehicles, and one I stayed in didn't even allow them to use the washrooms.

Providing travellers are prepared to make the necessary mental adjustments, staying in *ger* camps in Mongolia is a delightful experience.

It's worth saying that in the countryside the accommodation needs of most tourists are catered for by tour companies, which arrange for them to stay in *ger* camps. Backpackers may need small hotels, but they usually prefer to camp or stay at private *gers* (see GER TO GER, page 238). Hotels in the countryside therefore tend to be back-ups should other arrangements fail, although they are improving in quality. Note that booking small hotels in the countryside direct is not recommended – it is better to go through a tour operator in Ulaanbaatar (see pages 237–9). You can try to contact hotels yourself, but note that answers may arrive too late, or not at all.

CAMPING IN THE COUNTRYSIDE Most tour companies provide camping gear – everything you are likely to need. Otherwise, as an individual traveller you will need to bring your own equipment. You can camp almost anywhere in Mongolia; the choice is vast – but you will need permission within national parks from offices, locally, or in advance from the head office in Ulaanbaatar. If you want to use *ger* camp or hotel facilities, it is polite to ask and possibly there will be a small fee.

FURTHER INFORMATION Mongolian Hotel Association (MHA) (*Mongolian Children's Palace, Genghis Khan Av, Ulaanbaatar 210524; mail address: Central Post Office, PO Box 578, Ulaanbaatar;* \ *+976 11 311751*) was founded in 1997 by the growing number of Mongolian hoteliers. Priorities are upgrading hotel facilities and services by officially licensed hotels and organising training schemes. The recently established Hotels Network Information and a Travel Service Centre is operated by MHA.

TRADITIONAL MONGOLIAN FOOD

Traditional Mongolian food has two main ingredients – meat and flour, in some shape or form. The most popular dishes are *buuz* (small, steamed meat dumplings) and *huushuur* (flat meat-filled fried pancakes). There are also soups, plain steamed buns (*mantuu*) and salads (usually potato, cabbage or carrot), although increasingly green-leaf salads are finding their way on to menus. Mongolia is becoming a nation of urban gardeners (at least in the capital), producing lettuce on 30,000 private vegetable plots, much to the surprise of visitors who expect all Mongolians to be carnivores. In the past, Genghis Khan and his warriors survived on meat but many people forget that in ancient times, as well as today, Mongolians have supplemented their protein diet with local herbs and greens when they could find, or grow, them!

Out of necessity, Mongolians have found creative ways to use the milk of sheep, cattle, goats, camels and horses. *Öröm* is clotted cream; *aaruul* are the dried curds seen soaking up the sun on the *ger* tops in summer; and *tsötsgii* is cream. *Tarag* is a delicious sour-tasting yoghurt drink. *Shar tos* is made from melted butter and *tsagaan tos* is a mixture of boiled *öröm* with flour or fruit. Dried products are prepared during spring and summer to last over the long winter. One speciality is to cook the whole carcass of a goat, filling it with hot stones and roasting it on a spit over an open fire. Whole marmot is cooked in the same way.

Meat is usually mutton, boiled, fried in pancakes or served as dumplings. It can be fatty and taste strongly of sheep but it supplies the vitamins that are needed. A variation on this is *borts* – dried meat, usually beef and sometimes goat or sheep – similar to the South African *biltong*. It will keep for months and can jazz up otherwise dreary rice and noodles. The soldiers of the Mongol Empire used to keep dried meat under their saddles and chew a piece of it as they rode along. The strips of meat are incredibly dry and brittle but will soften up if broken into manageable pieces and stewed in boiling water. Beware of toothache if a piece of meat is trapped between your teeth. Travel with a good supply of strong toothpicks. During the summer, most families in the countryside dry large

IN DEFENCE OF MONGOL FOOD   *Natalie Teich*

People have maligned Mongolia with regard to food. I was very tempted to bring a lot of dried provisions with me in expectation of mutton, mutton and more mutton. But in fact, although there was a lot of mutton, there was also chicken and occasionally beef (particularly tongue), sometimes eggs, and rarely cheese or yoghurt (I am not sure why the last two were not more frequently served). There was an abundance of coleslaw and gherkins, carrot salad and potatoes. Spaghetti was often served as an additional source of carbohydrate and arrived on all occasions with the ubiquitous rice. Desserts were prepared cakes, biscuits and canned fruit salad. Vegetarians will have no trouble surviving, especially if they eat fish. Some fresh fruit is available in the markets in Ulaanbaatar, but I found none outside the capital. When visiting nomadic families we were invited to share their hard cheeses, sour milk drinks, occasional yoghurt and rare fermented mare's milk (this last one is usually much more readily available, but it had not been the best weather for the fermentation, so it was an exceptional offer – either that or the sensitive Mongolians were worried what it might do to our digestion).

quantities of meat in preparation for the winter and, if asked politely, will be happy to sell you some.

Summer in Mongolia is known as the 'white season' and herders and nomads work around the clock to process milk – turning it into cheese and a variety of other products to last them through the winter. Rock-hard curd, fermented mare's milk, distilled milk resembling vodka (*arkhi*), soured cream, milk skin – the list is endless. Fermented horses' or camels' milk, known as *koumiss* or *airag*, is, most definitely, the most popular – a slightly fizzy, cheesy beverage which is both refreshing and thirst-quenching after a long day's ride. However, it is important not to overdo the intake of dairy products, as travellers are known to become ill. Mongolians attribute the problem to foreigners' guts! Below are a few of the common foods and drinks:

- **Aarts** Dry white cakes made from the residue after straining whey. They are eaten with milk and sugar or coated in flour and boiled in water. Said to be very healthy for young children.
- **Buuz** Large dumplings made of dough, filled with meat, onion and garlic and steamed for 20 minutes. *Buuz* are served particularly in large quantities at Tsagaan Sar, the Mongolian New Year, when people may prepare as many as 1,000 dumplings for their guests.
- **Bansh** Smaller version of *buuz*, which are boiled in a soup.
- **Airag** Fermented mare's milk is the classic Mongolian drink. It is said to clean the system, but if you are not used to drinking it, make sure not to drink too much or your system will indeed be cleaned out!
- **Nermel** A home-distilled drink which is pretty lethal – a white spirit made from milk. It comes in many flavours and strengths and although it does not appear to be strong, be warned: a small amount may make you drunk very fast. *Nermel* means 'distilled' in Mongolian.

Country markets provide a variety of fresh and tinned food. Outdoor 'container' markets are found in every provincial centre, usually sited on or near the main central square. Local food stalls, usually located next to bus stations and in markets, provide take-away snacks and tea. The daily dish, mutton and noodles or boiled meat and dumplings, costs around T2,500. Supermarkets in Ulaanbaatar provide all sorts of fresh food, meat, vegetables and other products (see page 250). Restaurants in the capital are listed on pages 242–6.

FESTIVALS AND SPORTS

NAADAM Held annually in July, the great Naadam Festival is a thrilling three-day sporting event that has been happening for centuries. In Genghis Khan's time it happened at different times of the year, particularly in summer. Since 1922, when Sükhbaatar ordered a *naadam* to mark the first anniversary of the revolution on 11 July, it has been held annually – from 11 to 13 July. The festival highlights Mongolia's 'three manly sports' – horse racing, wrestling and archery. It continues to bring together Mongolia's sporting men and women from the remotest regions to compete at national level in Ulaanbaatar. It is also a celebration of the ordinary people – herders who ride into town and urbanites who leave their flats and offices to watch the games. The combination of people and events presents an unforgettable spectacle to the visitor: colourful silken tunics, fresh-faced nomads, thundering hooves, flying arrows, wrestling bouts, which thrill and entertain thousands of spectators. Mongolians like to show off centuries of tradition and celebrate the moment with plenty of *airag*. It is a time when people remember their glorious past and are proud of their equestrian skills, the stamina of their horses and the strength of their arms.

Although the main events are known as the 'three manly sports', women also compete (except in the wrestling contests) with just as much courage and daring as the men. These are the qualities that over the millennia produced the warrior nation of Genghis Khan. The root of the word '*naadam*' (game(s) festival) comes from '*naadakh*', meaning 'to play' or 'to have fun'. Outside the capital, smaller games, or mini *naadams*, happen throughout the summer months. Visitors often come across them unannounced, which is a bonus, since you can get much closer to the action than you can during the national games held in Ulaanbaatar. See also pages 261–4 for a description of Naadam (games) and the sports involved.

Mongolian festivals bring herders into the towns and their environs from isolated encampments to gatherings where they have the opportunity to participate in the events, to barter, flirt, mix, feast, sing and enjoy life to the full.

History of Naadam The history of the games began centuries ago at the time of the Hunnu or Hun Empire (3rd century BC) when hunting and other events were wilder and more primitive. Later, during the Mongol Empire (13th–15th centuries) the games lost some of their original glamour and impetus when the court of Kublai Khan moved to Peking and when the Mongol Empire disintegrated. However, in the 17th century the tribes regrouped at Shireet Tsagaan Lake to celebrate the Danshig Naadam – a *naadam* of seven banners – accompanied by Buddhist religious ceremonies. The latter were stopped in 1921, making it a 'games only' festival.

In the 21st century there is a renewed interest in traditional folk activities. In the capital, towns and provincial centres, as well as in lonely *gers* in the remotest areas, you will, most likely, discover a lifestyle, arts and music that reflect the true national identity and culture of the Mongol people.

Order of events for the National Naadam The opening ceremony raising the horse-tail banners in the presence of the president begins at 11.00 at the Naadam Stadium. You need tickets to get into the stadium events, best booked in advance through a tour company. Tickets cost T36,000 and are very difficult to get at the last minute. The horse races are held just outside the capital, at Yarmag, in a broad valley about 10km along the road to the airport – races begin at one end of the valley and contestants gallop the required distance towards the crowds who watch at the finishing post. There are plans in the future to hold the horse races at alternative locations. There is no cost. Buses or taxis are available from the city centre to take you there. If you are travelling outside an organised tour with your own car and driver, you will need a vehicle permit (obtained in advance from the traffic police in Ulaanbaatar). The driver should be able to arrange this. Wrestling competitions begin at noon in the central stadium and archery is held in another open stadium nearby.

TSAGAAN SAR Tsagaan Sar is a family festival which is celebrated on the first day of the lunar new year to put some cheer in the endless winter months and mark the beginning of spring. This could be any date from late January to early March. Each year is named after one of the following 12 animals – mouse, cow, tiger, hare, dragon, snake, horse, ewe, monkey, chicken, dog or pig. The animals are alternately male and female. You need to plan well in advance if travelling to Mongolia in winter, as most

Mongolians take this time off to be with their families. You also need special winter clothing to deal with temperatures as low as –30°C (see page 192).

Celebrations are not unlike Scottish Hogmanay, when neighbourly visits take place home to home – or *ger* to *ger* – in the Mongolian countryside. The celebrations happen over several days, with feasting on the night of the new moon. Everyone dresses in their best clothes to visit family members. During the holiday, people are glued to their television sets to watch the national wrestling competitions. There are some horse races but the maximum distance is 9km.

Throughout the ages the festival has been celebrated in the traditional way – family ties are renewed and in particular it is a time to honour the elderly. After the 1921 revolution many traditions, including Tsagaan Sar, were swept away but country people clung to their beliefs and fortunately for their culture the remoteness of the Mongolian hinterland protected such traditions. During the socialist period, Tsagaan Sar was transformed into the 'Spring Festival of Herdsmen' to suit the authorities after collectivisation in 1957. Since 1990 it has reverted to its old name.

As a sign of respect, the younger adults greet their elders in a certain way, with a special arm-hold embrace (*zolgokh*), which symbolises both support and esteem. The elders' forearms are supported palm-to-elbow by the younger person and, in return, the elder places his or her forearms (palms down) on top of the younger person's forearms in a gentle, arm-locked embrace. The gesture is accompanied by the exchange of a ceremonial pale blue or white silk scarf (*khadag*). Gifts are usually given and received with both hands, or with the right hand supported at the elbow by the left. The *khadag* is folded in a special way to show trust, as part of the greeting, with the folded edge facing the elder.

A typical three- or four-day Tsagaan Sar programme would offer the following: wrestling matches at the National Wrestling Stadium; a New Year's Eve dinner; horse racing in the countryside; and sightseeing in Ulaanbaatar, including evening performances of opera or ballet.

Customs and gifts If you receive an invitation from a Mongolian family to celebrate Tsagaan Sar with them, do not forget to buy a *khadag* (a blue silk scarf to present as a gift). Drape the *khadag* over your arms when greeting people, starting with the eldest. It is not necessary for men or women to remove their hats indoors when visiting a country *ger*. When offered a drink, always take a small sip or pass the cup to your mouth. Hot salty-milky tea is delicious and warming and so is Mongolian alcohol!

It is not a tradition to offer money or expensive gifts. Only children and other close relatives give money or special presents to their parents. Gifts between friends and relatives might be wine, cosmetic products, sweets and anything that is new and useful to the person.

Whole carcasses of lamb are cooked in advance, pans of *airag* and heated tea stand waiting, the table at the centre of the *ger* is decked with bread and dried cheese and piled high to symbolise prosperity. Steamed dumplings (*buuz*) filled with mutton appear as soon as you have drunk your welcome bowl of steaming salty-milky tea. Then the eating and drinking begins in earnest. The first piece of mutton is offered to the fire god and later choice pieces of mutton are served to the guests. Outside, cold weather and snow have long provided natural deep-freeze conditions to keep the meat fresh. Traditionally, after long bouts of feasting when alcohol flows freely, the Mongols settle down to hours of story-telling and, in this way, oral histories have been passed on from one generation to the next.

5

RIDING

HORSE RIDING Because horses and camels are so central to Mongolian culture, and essentially to tourism as well, this guide offers readers many different peoples' viewpoints and knowledge on the subject of riding, horse management and personal experiences on riding tours; likewise for camels – including how to buy and look after a camel for those who set out to cross the Gobi on foot. In the aimag chapters you will find further travellers' tales and information on expeditions, polo, and hunting with eagles in the west of the country.

Finding your horse The Mongolian horse tends to be small, around 13 or 14hh (hands high), and to the Western eye may look bony and undernourished. These animals have tremendous stamina however and are well adapted to the harsh environment where they have survived over the centuries. You can ride a Mongolian horse for 100 miles a day but you must rest it for the following two days. On a long-distance ride, 20–30km a day is the normal pace, depending on the terrain.

When selecting a horse:

- Avoid wild, nervous horses as either riding or pack animals
- Do not choose a horse that is too old, because it may not withstand hardships
- Ask the owner to walk the horse around. It should move well with a free, springy action
- Look at the horse's feet and mouth and judge for yourself whether it looks in good health
- If possible, ride the horse you plan to buy before settling your price
- Before saddling, brush the horse's back with your hand to ensure there are no sores and that the hair lies flat.

LONG-DISTANCE HORSEPACKING   *Danielle Bennett and Jay Harris*

Horsepacking is an adventurous and authentic way of experiencing the way of life in rural Mongolia. The people are friendly and welcoming, the horses are unique and admirable in their own environment. Always display proper guest etiquette. Unless you are very experienced with horses it is a good idea to get a guide to manage the horses, translate for you and help you find your way to the water hole. That being said, we went it alone. The horses are small at 12.1–13.2 hands (1.2–1.3m) but sturdy. Make sure you have enough horses to carry all your gear comfortably. On longer trips, it is a good idea to buy an extra horse to alternate riding and packing. You should rotate so every horse gets to be free of pack or person every few days. If you want to travel without a pack horse, unless you are taking an extremely short trip, make sure you don't have much more than 250lb (114kg) total on each horse. You can get a lot of supplies at Naran Tuul, the 'black market' in UB. Mongolian saddles are valuable as riding saddles and can double as pack saddles. They attract less attention and can be very comfortable if you ride with balance. Make sure the wither bars are an even slope; go for wide and not too sharp. Bring lots of rope, extra cinches, buckles and clips as this stuff is not readily available in the countryside. You might ask tour guides in UB if their families have any horses to sell. You can rent a jeep for the day, find a big herd and ask if they will sell a couple. Ask for a '*Nom-Hu*' horse; that means gentle and well trained. Make sure you ride your horse before you seal the buy. It is better to pay a relatively high price and get quality horses. Shoot for US$150–250 per horse.

Some other useful tips on how to get the most out of your horses when on expedition are as follows:

- Decide how many animals you need and for what purposes – riding horses, and pack animals
- It is a help to pack and load horses in pairs
- Keep pack animals at a steady slow pace to prevent chafing
- Allow more frequent rest periods if in hilly country
- Veterinary care is 90% prevention. Bring iodine to pour on to wounds
- Older, more experienced horses manage loads more easily
- To stop a runaway horse, turn its head to the side
- Pull on the reins sideways to halt (not straight back, as in Western riding style)
- Shout '*chüü*' to speed up your horse.

Tack and other equipment A horse harness comprises a head collar and leading rope, which is rarely removed from the horse, a bridle with a simple steel bit, and a Russian steel-framed or European saddle. Tack is held together by leather straps and pieces of rope and no two Mongolian bridles look alike. Mongolian saddles, contrary to expectations, can be quite comfortable if well padded. You will find all this kit in Mongolia (there is no need to bring your own if on a riding tour but do wear the right gear: chaps, breeches and riding boots (for riding balance) and to prevent chaffing), but if bound on an expedition – including very long journeys – you may prefer to arrive with your own saddle and other familiar tack. Australian saddles are available in Mongolia and these are the best – as advised by Lord Patrick Beresford, experienced Anglo-Irish horse expert and tour leader.

There are no topographic maps outside Ulaanbaatar, so get your maps there! There is a *sum*, or county seat, to get supplies about every two weeks by horseback, plan your routes around this and watering your horses at least twice a day. If you can't find water, ask. Herders always know where the water for livestock is. Don't forget your powerful water filters! There are two strategies for camping. You should either camp in a secluded area, keep your gear in your tent and your horses close by. Horse theft is not unheard of and it is always better to be safe than sorry. The second, and more stable, strategy is to ask someone if you can picket your horses and pitch your tent next to their *ger*. This will give you guest protection during the night and it will also give you the opportunity to meet local families. It is a good idea to carry vegetables; carrots and potatoes to contribute to the dinner stew if the family offers to cook for you. In more rural areas these veggies will be welcomed with delight. At night, picket at least most of your horses; you may hobble some but remember that they can go far with hobbles throughout the night and may be able to range beyond your protection. We always pick our campsite with an eye for the best fodder for the horses. They work hard during the day, so make sure they eat well at night. Remember, if you sell them in good condition, you will get a better return and they will have a better shot at surviving the winter.

Contact dbhwildryde@hotmail.com if you have any questions.

Other items to remember to take on a riding expedition (not a riding tour) are a head collar, a crupper (to stop the riding saddle from sliding forwards when going steeply downhill), saddlebags (two identically sized bags, preferably leather, for packing equipment) and several good lengths of rope (can be bought in Mongolia). You should take basic veterinary drugs like worming tablets, saddle-sore ointments and a couple of bandages. For information on food and other supplies to take, see pages 195–6.

CAMEL RIDING   With Ed Brown
For details of tour operators offering camel-riding trips, see page 166.

An encounter with camels   When I arrived in Mongolia with the intention of buying camels I had no idea what I was looking for. One month, 800km and a desert later, I was no wiser. I had lived, breathed, contemplated eating and certainly smelt of camel and yet to call them curious beasts is an understatement. Their bitter whines of complaint drill through your head, a kick from their back legs can send a man flying three metres, and their acrid smell pervades all clothes, food and even toothpaste. However, as beasts of burden they are unsurpassable. Whether they are carrying you, your bags or pulling a 500kg cart, their strength is awesome, their long legs eat up the kilometres, and if properly fed and watered their stamina will most certainly outlast yours.

The indigenous camels of the vast areas of the Gobi Desert are wild and when on the move they can cover up to 70km a day. Wild male Bactrians have been known to infiltrate domestic herds to mate with the females. Herdsmen do not like this with the result that the wild camels are chased away from water holes.

The amateur's guide to buying a camel   Naturally it depends on what you intend your camel to do and how far you plan on taking it, but various pointers can had no means of controlling the animal. Given the size of the horses, I was not too afraid, as if the horse wanted to throw me off, it wouldn't be very far to fall! I was very quickly won over by my little horse. It turned out that he was the fastest of the bunch.

Within half an hour of setting off, with sign language, the horseman had asked me if I wanted to go faster. Nodding my head, we charged off, galloping down the valley like wild things, leaving the others a long way behind. It was wonderful! My horse kept threatening to overtake the Mongolian's horse and I realised with some surprise that I wasn't at all worried at the speed. Rather than the hard, uncomfortable wooden saddles that most Mongolians use, we were treated to nice soft, comfortable Russian saddles. The stirrups were secure and gave solid support, giving the feeling of being glued to the horse's back. The friend who had had just the one lesson was also having a great time, although by the end of the ride she was having to urge her tired horse along!

The last couple of days were spent riding in the Terelj National Park, close to Ulaanbaatar. (This came as much as anything from nervousness at the idea of injury somewhere remote and far from a hospital.) We spent the rest of the afternoon galloping along the valleys nearby, screaming 'yahoo', like mad things, to encourage the horses to go faster. Still nervous of riding at home, those few lessons before going were all that were needed to have a fantastic time.

be taken to ensure that your camel will not fail its MOT (MOT = diagnostic check-up for those unfamiliar with the term!).

- Never completely trust the guy you are buying from.
- After discussions, bartering and vodka that will almost certainly go on for days, give in and trust him.
- The best time for buying camels is late summer, when they have spent the summer months fattening up away from the homestead. The drawback is that they haven't seen humans for a while and might therefore be a little skittish.
- Buy them in good time before you depart on the trip to make sure they are in good condition and will not rapidly waste once on the road.
- Officially, a camel's age can be determined by its teeth and its feet. I have no idea of the technicalities, but if you are mad enough to brave the flying green cud and go near its mouth, then at least it looks as if you have a clue. Never let on about your ignorance.
- If you are in a large group, or intent on taking your camels through inhabited places, just check how the camel behaves when surrounded by people.
- The Bactrian camel possesses two humps and when fully watered these humps should be fully erect. If they are not then this is a possible sign of an aged camel that should therefore be left alone.
- Once the deal is sealed (usually over a barbecue and vodka), tie a piece of brightly coloured material round your camels' necks so as not to lose them in the crowd.

Watering your camels Opinions differ as to how much water a camel needs and how often it needs to drink. Some say that a camel can go for seven days and often longer without water and when refuelling will drink up to 60 litres.

When we trekked with camels, we were walking on average 26 miles a day and tried, whenever possible, to water our camels at least once during the day. The

BECOMING TOP CAMEL – BACTRIAN CAMELS ON TREK

Benedict Allen

Camels are not always the easiest of animals to handle, but even the most brutish, spitting beast can be transformed into a loyal friend – well, in theory at least. The key is to understand the camel's one little weakness. It has only this one, for, unlike a horse, or any other livestock animal, the camel does not need daily provision of water and grazing. The camel comes as a self-sufficient unit, and a Mongolian camel can last the entire, harsh, Gobi winter without water, obtaining its moisture from snow or grazing. If it comes to a battle of wills, the camel's flat feet, humps, nostrils and even eyelashes ensure that it can survive in the desert a lot longer than any exasperated human. In short, the camel's loyalty cannot be bought; furthermore, the Bactrian is considerably taller and stronger than any Mongol horse, and has a formidable array of defences – it can bite (rare), box with its 'knees' (all too common), kick with all four feet (at the same time if necessary), and has a special weapon, the brisket or cartilaginous pad on its sternum. This it normally uses for resting its weight on when sitting – but it can also be usefully employed for crushing undesirables. So, if a camel is fed-up with its owner, it either battles, sits in protest or walks off in triumph – and the camel has an acute sense of direction. Furthermore, it has a photographic memory, so will have recorded the location of promising bushes it has passed. Jigjig, one treacherous camel of mine, abandoned me in the Gobi to amble 500km back home – arriving there three weeks later, and fatter than when it set off. So what can a human offer a camel? What is its one weakness? In a word, security. An animal adapted to the margins of existence, the camel has survival forever at the forefront of its mind. Its defence is its herd, and head of that herd is a leader, the 'top camel'. And essentially it is this formidable creature that a camel owner must become, if he is to be able to lead a camel train across the desert.

Becoming a top camel is a question of familiarising your potential camel team members with you – a stranger is outside the herd, and therefore another threat to a camel's security. This partly explains why tourists are always regarded with

longest the two camels went without water was three days and they were beginning to complain seriously by the end of the third. It goes without saying that if a camel eats and drinks regularly and well, then the further it will walk and the less it will sit down and complain.

Camel saddles and other equipment Try and get an all-inclusive package. Camels need saddles for both pack and people, they should have a good peg rammed through their nose and it is vital to have several strong leather hobbles. Camels have been known to move large distances when unhampered, so when camping for the night make sure the animals are properly hobbled. This allows them to move relatively freely but prevents an extra 2km walk each morning to go and retrieve them.

Hiring a camel-helper and guide Like many things, if you treat camels to the best of your abilities (easier said than done when trying to find good food and water every day in the desert), then you might almost become attached to them. However, the ultimate solution to all your camel worries is to rely on local knowledge and hire a Gobi guru. In any of the small desert towns you are guaranteed to find someone (however harebrained the trip might be) to come along and help with disdain by camels working the Egyptian pyramids. But, once your camel regards you as a familiar object, a companion, it will trust you to lead it away from familiar surroundings. Often the answer is to get the previous owner to walk with you for a couple of weeks, and effect a transfer of leadership (and other skills). Even then, a camel will be alert to any sign of nervousness on your part; once, I remember hesitating as I led my proud camel train up a dune, and the camels immediately anchored their feet in the sand, refusing to go on with me until I began humming contentedly again. The camels' natural neurosis is exacerbated in Mongolia, where nomads rarely go long distances, and camels hardly ever leave the surroundings they know. Furthermore, bred for milk, fur and carrying *gers*, they have a close relationship with their owner's family, which has nurtured them since birth.

The potential of your camels – the distance they might go, the load they might carry – depends on day and night temperatures, and the strength and fitness of the animals. Prime time is the late summer, when camels are fat from grazing, and their fur is thickening again. Generally, if walking for months, camels should have a weekly rest day, grazing time at dawn and dusk, and be watered every other day – they can go for five, but their strength starts to be depleted. They can carry 100–200kg without too much strain. Mongolians load them with double this weight, but seldom walk for more than a day or two. Travel with castrated males if possible – they are anyway easier to obtain than females, which are wanted for breeding – and whatever happens, don't mix sexes. Do not ride camels if alone with them – it's a long way to fall, and not easy to regain control if a member of the train is having a panic, due to loosening baggage.

With time, a camel if treated kindly will do whatever you ask – and with what appears to be genuine affection. It's true that, even after a few weeks, a camel may still spit at you – actually it's vomiting – and demand to be top camel itself. However, if you can tolerate all this, and more besides, a camel is the best of all possible friends. If it has chosen to stay with you, you know you have been given the greatest accolade of all – that of the status of a fellow camel.

the camels. We found Baatar, gave him US$4 a day, food and an extra sleeping bag, endless cigarettes and his return train fare home. In return, he looked after the camels superbly, fetched them every morning, watered them and found them good grass. He was also able to tell the bemused herdsmen what we were doing and ask where the next well was. This is hugely important for, equipped with only an out-of-date Russian map and limited Mongolian, a wrong turn could have meant serious problems. Finding someone that you feel you can trust is obviously the hard part, but whoever you choose, they might ask to draw up a 'contract' of some sort in the presence of the local aimag or *somon* governor. This is no bad thing, for everyone knows where they stand and what's expected from them – a definite plus point considering Mongolian camel-helpers aren't renowned for their initiative.

FITNESS   Personal fitness is one of the most important things to pack before setting out on a biking trip or any expedition that requires physical endurance. Run, walk or ride yourself into fitness for three months to a year by setting an easy-to-achieve daily fitness routine. Then when the going gets tough you are up to it. Strengthening the body does not happen overnight so prepare if possible before you launch yourself into strenuous holidays!

FISHING

Mongolia is now among the top fly-fishing destinations in the world. The rivers are rugged and wild and offer a marvellous variety of fishing in landscapes of unrivalled scenic beauty. The dry-fly take of Mongolia's famous *taimen* fish is like nothing else

THE FISH AND HOW TO CATCH THEM

TAIMEN (HUCHO HUCHO TAIMEN) The *taimen* is among the largest, most ferocious, freshwater fish in the world. The species is found only in a few inaccessible parts of Siberia and Mongolia. It is the fastest-growing freshwater fish in the northern hemisphere. A standard *taimen* averages over 1m in length and weighs around 9kg. Lucky anglers have landed specimens up to 75 inches – over 6ft (nearly 2m) long! (Mongolians record *taimen* by their length rather than their weight.) Because it is threatened with extinction the *taimen* is a highly valued trophy fish. It is described by experts as similar to fishing oversized Atlantic salmon. **All catches are returned to the river.**

Catching *taimen* The favourite Mongolian method is to fish for *taimen* under a full moon using a stout line, a hook and a dead mouse as bait. *Taimen* are caught by anglers using all manner of spinners, spoons and plugs and can also be caught on dead fish and on fly in clear water. Large dry flies can take smaller fish at dusk. Bring a set of both dry and wet flies, dummy mice and other fish imitations plus sufficient backing of more than 150m.

Some *taimen* are very large – up to 30kg – so you will need powerful equipment. Fly-fishermen are advised to bring a hefty 15ft fly rod (eight-, nine- or ten-weight). You may fish with either a two-handed or a single-handed rod (depending on your preference). Bring a leader, as heavy as practical: 14–20lb breaking strain. To date there are no nets large enough to land *taimen*. That is a tricky business and one where you need a fishing guide on hand to help. Remember to pack a wading stick, forceps or pliers to remove hooks from fishes' mouths, scales, a ruler and mousetraps!

LENOK (BRACHYMYSTAX LENOK) *Lenok* provides excellent dry-fly fishing for good-sized fish on light tackle. Like the *taimen* it belongs to the salmon family. The species is superficially like our rainbow brown trout, with a rich coral tinge. It's a wonderfully tasty fish. It reaches around 60cm (18–20ins) and weighs approximately 3kg. *Lenok* can be caught with all kinds of bait and streamers. A lucky catch reaches 75cm (30ins) and weighs 3.5–4.8kg (8–11lb).

ARCTIC GRAYLING (THYMALLUS ARCTICUS) Known to some as the 'lady of the stream', grayling, like *lenok*, makes excellent eating if you picnic on the river for lunch. (*Taimen* consider them an 'arctic delicacy' and devour them in quantities.) Fish grayling using small dries and nymphs.

CATCHING LENOK AND GRAYLING This includes a light fly rod (four- to six-weight) with a leader of 3–5lb (1.3–2.2kg). Use traditional river flies – the same flies you would use in the UK or Scandinavia. Czech nymphs and goldheads are good choices and have proved successful. Use a three- to five-weight rod and some hoppers to catch *lenok*, plus 4lb (1.7kg) leader material.

Anthony Wynn

A number of travel companies offer fishing tours to Mongolia, promising catches of giant *taimen* (*Hucho hucho taimen*) and other adventures, but all you need to catch fish on your own is a stout trout rod and a small box of flies. Once out of reach of Ulaanbaatar, the rivers are full of Arctic char and grayling. The char go up to 1.7kg (4lb) and the black grayling in the west are very fine fighting fish up to 0.9kg (2lb). If fishing wet, a black pennel or grouse and claret will catch both fish. Grayling will also come spectacularly to a bushy, dry fly.

If you have forgotten to bring a rod, copy the Mongolians, who catch char with a hook and line attached to the end of a long pole. Scratch about under the stones to find caddis flies, attach them to the hook and go dapping. This requires some skill.

The rivers run cold and gin-clear for the most part, except during the brief summer rains, when they can colour up. Wading is not necessary. To cook your fish, take some foil with you. Find some wild spring onions to stuff them, wrap the fish in the foil and bake them over a fire of dried camel or yak dung. Nothing could be more delicious.

To catch *taimen* the Mongolian way, take a very stout line and tie a wooden 'mouse' wrapped in marmot fur and festooned with hooks to the end of it. Wait until dark and light a fire by the riverbank over a deep pool. Throw the mouse out into the river and pull it back towards you. If you hook a fish, lash yourself to a friend, or a tree, and haul in. Some rural Mongolians regard fish as sacred (because they do not shut their eyes) and do not approve of fishing, but most of them have no objection. Be sensitive about this.

in freshwater fishing. Where else in the world is it possible to cast dry flies to fish weighing over 22kg?

Mongolia's northern central rivers flow via Lake Baikal, the Angara and the Yenisey to the Arctic Ocean, whereas the rivers of the northeast and east flow to the Pacific via the Amur, another great Siberian river. The lake basin in the west has no outlet to the sea. Mongolia has a small organised fishing industry on the eastern border at Buir Lake, at Ögii Lake in central Mongolia and at the western lakes in the Darkhad basin. Some 300 tonnes of fish are exported. Little is consumed in the country since the Mongols have no taste for, or habit of, eating fish.

Taimen, the biggest fish in Mongolian rivers, is related to the non-migratory *huchen* of the Danube and belongs to the salmon family. It has been described as prehistoric in appearance, with huge fins, the head of a conger eel and the teeth of a pike. Besides with flies, it is caught by using 'dummy' mice or, as the Mongolians do, by using dead mice, squirrel or marmot as bait. In late autumn, when migratory tundra mice cross the forming ice on the northern rivers and streams, giant *taimen* lie ready in wait below the frozen surfaces to snap them up for breakfast. In early spring *taimen* have even been seen catching young ducklings for dinner, such is their voracious appetite. Nobody knows where the land-locked *taimen* go in winter. It is thought they head for Lake Khövsgöl, the deepest freshwater lake in central Asia, or lurk in the hollows of the deepest pools.

Lake-fish catches consist mostly of the Yenisei white fish, a species related to the famous *omul* fish of Lake Baikal in southern Siberia. Otherwise the catch usually consists of *taimen*, *lenok* and Arctic grayling. Two species of grayling are common in rivers of northern Mongolia: the Arctic grayling (*Thymallus arcticus*)

5

and Mongolian grayling (*Thymallus brevirostris*). Roach, perch, pike and carp are also caught. Winter fishing produces burbot caught through holes in the ice. The Siberian sturgeon is a protected fish. One interesting and little-studied species of endemic fish is the Altai osman (*Oreoleuciscus potanini*).

Fishing, especially fly-fishing, is a new leisure sport in Mongolia. Most Mongols rarely eat fish because of their Buddhist traditions, but despite this the rivers near Ulaanbaatar tend to be over-fished. Further afield the majority of Mongolian waters have never seen a fisherman. Equipment is difficult to rent anywhere in the country, so it is recommended to bring your own gear. Should you arrive unprepared all you need when fishing for the pot is a strong handline and a lure (see box, page 217).

What does it take? The swish of the line and the fly is freed from the water, on the forward movement it droops on the spot where in all likelihood a giant trout lies waiting below the surface. A sudden jerk and the fly is taken. You have caught your supper. It is that easy to land a fish in Mongolia, which sounds rather unsporting; on the other hand you will never experience better and more thrilling fishing conditions.

SEASONS AND WEATHER You can push the seasons at both ends in spring and autumn depending whether you get an early or late winter. Most fishing happens from late August until mid October.

Spring fishing begins in May and June when the winter is over (one hopes) and rivers are at their lowest. Early spring is an idyllic time of year when the fishing is excellent and the hillsides are carpeted with alpine flowers. Dan Vermillion, an American who pioneered Mongolian *taimen* fishing in the early 1990s, reported during the caddis and mayfly hatches, 'This is a wild time for fish and fishermen alike, when grayling and *lenok* rise steadily and *taimen* cruise beneath them until they pick out their lunch.' According to Vermillion, this is when it is most difficult to decide whether to cast a mouse or a mayfly.

During the summer months of July and early August there is a low rainfall – not the ideal time for fishing. Autumn is also a beautiful time of year and the fishing is good. However, giant *taimen* may be fished throughout the season until early/mid October. Thereafter, temperatures plummet.

During winter from November to April (and sometimes until June) Mongolian rivers are ice-covered, so that anyone fishing for food chops holes in the ice over deep pools to catch fish 'Greenland' style with a long line. This technique is obviously not possible in shallow rivers which freeze through to the bottom in winter.

CONSERVATION POLICY AND INFORMATION Fishing camps recommend fishing with barbless hooks. It is common practice to release all trophy fish when caught. Other fish may be caught for the pot. For the best information on Mongolian native fishes see *The Mongolian Red List of Fishes* in the Zoological Society of London's Regional Red List Series. For further details, and for conservation measures, see the *Summary Conservation Action Plan for Mongolian Fishes* – funded by the World Bank and other organisations. Go to the ZSL website (*www.zsl.org*).

PERMISSION AND LICENSING Out-of-the way rivers are unpatrolled but that does not mean you don't need a licence. This means that tourists cannot pitch up and go fishing, although some 'pot' fishing is bound to happen with or without a licence.

Permits are also available for a day's fishing from local national park administration offices. For anglers, a fishing licence may be obtained from the Mongolian Ministry of Nature and Green Development (*Baga Toiruu 44, Ulaanbaatar;* \ *11 326617;* f *+976 11 328620*).

COOKING FISH FOR THE POT Grilled fish makes a pleasant change from mutton for the evening meal. Proceed with caution and respect for local beliefs and customs. If you are not part of a fishing group, take charge of the cooking yourself. Mongolians tend to obliterate fish by boiling it like meat, so that all that remains is a thin white soup with a vaguely fishy taste. Bring tin foil to wrap your fish in, add herbs and cook in the campfire embers. You will not easily order fish in a restaurant again!

FISHING RIVERS AND LAKES The best fishing rivers include the famous 'Five Rivers' area near Lake Khövsgöl – the Ider, Delgermörön, Bugsei, Selenge and Chuluut rivers. The Eg and Shishigt are also excellent fishing rivers.

Good lake fishing may be found at:

- **Terkhiin Tsagaan Nuur** (Great White Lake) in Arkhangai Province.
- **Lake Khövsgöl** in Khövsgöl Aimag. You may find *omul, lenok, umber,* roach, river perch, sturgeon and *taimen*. Fishing usually takes place from the shoreline or from bridges. The lakeshelf is very steep so don't attempt wading unless you have good local advice. Best spots include the bridge at Khatgal on the eastern shore.
- **Lake Ögii** in Arkhangai Aimag. The lake can be reached from the main road linking Tsetserleg with Ulaanbaatar and can also be reached on a day trip from Karakorum, in the Orkhon Valley.

PROFESSIONAL FISHING CAMPS Most fishing camps are organised by top fly-fishing tour operators and are specifically set up for clients, often in very out-of-the-way sites on choice rivers. Some of these 'private' camps are located in river valleys four to five hours' journey southeast of Lake Khövsgöl; they are not geared to casual drop-in visitors who might turn up expecting to hire equipment for a day's fishing.

Helicopter transport is used to reach some of the more remote fishing camps, which provide a high standard of comfort (baths, showers, plenty of hot water and good meals, with freshly baked bread and, naturally, fish menus). Stoves warm the *gers* at night. Days are spent on the river. There are also marginally less-comfortable tented camps. It is possible to 'go it alone' and travel with tents in search of new waters, but this needs careful planning.

GENERAL EQUIPMENT Fishing is a new sport in Mongolia, so for those who are keen to fish the best advice at present is to come prepared and bring your own rod, although this situation should change in a few years' time. Fishing rods and equipment are difficult to buy or hire anywhere in the country, so bring what you need. Rods should have a 2½lb test curve. Bring lines of at least 18lb breaking strain, big fixed-spool reels or multipliers, a good selection of spinners and spoons and plugs, including heavy sinking deep-diving plugs (10–12ft) and big splashy surface plugs with a good vivid action. High-quality reels such as Shimano's Aero GT or Stradic are recommended. Rods must be packed in travelling tubes for transport in the luggage compartment of the aircraft. For recommended tackle for specific species, see box, page 216.

WINTER SPORTS

SKIING Downhill skiing is in its infancy in Mongolia although there is some opportunity for development. Snow cover in the northern and central regions lasts throughout the long winters, some seven months of the year, although not in the warmer south where it falls periodically or not at all. The best months for skiing are January and February The most accessible skiing areas are just outside Ulaanbaatar at the Terelj resort and at the new Bogd Khan Swiss-owned Sky Ski Resort outside Ulaanbaatar where the snow is man-made and skiing takes place up to 22.00 on floodlit slopes. You can hire skis and boots.

ICE SKATING Many Mongolians are keen ice skaters. Although it is possible to buy ice skates in Mongolia, it would be more reliable to bring your own. For more details on skating contact Mr Darjaa (11 458964).

DOG SLEDDING For further information, contact Frenchman Joel Rauzy in Terelj resort (via tour companies Panoramic Journeys and Nomad Tours and Expeditions; see pages 165 and 238) and see box, page 272.

MEDIA AND COMMUNICATIONS

TELEVISION, RADIO AND NEWSPAPERS Television is available to all who have a TV set (and an electricity supply now greatly helped in the countryside by solar panels) – that is, essentially, the urban population. In the countryside families will gather in the *ger* that has a TV set and you are lucky to have both television and a constant electricity supply along with good reception so that viewing is not interrupted Most standard hotels in Ulaanbaatar have a television in the bedroom, some connected to world programmes via satellite. Guesthouses and small hotels have televisions in the reception/lounge area. Mongolian Television broadcasts European (English, German, French, Russian) and American TV news.

To illustrate just how far and how fast the world has come, telegraph lines for commercial telegram traffic were operated between Russia and China in the 19th century – the main line running from Kyakhta via Urga (Ulaanbaatar) to Kalgan was built by a Dutch company, and a western line was built by the Russians from Kosh-Agach (Altai) to Khovd in 1913. Radio was first broadcast in 1934 through wired loudspeakers in urban housing and did not operate as 'wireless' until later.

Radios have played an important role in rural communications to help, for example, women in isolated situations by providing vital communication links and education programmes. The rural population, with battery-powered receivers, depended on radio broadcasts for home and foreign news. Satellite phone communication works for most areas around UB but in the more remote regions of Mongolia it is often difficult to get a signal for your satellite phone. Batteries can be

---

MOBILE PHONE AND CAMERA BATTERIES

Ger camps nowadays have solar or generator systems and tourists will have access to electricity at times in order to recharge mobile phones and camera batteries. Bring several fully charged camera batteries, do not rely on your mobile phone and invest in a wind-up torch and/or bring extra torch batteries when travelling in remote areas of the countryside.

INSIDE MONGOLIAN TV AND MEDIA   *Sarah Georgiana Head*

I was given the opportunity to gain an insight into the little-known world of Mongolian television and radio, on a three-month programme with i-to-i. The impressive building which was the Mongolian National Television and Radio headquarters became my home for the summer of 2005. The vast building is marked by the proud red television mast positioned alongside, making it a visible landmark across the whole city. It stands to the north of Ulaanbaatar surrounded by a *ger* district although only a stone's throw from the commercial Bayangol shopping and residential district.

I worked in an unpaid role for the national MN news agency where I worked on the English-language news programme *MM Today*. Since the end of the communist era, the learning of English has become increasingly important to Mongolia. The programme was therefore designed as an English-language tool as well as a means to inform expats of domestic and local news and events. *MM Today* was pre-recorded and broadcast at 21.00, three days a week. A typical day would be spent researching possible stories to be broadcast. This proved difficult as only one computer was linked to the internet and reserved mostly for the international news programmes – a concept which is hard to fathom in the internet-dominated environment that we are usually surrounded by. I spent my time working alongside young Mongolian journalists, who were the first generation to be taught English at school. I would assist in the lengthy editing process, ensuring the news was grammatically correct. We would then make the journey down the long corridors to the news studio located in the basement where we would record the out-of-vision footage and present the programme.

Working on *MM Today* gave me an extraordinary insight into the current affairs and media world of Ulaanbaatar. The programme worked closely alongside the two main English-language newspapers, *The Mongol Messenger* and the *UB Post*. It provided a gateway into a fascinating world that is inaccessible as a tourist. My experiences working for Mongolian National TV provided an extraordinary view of a unique country allowing me to understand the political, economic and social goings on of the country. I was able to experience and embrace the Mongolian way of life. Living in the Bayangol district in a small apartment with two Mongolian students and working with young Mongolian journalists, I learnt a great deal about the country, its media and most importantly, its people. For further information see the i-to-i website (www.i-to-i.com), the host organisation.

Mongolian National Television (www.mnb.mn) is the oldest broadcaster in Mongolia and continues to have the widest outreach, broadcasting to the remotest parts of the country. Since 2003, a number of other broadcasting channels have appeared, including TV 5 (www.tv5.mn) – which focuses on entertainment and sport, and TV 9 (www.tv9.mn) – a privately run channel with an emphasis on politics and news.

problematic and people often resort to recharging them via car batteries if there is no other means. Small solar chargers work but what flummoxes people is that they forget to bring the correct leads and plugs that adapt and connect to their specialist equipment, be it phones, cameras, battery chargers or satellite phones. Ordinary cell phones also operate but signals are variable and some don't work at all.

Newspapers/media (in English) Among Mongolia's many local newspapers are two weekly papers published in English: *The Mongol Messenger* (c/o Montsame News Agency, PO Box 1514, Ulaanbaatar; ☎ 11 327857; e *montsame@magicnet. mn, monmessenger@mongolnet.com; www.mongolmessenger.mn*) and the *UB Post* (*20 Ikh Toiruu, Ulaanbaatar;* ☎ 11 313427; e *argamag@magicnet.mn; www.ubpost. mongolnews.mn*), both available in Ulaanbaatar at the Central Post Office, street vendors and leading hotels, costing T600. Both provide online information on subscription or will post to overseas subscribers.

To follow Mongolian daily news in English, Email Daily News (EDN) provides an email service: edn@pop.magicnet.mn.

TELEPHONE Mongolians jumped straight on to mobile phones and have almost avoided land lines. All 335 districts in Mongolia have mobile phone services, broadband internet services are available in 34 district centres, and the distance herders have to travel to make a call has fallen by more than half.

Mobile phones have taken life to new levels of communication which was unheard of only a decade ago. Outside Ulaanbaatar it is often difficult to connect telephone calls of any kind so come prepared with roving facilities and battery chargers for your own equipment. It is better to plan on that basis and understand that although there are many satellites in operation, signals are not reliable everywhere. **Mongolian Telecom** (*PO Box 1166, Sükhbaatar Sq 9, Ulaanbaatar;* ☎ 11 320597; e *contact@mtcome.net; www.mng.net*) provides telecommunications services throughout the country.

Mobile operators are Mobicom Corporation (GSM) (the first mobile operator), Skytel (CDMA), Unitel (GSM) and G-Mobile (CDMA) (established in 2007 and focusing on development in rural areas).

Telephone codes The international code for Mongolia is 976. People essentially operate on mobile phones – especially in UB and in towns. Landlines are also used and usually have eight digits. If calling within the same region, the two-digit area code can be dropped for landline to landline calls.

Arkhangai	33	Dornogobi	52	Khovd	43	Sükhbaatar	51
Bayankhongor	44	Dundgobi	59	Khövsgöl	38	Töv	27
Bayan-Ölgii	42	Gobi-Altai	48	Orkhon (Erdenet)	35	Ulaanbaatar	11
Bulgan	34	Gobi-Sümber		Ömnögobi	53	Uvs	45
Darkhan-Uul	37	(Choir)	54	Övörkhangai	32	Zavkhan	46
Dornod	58	Khentii	56	Selenge	36		

Emergency and other useful numbers The following numbers are primarily for Mongolian speakers, so you'll need a translator standing by!

Fire station ☎ 101
Police ☎ 102
Traffic police ☎ 321008
Ambulance ☎ 103
Central railway station enquiries ☎ 194
International telephone enquiries ☎ 106116 (operator speaks English)
Ulaanbaatar telephone directory enquiry ☎ 109

Satellite phone When I travel I use the Inmarsat mini M satellite phone. If you take a satellite phone, you will need to purchase a licence from the Ministry of

Infrastructure (*Government Hse ll, 12a United Nations St, Ulaanbaatar 46;* ✎ *11 321713;* f *11 310612*) before bringing it into Mongolia.

POST The Central Post Office (CPO) in UB is fairly reliable, and letters take around a week to arrive in London, for example, although it may take longer to reach other destinations. Stamps cost as follows:

All letters and postcards to any country cost around T1,500, postcards slightly less, T1,000, and packages are charged at a rate of T15,000 per 100g. Stamps may also be purchased at large hotels.

Mongolian stamps are particularly splashy and colourful, and well worth collecting. Genghis Khan features as well as well-known celebrities – even Princess Diana had a Mongolian stamp in her honour. The Mongolian Stamp Company (*PO Box 794, Ulaanbaatar;* ✎ *11 360509*) was set up to cater for stamp collectors worldwide.

SEND US YOUR SNAPS!

We'd love to follow your adventures using our Mongolia guide – why not send us your photos and stories via Twitter (@BradtGuides) and Instagram (@bradtguides) using the hashtag #Mongolia. Or you can email your photos to e info@bradtguides.com with the subject line 'Mongolia pics' and we'll tweet and instagram our favourites.

Part Two

THE GUIDE

6

Ulaanbaatar

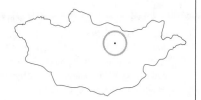

Ulaanbaatar (UB) is a thoroughly modern, concrete city, teeming with people and humming with taxis and buses, where only 100 years ago men on horseback drove camel caravans and mule wagons along unpaved streets past hundreds of temple buildings, bells on the animal harnesses ringing loudly to attract attention to imported wares sold by Chinese, Russian and Mongol traders in the open-air markets. Today it is the general base for all business and development and it is the natural headquarters from which to plan all major travels to the countryside. Tourism operates essentially from the capital. Make the most of this opportunity and organise events in advance if travelling outside a tour group. International companies, UN and other development agencies are located in the capital, and political and government life is centred here.

Until recently, change happened slowly in Mongolia. Fifty years ago there were few buildings in the capital over five storeys high and the population was under 50,000. Since the beginning of the 21st century, mostly as a result of a recent mining 'boom', businesses, new buildings, hotels, restaurants and supermarkets have transformed the city from a fairly sleepy trading town into a buzzing modern capital. Over time UB has developed from an unindustrialised settlement to an increasingly international city.

ULAANBAATAR TODAY   *Bill Manley*

The mining boom, while temporarily slowed by lack of clarity for investors, has changed the scene of Ulaanbaatar. There are many more foreigners stationed here for two to three years and consultants who fly in and out. The result is that almost every type of restaurant has opened for business, generally at expatriate prices (the same as being back home). Salaries have increased by over 30% in the last two years and inflation is on average between 15–20%, so while almost everything you could possibly want is available, prices have escalated.

Tourism is still trying to make its year's income from about four months in the summer, so again we see budget travellers arriving in UB only to find their budgets are too small to do everything they expected to do. Tourists seeking high-end facilities seem to be on the increase and appear unaffected by prices. Last season most tourists came from the Netherlands, France, Italy, Singapore, Australia, Korea, Japan, Taiwan and the USA.

Watch out: pickpockets are on the up and up, especially between the Central Post Office and the State Department Store. They are now organised into more aggressive larger groups and face little or no intervention from the authorities.

The usual Mongolian greeting is *Sain bain uu?* (How are you?) and the expected answer is *Sain, ta sain bain uu?* (Fine, how are you?), to which the response is *Sain bainaa!* (fine!). This is usually followed by two key questions: *Ta khaanaas irsen be?* (Where have you come from?) and *Ta khaashaa yavakh ve?* (Where are you going?). When saying goodbye (*Bayartai*) Mongols may say *Sain yavaarai* (Have a good journey), to which the response is *Sain suuj baigaarai* (Stay well!).

Soviet-style apartment blocks mixed with modern developments and government buildings line long avenues, cut by ring roads and traversed by the main railway line between Moscow and Beijing (the Trans-Siberian/Trans-Mongolian Railway). The population has officially surpassed one million people (2013), and unofficially well over that number, reflecting the drift of incoming herders who settle on the outskirts of town in growing makeshift *ger*-compounds. The city has the conveniences of modern life and yet if you want to escape for a few hours the countryside is only a bus ride away.

Ulaanbaatar is situated in the broad mountain valley of the River Tuul, surrounded by pine and fir forests that cover the hillsides. For much of its history

TAXI RIDE: UK TO UB   *Sam Glover*

Our quest was an unusual one: to nurse a vintage London taxi from the UK to UB (Ulaanbaatar) via a sizeable chunk of central Asia. The plan was hatched, developed and – wherever possible – realised in bars, which helped to keep all forms of organisation to a bare minimum.

The taxi that was to be our temporary residence was purchased for £150, having rested in a garden since retiring from the cab circuit with an estimated 850,000 miles under its belt. Slapdash modifications to prepare it for the abuse that lay ahead included a roof rack, capacious fuel tank, chunky off-road tyres, crude under-body armour and a double bed that was almost large enough to sleep both of us comfortably. Into its homely rear, we threw a minimum of tools, spares, clothing, pot noodles and camping impedimenta.

Significant parts of our steed began to expire and/or detach *en route* to Dover, and continued to do so with alarming regularity from thereon. Breakdowns through Europe were an almost daily occurrence, prompting us to claw back time by heading due east across Ukraine and Russia, rather than south into Iran as planned. We took a relatively sedate pace, spending time in the places that took our fancy, and chugging through those that did not. After just under six weeks, we reached the Tashanta-Cagaanuur (Tsaagaanuur) border crossing into Mongolia.

It took us more than six hours to exit Russia, but only 30 minutes to enter Mongolia. The fact that it was almost going-home time for the officials, and that the 'Mongol Rally' fraternity were beginning to filter into the country, could well have been beneficial to our cause.

Geography-keen thieves had lightened us of our detailed military maps in Chelyabinsk, leaving us with nothing but a small-scale tourist offering by which to navigate. Attempting to take the lesser-trodden northerly route to UB, we quickly discovered that its markings bore no resemblance to the bewildering array of tracks that lay before us. The cab did not fare at all well on terrain that varied from

Ulaanbaatar was known as Urga, a name that originated from the word *örgöö*, meaning 'a temple *ger*'. In the mid 17th century, the monk Zanabazar, who became Mongolia's first religious leader (Öndör Gegeen), established a mobile capital. His residence moved from place to place along the Orkhon, Selenge and Tuul river valleys. In 1778, long after Zanabazar's death, the mobile capital of Mongolia finally settled on its present site. Thus Ulaanbaatar was once a felt-tented capital made up of thousands of *gers* and temples; indeed, it was known as Ikh Khüree Khot, the Great Monastery Town. Brick and stone temples were not constructed until 1837. In 1911, the city was renamed Niislel Khüree (Capital Monastery), when it became the political capital of autonomous Mongolia. In 1924, after further political upheaval, the city was renamed Ulaanbaatar after the revolutionary leader, Sükhbaatar. During the 20th century, most of the felt encampments gave way to high-rise apartment blocks and government buildings in the Soviet style. Most temple buildings were either destroyed or closed during the religious purges of the 1930s; one exception was Gandantegchinlen Monastery (see pages 253–5).

In the 21st century there have been huge changes and development as mentioned, built around the new mining industry. The *Guardian* newspaper in the UK declared on 7th November 2011 that Mongolia was fast becoming 'the centre of the planet's greatest resource boom … On the brink of one of the most dramatic

Amazonian to lunar, sustaining significant damage about its hull. After three days of misdirection in a massive valley, a lack of diesel forced us to limp to Ölgii – a bustling Kazakh frontier town in all but location, where local mechanics helped us to patch up our disintegrating chariot.

The southerly route to UB proved slightly more navigable, but rear suspension collapse combined with the detachment of a front wheel eventually heralded curtains for the cab. With limited time remaining, we opted to donate its remains to locals, and hire a chauffeur-driven UAZ (a Russian off roader) to take us the rest of the distance.

There can be few more fascinating, beautiful and – above all – friendly countries to explore than Mongolia. However, attempting overland travel in anything other than a rugged 4x4 is not to be recommended. One of the country's growing number of few metalled roads heads south to UB from Ulaan-Ude, Russia. If, like us, you find yourself bound for the capital in a woefully unsuitable vehicle, we wholly recommend that you go this way. My advice to anyone planning a similar road trip is thus: allow yourself plenty of time, don't plan a definite route until you get there, and never stop smiling!

STATS

Cost each	£2,000
Mileage covered	7,000
Time taken to UB	seven weeks
Prior visas required	Russia, Mongolia
Serious breakdowns	Ten+
Impromptu appearances on Russian television	four
Hours spent in a Chelyabinsk police station	21½
Website	www.slightlycliveracing.com

transformations in human history.' On the ground things are sometimes seen differently and not everyone is on the receiving end of the benefits. But undeniably the country is changing fast.

GETTING THERE

BY AIR On arrival at Chinggis Khaan (Genghis Khan) Airport [off map, 232 D7], transfers for groups to UB are usually pre-arranged involving a tour company and the transfer cost by minibus/taxi is US$20. What used to be about a 30-minute drive from the airport to the centre of town may now take a matter of hours due to heavy traffic jams – so allow plenty of time to get to and from the airport. A new airport road is under construction as this book goes to print.

If you are not being met at the airport, transport into the centre of town (18km) is easily arranged. Taxis are available outside the airport; the cost is approximately T20,000 – locals pay less, around T30,000 for a pre-arranged collection. Yellow taxis are metered and taxis usually meet international flights; it is possible the Mongolian

A GOLDEN JOURNEY: BEIJING TO UB, PART 1   *Hallie Swanson*

Beijing to Ulaanbaatar is one of the world's great train rides. Our cosy compartment had bunk sleeping berths that were surprisingly comfortable and a big window to watch the world go by. This epic transition from Beijing's crowded concrete cityscape to the brilliant blue skies and timeless landscape of Mongolia reveals the extraordinary distances and challenges the Mongols had to face on their quest for world rule. I wake at dawn to a new world, where camels dot the horizon and majestic dunes undulate into the distance. As the train rumbles on towards Ulaanbaatar (UB) I look forward to exploring this mystical country.

First impressions: UB is a sprawling, rollicking boomtown, liberated in 1990 after 70 years of socialism and now enjoying all the pleasures of freedom and democracy and some of its shortfalls too. It's chaotic and crowded, its streets a jumble of motorbikes, jeeps, UAZ vans, overloaded lorries and massive Hummers all vying for supremacy. Gleaming new office buildings rise above the fray, signalling UB's status as one of central Asia's most dynamic emerging markets thanks to a fast-growing mining industry that is both a blessing and a curse for the country.

The nightlife in UB is buzzing. You can be at a bar arm-wrestling with a nomadic herdsman who just rode in off the steppes or chatting with an Armani-suited Ukrainian hot off his private jet. UB's breathless pace and 'anything goes' attitude are part of its charm, but we didn't come to Mongolia to hang about in a city, and it's a relief to toss our bags in the back of our sturdy UAZ van and head for the hills. In our modern world it's hard to imagine a place where architecture hardly exists, where man's presence is so muted that it blends into the background rather than making its mark. In Mongolia, nature still rules. It's a humbling, profound experience. We head north to Lake Khövsgöl via the Orkhon valley and some interesting camps on the way. (See box, *Golden Journey, part 2*, on page 354.)

Our family trip was arranged by Panoramic Journeys UK (www.panoramic journeys.com).

drivers speak some English but don't bank on it – however, drivers understand hotel names and will get you there!

The airport bus into town costs US$5 (recommended for those who speak Mongolian or who are keen to pick up the language). Local public buses also travel to and from the airport but they are infrequent and often very crowded; the cost is T600. There are plenty of Mongolians keen to practise their language skills and eager to help new arrivals at the airport and in town, as those travelling on their own will find.

ORIENTATION

Ulaanbaatar is not an easy city to find your way around since street names and signposting are haphazard, but it is being improved. Signs are written in Cyrillic and addresses follow a local system that confuses even the Mongolians. Most people give directions not by street name and number but by saying that, for example, it's next to such-and-such a building with green walls. I recommend buying a large-scale city map of Ulaanbaatar on arrival to help find your way around and, if language fails, try the 'finger pointing' system with the map, used by travellers the world over. Maps of the city are now available in most tourist hotels, bookshops and at the Map Shop [232 B4] located on Ikh Toiruu 15 (outer ring road).

Public toilets are few and far between in the city so you will have to nip into a café or hotel and ask to use their conveniences. See box, page 254, in preparation for needing a loo when you are out and about in Ulaanbaatar.

The map of the city provided in this guide (see pages 232–3) lists the street names, in transcribed Mongolian. In the main text street names are referred to in English and transcribed Mongolian.

FROM GENGHIS KHAN SQUARE

North To the north of the square you will find Sükhbaatar district, with *ger* settlements sprawling to your left and right. The State Palace or Parliament Buildings (Töriin Ordon), along with the giant statue of Genghis Khan, dominates the north side of the square. There are good restaurants in the area; further north are several universities. On the northwest side is the National History Museum and a block to the north is the Natural History Museum. Nearby you will find the police station.

South On the south side of Peace Avenue, below Sükhbaatar Square, stands the State Library and a bit farther on the 'Wedding Palace', where marriages take place. Beyond these buildings is the famous Children's Park, and nearby is the Choijin Lama Temple (a five-minute walk from the square). The tall Blue Sky Tower Hotel stands just south of the square and dominates the skyline along with the nearby Central Tower building; both have views in all directions across the city. The multi-storey Bayangol Hotel is not far away, across Chingisiin Örgön Chölöö. A little further south (a half-hour walk from the square, or a short taxi ride) is the Winter Palace of the Bogd Khan.

East On the eastern side of the square you will find the National Opera and Ballet Theatre, the Palace of Culture housing the Art Gallery and, nearby, the Institute of Technology. The Ulaanbaatar Hotel is behind the theatre. The Chinggis Khan Hotel is farther along Enkhtaivny (Peace Avenue), after a number of embassies, including the British Embassy.

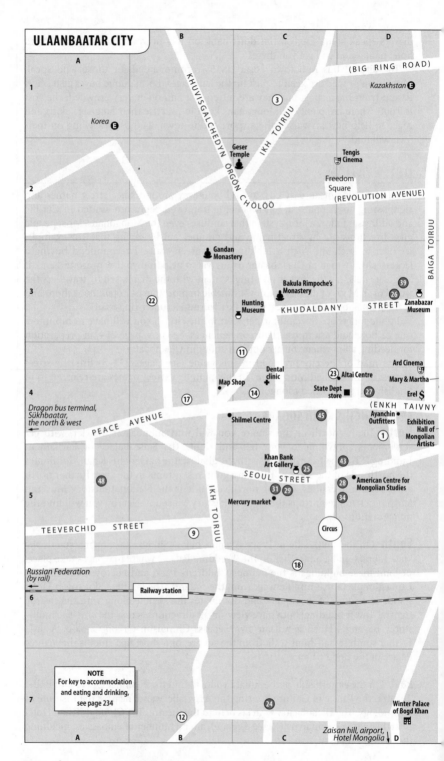

ULAANBAATAR CITY

A　B　C　D

(BIG RING ROAD)

Kazakhstan 🄴

Korea 🄴

③

KHUVISGALCHEDYN ORGON CHÖLÖÖ

IKH TOIRUU

Geser Temple

Tengis Cinema

Freedom Square
(REVOLUTION AVENUE)

BAIGA TOIRUU

Gandan Monastery

Bakula Rimpoche's Monastery

39
26

Zanabazar Museum

22

Hunting Museum

KHUDALDANY　　STREET

11

Ard Cinema

Dental clinic

23 Altai Centre

Mary & Martha

Map Shop

14

State Dept store

27

Erel $

17

45

(ENKH TAIVNY

Shilmel Centre

Ayanchin Outfitters

1

Exhibition Hall of Mongolian Artists

Dragon bus terminal, Sükhbaatar, the north & west

PEACE　AVENUE

Khan Bank Art Gallery

25

43

48

SEOUL　STREET

28

American Centre for Mongolian Studies

IKH TOIRUU

31　29

Mercury market

34

TEEVERCHID　　STREET

9

Circus

Russian Federation (by rail)

18

Railway station

NOTE
For key to accommodation and eating and drinking, see page 234

24

Winter Palace of Bogd Khan

12

Zaisan hill, airport, Hotel Mongolia

A　B　C　D

232

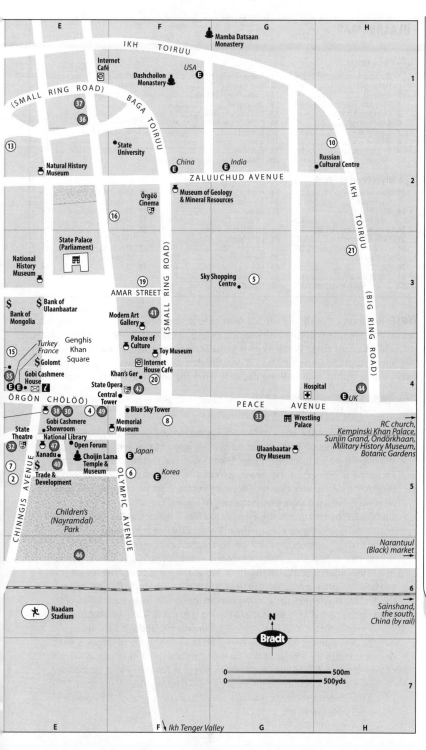

Mamba Datsaan Monastery

IKH TOIRUU

Internet Café

Dashchoilon Monastery

USA

(SMALL RING ROAD)

BAGA TOIRUU

37

36

13

State University

China

India

Natural History Museum

ZALUUCHUD AVENUE

Russian Cultural Centre

10

Örgöö Cinema

Museum of Geology & Mineral Resources

IKH TOIRUU

16

State Palace (Parliament)

21

National History Museum

19

Sky Shopping Centre

5

AMAR STREET

(SMALL RING ROAD)

(BIG RING ROAD)

$ Bank of Mongolia

$ Bank of Ulaanbaatar

Modern Art Gallery

41

Palace of Culture

Toy Museum

Turkey France

Genghis Khan Square

$ Golomt

Internet House Café

15

Khan's Ger

20

Gobi Cashmere House

State Opera

42

Hospital

44

ÖRGÖN CHÖLÖÖ)

35

Central Tower

PEACE AVENUE

UK

38 30

4

49

Blue Sky Tower

33

Wrestling Palace

RC church, Kempinski Khan Palace, Sunjin Grand, Öndörkhaan, Military History Museum, Botanic Gardens

Gobi Cashmere Showroom

Memorial Museum

8

State Theatre

National Library

32

Open Forum

Ulaanbaatar City Museum

47

Xanadu

Japan

CHINNGIS AVENUE

7

40

Choijin Lama Temple & Museum

6

Korea

2

Trade & Development

OLYMPIC AVENUE

Children's (Nayramdal) Park

46

Narantuul (Black) market

Naadam Stadium

Sainshand, the south, China (by rail)

N

Bradt

0   500m
0   500yds

Ikh Tenger Valley

ULAANBATAAR
For listings, see pages 239–46

🛏 Where to stay
1	Backpackers' Hostel......D4	11	Gana's Guest House......C4	21	Undruul.............................H3
2	Bayangol.............................E5	12	Idre's Hostel.....................B7	22	White House....................B3
3	Bishrelt............................. C1	13	Lotus Guest House.........E2	23	Zaya's Guest House........C4
4	Blue Sky Tower................E4	14	Narantuul..........................C4		
5	Chinggis Khan................G3	15	Nassan's Hostel................E4		**Off map**
6	Continental......................F5	16	Puma Imperial..................F2		Hotel Mongolia................D7
7	Corporate..........................E5	17	Ramada..............................B4		Kempinski Khan
8	Edelweiss.......................... F4	18	Sarora.................................C6		Palace...............................H4
9	Evergreen......................... B5	19	Tuushin..............................F3		Sunjin Grand....................H4
10	Flower...............................H2	20	Ulaanbaatar......................F4		

✴ Where to eat and drink
24	Bangkok Thai....................C7	33	Hazara................................G4	43	Oriental Treasures.......D5
	Bayangol.....................(see 2)	34	Ikh Mongol........................D5	44	Papa Café..........................H4
25	BD's Mongolia	35	La Boulange/Michael's	45	Planet Pizza......................C4
	Barbecue....................... C5		French Café.....................E4	46	Seoul.................................. E6
26	Buddhist Centre Café....D3	36	Le Bistro Français............E1	47	Silk Road........................... E5
27	Café Amsterdam.............D4	37	Le Triskell..........................E1		Taj Mahal...................(see 2)
28	Café Ti-Amo.....................D5	38	Los Bandidos....................E4	48	The Bull.............................A5
29	California...........................C5	39	Luna Blanca.......................D3		Veranda................(see 47)
30	City Café............................E4	40	Millie's Espresso...............E5	49	Zen......................................E4
31	Fashion Café.....................C5	41	Modern Nomads..............F3		
32	Grand Khan Irish Pub.....E5	42	Monet................................ F4		

West Bordering the square on the west side is the main post office, along with banks, government buildings, airline offices and many small cafés and restaurants. A few blocks west along Peace Avenue is the State Department Store (Ikh Delger or 'Big Shop'), and the souvenir Mary & Martha shop is tucked away in a nearby small street – also within easy walking distance from the square and easily located as it

---

GENGHIS KHAN SQUARE

The square lies at the heart of the city surrounded by government buildings and banks. Although it was renamed in 2013, many Mongolians in the capital still refer to it by the former name, Sükhbaatar Square. The Mongolian Stock Exchange is housed in the peach-coloured building on the square, which used to be a children's cinema. There are hotels, theatres, cinemas and cafés all in easy walking distance from the central square. The square itself is further surrounded by two ring roads: Baga Toiruu (the inner or smaller ring) and Ikh Toiruu (the outer or greater ring). The major avenue, Peace Avenue (Enkh Taivny Örgön Chölöö) borders the south section of the inner ring and runs east–west through the capital. Other avenues cross the smaller ring road on the west side to join the outer circle. Within the inner ring on the north side of the square you will find the Töriin Ordon (State Palace) buildings of the Mongolian parliament, the Ikh Khural. A large equine monument to the revolutionary hero Sükhbaatar stands at its centre, at its base the following statement: 'If we are able to unite our strength, then for us nothing will be impossible and we shall attain the heights of happiness for all.' However, a huge seated statue of Genghis Khan now dominates the square at the front of the Parliament Buildings. A festival of traditional costumes, the Deel Festival, is held in July every year, taking over the space with music, circus performances and dancing. The tourist office [233 E4] on the southwest corner will offer advice, plan trips, arrange transport and answer all your questions.

is well signposted from Peace Avenue. New shops are springing up in the centre of the city all the time, well advertised by designer brands. The industrial part of town is across Peace Bridge, south of the railway line, a taxi ride away. The railway station is situated in the southwestern suburbs in Bayangol district [232 B6]. Beyond the outer ring road, to the northwest, you will find Gandan Monastery, Mongolia's largest Buddhist monastery, which is worth visiting (see pages 253–5).

GETTING AROUND

Public transport within the capital is extensive, cheap and generally reliable but the UB traffic congestion is very bad at times.

BY BUS The UB city bus lines mainly follow the central east–west axis of the city and the inner and outer ring roads connecting the suburbs to the centre.

Public bus service Bus tickets cost T500 for adults and T200 for children, irrespective of the length of the journey (although you must pay again if you change buses). Tickets are sold at the back of the bus, checked by the conductor and may be checked again when you're getting off the bus at terminals. Passengers usually pay for their fares in cash and alight through the middle or front doors. Expect overcrowding at rush hour and watch out for pickpockets! Below is a list of some of the city buses and their routes.

No 25 Operates frequently & runs to the northwest districts from outside the Ard Cinema, opposite the MIAT (Mongolian Airlines) offices.

No 22 Runs from outside the Ard Cinema to a terminus 5mins from the airport.

No 11 Runs to & from the airport (18km southwest of the city) and stops outside the Bayangol Hotel.

No 16 Runs from the park opposite the Ulaanbaatar Hotel to a *ger* compound north of the city.

No 18 Runs from the park opposite the Ulaanbaatar Hotel to a valley on the west side of the city.

No 7 Runs from the Ard Cinema to the southern districts of the city & terminates in the Zaisan valley.

Nos 14, 15 and 20 Leave from Genghis Khan Square to different parts of town.

Trolleybus The city also provides a trolleybus service (tickets cost a flat-rate T300). Numbers 2 and 4 run between Genghis Khan Square and the long-distance bus station [232 B5], which is located on the western side of town near the railway station. The line traverses the city from east to west. Trolleybuses 2, 5 and 6 start at the eastern end of Peace Avenue and terminate at or near the railway station. Number 2 continues to the suburbs in the western district. Trolleybus 4 starts at the railway station and terminates at the Botanical Gardens.

Minibus Private minibuses began operating in the mid-1990s and are useful in the late-night hours when public transport stops running after 22.00. The modest cost of tickets varies, and is calculated on a journey basis.

BY CAR Driving in Ulaanbaatar can be difficult on account of the inadequate street lighting and a shortage of traffic signs. People usually hire cars with drivers. To arrange day trips, it is best to negotiate with a taxi driver, or to use a tour company, which will provide a car and driver at US$100 a day. Mongolian drivers negotiate the terrain with incredible ability and Formula One confidence. The roadworthiness of vehicles in Mongolia leaves much to be desired, but the drivers on the whole are exceptionally skilful, especially over long distances when they turn out to be excellent mechanics too! There has been a dramatic increase in the number of vehicles on Mongolian roads in recent years.

BY TAXI Short taxi rides in and around UB, to and from your hotel to inner-city sights and restaurants, will cost around T7,000. Taxi ranks may be found outside the large hotels (eg: the Ulaanbaatar Hotel), in front of museums such as the Zanabazar Museum, or outside the railway station during the main tourist season. When taxis are free they are readily hailed at any point. People tend to hail any passing car if they are stuck, and negotiate a ride. However, if you don't speak any Mongolian, this system presents difficulties and is not advisable. Some people ask the hotel receptionist or a Mongolian friend to write down travel details on a piece of paper to show the driver. The taxi fare is worked out on the basis of around T700 per kilometre.

Taxi companies include **City Taxi** (✆ *11 343433/344499; 24hrs*), **Han Gug** (✆ *11 451617* m *961 11501; daytime*) and **Taxi Ulaanbaatar** (✆ *11 311385*). **Help Taxi** (✆*996 52371*) is reliable: the owner-operator Sukhee speaks English; it is a bit more expensive but still good value by UK standards. Currently the starting price is T5,000. Safer than most; used by expats.

HIRE COSTS To hire a **bus**: 40 passengers during the tourist season costs US$120 per day plus petrol; 22 passengers during the tourist season costs US$80 per day plus petrol.

A comfortable **jeep or minibus** costs T700 per kilometre plus petrol. Current petrol prices are T1,500 per litre (95 grade); T1,250 per litre for diesel.

It is not an easy thing to hire a **car** and drive around. Rally drivers do so with difficulty. So you are better off to stick with a Mongolian car and driver (from US$100 per day) because apart from the road conditions, finding your way around tends to frustrate most people. If you decide to hire a 4x4 Japanese, Russian or Korean vehicle daily hire is around US$230 for a Land Cruiser plus petrol. For further information see www.sixt.mn or www.mongoliacarrentals.com.

An international driving licence is needed. Expats are required to obtain a local licence; be sure to have good insurance coverage.

TOURIST INFORMATION

The **Centre for Tourists** (CIT) [232 D4] (70 101011/11 320493; e info@ mongolianguideschool.com; www.touristinfocenter.mn) is located off Genghis Khan Square in the Erel Bank building (across the street from the Flower Centre on Peace Avenue). Also worth contacting is the **Mongolian Tourism Association** [233 E4] (Genghis Khan Sq, Trade Union Confederations Bldg 309; 11 327820; e info@ travelmongolia.org; www.travelmongolia.org).

LOCAL TOUR OPERATORS

Many independent travellers deal directly with Mongolian tour companies via the internet and book their flights and tours online. The main difference between booking via a foreign travel company (ie: in your home country) and booking via the internet is the price; obviously foreign companies add a percentage to the price quoted by the ground operator. Things to consider when booking directly are ease of payment, insurance risks and reliability. Independent travellers use Mongolian companies on the spot and settle by cash (usually in US dollars or local currency); see the list below. Recommend are smaller environmentally conscious travel companies, often family run, that cater for individual needs.

In the following, the Classic Tour (Mongolia's Golden Circuit) refers to a tour to one or more of the best-known areas such as the South Gobi, Lake Khövsgöl and the Orkhon valley; tours normally include, among other things, sleeping in a *ger* and visiting nomadic families.

Active & Adventure Tours Bldg 7/1-102, Erkhuu St, 7th Khoroo, 11th Khoroolol, Sükhbaatar district; 11 354662; e info@tourmongolia.com; www.tourmongolia.com. Tours that respect local tradition & culture, & aim to provide travellers with a real experience of nomadic life.

Ar Mongol Travel Group The Trade Union Confederations Bldg, Room 309, Genghis Khan

Sq; 11 327820; e info@travelmongolia.org; www.travelmongolia.org

Blue Bandana Expeditions PO Box 308, Ulaanbaatar 46A (office inside the Seven Summits outdoor shop, opposite the post office and behind the Zorig statue); 11 329456; m 991 77029; www.activemongolia.com. Good & helpful company; youth tours throughout Mongolia.

Destination Mongolia e info@ destinationmongolia.com; www. DestinationMongolia.com. General/cultural & camel tours for groups.

Discover Mongolia Metro Business Centre, Baga Toiruu, 6th Khoroo; ☎70 120011; e info@ discovermongolia.mn; www.discovermongolia. mn. Offers tours to the Gobi & other areas.

Genco Tour Bureau Bayangol Hotel B-201, 5 Chinggis Khan Av; ☎11 328960; e info@genco-tour.mn; www.genco-tour.mn. Homestays with nomadic families, special-interest tours, fishing, trekking & cycling.

GER TO GER 1st Fl, 5/3 Baruun Selbe, 1 Khoroo, Ulaanbaatar; ☎11 313336; www.gertoger.org. This innovative foundation will change the way many people travel in the future, not taking tours but learning the language & living with families. A cultural exchange experience.

Great Genghis Expeditions CP Box 675; ☎11 310455; e greatgenghis@magicnet.com; www.greatgenghis.com. Offers high-quality tailor-made tours with personal service for small-to-medium groups. Botanical & wildlife conservation tours team up with Mongolian scientific experts.

Happy Mongolia ☎Daka +976 9984 4844; e happymongolia@gmail.com; www. happymongolia.net. Specialises in small personally operated tours in Terelj Resort & around Ulaanbaatar.

Housgol Travel ☎11 460368; e info@ housgoltravel.com; www.hovsgoltravel.com. Offers tours to Khövsgöl & reindeer people as well as other northern destinations.

Hovd Tour 301 Peace Av; m 991 49087; e info@ hovdtour.mn; www.hovdtour.mn. Specialists in rally events such as the Mongol Rally.

Jules Vernes Mongolia ☎11 310659; e julesverns@mongol.net; www.tripmongolia. com. Offers fishing & adventure tours.

Juulchin Tourism Corporation ☎11 328428; e info@juulchin.com; www.juulchin.com. Oldest tour company in Mongolia with lots of experience & services.

Juulchin World Tours Corporation Marco Polo Palace, Jamyan Gunii St 5/3; ☎11 319401; e info@ juulchinworld.com; www.juulchinworld.mn. A leading tour operator offering classic, cultural, business, adventure & sports tours, with a trusty network of hotels, camps, restaurants & local transport services.

Karakorum Expeditions Gangariinn Gurav Bldg, 1st Fl (southwest side of State Circus), PO Box 542, Ulaanbaatar 46; ☎11 315655; USA voice: +1 212 658 9938; e info@GoMongolia.com; www.GoMongolia.com. Offers active adventures & cultural journeys. Founded & run by Australian Graham Taylor.

Kazakh Tour Social Services Bldg, 2nd Fl; PO Box 111, Main Square, Bayan-Olgii; m 994 22006/29696; e dosjan@yahoo.com; www. kazakhtour.com.

Nature Tours ☎11 312392; www.naturetours. mn. Has been around since the 1990s. Well-known tour operator that offers a good selection of tours.

Nomadic Expeditions ☎11 313396; e badral@nomadicexpeditions.com; www. nomadicexpeditions.com. Offices in the USA: 1095 Cranbury-South River Rd, Suite 20A, Jamesburg, NJ 08831; ☎+1 609 860 9008 or 1 800 998 6634; e info@ nomadicexpeditions.com. One of the leading tour operators offering several trips: trekking in nomadic style, horseback expeditions & sport fishing. See ad on page 302.

Nomadic Journeys PO Box 479, Ulaanbaatar 13; ☎11 328737; e infomongolia@nomadicjourneys. com; www.nomadicjourneys.com. Swedish office: Eco Tour Production Ltd, Norra Kustvagen 17, 620 Gotland, Sweden; ☎+46 498 487105. Offers special low-impact tours; experts in fishing & conservation with affiliated *ger* camps in special locations. Run by Jan Wigsten, an expert on Mongolian journeys & tourism.

Nomads Tours & Expeditions Peace and Friendship Bldg, 3rd Fl, Suite 8–9, Peace Av; ☎11 328146; e info@nomadtours.com; www. nomadstours.com. For a wide range of soft adventure trips & cultural visits. Julia Roberts travelled with this company (1999). Nomads own & run a luxury *ger* camp called Tuul Riverside Lodge (*www.tuulriverside.com*), situated just east of the capital.

Off the Map Bayan Zurkh District, 13th Microdistrict, Bldg 4, 184 Ulaanbaatar; ☎11 345715; m 997 54387; e info@mongolia.co.uk; www.mongolia.co.uk. A reliable & excellent tour company working year round with classic, motorbike, mountain bike & adventure tours throughout Mongolia; good for those with children. A UK/Mongolian family-run company (Catherine & Enkhbold Darjaa) offering tailor-made tours for small groups & adventure holidays.

Selena Travel ☎ 11 363499, 7018 3499; e sales@selenatravel.com; www.selenatravel. com. The tourist company for adventurous budget travellers & organises a special 2-day 'Nomads Day Festival' in Gün Gulüut Reserve south of the capital in Sep.

Shuren ☎ 11 312339; e shuren@magicnet.mn. Classic/group/budget tours.

Tseren Tours Baruun Selbe 14/1 (opposite the east entrance of the State Dept Store); ☎ 11 327083; m 991 11832, 997 40832 e info@ tserentours.com; www.tserentours.com. Specialist in sporting & adventure tours, especially biking.

Family-run company founded by Tseren & Ric – a Mongolian/Dutch couple.

Tsolmon Travel Chinggis Av Hse C61, Sükhbaatar District, Ulaanbaatar 11; ☎ 11 322870; e info@tsolmontravel.com, tsolmon@ tsolmontravel.com; www.tsolmontravel.com. Fishing, birdwatching, camping & horseriding.

Wind of Mongolia m 9909 0593; e info@ windofmongolia.mn; www.windofmongolia.mn. Cultural journeys & adventure trips in the heart of the Mongolian steppes. See ad in 2nd colour section.

 # WHERE TO STAY

When travelling independently in Mongolia I usually stay at either the Edelweiss Hotel or the Bayangol. Another of my favourite hotels is the Hotel Ulaanbaatar, the first place I stayed when visiting Mongolia in 1978. Back then it was known as Hotel A and foreign tourists had only one other choice, Hotel B, which no longer exists. Things have moved on considerably since those days and Ulaanbaatar offers new exciting choices such as the Blue Sky Hotel in the centre of town. Several new five-star hotels are due to open in 2014 – at the time of writing: the Hong Kong-owned Shangri-La Hotel; the US Hyatt group has planned two new hotels – one in UB and the other in the nearby resort of Terelj; and a UB Hilton Hotel is due to open soon. A selected number of hotels of differing prices are listed below. For visitors on business trips a number of these hotels – Ulaanbaatar, Bayangol, Continental, Flower and others – have business centres with all the necessary communications facilities and conference rooms. Other top hotels include the Kempinski Khan Palace Hotel and the Corporate Hotel. The larger hotels all have restaurants and bars and many have shops too, so that you can buy presents and send postcards without a problem. The receptionists will take endless time and trouble to help travellers, book theatre tickets and generally assist in 101 different ways. For those on a budget the guesthouses offer good-value accommodation at low prices, especially in hostel dormitories. Serviced apartments are available to rent (see *Serviced apartments*, page 242).

COSTS There are many hotels to choose from depending on what you want to pay. They range from US$15–30 for a single room at a hostel (less if you are prepared to share a dormitory at US$10), to a double room with bathroom at a top hotel for US$200 plus; de luxe suites range from US$250 per night and presidential suites cost from US$500–2,000+. Credit card payments are accepted in most hotels listed below, but not in the hostels, where bills are normally settled in US dollars or local currency. The prices given are subject to change and quoted at high-season rates. They exclude breakfast unless stated.

It is easy to book hotels online. If travelling independently check the latest figures (and discount deals) online.

LOCATION Most hotels are easily located on an online map – available on your phone or on the hotel's website. Just in case you (like most of us) are confused when finding your way around UB, arrive with a good map of the city. The way that people locate places in Mongolia is not by street addresses (which may be written in Mongolian Cyrillic to add to your confusion) but by referring to buildings and other landmarks, as mentioned in *Orientation*, pages 231–5 – it's worth repeating this many times. A street map will help so again, as mentioned, be sure to buy one before arriving or be confident that your internet connections will work – that is if you intend to rely on your mobile phone, GPS and other internet services. For location of listings, see map on pages 232–3.

UPPER RANGE $$$$

⌂ **Blue Sky Tower Hotel** (200 rooms) Peace Av 17; ☏ 701 00505; www.hotelbluesky.mn/en/. Excellent central location south of Genghis Khan Square. Good restaurants (Western, Japanese, Chinese, Korean) in the hotel & within walking distance. Its Bliss Fitness Centre is fully equipped. The choice for business travel; terrific views from the top (25th) floor bar, although rooms pricey. At this level service needs careful attention.

⌂ **Chinggis Khan Hotel** (178 rooms) Tokyo St, Khoroo 1 District; ☏ 11 313380; e chinggis-hotel@ magicnet.mn. This is a grand hotel of immense proportions & modern-style architecture, with lots of glass & chrome; it attracts tour groups & businesspeople. The restaurants are fairly pricey – main courses cost T5,000–6,000, desserts T2,000, beer T1,800–2,300. The hotel has a swimming pool, gym, sauna, several restaurants & bars. The café in the entrance hall serves hot chocolate & other drinks. The hotel has access to a large supermarket at the back of the building.

⌂ **Continental Hotel** (37 rooms) Embassy St, Peace Av (just south of Genghis Khan Sq beside the Japanese Embassy); ☏ 11 323829; e continental@magicnet.mn; www.ulaanbaatar. net/continentalhotel. A large modern hotel where diplomats & foreign groups stay. Facilities & services include a business & travel centre; banquet room; sauna & massage; swimming pool; comfortable rooms & prompt service. The Venus Restaurant & Bar serves European food.

⌂ **Corporate Hotel** 9–2 Chinggis Av; m 991 94807; e mail@corporatehotel.mn; www.

corporatehotel.mn. Located in the city centre with most visitor sites within walking distance. Offers luxurious suites, apartments & standard rooms. Provides b/fast buffet, internet, sauna & fitness.

⌂ **Kempinski Khan Palace Hotel** (102 rooms) East Cross Rd, Peace Av, Bayanzürkh District; ☏ 11 463463 e reservation@khanpalace.com; www. khanpalace.com. Located along Peace Av, the main road of the city, this new luxury hotel offers traditional rooms & suites & traditional Mongolian hospitality. In only a 7-min drive, you'll reach Genghis Khan Square, the Central Post Office, the National History Museum, the Natural History Museum, the Sky Shopping Centre & the State Department Store.

⌂ **Narantuul Hotel** Chingiltei District; ☏ 11 330565; e info@narantuulhotel.com; www. narantuulhotel.com. Fairly new 3-star hotel, close to the State Department Store & Gandan Monastery.

⌂ **Ramada Hotel** (128 rooms) 35 Peace Av & Amarsanaa Rd, nr Ganden Monastery; ☏ 701 41111. This large hotel is situated near the heart of the city conveniently near the railway station & provides full hotel services with restaurants & has a health & fitness centre. Built in 2011.

⌂ **Tuushin Hotel** Amar St; ☏ 11 323162; www. bestwestern.co.uk. Located in the heart of UB, the Tuushin belongs to the Best Western Premier chain. There are 3 restaurants, a spa & fitness centre.

⌂ **Ulaanbaatar Hotel** (119 rooms) Sükhbaatar Sq 14; ☏ 11 320620; e ubHotel@magicnet.mn; www.ubhotel.mn. Lots of comings & goings at this hotel, which is an excellent place to stay as it is centrally located. Rooms are large & airy, & there is

---

ACCOMMODATION PRICE RANGES

Approximate price per person in a standard double room.

$$$$	Upper range	US$120–200
$$$	Mid range	US$90–120
$$	Budget	US$50–90
$	Guesthouse/hostel/country hotel	Less than US$50

something of an old-world style to the décor. Good business centre, large dining room, private rooms for entertaining & several bars & a dance area. Private concerts & special parties are celebrated here.

MID RANGE $$$

🏠 **Bayangol Hotel** (198 rooms) Chinggis Khan Av 28, PO Box 43; 📞 11 312255; e bayangol@ magicnet.mn; www.mongoliaonline.mn/ bayangol. This multi-storey building is one of the busiest & largest hotels in UB, frequented by tour groups & the business community. Its Casablanca Bar is among the city's nightspots; the foreigners' restaurant is usually full. Although fairly austere-looking in terms of architecture, the Bayangol is a lively, fun place to stay.

🏠 **Bishrelt Hotel** (16 rooms) Khuvisgalchdyn Örgön Chölöö 3/1; 📞 11 313789/310063; e bishrelt@magicnet.mn. This 5-storey building left of the Chandmani Centre is a good, small hotel with comfortable rooms. Well located, it caters for tour groups & individual travellers. The restaurant serves Bulgarian food.

🏠 **Edelweiss Hotel** (20 rooms) Peace Av, 15A/5; 📞 11 312186/325091; e edelweiss@ mongol.net. This is one of my favourites. Small & intimate, it has an easy-going atmosphere. A good place to hold quiet meetings & to entertain guests is in one of the hotel's restaurants, serving European & Asian food. There is a sauna on the ground floor (🕐 15.00–21.00). Helpful reception.

🏠 **Sunjin Grand Hotel** Enkhtaivan Av; 📞 11 457711; e jonghwan-j@hanmail.net; www. sunjingrandhotel.com. Located east of the Kempinski Khan Palace Hotel around 20mins from the city centre (& off map), the Sunjin's location is probably a drawback. Has good business centres & meeting rooms. Good restaurant with Korean chefs serving European & Korean dishes.

🏠 **White House Hotel** Amarsanaa St; 📞 11 367872; e chono@magicnet.mn; www. whitehousehotel.mn.

BUDGET HOTELS $$

🏠 **Evergreen Hotel** Teeverchid St 6, nr railway station; 📞 11 242525; e info@evergreen.mn. Well-run reasonably priced, charming hotel.

🏠 **Flower Hotel** (184 rooms) Khökh Tenger (Blue Sky) St 12; 📞 11 458330; e flower@ magicnet.mn. Near the British Embassy, the Flower

caters for large groups. Prices are competitive, the food is good & receptionists are helpful.

🏠 **Puma Imperial** Centrally located on University St off Sukhbaatar Sq; 📞 11 313043; e puma_imperial@mbox.mn; www. pumaimperialhotel.mn. Frequented by diplomats & journalists.

🏠 **Sarora Hotel** Seüliin Gudamj (Seoul St) 12/b; 📞 11 327831; e sarora@magicnet.mn.

🏠 **Undruul Hotel** Peace Av; 📞 11 455108; e undruul@magicnet.mn.

GUESTHOUSES/HOSTELS $

🏠 **Backpackers' Hostel** Seüliin (Seoul) Av, nr the State Department Store, Peace Av; 📞 11 315398/328410. Will pick up at the airport; located nr the Mercury Market for food shopping. Fax & email service, laundry & travel service; café food.

🏠 **Gana's Guest House** 📞 11 321078; e ganasger@magicnet.mn. Nr Gandan Monastery in the suburbs of a *ger* compound. Slightly run-down but cheap & cheerful.

🏠 **Idre's Hostel** Narnil Guur Bldg 22; 📞 11 325241; 9911 2575. Within walking distance from the railway station. Friendly place, English spoken; hot showers; TV, free Wi-Fi.

🏠 **Lotus Guest House** North of Genghis Khan Sq, Baga Toiruu 17–15. Friendly staff; dorms & twin rooms, also 2 fully furnished apartments. Provides airport collection, b/fast & laundry service.

🏠 **Nassan's Hostel** Nr Genghis Khan Sq; Chingeltei District, I-R Khoroo, I-R40 Myangat, Baga Toiruu, Bldg A-4, 3rd entrance, door #13; 📞 11 321078; e nassantours@mongol.nt; www. nassantour.com. Helpful & friendly; will arrange travel & help organise onward journeys, provide guides & transport. Guests can use the kitchen to prepare their own food.

🏠 **Zaya's Guest House** Tserendorj St (building 63) nr State Department Store, off Peace Av; 📞 11 331575; e backpackza@hotmail.com.

AIRPORT HOTEL

🏠 **Hotel Mongolia** A conveniently located out-of-town hotel 20mins' drive from the city centre & 40mins' drive from Ulaanbaatar International Airport, Buyant-Ukhaa; 📞 11 710154; www.hotel-mongolia.com. The hotel is designed in the form of a mock castle, and is located close to Gachuurt village. It is situated on the banks of the Tuul river and its architecture is reminiscent of buildings in the ancient

6

capital of Karkorum and surrounded by a fortress wall with four gates. **$$$$**

SERVICED APPARTMENTS

🏠 **Tsolmon Travel** Contact Mrs Navchaa; 3 Khoroo, 5 Khoroolol, Hse 37, Entrance 1, 2nd Fl, Sükhbaatar District, Ulaanbaatar-14252; ☎ 11 322870; m 990 11303, 991 14910; e tsolmon@ magicnet.mn; www.tsolmontravel.com/serviced apartments. Offers serviced apartments for one week, one month, one year & other times by arrangement. Short-term apartments (1–3 rooms) up to US$1,700/month for 1 year; 1 room 1 person US$40/day, 2-room apartment US$60/day; 3-room apartment for 4 persons US$144/day. Additional services include laundry, tours & meals.

GER ACCOMMODATION Many *ger* compounds surround the city. They are seen but generally not visited by tourists who are itching to leave UB & get out into the countryside to experience the life of the nomads & stay in a *ger*!

Family *gers* & *ger* camps provide warm hospitality & comfortable, rudimentary accommodation; prices range from US$45–55/ night, including 3 meals. They top the list for the unique experience they offer. Private *gers* & *ger* camps welcome visitors during the tourist season Jun–late Sep. Some camps remain open in winter, while others close.

✖ WHERE TO EAT AND DRINK

The majority of Mongolians eat meat with lots of fat, which sustains them through the long cold winters, especially if they live in the countryside where people kill their own food. However, there are a number of newly opened international restaurants in the capital, including French, Italian, Indian, Chinese and Korean. There are also a number of 'foreign' cafés but they open and close quite frequently.

The many options available vary from a quick take-away to fine dining. UB now has a variety of top-quality and reasonably priced restaurants. You can get a delicious pizza for around T5,000. A night out may cost from T16,500 to T33,000, not including drinks. Be aware that fresh vegetables are difficult to get especially in the winter months. The city is full of Chinese and Korean restaurants that modify their menus to international tastes. Mongolian dishes like *buuz* (meat dumplings) are popular. A low budget meal costs from US$0.25. Students eat at college cafeterias, costing around US$ 1.50. Reasonable middle-range eating places include the California Restaurant on Seoul Street near the State Department. Top-range restaurants listed below include Los Bandidos near Genghis Khan Square; Monet, Zen and Hazara Indian (with vegetarian options) all on or near Peace Avenue; along with excellent Chinese, Korean and Japanese restaurants at the Blue Sky Tower.

Restaurant hours in Ulaanbaatar are normally noon–14.00 for lunch and 18.00–20.00 for dinner. Cafes serve breakfast from 07.00–10.00. Street food is available during the day. Most hotels serve meals at similar times as mentioned. For location of listings, see map on pages 232–3.

RESTAURANTS There are many more restaurants than those listed below, catering for all tastes; for example, KFC (Kentucky Fried Chicken) the fast-food chain recently opened in UB with people queueing up to 40 minutes to get a taste of 'original spiced chicken'. KFC is located on the west side of the Central Library. Major hotels like the Kempinski serve wonderful Japanese food and high-quality beef & seafood; dishes tend to be pricey (ranging from T50,000–69,000).

✖ **Bangkok Thai** Cnr of Genghis Khan Sq; ☎ 11 325588. In the building housing the Mongolian Artists Exhibition Gallery across the road from the Democratic Party HQ & Central Post Office. You go in some wooden doors downstairs, turn left & go upstairs. There is scant signage outside with no signs on the front door or stairway. Good Thai food. The menu also includes chicken curries, noodle dishes & salads; recommended for vegetarians. Credit cards accepted.

✗ Bayangol Restaurant Bayangol Hotel, Chinggis Khan Av 05; ✆ 11 326794/312255. After so many years, still one of the best restaurants in Mongolia, with character as well as good food. The Casablanca Bar is located on the ground floor, serving a wide range of food, mainly Western, in a large well-designed conservatory.

✗ BD's Mongolia Barbecue Western end of Seoul St, west of the Naran Dept Store & Ayanchin outfitters; ✆ 11 311191. 1st US franchise restaurant to open in Mongolia. Features unlimited 'create your own stir-fry' from a buffet of meat, sauces, spices & (most importantly) the largest selection of vegetables in the country; impressive salad bar; desserts; good service. Credit cards accepted.

✗ California Seoul St, opp Aeroflot office; ✆ 11 319031; ⏲ noon–23.00 daily. International cuisine & grilled meat (as opposed to boiled); serves a variety of steaks, burgers, pizzas & excellent salads of alarming proportions. Good wines & one of the few places in Mongolia to find Perrier water; iced-teas; cheesecake or ice-cream sundaes for dessert.

✗ Grand Khan Irish Pub Seoul St; ✆ 11 336666/330993/330995; e info@gk-irishpub.mn; ⏲ 11.00–midnight daily. This is *the* place to hang out. Good food, excellent beer, vibrant atmosphere & an unrivalled location adds to its popularity with trendy Mongolians & foreigners alike. Draught Guinness from Ireland is on tap (of course), at around T6,000 a pint.

✗ Hazara Restaurant Peace Av 6, Bayanzürkh District; ✆ 11 455071; ⏲ noon–14.30 & 18.00–22.00 daily. Northern Indian cuisine, with an excellent lunchtime menu. A good place to eat for vegetarians. Special dishes include vegetable curries, tandoori chicken & kebabs.

✗ Ikh Mongol Restaurant Next to Natsagdorj Library & State Circus; ✆ 11 331206/305014; ⏲ 11.00–23.00 daily. Doubles as a pub & restaurant, serves European & local food, grilled meat & homemade beer.

✗ Le Bistro Français Opp Mongolian State University, Ikh Surguuliin Gudamj; ✆ 011 320022; ⏲ 11.00–midnight daily. Good French food & wine including snails, salads, steak & a great

chocolate mousse. The service is some of the best in UB – the staff actually come & check on you instead of waiting to be called over. Cosy in winter; in the hot weather the open-air conservatory area is cool & relaxing. Credit cards accepted.

✗ Le Triskell North of Genghis Khan Sq, Bldg 4 Sukhbaatar St, a few doors down from Le Bistro Français; m 9903 4308; 771 21919; e denkhjargail@yahoo.com; ⏲ 09.30–midnight daily. Specialises in crêpes of all sorts. More casual than the bistro, the sort of place where you can also go for a snack or drink if you don't want a full meal. On the menu: quiche Lorraine, duck, snails.

✗ Los Bandidos Restaurant Peace Av, opp Peace & Friendship House; ✆ 11 318174/314167; ⏲ 08.30–midnight daily. Mexican & Indian food. Menu includes curries, nachos & its famous fajitas.

✗ Luna Blanca Nr Genghis Khan Sq, Apt M100, Gutliin 22, west of the Parliament building, across the road from the CIA; ✆ 11 327172; www.lunablanca.org. Very good vegan food. Service can be a little slow but it's worth the wait; not just for vegans. Better to go for lunch or early dinner as it closes quite early (around 23.00) especially in winter.

✗ Modern Nomads Baga Toiruu, opp Children's Palace; ✆ 11 318744; e info@ modernnomads. mn; ⏲ 10.00–23.00 daily. Designed for tourists who want to experience Mongolian food; serves traditional *buuz* (steamed mutton dumplings), *khuushuur* (fried mutton dumplings) & traditional milky salty tea.

✗ Monet Central Tower Bldg, 2 Genghis Khan Sq; ✆ 11 310707; www.onetrestaurant.mn. Probably the most expensive fine dining restaurant in UB with excellent views across the city (only Blue Sky is taller); food & service are very good. Next door (on 17th floor) is the Sky Lounge – a good place to meet for drinks; hosts expat get-togethers every Wed evening. There are also a number of restaurants on the 3rd floor, including a Japanese restaurant & *sake* bar.

✗ Oriental Treasures Tserendorj St (generally referred to as 'Beatles Street' by expats since they put up the Beatles monument), between State Dept Store & Circus. Easy to spot due to the curtains of lights in the windows. Review: 'Best dumplings I've ever tasted.'

✗ Planet Pizza Tserendorjiin Gudamj; ✆ 11 319394; ⏲ 10.00–23.00 daily. On the street opposite the State Dept Store running down to Seoul Street on the right-hand side, this is a tiny Mongolian-run restaurant where you can eat in or take away. Good-quality Domino's-style pizzas (very cheesy with a thick crust) in 3 size options. A chance to practise your Mongolian food vocabulary as staff don't all speak English.

✗ Seoul Restaurant Round bldg in Nairamdal Children's Park; ☎ 11 329709/315394; ⏰ noon–23.00 daily. Korean food & has been a long-standing favourite of Mongolians & foreigners alike.

✗ Silk Road & Veranda restaurants (Veranda is upstairs) Off Chinggis Khan Av, nr State Library on Jamiyan Guunii Gudamj; m 919 14455 (Silk Road); ⏰ 11.00–midnight daily. Italian & international cuisines. Serves wonderful BBQ-style meals in a pleasant setting with views over the Choiijin Lama Temple. Portions are large & tasty.

Diners can choose between steaks & kebabs, a range of salads & toasted sandwiches & wraps. There is a small club downstairs.

✗ Taj Mahal Restaurant Bayangol Hotel, Tower A; ☎ 11 311009/326875; ⏰ 11.00–22.00 daily. Serves delicious Indian food in comfortable surroundings. The menu has many vegetarian options as well as some excellent meat dishes. The set-lunch *thalli* includes several curries, rice, bread, salads & a dessert – good value for money.

✗ The Bull Korean hotpot restaurant with three branches. **Bull 1** (only branch marked on map) on Seoul St; **Bull 2** next to Rokmon Bldg; **Bull 3** in new Blumon Bldg next to university & Urgoo 2 cinema; all ⏰ 10.00–midnight daily. Very central. Pick a soup & cook your own meal. The food is tasty & delicious. No need to book – it is come in, cook & eat.

A VEGETARIAN IN MONGOLIA – ÜGÜI MAKH! (NO MEAT!)

Sam Strauss

Being a vegetarian (*tsagaan khoolton*) is hard in Mongolia, for it is not an exaggeration to say that the Mongolian diet revolves around meat, mutton especially. In fact, most Mongolians will have meat for breakfast (some form of sausage or paté), lunch (usually steamed *buuz* – mutton dumplings) and dinner (pieces of fried or boiled meat or more dumplings). Being offered pieces of white fat or lard is not uncommon. Even for non-vegetarians this amount of meat and the way it is prepared, very fatty and gristly, is unpalatable for most visitors. In the past, fish did not feature in the Mongolian diet owing to a traditional dislike – among nomads it is assumed that only those poor enough to own no animals would stoop to eating fish. Being landlocked and with large rivers and lakes confined to the far north of the country also restricts fish supply, although tinned Baltic sprats and tuna are stocked in the bigger supermarkets.

The Mongolian climate means that with the exception of carrots, potatoes and white cabbage, very few vegetables can be cultivated. These, along with cucumber and beetroot, are generally pickled in vinegar to make Russian-style salads – a legacy of the Soviet era, and a way of preserving food where there are often no refrigerators and where it must be stored for a long time.

There are two ways of surviving as a vegetarian in Mongolia – by cooking or by eating in restaurants (a number of vegetarian restaurants have sprung up in the city – such as Luna Blanca, see page 243). Visiting the countryside can be problematic unless you want to live off carrot and beetroot salad, so it is best to stock up on your own supplies before you leave UB.

COOKING The Sky Centre supermarket behind the Chinggis Hotel is by far the best place for buying food in UB. Unless you visit in the middle of winter when it is difficult to get supplies in from China, this is stocked with most Asian vegetables and many Western food brands, for example dried pastas, sauces and tinned

✕ **Veranda Restaurant** In same building as Silk Road nr Monnis Tower; ☎ 11 330818; m 940 44455, 990 84455, 944 99501. One of the few places in UB where it's a good idea to book in advance due to its popularity & convenient location in the centre of town. Pleasant sitting on upstairs terrace outside in summer. The food is Mediterranean with a wide range of choice. The chicken soup is excellent.

✕ **Zen Blue Sky Hotel & Tower** Peace Av, off Genghis Khan Sq; ☎ 701 09559; www. hotelbluesky.mn. Japanese restaurant. As one expat put it: 'in my personal opinion this is the best. I was a bit worried about eating sushi so far from the sea, but have become a regular.' The top-floor bar has great (but expensive) views of UB. Also in the Blue Sky Tower are excellent Korean (☎ 701 09449) & Chinese (☎ 701 00505) restaurants on the 3rd floor.

CAFÉS

▭ **Buddhist Centre Café** Khudaldaany Gudamj, opp Zanabazar Museum of Fine Art. Bright & welcoming, this small café inside the Buddhist Centre is well worth a visit. Order a tea, apple juice or hot chocolate, as well as one of the delicious homemade cakes, then snuggle into one of the *ger*-style sofas with a good book.

▭ **Café Amsterdam** Peace Av, left side of State Dept Store; m 8891 1832; ⊕ 08.30–22.30 daily. Popular with expats & foreigners, a fun place to meet for coffee; delicious toasted cheese sandwiches. Screens films 20.00 Wed. Wi–Fi connections.

▭ **City Café** 1st Fl, Union of Mongolian Artists Bldg; ☎ 11 328077; ⊕ 08.30–20.00 Mon–Fri, 10.00–midnight Sat/Sun. Coffee, bakery, hotpot & drinks as well as internet access. Great location.

▭ **Fashion Café** Seoul St, nr California Restaurant. Trendy fashion-themed restaurant &

goods. It also has a large section devoted to dried fruit and nuts (perfect for expeditions), and sells tofu and other soy products.

The Mercury Food Market near to the Mongolian State Circus also sells a wide range of fruit and vegetables, although prices are high and Westerners are likely to be overcharged because of an inability to bargain – it's best to take a Mongolian friend with you if you want to shop here for hard-to-get speciality items. The UB Mart is a handy smaller market (opposite KFC!).

Local shops and supermarkets rarely stock more than the ubiquitous pickled vegetables and piles of onions, cabbages and maybe a few shrivelled apples. However, it is possible to find street stalls selling bags of seeds, nuts and dried fruit all year round (look in the Bayangol/3rd micro-district).

EATING IN RESTAURANTS This can be tricky in those serving traditional Mongolian food, although if desperate it's possible to 'create' your own fairly balanced meal by asking for rice, a fried egg and some salad. Restaurants serving other cuisines are far easier options. Places such as Millie's, Café Amsterdam and California (see *Where to eat and drink* listing, pages 242–6) have good salads and pasta, while the Thai and Indian restaurants have a range of vegetarian dishes. It is also worth trying some of the Korean restaurants behind the State Department Store. Although very few of these have menus printed in English, most of them display pictures of the various meals, with tofu featuring strongly.

A CAUTIONARY NOTE! This is not the place to come if you are vegan, as most protein, excluding meat and fish, comes from eggs and dairy products and almost all salads are liberally covered in creamy dressings. However, should you still be tempted to visit, shop at the Sky Shopping Centre for vegetables, soy products and nuts. Aside from Luna Blanca, BD's Mongolian Barbecue is probably the only restaurant that can properly cater for vegans, as here you can pick what you want to eat yourself.

6

bar with informal & fun atmosphere. Inspiration comes from the multi-screens showing constant footage from the Fashion TV satellite channel, & stacks of *Vogue* magazines. A little incongruous with the fashion theme, the menu includes comfort food such as chicken & mashed potatoes & the best milkshakes in Mongolia.

La Boulange/Michel's French Bakery Just north of Peace Av, nr State Dept Store; 11 329002; m 992 37181, 991 69970; ⊕ 08.00–20.00 daily, closed Jan. A favourite place to buy cakes & croissants; great meeting place for the French community in UB.

Millie's Espresso 1st Fl, Jamyan Gunii St, due south of Sukhbaatar Sq & Peace Av; 11

330338; ⊕ 09.00–19.00 Mon–Sat. Popular with tourists; serves pizza, moussaka, pastries & good coffee.

Café Ti-Amo Seoul St, next to Platinum Centre & Sky Dept Store; 701 12422; ⊕ 09.00–19.00 Mon–Sat. Good lattes, relaxed atmosphere, b/fast & lunch.

Papa Café On far side of British Embassy (from centre town), northside of Peace Av; 11 461687; e papacafe2010@gmail.com; ⊕ 10.00–21.00 Mon–Sat. Provides a healthy, safe, hangout place for expats & others; community based for all ages. It runs as a model of integrated business: provides employment, gives training & develops skills for those involved.

ENTERTAINMENT AND NIGHTLIFE

BARS AND CLUBS Nightlife centres on the bars and discos where food as well as drink is often also available and live music predominates. Club life takes off on specific nights: Wednesday, Friday and Saturday evenings when the **Grand Khan Irish Pub** is buzzing. In fact, it's buzzing most evenings. It's a great nightspot and offers food (see page 243).

Most places serve cocktails and other drinks; beer, the most popular drink, costs T5,000, vodka is around T6,500; prices may vary from place to place.

Many places listed below stay open to midnight and later. A huge number of bars have opened and it is difficult to keep track of them. The most famous nightclub in centre town is the **Vegas Club** situated in the Blue Sky Tower of Genghis Khan Square. The main clubs are **Metropolis** – connected to the Chinggis Hotel by the Sky Shopping Centre; **Brilliant** – in the 19th district; **Medusa** – to the right of the Tengis Cinema; and **Silence** – across the road from the Medusa.

MODERN MUSIC – FROM POP AND ROCK TO RAP

Gunjiimaa Ganbat

Soyol Erdene were the first professional rock band in Mongolia in the 1970s. B Naranbaatar, a founding member of the group, went on to work in Buryatia, Siberia, with the well-known Ensemble Baikal – one of the most popular folk-song ensembles. Örgöö, a popular rock band of the 1980s, are back in fashion after some time in oblivion. I Bolooj is still the leader of the eight-man group.

B Sarantuyaa (known as Saraa) was the top pop idol of the 20th-century all-female group Lipstick, famous for their hit song 'Uchralyn Blues' (Rendezvous Blues), who were contracted to perform as part of election campaigns in 2000. Since then they have been replaced in popularity by the girl band, Gala.

The rap singer Gee is famous for his protest songs about serious environmental concerns. See his YouTube videos that show him performing with the Mongolian folk band Jonon and other singers.

The singer D Oyuuntülkhüür introduced Mongolian music to Japan and has been recognised for her charity work; her concerts in UB attract large audiences.

While working at the *Mongol Messenger* newspaper for three months, I was lucky enough to be 'adopted' by a group of Mongolians around my own age (mid-twenties). I say 'adopted' because we met completely by chance and yet I ended up seeing them almost every day for the duration of my stay, and 'lucky' because we became firm friends; they turned out to be some of the nicest people I have ever had the good fortune to meet and we are still in touch today.

For anyone visiting Mongolia for a substantial period of time, making friends with locals is a fantastic way to experience the unique culture this country has to offer. This is especially true given the language barrier (virtually no-one outside UB will speak English) and the relatively underdeveloped state of the tourist industry and general infrastructure – a lack of road signs, public transport, etc, can render the countryside almost impenetrable to travellers.

As Mongolians are so hospitable and friendly, all it takes to 'make contact' is a little bit of trust on your part. We in the West seem to be naturally suspicious of strangers who approach us, yet in Mongolia this is a frequent occurrence and little harm can come from having a drink or lunch with someone who chats to you in a bar or club (the usual rules of common sense apply of course). It is quite normal (especially for Western girls) to be approached by Mongolians who are being genuinely friendly and are totally benign. However, male tourists should exercise some caution when talking to Mongolian girls in bars and clubs as young Mongolian men can be very territorial and are inclined to see Western men as being 'predatory'. Late-night fights, fuelled by vodka, are not infrequent at these venues.

Given the usual perception of Mongolia as being so isolated and remote, it is astounding to see young, urban Mongolians dressed in the latest fashions and listening to recently released music, courtesy of Fashion TV and Russian MTV. This is something to bear in mind if you intend to socialise – don't embarrass yourself by wearing your hiking boots and North Face jacket in UB; clothes that you would wear to go out at home are surprisingly appropriate here! In fact, young affluent Mongolians are brand obsessed and are all kitted out in Calvin Klein underwear and Puma trainers (mainly fakes because no luxury goods are actually sold in Mongolia). As many young Mongolians study abroad, don't be surprised to hear them speaking a variety of languages, including French and German, as well as English. They are also responsible for the assimilation of many 'Americanisms' into the Mongolian language. Given that most Mongolians live with their parents until they get married (with correspondingly few responsibilities for the urban affluent), the Mongolian youth often lead a somewhat hedonistic lifestyle, partying late and drinking heavily most nights of the week – the perfect excuse to join in and have fun!

6

THEATRES Music, poetry and folk tales play a large role in Mongolian cultural life and are woven into opera and ballet productions. The dress code is casual/smart, similar to theatre dress around the world.

National Theatre [233 E5] Large, red-walled building on Chinggis Av, next to Bayangol Hotel; 11 323402. The National Folk Song & Dance Ensemble is based here & puts on classical

Mongolian & international theatre productions & traditional *khöömii* (overtone or throat-singing) accompanied by the *morinkhuur* (horse-head fiddle). Tickets T7,000.

Mongolian Song & Dance Ensemble, known as Tümen Ekh [233 E5] Exhibition centre in Children's Park; ✆ 11 322238/327916. The entertainment starts at 18.00 on Tue (spring & summer). Tümen Ekh Dance Ensemble consists of 35 artists who perform traditional folk dances, accompanied by Mongolian musical instruments, & overtone singing (*khöömii*). Tickets T7,000.

National Opera & Ballet Theatre [233 F4] Southeast cnr of Genghis Khan Sq; ✆ 11 322854/323339. The theatre celebrated its 50th anniversary in 2013. It stages Mongolian & classical concerts & opera, the latter having included *Chinggis Khan* by B Sharav, Tchaikovsky's *Eugene Onegin* & in 2013 a musical after Shakespeare's *Romeo and Juliet*. Performances begin at 17.00. Tickets from T7,000.

Puppet Theatre [233 E5] Left side of National Theatre; ✆ 11 321669; ☉ Jul–Sep. Tickets T7,000.

CINEMAS Not many tourists go to the cinema inp. Ulaanbaatar, as the theatre performances of traditional music and folk dance are more popular. However, it is worth experiencing a Mongolian film – with themes of romantic love and traditional life centred on Genghis Khan. Look at the back page for 'What's on' in the *Mongol Messenger* or *UB Post*. Alternatively ask the receptionist at your hotel to check the film listings for you.

🎬 **Ard Cinema** [232 D4] Opp MIAT offices, town centre; ✆ 11 327193. Inside the building there is a bingo hall & a place to change money upstairs. Shows Mongolian films &, occasionally, translated or dubbed foreign films. Tickets cost T2,000.

🎬 **Örgöö Cinema** [233 F2] In 3rd district beside Nomin supermarket; ✆ 11 367445/324187. This cinema shows English films. Tickets T2,000.

🎬 **Tengis Cinema** [232 D2] Revolutionaries' Av (Khuvisgalchdyn Örgön Chölöö) & inner ring road; ✆ 11 312178/326575; www.tengis.mn. Latest releases. Tickets T2,500.

SHOPPING

In general, shops open 09.00–18.00 weekdays and Saturdays. Most are closed on Sunday. Markets open later (10.00) and stay open in the evenings to 20.00.

Most visitors want to buy Mongolian cashmere: the State Department Store (walking distance from Genghis Khan Square) has a good selection; Cashmere House, at 5 Peace Avenue, offers high-quality cashmere and yak wool garments and items like gloves and scarves.

Mongolia produces many specialist items based on natural products – from exotic cashmere garments to puzzles and games. Mongolian watercolour paintings are of exceptional quality as are jewellery and leather goods. The souvenir industry is developing in the countryside, so please save some shopping space for local traditional products when travelling outside the capital. Buy your cashmere in Ulaanbaatar or Bayan-Olgii. Mongolians tend not to barter so don't quibble over prices, even in the open markets. Finally, don't leave shopping until the last minute at the airport, or you may be disappointed. The best souvenir shop in Ulaanbaatar is the Mary & Martha shop next to the State Department Store – see box, opposite page. At the State Department store you may buy Mongolian *deel* or tunics, or have tunics or jackets tailor-made and posted.

WHAT TO LOOK FOR
- Cashmere jumpers
- Camel-hair waistcoats

MONGOLIAN FASHION

Mongolia has a thriving fashion industry and Mongolian designer labels are gaining access to international markets around the world. It has been the case in the recent past that raw materials – especially cashmere – left the country to be turned into fashion garments abroad – in China, Italy, Germany, Scotland, the USA and elsewhere. This is no longer the case. The Gobi factory is based in UB; a new cashmere factory opened in Erdenet in 2013. New home markets have developed in UB and in the countryside, where felt and other hand-crafted items are made for the local tourist market. Many souvenir items, ranging from gloves and slippers to headscarves and handbags, are on sale in market towns or in local aimag museums, and are exported around the world. Many young Mongolian artisans are teaming up with overseas designers like the UK's Clare Ed, and marketing their products this way (see box, page 71).

Shilmel Zagvar Fashion Center [232 B4] (*Golomt Town, Enkhtaivan Av, Ulaanbaatar 24;* ☏ *11 331612;* e *shilmelzagvar@yahoo.com;* ⏰ *10.00–18.00 daily) stages a fashion show every Wednesday at 16.00. Its website (in Mongolian) will give an indication of what's on show: www.shilmelzagvar.mn.*

- **Wooden puzzles** Some of the best presents to bring home. Traditional Mongolian board games – but you will need to play with Mongolians first in order to learn them.
- **Mongolian-style silk tunics (*deel*)** Made to measure at the State Department Store in the centre of Ulaanbaatar.

MARY & MARTHA – SOUVENIR SHOP IN ULAANBAATAR

Bill Manley

The only registered fair trade (WFTO) shop in Ulaanbaatar, Mary & Martha (*http://maryandmarthamongolia.blogspot.com/*) works with over 100 artisans from all over Mongolia with products in leather, silk, felt, embroidery, all sorts of jewellery, handmade cards, paper cut products, hand knits from yak and camel hair, yarns from herders ... the list goes on. The shop has seen business increase greatly from the mining and diplomatic staff as well as tourists wanting to shop in a known situation – while other 'souvenir' shops like the State Department Store have seen sales stagnate. All the staff speak good English and even a little Russian, Korean and Japanese and offer Western-style service. From a social responsibility point of view, Mary & Martha gave away over US$10,000 in 2012: to groups or projects such as the CR Alcoholics Recovery programme; to help small business with loans, initiatives and training schemes; to support to local authorities for homeless people (Adults Underground). M&M has also helped to provide machinery and tools for artisans and has helped individuals with health and medical issues.

Mary & Martha sits in a small side road in between the post office and the State Department Store, near Gobi Cashmere and immediately next to the French Bakery.

- **Jewellery and silverware** Finely crafted in Altaic-knot designs (reminiscent of Celtic patterns).
- **Paintings** Mongolian landscapes in oil and watercolour, and Mongol *zurag* paintings (realistic, classical, nomadic lifestyle and landscape art).
- **CDs** Traditional Mongolian music – look for a CD of the extraordinary sound of overtone singing, unique to Mongolia.

ESSENTIAL ITEMS AND CASHMERE

⛩ **State Department Store** [232 D4] 5th Fl, 44 Peace Av; ☏ 11 319232; www.nomin.mn; ⏰ 09.00–22.00 daily. Huge range of cashmere, electronic goods, mobile phones, traditional clothing, souvenirs.

⛩ **Buyan Cashmere Shop** [232 D4] At State Dept Store on Peace Av; ☏ 11 325423

⛩ **Gobi Cashmere House Boutique** [233 E4] Peace Av 5; ☏ 11 326867; e cashmerehouse@magicnet.mn

⛩ **Gobi Flagship Shop** Next to Gobi factory, Industrial street, 3rd Khoroo, Khan-Uul District; ☏ 11 343051; e marketing@gobi.mn; ⏰ 10.00–22.00 Mon–Sun. Go there by taxi, as it is difficult to find.

SOUVENIRS, CAMPING AND OTHER ITEMS

⛩ **Mary & Martha Shop** [233 E4] 1st Khoroo Bldg 10, east of Broadway Restaurant, off Peace Av, beside French Bakery; m 99 725297; www.mmmongolia.com; ⏰ 11.00–19.00 daily. Hand-crafted fair trade gift shop. See ad, page 226.

⛩ **Khan's Ger** [233 F4] Right side of the Youth Federation Bldg, behind Ulaanbaatar Hotel, nr small ring road (Baga Toiruu); ☏ 11 328410. Souvenirs, traditional arts & crafts.

⛩ **Map Shop** [232 B4] Ikh Toiruu 15; ☏ 911 56023/48698; e caen@mongol.net

⛩ **Xanadu** [233 E5] Marco Polo Plaza; ☏ 11 319748; www.xanadu.mn. Bookshop & provider of fine wines.

⛩ **Ayanchin Outfitters** [232 D4] West of Parliament Hse & east of Golmot Bank on Seoul St; ☏ 11 319211; e ayanchin@magicnet.mn; www.ayanchin.com; ⏰ 10.00–19.00 Mon–Fri, 11.00–18.00 Sat/Sun. Supplies everything you need for fishing, hunting & camping trips.

GENERAL SHOPPING IN ULAANBAATAR   *Nicolle Webb*

There are numerous places in UB to buy food, clothes and other essentials. They range from little kiosks and small shops to larger shopping centres and markets. The huge, open-air central market **Naran Tuul** is commonly called the 'Black Market' [off map, 233 H6] (not an illegal market) where you can find almost anything you need. It is always very crowded (watch your handbags and wallets). In the centre of the city there is a large food market called the **Mercury Market** [232 C5] (also known as the New Circus Market) located off Seoul Avenue, which offers a wide range of fruit, vegetables, meat and imported foodstuffs. It is also where most foreigners shop, so prices are higher. The **State Department Store** [232 D4] (Ikh Delgüür) offers many of the same products as the Mercury Market. For those who don't want to pay top prices for everything there are alternatives. For bulk value, the **Container Market** [232 D2] near the Tengis Cinema offers the best deal on almost all the foodstuffs you need. Household necessities, toys and beauty products are available there as well. Small food markets in the various city districts offer competitive pricing and a good variety of products. Finally, there is the new **Sky Market** [233 G3] behind the Chinggis Khan Hotel that has everything from frozen smoked salmon to leopard-skin steering-wheel covers and bowls of tropical fish.

Jane Grendon

The New Way Life NGO, Mongolian Quilting Centre (*www.mongolianquilts. org*) was established in 2003 by Selenge, a young lawyer who came into contact with disadvantaged women struggling to survive in Ulaanbaatar during the 1990s. Unemployment was high and alcohol was a big problem. Women bought bags of fabric scraps to burn, which made poor fuel; Selenge saw a better use for them and taught women how to piece the scraps together to make quilts which could be used in the home or sold. Selenge had spent some time in America, and while there she had been introduced to patchwork and quilting and saw the support that a community of women can give other women.

At first, women worked in a cramped basement with no natural light or ventilation. Selenge soon realised she needed more practical help, so using the internet she looked for quilt teachers. As a result Maggie Ball, a quilt teacher living in America, went to work with them in 2004. She suggested that Selenge should also contact the Quilters Guild of the British Isles and appeal for more teachers. And that is how Lesley Coles (a quilt teacher) and I became involved.

In the summer of 2006 we spent four wonderful weeks in Mongolia teaching and travelling. Quilting is a new activity in Mongolia and the women were eager to learn. They already had sound sewing skills and most of them own hand-cranked sewing machines. Language wasn't a problem because sewing is a visual craft. They have a tremendous sense of fun and we laughed a lot. They learnt quickly despite poor working conditions and a lack of good tools.

We returned in 2009 to do more teaching and travelling. Selenge receives grants to extend skills and create income in rural communities. Lesley was keen to be involved with this outreach and we travelled overland to work in Mörön and Bulgan. Selenge made our journey a sightseeing tour. We were welcomed into the homes of local herders, told them about what we were doing and taught women some patchwork skills. They were especially pleased to be able to use scraps of material to make small gifts. The interest and generosity of these people was humbling.

With the help of money raised by Maggie in 2009, Selenge was able to purchase permanent premises on Seoul Avenue opposite the Mongolian barbecue restaurant. This now includes an office, a workroom and a shop, which gives them the opportunity to sell direct to tourists or locals. Their goods are also on sale in the State Department Store.

Despite escalating costs and particularly severe Mongolian winters, Selenge is determined that the centre will become self-sustaining and is working hard towards that goal. The problem of women needing to support their families has not diminished and although many women have been drawn into this project we expect many more will be helped as the centre grows in strength.

Ulaanbaatar **SHOPPING**

6

ART Modern Mongolian art is shown at the Palace of Culture [233 F4], located on Genghis Khan Square, which also exhibits classical Mongol *zurag* works; for art at other galleries and museums in the city see *Art galleries* listings below provided by the Arts Council of Mongolia. The exhibition hall of the Union of Mongolian Artists [233 E4], which puts on changing art exhibitions, is located near the Central Post Office on Chinggis Avenue, south of Genghis Khan Square (*11 327474*), and in the Marco Polo Plaza Gallery (*11 330269*) in the Palace of Culture. The

Artists Union helps to promote and sell works. One group is Oron Zai (Space) Art Society. Its members, painters, sculptors, graphic artists and craftsmen, are mostly teachers at UB Art College. Oron Zai may be contacted via D Erdenebileg, Art College, Ulaanbaatar (✆ *11 210646*). To follow the works of individual artists who show works at 'Space' exhibitions, Google: 'Oron Zai (Space) Art Society'; different names and exhibitions will come up – changing all the time.

Galleries exhibiting paintings for sale are found beside Gandan Monastery, and at locations near the State Department Store on Peace Avenue. Hotel lobbies are now a favourite place to find small works – prices vary from around US$20 to US$200 for the work of unknown artists.

Art galleries

Art Gallery of the Union of Mongolian Artists [233 E4] ✆ 11 327474; www.uma.mn; ⏱10.00–18.00 daily; entrance free

Khan Bank Art Gallery [232 C5] Khan Bank new building, Seoul St; ✆ 11 332333/333264; e artgallery@khanbank.com; ⏱ 09.00–18.00 MonFri; entrance free

Modern Art Gallery [233 F3] ✆ 11 327177/ 331687; ⏱ 09.00–17.00; entrance adults T2,000, children T500, students T1000

Valiant Art Gallery [232 D4] Altai Center, west side of State Dept Store; m 990 80644; www.

mongolianartgallery.com; ⏱ 10.00–18.00 Mon– Fri, 11.00–18.00 Sat/Sun

Zanabazar Fine Art Museum [232 D3] ✆ 11 326061/326060/326837; www. mongolianationalmuseum.mn; ⏱ 09.00–18.00 Mon–Fri; entrance adults T2,500, children T200, students T400. More information on Zanabazar himself is available at www.zanabazar.mn.

Xanadu Art Gallery [232 D4] North of State Dept Store, beside Tedy Center; ✆ 11 310239; m 991 10873; www.xanaduartgallery.org; ⏱ 10.00–19.00 Mon–Fri, 11.00–19.00 Sat; entrance free

OTHER PRACTICALITIES

BANKS Banks stay open 09.00–17.00 Mon–Fri & a limited number of branch offices open on Sat. Other banks include Khaan Bank, an agricultural bank with a wide network of branches – even in remote villages; Xas Bank-SME, a micro finance-focused bank; Capital Bank – SME bank. The Savings Bank formally declared insolvent in July 2013 put its branches under the State Bank of Mongolia.

$ Bank of Mongolia (Mongol Bank) – Central Bank of Mongolia [233 E3] Baga Toiruu 3, 15160, behind the MIAT ticket office; Khudaldaany St 6; ✆ 11 322166; e adm@mglbank.com.mn; www.mongolbank.mn

$ Bank of Ulaanbaatar [233 E3] Baga Toiruu 15, across the street from Government Hse; ✆ 11 312155

$ Golomt Bank [233 E4] Genghis Khan Sq 3, next to Mongolian Stock Exchange; ✆ 11 311530/327812/311971/326535; e mail@ golomtbank.com; www.golomtbank.com. Travellers' cheques; cashes Amex, Visa, MasterCard, City Co-operation.

$ Trade and Development Bank [233 E5] Cnr Khudaldaany St & Baga Toiruu; ✆ 11 312362; e tdbmts@magicnet.mn; ⏱ 09.00–12.30 & 14.00–15.30 Mon–Fri. Accepts Amex, Visa, MasterCard, credit-card cash advances. Multi-storey modern building with a new room on one side (outside) that caters especially for foreigners.

COMMUNICATIONS
Post

✉ **The Central Post Office (CPO)** [233 E4] ⏱ 08.00–17.00 Mon–Fri, 08.00–14.00 Sat; telephone services 24hrs. The post office is fairly reliable, although letters take a long time to reach their destinations. It is open at different times for different services, eg: parcels and stamps. In addition to postal services there are reasonably priced postcards for sale.

Internet Internet cafés in Ulaanbaatar have sprung up between new dance clubs & bars; internet access costs around T800 per hour. Most of the larger hotels have full business centres, including internet access.

@ **Internet Café** [233 E1] Solongo Restaurant Bldg; e bodicom@mongolnet.mn; ⏱ 10.00–19.00 Mon–Fri, 11.00–18.00 Sat

@ **Internet and information** [233 E5] Central Library; e ubpic@magicnet.mn; ⏱ 09.00–17.00 Mon–Sat

@ **Internet House Café** [233 F4] Youth Federation Bldg, Baga Toiruu (small ring road) behind Ulaanbaatar Hotel; e byambaa@mongol. net; ⏱ 09.00–17.00 Mon–Sat

Mobile phones GSM 900 network is operated by Mobicom & Unitel companies. CDMA is operated by Skytel company. Aimags (provinces) are covered with mobile phone networks. G-mobile & F-zone are new operators. Satellite & cellular phones are available to hire & to buy; for example, Iridium satellite phones, from Monsat LLC (*New Horizon Bldg, Olympic St 6;* ✆ *11 32370;* m *990 96062;* e *monsat@mcs.mn; www.monsat. mcs.mn*).

FOREIGN EMBASSIES AND CONSULATES

@ **China** [233 F2] CPO Box 672, Zaluuchuud Av 5; ✆ 11 320955; f 11 311943; e chinaemb_mn@mfa. gov.cn; http://mn.china-embassy.org

@ **France** [233 E4] Peace Av 3; ✆ 11 324519; f 11 319176; e contact@ambafrance-mn.org; www. ambafrance-mn.org

@ **Germany** Negdsen Undestnii Gudamj 16 (behind Mongolian National University) [233 F2];

✆ 11 323325; f 11 323905; e germemb_ ulanbator@mongol.net, info@ulan.diplo.de; www. ulan-bator.diplo.de

@ **India** [233 G2] Zaluuchuud Av 10; ✆ 11 329522; f 11 329532; e info@indianembassy.mn; www.indianembassy.mn

@ **Japan** [233 F5] Japan Olympiin Gudamj 6; ✆ 11 320777; f 11 31333; e eojmongol@magicnet. mn; www.mn.emb-japan.go.jp

@ **Kazakhstan** [232 D1] Zaisan St 31/6; ✆ 11 345408; f 11 341707; e info@kazembassy.mn; kazakhstan.visahq.com/embassy/Mongolia

@ **Korea** [233 F5] Republic Olimpiin Gudamj 10; ✆ 11 321548; f 11 311157; e kormg@mofatgo. kr; www.south-korea.visahq.com/embassy/ Mongolia/

@ **Russia** Peace Av A-6; ✆ 11 327191; f 11 327018; e embassy_ru@mongol.net; www. russianembassy.net

@ **Turkey** [233 E4] Peace Av 15160; ✆ 11 311200; f 11 313992; e turkemb@mongol.net, embassy. ulaanbaatar@mfa.gov.tr; www.turkey.visahq.com/ embassy/Mongolia/

@ **UK** [233 H4] Peace Av 30; ✆ 11 458133; f 11 458036; e britemb@mongol.net; www. britishembassy.gov.uk/servlet/, www.british-embassy.net/mongolia.html

@ **USA** [233 F1] Ikh Toiruu 59/1; ✆ 11 329095, main switchboard 700 76001; f 11 320776; e esyam@mongolianembassy.mn; www.us-mongolia.com. In US ✆ +1 202 333 7117; f +1 202 298 9227

WHAT TO SEE AND DO

MAIN BUDDHIST MONASTERIES AND TEMPLES The three main temples are Gandantegchinlen (Gandan) Monastery (the major monastery of the city), Bogd Khan Palace Museum and the Choijin Lama Temple/Museum. Ulaanbaatar is also the home of several important religious institutions, including the *ger*-shaped Dashchoilon Monastery, whose abbot is the country's second most senior religious leader. Mongolian and Tibetan traditional medicines are taught and practised and there is a Buddhist centre of astronomy and astrology. Nuns have their own monastery called the Tögsbayasgalant süm (temple). Buddhism in Mongolia follows the Yellow Hat school, although a Red Hat monastery may be found at Namdoldenchinlin in Bayanhoshuu district.

Gandantegchinlen Monastery [232 B3] Located in the western region of the city, off Peace Avenue, this monastery is one of the most important visitor sites in the city (✆ *11 360023;* ⏱ *09.00–11.00 Mon–Sat, 09.00–13.00 Sun*). It is the centre of Mongolian Buddhism, known as 'Gandan' Monastery for short. The abbot is the senior Buddhist in Mongolia today, who studied at the Dalai Lama's religious academy in India and has the title of Gavj. Gandan's Sanskrit name means 'Paradise of Mahayana' or, more loosely translated, it means 'place of all joy'. The monastery comprises a complex of buildings on the hillside northwest of the city centre, near the television tower. It is easily recognised from a distance by its multi-storey temple, housing a 23m statue. Before the 1921 revolution, Mongol herders traditionally sent one of their sons to study Buddhism. Most of the monasteries were destroyed in the 1930s, but Gandan escaped. As a teaching monastery, Gandan houses the Mongolian Buddhist University. It has a large library of rare books and manuscripts in Mongol and Tibetan on Buddhist philosophy, astrology and medicine. Visitors can attend services. No photography is allowed inside the temples.

There are five temple buildings in the complex:

The Temple of Vajradara (Ochirdar) Built between 1840 and 1841 in stone and brick, with a tiled roof. Most important religious ceremonies are held in this temple. The statue of Vajradara, sculpted in 1683 by Zanabazar, is to be found here.

The Temple of Zuu (The Jewel Temple) Built in 1869 to house the remains of the young seventh Bogd Gegeen, who died in his teens. 'Zuu' means Buddha.

The Temple of Didan-Lavran The former library of the fifth Bogd Gegeen. The 13th Dalai Lama stayed here when fleeing Tibet in 1904. Another temple was built in 1924 to house the library of the monastery, which contains a collection of over 50,000 rare books and manuscripts and can be visited only by special permission from the head monk of the library temple, which can be arranged in advance, ie: by special request through a local tour operator.

The Temple of Megjid Janraiseg (Avalokiteshvara) Built in 1911–12 to commemorate the end of Manchu rule in Mongolia, and perhaps as a plea for the healing of the Bogd Gegeen's blindness. It contained an immense statue of

UB LOOS   Sam Strauss

In case you need a loo when out and about during the day here is my list:

Open Society Forum [233 E5] Jamiyan Günii Gudamj. Off Chinggis Avenue, a small side street, directly opposite Choijin Lama Temple and next to the Silk Road Restaurant.
Marco Polo Complex Jamiyan Günii Gudamj. Off Chinggis Avenue, a small side street, directly opposite Choijin Lama Temple, location of Millies [233 E5].
UB Hotel Foyer [233 F4] East of Genghis Khan Square.
Buddhist Centre Café [232 D3] Khudaldaany Gudamj, opposite the Zanabazar Museum of Fine Art.

These are modern, Western-style toilets that work, have ample supplies of loo paper and are cleaned to standards you probably take for granted back home, but will really miss after a few days in Mongolia!

Loo paper appears to be a rarity in UB's toilets so it is advisable always to carry your own supplies (these can be purchased from most supermarkets). Given the lack of soap, or washing facilities in many cloakrooms (or even the loo itself outside UB), wet wipes prove indispensable.

Avalokiteshvara-Janraiseg, which was destroyed and taken in pieces to the Soviet Union in the 1930s. The statue was rebuilt in the 1990s by public subscription.

School of Advanced Religious Studies Housed in a fifth temple building. Monks from Mongolia and now from all parts of the globe gather here to study.

The Bogd Khan's Green Palace (or Winter Palace) [232 D7] (*Zaisan St (Zaisany Gudamj), south of Peace Bridge;* \ *11 342195;* ⊕ *10.00–17.00; closed Thu in summer & Wed/Thu in winter; no admission charge*) The European-style Winter Palace was built in 1905 by Tsar Nicholas II of Russia for the eighth Öndör Gegeen, Mongolia's only religious and political leader, who died in 1924. It stands next to a large temple complex with a very elaborate entrance gate within a wooden-fenced compound on the south side of Ulaanbaatar, not far from the river Tuul and Bogd Uul Mountain. In 1961, it became a museum and it now contains many treasures including works by Zanabazar, magnificent furs such as the Öndör Geegen's *ger* covered by snow-leopard skins, jewels and many gifts that were received by the Bogd Khan. There is a collection of stuffed animals (from his private zoo) and some erotic drawings.

The temples The temples of the Winter Palace are known as the 'temples of the monastery that spreads wisdom'. Visitors enter the complex of buildings via the visitors' entrance (see map). It is found on the left-hand side of the formal entrance: the stone screen (*yampai*), an ornate triple gate, which is closed. Entrance to the temples is free, although donations are accepted.

The temples include the Temple of Maharajas, where Mongolian musical instruments are housed, along with pictures, jewellery and precious stones; the Temple of the Apostles (Naidan), where prayers were said for the happiness and long life of the Bogd Gegeen, with two smaller temples to the east and west (with displays of appliqué on the left and painting on the right); the main temple (Nogoon Lavran or High Lama's Palace), where sculptures by Mongolian, Tibetan and Chinese artists of the 18th and 19th centuries are exhibited, and where the eighth Bogd Gegeen came to pray in private. To the south of this temple is the Jüdkhan Tantra Süm, which houses a portrait of the third Dalai Lama, Sodnomjamts. The side temples of the main temple used to house the Bogd Khan's library.

Choijin Lama Temple [233 E5] (\ *11 324788;* ⊕ *summer 10.00–18.00 daily. Check opening times if visiting out of the tourist season*) Built in the first decade of the 20th century for the Bogd Khan's younger brother who was also the state oracle. The temple/museum is situated in the centre of Ulaanbaatar not far from the Wedding Palace, directly below Genghis Khan Square, south of Peace Avenue. It has a fine collection of art and religious relics, including *tsam* masks and costumes used in religious dances. It is known as one of the most beautiful religious buildings in Mongolia.

The Principal Temple At the entrance of this 'temple that spreads compassion' is a sculpture of Buddha and his two disciples and the embalmed body of the tutor to the seventh and eighth Bogd Gegeens. In the middle of the temple is the throne of the Bogd Gegeen. Also to be found here are some important religious texts: 108 volumes of the Ganjur and the 226 volumes of the Danjur (Buddhist holy texts) as well as many paintings depicting the horrors awaiting sinners in the underworld.

Temple of the Makharaji Consecrated to the Four Guardians of the Four Directions of the World.

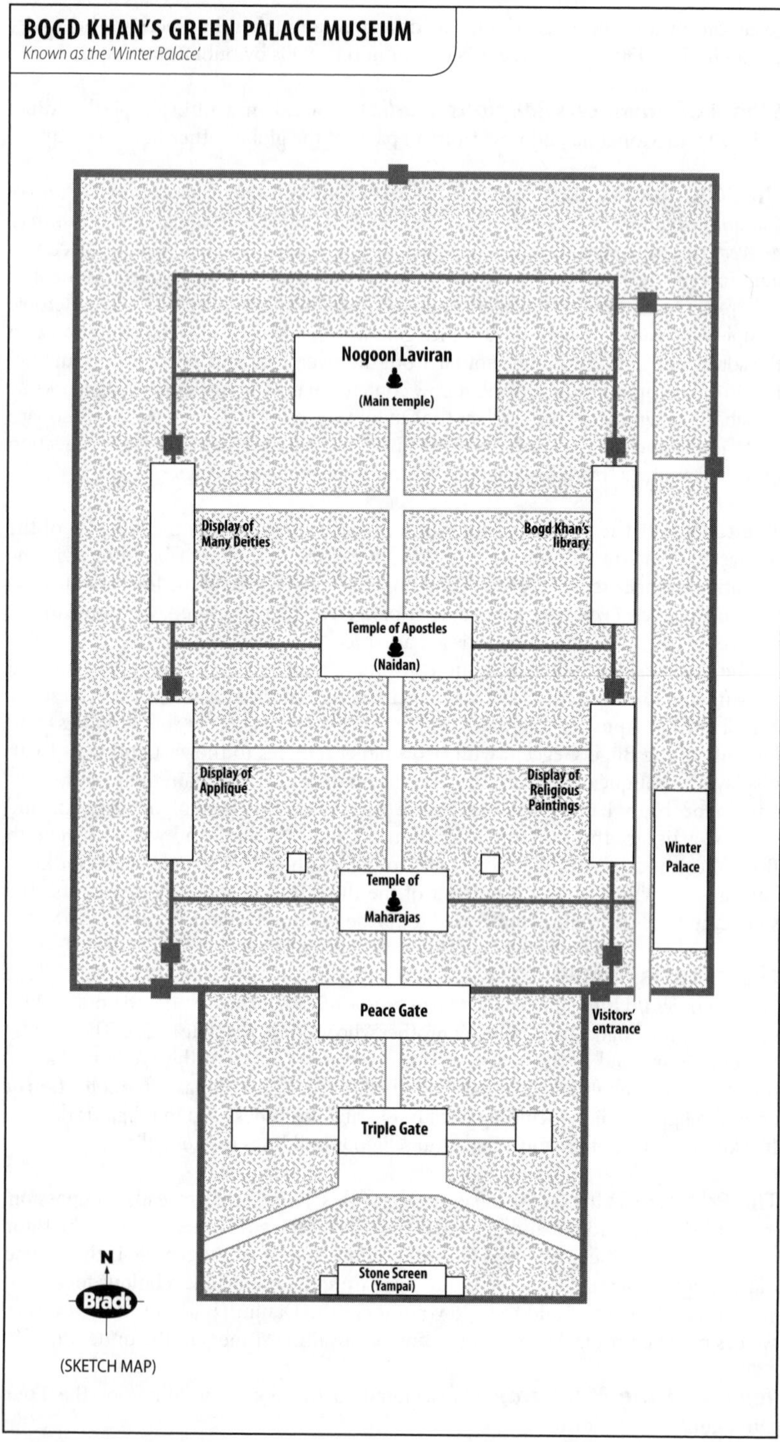

BOGD KHAN'S GREEN PALACE MUSEUM
Known as the 'Winter Palace'

Nogoon Laviran
(Main temple)

Display of
Many Deities

Bogd Khan's
library

Temple of Apostles
(Naidan)

Display of
Appliqué

Display of
Religious
Paintings

Winter
Palace

Temple of
Maharajas

Peace Gate

Visitors'
entrance

Triple Gate

Stone Screen
(Yampai)

N

Bradt

(SKETCH MAP)

The Temple of Zuu Consecrated to the Sakyamuni Buddha.

The Temple of Yadam Forbidden to ordinary believers, this temple was devoted to the gods of Yadam (a protective deity) and it was where Tantric rituals took place. Sculptures in bronze depict the doctrine of Tantric Buddhism. Here too is Zanabazar's statue of Sitasamvara.

The Temple of Amgalan (or Temple of Öndör Gegeen) Contains many sculptures, bas-reliefs of the 16 Arhad (enlightened ones) and many works of Zanabazar, including a self-portrait. Of particular significance is the statue of the goddess Tara, beloved by the nomads.

OTHER MONASTERIES AND TEMPLES Full addresses are not currently available for all the temples and monasteries described below, but with a taxi driver's help, the help of a Mongolian guide, and persistent asking, you should be able to find them. Generally, visiting hours are in the mornings from 09.00 to noon.

Mongolia is piecing together its heritage because so many temples and their contents were destroyed in the religious purges of the 1930s and little information on them remains. The elderly are counted on to remember the past – though even they are few now – and the process of interviewing the older generation to restructure the history of temple life is happening, but it will be some years before printed brochures with accurate details relating to specific temples, their history and contents are available.

The Monastery of Dambadarjaa (Dambadarjaalin Khiid)
About 7km north of Ulaanbaatar, this used to be known as the 'temple that spreads religion' and was built in 1795 on the northern outskirts of Ulaanbaatar by the Manchu emperor to house the remains of the second Bogd Gegeen (which were later transferred to Bogdyn Khüree at Dambadarjaa).

The Temple of Vajrayogini
The temple was inaugurated in 1995 and replaces an earlier temple built at the beginning of the 20th century. It is consecrated to Padmasambhava, the Indian Grand Master from Kashmir, who introduced Tantric Buddhism to Tibet in the 8th century. The doctrine of Red Hat Lamaism is based on the teachings of Padmasambhava. Part of the temple is Narokhajid, a school for nuns, which opened in 1995.

Dashchoilon Monastery
[233 F1] (⏰ *10.00–noon daily*) Located between the outer and the inner ring roads in the north of the city, the monastery was built in 1991 in the shape of a *ger*. This temple is also dedicated to Padmasambhava and follows the doctrine of Red Hat Buddhism.

Mamba Datsan
[233 F1] (📞 *11 358489*; ⏰ *09.00–noon daily*) Located northeast of the city, outside the outer ring road (Ikh Toiruu) in Batanzürkh district; specialises in teaching Buddhist medicine.

Bakula Rimpoche's Betüb Monastery
[232 C3] Located on the corner of Ikh Toiruu (outer ring road) and Revolutionaries' Avenue, near the Geser Temple. Founded by Bakula Rimpoche, the former Indian Ambassador to Mongolia and a high-ranking Buddhist. Inaugurated in 1999, this monastery is a symbol of Indian/Mongolian co-operation. The old form of Mongolian writing in cursive script is taught here.

Geser Temple [232 C2] (🕓 *09.00–noon daily*) Northwest of the city on the outer ring road (Ikh Toiruu). This temple, named after the Tibetan hero Geser Khan, is part of Gandan Monastery. The building is in Chinese style and is much frequented by local people. Medicinal herbs are sold on stalls there and fortunes told.

Namdoldechinlin Monastery (🕓 *09.00–11.00 daily*) Located in Bayanhoshuu district.

MUSEUMS There are a number of museums in the capital which are interesting, informative and well worth taking the time to visit. Most museums charge entrance fees. The standard rate for foreign tourists is currently around T2,500 though this varies slightly.

National Museum of Mongolian History [233 E3] (*Commerce St (Khudaldaany Gudamj) 2;* ☎ *11 325656;* 🕓 *10.00–16.00 Sun/Mon, 10.00–14.30 Tue, closed Wed, 10.00–16.00 Thu–Sat (during the tourist season; check opening times out of season; US$7 to take photos*) This museum, opposite the Golomt Bank, presents Mongolian history and culture from prehistoric times to the present day. It features the costumes and accessories of Mongolia's many ethnic groups, a collection of Mongol saddles and a replica of a traditionally furnished nomadic *ger*. Gift shop.

Museum of Natural History [233 E2] (*Khuvisgalchdyn Örgön Chölöö;* ☎ *11 315679;* 🕓 *summer 10.00–15.00 Mon, 10.00–16.30 Tue–Sun (check opening times out of season); admission adults/children T2,500/1,000*) This museum covers geology, zoology, botany, anthropology and palaeontology. Exhibits include the famous fighting dinosaurs, dinosaur nests, bone and fossil fragments of other ancient creatures, expedition material from anthropological digs and the American palaeontologist Roy Chapman Andrews' fossil finds in the 1920s. Don't forget to see the Golden Camel Museum on the second floor, which exhibits camel paraphernalia. Gift shop.

Zanabazar Museum of Fine Art [232 D3] (*Commerce St;* ☎ *11 323986;* 🕓 *summer & autumn 09.00–18.00 daily; winter & spring 10.00–17.00*) On the east side of Builders' Square (Barilgachdyn Talbai) along from the Trade and Development Bank, the museum is named after the religious leader Zanabazar (1635–1723). Its collection shows art from Neolithic times through to the Turkic period (6th–7th centuries AD), masks and paintings of the 13th-century Mongol khans to early 20th-century art. Highlights include figures of Buddha sculpted in bronze by Zanabazar; a silver, gold and pearl mandala; traditional Mongol *zurag* paintings by famous Mongolian artists; a section on appliqué wall hangings; and items of Mongolian ritual dances. Gift shop.

Theatre Museum [233 F4] (*Genghis Khan Sq;* ☎ *11 326820;* 🕓 *10.00–18.00 Sun– Wed & Fri/Sat*) Located within the Palace of Culture Building (third floor), the collection shows the history of Mongolian theatre from 1921 through a series of photographs and film. Theatrical costumes are also modelled and there are sections on puppets, the circus, folk music and dance as well as a good exhibit of *tsam* (Buddhist dance) masks.

Memorial Museum of the Victims of Political Oppression [233 E4] (*Genden St (Gendengiin Gudamj);* 🕓 *10.00–16.30 daily, 13.00–14.30 Sat*) Located between the Ministry of Foreign Affairs and the Wedding Palace, Sükhbaatar district. Designed by German-Swiss architects in the 1930s, the wooden building with its sloping roofs was once the home of Prime Minister Genden, a victim of the purges, shot in 1937 in Moscow. He was replaced by Anandyn Amar, who was also executed in the USSR, in 1941. It became a museum in 1996 and is dedicated to the Mongolians who lost their lives in the 1930s purges. Around 30,000 Mongolians died and records of personal belongings and political reports bring this tragic story to life. Genden's daughter was the curator.

Ulaanbaatar City Museum [233 G5] (*Blue Sky St (Khökh Tengeriin Gudamj)*; ⊕ *09.00–18.00 Mon–Fri*) Located in an old-style Russian house. The history of Ulaanbaatar, from its founding in 1639 to the present day, is shown through the collections, photographs, paintings and tapestries. Special items of interest include a panoramic view of the city carved on an elephant tusk and a famous series of woodblock prints by the artist Natsagdorj.

Military History Museum [off map, 233 H4] (*Lkhagvasürengiin Gudamj*; ⬧ *11 451640*; ⊕ *summer 10.00–17.00 Thu–Mon*) The east wing shows Mongolian history from the Stone Age to the 19th-century Manchu period, while the west wing houses post-1921 military history; paintings in Mongol *zurag* style depict the Battle of Kyakhta, fought in 1921. Various tanks and artillery are displayed outside.

Mongolian Hunting Museum [232 C3] (⬧ *11 360248/360879*; ⊕ *09.00–18.00 Mon–Sat*) This museum is found on the second floor of a two-storey yellow building (the Nature Palace) on the right side of the road leading to Gandan Monastery, Bayangol district. The museum exhibits many stuffed animals shown in their 'natural environment' depicted by artists. They include wild horses, wild camel and several different types of deer. There is a model of an ancient hunter's camp and many other interesting items such as *argali* (wild sheep) horns and equipment to do with hunting. Ask downstairs for a key if the door is locked. Opening hours are irregular.

Mongolian Toy Museum [233 F4] (⊕ *10.00–17.00 Mon–Sat*) Housed in a four-storey building behind the Ulaanbaatar Hotel off the small ring road (Baga Toiruu). Exhibits over 500 Mongolian and international puzzles and games.

Museum of Geology and Mineral Resources [233 F2] (⊕ *09.00–noon daily*) On the second floor of the Mongolian Technical University, this museum has a collection showing Mongolia's diverse minerals including interesting exhibits of agate and jade. It is divided into three areas: geology, mineral resources and mineral description.

GALLERIES Art exhibitions are held at the Hall of Mongolian Artists, located immediately south of Genghis Khan Square on Peace Avenue. Paintings are usually for sale. For current exhibitions look in the *Mongol Messenger* (English-language Mongolian weekly newspaper) or ask the hotel receptionist to find out what is on and how to get there.

The Art Gallery [233 F4] (⬧ *11 328486*; ⊕ *09.00–18.00 daily*) Located in the Palace of Culture on Genghis Khan Square, off Peace Avenue; this is the largest art gallery in Mongolia and features 20th-century paintings. Important works include *Black Camel* by Sengetsokhio, *Fighting Stallions* by Tsevegjav and *Tale of the Great Horse* by Tengisbold. One room is devoted to traditional Mongol *zurag* painting.

Paintings and photographic works are for sale. Contemporary works tend to fuse Eastern and Western traditions, combining the characteristics and the techniques of both. See also *Art galleries*, pages 251–2.

OTHER ATTRACTIONS

Nairamdal Park (Children's Park) [233 E5] (*Entrance T8,550*) This large park near the city centre has amusement rides for children, a maze, a pond and boat rides. Every evening at 18.00 during the summer tourist season there is a performance of traditional song and dance held in the theatre here. The park was renovated in 2010 and the roller coaster relocated within it.

Zaisan Memorial [off map, 232 D7] This tall memorial is dedicated to Mongol–Soviet comradeship-in-arms. It is situated on a small hill directly south of UB, the high ground providing wonderful views of the city. It is well worth climbing up to this viewpoint, especially at night to see the city lights and also the many new property developments in UB. Parking is limited on the narrow one-way access road.

Wrestling Palace [233 G4] (*Tickets around T7,000, tourist price*) On the east side of the city, south of Peace Avenue, near the British Embassy, the new Wrestling Palace, completed in 1998, is an imposing circular, domed stadium which seats 2,500 people. During competitions several hundred wrestlers wrestle in pairs, simultaneously, in the 770m² arena, until one pair remains to compete for the victory title. National tournaments are held during Tsagaan Sar (New Year) and Naadam (in early July) festivals, although during Naadam the main wrestling tournaments are held in the Central Stadium, or Naadam Stadium [233 E6], south of the city. For Naadam's three competitive sports – horse racing, wrestling and archery competitions – see pages 261–4.

Mongolian State Circus [232 C5] (☏ *11 320795; tickets US$7/T10,000*) Found in a blue-domed building on Seoul Street (Seüliin Gudamj), Bayangol district near the railway station. The programme includes acrobatic displays, high-wire balancing acts by trapeze artists, along with animal performances – tremendous fun and entertainment. Performances begin at 17.00. Acts include Daggy the Camel, water juggling, clowns Bungle and Fumble, and the Ace Contortionists Duo Sükhbaatar. Unfortunately, since the circus performers are frequently on a world tour, the number of shows has dropped, and much of the time there are no performances.

National Library of Mongolia [233 E5] (*4 Chinggis Av;* ☏ *7011 2396; www. mnlibrary.org*) The Mongolian National Library holds the country's largest collection of manuscripts and sutras (holy writings) as well as copies of more than three million books and other publications of historic and contemporary interest. The collection is represented in many languages from Chinese, Korean and Japanese to English, German and other European languages. The building provides reading rooms and there is a small museum dedicated to valuable rare manuscripts and books.

American Centre for Mongolian Studies (ACMS) [232 C4] (*Natsagdorj Library, East Entrance, Seoul St 7;* ☏ *7711 0486; www.mongoliacentre.org*) This non-profit educational organisation supports Mongolian studies and exchanges; it offers translation services and can help visitors to find guides and translators. ACMS supports field project research in providing fellowships; it helps to coordinate international summer school courses for language and other training.

Naadam are the national games, held annually in Ulaan Baatar on 11 July. The opening ceremony is reminiscent of an Olympic Games opening, with traditional gala, pomp and circumstance. There is a covered grandstand area for which you need tickets. Parachutists float down to land in the sports arena (a rectangular field), swinging on brightly coloured parachutes, with Mongolian flags, streamers and smoke trails flying behind them. The 'Mongolian Standard' – nine poles topped by white horse manes and flags – are individually carried by mounted horsemen who thunder into the arena and circle the stadium with great fanfare before ceremoniously placing their standards on the podium. Then, the president officially declares the games open.

A succession of colourful and musical performances begins – marching bands, dancers with feathers and streamers, and ceremonial traditional dances reminiscent of warriors and hunters. These are accompanied by drummers situated around the field and by more traditional musicians playing horse-head fiddles and *yatags*, instruments like zithers (for details on musical instruments, see page 109).

Next, the competitors arrive: archers clad in their traditional dress; jockeys, some as young as six or seven; and wrestlers – 100 or so, wearing brief costumes – stomp across the field. (Mongolians come in all shapes and sizes: some incredibly tall, others small and slender.) The burly wrestlers circle the 'Standard', bow and touch their heads or caps to the standard poles and prance around waving their arms in a birdlike way. Then they bow to one another and the wrestling contests begin.

Archery takes place in the afternoon, both men and women competing simultaneously, although in separate groups. There are small brick-like targets, composed of leather and positioned in lines along the ground at distances of up to 25m. After each shot the adjudicators, near the targets, make hand signals and whistle to instruct the archer of the accuracy of his/her shot. Only three arrows are allowed per person. Everyone wears traditional costume.

While waiting for the horse racing to begin, the crowd is treated to some equestrian events. The police and military clear the area of stray horses and cows and the race is on! Excitement rises as a storm of dust in the distance heralds the approaching riders, then all too soon, the event is over. The winner receives a prize but it is the horse who is the hero of the day!

The National Games – Naadam The most important sports in Mongolia are horse racing, wrestling and archery, known as the 'three manly sports'. They are the focus of the national Naadam, the Games, held annually in Ulaanbaatar on 11 July, to celebrate National Day.

Horse racing Two things set Mongol horse racing apart – the length of the race and the age of the jockeys. The Mongols, once the world's greatest riders and cavalrymen, are interested in stamina; horses therefore race in different categories (mares, geldings, two year olds, three year olds, etc) over distances between 15km and 30km. Since it is considered that it is the horse and not the jockey that wins the race, children aged six to 12, girls as well as boys, take part as jockeys, being far lighter than adults. They are supposed not to force the horse but only to guide it to the winning post. In the big races, jockeys over nine years old are barred. The reason is that the Mongols want to bring out the horses' willingness as well as their speed.

The youngest horses (two year olds) race over a distance of 15km; three to five year olds race 20–25km, and separate races are held for stallions. The big race for mature horses is over 30km, and many of the young jockeys ride bareback, which is a feat in itself. The winning horse is garlanded with blue ribbons and sprinkled with *airag* (fermented mare's milk), while its jockey is given a pat on the back and a prize and disappears into the crowds. Most prize money goes to the owner and racehorse trainer. A song called 'Bayan Khodood', meaning 'full stomach', is chanted when the last horse comes in – no disgrace for the horse or rider but the trainer is teased for not doing a proper job.

Around 100 horses, from all 21 aimags, compete in each of the five or six separate races at the Naadam in Ulaanbaatar. The winning five horses are given the title Airagiin Tav, that is, the 'airag five'. In other words, they are 'placed', as in English horse races, when the first three, not more, are 'placed', or the first four in handicap races. The most coveted prize in the rural Naadams is a motorbike. At the national games the prize money is good. For the jockeys, mud, dirt, tears and sweat characterise a horse race, while the roaring crowds and anxious faces fixed on the winning post resemble horse race-goers the world over.

Wrestling Wrestling has always been a favourite sport of Mongolians, as the new wrestling palace in Ulaanbaatar testifies. Radio and television broadcasts from the arena keep its audiences transfixed throughout the year – not only during the Naadam festival. Balance and agility are more important than brute strength. No agonising holds are used and wrestlers try to out-kick or throw their opponents. Bouts can be over in seconds.

A match is won when any part of the loser's body, except the soles of his feet, touches the ground. (New rules do not allow fingers or palms to touch the ground.) When this happens, the loser passes under the arm of the winner who then imitates a Garuda, raising his arms above his head, before meeting his next opponent. The final winner at the Naadam games becomes a national hero. During the summer months they wrestle on grass in the open air (see below).

The wrestling costume consists of the traditional long boots with upturned toes (*gutal*), a short jacket with long sleeves (*zodog*), tightly fitted across the back and open-chested, and short trunks (*shuudag*), like swimming briefs. The material used is top-quality silk, usually in red or light-blue colours for the trunks, and incised and ornamented leather for the *gutals*. There is a rumour that the reason Mongolians wear an open-fronted jacket is that long ago a lady wrestler, dressed as a man, took part in the games, and only when she had won did she reveal herself to be a woman.

Each contestant must have a second (*zasuul*), as in duels, who stands close by to advise him during the contest, to hold his hat and to announce his titles at the beginning of the third, fifth and seventh rounds. This announcement is made to encourage the wrestler and his fans.

Mongolian national wrestling has unique features: bouts are not limited by time, there are no weight categories, and many pairs of wrestlers meet simultaneously. This allows large numbers of competitors to take part in contests within a short period of time. Wrestlers are listed according to their title and rank: Falcon (*Nachin*) is awarded to a wrestler who wins five rounds in a nationwide competition; Hawk is the title after six wins; Elephant (*Zaan*) is given after seven wins; Garuda after eight wins; and Lion (*Arslan*) after nine wins. The title Titan (*Avraga*) is awarded to the Lion who has won a tournament in the past. There are several categories of

ARCHERY   *Ross Tokola*

The main body of the traditional Mongolian bow is made of two Mongolian rams' horns that are joined in the middle. It can also be built of layers of horn, sinew, bark and wood. The ends of the bow, where the string is notched, are made of wood, the glue is made of animal tendon, and leather is wrapped around the handle. It takes one year for the bows to be shaped properly before they can be used, which makes them all the more valuable. The arrows are also traditionally made. The shaft is made of wood, the fletching is made of bird of prey feathers, and the tips of competition arrows are made of bone.

There are three different kinds of archery practised in Mongolian tournaments. The kind that I practise, which is the most common one among Mongolian archers, is called *khalkh kharvaa*. In khalkh kharvaa, the target is a line of hand-sized camel-hide baskets that are laid on the ground 75m away for men and 68m away for women. At the beginning of a competition, each archer is assigned a firing line based on the number of years the archer has practised and the archer's skill, the more outstanding archers being the ones with the red ribbons hanging off the back of their hats on which each chevron symbolises a competition they've won. Each archer shoots four arrows in each of ten rounds during a competition in which the archers take turns firing down their line in each round. Because there are normally hundreds of archers competing, a competition usually lasts two days.

During the first 20 shots, in order to score a point, and you can only ever score one point per shot, it is enough to fire the arrow underneath the red ribbon above the baskets and 1m in front of the baskets. During the final 20 shots, in order to score a point, the arrow has to hit one or more of the baskets and can do so after hitting the ground within 1m of the target line. Mongolian archers take turns being judges for each other during rounds when they are not shooting and do so standing right next to the targets. The judges use signals to indicate to the archer who fired where the arrow hit, relative to the line of baskets. When an archer scores a point, the archers judging will indicate where the arrow hit, then raise both hands high in the air and sing. It is quite an experience watching the arrows come flying in. It is very important to pay attention when being one of the judges. The arrows take less than two seconds to reach the target and, rather than lobbing in, move in an incredibly straight line. The Mongolian bow is, arguably, the most powerful traditional bow in the world.

I began learning traditional Mongolian archery in the spring of 2004. I was taught by a very skilled champion archer called Byamba. I also had the help of a good friend of mine called Tümenbayar, who has translated for me and been a great support during my time practising archery in Mongolia. In summer 2004, I competed with the young archers in the youth Naadam (National Games) and earned sixth place, becoming the first foreign national to take part in the traditional archery competition in the history of the tournament. In 2005, I turned 18 and graduated to competing with the adults and masters. That year I took part in the Naadam and the State Archery Tournament. Later that year my family moved to England, where I now study philosophy at the University of London. I returned to Mongolia in 2006 to take part again in the summer Naadam and State Archery Tournament, held in commemoration of the 800th year of Mongolian Statehood.

I am continuing my studies at the University of Cambridge.

Titan: Oceanic Titan, Worldly Titan and the highest, Invincible Titan, granted to the Worldly Titan who wins a tournament for the second time. Mongolia's greatest wrestler, Invincible Titan Bat-Erdene, carried the Mongolian flag at the 2000 Sydney Olympic Games. Since his retirement in early 2000, Bat-Erdene has become a politician. He stood for president in the 2013 elections but was unsuccessful.

Archery What distinguishes Mongolian archery is that the archer does not aim at an upright bull's-eye target, but at targets made up of cork wrapped with leather straps, positioned flat on the ground. The arrow has to rise into the air and descend (like a javelin) to hit the ground targets without overshooting or undershooting. While this is happening, a wail goes up from the crowds and the cries 'mergen' ('good shot') and 'uukhai' ('hit') are followed by thunderous applause.

In the countryside there is less emphasis on archery and even in the city it doesn't draw as many crowds as the wrestling and horse events. Spectators stand nearby to cheer on the contestants. Judges stand near the targets to signal results by a sign language of hand movements and shouts of 'uukhai'. Prize money for the winner amounts to thousands – up to T500,000.

Archery has as ancient a history as wrestling and both are mentioned in *The Secret History of the Mongols*, the 13th-century Mongolian chronicle that describes the life of Genghis Khan. An ancient rock inscription records an arrow shot of 335 spans – estimated at about 500m. The Mongols used a compound bow (built of layers of horn, sinew, bark and wood) strung with bulls' tendons; the result was as powerful as the English longbow. The Mongols handled their bows on horseback and used what is known as the 'Parthian shot' – an arrow shot made by turning in the saddle to shoot back at the enemy while galloping away.

Rugby The latest, imported 'manly sport' in Mongolia is rugby – the game was first introduced to Mongolia in the Soviet period by the Red Army. The Rugby Union of Mongolia was established and played its first match in 2009. Summer 2013 saw a team of rugby players from Hertford College, Oxford, take on a Mongolian Students' XV (for further information e rugby@hertford.ox.ac.uk). Local and national local club sides compete at the National Sports Stadium in Ulaanbaatar.

7

Central Provinces

The more possessions you have the more you are robbed of your freedom.

Wilfred Thesiger, writer and explorer

The central provinces (aimags) – Töv, Övörkhangai and Arkhangai – offer some of the most exciting Mongolian landscapes and are the obvious choice for less-mobile travellers, or those with not much time on their hands. There is plenty to see, from Erdene Zuu Monastery in the Orkhon Valley to lesser-known temples and ruins. The valleys of Terelj, so close to the capital, are as wild and beautiful as the more distant parts of the country. Terelj village itself is not so exciting; there are clusters of *ger* camps and people trying to entice you to ride on horseback at the rates of the day or hour (around US$5 per hour) but as soon as you move out into the countryside all is peaceful – whether it be on horseback or on your own two feet. The ranges of the Khentii in the northeast and the Khangai in the west give rise to many rivers, including the Orkhon River, with its magnificent waterfall. The provinces' national parks and game reserves are full of wildlife and the vast steppe itself offers both cultural tours and exciting places to explore.

TÖV AIMAG

Töv literally means 'central', and although Ulaanbaatar (an autonomous municipality) lies within its boundaries, the aimag capital is the small town of Zuunmod. Owing to its proximity to Ulaanbaatar and the good local transport system to and from the capital, this aimag is an excellent place to start exploring the country through a series of day trips. If you are waiting for a visa extension or planning an expedition further afield, the Genghis Khan Statue Complex, focused on a massive steel equine sculpture mounted by the khan himself, with its museums and surrounding exhibitions, offers you a great day trip (see page 279) and is a conveniently short distance away from the noise and hassle of the capital.

The Töv landscape is predominantly forested mountain/steppe, where wild berries, mushrooms and medicinal herbs grow in abundance. In the central provinces there are over 30 clear-water rivers (good for fishing), among them the Kherlen and Tuul. A number of mineral spas and hot springs are found at Janchivlin, Bööröljüüt and Elstei. These springs are in the main totally undeveloped so please don't get your hopes up that you will be submerging in hot pools while looking at mountain goats clashing heads on the mountainsides, as you do in New Zealand. However, the heated indoor pool at the Terelj Hotel is magnificent. The hotel itself is newly developed and won a 2010 World Luxury Hotel award (*www.hotelterelj.com*). Another top hotel is due to open in Terelj in 2014 – the US Hyatt group has planned a 131-room hotel near Turtle Rock. Towns in Töv

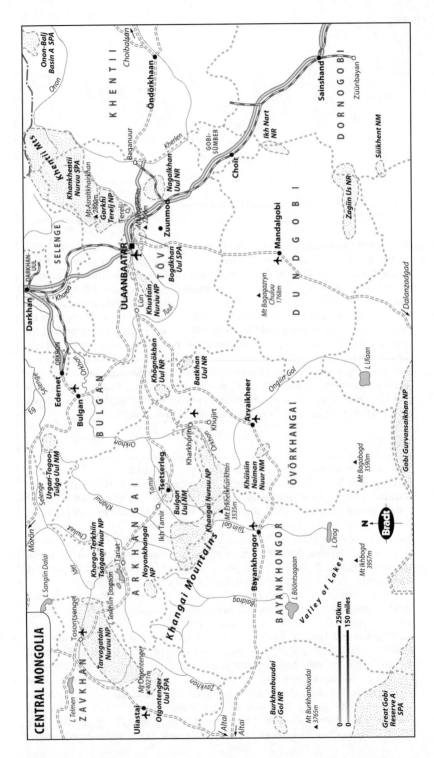

CENTRAL MONGOLIA

include the aimag centre Zuunmod, the former coal-mining town of Nalaikh and the peaceful settlements of Gachuurt and Khandgait. Resorts, besides the most popular resort of Terelj, include Nairamdal Zuslan (the Children's Centre), sometimes known as Bayangol, and the Nükht Hotel Resort, both of which offer accommodation and are close to Ulaanbaatar. A new Sky Ski Resort [map page 270] (*www.skyresort.mn*) opened in the Bogd Khan area outside UB in 2009 with the result that snow boarding in Mongolia became popular overnight. It is some 13km south of Ulaanbaatar and can be reached by car via the Zaisan road or by crossing the Marshall Bridge and turning east. A golf course is planned for the future in the same resort.

ZUUNMOD Located 40km south of Ulaanbaatar, Zuunmod is a relaxed town of around 17,000 people. It makes sense to stay a night here when hiking in the mountains or visiting Manzshir Monastery nearby. The town is laid out around the central park with a post office, theatre, cinema and administrative building. It is a small sleepy town with two museums (described overleaf) and the small monastery (*khiid*) of Dashichoinkhorlin, located southeast of the town. It is not of the same standard as the Manzshir Monastery but it is still worth a visit.

Getting there from Ulaanbaatar
By car Accessible without 4x4. From Ulaanbaatar take the airport road and drive 40km to Zuunmod.

By minibus Operates from Ulaanbaatar bus station between 08.00 and 18.00. Cost T1,500; buses run every half-hour.

BRIEF FACTS: TÖV AIMAG

Area 77,400km²
Aimag centre Zuunmod
Districts 27
Elevation of Zuunmod 1,529m
Livestock and crops Horses, cattle, sheep, potatoes
Ethnic groups Khalkh, Kazakh and Barga
Distance from Zuunmod to Ulaanbaatar 40km
Average temperatures July 15.6°C, January –20.4°C

HIGHLIGHTS
* Terelj Resort
* National parks and cultural sites: Manzshir Monastery in the Bogdkhan Uul Strictly Protected Area and Günjiin Süm (temple) in Gorkhi-Terelj National Park (although the temple is derelict, the walk to get there is worth it!)
* Wild horses at Khustain Nuruu National Park
* Eco-*gers* in Khankhentii Strictly Protected Area
* Genghis Khan Statue Complex
* Skiing and golf in the Bogd Uul
* Walking, hiking, wild flowers, meditation, horseriding: Terelj, Bogdkhan Uul SPA
* 'Nomads Day Festival' at Gun Galuut Reserve

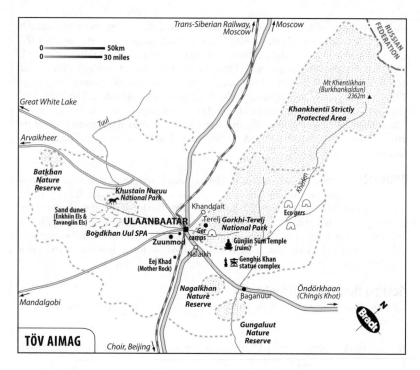

By local bus From Ulaanbaatar long-distance bus station to Zuunmod bus station, west of the main street.

By shared taxi Shared taxis can be picked up in the tourist season on the main street in Zuunmod or from the bus stations in Ulaanbaatar. They are more comfortable and cost around US$20 one-way with an additional waiting fee, if requested, to visit Manzshir Monastery.

Where to stay In addition to the hotels listed below, there are *ger* camps in the area at **Öndör Dov** (☏ *11 455108; US$55, includes meals & hot shower*) and at **Ovooni Enger** (☏ *272 22011; 4-bed accommodation T60,000*).

⌂ Government Hotel Northeast of the town square & central park (opposite the Hotel Zuunmod). **$$**

⌂ Hotel Zuunmod A minute's walk northeast of the town square & central park; provides ordinary rooms at standard/cheap rates.

✖ Where to eat and drink

✖ **Dölgöön Café** East side of the central park.
✖ **Öndör Dov** *Ger* **Camp** Located 8k west of Zuunmod. The restaurant opens for tour groups;

meals include grilled or boiled meat, noodles & vegetables.

What to see and do in Zuunmod

Aimag Museum (☉ *09.00–13.00 & 14.00–16.00 Wed–Mon; entrance fee T2,500*) Situated in the southwest corner of the central park. Exhibits local geology, flora, fauna and historical photographs.

Ethnography Museum (⊕ *10.00–17.00 daily; entrance fee T1,500*) Down a small lane southwest of the central park (a five-minute walk); exhibits include some traditional artefacts with a fully furnished *ger* as the main showpiece.

Dashichoinkhorlin Khiid This monastery lies on the southeastern outskirts of town across a small creek, a 10–15-minute walk from the central park. Religious ceremonies are held at 11.00, though double-check times of ceremonies with the resident monks and ask permission to watch them.

SIGHTS AND SITES IN TÖV The holy mountains and the national parks are great recreational places for hiking, camping and looking at nature, besides many other activities like riding, rafting and, in the winter, cross-country skiing. The forests are full of birds such as the Ural owl and northern hawk owl among over 250 other bird species; wild fauna includes musk deer, ibex and roe deer. Such areas of natural interest are mainly contained in Töv's five national parks. They include Bogdkhan Uul Strictly Protected Area in the south; Gorkhi-Terelj National Park in the west and the adjoining Khankhentii Strictly Protected Area, which extends northwest into Selenge and Khentii provinces; and Khustain Nuruu National Park, 100km to the southeast – famous as the home of Mongolia's recently reintroduced wild horses.

The nature reserves include Batkhaan (located on the border of neighbouring Övörkhangai Province in the southwest) and Nagalkhaan Mountain Reserve in the southern Khentii Mountains.

Bogdkhan Uul Strictly Protected Area (⊕ *May–Oct; admission (you enter park to reach Manzshir Monastery) T5,000pp, includes entrance fee to museum; Taxi from UB to Manzshir return costs US$40; by bus – see page 441*) Located near Ulaanbaatar, just north of the town of Zuunmod, this protected area covers 41,651ha of mountain range with taiga vegetation and bare rock peaks; it encompasses forests of Siberian larch, birch, cedar, pine, poplar and fir trees. The forested area extends to grasslands, which form the major part of the reserve situated on the borderline of the forest/steppe zones. There is a buffer area of 13,433ha and a transition zone of some 12,216ha between the strictly protected areas and areas lived in by local people and visited by the public. Bogdkhan Uul became an officially protected area in 1778, and is Mongolia's earliest protected area, but it was first recognised as a sacred mountain as long ago as the 12th century when logging and hunting were prohibited.

Special attractions include Manzshir Monastery, near Zuunmod; a winter camp of nomads; and the peak, Tsetsee Gün (2,256m). Seventy families, including rangers, live in this quiet reserve and many tourists visit it. Wildlife includes 47

THE FOUR HOLY MOUNTAINS

Four 'holy mountains' surround Ulaanbaatar ('Uul' means 'mountain'). They roughly correspond to the four points of the compass. They are Chingeltei Uul in the north; Bogdkhan Uul in the south; Bayanzürkhkhairkhan Uul (Bayanzürkh for short) in the east; and Songinokhairkhan Uul (Songino), in the west.

Bogdkhan Uul is considered the most magnificent of the holy mountains. It is possible to climb its highest peak, Tsetsee Gün (2,256m), but you need a permit to do so from the park authorities: contact the parks office (*Commerce St 5 (Khudaldaany Gudamj), Ulaanbaatar;* ☎ *11 312656*).

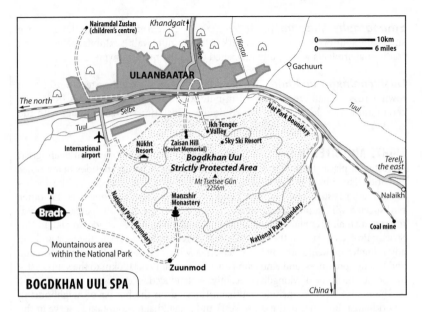

BOGDKHAN UUL SPA

mammal species, among them Siberian roe deer, Russian flying squirrel, Eurasian red squirrel, long-tailed ground squirrel and Siberian chipmunk. Some 116 bird species include black-billed capercaillie, hazel grouse and red crossbill. There are four species of reptile and over 500 vascular plants. The park has been nominated as a biosphere reserve by UNESCO and is a World Heritage Site. For hiking permits and further information contact the administration of Bogdkhan Uul Strictly Protected Area (*Commerce St 5 (Khudaldaany Gudamj), Ulaanbaatar;* ☏*11 312656*).

Getting there Bogdkhan Uul is easily accessible from Ulaanbaatar by bus, or by taxi to Zuunmod; cost T1,500 (bus); US$20 taxi one-way. You can hike across the mountains (camping *en route*) from the Nükht Hotel Resort (see below), situated in a mountain valley 16km outside the capital.

 Happy Mongolia (*happymongolia@gmail.com; www.happymongolia.net*), run by an entrepreneur called Daka, offers short tours near Ulaanbaatar and a day tour takes five hours from Tsetsee Gün to Manzshir Monastery – you can stay with a local family for US$35 per person including three meals.

🏠 *Where to stay*

🏠 **Chinggis Khan Khüree *Ger* Camp and Restaurant** ☏ 11 379923/311783. This camp lies at the western entrance of the Bogdkhan Strictly Protected Area, along the main Ulaanbaatar–Zuunmod road 25km from UB. Beside the *ger* camp there is a small museum which houses the costumes, weapons & armour formerly used when making an epic film on Genghis Khan; the camp's restaurant is well known & decorated in the same theme. **$$–$**

🏠 **Nükht Resort** Nükht Hotel (director Mr Gankhuyag); ☏ 11 325417/310421; **e** mail@ corporatehotel.mn; www.corporatehotel. mn/nukht. The hotel & other facilities are located 16km southwest of Ulaanbaatar off the main airport road, at the head of a secluded mountain valley. The resort provides accommodation for large groups at the hotel; also *ger* accommodation, with hot running water, showers & restaurant facilities. It is a convenient place to stay for local sightseeing & during the Naadam (national games), as the horse races take place nearby. Overnight hiking arrangements can be organised by the resort. **$$**

🏠 **Tuul Riverside Lodge** ☎70119370; e info@ ┊ A luxury *ger* camp lodge to the east of the capital.
tuulriverside.com; www.tuulriverside.com. ┊ Run by Nomad Tours & Expeditions. **$$$$–$$**

Hiking to Tsetsee Gün Uul Tsetsee Gün is the highest point (2,256m) in the Bogdkhan Uul Strictly Protected Area. A hiking permit is required (see above). The park entrance fee costs T1,500 per person and T4,000 per vehicle; tickets are available at the park gate and are also obtainable at Manzshir Khiid.

There are many different approaches to the summit though note that there are no marked routes.

Manzshir Monastery This monastery is located 45km from Ulaanbaatar and 5km northeast of Zuunmod. It was established in 1773, and dedicated to Manjusri, the Bodhisat of Wisdom. There were over 17 temples at one time, inhabited by 300 monks, but the monastery was almost completely destroyed during the Stalinist purges of the 1930s. One object that was indestructible was a huge bronze cauldron said to have provided food for 1,000 monks at a single sitting; a recipe called for the meat of ten sheep and two cows. The site has spectacular views and it is well worth visiting. A wooden balconied temple building has been restored and next to the reconstructed museum are ruins of Togchin Temple, one of an array of 17 temples that stood on the spot, built in the mid-1700s in Tibetan-style architecture. A resident community of monks is helping to bring the place to life again. There is a small museum showing Buddhist relics, *tanka* (religious) paintings and musical instruments.

To walk from Manzshir Monastery across the mountains to Ulaanbaatar via the Ikh Tenger Valley takes around ten hours; a two-day walking tour is advisable; you need to follow a map and preferably walk with a guide. Watch out for sudden changes in the weather (thunderstorms and icy winds in summer, deep snow in early winter). It is wise to inform someone of your journey, for safety reasons, before setting out.

Gorkhi-Terelj National Park *(Entrance fee T3,000)* Northeast of Ulaanbaatar,
Terelj has long been a holiday resort for people from the capital. The entrance to the park is 16km from Terelj village on the main UB–Terelj road. Established as a national park in 1993, the area covers 293,168ha; precious stones have been mined there for over 100 years and continue to be mined. Parts of the park are permanently inhabited by local herders who keep livestock in the buffer zones.

Terelj Resort Lying in the valley of the Terelj River 80km northeast of Ulaanbaatar, this resort is part of the Gorkhi-Terelj National Park. It is one of the most visited areas in Mongolia on account of its magnificent scenery and its proximity to Ulaanbaatar. During the summer season there are great opportunities for hiking, rock climbing, swimming, rafting, riding and birdwatching. In winter frozen rivers provide skating and the snow-covered valleys are ideal for cross-country skiing. Also here is the **Ariyapala Meditation Centre**. Tours are offered to the centre – a temple-style building set apart on a mountainside in Terelj area 1km from Turtle Rock – by Selenge Travel (*www.selenngatravel,com/tours*). The resort provides good accommodation with first-class hotels like the Terelj Luxury Hotel (see page 272).

Getting there To get to Terelj, the bus departs from UB long-distance bus station daily at regular intervals and returns to UB, from a stop beside the UB2 Camp, at around 20.00. Otherwise take a taxi (the road is paved so a jeep is unnecessary) and pay US$35 one-way. You might be charged more if the return journey is empty. If you are on a day trip, pre-arrange waiting time (US$5) and return cost at the long-distance bus station in UB (many taxis leave from there on Sundays in summer).

 ## Where to stay

☐ **Terelj Luxury Hotel** m 9999 2233; e reservation@terelj.hotel; www.tereljhotel.com. Located in Gorkhi-Terelj National Park, guests are collected at the airport in Ulaanbaatar & chauffeur driven to the hotel some 70km distance. *High season (Apr–Sep & Dec)/low season (Jan–Mar & Oct–Nov)* **$$$$**

The *ger* camps here are mainly clustered around Terelj village and prices range widely. Eco-*gers* are situated further afield in the visitors' zone of the quieter, more remote Khankhentii Strictly Protected Area, a far cry from the bustle of Terelj

---

DOG SLEDDING – EASTER SATURDAY

Richard Austen

Some friends and I celebrated Easter 2005 by dog sledding in Terelj, a national park within easy driving distance from Ulaanbaatar. The organiser – a Frenchman called Joel Rauzy – assured us that there was still enough ice and snow on the river. So off we set. It sounded strange to hear the commands to the dogs called out in French – *à gauche, à droit*, etc! Originally Joel imported a few pure-bred huskies from Alaska, but now has some with a bit of Mongolian mutt in them as well – including one that is half greyhound. They are very strong and on one or two occasions it was nigh on impossible to hold back the team of four dogs.

It was a fantastic day out – there were little patches of snow still on the mountains and the sky was the bluest you could imagine. After we left Terelj village, we didn't see another soul for the entire trip. We travelled fairly quickly – up to around 15km/h and Joel estimated that we covered around 40km in each direction. The ice changed as we went along – in some places it was still solid with snow on it – in other places it was very definitely melting. On one stretch on the outward run we found ourselves in surface water around six inches deep, which left us with damp feet. Panic not – there was at least a foot of solid ice underneath the surface water.

We did not see much in the way of wildlife, but we did see plenty of wolf tracks, some very fresh – Joel pointed out that they always seem to follow old sled tracks, perhaps hoping for a tasty tourist meal. He also said that on a recent trip he had seen bear tracks.

After around three hours we came across a place with surface water as far as one could see, so Joel decided this would be the lunch stop. No quick sandwich in British fashion. He produced a barbecue grill from his sled and we built a fire and had barbecued mutton and a vegetable salad. As we were eating we noticed that the surface water from upriver seemed to be moving downriver. Within minutes our picnic site was awash, the poor dogs were up to their knees in water and the fire was extinguished. We got moving back down river pretty fast – wondering how much more water we would have to deal with on the way back. But in the event we got back more quickly than we had come and with no incidents – having finally become quite expert (!?).

For further information on dog sledding in Terelj visit www.nomads.mn and www.panoramicjourneys.com.

village itself. Local people are enormously generous and entertaining; the warm bowls of tea and the friendly welcomes just 'do it' for most visitors.

Activities in Gorkhi-Terelj National Park

Hiking You will need a compass and good maps or arrange to go with an experienced guide. Look out for 'Turtle Rock' (Melkhii Khad) in a side valley off the main UB–Terelj road, and nearby the rock formation of 'Old Man Reading a Book' (a rock shaped like a figure, perched on top of a hill). There are easy, well-worn flat paths where you can stroll along the Tuul and Terelj riverbanks in the direction of the Khentii Mountains with wild alpine flowers in the early summer including edelweiss and irises. You can also walk to Altan-Ölgii Uul (2,656m), the source of the Akhain River, and walk in the Bagakhentii Nuruu (mountains) north of the Akhain River.

Horseriding You can ride to Khagiin Khar Nuur, a 20m-deep glacial lake about 80km along the Tuul River from Terelj's *ger* camps. For long treks both experience and a guide are necessary, plus your own camping gear if travelling independently; organised tours provide all the necessary equipment and horses. You can hire horses from most *ger* camps, but expect to pay tourist prices: US$5 per hour; and from US$12 per day. Alternatively, if you make no arrangements and want to ride on the spur of the moment, local Mongolian families living in the area also have horses and may hire them out for an hour or more at the standard rate (US$5 per hour). For arranged tours there is a **Riding Club** in Terelj and details may be found via Selena Travel (*www.selenatravel.com*). To check the location and see what kit to bring on a riding trip arranged by www.stonehorsemongolia.com visit YouTube (*www.youtube.com/watch?v=ltlJ2sOx4as*).

Rafting The Tuul River provides excellent rafting; the best section is a 40km stretch from Dörgöntiin Gatsaa (north of Terelj *ger* camp) to Gachuurt (near UB).

Skiing There are no set trails for cross-country skiing; bring your own skis and ask local owners of *ger* camps to recommended safe areas. For organised weekends to Terelj, including winter skiing tours, contact Terelj-Juulchin and other tour companies based in UB (see pages 237–9). For a skiing experience in the new Ski Centre in the Bogd Khan Reserve see page 267.

Günjiin Süm Located within Gorkhi-Terelj National Park, 30km north of the main resort area, at Baruunbayar. To get there, hike directly over the mountains (with tour guide); the easier/longer route is along the Baruunbayar River (two days' trek, one day on horseback).

The temple was built in 1740 by Efu Dondovdorj (grandchild of the Tüsheet Khan) to commemorate the death of his first wife, the youngest of six daughters of the Qing emperor, Kangxi. The princess, a great beauty, died tragically following a long illness brought on by the discovery that her newborn son had been secretly murdered and replaced (for reasons of state) by another child (the son of her husband's Mongol concubine). The princess's child was supposed to succeed the Bogd Geegen to become the country's spiritual leader and ruler, but this was not to be. The deception broke the Manchu princess's health and heart. The temple was not destroyed during the religious purges of the 1930s, although it has been neglected over the years. Some original monastery walls remain around the small main temple. The site is under-developed at present with no signs and no facilities.

Khankhentii Strictly Protected Area Located in Töv, Selenge and Khentii aimags, this protected area covers over 1.2 million hectares of the desolate and wild Khentii Mountains, stretching northeast from just outside Ulaanbaatar to the Russian border. Perennially snow-covered mountains and dense forests at the core of this remote wilderness area are uninhabited and accessible only by foot or on horseback. Several peaks rise above 2,500m. The highest is Asraltkhairkhan (peak), rising to 2,800m. The headwaters of three major river systems spring from the protected area: the Tuul, which flows into the Orkhon and Selenge to Russia's Lake Baikal and continues to the Arctic Ocean; and the Onon and Kherlen rivers which flow east to join the River Amur before entering the Pacific Ocean. The reserve contains 10% of Mongolia's forests and defines the southern edge of Siberia's taiga. Hot springs used for medicinal purposes lie along the Onon River, and elsewhere, in the protected area. Eco-*gers* developed for tourism by the park and the local people provide limited but very select accommodation.

 Eco-*gers* in the Khankhentii (*For bookings & further details contact T Selenge;* \ *11 329323;* e *gtznaturecom@magicnet.mn*) An eco-ger project is run by the Khankhentii Strictly Protected Area's administration. Three secluded *gers* are situated about 10km apart in the park: one at Sain Ovoo (junction of the Tuul and Baruunbayan rivers); one at Buutin Khoshuu in Baruunbayan Valley; and one at Khalzangiin Adag (further up the Tuul River). The cost is US$25 per person, excluding food; horse hire costs from US$12 a day, including guide. A small percentage of the money received is kept by the park for administration purposes, otherwise it benefits the local people.

Nomadic Journeys (see page 238) runs several **ecotourist camps**, including one at Jalman Meadows (see below). They are small, family run and eco-friendly with a maximum of 14 *gers* that allows simple wind and solar energy to provide for cooking and heating without the hum of a noisy generator. *Gers* are candle lit.

▲ **Jalman Meadows *Ger* Camp** \ 11 328737; e infomongolia@nomadicjourneys.com; nomadicjourneys.com/jalman-meadows. 120km northeast of Ulaanbaatar at the headwaters of the Tuul River. Booking restrictions apply. **$$$$**

Ger camps in the Gorkhi-Terelj and Khankhentii areas Some *ger* accommodation is difficult to book – either they are unknown on the internet or have agreed to run their *ger* facilities for a local tour company. Where possible book ahead in the summer season as dropping in won't work due to prior reservations. In winter check with local people and with the park authorities whether the camps are open. As mentioned, some open for individuals, while others cater exclusively for organised tours.

▲ **Bolor *Gers*** 10km along the road from the main Gorkhi-Terelj park entrance. Provides food, or you may bring your own food & cook it there. No telephone. **$**

▲ **Buuveit Camp** www.tsolmontravel.com/ our-camps/buuveit-camp. 65km northeast of the capital; open year-round. The camp is surrounded by rocks & mountains. There is a restaurant, bar & souvenir shop. Offers local countryside tours. **$$**

▲ **Dinosaur Camp** \ 11 313031/458623; m 991 50876; e dinosaur@mol.mn. A *ger* camp surrounded by concrete dinosaurs, located on the way to Terelj village beside the main UB–Terelj road.

▲ **Gorkhi *Gers*** 15km along the main road from the park entrance in a secluded valley 5km west of main road, past Turtle Rock; no telephone. **$$** with/without 3 meals.

▲ **Guru *Ger* Camp** Terelj; \ 11 319401; www. juulchinworld.mn; ☺ closed in winter. Run by Juulchin World Tours. 40 gers, 200-seat restaurant, modern showers; activities include mini naadam, visiting nomadic families, constructing a ger;

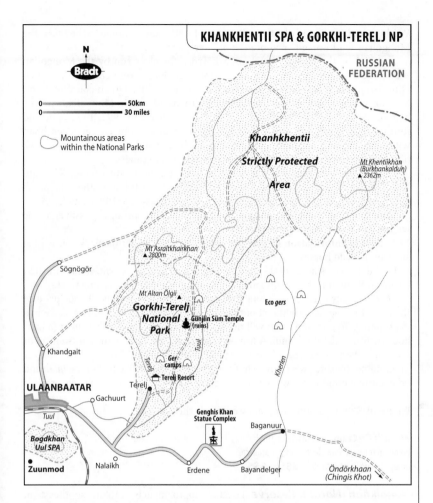

RUSSIAN
FEDERATION

N

0 ___ 50km
0 ___ 30 miles

Mountainous areas
within the National Parks

Khankhkhentii

Strictly Protected

Area

Mt Khentiikhan
(Burkhankalduh)
▲ 2362m

Sögnögör

Mt Asraltkhairkhan
▲ 2800m

Eco *gers*

Mt Altan Ölgii

Gorkhi-Terelj
National
Park   Günjlin Süm Temple
(ruins)

Khandgait

Ger
camps
Terelj Resort

ULAANBAATAR
Terelj
Gachuurt
Tuul

Genghis Khan
Statue Complex

Baganuur

Bogdkhan
Uul SPA

Zuunmod   Nalaikh   Erdene   Bayandelger   Öndörkhaan
(Chingis Khot)

easy access to Turtle Rock, Günj Temple & Aryabal Meditation Temple. And golf! **$$**

Khan Terelj Tour Camp m 997 22835/966 54989/991 84036. 50km from Ulaanbaatar. Capacity of 70 tourists. Restaurant, bar, karaoke, snooker, table tennis, horseriding, yak riding & camel riding, trip to Aryabal Monastery, frog rock, dinosaur statue, trekking. **$$**

Miraj Gers ✆11 325188. 14km along main road from the Gorkhi-Terelj park entrance. Good place for hiking. Hot showers are available. Horse for hire at standard rates of US$5/hour or US$12/ day. **$**

San Gers 18.5km along main UB–Terelj road, frequented by Mongolian visitors. **$**

Temüjinii Otog Gers ✆11 456087. 15.5km along main road from park entrance, near the concrete dinosaurs. *Gers* with hot showers. Children welcome. *US$25 without meals.* **$$–$**

Tsolmom Ger Camp ✆11 322870. 13km along the main road from the Gorkhi-Terelj park entrance, in a secluded valley 3km east of the main road. *Food costs US$20 pp for 3 meals.* **$**

UB2 ✆11 309016. 27km from the park entrance next to Terelj village. Large hotel complex. Good restaurant serves Mongolian food. **$$–$**

Other reserves in Töv Aimag

Khustain Nuruu National Park Located about 100km west of Ulaanbaatar, this park is part of UNESCO's 'Man and the Biosphere' reserves included in its

World Biosphere listing of Nature Reserves. Its 50,620ha is home to the *takhi*, the Mongolian wild horse (for more details, see pages 277 and 366). It is now run as an NGO by the Hustai National Park Trust; formerly run by the Mongolian Association for the Conservation of Nature and the Environment and the Dutch Foundation Reserves for the Przewalski Horse set up by a Dutch couple Mr and Mrs Jan Bouman and their friend Annette Groenveld; and in Mongolia, with the help of the Mongolian scientific researcher Tserendeleg, in 1992. The steppe and forest-steppe environment is also inhabited by maral, steppe gazelle, deer, boar, wildcat, wolf and lynx; there is interesting birdlife including Eurasian eagle-owl, boreal owl and Eurasian nightjar as well as migratory cranes.

The park is easily reached. You can take a local bus to the turn-off for Khustain Nuruu along the main UB–Kharkhorin road, signposted 10km south of the park's entrance. It is best to have your own transport (jeep); cost US$100 round trip.

Note that it is worth spending a night at Khustain Nuruu, if possible, as the wildlife is best seen at dusk and dawn.

The **Takhi Information Centre** inside the park has poster displays that tell the story of the wild horses' return to Mongolia.

Park entry costs around US$10, less for locals. To see the wild horses in their enclosures you must be accompanied by a park guide; keep to existing tracks.

There is plenty to do, from hiking to horseriding; horse hire costs T14,500 per day; there are Turkic graves southeast of the park which you can ride or drive to see in a day's outing. To go fishing, you will need your own transport to drive 30km (a half-hour's drive) to the River Tuul. A fishing permit, obtainable from the park's office (or the Central Parks Office, Baga Toiruu 44 in UB), costs from US$50–100. Eco-volunteer programmes (of three weeks) help to fund research projects like that of the *takhi* and other current projects; see www.ecovolunteer.org or http://en.cybelle-planete.org.

 Where to stay   Camping is not allowed inside the park.

⌂ **Moilt *Ger* Camp**   m 9981 1918. On the border of the park. Provides accommodation for groups & long-staying visitors. **$$$$–$$$**

Nagalkhan Nature Reserve   Located approximately 110km southeast of Ulaanbaatar, this area of some 3,076ha is designated to protect the southernmost limit of the Khangai and Khentii mountain ranges. It is not a particularly well visited area, nor is it developed for tourism.

Batkhan Uul Nature Reserve   This reserve, located on the western border extending into Övörkhangai Aimag, is described in on pages 143 and 291.

Güngaluut Nature Reserve   A reserve of 370,000km² of grassland, lakes and rivers 130km east of Ulaanbaatar with a well established *ger* camp situated by a river. Conditions are isolated; there is nothing to do if you don't like hiking or arranging your own programmes. You will find bar-headed goose, black stork, and orange-flanked bluetail among other bird species.

The **Nomads Day Festival** is held annually in mid-September at Güngaluut Nature Reserve. It brings together some exciting displays of horsemanship and traditional nomadic skills, such as felt and rope making; there are competitions, music and feasting – a two-day treat, well worth being there! Book with SelenaTours. com (**e** *nyama@selenatravel.com; www.mongoliagercamp.com*) or Step Nomads

above Riding through Övörkhangai in Orkhon Valley in winter (NL/AWL) pages 281–92

above, left & below The Naadam Festival highlights Mongolia's 'three manly sports' — horse racing, wrestling and archery — but also celebrates centuries of tradition (PJD/S), (G) and (PJ) pages 207–8

above left   The Altai Eagle Festival is held in Ölgii in October: eagle hunters parade on horseback proudly displaying their well-trained golden eagles (AP/AWL) page 398

above right   Archery at Altai Eagle Festival (DDS/AWL)

below   Lassoing a horse on the steppes in the traditional way, using a long pole with a rope noose at its end (G)

above   The largest of Mongolia's national parks, Gobi Gurvansaikhan covers more than two million hectares and plays host to an array of wildlife (DDS/AWL) pages 313–16

above left   The only wild horse to survive in modern times, Przewalski's horse have been successfully reintroduced in Mongolia having become extinct in the 1960s (JK) pages 130–1

below left   More than 90 rivers and streams flow into Mongolia's deepest lake, Lake Khövsgöl, which contains two per cent of the world's fresh water (G) pages 353–5

below   The Darkhad Valley northwest of Lake Khövsgöl sets a boundary between the steppe (south) and the Siberian taiga (north) (MP/S) pages 358–9

above   Hunted for its meat and shy around humans, the Bactrian camel is very much under threat — only about 1,000 remain today in the Gobi National Park (JK) page 127

right   Deer stones — cultural monuments dating from the Bronze Age — are scattered across Mongolia's landscapes, often located at burial sites (BB/S) page 371

below right   Steppes make up the heart of Mongolia both geographically and economically, offering important grazing for livestock herds (PH/AWL) pages 121–3

below left   The spectacular Orkhon Khürkhree waterfall located on the Orkhon River (PH/AWL) page 290

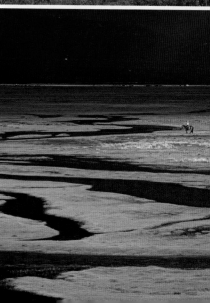

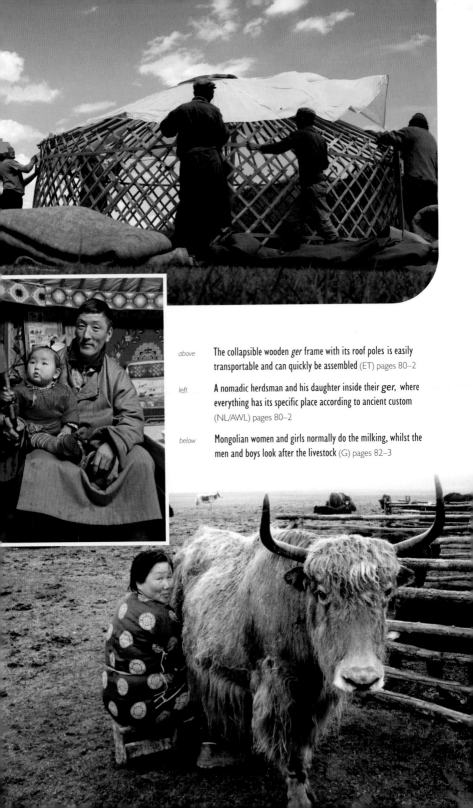

above The collapsible wooden *ger* frame with its roof poles is easily transportable and can quickly be assembled (ET) pages 80–2

left A nomadic herdsman and his daughter inside their *ger*, where everything has its specific place according to ancient custom (NL/AWL) pages 80–2

below Mongolian women and girls normally do the milking, whilst the men and boys look after the livestock (G) pages 82–3

above   Cow hides are used to make leather bags to hold *airag* (fermented mares' milk) (ET) page 83

above right   The traditional — and unusual — spiked hat worn by Mongolian men is now most often seen at festivals such as Naadam (SS) page 71

right   The traditional dish of Ul Boov, served at Naadam (G)

Wind of Mongolia

Your customised tour operator in Mongolia.
A new way to discover Mongolian's nomadic world.
Cultural journeys, adventure trips or more classical
route through the heart of Mongolian steppes.

(m *9134 3497*; e *booking@steppenomads.com*). The price is US$50 per day, which does not include accommodation so you need to arrange this separately, eg: through Mongolia Ger Camp (m *9134 3498*; *www.mongoliagercamp.com/nomads_day_festival.html*) or Nomadic Journeys (✆ *11 328737*; e *infomongolia@nomadicjourneys.com*; *www.nomadicjourneys.com*).

Nomads Day Festival shuttle bus services are available from UB.

ECO-VOLUNTEERING – WILD HORSES AT KHUSTAIN NURUU

Lindsay Perry

As an eco-volunteer at Khustain Nuruu (in 2006) I was able to observe the horses in their natural habitat: rocky mountain steppe with occasional birch forest. The horses live in family groups or harems; each group has a dominant stallion, mares and young horses. The study I was involved in looked at the home range of the harems, and looked into how the harems used their time, where they went and what they ate.

We usually observed them in the morning, starting at 06.30 when the horses came down to the valley to drink from the stream, and then followed them until midday. Sometimes this could be a breathless climb up and down ridges desperately trying not to lose track of them in the trees or beyond a ridge, behind a rock … sometimes they would idle their way to a favourite spot at a high altitude out of the sun and snooze there for the full observation period. Manlai, the first horse born in the park, was a big fan of snoozing by a pile of rocks with a fabulous view of the valley. Most of these horses were born at the park although a few were oldies from the original zoo groups. One old Dutch stallion seemed to shun the wild life after he lost his harem to a younger stallion. In his dotage he hung around the tourist camp, scratching on the fence, posing for photographs and occasionally making off with the riding horses (geldings!), causing much consternation in camp as the rangers doggedly trek into the park in search of them!

Bachelor stallions, a fluid group of 40 or so horses, come and go throughout the day. Sometimes they shadow a harem for a while, gathering courage to make a move on a stallion. They reminded me of adolescent boys, hanging out in groups, safety in numbers, smoking cigarettes behind the bicycle shed – they were for the most part gangly and awkward. They travelled in groups that seemed to interchange at will. I saw few real fights, although missing ears and manes bore witness to their occurrence, but most advances were settled with a stomping trot and a few squeals. Mares were entirely unconcerned by these antics and rarely changed home range, even when a new stallion took over. A total of 195 horses now roam the steppe at Khustain Nuruu – other sites include Takhiin Tal in the remote Gobi-Altai and Khomiin Tal in the far west near Khar Us Nuur National Park.

The volunteers stay in *gers* at the tourist camp on the edge of the park. I found our hosts to be friendly and kind and always made a huge effort to show us Mongolian culture and ways of life. We visited the rangers and their families (I got quite fond of the milky tea!) and went to see a nearby naadam (games) to watch the tiniest children gallop across the finishing line. Eco-volunteering is an excellent way to help support the park's activities and to gain an insight into the lives of the wild horses and the Mongolian way of life.

For further information see www.hustai.mn and www.treemail.nl.

Towns and other attractions in Töv Aimag

Khandgait This small village lies 40km north of Ulaanbaatar in an area of cow pastures, hills and pine forests, with meadows of wild flowers. Less touristy (and cheaper) than Terelj, and lacking in facilities, it is not in the national park so camping is permitted. There's plenty to do: activities include hiking, walking, rock climbing, fishing, and ice skating and skiing in winter.

There's a lack of scheduled transport to Khandgait. The first half of the road from UB is paved, the second half is pretty rough. It continues north from Khandgait to smaller valleys, where there are wooden huts, once used as summerhouses, but now abandoned. To get there, take a taxi or share a minibus; a taxi is easier and costs around US$40 return, plus US$5 waiting time. There is no tourist accommodation so you will need to bring a tent if staying overnight.

Gachuurt Located 21km from Ulaanbaatar, Gachuurt is a pretty village in quiet surroundings. It offers no hotel or restaurant facilities but there are plenty of sporting opportunities like horseriding, fishing, hiking and rafting in the area. To get there, buses leave every hour from the long-distance bus station in UB (unreliable) or you can take a taxi. The paved road continues beyond Gachuurt to Sansar, but there is no public transport out there.

Where to stay and eat In addition to staying at Hotel Mongolia, you can **camp** outside the village or stay with local people – private *ger* accommodation may be arranged on the spot.

There's also a *ger* camp 3km up the Tuul River from town (*US$10 pp/day, meals an extra US$10*). Horse hire costs US$12 per day. Contact Gana's Guest House in Ulaanbaatar for bookings (✆ *11 321078*; e *ganasger@ magnicnet.mn*).

Hotel Mongolia (50 apts & 48 modern, well-equipped *gers*) Bayanzürkh District, Gachuurt Village, Ulaanbaatar; ✆11 315513; e info@hotel-mongolia.co; www.hotel-mongolia.com. Called Mongol shiltgeen in Mongolian (Mongolian castle), the hotel is built after the model of an ancient Buddhist temple. It is conveniently located 20mins' drive from the city centre & 40mins' drive from Ulaanbaatar International Airport, Buyant-Ukhaa. The northern main gate leads directly into a spacious lobby with high brick walls, which remind one of an ancient 'Forbidden City'. All rooms have their own modern bathroom, with running hot & cold water, telephone, TV & minibar. It has a good restaurant & a price range of *gers* to choose from, including the Khan Suite at US$286. **$$$$–$$$**

Nairamdal Zuslan or Bayangol (Children's Centre) (✆*11 332776; admission US$30 children, US$80 adults, inc accommodation, meals, guides & transport from the city; ☉ all year, though it might be full in summer*) Located in the foothills 30km northwest of Ulaanbaatar, Nairamdal Zuslan is situated at a lower altitude than Terelj's resort and has milder weather during the winter. The scenery is spectacular and it is a good place to go if you are travelling with children. There is a small hotel where you can stay with your family; prices are reasonable and services are good. It is advisable, however, to book in advance.

Activities include cultural displays, archery competitions and horseriding in summer; cross-country skiing in winter. A skiing area with lifts is currently being developed.

Nalaikh Located 35km southeast of Ulaanbaatar, Nalaikh is a depressed coal-mining town that supplied Ulaanbaatar in the early 1900s. In 1950, the Kazakh minority people from Bayan-Ölgii were brought here to work in the state mines and stayed on after state mining stopped in 1990. Small-scale mining continued by 'ninjas', self-employed labourers. There is a small mosque that may be visited off the main road on the outskirts of town.

Buses depart to Nalaikh from UB long-distance bus station every half-hour (daytime only) and cost T400. It is safer and more reliable to take a taxi (US$35 return). Jeeps are approximately T700 per kilometre; Japanese jeeps can be more expensive at T850 per kilometre.

 Where to stay

🏠 **Chinggis *Ger* Camp** 25km from Ulaanbaatar on a paved road & 4km unpaved road. This lovely tourist camp, owned by Samar Magic Tours, lies on the bank of the Tuul River. **$$$**

🏠 **Chinggis Tourist Traditional Lodge** 3km from the new 40m Chinggis Khan statue (see below). **$$**

Eej Khad (Mother Rock) Eej Khad stands near the village of Khöshigiin Ar, 15km south of Zuunmod near Mount Avdarkhangai. According to the local people this rock is said to have special spiritual powers and a popular cult has sprung up around it. The story is that a virtuous young girl and her flock of sheep were transformed into rock. Rumours are that the rock can heal the broken-hearted. Visitors place silk scarves on the rock along with other offerings. There is nowhere to stay nearby but you can camp, although it is not recommended on account of the litter that surrounds the rock, and the stray dogs it attracts. Apparently since the ground is sacred nothing can be removed. A return trip by jeep from UB costs US$50.

Enkhiin Els and Tavangiin Els These belts of sculptured sand dunes lie in the area of Ikh Khairkhan Mountain (1,668m), and are described as old beaches in an ancient landscape.

To get there, hire your own vehicle and drive 102km on a paved road from Ulaanbaatar to Enkhiin Els (Moltsog), and from there on unpaved tracks 30km south to the dune area. A return trip by jeep from UB costs around US$100.

Day trips

Genghis Khan's Statue Complex An enormous statue to honour Genghis Khan (1162–1227) was built at Tsonjin Boldog on the banks of the River Tuul – some 54km (an hour's car journey) from Ulaanbaatar. It stands 40m tall, and was designed by the sculptor D Erdenebilig in 2008. The statue faces northeast and the Great Khan mounted on his steed looks in the direction of his birthplace, Dadal in the Khentii Mountains. The edifice, coated with stainless steel, is entered via an exhibition hall, from where visitors may take an elevator and walk to the horse's-head area to look out on a panoramic view of the surrounding countryside. In other words you can get inside this 'Trojan horse'. The many *ger* tents that surround the statue hold art and craft exhibitions. A golf course, a spa and hotel are planned by Genco Tour Bureau (*Bayangol Hotel, room 4;* m *962 02042;* e *info@genco-tour.mn; www.genco-tour.mn*), developers of this innovative, extraordinary complex, which is set in its own grounds of 500 acres and makes a great day trip from the capital.

The 13th-century 'Chinggis Camp' This theme park is located around 80km south of Ulaanbaatar. It is a Middle Ages-style Mongolian camp that offers insight into arts and crafts of the 13th century particularly, with traditional costumes, theatrical shows (summer only) and, along with the entertainment, food and drink. On the way you might also take in the Genghis Khan Complex (above). Arrange own transport.

SUGGESTED ITINERARY
Horse trek in Gorkhi-Terelj National Park To experience the openness and hospitality of the Mongolian people and to see some magnificent landscape it is possible to ride and hike in mountains that lie just 80km from the capital in Gorkhi-Terelj National Park. This ten-day itinerary is organised by Off the Map Tours (*www.mongolia.co.uk*).

To climb Khürel Togoot (Bronze Pot) and to hike and ride in the Altan Ölgii Mountains, you start from Ar Khurakh *Ger* Camp and ride through wooded grasslands to Khalazan Bürged. Having camped there, you then continue on horseback for a day to Tögöl Mod, from where an early-morning start on foot (leaving the horses at the camp) gets you to the top of the 500m 'pot'. The climb is on loose shale, so bring good boots. The alpine scenery is breathtaking. Returning to camp, the next day you ride on to the Zaan (Elephant) River and up and over Khavirgan Davaa (a mountain pass). This brings you to the far side of the Altan Ölgii Mountains. Tether the horses

---

RIDING TOURS: WHAT TO EXPECT

For those who prefer the comfort of a bed each night rather than crawling into a two-man tent, tour companies now offer a 'luxury' horse trail in Mongolia, but with prices to match. You still experience the wonderful riding over wide-open spaces, meeting the nomadic people who live here, but at night you stay in a spacious *ger*, on a made-up bed with a stove for warmth on cold nights. The UK-based horse-riding specialists In the Saddle, for example, run such riding tours in the Khan Khentii Special Protected Area, northeast of Ulaanbaatar. You normally stay two nights at each *ger* camp, some of which are set up as private camps and others are semi-permanent *ger* camps. A more varied menu is offered than on a basic camping trip and the group size is smaller – up to eight riders. Horse tours can also be tailor-made for private groups.

TERRAIN Landscape of the Khan Khentii offers riders two strikingly different areas. Heading northeast from Ulaanbaatar towards the northern wilderness, the first part of the journey is over the open grasslands, but, should you head north to ride in the Gorkhi-Terelj National Park and Khan Khenti Special Protected Area, you will experience mountain forest taiga.

Gobi riding tours take you south of the capital Ulaanbaatar beyond the Bogdkhan Mountains, through grassland steppes, sand dune areas and the giant rock formations of Zorgolkhairhan Uul. There are no rivers or forests in these semi-arid areas, although you may be lucky enough to see a variety of birdlife and animals. This is the area of the best horse trainers in Mongolia.

In the Saddle offers tours to the above mentioned areas, camping in two-man tents; most rides use a large communal *ger* tent for evening meals. Costs start at US$1,950 and go to around US$3,500 per person sharing.

In the Saddle ☏ +44 1299 272 997; e *rides@inthesaddle.com; www.inthesaddle.com*)

and leave them with a guardian, then climb the west flank on foot, to the flat summit from where there are marvellous views over the surrounding countryside. The return ride brings you to Günjiin Temple ruins, from where you ride downhill to the Baruun Bayan River, the winter quarters of several nomadic families. Having paid a visit to them, you then return by jeep to Ulaanbaatar.

Tseren Tours and Karakorum Expeditions (see pages 238 and 239) offer biking and hiking tours to Terelj. Indeed, most tour companies based in Ulaanbaatar (see pages 237–9) will provide itineraries to Terelj and the environs.

ÖVÖRKHANGAI AIMAG

BRIEF FACTS: ÖVÖRKHANGAI AIMAG

Area 62,900km²
Aimag centre Arvaikheer
Districts 19
Elevation of Arvaikheer 1,913m
Livestock and crops Horses, cattle, goats, sheep, wheat
Ethnic groups Khalkha
Distance from Arvaikheer to Ulaanbaatar 430km
Average temperatures July +15.3°C, January –14.7°C

HIGHLIGHTS
* Erdene Zuu Monastery
* Hot springs at Khujirt
* Orkhon waterfall and river valley
* Archaeological sites

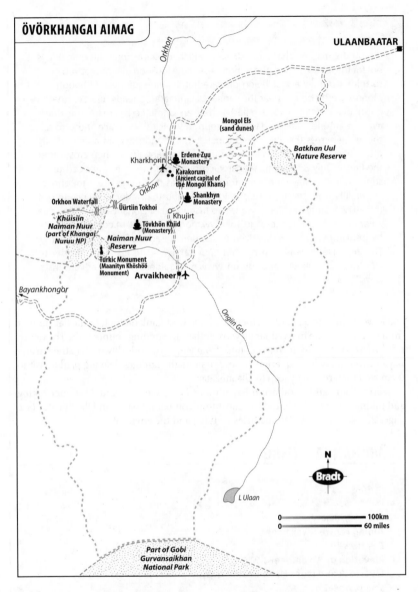

ÖVÖRKHANGAI AIMAG

ULAANBAATAR

Orkhon

Mongol Els
(sand dunes)

Batkhan Uul
Nature Reserve

Kharkhorin   Erdene Zuu
Monastery

Karakorum
(Ancient capital of
the Mongol Khans)

Orkhon

Shankhyn
Monastery

Orkhon Waterfall

Üürtiin Tokhoi

Khujirt

Khüisiin
Naiman Nuur
(part of Khangai
Nuruu NP)

Tövkhön Khiid
(Monastery)

Naiman Nuur
Reserve

Turkic Monument
(Maanityn Khöshöö
Monument)

Arvaikheer

Bayankhongor

Ongiin Gol

N

Bradt

0   100km
0   60 miles

L Ulaan

Part of Gobi
Gurvansaikhan
National Park

Övörkhangai Aimag ('the front or southern slopes of the Khangai') occupies mountains and valleys, steppe and desert. The northwestern part of the province is dominated by the Khangai mountain range. The Orkhon River, which rises in the Khangai, flows through a beautiful river valley and is often referred to as the cradle of Mongolian civilisation because of its historical links with the Mongol khans. Genghis Khan based his winter camp along the riverbanks and at the height of the Mongol Empire in the 13th century, after Genghis's death, his son and successor Ögödei Khan built the city of Karakorum beside the Orkhon. Natural sights include the Batkhan Uul Mountain Reserve, which crosses into Töv Aimag and is worth visiting for its birdlife. The province's southern territory, past Arvaikheer, is lonely desert steppe and less inhabited except by herders with their large flocks of sheep and goats. The wealth of the aimag does not come only from its livestock, as the province has valuable gold mines, a large coal mine and a flour mill. The province is easily accessible by jeep from Ulaanbaatar. Places of cultural and historical interest are concentrated mainly in the north where the Orkhon River valley is ideal for biking, riding, camping and adventure travel.

Private *gers* and *ger* camps provide traditional accommodation at US$45–50 (including meals) per day. A typical dinner would be barbecued mutton; beer costs T3,000. *Ger* camps in the region include Kublai Khan, Chandmani, Möngön Mod and Anar. Camping is popular along the Orkhon River.

ARVAIKHEER Located in the southern part of the Khangai mountain range, Arvaikheer means 'barley fields'. It is a friendly service town with limited tourist facilities, though this doesn't stop some travellers from stopping over here to eat, sleep and prepare for their onward journey. Arvaikheer has a number of bars, a post office, cinema and a theatre. There is a good, daily market for food supplies. Local visitor sites of note include two museums and a large monastery (listed below).

Getting there (from Ulaanbaatar)
By road There is a paved road from Ulaanbaatar to Kharkhorin and on to Arvaikheer; it continues west to Bayankhongor (centre of Bayankhongor Aimag, pages 332–3). The bus for Bayankhongor leaves Arvaikheer petrol station between 15.00 and 16.00 daily. From Ulaanbaatar to Arvaikheer costs T18,000 by bus; T20,000 by minibus; otherwise hire a jeep and driver in Ulaanbaatar and expect to pay T1,000 per kilometre, approximately from US$400 in total; limited jeep transport is available locally.

By air There are scheduled flights from Ulaanbaatar on Hunnu Air, Eznis Airways and Aero Mongolia (a one-hour flight), with some direct flights to Kharkhorin: Kharkhorin airport is small, located 4 km north of the town.

Where to stay
Hotels
Altan Ovoo Hotel ╲2755 2360. A block south of the square next to Bayan Bulag Hotel. Has de-luxe rooms with showers. **$$**

Arvaikheer Hotel ╲1322 22375; m 993 29212. Café, bar, laundry service. **$**

Bayan Bulag Hotel/B&B ╲1322 23374; m 993 29677/27853. A block south of the square. Has a restaurant & bar (with billiard table), serving local food & beer. **$**

Khangai Hotel m 993 29999. West of the town square. Bar & snooker. **$**

Kharaa Hotel ╲1322 23655/26020; m 993 29695. B&B, internet, laundry, snooker & billiards, bar, restaurant. The restaurant (🕐 *10.00–23.00*) serves local dishes. **$$**

Munkhsunder Hotel Located in the southeast. Café, bar, laundry service, garage, snooker. Restaurant serves European & Mongolian food. **$$**

Orkhon Hotel ╲27 552434. On the outskirts of town. A good hotel with en-suite rooms & bathrooms. **$**

Time Hotel ╲1322 22866/22867. B&B, garage, bar/restaurant. **$**

Local *ger* camps
Hot Springs Khuremt, 28km from Arvaikheer. Location offers natural hot springs. There are over 30 different springs. **$$$**

Tsagaan Suvarga m 883 25051/993 28604; e ayurzana_unudelger@yahoo.com. 30km from Arvaikheer City. Riverside location with 40 beds. Offers guided tours to Kharkhorin, Erdene Zuu, Bat-Ölzii, Orkhon Waterfall. Horseriding, visit herders' families. **$$**

➤ **Tsaidam** ✆ 27 319233; **m** 991 68971. This lovely small camp is situated between Kharkhorin & Lake Ögii (about 25km from each). Good hot shower; restaurant offers Mongolian dishes. **$**

➤ **Tsengüün Khüree** ✆ 27 325357; **e** atartravel@magicnet.mn. This camp is one of the biggest in the area with a 120-person capacity; offers horse trekking & local tours. **$**

✕ **Where to eat and drink** Bayan Bulag and Altan Ovoo hotel restaurants (see page 283) charge US$10 on average for a meal. Hotels will also pack picnic lunches for US$8 per person; order ahead of time. Otherwise, food supplies can be bought at the shop in the Khangai Hotel (**m** 993 29999) or at the local market on the town square.

Local canteens (*guanz*) and noodle stalls near the square supply fast food such as meat and noodle soup from T1,500–2,500.

✕ **Bayan Bulag Restaurant** ✆ 1322 23374/23891; **m** 993 29677/27853. Located in the Bayan Bulag Hotel; European, Chinese & Mongolian food. *T6,000.*

✕ **Chinggis Restaurant** Located in the Central Market; ◷ 10.00–22.00. Asian, European & traditional Mongolian food. *T6,000.*

✕ **Kharaa Restaurant** ✆ 1322 23655/26020; **m** 993 29695. Located in the Kharaa Hotel; ◷ 10.00–23.00. Chinese & Mongolian food. *T6,000–14,000.*

✕ **Time Restaurant** ✆ 1322 22866/22867. Located in the Time Hotel; European, Chinese & Mongolian dishes. *T2,500–5,000.*

✕ **Tüshig Restaurant** ◷ 10.00–22.00. Mongolian, European & Korean meals. *T6,000–10,000.*

♀ **Leader Bar** Centre of town; ◷ 11.00–midnight. Karaoke.

♀ **Ongi Bar** Centre of town; ◷ 11.00–midnight. Karaoke.

Shopping

⊞ **Central Market** ◷ 09.00–18.00. Located in the centre of Arvaikheer, you can buy food, clothes & electrical goods.

⊞ **Öguöömör Centre** ◷ 10.00–20.00. Located in the west of the city, selling mostly groceries.

Communications

🖳 **Internet** In the post office; ◷ 09.00–20.00; T800/hr.

🖳 **Internet café** In the Central Market; ◷ 10.00–18.00; T800/hr.

ORKHON VALLEY – UNESCO WORLD HERITAGE SITE

The Orkhon Valley was listed by UNESCO in 2004 (*www.unesco.org*) as one of its World Heritage Sites in Mongolia, along with the Great Lakes Area in Uvs Aimag (in 2003) and the Petroglyphs of the Altai (in 2011).

One reason this beautiful river valley in Arkhangai Aimag was selected is that it clearly demonstrates how a strong nomadic culture led to the early growth and development of ancient trading routes and archaeological remains dating back to the 6th century. The control of this valley was of strategic importance. The valley is principally known as the site of the Mongol khans' capital Karakorum in the 13th–14th centuries (see opposite page). Despite the fact that the capital moved to Beijing in 1264, the Orkhon Valley has dominated the country as a centre of nomadic culture – illustrating even today how nomads respect nature and live in harmony with it. The valley is an outstanding example of various significant stages of development in human history, from trading posts to capital. The World Heritage Site includes a core zone on both banks of the River Orkhon and a buffer zone of over 14,000ha.

What to see and do in Arvaikheer

Aimag Museum (⊕ *09.00–noon & 15.00–18.00 Mon–Fri; entrance fee T2,800*)
A five–ten-minute walk south of the square, the Aimag Museum's exhibits include stuffed mountain/desert animals, fossils and local artwork.

Gandan Muntsaglan Khiid (*Entrance fee T2,800*) North of the town square, this monastery was built in 1991. It has a collection of fine *tanka* (religious scroll paintings); 50 monks are resident; visitors are welcomed and a shop, to the left of the temple, sells religious items.

Zanabazar Memorial Museum (*Entrance fee T2,800*) Near the Aimag Museum, south of the square beside the park, this museum displays works by Zanabazar (1635–1723; see page 113), the first religious leader of Mongolia and an extremely accomplished Buddhist artist and sculptor.

SIGHTS IN ÖVÖRKHANGAI AIMAG

Kharkhorin Located 373km southwest of Ulaanbaatar, this modern, agricultural service town is built near the site of ancient Karakorum, the great Mongolian capital, established in 1235. Kharkhorin offers limited tourist facilities and most groups stay in *ger* camps around the town, buying picnic and other food supplies in the central market. The indoor market sells clothes, hats and a limited supply of camping equipment. East of the markets there are cafés and restaurants serving simple but edible dishes for around T1,000–1,500. Fresh drinking water can be found on the western outskirts of the town for which you must pay the person who runs the tap a fee of around T500 per 2.5 litres.

Karakorum Located in the Orkhon Valley in northern Övörkhangai Aimag, Karakorum was formerly a great capital city built by Ögödei Khan (Genghis's successor and third son) in 1235. It existed primarily as a focus for the expanding empire, was the hub of political and administrative life and housed a treasury for tax and plunder. Foreign envoys, merchants and prominent clerics travelled to Karakorum for an audience with the Mongol khan. The imperial palace consisted of a walled compound known as the 'Palace of the World', situated in the southwest corner of the city. In its halls, audiences, banquets and receptions were held for guests like William of Rubruck (1215–95), a Franciscan monk from Flanders who reached Karakorum in 1253 in search of a group of Catholic monks whom the Mongols had abducted. He stayed for a year in Karakorum and during that time he engaged in religious debates and wrote about life in Mongolia at the court of the khan.

The city was strategically located at the crossroads of traditional routes, creating a staging post for migrating nomads and merchants' caravans. It was surrounded by a mud wall, and Friar Rubruck mentions four gates selling different wares: millet and other grains were sold at the east gate, sheep and goats were marketed at the west gate, oxen and carts at the south gate, and horses at the north gate. Sophisticated art was produced by craftsmen who included a French silversmith, Guillaume Bouchier. He designed a famous drinking fountain: mare's milk, wine and other alcoholic beverages gushed from the mouths of dragons who guarded an elaborately designed evergreen tree topped by the figure of an archangel blowing a trumpet. Within this large piece of sculpture, it is thought, was a person (or persons) who hand-pumped its liquid output, poured in through other channels to hidden containers at its base.

When Kublai Khan moved the Mongol capital to Beijing in 1264, Karakorum lost its international influence. Karakorum was razed to the ground in 1380 by soldiers of the Ming Emperor. Sculpted rocks in the shape of turtles marked the boundaries of the ancient city, and a few of these survive. They acted as the bases for inscribed memorial slabs (now missing). However, the bricks and stones from the ruins of Karakorum were used to build the monumental walls of the Erdene Zuu Monastery nearby, so in that way the old city lives on. It is worth visiting the spot if only to sense the history.

Erdene Zuu Khiid (⊕ *09.00–21.00 daily; museum closes at 17.00*) A 2km walk from the centre of Kharkhorin, entrance to the monastery grounds is free, but to enter the temples you must buy a ticket (T4,000), which includes a guided tour. The shop located inside the compound (see map) is well stocked with souvenirs, and there are computers, with email access and a telephone line that travellers can use. You pay additionally to take photographs and video.

Erdene Zuu probably means 'Precious Buddha', since the main object of veneration at Erdene Zuu is the Zandan Zuu (Sandalwood Buddha). It is Mongolia's oldest Buddhist monastery, founded in 1586 by Abtai Khan, and was one of the few monasteries to survive, partly intact, the destruction of religious establishments in the 1930s. The colossal grey brick walls (400m x 400m) that enclose the monastery compound were constructed using the stones and bricks from the ruined capital of Karakorum city. The walls are extremely thick and every 75m or so they bear huge stupas, funeral monuments or relic holders of Buddhist saints. Each wall has a gateway at midpoint. In total there are 108 similarly sized, white-painted stupas that tower above the walls (108 being a symbolic, sacred Buddhist number). They are placed at slightly irregular intervals (see map). Heavy damage was inflicted on the temple buildings in 1731 by Manchu forces but they were later repaired. From 1941–90 the religious life of the monastery was virtually shut down, and Erdene Zuu became a national museum with no monks in residence. A few special visitors were shown around. Religious life began again during the 1990s. In 1997, the government decided to restore the monastery.

At its height Erdene Zuu had around 100 temples as part of the monastery complex, with 1,000 resident monks, who lived in nearby *gers*. Five temples, stupas, some small buildings used for prayer and some tombs remain. A surprising number of statues, masks and Buddhist scroll paintings (*tankas*) somehow survived the religious purges in the 20th century – hidden or buried in the nearby mountains or stored in local homes at great risk to the owners. An important building that survived is the large golden-topped stupa, which stands almost opposite the main entrance and is surrounded by eight smaller stupas and some side buildings near the white, Tibetan-style temple building (see map). Religious ceremonies are held in this temple and the public can attend some of them. The monastery houses some of the most precious of Mongolia's art treasures, the works of 16th- to 19th-century Buddhist masters, among them, Zanabazar (see page 113). Starting at the main entrance there is a religious pathway, used by monks on their meditation walks.

Temples, buildings and relics

Dalai Lama Süm All on its own, this is the nearest building to the main gate. It was built in 1675 to commemorate the visit of Abtai Khan's son Altan to Tibet to pay his respects to the Dalai Lama. This red-brick and gold temple was at one time the museum's archive office. It consists of two small chapels and contains a statue of

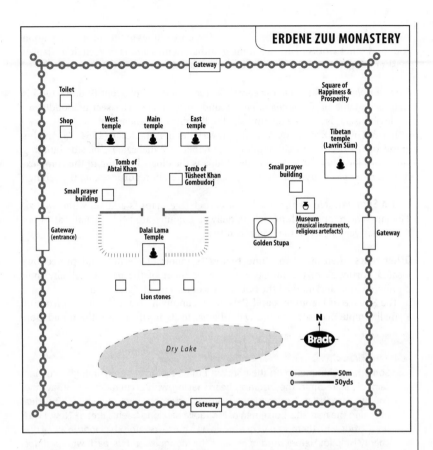

ERDENE ZUU MONASTERY

Gateway

Toilet

Square of
Happiness &
Prosperity

Shop

West
temple

Main
temple

East
temple

Tibetan
temple
(Lavrin Süm)

Tomb of
Abtai Khan

Tomb of
Tüsheet Khan
Gombudorj

Small prayer
building

Small prayer
building

Gateway
(entrance)

Dalai Lama
Temple

Museum
(musical instruments,
religious artefacts)

Golden Stupa

Gateway

Lion stones

N

Bradt

Dry Lake

0 ——— 50m
0 ——— 50yds

Gateway

Zanabazar, some *tankas* and figures of protective deities. The Golden Stupa stands
on its own near the centre of the monastery; built by the fourth Bogd Gegeen in
1799, it is surrounded by eight lesser stupas.

Inside a low-walled courtyard in the southwest corner are three main temples:

West Temple Dedicated to the Buddha, this temple houses statues representing
Buddhist deities, with a central altar dedicated to Sakyamuni (Historic Buddha),
Sanjaa (Buddha of the Past) and Maitreya (Buddha of the Future). The last is
one of the most popular bodhisattvas, a deity who delays his own attainment of
nirvana (state of bliss) in order to minister to others. Buddhist artefacts include
the golden wheel of eternity, eight auspicious symbols – an umbrella, fish,
vase, flowers, cards, lucky diagram, victorious banner and wheel – and delicate
pieces of sculpture from the 17th–18th centuries. Folk art includes *balin*, baked
and highly decorated figures of wheat-dough and mutton or goose fat as altar
ornaments, with colourful multi-layered medallions incorporating small gods
and other symbolic figures.

Main Temple The entrance to the main temple is flanked by protective deities:
on the left is Gongor, also known as Sita Mahakala, while on the right is Baldan
Lkham (Sridevi). Inside the temple the central statue is of the child Buddha. To his
right is the Buddha of Medicine, Otoch (Manla in Tibetan) and, to his left, Amida

(Amitabha), the Buddha of Infinite Light. There are statues to the sun and the moon gods and other works of art including guardian figures and *tsam* (religious dance) masks dating from the 16th–17th centuries, including works by Zanabazar.

East Temple In this temple the central statue is of the adolescent Buddha. On his right is a statue of Tsongkhapa who founded the Yellow Hat sect of Buddhism, while on his left is a statue of Janraisig, the Buddha of Compassion.

In front of the three temples are the gravestones of Abtai Khan (1554–88) and his grandson Tüsheet Khan Gombodorj (the father of Zanabazar). The side building (see map) located next to the Golden Stupa is the oldest building in the complex. It has a *mandala*, a mystical diagram used for meditation purposes, on the ceiling.

Lavrin Süm Located in the northwest corner (see map) is a large, white-walled, Tibetan-style temple building where daily ceremonies are held – usually at 11.00; times may vary so ask at the visitor centre.

Other relics There are two **stone turtles** (symbols of eternity and protection) located northwest of the monastery as a reminder of the past. Originally they numbered four, and marked the boundaries of the city of Karakorum.

The **Square of Happiness and Prosperity**, an open area, is located in front of a small temple dedicated to the Dalai Lama; to its northeast are the foundation

---

HELP FOR HEROES: A CHARITY RIDE   *Jane Shortall*

Something shimmered on the horizon. 'I think the horses are coming!' someone said. We stared into the distance, hearts racing with excitement as we saw the line of riders and horses coming towards us across the vast, open plain. The idea of seeing the nomadic horsemen of Mongolia had long been a dream. Now, I was here to ride with them, as part of a group on a horse trekking challenge in aid of the charity Help for Heroes. And here came the Mongolian riders, each with perhaps half a dozen horses roped together. Wearing traditional Mongolian, brightly coloured *deels* – gold, royal blue, green, dove grey, gold sashes tied around their waists – and terrific black boots, they cantered up and with a debonair flourish, brought all the horses to a halt and sat looking at us. Mongolian horsemen with a herd of Mongolian horses; a colourful, breathtaking, extraordinary sight, like a sketch from the cover of an old novel or a poster for an adventure film in faraway places. The land of blue sky, the vastness of Mongolia spread out behind them. The adventure of a lifetime lay ahead for us. I was not alone in being moved by some wild, primitive emotion, as one of our group quietly said 'there is no camera that can capture this'.

Even though we had been travelling for days – a long flight to Ulaanbaatar, a quick hotel stop with hardly any time to sleep and then a riotous eight-hour journey in a massive truck on unbelievable roads, with the possibility of a two-hour horse ride on our first evening – all tiredness vanished. A Mongolian rider took a good look at each of us, pointed to a horse and helped us up on to some of the strangest saddles we had ever sat on. And we were off, flying across Mongolia's breathtaking scenery, with a stupendous close-up of its wildlife. We rode where edelweiss carpets the ground, saw herds of yaks and goats roaming free, vultures devouring a carcass, families of eider ducks, enormous cranes and thousands of small ground squirrels. And everywhere, herds of horses.

stones on top of which a gigantic *ger* was constructed. The *ger* is thought to have accommodated up to 300 people during the assemblies of local khans in the heyday of the Mongol Empire.

The **Phallic 'Rock'** is a standing sculpture that is about a half-hour's walk from the monastery and can be seen from the main Ulaanbaatar road, a kilometre from Kharkhorin. As the name suggests, it is in the shape of a phallus. It was meant to warn monks to keep away from women: one story has it that the stone represents the phallus of a womanising monk who was castrated. Many visitors take the opportunity to go for a walk and see it, particularly women who want children; you can't get lost as the path is clearly worn.

Khujirt Hot Springs Located on the banks of the River Khujirt, 90km from Arvaikheer, southeast of Erdene Zuu Monastery, this is a health spa, opened in 1941, that grew up around the hot-water springs. The spa is frequented by local people, and now welcomes foreign visitors. Water temperatures can reach 55°C. If you visit you may see a local doctor who will take your pulse and blood pressure and advise you to keep warm and to avoid alcohol for at least two weeks! A new hotel is under construction as part of tourist development in the region. There is a *ger* camp nearby which offers accommodation and meals for around US$50; you will need your own transport to get there and most people pass through Khujirt on their way to the Orkhon Waterfall.

With amazing good luck, we witnessed a stallion rounding up his herd. Turning back to collect some straying mares and foals, he suddenly upped his speed by several gears, giving us a thrilling close up of powerful muscles and huge, strong back legs as he thundered by. On a boiling hot day we met nine people, three generations of a family, squeezed into an old Russian van, who smiled and waved as they cheerfully told us they had come all the way from the Gobi, to see the Orkhon Waterfall.

A memory that will stay with me forever is waking at 05.30 with the first light and watching the sun rise, having seen a dazzling display of stars the night before. I thought I was the only one awake, walking in the silence, but one of the horsemen was walking along a ridge opposite. One of them always watches the horses; there may be wolves about. Mongolia, a seemingly never ending vista of land and blue sky, a place with no fences, is simply glorious. The Mongolian people are survivors of the highest order. Living by the seasons, they can and do move house in half a morning, taking down their *ger* and re-assembling it elsewhere, as families and livestock move to richer pastures. Being invited into their home, experiencing their hospitality, seeing how they live in harmony with their land and animals, moves all emotions to another level. It was a privilege for me to meet, to travel with, to be fed and cared for by the Mongolian team who accompanied our group. For me it was all about the horses. To see the dazzling riding skills of the Mongolian horsemen was the dream of a lifetime. They can perch on the back of the saddle, turn completely around, sit sideways, even stand up. I saw one retrieve a dropped strap without slowing down, an ankle hooked around his colourful silver birch saddle and his head almost touching the ground. Mongolia and its horsemen; the stuff of legend.

Jane raised money for the UK charity Help for Heroes (www.helpforheroes.org.uk).

Orkhon Khürkhree You'll need your own transport to get to these waterfalls, 80km west of Khujirt (GPS: N46° 47.234', E101° 57.694'). Formed by volcanic eruptions (or earthquake) about 20,000 years ago, the waterfall cascades from a height of 20m. It tends to dry up in summer. It is a scenic, tranquil spot and the surrounding nature is undisturbed, since so few people live here. As such, there are opportunities for good walking or riding in the area. Downstream there is a deep gorge and 10km away are the cold springs of **Uürtiin Tokhoi**, where there is a second, smaller waterfall (with a 4.5m drop).

Shankhyn Khiid (*Entrance fee to main temple T2,800*) You'll find this monastery in Shankh village, on the main road halfway between Kharkhorin and Khujirt and about 20km south of Erdene Zuu Monastery in the Sarnai River valley. The main temple (of three) has been restored and houses a small community of monks. Ceremonies take place in the main temple at 09.00; visitors are welcome. Historically the monastery was known as the Western Monastery. Its full name is Shankhyn Baruun Khüree or Ribogandanshaduulin Khiid, one of several monasteries built in the early to mid-1700s, during the lifetime of Zanabazar. It was a monastery of importance and once housed Genghis Khan's military black banner. Previously home to 1,500 monks and surrounded by wooden buildings, it was closed in 1937, the buildings and their contents destroyed and the monks dispersed. There is a story that five monks continued their religious practices in secret for many years, meeting in a local *ger*. When the monastery reopened in 1990, one of them returned; local people are fund-raising to build a stupa in his honour.

These remote temples and monasteries are best reached on foot and are often incorporated in riding or hiking tours as somewhere interesting to stop and see on a day's journey. One monastery worth mentioning is **Dövkhön (or Tövkhön) Khiid**, located in the forested hills of Bat-Ölzii district, 68km from Erdene Zuu. It is famous for its cave and a smaller meditation rock chamber used by Zanabazar.

THE GENGHIS KHAN POLO CLUB   *Jim Edwards and Christopher Giercke*

Polo requires skill, balance and fearless riding – all of which the Mongol horseman has in abundance. They are polo naturals. What is more, Mongolia has all the essential resources – hard flat land and millions of free-roaming horses, so all that was needed were polo sticks and balls.

First, we taught them how to make polo sticks using the branches of willow trees. Polo balls are also made of willow wood and are supposed to be roughly 3½ inches in diameter and to weigh 4½ ounces. Homemade balls are none the worse for three good coats of white paint. The club was formally registered with the authorities when Mongolia's first polo tournament took place as part of the 1997 Naadam Festival, featuring the 'three manly sports' to which polo was added – a possible fourth!

Our game (adapted to Mongolia) has two rules:

* No hitting the person or pony with a stick
* No hooking sticks above the waist

There was a third rule – no crossing – but it was abandoned. It also became obvious that Mongolian polo has no boundaries!

We were surprised by how much local spectators threw themselves into the game. To get started we presented the club members with 30 polo shirts and

Mongol Els Lying on the eastern border of Övörkhangai Aimag on the Ulaanbaatar road (270km west of the capital) in Bürd district, Mongol Els is a belt of sand dunes covering an area of around 2,800km². Many people stop there on their way to Arvaikheer, and the magnificent dunes, surrounded by hills with willow trees, streams and bushes, are worth stopping for. The dunes liven up a stretch of otherwise uninteresting road and give the visitor a taste of the desert. You can hire horses and camels to ride in the region and around the dunes.

Bayangobi *Ger* Camp offers accommodation for around US$50 per person, including meals. For reservations contact Juulchin Foreign Tourism Corporation (*Genghis Khan Av 5B, Ulaanbaatar;* ☏ *11 328428;* e *juulchin@mongol.net; www.mol.mn/juulchin*).

Batkhan Uul Nature Reserve Located on the northwest border of the aimag extending into Töv Aimag, this mountainous area is part of the Khangai and Khentii mountain ranges. Visitors driving west from Ulaanbaatar often stop to camp and enjoy the scenery, as the area is conveniently near the main road from Ulaanbaatar to Arvaikheer. Bayangobi *Ger* Camp (see above) is nearby.

Khangai Nuruu National Park This remote mountainous forest region, in the northwest corner of the aimag, extends into Bayankhongor Aimag and is described there (see page 334). Apart from the Eight Lakes area (described below), the park is not well visited because of transport difficulties.

Eight Lakes (Naiman Nuur) Some 100km from Arvaikheer, the lakes were formed by volcanic eruptions centuries ago. Some 70km southwest of Orkhon Waterfall, the Eight Lakes are part of the Khangai Nuruu National Park and lie in a long and broad valley which divides the Gobi-Altai from the Khangai mountain range. Access is difficult as earth roads are often impassable due to marshy ground made worse in bad weather conditions.

50 balls (bought at Harrods in Knightsbridge!) and a number of Indian pith helmets, which we brought with us from Nepal.

In international polo the most dangerous thing is considered to be horse collisions; however, in Mongolia the horses swerve naturally to follow the ball and somehow also succeed in avoiding holes and rocks on the practice grounds. Their horse-herding instincts have replaced brakes. The polo ponies (ordinary Mongolian range ponies) are very agile and athletic, like the riders.

It is advisable to hold the polo stick close up to the heart and upright when not in play. Accuracy and command of the ball in forward play is extremely difficult. The idea is to hit a clean shot and follow up the ball to position it for a goal shot. The whole secret of direction lies in making the head of the stick travel along the line of the ball. Also, you want to aim to hit the ball before you get to it, so a player should try to foresee every stroke. It is best to hit the ball close beside one's leg, leaving room to swing the stick.

Although we don't know if Genghis Khan ever played polo, the sport certainly originated in the great Mongol warrior's empire. We are thrilled by the way polo has been received in Mongolia, and as a result we have developed a camp and training grounds for visitors. We are expecting to play a number of entertaining tournaments in the future. See www.genghiskhanpolo.com.

ACTIVITIES

Mountain biking in the Orkhon river valley A ten-day biking holiday is offered by Off the Map Tours (*www.mongolia.co.uk*). The itinerary takes you from Kharkhorin along the Orkhon River valley and back again. You will bike along typical dirt roads and tracks across rolling hilly countryside and camp by rivers and mountain streams, where you can experience the vastness of the steppe scenery and the beauty and silence of the mountains. You will also eat outdoors around campfires and in local restaurants and spend some well-earned rest in a hot, open-air spring bath. Furthermore, you will also have the chance to meet with nomadic families, drink fermented mare's or cow's milk vodka and salty-milky tea with yak-herding families and see their yaks grazing on the high pastures above Khayasaan Gorge. The itinerary also offers the chance, when biking along the River Orkhon, to stop at a magnificent waterfall where you can rest your weary muscles, before continuing along the valley floor to Khujirt, where you will find more hot spring baths to recuperate in and where you can relax and totally let go.

Polo in the Orkhon Valley This sport has become a huge success, for both local players and spectators. It is not considered an elitist sport in Mongolia, nor is it wildly expensive to keep horses to play polo, as it is elsewhere in the world. Camel polo is a spectator sport in Mongolia with organised events. In 2002 parliamentarian Oyunbaatar Tserendash founded the Mongolian Camel Federation. His son Temuhiin is involved in match arrangements and fundraising to help save the wild Bactrian camel.

The Genghis Khan Polo Club (see box, pages 290–1) originated from an impromptu game played on a trip to Mongolia in 1997, when Jim Edwards (founder of World Elephant Polo), his son Kristjan and their friend the film-maker Christopher Giercke founded the club with 12 members and a group of 'would-be' Mongolian players. They discovered that Mongolian riders possess two great characteristics: remarkable co-ordination and extraordinary flexibility in the saddle. The club is now firmly established under the guidance of Christopher Giercke, his Mongolian wife Enkhe and their three children, Ich Tenger, D'Artagnan and Allegra, in a beautiful part of the Orkhon River valley.

ARKHANGAI AIMAG

Arkhangai means 'Back of the Khangai', or 'Northern slopes of the Khangai'; it is also known as the 'wet province' which doesn't sound very promising, though in fact it is one of the most beautiful of Mongolia's provinces, with mountains, cliffs, fast-flowing rivers and lush, green forests. It is situated in central Mongolia in the northern territory of the Khangai Nuruu, where ranges like Suvargakhairkhan rise above 3,000m. Forests cover one-sixth of the aimag and pastures about 70%. Yaks thrive on the high mountain pasture and live on the hillsides, their long, hairy coats helping protect them from the harsh winter weather. Nature, along with the opportunity for adventure travel to lakes and rivers, is the main attraction of this province.

TSETSERLEG Tsetserleg (meaning 'garden') is situated at the southern foot of Bulgan Mountain, the site of Zayain Khüree Monastery. The town is laid out with spacious streets and has more charm than most other aimag centres. Peaks of the Khangai range are seen in the south and Bulgan rises sharply to the north. Behind the main museum, a path leads to a small, unoccupied temple in the hills which is worth visiting for the view. Tsetserleg is an excellent place to use as a base if you are touring

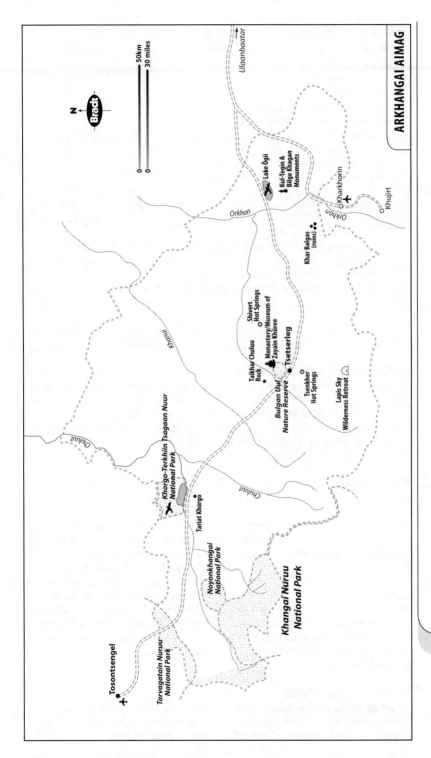

BRIEF FACTS: ARKHANGAI AIMAG

Area 55,300km²
Aimag centre Tsetserleg
Districts 19
Elevation of Tsetserleg 1,631m
Livestock and crops Horses, yaks, potatoes, hay
Ethnic groups Khalkha, Ööld
Distance from Tsetserleg to Ulaanbaatar 463km
Average temperatures July 14.3°C, January –14.9°C

HIGHLIGHTS
- Ögii Nuur – lake
- Chuluut River – fishing
- Terkhiin Tsagaan Nuur (Great White Lake) – sightseeing, hiking and camping
- Tsenkher and Shivert – hot springs
- Turkic (6th–8th century), Uighur (8th–10th century) – archaeological sites

the Mongolian lakes – Ögii and Terkhiin Tsagaan Nuur (Great White Lake). It is a busy town where you can pick up supplies at the daily market for your journeys.

Getting there from Ulaanbaatar

By road Most tourists travel to Tsetserleg by public bus/minibus or private jeep. Buses run between UB and Tsetserleg daily leaving around 08.00 (or later, sometimes waiting until the bus is full). The fare is T18,000, with a travel time of approximately nine hours. To hire a jeep with a driver costs from T500–800 per kilometre depending on the sort of jeep (which works out at US$230 from UB, cheaper if travelling in a shared jeep).

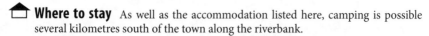 **Where to stay** As well as the accommodation listed here, camping is possible several kilometres south of the town along the riverbank.

🏠 **Hotel Buyan** located in the centre, opposite the police building ; ☎701 70299; m 9696 0299. One of the better hotels. *Rooms with bathrooms* **$**
🏠 **Hotel Sasa** 2–3mins' walk east of the town square; no telephone. Has a friendly atmosphere & good service.
🏠 **Hotel Sundur** ☎1332 22359. South of the town beside the market on the UB road. Simple, cheap rooms; billiard table, showers, laundry service & a restaurant. The hotel will arrange transport & taxi service. **$**

🏠 **Hotel Zamchin** ☎1332 21096/21196. Located in the southwest part of town; has restaurant, bar, sauna, free internet for guests. **$**
🏠 **Fairfield Guest House B&B** ☎guesthouse: 7033 3036; café: 7033 3096; e workers@mongol. net; www.fairfieldmongolia.co.uk, www. fairfield.mn. Located on the east side of town; excellent place to stay. English-speaking staff serve good coffee. Also has a restaurant (see following listing). **$**

✕ Where to eat and drink

✕ **Fairfield Restaurant/Café/Bakery** On the east side of town; ☎7033 3096 e twonomads@ magicnet.mn; ⏰ 09.00–18.00 Mon–Sat (closed

Sat in winter). Run by Mark & Gill Newham. Many foreigners & locals eat here. Fairfield was the brainchild of Roger & Caroline Whiting back in 1993 when they move to Mongolia to teach English, the bakery was added later with the help of Mark & Gill Newman & friends – & since that time both the guesthouse (above) and the café/bakery have thrived. They serve excellent, low-cost meals including pizza, lasagne, stews & burgers, all at local prices (T800–2,000). The bakery (*same opening times*) supplies Western bread, cakes & pastries to order for foreign groups.

✕ **Naran Centre** ☎ 1332 22869. Located on the east side of town; restaurant/bar.

Shopping

🏬 **Art Shop** Contact Oyuun; 📱 993 39902; ☉ 10.00–18.00. Located to the left of the post office, sells Mongolian antiques, paintings & souvenirs made by local artists.

🏬 **Main Market** ☉ 10.00–18.00. Located in the town centre.

🏬 **Tansag Trading Centre** ☉ 09.30–20.00. Located on the north side of town by the main road for groceries.

What to see and do in Tsetserleg

Arkhangai Palace Museum (☎ *1332 22281*; ☉ *09.00–18.00 Mon–Fri; entrance fee around T4,500*) This museum is housed in the temple buildings of the former Zayain Khüree Monastery, built in 1586 and expanded in 1631. In the 17th century, the monastery was one of the most active in Mongolia. It had five temples and housed 1,000 monks, and on ceremonial occasions over 4,000 monks were known to have participated in events there. Two of its main temples were destroyed in the religious purges of the 1930s; it survived destruction to be used as a storehouse. Three temples remain: Gandan, Niser and Lavran; their architecture is a mixture of Mongolian and Tibetan styles. The museum exhibits Buddhist ritual objects and features a collection of traditional Mongolian costumes, traditional tools, a *ger*, musical instruments, saddles and weapons, and a collection of 20th-century paintings by local artists.

Buyandelgerüülekh Khiid This is the main active monastery, located just north of the town square. Regular services are held in the mornings in the main hall or in a neighbouring *ger*; if you want to attend, ask the monks.

To learn more about Buddhism and Mongolian temples visit: www.zanabazar.mn/zanabazar.html.

WHAT TO SEE AND DO IN ARKHANGAI AIMAG

Terkhiin Tsagaan Nuur (*Entrance fee T3,000 pp per day plus T4,500 for a vehicle; fishing permit from US$10 per day; arrange with park rangers*) In the northwest part of the province, Terkhiin Tsagaan Nuur ('White Lake of River Terkh') is a beautiful body of water surrounded by extinct volcanoes. The lake covers 16km x 20km, and is 10m deep. Some parts of its shoreline are sandy and in summer the water is warm enough to swim in. The area offers excellent opportunities for fishing (pike and perch). It is also possible to hike from the northeastern shore to Khorgo Uul Volcano (2,965m). A local guide will help you to find the best route. On the way there are caves worth exploring. You may also spot deer, *argali* (wild sheep) and wild boar. The lake, the surrounding volcanoes, and the animal and birdlife are now protected within the 73,000ha **Khorgo-Terkhiin Tsagaan Nuur National Park**. Birdlife includes swan goose, Pallas's fish eagle, saker falcon, hooded crane and common merganser.

Where to stay

🏠 **Khatan-Ugii *Ger* Camp** (UK contact) www.coxandkings.co.uk. Small quality camp of 15 *gers*; can accommodate 60 people for dining.

🏠 **Khorgo *Ger* Camp No 1** Zürkhiin Gol Valley, northeast of the lake. Run by Tsolmon Travel Company (see page 239). Hot showers are available. **$$$**

⌂ **Khorgo *Ger* Camp No 2** www. tsolmontravel.com/en/our-camps/khorgo-camp. Sister camp of the above, lying in the southwest. **$$$**

⌂ **Tariat Village Hotel** Short distance from the main east–west road (see map). This is the nearest hotel, lying some 6km east of the lake. You need your own transport. **$**

⚠ **Camping** Allowed in the pine-forested area on the eastern lakeshore or beside the beach on the northeastern corner of the lake. **$**

Archaeological sites There are many archaeological sites in this aimag, belonging to different times: from Paleolithic and Neolithic periods to Bronze and Iron Age periods that cover the historical times of the Xiongnu, Turkish, Uighur and Qidan peoples to the Mongolian period of Genghis Khan onwards. The Tamir River site was excavated in 2005 with the help of the Silk Road Foundation working with the Mongolian National Museum. Where the Orkhon River meets the Ordos Mountains was once a centre of four great cultures, Xiangnu, Turk, Uighur and Mongol. Near where the Tamir River and Orkhon River meet excavations at three different sites unearthed Xiongnu (3rd century BC to 1st century AD) burial grounds. See www.silkroadfoundation.org/excavation/arkhangai/index.htm.

Khar Balgas On the eastern bank of the River Orkhon, 46km northwest of Kharkhorin, are the ruins of an ancient Uighur city founded in AD751. This was the capital of the Uighur khanate which ruled Mongolia from AD745–854. Now only the city's outer walls and gateways remain. Khar Balgas was a typical trading centre and routes between it and many other trading centres like it criss-crossed central Asia – described in 1889 by Russian explorer N M Yadrintsev. Archaeologists say the city would have had lookout towers, stables and storehouses. You can see the underlying layout of the town including the ruler's palace and a Buddhist stupa, which shows the religious significance of Buddhism in the city, in addition to its military and commercial links. Other ruins show an ancient water system that channelled water to Khar Balgas from several kilometres away.

Monuments to Bilge Khagan and Kul-Tegin (leaders of the Turkic Empire)

Khöshöö Tsaidam Around 20km northeast of Khar Balgas and 47km north of Kharkhorin are the most famous of Mongolia's stone stelae. Both stelae date from AD732, are roughly the same size (approximately 3.30m high x 1.30m wide) and both bear inscriptions in Turkic runes and Chinese script. Both, too, are dedicated to the Turkish khans who ruled Mongolia between the 6th and 8th centuries. One honours Bilge Khagan (Bilgä-Kagan) and the other General Kul-Tegin (Köl-Tegin), Bilge's brother. They were discovered in 1889 by the Russian explorer, N M Yadrintsev. The inscriptions were recorded and further studied by members of several other late 19th-century Russian expeditions. The National Museum of Mongolian History exhibits a copy in its entrance hall.

The two stone monuments are found close to one another in the Tsaidam district of the Orkhon River valley. Bilge Khagan's monument is 1km southeast of Kul-Tegin's monument, at one kilometre's distance.

Examples of rock art, gravestones and deer stones have been well recorded, the last at Altan Sandal Uul (mountain), Suman Gol (river) and in Bayanbulag (spring) in Tariat sum (district); and at Bugat, Khuruugin Üzüür ('fingertip') and in Ikh-Tamir sum (district). An archaeological trail for tourists and an interpretive centre on the Orkhon Valley and its archaeology are much needed for visitors.

Taikhar Chuluu Around 2km north of the town of Ikh Tamir, 22km along the main road west of Tsetserleg, this massive granite rock (possibly a volcanic plug) towers above the surrounding flat country. Legend relates it was put there by Baatar, a giant Mongolian hero who crushed a fierce serpent to death by placing the rock on top of it. This gigantic, sheer-sided boulder is impossible to climb. It is also a sacred rock. According to the local people Tibetan inscriptions were carved on the rock but sadly they are covered by graffiti markings (of the recent past), which have destroyed them.

Close to the rock there is an excellent *ger* camp (*US$65 inc meals*) run by Mongolian Outdoor Safaris (↘ *11 311008*).

Tsenkher Hot Springs These springs lie south of Tsetserleg in Tsenkher district, a ten-hour drive or two-hour flight plus a four-hour jeep ride from UB. The springs and streams are well developed and jointly owned by a Japanese company. The waters are supposed to have curative properties for joints and other ailments.

FIVE-DAY TRIP TO THE GREAT WHITE LAKE   Polly Gotthard

There are no great whites there but it is a very pretty place and although it was a five-day trip, I spent four of those travelling. We started off on a local bus for nine hours to a place called Tsetserleg where I stayed at a very run-down hotel. On my wanders about town I was shown around a disused monastery by an old monk. It turned out that he learnt Tibetan and Sanscrit in 1992 at Baldan Baraivan, the monastery in eastern Mongolia where I had worked on a restoration project in 2004. Small world. He and a friend gave me supper, *aaruul* – hard dried curds which I can only eat small amounts of at the best of times, so I ended up breaking off small amounts of it and hiding them in my socks to smuggle them out without seeming rude!

The next day, an eight-hour jeep ride took us to the lake, along with other passengers, a couple of nice Mongolian lads who worked at one of the *ger* camps on the lake. The clouds were dark and looming as we left town, and pretty soon we were in a sand/hail/snowstorm for about an hour, but it cleared without the jeep breaking down, which was a bonus (its radiator was refilled with water three times but that doesn't count). We stopped off at a tea house for tea, biscuits and more *aaruul* and vodka, and arrived at sunset in the freezing cold!

Woke up the next day to a cloudy, dismal day, but I managed to motivate myself to go for a walk. The lake was really lovely, even more so when the sun came out from behind the clouds. Pottered back to the *ger* camp and found some 'crazy Russian pilots' and one of them took me on a tandem flight (despite him speaking no English and me no Russian), which was awesome – especially considering all my joints remained intact. I later discovered one of their friends broke his arm that day. Had I known that ... Then off for a few hours' horseback riding before joining a Russian party later on that night, which turned a bit silly when people discovered it was my birthday!

The next day, travelling back to Tsetserleg by jeep, with a newborn on one side and a drunk on the other, I arrived and immediately checked into a nice British-run guesthouse (the Fairfield Guest House, see *Where to eat*, pages 294–5) I'd spotted on my travels around town, and feasted on lasagne before sleeping for 12 hours.

Outdoor pools are attended by staff who can cool or heat the water via a water-gate system; there are also indoor pools. Men and women bathe separately. Electricity is generated using sunlight and the temperature difference between the hot springs and the river water. It is an excellent place to relax.

Nearby **Tsenkher Hot Springs *Ger* Camp** (✆ *11 358005*) sleeps up to 60 people and costs US$45+ per day including meals such as stone-grilled mutton, greenhouse vegetables, eggs (when available) boiled in the hot springs, and fermented mare's milk or cow's milk vodka.

Shivert Hot Springs
Located in a valley some 50km northwest of Tsetserleg (see map), you will need to ride or hike to get to these springs, and you'll need a 4x4. Allow plenty of travel time. The hot springs are natural chlorine- and potassium-compound springs and are currently very undeveloped. Apart from the springs the region has interesting deer stones (see box, *Deer stones*, page 359) and is an attractive place to camp, ride and hike.

Lake Ögii
This lies off the main Ulaanbaatar–Tsetserleg road as you enter the province, about 150km from Tsetserleg. It is a wonderful area for fishing, camping and birdwatching – the types of birds you may see include Dalmatian pelican, swan goose, Baikal teal, Pallas's fish eagle, lesser kestrel and Siberian crane, among other crane species – white-naped, hooded and common; you may also see great bustard and relict gulls. See *Suggested itinerary*, pages 162–4, for further details.

| YOGA | *Carroll Dunham and Thomas Kelly* |

As you wear out the saddle stirrups – contemplate – turn back and look at your tracks.

Dendevyn Pürevdorj

Lapis Sky Wilderness Retreat is a unique experience not only because of its stunning geography, but due also to the special relationship with the local nomad community, its unusual hosts and the focus of spirit and rejuvenation through the wilderness, reflection and the horse. Base camp is located 42km south of Tsetserleg (47 15′59′N 101 8″48 E), nestled in the Bunkhan Valley beside the Tamir River below the sacred Bayon Öndör Mountain in the Khangai range of central Mongolia. Visitors experience a combination of monasteries and nomads, horses and *gers*, wide green grasslands and mountains, lakes and deep quiet. They visit some of the most extraordinary Buddhist monasteries in Mongolia, and find time for yoga practice.

In Bunkhan camp summer *gers* are equipped with wood stoves against the evening chill. Tasty meals are prepared by nomad staff on the stoves using the best of local fresh ingredients, dairy products, meat, fruit and vegetables, adapted to suit Western diets, vegetarians and vegans. Meals are relaxed and served in the large dining *ger*, where wines and spirits are available. Pranayama meditation and yoga sessions take place in a traditional Mongolian tent in a cottonwood tree forest with the sound of a rushing river, and the bustle of morning photography workshops. Bathing is simple – hot water from the wood stoves, solar showers in the shower *ger*. Afternoons are spent horseriding using comfortable Western saddles. Beginners can be led by experienced nomad horsemen or visitors may prefer to explore the surrounding countryside on foot.

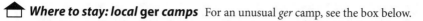

Where to stay: local ger camps For an unusual *ger* camp, see the box below.

Khatan Ögii e khatan@ugiitour.mn; www. ugiitour.mn. The camp is next to the lake & it is 120km from Tsetserleg city & 70km from Kharkhorin. **$**

Ögii (also Ugii) Tour Camp e Tseegii0711@ yahoo.com. This relatively small camp (10 *gers*) is on the northern shore of the lake.

National parks and protected areas

Noyonkhangai National Park (*Entrance fee US$2; paid to a ranger, if & when you meet one*) Located on the western boundary of the province (see map) in a very remote mountain habitat, this area has been a national park since 1998, largely thanks to its curative mineral waters and wildlife. Access is difficult, on account of poor road conditions in Khangai sum (district). To get there by jeep, drive to Noyonkhangai village, which lies outside the park's boundaries on the north side. This area is not frequented by tourists and there are no tourist facilities. There is no fencing; there are no park gates and no offices *in situ*.

Bulgan Uul Nature Reserve (*Entrance fee US$2, paid to a ranger*) Covering an 18km² area of mountain range immediately north of Tsetserleg, this has been a natural reserve since 1985 because of the diversity of its birdlife. The mountains, whose northern slopes are larch covered, reach almost 2,000m. Pictographs and carvings of deer and other animals dating from the Bronze Age are found on rocks in the area.

Some guests enjoy the bracing waters of the crystal-clear Tamir River on raft floats while others enjoy fly fishing.

After forays around the camp, and honing riding skills, visitors can prepare for a three-day expedition/horse pilgrimage to Mandal Mountain, camping out along the way. Informal polo matches are set up with local horsemen, yak-cart picnics and later on bonfire evenings with traditional Mongolian music take place under the clear star-studded night sky.

If you yearn to be immersed in the raw magic of Mongol wilderness and ride with the nomads this is the place for you. 'Rustic simplicity, stunning essentials' describes the camp at Bunkhan in the 'Valley of the Graves of the Ancestors' – rich with ancient grave sites. The *gers* are all handmade by Toro at his community workshop and are erected every summer and taken down in autumn leaving no trace behind. A combination of museums and monasteries, guides and experts in anthropology and history help to enrich the experience.

Lapis Sky Wilderness Retreat was established by two Americans – anthropologist, Carroll Dunham and her husband, award-winning photographer, Thomas L Kelly – both National Geographic guides, in partnership with Narangerel Ailaikhuu, a local school headmistress and her husband Toro, *ger* maker and politician. Lapis Sky is an example of social entrepreneurship community-based ecotourism.

For further information and costs, contact National Geographic Adventure Tours at Lapis Sky Camp (*www.nationalgeographicadventures.com*). For yoga or Buddhist meditation retreat programmes and costs e info@wildearthjorneys.com.

See also www.wildearthjourneys.com.

7

Tarvagatain Nuruu National Park Located on the western border of the aimag with Zavkhan Aimag, the national park extends into Zavkhan and is described on page 378.

Khangai Nuruu National Park Covering a remote mountainous area in the southwest part of the aimag, extending into Bayankhongor Aimag (see page 146).

Activities Some of the best fishing takes place in this aimag. The rivers Tamir and Chuluut rise in the Khangai Mountains and flow north with the Orkhon River (which runs through the western part of the province) to join the great Selenge River which flows into Lake Baikal in southern Siberia and from there to the Arctic Ocean.

Ayanchin Outfitters in Ulaanbaatar (*Seoul Av, nr State Dept Store; www. ayanchin.com*) provides a good standard of fishing gear and other camping equipment.

Travelling back to Ulaanbaatar by jeep one winter day, motoring carefully across the snowy plains, my eye spotted a dark speck in the distance, larger than the size of a yak. It transformed into a colourful herd of ponies and riders about to start a race, unusual for the time of year as racing normally takes place in summer. The warm breath of shaggy ponies clouded the clear air. They were ridden by children aged between five and 12, some of whom were being led to the start by anxious-looking parents. The youngest laughed and joked while their elder brothers and sisters appeared to be more serious. An announcement from a nearby van called them to order. Finally, around 100 children mounted their winter-coated ponies, assembled and dutifully trotted out of sight behind a hill to the start.

They then turned to gallop back at full pace through the snow fields, cutting a path over the frozen surface and churning up a plume of shimmering snow particles that were carried on the wind as the ponies swept into sight. Sheepskins were bound to the legs of some jockeys to prevent chafing, while others rode bareback. Their riding skills and energy were extraordinary to witness. There was huge excitement among the racing crowd, who were brilliantly attired in silk fleece-lined *deel* – the traditional knee-length Mongolian tunic, worn by men and women. The colours contrasted fantastically against the white snow – tunics of green, purple and deep red, tied at the waist by saffron sashes. Since it was mid-February, most nomads wore fox-fur hats. Many had ridden for miles to attend the meeting. I was surprised to see several herders pull out binoculars to scan the distant hillside for the first sign of the oncoming riders. When they did appear, the crowds roared and cheered. Many parents tried to run on to the course to encourage the young riders but were held back by race officials. The trainer of the winning horse, ridden by a child of seven, is now the happy owner of a motorbike. The atmosphere differed little from the excitement experienced by enthusiastic race-goers anywhere in the world.

SUGGESTED ITINERARY

A riding/driving holiday For this itinerary you will need to work out timing and logistics with a Mongolian travel company in advance, or with a guide/translator and driver on the spot. Allow 10–14 days for this tour, which begins with a drive by jeep from Ulaanbaatar to the Great White Lake stopping *en route* for the night at Khustain Nuruu, the wild horse reserve 100km west of UB. From there, continue the next day by jeep to the Orkhon Valley, paying a visit to the famous Buddhist monastery of Erdene Zuu. From here you can arrange horses to ride north into Arkhangai Aimag, where you'll find yourself galloping across unfenced pastureland under the craggy granite mountains of the Khangai range. Ride and camp for a few days before handing the horses back. Stop in Tsetserleg to sightsee and camp overnight beside the sacred rock, Taikhar Chuluu, then continue by jeep to the Great White Lake in the northwest, spending a day hiking around the lake. To ease stiff and aching joints take an open-air bath in the hot mineral springs at Tsenkher, before finally returning to Ulaanbaatar via the sand dunes at Mongol Els, where you may hire a horse or camel to experience riding in desert conditions.

Sightseeing in the Chuluut area As with the above, costs and logistics for this trip can be worked out in advance with a tour company or on the spot with a

7

guide/translator and jeep driver. This itinerary begins with a jeep ride to Arkhangai (150km west of Tsetserleg); camp beside the Chuluut River. Visit Chuulut river gorge with its dramatic scenery and camp there, spending a few days fishing or birdwatching. From there, drive (45km) to Tariat village and trek to the volcanic crater above the Great White Lake, where you can pitch your tent by the lakeside, relax on the sandy beach by the lake, allowing plenty of time to take in the scenery before driving back to Ulaanbaatar via the sand dune area at Elsentasarkhai (Mongol Els), where you may ride a camel or hire a horse for the day.

8

Southern Region: Gobi Aimags

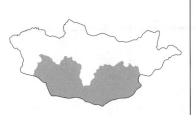

Gobi, a term first noted on a French map in 1706, is defined in many different ways: as a gravel landscape without water, as a 'treeless terrain without marmots and little surface water', as a desert area waiting to be watered. It encompasses the world's most northerly desert (the sand dunes in Uvs aimag), and it shelters frozen snowmelt throughout the summer in a canyon in the South Gobi. The topography of this vast territory is predominately a closed drainage depression. The landscape includes mountain ranges, springs, forests, sand dunes and steppes. Towards the west the Altai peaks rise to over 4,000m. The ground is rich in copper, molybdenum, gold, tin, iron ore and coal; forests of poplar, elm, willow and aspen grow in the mountains and near oases; feather grass and leek cover the plains. Few plants grow in the bare soils of the semi-desert and sand dunes are almost devoid of plant life though a bushy shrub called *zag* thrives in places where there is enough groundwater. The Gobi may also be described as land waiting to be watered, as with the slightest amount of precipitation shrubs and wild flowers bloom and flourish. Fierce sand and windstorms are common and nearly all the region's soil has been removed by prevailing northwesterly winds and deposited in north central China as loess (fine silt). There are many types of Gobi – at least 33 – and they mostly differ from one another, usually based on location, minerals and water supply; often named after local features.

The landscape commonly known as 'Gobi' stretches 3,000 miles along Mongolia's southern border and extends to parts of the far northwest, running between the Altai and the Khangai mountain ranges, as well as south into northern China. Principally the Gobi spans six Mongolian provinces (aimags): Ömnögobi, Dornogobi, Dundgobi, Bayankhongor, Gobi-Sümber and Gobi-Altai. It is a wide-open place of huge extremes: mostly it is one huge gravel plain quite unlike any other desert on earth. Of the total Gobi area only 3% is the sandy desert type. Despite these arid conditions, wildlife abounds.

Two hundred million years ago the Gobi was an inland sea. During this period, western Siberia and the Jungarian plains formed one vast sheet of water. Warm, damp conditions prevailed with abundant vegetation. The site of this ancient inland sea was discovered to be a treasure trove of fossilised dinosaur bones. In the 1920s the American palaeontologist, Roy Chapman Andrews, made some exciting dinosaur discoveries including fossilised dinosaur eggs and later expeditions have discovered giant prehistoric animals (see box, *Dragon bones*, pages 316–17).

These days, however, the Gobi is more famous as a place of huge, mostly untapped, mineral wealth. Overall, the region is very sparsely populated but the modest and plain life of the people living there inspires respect. But the Gobi is a changing place – and this is due to new mining interests. Where once there were few or no roads, today the south Gobi region around the big copper and coal mines is buzzing. New airports, new roads, and new rail links are to come. What was part of the Gobi's

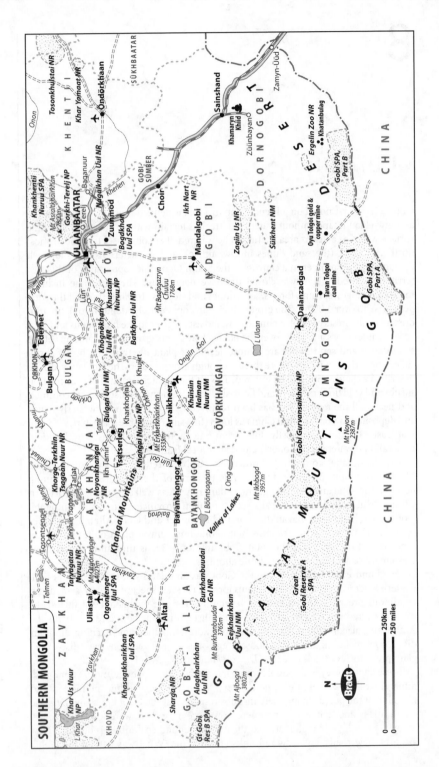

SOUTHERN MONGOLIA

N

Bradt

| 0 | 250km |
| 0 | 250 miles |

CHINA

CHINA

charm is being, as many locals see it, trampled upon. Wildlife is disturbed, people feel out of it, so the transition story reads. The changes are very real. The mining companies involved, like Rio Tinto, are making an effort to help people and wildlife of the region. Projects run by Flora and Fauna International led by Dr Tony Whitten and Dr Pippa Howard are an example of an integrated approach towards the protection of species, alongside development. Elsewhere, away from the mines, there are few roads and most places are entirely undeveloped: that is part of their charm but the charm may fast disappear as traffic increases. Behind the romance of the desert is the harsh reality of an inhospitable land. A mixture of foolhardiness and bravery is needed to travel long distances in the Gobi, as explorer Benedict Allen discovered on his 1,000-mile trek from the northwestern border of Mongolia to where the Trans-Mongolian railway cuts through the southeastern end of the Gobi (see pages 214–15).

TRAVEL RISKS

Do not go into this country unprepared or underestimate the hazards of getting lost, even in broad daylight. When the sun goes down and the distant mountain profiles disappear into darkness, you very easily become disoriented, especially on a moonless night. Individual travellers should take good maps, a torch, a compass, plenty of water and some food if travelling by jeep. In the Gobi vegetation clings to the slightest root and precipitation is truly a matter of life and death. Desert terrain is a mixture of great fragility and extraordinary toughness, like the people who inhabit it.

Another thing to watch out for is estimated distance. In a desert such as the Gobi, mountain ranges appear to be much closer than they actually are. Mirages, too, tantalise and look so real that you might even start preparing your water bottle for a refill. This terrain is deceptive. Ancient travellers have long bemoaned the strangeness of the Gobi with its whispering sands and unaccountable, shrill, eerie noises. Desert caravans along the old trade routes frequently complained they lost people who wandered off following the hum of human voices that were completely imaginary.

Sudden desert storms are also a real hazard. These freak meteorological incidents last from moments to hours and can literally destroy a campsite. Dust storms, flash floods and sudden cold snaps are unpredictable and happen mostly during the winter and spring months, but can happen at other times of year including summer.

ÖMNÖGOBI AIMAG

Ömnögobi is more commonly known to foreigners as the South Gobi. It is part of Mongolia's Golden Circuit, referred to in this guide as one of the classic routes. The aimag (province) has many visitors, despite being the hottest and driest region of Mongolia: summer temperatures reach 38°C and annual precipitation is 130mm. Mountains capture what little surface moisture there is as snow which melts into streams and supplies much-needed water for wildlife, livestock and the human population. Apart from the extensive Gurvansaikhan Nuruu range, known as the 'Three Beauties', the aimag is predominately flat. The desert supports thousands of black-tailed gazelles, but it is too dry to graze large domestic herds of cattle and sheep that thrive on the province's steppe further north. The Gobi is home to a quarter of Mongolia's domestic camels; they include Gobi red and Gobi brown camels, both native stock, prized for their high productivity and endurance, though their numbers are now in decline. Sadly, the wild camel appears to be endangered. The Gobi is famous for its cashmere goats; there are three species: the Gobi *gurvansaikhan* (brown goat), the *gurvantes* (blue goat) and the *buur nomgon* (red

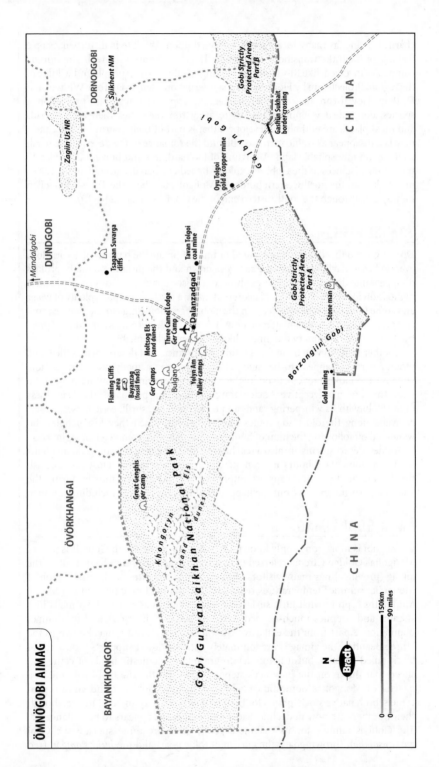

ÖMNÖGOBI AIMAG

BAYANKHONGOR

ÖVÖRKHANGAI

DUNDGOBI

DORNODGOBI

CHINA

Mandalgobi

Zagiin Us NR

Süjikhent NM

Tsagaan Suvarga cliffs

Flaming Cliffs area

Bayanzag (fossil finds)

Moltsog Els (sand dunes)

Ger Camps

Bulgan

Three Camel Lodge Ger Camp

Yolyn Am Valley camps

Dalanzadgad

Great Genghis ger camp

Khongoryn Els (sand dunes)

Gobi Gurvansaikhan National Park

Tavan Tolgoi coal mine

Oyu Tolgoi gold & copper mine

Gashüün Sukhait border crossing

Gobi Strictly Protected Area, Part B

Gobi Strictly Protected Area, Part A

Stone man

Borzongiin Gobi

Gold mining

CHINA

N

Bradt

0   150km
0   90 miles

goat). South Gobi's goats yield tonnes of soft, raw cashmere wool annually. Apart from the livestock industry, the South Gobi has a flourmill and factories for wool scouring and candle making, set up recently with the help of foreign investment. The aimag has mining interests in the extreme south near the border with China. Small farms produce potatoes and vegetables. Future plans for the province include upgrading the airport, possibly enabling direct flights to/from China and elsewhere, as part of tourism development.

DALANZADGAD The town is located roughly 600km from Ulaanbaatar at the eastern extremity of the Altai mountain range. The town is Mongolia's most southerly aimag centre, with a population of around 20,000. It is typical of many centres with white, stone administrative buildings with green roofs; the town is surrounded by *ger* compounds. There is more to this Gobi centre than meets the eye – it is being transformed into a new mining town. Despite the changes a real sense of community exists and the local government has made a big effort to make the town attractive by planting trees. Beyond the town, on three sides, is endless flat steppe, while to the west are the Gurvansaikhan Mountains (the 'Three Beauties').

Among the facilities are shops with a good supply of Western foods; a well-stocked pharmacy; and, if you run out of battery on your mobile phone, a telephone exchange where international calls can be made and emails can be sent. Hotels include the Khan Uul Hotel and Dalanzadgad Hotel (see page 309). Bars and nightclubs complete the scene – along with banks and improved conditions at the now very busy airport. Entertainment includes traditional throat singing (*khöömii*) and folk dancing, which take place during festival times when the town comes alive. Dalanzadgad has a theatre and supports a group of local singers.

Getting there from Ulaanbaatar
By air Aero Mongolia, Eznis and Hunnu airlines fly from Ulaanbaatar to Dalanzadgad. It is advisable to book well in advance and *confirm your flight* since double bookings are a problem. There's a luggage allowance of 15kg per person; the flight time is 90 minutes. The airport is located north of Dalanzadgad (✆ *53 2657*).
For the summer schedules see: www.touristinfocenter.mn.

BRIEF FACTS: ÖMNÖGOBI AIMAG

Area 165,400km²
Aimag centre Dalanzadgad
Districts 15
Elevation of Dalanzadgad 1,465m
Livestock Goats, sheep, camels
Ethnic groups Khalkha
Distance from Dalanzadgad to Ulaanbaatar 553km
Average temperatures July 21.2°C, January –15.4°C

HIGHLIGHTS
* Gurvansaikhan National Park
* Yolyn Am Valley – country museum, gorge and glacier
* Bayanzag – dinosaur bones
* Khongoryn Els – sand dunes
* Minerals and mining

8

By road It is 553km from Ulaanbaatar to Dalanzadgad and it is possible to cover the distance in one day if you start very early. Buses leave Ulaanbaatar daily at 08.00 from the Eastern Bus Station at Naran Tuul ('Black Market') for the South Gobi, stopping *en route* at Mandalgobi in Dundgobi Aimag. The bus arrives and leaves from beside the hospital on the main UB road out of town in Dalanzadgad; tickets cost around T22,000 (US$15) and can be purchased at the bus office (℡ 53 3708) beside the hospital, or in Ulaanbaatar at the long-distance Eastern Bus Station.

If hiring a car, try not to complete the trip in one go since the road conditions are poor albeit improving. Instead, break the journey either by camping, or staying overnight in a local family *ger*, or at a hotel in Mandalgobi (see page 326). Petrol is available at Mandalgobi.

NEW DEVELOPMENTS IN SOUTH GOBI

The economic opportunities created by the new mining industry are changing the face of this province, because alongside mining development are the issues of the migration of nomads to cities (away from the Gobi) and immigration of casual labour from China, Korea and other countries. New services and a better infrastructure are being developed. Mining towns such as that at Oyu Tolgai have been built from scratch by the Mongolian government and companies involved, like Rio Tinto. Some of these buildings will not be long term but certainly used for the lifetime of the mine – they include public service buildings, schools, hospitals and housing. Power and water are needed and the national government rather than local government is responsible for this and for providing roads. Thus the mining areas are undergoing mega improvements while the rest of the countryside in fact remains basically undeveloped. But there are trade-offs and these include improved services in banking and many new businesses in the capital and in specific areas of the countryside.

There are 150 million tonnes of coal reserves at Ovoot Tolgoi to the southeast of Dalanzadag and even larger coal deposits at Tavan Tolgoi due east of the aimag centre. Copper and gold are in huge deposits, currently being mined at Oyu Tolgoi – where the mine-life is estimated at 35 years. There are further gold deposits in the region at Olon Ovoot. These deposits are spread through the *soums* (local districts) of Manlai, Mandakh, Bayan-Ovoo, Khanbogd and Khantanbulag.

New paved road networks – non-existent in the past – are now the responsibility of different government departments and are improved or newly paved between UB and Dalanzadgad and between Sainshand along the main north–south railway line to Tsagaan Suvraga. There is also a road from Zamyn Üud on the border with the People's Republic of China that links to the mining areas. Railway branch lines from Airag on the main north–south line are planned (not yet constructed) to Tavaan Tolgoi, Dalanzadgad and further west to Naryn sukhait and Shiveenkhuren. The airport is much improved at Dalanzadgad with a new private airstrip at Oyu Tolgoi. Needless to say the population in the mining areas, at Khanbogd for example, is expected to increase to around 45,000 by 2015. This is a dramatic rise given that ten years ago the population was under 5,000. Keep a watch on future developments in this area.

Where to stay Most organised tours stay outside the town in *ger* camps (see list below). Note that standard *ger* camps in the Gobi cost US$45–65 including meals. This is the country's most-visited aimag.

Two new *ger* camps have been developed at **Borzongiin Gobi**, 700km from Ulaanbaatar. There are plans to fly direct to Borzongiin Gobi but it has not yet happened; to reach the camps you must fly to Dalanzadgad and travel the 70–110km from there by jeep.

And, don't forget to check www.gertoger.org.

🏠 **Bayangovi** ✆1532 3130. B&B, in the east of the city centre. **$$$**

🏠 **Dalanzadgad Hotel** (32 beds) ✆1532 4455; m 998 77613. B&B, the biggest hotel in Dalanzadgad, located in the northeast, with bar, restaurant, nightclub, sauna. **$$$$**

🏠 **Devshil Hotel** ✆153 3786. **$**

🏠 **Gurvansaikhan Hotel** ✆153 3830. Good value. **$**

🏠 **Khan Uul Hotel** (28 rooms) located in the centre; m 969 60299. This luxury hotel has suites and standard rooms. **$$$**

🏠 **KherlenOne** (5–6 beds) ✆1532 3918. B&B to the west of the city centre. **$**

🏠 **Mongol Baigal Hotel** ✆1532 23830. B&B, located in the north of the city, meal available if you order. **$$**

🏠 **Oyut** (8 rooms, 2 gers) m 995 32212. B&B, in the southeast of Bor Square, with 20 beds available. **$**

🏠 **Tüvshin Guest House** (4 beds) ✆1532 22240. B&B in the north of the city centre. Café (🕐 11.00–19.00) serves Mongolian, European, Asian food. **$**

🏠 **Undraga** (2–3 rooms) ✆1532 3870. A nice, clean little hotel. *US$10 (T14,300) pp per night.*

Ger *camps near the city*

⛺ **Kherlen** ✆1532 23918. 2 *ger* camps west of the city. **$$**

⛺ **Mazaalai** *Ger* Camp ✆1532 23040; m 991 79188; 🕐 summer only. East side of the city. Restaurant, bar, souvenir shop, sightseeing. **$$$**

Ger *camps in Ömnögobi Aimag*

⛺ **Chinggis Bulls** m 992 59903. This camp has 15 *gers* only but offers a decent service & good local food.

⛺ **Duutmankhan** *Ger* Camp Nr the Khongor Els (sand dunes). **$$$**

⛺ **Gobi Discovery 1 & 2** ✆11 312769; e gobidiscovery@magicnet.mn. Both camps are close to Dalanzadgad, between them boasting a capacity of 150 people. Ideal for group tours.

⛺ **Gobi Mirage** *Ger* Camp e gobimirage@mol. mn. Located nr Gobi Gurvansaikhan NP, with 25 *gers*, this is a medium-sized camp with friendly service & decent food. Ask the manager to advise on local tours.

⛺ **Khavtsgait** *Ger* Camp Nr Yol Valley, 40km west of Dalanzadgad; ✆11 311521. Sleeps 100; well situated with good activities including camel rides in the vicinity. **$$$$–$$$**

⛺ **Mongol Baigal** *Ger* Camp 22km from Dalanzadgad. 25 *gers*, basic arrangements with food on request. **$**

⛺ **Three Camel Lodge** m 9815 0802; e info@threecamellodge.com; www.threecamellodge. com. The camp is operated by Nomadic Expeditions (see page 238 & ad on page 302) & considered one of the best (& priciest) in the area, with good service & live entertainment. Located nr Gobi Gurvansaikhan NP. **$$**

⛺ **Turbaaz, Juulchin Gobi** *Ger* Camp 1 & 2 35km from Dalanzadgad; ✆11 312769. There are some direct local flights in summer from Ulaanbaatar to the landing strip at this camp, which sleeps 100 & is popular with organised tours, though the site itself is uninspiring. **$$$**

⛺ **Tüvshin** *Ger* Camp 42km west of Dalanzadgad; ✆11 326419. Sleeps 110 in 42 gers. Has good showers, a restaurant & bar. The site was chosen for practical reasons rather than aesthetic ones. **$$$$–$$$**

🍴 **Where to eat and drink** There is no shortage of places to eat in Dalanzadgad, including the simple lunchtime roadside eating houses with fixed meals near the Trade Centre.

Typical hotel food consists of well-flavoured noodles with meat and vegetables, with a breakfast of cold meats, scrambled eggs, tea and toast. Picnic packages generally include cold noodle salad, meatballs and a litre bottle of spring water per person. The cost is roughly US$15 per day for three meals.

Eating in local places is very reasonable and costs from T4,000–10,000, depending on the menu.

✗ **Bayanbulag Restaurant/Bar** Dalanzadgad Hotel; ☏ 1532 24455; m 998 77613; ⊕ 09.00–21.00. Mongolian, European & Asian menu.
✗ **Gobi Restaurant** ⊕ 10.00–20.00. Located in the city centre, on the left of the Bayan Uul Centre. Mongolian, European menu.
✗ **Mazaalai Bar/Restaurant** Next to the Bayan Uul Centre; ☏ 1532 23040; m 991 79188; ⊕ 09.00–midnight. Mongolian, European menu.

✗ **Michid Café** Next to the Mongol Baigal Hotel; ⊕ 09.00–21.00. Mongolian, European menu.
✗ **Namuun Café** By town hall; ⊕ 10.00–19.00. Mongolian, European menu.
✗ **New Time Café** To the left of the city centre; ⊕ 10.00–18.00. Mongolian, European menu.
✗ **Oyut Bar/Restaurant** In the southeast of Bor Sq; m 995 32212; ⊕ 08.00–midnight. Mongolian, European menu.

Nightlife
☆ **Bayanbulag Nightclub** Dalanzadgad Hotel; ☏ 1532 24455; m 998 77613; ⊕ 18.00–midnight
☆ **Mineral Nightclub** By town hall; ⊕ 16.00–midnight

☆ **New Time Nightclub** To the left of the city centre; ⊕ 18.00–midnight

Shopping
🏬 **Bayan Uul Shopping Centre** In the west of the city centre; ⊕ 10.00–20.00. Provides food, clothes, electronics.
🏬 **Evsel Souvenir Shop** Located on the west of the Bayan Uul Shopping Centre; ⊕ 10.00–19.00. Handicrafts & paintings by local people.

🏬 **Nunjig Shopping Centre** In the south of the city centre; ⊕ 10.00–20.00. 2-storey grey building. Food, clothes, electronics.

Other practicalities
Changing money ITI Bank (☏ 53 2330; ⊕ 09.00–17.00 Mon–Fri) is at the eastern end of town and changes US dollars. Khan Bank in the town centre is open similar hours; with ATM.

Taxis Taxis cost T3,000–7,000 to anywhere within city centre, anytime.

Telephone (or communications centre) This is on the main street opposite the Trade Centre. It's open 24 hours a day. You can dial direct to Ulaanbaatar and send emails and faxes worldwide. International calls are expensive, costing around US$8 for a two–three-minute call.

Post office The post office (☏ 53 2232; ⊕ 09.00–20.00 Mon–Sat, closed 13.00–14.00) is at the eastern end of town. It is a reliable and friendly service. Stamps for local mail (to UB) cost T300 for postcards, around T400 for letters; letters and postcards abroad cost from T1,500.

Medical services The hospital is situated on the main road to UB; there are English-speaking doctors and a range of Western medicine is available.

Electricity Supplies are generally adequate in Dalanzadgad and there are, in addition, small generators for emergencies. In remoter areas of the Gobi power gets switched off between 11.00 and 18.00.

Interpreters There are a number of young people in Dalanzadgad who are willing to act as interpreters if you need their help; the local rate is US$7 per day.

Internet
🖻 **Post office** 🕘 09.00–18.00 Mon–Sat; T800/hr.

🖻 **Library** To the south of Bor Sq; 🕘 09.00–18.00 Mon–Fri; T800/hr. Two-storey white building.

SIGHTS IN ÖMNÖGOBI AIMAG

Yolyn Am Around 45km west of Dalanzadgad in the Gurvansaikhan Mountains is Yolyn Am Gorge. Yol in Mongolian means 'bearded vulture' and Yolyn Am means 'Vulture's Gorge'. This magnificent mountain valley has a 40km-long canyon containing a small area of frozen snowmelt at the far end. In the streams you may see grey-necked buntings and rosefinches, along with Mongolian trumpeter finches. You enter the valley on a winding mountain road that takes you to the start of the gorge. Here there is a car park (and a WC – a simple pit latrine which is clearly visible as it is situated in a prominent position above the car park!). Over the winter months the river water builds up a thick layer of ice, which thaws slowly. In addition, the cliffs of the canyon rise so steeply that they block the sunlight to the river below, so that parts of it remain frozen throughout the year, although in particularly hot years it melts completely. This sunless canyon, although cold and dark, has a particular beauty as you'll find when you follow the narrow path that hugs the river, broadening in places between the rocks, while buzzards and eagles wheel and glide in the blue skies above and gerbils and picas hide among rocks.

Yolyn Am Valley Museum (*Entrance free, though there is an entrance fee of T1,500 for the park*) West of Dalanzadgad, within the Gurvansaikhan National Park at the entrance to Yolyn Am, is a museum containing a small but excellent collection of stuffed animals and birds, the handiwork of the museum's director and owner. The hall features a spectacular eagle with its huge wings outstretched hanging over a collection of various mountain/steppe species including ibex, steppe fox, Siberian dog (*korak*), wild goat and different types of rodents such as the hairless mouse, the principal protein in the eagles' diet. The museum also houses a small collection of dinosaur remains, eggs and bones, while antelope antlers and *argali* horns line the corridor walls. A hunter's tent and camping equipment from the 1920s is exhibited with traps and an ancient musket, along with an assortment of wolf, fox and antelope skins. In the final room is a model of the Gobi landscape in which displays of Mongolian gazelle and wild ass feature. You can also shop here for postcards and there's a small collection of books and watercolour paintings that can all be purchased at a desk near the exit.

Khongoryn Els Lying around 180km from Dalanzadgad, the dunes of Khongoryn Els are also known as the 'singing sands'. You will need to hire a jeep (around US$100 round trip) or join an organised tour to reach the dunes, which are well worth a day's outing. Swept into constantly varying shapes by the wind, part of their attraction is the impressive colours that the yellow-white sands take on with the changing light of day.

8

The 'singing' sands – a humming sound when the wind blows – has been scientifically explained by a French team. The sound happens because each grain is coated in a salty veneer, causing the sand to make a booming sound, or 'sing'. The sounds also depend on heat, ie: the weather, and on an avalanche movement set up by the sand particles themselves moving in unison.

When the wind blows over the dunes it makes strange sounds like the high-pitched tone of an aeroplane engine about to take off or land. These dunes are the largest accumulation of sand in the Gobi Gurvansaikhan National Park, covering 965km². They rise abruptly from the plain, reaching a height of 800m and extend over an area 6–12km wide by 150km long. The dunes are bordered by lush green vegetation supported by a small river, the Khongoryn Gol, which is fed by underground sources from surrounding mountains. Nomads graze their camels and horses in this area at the northern limit of the dunes. Watch out for saker falcon, Palas's sandgrouse and the saxaul sparrow; you might see corsac fox or red fox.

Bayanzag – the Flaming Cliffs The red sandstone cliffs and canyons of Bayanzag ('Rich in Saxaul'), 65km northwest of Dalanzadgad, are where the

MINING AT OYU TOLGOI

Located in Mongolia's south Gobi desert, 550km south of Ulaanbaatar and 80km north of the Mongolian–Chinese border, the Oyu Tolgoi copper project now sits in the same area where, in the time of Genghis Khan, outcropping rocks were smelted for copper.

The Oyu Tolgoi mine delivered its first production in 2013 and is due to be in full production by 2021, and will continue to supply copper to its Chinese neighbour for decades ahead. Oyu Tolgoi is set to become the world's second-largest producing copper mine and is estimated to contribute (when full production is reached) around one third of Mongolian GDP. It has a projected mine life of 50 years, producing copper using leading-edge underground mining technology. On average it is expected to produce up to 160,000 tonnes of copper in concentrates in 2014 and this figure should rise to 450,000 tonnes of copper per year in the future. Gold production is a byproduct of the mine and 330,000 ounces of gold per year is forecast during the life of the mine.

Mongolia's leadership is supportive of foreign investment and the country's leaders have committed to develop infrastructure needed to attract future investment. This involves new road and rail networks, electricity supplies and water – all difficult to build or obtain in the Gobi. Oyu Tolgoi would like to become a model for future development – ie a long-term, sustainable project developed with the Mongolian government and local communities.

Oyu Tolgoi was initially pioneered in 2001 by Ivanhoe Mines at Turquoise Hill in the south Gobi and further developed by the giant global mining company RioTinto. Oyu Tolgoi reached a long-term investment agreement with Mongolia, which paved the way for additional investments. In 2014 operating as Oyu Tolgoi LLC this huge copper mine is jointly owned by Rio Tinto's Turquoise Hill unit and by Mongolia, whereby the country has a 34% stake in the mine.

American palaeontologist Roy Chapman Andrews (see page 319) first discovered fossil beds of dinosaur bones and the first ever recorded dinosaur eggs in 1922 – discoveries which made world headlines. Subsequent expeditions by the American Natural History Museum followed and, though they were discontinued during the socialist period, they have now been resumed. Scientists say that the dinosaurs were buried under the soil by sudden landslides. The barren cliffs look strikingly flame-like, especially at sunset. Look out for the desert wheatear and Asian desert warbler.

Nearby there are two areas worth exploring: the dunes at Moltsog Els (22km northeast of Bayanzag) where, alongside, there's a stand of saxaul; and a site called Tögrögiin Shiree, northwest of Bayanzag, where the dinosaur protoceratops was discovered. These areas can be reached only by jeep, a day's outing with jeep and driver costing around US$100 (T142,500).

National parks and protected areas

Gobi Gurvansaikhan National Park (*Entrance fees T3,000 pp per day & T10,000 per vehicle per day*) This park covers over two million hectares and lies within a few kilometres of Dalanzadgad. It extends 380km from east to west and some 80km north to south. The park is the largest of Mongolia's national parks and the second-largest protected area in Mongolia. It comprises gravel and rubble plains, salt wetlands, dry valleys, springs and oases. Surprisingly, despite the barren landscape and hostile

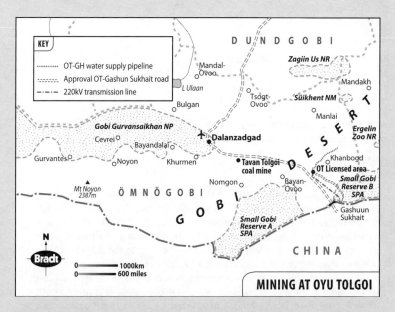

Southern Region: Gobi Aimags   ÖMNÖGOBI AIMAG

8

Mongolia's people and leaders are eager to deepen and diversify the country's economy with sustainable development. For its part, the mine's primary financier Rio Tinto has made public its commitment to the investment in Oyu Tolgoi and Mongolia.

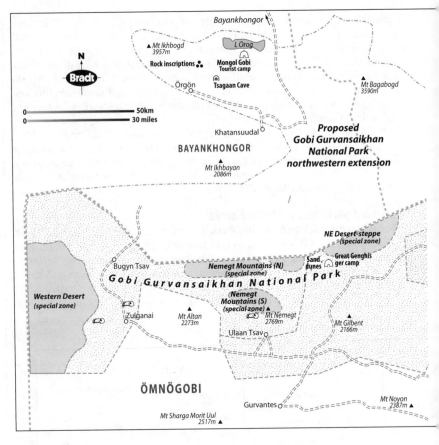

climate, the Gobi Gurvansaikhan provides a home to a wealth of wildlife. Fifty-two mammal species have been recorded in the park including wild ass, pikas, hamsters,

SAXAUL

Saxaul (*Haloxylon ammodendron*) is the perfect plant for the Gobi: it burns like coal, it tolerates salt water and droughts and it provides fodder. The Gobi's terrain supports 4.5 million hectares of this woody desert shrub, which grows, very slowly, up to a height of 4m and is dependent on underground water sources. Known as *zag* in Mongolian, saxaul is crucial to the desert ecology. Mature saxaul (ie: 25 years and over) is a natural desert stabiliser, preventing wind erosion and the expansion of desert sands. Under favourable conditions saxaul survives for several hundred years. However, there is concern about its recent decrease. Diminishing rainfall, intensive use as camel pasture and overuse as a source of fuel are the main reasons for its decline. Old *arats* (herdsmen) can remember times when it was difficult to ride a camel through *zag* country and when it was difficult to spot free-ranging camels between the branches. Another bush that thrives in the Gobi is *Reamuria songorica*, which is abundant in low-lying areas and plains.

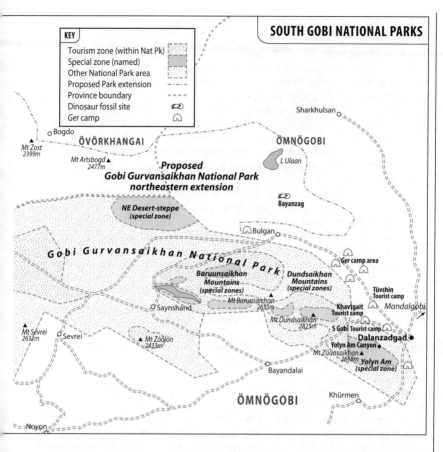

KEY

Tourism zone (within Nat Pk)
Special zone (named)
Other National Park area
Proposed Park extension
Province boundary
Dinosaur fossil site
Ger camp

gerbils, jerboas, Gobi bear, wolf, snow leopard, wildcat, *argali*, ibex and gazelles. There have also been 246 kinds of birds recorded: the majority are resident breeding birds. Look out for kestrels, lammergeier, vultures, saker falcon and altai snowcock. Part of the park is a strictly protected area, although it welcomes visitors in non-restricted areas and ecotourism is one of its strengths. In the mountains you might find snow leopard trails although it is virtually impossible to spot them. Their haunts are known and it's easy to see their droppings. Keep a look out for ibex and *argali* (wild sheep) on mountain climbs. Views to the distant horizons from the summits are stunning. The foothills of the mountains consist of red cretaceous sandstone which has eroded into gorges. The shortage of water limits the living conditions for people and animals. Drinking water comes from wells and domestic animals are watered in the Gobi by means of hand-drawn water, bucketed into wooden troughs.

One thousand families (around 5,000 people) live within the national park, either as nomads or in small settlements. Their livelihood depends on their camel and goat herds, totalling over 250,000 animals. A number of herders supplement their income by undertaking park activities such as monitoring, research, or collecting park entrance fees.

The peak tourist season tends to be between mid-June and September when the climate is more favourable – a slightly longer season than other parts of Mongolia. The park welcomes between 3,000 and 5,000 foreign visitors each year, the majority from east Asia, Australia and western Europe and most arriving through Mongolian tour operators. There remains a lack of tourist infrastructure.

 Where to stay For accommodation, you can base yourself in one of the *ger* camps around the park or in the hotels in Dalanzadgad.

DRAGON BONES

Ancient cartographers filled in unknown areas of their maps with the words: 'Here be Dragons'. In the 1920s, this notice appeared across maps of the Gobi. From 1921 until 1930, five expeditions were launched by the American palaeontologist Roy Chapman Andrews. One of the expeditions' aims was to search for the origins of man. What Chapman Andrews discovered was a treasure trove of fossils or 'dragon bones', as the Mongols and Chinese called them. This surprisingly rich discovery yielded the first nest of dinosaur eggs, which made front-page headlines worldwide.

Until then the Gobi had held little interest for scientists. In the early 20th century, travellers avoided this harsh, upland desert area. Furthermore, the political situation between Mongolia and China was turbulent, if not dangerous at the time. The Mongols were trying to defend themselves against the territorial ambitions of the Chinese; indeed, a driver on the 1921 expedition was shot by Chinese soldiers. That year, the Bolsheviks helped the Mongolian revolutionaries to power. Afterwards the civil war between the Bolsheviks and the Tsarists continued in Russia but not in Mongolia.

All this was far from the minds of 'dragon collectors', whose finds surpassed all expectations. Even the expedition drivers helped on the dig as excitement mounted over the finding of teeth, skulls and claws, many of which were revealed just beneath the surface of the sands. Chapman Andrews's Asiatic expeditions were initially budgeted at a total of US$250,000, though they ended by costing the American Natural History Museum and its sponsors US$10 million.

The park's staff welcome all visitors and are happy to help, where possible, with transport and accommodation. They also welcome enquiries from foreign tour operators, travel agents, tourism organisations and the media to help facilitate interesting programmes. For further information contact the South Gobi Areas' National Parks Administration (✆ 53 3973).

Zagiin Us Nature Reserve In the far northwest corner of the province extending north into Dundgobi (described in *Dundgobi Aimag*, pages 327–8).

Small Gobi Reserve Strictly Protected Area (Parts A and B) Located along the southern border with China, this strictly protected area is designated to preserve the main habitat for rare and very rare wildlife such as *khulan* (wild ass), black-tailed gazelle, *argali* (mountain sheep) and ibex. About 50% of the khulan population of Mongolia inhabits this area. It is not open to tourism.

Activities
Camel trekking One of the best ways to experience the Gobi is from the back of a camel. They are surprisingly easy to ride, so don't be put off; it may even turn out to be the highlight of your journey. Do take care when mounting: too many accidents have happened this way, including falling over the other side in the excitement of it all – nothing to do with the camel. One of the best places to go is to climb Khongoryn Els, the huge sand dunes. You don't have to gallop like Lawrence of Arabia; a quiet stroll will give you the same feeling of floating along. Camels have a rocking motion and after a while when you know the temperament of your camel, you may be able to control the direction you want to go in. They are quite obstinate with definite minds

American palaeontologists had to wait until the communist period ended in 1990 before returning. A team under Professor Malcolm McKenna, his wife Priscilla and two colleagues from the American Museum of Natural History, Dr Mark Norell and Dr Michael Novacek, returned to the Gobi, and in 1991 they retraced some of the steps of the earlier Chapman Andrews route. As McKenna said, 'We spent hours on our hands and knees finding thousands of "little chaps" that would not make the headlines.'

FIGHTING DINOSAURS One of the world's most famous fossil finds is two dinosaurs interlocked in mortal combat. It is likely the plant-eating protoceratops was stalked by the meat-eating velociraptor, a dinosaur with savage jaws and a long pointed tail. It is thought they were preserved in their dying moment by a collapsing sand dune that buried them alive.

In an exhibit in New York at the Natural History Museum, artists have created the appearance of what these dinosaurs looked like from their fossil remains. No details have escaped their re-creation: even the skin patterns of the pebbly skinned protoceratops are accurately portrayed as far as we can tell from the fossil remains, which were etched on the surface of sandstone rocks in the Gobi. Virtual reality takes a further step in showing us (in terrifying reality) video footage of a *Jurassic Park*-style battle between the fighting dinosaurs in a superbly reconstructed landscape of the late Cretaceous Period. For further information, see www.amnh.org, and the dinosaur sections earlier in this chapter.

of their own. But fear not, for there are usually people alongside to help you. The standard cost of camel rides is around US$7 per hour (tourist price).

Camel trekking is easily arranged. Day rides can be organised through a guide or directly with the camel owners if you speak some Mongolian. The price of a 15-day camel-riding holiday is roughly US$2,450 per person, reduced to US$2,250 if you are a party of six or more.

Horseriding Tour companies offer horseriding tours complete with your mount, pack animals, tents and food. Guides, cooks and translators will make all the necessary arrangements and travel with you. However, local herdsmen are taking advantage of the growing market by offering individuals horserides. You may even try out their traditional wooden saddles, though most visitors find them too uncomfortable. To hire a horse costs US$5 per hour; or it's US$12 per day with a guide.

Dinosaur hunting Mongolia is second in importance to the USA for its dinosaur records, listing 40 species to the US's 64. China comes next with 36 species and the UK with 26. You need a permit to dig for dinosaur remains and it is strictly forbidden to take them out of the country. Twelve to 15 fossil egg types have been found in the Gobi. Some belong to dinosaurs, others to crocodiles and others possibly to birds. Dinosaurs and their eggs have been excavated in Bayanzag, Tost, Nemegt and Khermentsav.

Among the seven large sub-orders of dinosaur, five are represented in Mongolia, and range in age from 100 million to 65 million years. One unique find consisted of the skeletons of two dinosaurs, protoceratops and velociraptor, locked in combat. Prior to that time Mongolia was part of a warm inland sea and marine life dominated. This stage ended about 200 million years ago with

That Mongolia is one of the world's greatest fossil fields is thoroughly confirmed. It will require 100 years of work by many expeditions to exhaust these huge deposits.

Roy Chapman Andrews, American palaeontologist

The Mongolian Gobi is a paradise for palaeontologists. One of the major attractions has been the accessibility of fossils near the surface in areas like the famous Flaming Cliffs where, in the 1920s, American palaeontologist Roy Chapman Andrews discovered huge fossil finds including the first-ever nest of fossilised dinosaur eggs.

Nine years after a communist government came to power in Mongolia in 1921, Andrews's expeditions were stopped. This signalled the end of all Western exploration from 1930 until 1990. In the early 1990s, at the invitation of the Mongolian government, American scientists Malcolm McKenna, Mark Norell and Michael Novacek of the American Museum of Natural History gained access to remote regions in the Gobi where they found numerous new fossils which included a complete protoceratops skeleton, oviraptor eggs, velociraptor claws and a collection of ancient mammals. One significant discovery was the skull of a juvenile hadrosaur, possibly the first hadrosaur found at the Flaming Cliffs area in the South Gobi.

Man and dinosaurs never walked the earth together. To give this statement some perspective, palaeontologists take as an example the hands of a clock. If the history of dinosaurs is measured from 12 to 5 o'clock, when they became extinct, human history is recorded in the last three seconds before 5 o'clock. (See box, *Dragon bones*, pages 316–17.) As such, almost our entire knowledge of these creatures and the violent world they inhabited comes from these fossils. Bone by bone a new picture is emerging to describe what prehistoric life was like in the Mongolian Gobi.

There is a widely accepted theory that today's birds may well be the descendants of small meat-eating dinosaurs. Scientists now think that oviraptor, velociraptor and other theropod dinosaurs are the relatives of modern birds. In other words, birds are living dinosaurs. Apart from key skeletal features, it is thought that behaviour like brooding and nesting first arose in dinosaurs. The presence of protofeathers in these primitive animals indicates that they and birds all descend from a common ancestor.

The excavations in the Gobi so far have confirmed that flightless creatures the size of small turkeys wandered the Mongolian steppe 80 million years ago. What we as yet do not know is when they first took off and flew, or evolved beaks instead of jaws and wings instead of claws. Further excavations will be necessary before we have the answer to these questions.

the shrinking of the seas, although the Gobi remained a lake area surrounded by lush vegetation. Segnosaurus is exclusively a Mongolian predatory dinosaur. Another species, saichania, the armoured dinosaur, is named after the Gobi's Gurvansaikhan Mountains.

Amateur enthusiasts are welcome to contribute to this fascinating search, but most are sensible enough to leave a find where it is and seek expert help. Do not

Southern Region: Gobi Aimags   ÖMNÖGOBI AIMAG

8

pocket any fossils, even the tiniest ones, as souvenirs. It is hard to stop people doing this … though the Customs do try.

SUGGESTED ITINERARIES A typical short trip to the South Gobi might begin with a flight from Ulaanbaatar (UB) to Dalanzadgad; arrange a car and driver to meet you at the airport; check into a *ger* camp or homestay (see options at www.gertoger. com). In the morning drive by jeep to Yolyn Am and its museum. Overnight with a herding family, enjoy the experience of sitting around a campfire or *ger* stove eating local food and tasting salty-milky tea. Next day drive through the Gobi Gurvansaikhan National Park to the sand dunes of Khongoryn Els, returning via the Bayanzag Flaming Cliffs at sunset. Stay overnight with a local family or at a *ger* camp; return from Dalanzadgad to UB.

DORNOGOBI AIMAG

Dornogobi Aimag means 'Eastern Gobi'. It is classic Gobi country – flat, arid landscape, with a few shallow lakes, streams that dry out and springs. The harsh living conditions are reflected in the sparse population. In a wet year short grass sustains some domestic herds of sheep, camels and goats, although many animals die in years of drought. There are little economic growth prospects, although this could change as the USA has expressed interest in local oil reserves. The infrastructure is poor, the roads are bad and there are few tourist facilities. This is not a well-visited province. It is a place that travellers pass through on the Trans-Mongolian railway, which connects China to Russia. Sainshand and Zamyn-Üüd, the towns of importance, are located on this line. The newly created (1994) aimag of Gobi-Sümber is located to the northwestern end of Dornogobi province, at Choir, a former military town, which is described later.

SAINSHAND Sainshand sits on the main railway line to China not far from the Chinese border.

The name means 'Good Spring' and it is a good place to stop and stock up with fuel, water and food supplies before heading into the Gobi. The population is 20,000.

BRIEF FACTS: DORNOGOBI AIMAG

Area 115,000km²
Aimag centre Sainshand
Districts 14
Elevation of Sainshand 938m
Livestock Goats, sheep, cattle, horses
Ethnic groups Khalkha
Distance from Sainshand to Ulaanbaatar 463km
Average temperatures July 23.2°C, January –18.4°C

HIGHLIGHTS
* Khalzan Uul – curative springs
* Senjit Khad – rock formation
* Tsonjiin Chuluu – volcanic rocks
* Burdene Bulag – dunes and mineral springs
* Petrified trees – at Tsagaan Tsav and Süikhent

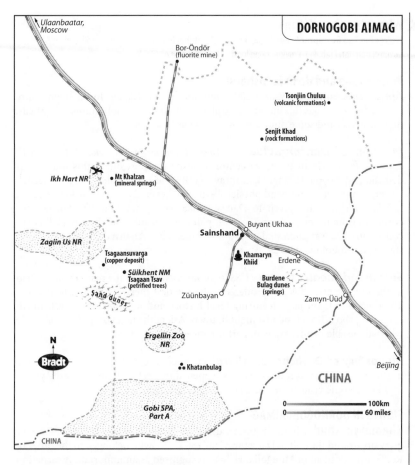

Ulaanbaatar, Moscow

Bor-Öndör (fluorite mine)

Tsonjiin Chuluu (volcanic formations)

Senjit Khad (rock formations)

Ikh Nart NR

Mt Khalzan (mineral springs)

Buyant Ukhaa

Sainshand

Zagiin Us NR

Tsagaansuvarga (copper deposit)

Khamaryn Khiid

Erdene

Süikhent NM
Tsagaan Tsav (petrified trees)

Burdene Bulag dunes (springs)

Sand dunes

Züünbayan

Zamyn-Üüd

N

Bradt

Ergeliin Zoo NR

Khatanbulag

Beijing

CHINA

Gobi SPA, Part A

0   100km
0   60 miles

CHINA

Getting there from Ulaanbaatar

By train Rail is by far the best way to travel here. At least one train stops at Sainshand every day in summer. A ticket from Ulaanbaatar costs around US$50 soft seat/sleeper and US$15 hard seat/sleeper, although the local schedules are often at awkward hours such as 04.00. Local trains connect Sainshand with Choir and Zamyn-Üüd, the border in the south. The Trans-Mongolian express train also stops at Sainshand station (☎ 63 3899).

By road Private jeeps and minibuses ply this route. There is no public service. Tourism operates via tour companies on the whole. Individual travellers need to ask locally in order to make their own transport arrangements.

 Where to stay

🏠 **Ikh Goviin Naran Hotel** Just off the main through road at the centre of town. Provides rooms & food at reasonable rates. **$**

🏠 **Od Hotel** Centre of town. Provides dormitory rooms at low prices, otherwise there is plenty of space to camp outside the town if you bring a tent. **$**

⛺ **Tavan Dokhio Tour Camp** This camp is just outside Sainshand next to the Kamariin Temple. With 15 *gers*, this could be a good alternative to the hotels in the town. **$**

8

✗ Where to eat and drink

✗ Ergeliin Zuu Restaurant Beside the Ikh Goviin Naran Hotel (above). Provides good local dishes including dumplings, grilled meat & stews. *Starting at T3,000.*

What to see and do in Sainshand

Aimag Museum (⊕ 09.00–17.00 daily; entrance fee T2,300) In the town centre beside the post office, this museum's exhibits include stuffed Gobi animals, seashells, marine fossils and some dinosaur fossils. It's worth a visit.

Museum of Danzanravjaa (⊕ 10.00–17.00 Mon–Fri (closed for lunch); entrance fee US$1) In the town centre opposite the post office, this museum is dedicated to Noyon Khutagt Danzanravjaa (1803–56), Mongolian religious leader, writer, composer, painter and physician who was revered as a sage by local people. Exhibits include gifts given to Danzanravjaa by Chinese and Tibetan leaders, costumes from his plays and some of his paintings. In addition, there is a wild herb collection as he was interested in traditional medicine. An urn containing his ashes stands in front of his statue.

Sainshand Theatre Group (US$10 for tourists) Just off the main through road in the town centre, this is considered to be the best theatre outside Ulaanbaatar. The theatre puts on plays featuring local history and folklore, and is well worth enquiring about if you spend a night in town. Ask at the hotel or find a local guide who will be able to advise you of performances.

Monastery of Dashchoilon Khural On the airport road at the entry to the north of the town, this monastery was reopened in 1991 and today friendly young monks welcome visitors. Services are held in the mornings.

SIGHTS IN DORNOGOBI AIMAG

Khamaryn Khiid About an hour's drive south of Sainshand, this monastery grew up around the cult of Danzanravjaa (1803–56), who belonged to the order of Red Hat Buddhism in Mongolia. He was recognised as an important incarnation around 1811. Danzanravjaa had a large following, and he was also a writer, a martial arts expert and an architect besides being a composer, poet, painter and physician. He created the original monastery and built the local theatre, and his play *Life Story of the Moon Cuckoo* is still performed. His life ended tragically

EARTHWATCH AT IKH NART RESERVE

Earthwatch scientists have researched archaeological sites at Ikh Nart Reserve and are involving volunteers in summer field trips.

The semi-arid grassland of the reserve with its rocky outcrops is home to *argali* sheep, kestrels, vultures and other animals; herds of Mongolian gazelles and goitered gazelles wander freely through the reserve. Volunteers should not expect to do excavation or be involved in active dig sites, but instead they are required to survey and document the landscape to help determine where such sites will need to be in the future. Fieldwork is a remarkable opportunity to be involved in designing an ongoing archaeological investigation.

For further details to participate in volunteering go to www.earthwatch. org/exped/wingard_archaeology.html.

when he was assassinated by a rival. Many myths and stories about this talented monk have become local legend. Today, however, there remains only a monastery and the meditation caves and retreats in the surrounding area, which were formerly used by Danzanravjaa and his students.

Senjit Khad Located 95km northeast of Sainshand, this interesting, natural rock formation is in the shape of an arch. You'll need your own transport here; a jeep and driver for the day costs US$100.

Tsonjiin Chuluu In the northeast corner of the aimag, 160km from Sainshand, this is a six-sided basalt pillar of volcanic origin that resembles a set of organ pipes standing on the steppe. Similar basalt columns are found in Gobi-Altai Aimag and on the banks of the Tamir River in Arkhangai Aimag. As with the above, you must have your own transport; the jeep costs are similar to those above.

Burdene Bulag Mineral Springs Located about 30km southwest of Erdene (railway station) are some of the largest sand dunes in the Gobi; the dunes are easily accessible but a guide is needed to find the cold-water springs; jeep cost as above.

Cliffs of archaeological interest Located in the area around Khatanbulag near the ruins of Demchigiin Khiid; ancient archaeological artefacts and rock drawings showing Gobi animals can be found here. Your own jeep transport is necessary as is a guide who knows the area; jeep cost as above.

Petrified trees at Süikhent The petrified trees at Süikhent, 130km west of Sainshand, are worth visiting. Tsagaan Tsav in Mandakh district, around 40km north of Süikhent, is a particularly good area to see these rare trees and is often visited by tourists. The petrified trees lie on the desert surface and many more exist beneath the sands. The petrified tree area at Süikhent is 500m long by 80m wide and the logs can measure up to 20m long by 1.5m in diameter. You will need your own jeep transport as well as a guide; jeep costs are as above.

Nature reserves

Ikh Nart The reserve of 43,740ha is situated in the midwestern part of the province close to the boundary with Dundgobi aimag. It protects the northeastern limit of the *argali* (wild sheep) habitat and was designated to extend their territory and to protect the natural environment. It is an off-road area where you will also find Pallas's cat, grey wolf, corsac and red fox and Eurasian ibex. In rocky uplands live steppe eagle, lammergeier, black vulture and saker falcon, among other bird species.

Ergeliin Zoo Nature Reserve This area of 60,910ha is situated on the southwest border of Dornogobi with Dundgobi Aimag. Many famous dinosaur fossil finds have been discovered here. People refer to the region as 'Altan Uul' (Golden Mountain). Tourists visit the area with their own transport and guides; they are cautioned not to keep any fossil finds and to leave bones and other objects where they are.

Gobi Strictly Protected Area, Part A This occupies the southern border area of the aimag – the protected area straddles territory of both Ömnögobi and Gobi Altai aimags and affords protection to some of Mongolia's rare species such as wild ass and *argali* sheep. It extends west into Gobi Altai Aimag (see pages 342–4).

Towns

Zamyn-Üüd Located on the border with China, Zamyn-Üüd is the town with the highest temperatures in Mongolia. It is prospering thanks to cross-border trade and the railway line which runs through the town connecting it with Ulaanbaatar, Beijing and Moscow. There are several hotels: Jintin Hotel, Tsagaan Shonkhor Hotel and Bayangol Hotel, providing standard rooms at US$15 per room. Restaurants in the town serve mainly Asian food at reasonable prices of around T600–700 with rice; hotel restaurants serve European meals and charge roughly US$10.

GOBI-SÜMBER AIMAG

This aimag was created in 1994 from the northern part of Dorngobi Aimag. The former Soviet army camp No 10 at Sümber was handed over to the Mongolian authorities in 1991. Sümber has a station on the Trans-Mongolian railway. Local resources include coal, tin and fluorspar, mineral pigments and ornamental stones.

Choir, the aimag centre and main town, is also on the railway line in the northwest corner of the province, halfway between Ulaanbaatar and Sainshand. It is a good fuelling stop. You can explore the nearby springs at Khalzan Uul. Choir Mountain, nearby, is part of a granite belt which offers good hiking.

GETTING THERE FROM ULAANBAATAR

By train Choir is a local stop from UB on the Trans-Mongolian line. It costs approximately US$7 per ticket, whereas by jeep you can expect to pay roughly US$100 (different rates if you are touring and sharing a jeep).

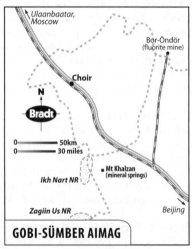

GOBI-SÜMBER AIMAG

 WHERE TO STAY AND EAT

🏠 **Dornogobi Hotel** (52 rooms) In the centre of Choir; www.mongolianhotels.net. This is the best in town. **$$$**

🏠 **Altan Gobi Hotel** Choir, near the station. The hotel restaurant provides local dishes & will pack picnics (US$5) if asked ahead of time. **$**

ACTIVITIES AND ITINERARIES

Genco Tour Bureau (*Bayangol Hotel B-201, 5 Chinggis Khan Av, Ulaanbaatar;* ☏ *11 328960;* e *genco@magicnet.mn; www.mol.mn/gtb*) This company can organise the following three- to four-day itinerary, which begins with a drive by jeep from Sainshand to Bürden

Bulag to visit the dunes and drink from the springs there. Camping overnight, the next day you can look at the fossil remains in the rocks at Ergeliin Zoo Nature Reserve, located 30km northwest of Khatanbulag district centre and from there drive to the petrified forest area and camp. *En route* back to Sainshand, stop to look at the saxaul groves southwest of the town; if you're lucky, you may spot some black-tailed gazelles. For the more adventurous, buy your own camels and cross the Gobi on foot. See box, *Crossing the Gobi and beyond* (pages 328–9). See also box, *Looking after your camel*, page 338.

SIGHTS IN GOBI-SÜMBER AIMAG
Khalzan Uul Spring Around 50km south of Choir, the centre of Gobi-Sümber Aimag, and 150km north of Sainshand on the western slope of Khalzan Mountain, the locals believe the natural mineral waters issuing from this spring are a cure for many diseases. The water has a sour taste and is used as both a digestif and a popular treatment for liver problems and gall stones. The composition of the water includes carbonic gas and radioactivity and is similar to the famous springs at Yessentuki in the Russian Caucasus.

DUNDGOBI AIMAG

Dundgobi means 'Middle Gobi' and consists mainly of steppe, dry plains and unusual rock formations. The north is relatively green, but going south the land gradually turns into the semi-desert of the arid Gobi. Throughout the province there are hundreds of graves of ancient warriors, easily spotted as they are usually under small piles of rocks. These rock mounds are sacred, respected and left untouched, even though the graves may contain bronze or gold objects. Many are thought to pre-date Genghis Khan's era.

The area is little visited as most visitors fly straight from Ulaanbaatar to more developed tourist areas. New road networks are opening up this aimag, as the final section of a 300km highway from Dundgobi to Ulaanbaatar was completed in 2013.

MANDALGOBI Mandalgobi is in the centre of the province with a population of around 11,000 people. It is a useful stopover where you can refuel and buy supplies.

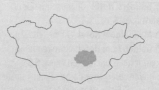

BRIEF FACTS: DUNDGOBI AIMAG

Area 74,700km²
Aimag centre Mandalgobi
Districts 16
Elevation of Mandalgobi 1,393m
Livestock Camels, goats
Ethnic groups Khalkha
Distance from Mandalgobi to Ulaanbaatar 260km
Average temperatures July 18.8°C, January –18°C

HIGHLIGHTS
* Bagagazryn Chuluu – sacred rock
* Ikhgazryn Chuluu – sacred rock
* Tsogt Taijiin Chuluu – rock inscriptions
* Birdwatching – in the hilly northwest area of the aimag

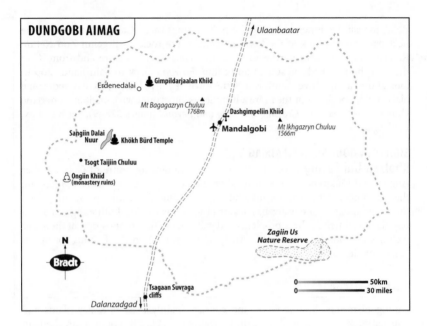

Climb to the top of a nearby hill for a view of the town. A monument there is dedicated to the 'everlasting friendship' between Mongolia and the former Soviet Union.

Getting there from Ulaanbaatar

By road Mandalgobi is on the main Ulaanbaatar–South Gobi route, so many cars, trucks and buses pass through. It is a desolate, unattractive, dusty and dry-looking town of concrete buildings and nearby *ger* compounds.

By air Scheduled flights, continuing to Dalanzadgad in the South Gobi.

Where to stay   Hotels have adequate rooms & charge from US$20 per room.

Builders' Hotel On the south side of Mandalgobi. **$**

Mandalgobi Hotel On the central park in. **$**

Golden Gobi Hotel Town centre, an eccentric hotel, pricey, with sauna. **$$**

Bayanbulag Tour Camp Slightly smaller camp with 15 *gers* located nr to the Gobi Pearl. Offers similar services.

Gobi Pearl Tour Camp The camp offers comfortable 30 *gers* & horse/camel treks.

Ongi Tourist Camp Located around 335 miles from Ulaanbaatar at Sainkhan Ovoo; ☎ 11 680450; m 99096841; e info@mongoliansecrethistory. mn; www.mongoliansecrethistory.mn. 45 *gers* accommodate up to 90 guests; restaurant; riding & tours arranged.

✗ Where to eat and drink

✗ **Delgerkhangai Restaurant** Within walking distance south of the central park; ⏲ 10.00–20.00 daily. Serves Mongolian dishes from T2,500; local

canteens (*guanz*) serve fast food & salty-milky tea for T700.

What to see and do in Mandalgobi

Aimag Museum (⏲ 10.00–16.00 *daily; admission around T3,000*) In the town centre, this museum has a natural history section that displays stuffed animals, as well as an ethnography and history section with a bronze Buddha by Zanabazar and some Buddhist scroll paintings.

Dashgimpeliin Khiid Northeast of the town centre off the road to Ulaanbaatar, this monastery was rebuilt in 1991. The temple consists of one small building and the monks' *ger* but it is still an active place of worship and the monks welcome visitors. Services are held in the mornings.

SIGHTS IN DUNDGOBI AIMAG

Zagiin Us The reserve of 273,606ha extends south into Ömnögobi Aimag. It's a valley area composed of saline soil with dry, circular salt marshes and sand dunes,

---

TREE PLANTING IN THE GOBI *Mo Strangeman*

Joining Byamba's tree-planting project in Mandalgobi gave me a unique chance to share in Gobi life. Byamba and her local helpers gather seeds and plant and nurture various hardy, local types of trees and bushes, watering them daily by hand. Water supplies are precious, erratic and expensive and much of it arrives by truck. In my mind's eye I see Byamba holding the garden hose aloft in the evening light, draining the last drops of water along a sapling trench. It takes a great deal of work and hours of transport by tractor to lift and transplant the saplings to where they are most needed. They are then planted next to more established plants that provide protection and support in the sandy terrain, which is so prone to dryness. However, I soon caught Byamba's vision and could see how, after some years of growth, huge tracts of land are now alive and green, which is why the project aims to continue to plant and replant over numerous hectares, annually.

The dry climate and harsh winters make it a real challenge but Byamba has developed this successful project from her agricultural training, experience and her own personal drive. The fun and laughter we had was so liberating; it fulfilled one of my long-held dreams – to stay in traditional *gers*. The hospitality we received was outstanding. The hardworking herdsmen and their families were always so ready to give and it touched me every time. Their meaty dairy diet takes some adjusting to. After supper we'd sing traditional songs together under the vast domed sky – from the Pole Star right down to the horizon. We were also surrounded by the nomads' herds of camels, horses, sheep and goats, who joined in with their own animal noises. What sounds! I loved the sense of this closeness contrasted to the enormous space of land and sky that is Mongolia.

I have discovered a country and people whose path through life is treasurable, with ancient sharing ways and deeply held Tibetan Buddhist traditions, which remain embedded in this still horse-led culture. Despite all the hard work there was time to visit the local *naadam* (festival) where we witnessed thrilling horsemanship, wrestling, archery, traditional throat singing and dancing, while children played games using sheep's ankle bones. The pride and skill of the horsemen, wearing their colourful tunics, was something special to see – and that sense of belonging to the land which still motivates their lives. All I knew was that I wanted to support such a project. '*Bayarlaa*' – thank you, Byanba. For further details go to www. gobioasis.com.

a mixed landscape of special ecological interest. Saxaul, or *zag* as it's known in Mongolian, grows in this semi-desert, and it is also the northern limit of the black-tailed gazelle's distribution range and the western extension of the white-tailed gazelle's range. It is an area popular for viewing wild animals and for its sand dunes, which are visited by tourists. You will need your own transport. The usual entry fees of US$1 per person and US$3 per vehicle apply.

Bagagazryn Uul – Bagagazaryn Chuluu Situated about 60km northwest of Mandalgobi in a remote area of desert plain, the rocks here are worshipped by local people. Genghis Khan is said to have camped in the area too. The highest peak is Bagagazryn Uul (1,768m), which takes about five hours to climb. This mountain also contains a cave with an underground lake. There are plenty of mineral springs in the area as well as rocky hills topped with *ovoos* (rock shrines). Animals of this area include *argali*, fox and grey wolves, with falcons and eagles circling the rocky heights.

You need your own transport. Hiring a jeep and driver for the day costs US$80, cheaper if organised for several days.

CROSSING THE GOBI AND BEYOND   *Faraz Shibli*

I peered down through sweat-soaked eyelids at my dark brown, sun-peeled hands. Between my left thumb and index finger squirmed a blood-sucking tick, swollen to nearly the size of a golf ball, freshly plucked from the genitals of one of my camels. In my right hand was a lump of dried camel faeces, just scooped from the ground to serve as fuel for the campfire. This was comfortably my most bizarre summer holiday to date.

I was part of a 12-strong expedition team crossing 1,600km of the Gobi on foot from May to July 2011. Using 12 Bactrian camels to carry our provisions, the journey brought us across six aimags, or provinces, from the southwest to the southeast of Mongolia. We came from ten different countries and most of us had met on the internet, making it as much a social experiment as a desert expedition. Even our camels were found online! Our leader viewed them via webcam, inspecting their humps, feet and teeth, and arranged to have them fattened up for months before we arrived. To support us, we had a crew of four locals, including a translator and a cook, who would meet us along the route in a rickety Russian van.

We began our trek on the colossal plains of Khovd Aimag. In the far distance to the north and the south stood row upon row of dark, jagged mountains, like the plates of huge, sleeping dinosaurs' backs. These were the Altai Mountains, home to an abundance of wildlife. Herds of semi-wild horses galloped past us and steppe eagles soared above our heads as we walked; wolves howled in the hills as we slept. *Gers* appeared on the horizon from time to time, like sparsely dotted daisies on the parched, yellow-green grass.

As we dropped deep into the South Gobi, grass turned to gravel, gravel turned to sand and the mountains slowly disappeared. Little existed above knee-height, leaving the cloudless, blue sky completely unobstructed, a huge blanket above our heads. As temperatures soared to 45°C, we zigzagged thirstily from well to well, many of which were dry. Meanwhile, sandstorms and violent twisters beat our tents, battered our clothes and covered everything we ate in sand.

The toll of walking just under a marathon a day in these conditions began to show. Our numbers slowly dwindled as team members suffering from

Ikhgazryn Chuluu Some 70km northeast of Mandalgobi, this 1,556m granite rock formation is sacred and has long been worshipped by local people as a place of pilgrimage. In the 19th century, two monks who lived here made rock drawings, which have become a tourist attraction in their own right, although it is a very remote place. There are no facilities here and you will need your own transport. Watch out for saker falcon and lesser kestrels; you may also see ibex and *argali*.

Tsagaan Suvraga This is an eroded landscape that was once beneath the sea. It lies 115km southwest of Mandalgobi near the aimag border with Ömnögobi Aimag. Rich in marine fossils and clam shells, some of the chalk mounds are up to 30m in height. Rock paintings dating from 3000BC exist in the area, though they're very difficult to find without an expert guide and you'll need your own transport. There are large copper deposits in this area.

Birdlife at Sangiin Dalai Nuur Located 65km north west of Mandalgobi near the settlement of Sangiin Dalai Khiid (not far from Baga Gazaryn Chuluu), this

tiredness and injury were evacuated one by one. Some were even kicked by our camels. But our spirits were lifted by the people we met on the road: dainty women on tiny horses, wind-burnt boys on rusty motorbikes and nomads moving to pastures new. I learnt to ride our camels, setting off from camp after supper to nearby *gers*, where I was greeted by open doors, milky tea and wrinkled eyes framed by honest smiles. We passed through a small town in the Gobi during the annual Naadam sporting festival, where we watched horse racing and wrestling, mingled with men snorting snuff and women dressed in brightly coloured *deels* and feasted on *aaruul* (dried cheese curds) and *airag* (fermented mare's milk).

When our trek finally came to an end at an *ovoo* outside Sainshand, two months after we had set off from Khovd Aimag, four of us had made it having walked the entire way. Unkempt and unwashed, we bade farewell to each other and our camels before selling them to a local herder!

I remained in Mongolia for one more month, buying a ticket on the Trans-Siberian/Trans-Mongolian railway. I trundled south to the border with China, then north again through the central steppes, sharing my third-class carriage with students, families and traders. I spent some time in Ulaanbaatar before taking a van further north until I arrived at a picturesque village, where I borrowed a tiny, semi-wild horse. I rode it further north still along the shores of Lake Khövsgöl, near the northern border with Russia.

I began my journey in the sun-scorched Gobi and could not have finished it in a more different place. On horseback, I climbed to high ground and gazed across the vast, motionless, cobalt-blue lake, its surface area larger than Luxembourg, to the pea-green, alpine forests beyond. Never before had I seen such a land of extremes.

In crossing the Gobi, Faraz and his team raised money for Edurelief, a charity that supports the educational needs of Mongolian children. For more information, please visit www.edurelief.org.

isolated area is remarkable for the birdlife (varieties of geese) that lives around the lake and its small island in the middle; falcons and eagles may be seen in the surrounding area. You will need a jeep and an experienced driver, as it is difficult to find. Travelling in this aimag involves going off the beaten track and usually off road. Transport costs by private jeep are as above.

Khökh Bürd Süm
Lying 120km west of Mandalgobi, on the island in the middle of Sangiin Dalai Lake, are the remains of the Khökh Bürd Süm. Built in the 10th century, this temple is on the same site as the ruins of a later palace, built around 300 years ago. The place is now abandoned but there are good camping spots around the lake. A health spa/sanatorium on the south side of the lake provides accommodation. Once again, you'll need your own transport; the cost of jeep hire is as above.

Gimpildarjaalan Khiid
Located 115km northwest of Mandalgobi near the camel-herding centre of Erdenedalai, this monastery was built in the 18th century to commemorate the first visit by a Dalai Lama to Mongolia in the 16th century. The monastery survived the destruction of the 1930s by becoming a warehouse and shop, reopening as a monastery in 1990. There is a spacious temple with a statue of Tsongkhapa, some large parasols and huge drums. The caretaker will open up for visitors if there are no monks around.

Ongiin Khiid
Nestling in a bend of the Ongiin Gol (river) in the extreme west of the aimag, about 240km from Mandalgobi and near the settlement of Saikhan Ovoo, this site comprises the remains of two monasteries: Barlim Khiid and Khutagt Khiid. Although there is little left, it is interesting to go there to explore the ruins.

You'll need your own jeep or minibus and driver as there's no public transport to here.

 Ger camps As well as the Great Gobi Camp, there's accommodation nearby at two *ger* camps: Saikhan Ovoo *Ger* Camp and Mongol Khan *Ger* Camp. Some 11km further away there's Saikhan Gobi *Ger* Camp.

- **Great Gobi Camp** ✆59 317233; e ongitour@ trip2mongolia.com; www.trip2mongolia.com.   Comfortable *gers* & good local dishes on offer; also horse & camel trips can be arranged.

SUGGESTED ITINERARIES Travel in this province mostly involves a through journey from Ulaanbaatar to the South Gobi, with a stop in Mandalgobi to refuel or to stay overnight. Other routes take you to desert oases, sand dunes and rock formations chiselled and sculpted by the wind and sand. Visit the cliffs at Tsaagan Suvraga or the sacred mountain of Kharaat Uul in the southeast of the province where people come every year to celebrate the autumn moon.

It is now possible to ride motorcycles in Mongolia without having to organise the whole thing yourself from scratch. Off the Map Tours (*www.mongolia.co.uk*, see page 238) will lead you to some of the best bits of Mongolia, riding on one of its Yamaha WR250 motorcycles.

BAYANKHONGOR AIMAG

Bayankhongor is a province of hot springs, dinosaur fossils and contrasting landscapes. Khongor in Mongolian means 'Light Chestnut' (as in the colour of a chestnut horse). The north is dominated by the Khangai mountain range, where fast-flowing rivers water the valleys and plains. Herding – camels, goats, sheep and horses – is the principal occupation of the nomadic and semi-nomadic population. The south is part of the Gobi Desert, where arid conditions make life hard. This region includes the mountains of the Mongol Altai range, the habitat of wild sheep and ibex.

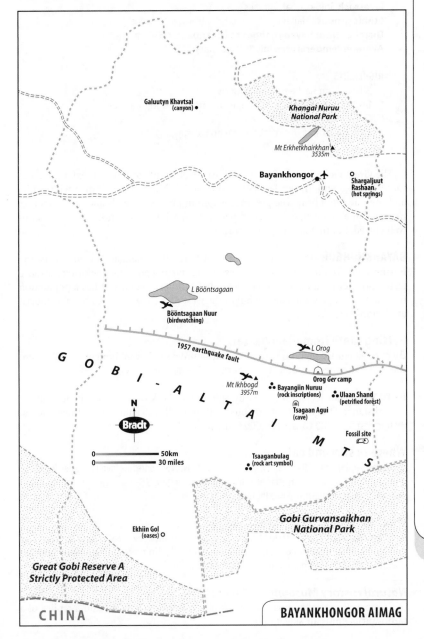

8

331

Area 116,000km²
Aimag centre Bayankhongor
Districts 20
Elevation of Bayankhongor 1,859m
Livestock Sheep, goats, horses
Ethnic groups Khalkha
Distance from Bayankhongor to Ulaanbaatar 630km
Average temperatures July 15°C January –18.4°C

HIGHLIGHTS
* Shargaljuut Rashaan – hot springs
* Birdwatching at Bööntsaagan Nuur and Ikh Bogd mountain
* Oasis life at Ekhiin Gol
* Well water and *The Beatles* – (see box, pages 334–5)

The Great Gobi Strictly Protected Area A (off-limits to tourists) extends across the extreme southern border with China and is home to the native wild camel and the rare Gobi bear. The province is rich in precious metals and famous for its natural mineral springs. Medicinal plants grow wild. This remote province is not well visited, but that is part of its attraction.

BAYANKHONGOR The town is located where the Khangai Nuruu meets the northern part of the Gobi and provides a good starting point for exploring the more fertile northern region and the remote, dry, southern regions. It has a population of 23,000. A stupa stands on the hill to the west of the town; there are a few tourist attractions (see below).

Getting there from Ulaanbaatar
By air Scheduled flights on Tuesdays and Saturdays to Bayankhongor – see the Aero Mongolia summer schedule: www.touristinfocenter.mn.

By road Private jeep or minibus; by public bus, check the current schedules at the long-distance Dragon (Western) Bus Station in Ulaanbaatar – they leave daily at 08.00; cost T25,000 (bus); T30,000 (minivan).

 ## Where to stay and eat
🏠 **Hotel Negdelchin** (30 rooms) www. mongolianhotels.net. On the airport road on the right side as you enter town, opposite the truck station. Food prices are from T2,500 per dish of meat or stew. **$$–$**

What to see and do in Bayankhongor
Aimag Museum (⊕ *09.00–17.00 Mon–Fri; entrance fee US$2 (tourist rate – less for locals)*) This museum exhibits Buddhist art, including two statues of the popular goddess, Tara, *tanka* paintings, and *tsam* masks and costumes.

Natural History Museum (⊕ *09.00–17.00 daily; entrance fee T2,000*) Southeast of the central park this museum has exhibits of dinosaur fossils and a replica of a tarbosaurus dinosaur skeleton.

Lamyn Gegeenii Dedlen Khiid On the main street in the centre of town, this is a new monastery that has replaced the original of the same name that stood 20km east of Bayankhongor. The original once housed up to 10,000 monks but was completely destroyed in the 1930s. Today, the new monastery, established in 1991, has a new community of monks. The principal brick-built temple is in the shape of a *ger* and the central hall contains a statue of Sakyamuni (Historical Buddha).

GOBI SURVIVAL BAR
Christine Sapiepha Freemantle

We were eight 'tourists' with a BBC film crew doing the 'adventure tourism' segment for a series called *The Tourist*, made during two visits to Mongolia. Once we had crossed the Mongol Altai Mountains we joined up with the camels and the real adventure began. It was probably the first time that I had been in an environment where nothing passed through the human mind: no roads, no overhead wires, no villages, no petrol stations, no aeroplanes. No sound but the wind. Nothing but the endless plain, with rose, yellow and silver tufty bushes, high cloud, bright sun and rain in the distance. Nature alone rules, unobstructed by man's intervention. Our objective was the Mother Mountain about 40km away. There was a swampy area that we had to ride around and the directions were, 'when you get to the dead camel, turn right'. It was so exhilarating that I started to sing and one of the camel drivers dropped back and rode beside me so that he could whistle and sing too. It's a morning I shall never forget.

We camped for three days at the base of Mother Mountain, Eej Khairkhan, near a cave where a Buddhist lama had spent 11 years hiding from the communists, following the anti-religious purges of the 1930s. One afternoon we rode further into the ravines on the other side of our campsite where we saw a fairly recent pug mark of a snow leopard and some tiny hoof marks, probably gazelle. No sign of a kill, but ... We then came to a particularly beautiful valley with small trees with silver bark and golden leaves, and tall, pale, gold tufts of grass, greenish at the root. There was a wonderful sweet smell and dark cliffs on both sides. I wondered if the perfume came from the sand jujube (*Eloeagnus latifolia*) as described by Cable and French in their book *The Gobi Desert*.

Our journey home was quite rough: we were caught by the first blizzards of winter as we struggled to drive back across the Gobi-Altai. One of the trucks was not a 4x4 and had to be dug out over and over again – hard work at 9,000ft in a driving cross wind. And when we finally took off for Moscow three days later, we had landing problems at Novosibirsk.

Lessons from the trip: learn some songs, like old ballads that tell a tale, to sing around the campfire in the evenings. Make your own survival rations, ie: my Gobi Bars (see below). One other piece of advice: try to travel with those of a like mind and with a well-grounded leader who speaks Mongolian and keeps a firm grip on the consumption of alcohol. Learn some Mongolian and familiarise yourself with the Cyrillic alphabet.

My recipe for Gobi Survival Bars: ingredients – dark chocolate, some instant coffee granules, some sultanas soaked in brandy or whisky, chopped hazelnuts and almonds; method – melt the chocolate, stir in the ingredients, spread the mixture about two inches thick on foil to harden. Before it gets brittle, cut into Mars bar-size lengths and wrap individually. This really will take you through a blizzard and many hours marooned on airport tarmac.

Southern Region: Gobi Aimags **BAYANKHONGOR AIMAG**

8

SIGHTS IN BAYANKHONGOR AIMAG There are two protected areas in this aimag: Khangai Nuruu National Park in the extreme north, and part of the Great Gobi Strictly Protected Area in the far south. The southern area is not frequented by tourists since it is a strictly protected area on the border with China and is set up to protect wild animals such as the *mazaalai* (Gobi bear), *khulan* (wild ass) and *argali* (wild sheep). (See box, *Ekhiin Gol*, page 336.)

Khangai Nuruu National Park The national park spreads over an area of 888,500ha at the heart of the Khangai Mountains – the second-highest in the country – and straddles the Arkhangai and Övörkhangai aimags. It was declared a protected area in 1996. The area is fed by the Orkhon – one of Mongolia's largest rivers – and is well watered (indeed, prone to flooding and even snow in summer). Its landscape is characterised by lakes, forests and meadows, and the mountain forest and steppe zones include regions that are important for semi-nomadic herders.

Shargaljuut Rashaan Located northeast of Bayankhongor town, between the peaks of Myangan Ugalzat Uul (3,483m) and Shargaljuut (3,137m), this well-known health spa consists of over 300 springs that vary in temperature from very hot to icy cold. The waters are diverted to pools and baths (indoor and outdoor) and, for the sake of privacy, to individual *gers*. The hot water is thought to cure all kinds of ailments, especially rheumatic complaints and skin disorders. Many Mongolians come for treatments and stay at the nearby sanatorium, a Soviet-style concrete block

---

GOBI CHANGES: WELL WATER AND 'THE BEATLES' *Barry Jiggens*

It is just over ten years since my first visit to Mongolia, and in a very real sense that introductory dose of hospitality, wilderness and traditions remains coursing through my blood. The Gobi has become part of my DNA!

In 2003 Mongolia was recovering from a prolonged period of *zud*. Many districts were in decline as the modest economic activity that sustained them came almost to a halt. Today Mongolia is wrestling with other demons. Large swathes of the Gobi have become copper, gold and coal mines, providing raw materials for the Chinese middle classes to the south. The number of apartment complexes and cranes in Ulaanbaatar attest to the fact that some people are benefiting from the mining boom, but many Mongolians have yet to see an improvement in their quality of life.

In the countryside, where scarce resources are being devoured by mining, the traditional Mongolian way of life is also under strain. Where once there were boundless plains for grazing herds and for wildlife, there are now fences and other obstacles for wandering animals. Where once there was enough water for small desert communities, the influx of workers and the demands of mineral extraction have exhausted or compromised the quantity and quality of reserves. Mongolia is at the crossroads.

In 2003 I began collecting and sending blankets from Australia to Mongolia, to help struggling Gobi hospitals and schools. In 2006 I sent 10,428 pairs of shoes and boots for disadvantaged children in Ulaanbaatar and in the countryside. In 2009 I established MongoliAid International Inc, a registered charity in Queensland, Australia. In February 2013 we sent 7,000 blankets to Mongolia once again, bringing our tally since 2003 to 31,000 blankets.

Nevertheless I do have a confession to make.

of a building. As well as the hotel at the sanatorium there is a *ger* camp; the cost for either is around US$35 (tourist price). Otherwise camp along the valley.

Galuutyn Khavtsal Around 38km northwest of Galuut village and 85km from Bayankhongor, this is a 25m-deep canyon that is only 1m wide in places. Nearby are many deer stones (see box, page 359) and rock inscriptions. To reach here your own transport is essential, while a jeep and driver for the day costs US$100; it's cheaper if organised for several days.

Tsagaan Agui (*Entrance fee T500*) This cave is supposed to have sheltered Stone Age people around 700,000 years ago. It is found some 150km south of Bayankhongor in the Bogd Uul area of Orog Nuur. Transport costs are as for Galuutyn Khavtsal.

Bayangiin Nuruu This is a canyon with rock engravings and petroglyphs, some of which are 5,000 years old, around 150km south of Bayankhongor town near Tsagaan Agui. As above, you can get here only by private jeep.

Orog Nuur Set in the foothills of Ikh Bogd Uul (3,957m), 110km south of Bayankhongor, this saltwater lake is good for birdwatching. Here you will find Dalmatian pelican, swan goose, Pallas's fish eagle, Pallas's sangrouse and Henderson's ground jay. The summit of Ikh Bogd Uul is accessible by jeep (take a guide) and provides stunning views.

Mongolia is not my only love. I also believe in the power and in the magic of The Beatles. Beatles songs are not merely tunes – they can be received as medicine and mantra. They invigorate the body, nourish the soul and stimulate the mind. The Beatles have become a part of my Mongolian experience.

Since 2008 my Mongolian friends Bodio and Mönkhtuyaa from Mongol Khan Expeditions, and I, had been planning a special water project for the people of Bayangobi, a small Gobi *soum* in Bayankhongor province. On 18 June 2012, the US$140,000 Bayangobi Water Project was opened to coincide with the 70th birthday of Sir Paul McCartney.

Ever since my first visit in 2003 I had noticed Bayangobi residents spending hours each day collecting water from one of two dirty and broken wells, or from the small stream polluted by the waste products of drinking goats, sheep and other animals.

The Bayangobi Water Project sunk a pipeline nearly 100m below the dry Gobi terrain. The underground reserve has enough water to last at least 100 years. It is pumped from the ground, filtered and stored in a vast tank within a secure brick building. From there it is pumped to three other water distribution centres along a central pipeline. For the first time ever, the Bayangobi school, hospital, and kindergarten buildings have water delivered to them. Bayangobi school even has a spectacular water fountain for special occasions.

To keep this project, and other water projects, up and running, MongoliAid has set up a term deposit. The interest will be used for construction, maintenance and repair. Anyone from around the world can help MongoliAid provide water security for vulnerable Gobi villages. All you need is love (sounds like a song title!) and our bank details. Your donation will let Gobi culture 'Get Back' to where it once belonged. For donations: www.mongoliaid.org.au.

8

You can stay here at both the **Orog *Ger* Camp** and the **Mongol Gobi Resort**, which provide standard *ger*-camp accommodation (*around US$45 per night exc food; meals US$20*). Once again you'll need your own transport; for the cost of hiring a jeep and driver, see above.

Nogoon Tsav These small hills ('*tsav*' means 'hillocks') lie in the extreme southeast of the aimag, around 145km from Bayankhongor as the crow flies (see map). Be warned that it may take much longer than you think to travel across this type of country, either off track or on dry, rutted routes. At the end your reward is a valley 2m wide by 10km long, which is renowned as an area of dinosaur fossil finds. Unsurprisingly there is no public transport here so you will need your own; the costs of hiring are as above.

Birdwatching sites Located 90km southwest of Bayankhongor town, the large saltwater lake of **BÖÖntsaagan Nuur** is home to many species of birds including relict gull, whooper swan, graylag goose, Houbara bustard, Pallas's fish eagle, Pallas's sandgrouse and damoiselle crane. There are also interesting volcanic formations,

---

EKHIIN GOL — *Lucia Scalisi*

This little Eden in South Gobi is marked as a 'look out' on most maps of Bayankhongor Aimag. The tiny oasis, developed in the 1970s, was actually originally a successful 'greening of the desert' project that was abandoned 20 years later for economic reasons – though not by the families living there. Those that had moved to work there remained and with a little effort everything continues to grow in abundance. Harvest time sees bumper crops of melon, marrow, peppers, tomatoes and even grapes flourishing amid marigolds, sunflowers, anemones and *Amaranthus caudatus*.

Country idyll though this may seem, it is a good six hours' drive from the dusty town of Shinejinst – where simple accommodation is available in the administration building if the wind and dust get too much for tents – travelling south towards Segs Tsagaanbogd, the highest peak in the province on the border with China.

Remarkable though Ekhiin Gol is, the main reason for heading there is that the region is home to the dwindling population of *mazaalai*, the Gobi bear. In this strictly protected area access must be undertaken with your own vehicle. Driving is made complicated as rarely used routes disappear under the desert dust.

You are unlikely to spot *mazaalai* because this small bear verges on extinction at around 35–45 individuals. It is possible, though, to see the small, grassy oases in which it makes its home. The local ranger is tuned in to spotting pawprints and recently used nests. With several oases in this region, it would be impossible to locate them without an experienced guide.

It is a sparse landscape, also inhabited by *argali, khulan* (wild ass) and gazelle. Tiny finches flit through the tall grasses, desert grouse flushed from hiding fly up the cliffs to scold from on high. Evidence of wolf and camel – both wild – can be found, and of the border guards who trek 20km through the mountains to the watering holes. New Gobi traffic is another reason the area gets trampled and the bears hide out in the surrounding hills.

CAMBRIDGE MONGOLIAN DISASTER APPEAL (CAMDA)

Tribute to John Pirie – CAMDA founder

John Pirie, an Englishman with a heart for horses, founded CAMDA in 2000 in the aftermath of a terrible *zud* the previous winter. Since then CAMDA has continued to supply funds and on-the-ground support to herders and their animals. As John said, 'The generosity of the British public is legendary when they understand precisely to what they are being asked to give.' CAMDA supports the survival of the nomadic, herding community, millions of whose livestock were wiped out by recent severe winter weather. John wrote the following specialist box for this guide before he died in February 2010.

Why Horses? Without his horse, a herder cannot do his job; his wife and small children cannot milk the livestock; or older children get to school (Mongolia has one of the highest literacy rates in the developing world). No charity can change the climate but in some key areas horses are prey to parasitic infection, and all horses need water, and in the winter, supplementary fodder: typically hay, harvested when the steppe grasses are high.

During the long years of socialist governance, gas-guzzling Soviet tractors harvested swathes of steppe grass for winter fodder; with the end of Russian dominance, the price of fuel quickly rose beyond the point the herder community could keep the tractors operating. CAMDA relieved the situation by making available through the co-operative more than 20 units of horse-drawn mowers from China (two horses to a unit). Simultaneously, with the help of Imperial College, London, we came up with a mower drawn by a single horse and with a fuel-efficient auxiliary motor, designed to be manufactured within Mongolia. In the desert region of Mongolia, where water tends to be in shortest supply, CAMDA has reopened a chain of disused, shallow wells in the rural areas to shorten the distance travelled by herders with livestock (horses being in most frequent need) getting them to water.

The project of which we are perhaps most proud is the establishing in three provinces of mobile veterinary teams to get round to herders' horses on their home ranges twice a year, chiefly to immunise them against parasitic infection. Many herders have told CAMDA the money they were otherwise laying out on vets' fees before CAMDA-funded vets arrived is now enabling them to meet school fees.

Despite some improvements in the overall Mongolian economy, the need for healthy horses in Mongolia and herders with a livelihood to manage families and animals alike is as great as ever; greater when the needs of mounts for tourists are taken into account.

In 2013 ten wells were refurbished in Gobi Sumner and Övörkhangai aimags. In Khövsgöl Aimag 20 new wells were dug to meet the needs of livestock concentrations. If you would like to help this work, go to www.camda.org.uk.

8

canyons with streams and ancient cave paintings in the area. Your own transport is needed; costs are given above.

Ikh Bogd Mountain, part of the Gobi Altai range, rises to 3,957m. Birdlife there includes Altai snowcock. You may see *argali* and Siberian marmot.

Although its role as a beast of burden is slowly declining due to the increasing prevalence of the car, the two-humped Bactrian camel is still used by nomads to carry heavy loads over long distances. As for carrying you or your luggage on a trek across the Gobi, it can be a fantastic or frustrating companion, depending on whether or not you care for it properly!

The Bactrian camel's ability to walk for several days without water makes it perfectly suited to desert travel, but it should be allowed to graze every day. Camping in areas with sufficient long grass or shrubs is ideal, as it can spend the evenings and mornings grazing. But this can be tricky in certain parts of the Gobi; you may have to camp slightly short of, or beyond, where you would otherwise wish to stop to ensure your camel is properly catered for, and you may need to allow it an impromptu lunch break during the day if you happen upon an area of good grazing among otherwise barren land.

Like us, camels come in different shapes and sizes, and younger, stockier camels will generally be able to carry more weight. Also, the greater its load and the longer distances you require it to walk, the more often it will need to eat, drink and (on a particularly long and arduous trek) take the occasional rest day.

Not allowing your camel enough food, water and rest can lead to tiredness, agitation and worse. It will refuse to carry weight and may well spit cud or kick out at you. Uneven loads can also irritate or even frighten your camel, causing it to kick out or stampede. If walking with multiple camels and covering long distances with limited grazing and drinking opportunities is a must, forming a 'camel train' can help. Loosely tie the lead of each camel to the saddle or load of the camel in front; camels are usually calmer and more willing to walk when following one of their own.

Despite the lack of infrastructure in Mongolia, you might occasionally come across tarmac roads. Be aware that camels have padded feet, not hooves, and walking on hard surfaces for long periods of time can lead to foot and leg injuries. Try to stay off-road.

A camel is controlled by combining verbal commands with gentle tugs on its lead. In Mongolia, a camel's lead is tied to a wooden peg that is inserted through a piercing in one of its nostrils. Care must be taken not to tug too hard on the lead, so that its nose peg does not fall out. Reinsertion of the peg can cause distress to the camel and is a difficult and daunting task for the novice camel handler. Overzealous use of the lead can also result in injury and infection of the camel's nose, attracting flies and maggots; smooth, plastic nose pegs can be used as a safer alternative. Harnesses can also be used instead, but some argue that nose pegs allow for greater control.

Some areas through which you travel may be infested with ticks, which will take great pleasure in attaching themselves to you and your camel and can cause infection. On a long trek, inspecting your camel (particularly its underbelly) for ticks is worthwhile. They can be removed by hand.

At the end of a day's walking, you should hobble your camel by tying its lead to one of its front legs, allowing enough slack for it to walk around and graze, but not run. If you do not, be prepared to spend hours searching for it, as camels have a habit of wandering! At bedtime, its lead can be staked to the ground.

Daunting though this all may seem, a Bactrian camel properly cared for can make a jolly, characterful and useful companion on a trek across the Gobi.

Rock paintings Tsagaanbulag is a white rock that features drawings of a helmeted figure, believed by the locals to have been made by aliens. It is the only one of its kind among other rock paintings in the area. To get there you will need a jeep and driver; standard costs to hire a jeep are given on page 335.

Fossil sites Dinosaur fossils are found in Bugiin Khöndii (Demon's Valley) – many of the fossils from here are exhibited at Ulaanbaatar's Natural History Museum – Yasnee Tsav and Khermen Tsav (which neighbours Ömnögobi).

Ulaan Shand, a petrified forest 66km southwest of Bayangobi, is also interesting for its fossil finds, though as usual you are not allowed to pick up one – even the smallest – to take home as a souvenir.

Oases Ekhiin Gol lies at the eastern side of the Tsuvliur Mountains and covers an area 17km long by 5km wide. It is said to be the hottest place in Mongolia, with a maximum air temperature of 42.2°C. Annual precipitation is 13.4mm. Travelling south towards the Gobi there are many oases such as Jartyn Khöv ('*khöv*' means 'pool'), Daltyn Khöv, Burkhant and Zuunmod. As usual your own transport is essential, with private jeep costs as above.

SUGGESTED ITINERARIES Gobi Camels' *Ger* Camp (*US$45 pp per day inc meals*) is a good base, located in a sheltered valley in the heart of the Gobi about 200km south of Bayankhongor. This remote *ger* camp is owned and run by Great Genghis Expeditions (see page 238). To the north of it, Ikh Bogd Mountain towers above the camp while to the south endless desert plains stretch to the horizon. Your accommodation is in traditional *gers* and a large dining *ger* is set up where the staff serve meals including barbecued meat and other Mongolian dishes. The camp provides all the things you need for both a comfortable stay and to explore the area: the tour guides and camp staff are professional and experienced pioneers of adventure and cultural travel in this area, and hot showers are available when you arrive back tired and dusty after a day spent looking at rock drawings or visiting a local camel herder.

GOBI-ALTAI AIMAG

Gobi-Altai is the second-largest aimag in Mongolia and is a land where the parched steppe grasslands of the Gobi meet the rocky landscape of the foothills and mountains of the Altai range. There is great natural beauty but it is a hard place to live both for people and livestock. The most settled part is the northeast

> ## CROSS-BORDER CONSERVATION
>
> Wild Bactrian camels know no frontiers. They wander south from a protected area in the Great Gobi in Mongolia across the border area into China where, currently, they are completely unprotected. It is interesting to note that the narrow paths of age-old migratory routes are etched into the hard desert ground. It is one of the most exciting things to sense from the narrow, hard-worn trails that this wild species continues to survive in these deserted hills and plains. But at this stage, both the wild camel and the Gobi bear need help if they are to continue to survive. Food for the Gobi bear is running out due to climate changes which have raised the ground temperatures by 2°C. We have a lot to learn from ancient migration routes of both mammals and birds.

8

corner, where melting snow from the Khangai Nuruu provides irrigation and water supplies. Many plants and animals of this region are listed in the Red Book of Mongolia's rare and endangered wildlife species, among them Przewalski's horse, the Mongolian wild horse or *takhi*.

ALTAI Altai is an attractive, off-the-beaten-track town with a population of 17,500. It's an exciting place to visit, and serves as a stopover to and from Khovd for those on their way to the national parks and the wild horse reserve at Takhiin Tal, which is not often visited owing to its remote location and lack of facilities of any kind. *Ger* settlements – fenced compounds – surround the town, where local people, especially the children, are excited to see foreign visitors. You will find a delicious cheap sherry wine in Altai hotels.

Getting there from Ulaanbaatar
By air Scheduled flights (just over two hours' flying time) are offered by Aero Mongolia (*www.aeromongolia.mn*) Monday and Friday; Eznis (*www.eznisairways.*

WILD BACTRIAN CAMEL   *John Hare*

The wild Bactrian camel (*Camelus ferus*) or *khavtgai* is more endangered than the giant panda. There are approximately 450 wild Bactrian camels in the Mongolian Great Gobi Reserve A, south of Bayan Toroi, and around 600 additional camels further south in Xinjiang province in China. It is an amazing creature that lives in some of the world's harshest environments.

In the Mongolian Gobi its main enemies are illegal miners and the wolf. Further south in China, the threats are from illegal miners, wolves and hunters. In the Chinese Gashun Gobi there is no fresh water and this former nuclear test site holds herds of wild camels that have not only adapted to drinking saltwater slush, but have also survived over 43 atmospheric nuclear tests. Samples of skin taken from the remains of dead Bactrian camels have been sent to scientists in the Vienna Veterinary University for genetic DNA testing and in every case the results have been remarkable. Each skin sample has shown two or three distinct genetic base differences from the domestic Bactrian camel. In 2008 as a result of these tests, the wild camel was declared a new and separate species and is recognised as such by the International Union for the Conservation of Nature (IUCN).

The separation from any other known form of camel took place 700,000 years ago. This wild stock, descendants of the primordial camels some of which crossed the Bering Strait sometime in the Pliocene Era (about four to three million years ago), are worth saving. It was those primordial camels going west out of the Arizona desert that probably pioneered the three modern camel species, the wild camel (two humps), the Bactrian (two humps) and the dromedary (one hump). It is likely that the others who ventured south into South America gave rise to the remaining four species of the zoological family of camelids, usually known communally as llamas (individually: the guanaco, the alpaca, the vicuna and the llama proper).

The most obvious difference between the three camel species is the number of humps, localised fat deposits which, like fat in any other species, provide a source of energy. In the hotter climates of southwest Asia (and Africa) a 'mutant' with only one hump, the dromedary, became the dominant species and disappeared into the wild over 2,000 years ago. The severity of extreme winter temperatures has an effect on other aspects of body conformation. The domestic Bactrian has *com*) flies Monday and Wednesday, but schedules are forever changing; check the airlines online or via a booking agent.

By road Buses from the Dragon Bus Station in UB depart Tuesday, Wednesday, Friday and Sunday at noon and cost T34,000 (bus), T37,000 (microbus).

Getting around Private transport is needed for getting about. Tourist information is available from tour and local guides. To find a guide, ask at hotels or *ger* camps.

🏠 **Where to stay and eat** Both of the following hotels serve food at local prices, with meat dishes around T2,500.

🏠 **Altai Hotel** Main street on the west side of town; provides simple comforts & adequate meals. **$**

🏠 **Birj Hotel** Centre of town. Standard countryside hotel. **$**

generally a more massive body than the dromedary, is set on shorter legs and clad in longer, darker hair – all useful attributes in conserving heat. Both species have a long gestation period (the dromedary 12–13 months, the Bactrian 13–14 months) and at most one calf is born every other year. With puberty late at four to five years and low calving rates, it is incredibly time-consuming to build up a declining camel population, domestic or wild. Compared with its domestic cousins, the wild Bactrian is greyer, slimmer and with smaller-sized humps. It also has a different shaped skull, which is the meaning of the word *khavtgai* – flat head. But the fact that the dromedary foetus commences development with two humps but is born with only one points to a long-term development from the double-humped camel and makes these remaining wild camels exceptionally important.

Back in 1877, it was Przewalski, the distinguished Russian explorer, who took three skins and a skull of a 'wild' Bactrian to St Petersburg and introduced the wild camel to the outside world. But the Petersburg zoologists could not determine whether Przewalski's specimens were original wild stock. Today there are more sophisticated methods to draw on and DNA tests have conclusively solved the problem. In Mongolia, as mentioned, there are thought to be around 450. What is quite clear is that they are all under ever-increasing threat. Only the wild camels in the Gashun Gobi in Xinjiang are completely isolated from domestic camels. This lack of an opportunity to hybridise is what makes their survival so vital. It is these remaining herds in China and Mongolia that the Wild Camel Protection Foundation is striving to save by establishing the Lop Nur Wild Camel National Reserve in China and the Breeding Centre in Mongolia. In conclusion, the wild camel is not a Silk Road runaway – it is a scientifically proven separate species and one which has survived against all odds for a very long time – over 700,000 years. It's up to our generation to ensure its future.

Should you wish to make a donation or to help in any other way please contact the Wild Camel Protection Foundation (School Farm, Benenden, Kent TN17 4EU, England; ☎ 01580 241132; www.wildcamels.com).

Kai is Altai's own distinctive form of throat singing, a magical technique in which a single vocalist produces spectral overtones and undertones to form multiple melodies. Used in epic performance and in shamanic and Buddhist rituals, this is perhaps the oldest form, combining kai with sounds of the natural world, a range of traditional instruments and their own songs. To find an authoritative connection see www.innerasianmusic.com/sales.htm.

See also *Mongolian Music, Dance and Oral Narrative: Performing Diverse Identities* (with CD) by Carole Pegg, Washington University Press.

What to see and do in Altai

Dashpeljeelen Khiid On the outskirts of town off the airport road, this is a new monastery, founded in 1990. It has a small community of monks and visitors are welcome to attend their morning ceremonies.

Aimag Museum (⊕ *09.00–17.00 daily; admission T3,000*) On the main street, this is a typical small museum exhibiting Buddhist statues, scroll paintings and featuring a Mongol warrior's dress, a shaman costume and a drum.

Theatre In the centre of town on the main street opposite the museum, the theatre holds occasional performances; tickets US$5–10 (tourist price).

NATIONAL PARKS IN THE GOBI-ALTAI The national parks of the Gobi-Altai are not well visited because they are so remote and there are no visitor facilities. In addition, the strictly protected areas are off-limits to tourists except those with permission to help with research programmes.

Great Gobi Reserve Strictly Protected Area Great Gobi is actually a mistranslation: 'Large Gobi' is more correct, but the name Great Gobi has stuck and it sounds better! This huge strictly protected area is not open to tourists.

The area covers 4.4 million hectares and is divided into two sections: A and B. It is a UNESCO Biosphere Reserve, nominated by the United Nations. Part A,

BRIEF FACTS: GOBI-ALTAI AIMAG

Area 141,500km²
Aimag centre Altai
Districts 18
Elevation of Altai 2,181m
Livestock Goats, camels, horses
Ethnic groups Khalkha
Distance from Altai to Ulaanbaatar 1,001km
Average temperatures July 14°C, January –18.9°C

HIGHLIGHTS
* Climbing the Altai peaks
* Visiting the national parks – ecotourism
* Sighting rare wild animals such as *argali*

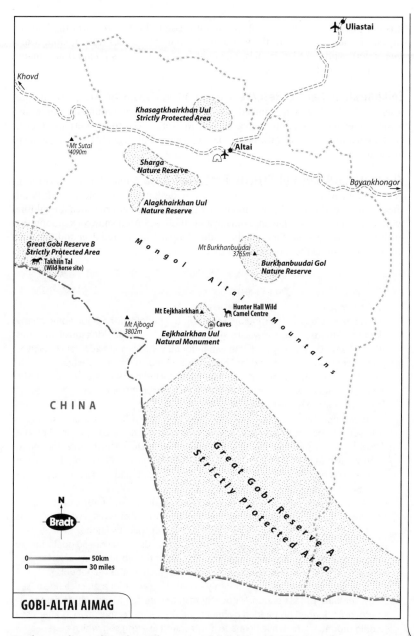

Map labels:

Uliastai

Khovd

Khasagtkhairkhan Uul
Strictly Protected Area

Mt Sutai
4090m

Altai

Sharga
Nature Reserve

Bayankhongor

Alagkhairkhan Uul
Nature Reserve

Great Gobi Reserve B
Strictly Protected Area
Takhiin Tal
(Wild horse site)

M o n g o l

Mt Burkhanbuudai
3765m

A l t a i

Burkhanbuudai Gol
Nature Reserve

Mt Eejkhairkhan

Hunter Hall Wild
Camel Centre

Mt Ajbogd
3802m

Caves

Eejkhairkhan Uul
Natural Monument

M o u n t a i n s

CHINA

G r e a t   G o b i   R e s e r v e   A
S t r i c t l y   P r o t e c t e d   A r e a

N

Bradt

0   50km
0   30 miles

GOBI-ALTAI AIMAG

8

in the southeast, lies along the national border with China and extends into Bayankhongor Aimag. You need special permission to enter its territory. The protection of the area contributes greatly to the survival of the Gobi bear and the wild camel.

Part B (sometimes referred to as Jungarian Gobi B, Jungaria being on the Chinese side of the border), the smaller part at 881,000ha, lies in the southwest part of the aimag along the national border with China and extends into Khovd Aimag.

It is not possible to visit without special permission. Both parts form the fourth-largest biosphere reserve in the world, protecting wild horses (*takhi*), Gobi bears (*mazaalai*), wild Bactrian camels, saiga antelopes, wild asses (*khulan*) and many small, unusual rodent species.

Eejkhairkhan Nature Reserve Located 150km south of Altai, this nature reserve of 22,475ha is designated to protect the local environment. There are some interesting rock pools and caves with well-preserved rock paintings of ibex, horsemen and archers near the base of Eejkhairkhan Uul. A guide is needed to help locate them.

Khasagtkhairkhan Uul Strictly Protected Area Situated in the northern part of Gobi-Altai, this is an area of 27,448ha designated to protect *argali* (wild sheep) and the Mongol Altai mountain environment. This is a rich area for wildlife with lesser falcon, saker falcon, Himalayan griffon and Altai snowcock among the birdlife; goitered gazelle, Siberian ibex, snow leopard, *argali*, red deer and Siberian marmot are among the other animals there.

TRANSFER OF MONGOLIAN FIELD NOTES FROM THE GOBI TO HOME

Jane Blunden

I can't believe this. I am sitting on a camel in the middle of the Gobi typing on my laptop with frozen fingers. We arrived here on roads you shouldn't travel on at this time of year. On the way we passed abandoned vehicles and had to dig ourselves out of snowdrifts. We stayed last night with a herdsman's family where warmth, good food and drink revived our little band, including Gallchüü and Enkhbold, my guide and driver. This morning we set off at first light, and leaving the ice and snow behind we drove further south and into the Gobi.

It was perishing cold as we set off, around –20°C with a piercing wind, but as the sun climbed in the sky the day warmed up. Had we been marooned on the roadside in the pale light of dawn, I had faith enough in my protective clothing to know it would save me from freezing to death. But just to make doubly sure the cold stayed on the outside, our kind hosts of last night made me a special present of a pair of hand-knitted camel-wool socks.

As we moved into the Gobi there were sand dunes and forests of the hardy saxaul bush to left and right, as well as huge expanses of open land where nomads raise herds of domestic camel, horses and goats for their livelihood.

My host herds 100 camel and 30 horses and tends more than 50 goats and 70 sheep, in a herding operation which in this part of the world is considered small. I was brought to this wild place as part of my research for this guidebook.

To ensure the link went as smoothly as possible I went for a practice ride to see how the camel and I bonded. My new herdsman-wrestler friend, whose name was Pürevbish, donned his padded overcoat and coaxed my camel on to its knees so I could mount; all the while he made a soft sound like 'sög sög' which he repeated several times while pulling on a rope attached to a peg in the camel's nose. The animal responded by swaying and gently dropping to the ground. On I climbed and the two of us rode off, out into the wide Gobi.

Hot *buuz* – Mongolian dumplings – were waiting for us on our return. The herdsman's family had gathered and relatives arrived, for the winter festival of Tsagaan Sar. The hostess greeted her guests outside the family *ger* and each person

Sharga Nature Reserve Located in the eastern part of Gobi-Altai this reserve is designated to protect the habitat of the highly endangered saiga antelope. These small, snub-nosed antelopes have short legs and light-coloured coats and survive in remote, semi-arid desert conditions. Since it is located just south of the Altai to Khovd road it is possible to visit the reserve. There are limited tourist facilities and the usual entrance charges apply.

Takhiin Tal – the *takhi* release site Beside the Takhiin Shar Nuruu range near the border with China, this is the home of a number of recently released wild horses (*takhi*) from European and American zoos. The last sighting of wild horses in the wild was in this area in 1968; thereafter the species became extinct outside of captivity. Captive-bred *takhi* were reintroduced from reserves and zoos worldwide in an effort to save the species. The first shipments reached Takhiin Tal in 1992 and later shipments came in 1996 and 2002. It is hoped that the released horses will survive the tough Gobi climate.

Rarely visited by tourists, there are a number of *gers* with simple facilities here for visitors. A modern station building was set up at Takhiin Tal by the Austrian

was received with outstretched arms holding a blue scarf, which symbolises goodwill and eternity.

As the evening approached, I mounted the camel again, this time with my computer and satellite phone clutched between me and the first hump. I knew the plan. I handed Gallchüü the digital Olympus C-900 zoom, he gallantly took the shot and returned the camera card to transfer the picture. As a precaution, a friend stood alongside just in case the camel bolted. With a little more practice I could have typed the entire piece happily from this position and sent it whizzing across oceans and continents, photograph attached, without having to touch ground from the camel's back. But given the cold I finished the piece from the warmth of the *ger*.

Meantime the sun set on a magnificent Gobi day. Tomorrow we drive north when we shall stay with another herder's family.

EQUIPMENT REVIEW A few years ago the equipment to send pictures such as these would have been available only to professionals with the budget of a multi-national corporation behind them. The equipment I used is all available off the peg: an Apple laptop, an Inmarsat satellite phone and an Olympus digital camera. Given the cold in the Gobi, my equipment worked well overall, but I learnt a few lessons:

- Spare batteries for the phone and camera were essential.
- The Apple Mac gave excellent running for two hours on battery power.
- On the advice of Chris Bonington's report from his latest Everest expedition, I packed several yards of good-quality black cotton to keep sand away from the equipment or to shield the screen in bright light. He also urged thorough testing before departure.
- No amount of training matters, however, if equipment is damaged in transit. I managed to snap the mains connection to the Inmarsat socket. But thankfully a Mongolian computer engineer provided a car battery and connected the cigarette lighter lead to it, which did the trick, although the lead itself was damaged too and had to be 'bandaged' using my medical supplies.

The release of two wild bull camels from the Mongolian Breeding Centre at Zakhiin Us into the Great Gobi Strictly Protected Area (GGSPA) area A took place in September 2013. Some months later, in December, one of the wild bull camels was spotted by a ranger with a small harem of four females. Survival continues.

The Hunter Hall Wild Camel Centre is located at Zakhyn Us, 25km outside the boundary of GGSPA A in Gobi-Altai Aimag. Tourists are not allowed into the reserve area without special permission, but the wild camel site nearby offers this opportunity to visit. You will need your own transport, camping gear and basic food and water supplies; you may find a domestic camel to hire and trek to Mother Mountain to further explore the area, some 15km due west of the Wild Camel Centre. It is the only site in the world where wild camels have bred in captivity. For further information: visit www.wildcamels.com.

See also pages 340–1 and boxes *Looking after your camel* and *Crossing the Gobi and beyond*, pages 338 and 328–9.

government – and is the Takhi centre's base for management and conservation purposes. It includes conference rooms and laboratories for basic biology studies. The area is patrolled by a number of rangers working for the Specially Protected Area of Gobi B National Park. The recently arrived *takhi* are observed for between six months to one year in a large fenced area near the centre building, where behaviour studies are carried out before they are released to join a herd of *takhi* in a huge area of the park. The herd currently numbers some 78 (2013). Other wild animals there include saiga antelope, black-tailed or goitered gazelle and hundreds of wild *khulan*.

SACRED MOTHER MOUNTAIN – EEJKHAIRKHAN   *John Man*

This is a sacred area to Buddhists and was worshipped long before Buddhism. It is Mongolia's equivalent to Australia's Ayers Rock, rising abruptly from a sea of sand. Situated northwest of the Edren ridge and south of the foothills of the Mongol Altai range, its southwestern reaches are gravel plains. The Sacred Mother Mountain was declared a national monument in 1992. The area of the site is 216km². It takes 58km to circumnavigate it completely; there are no paths and the sand makes for hard going at times.

As a sacred place of pilgrimage 'Mother Rock' is visited by Mongolians seeking solace and wisdom. The peace and quiet allow the traveller to rest. The rounded shape of this huge granite mountain is surprisingly beautiful. The mountain appears to be alive with colour and movement; its lower slopes are covered, in places, with rose bushes.

The tracks of a snow leopard have been seen on the ground at Mother Rock. The leopard must have crossed the desert to reach the mountain and its water sources. Gazelles, goats and lynx have been recorded at the two known oases. Climbing the mountain, from a height you can see streams flowing between boulders on the pilgrimage trail, known as the 'Nine Pots'.

John Man is author of Gobi – Tracking the Desert, *published by Weidenfeld & Nicolson.*

ACTIVITIES IN GOBI-ALTAI AIMAG

Climbing Adventurous and experienced climbers are tempted here to climb the Altai and peaks such as Khüren Tovon Uul (3,802m) and Burkhanbuudai Uul (3,765m). The Burkhanbuudai Mountain area (521km²) was placed under special state protection in 1996 along with the snow-capped Sutai Uul (4,090m).

Sutai Uul Located on the boundary with Khovd Aimag, this is the highest peak in Gobi-Altai and provides excellent climbing – most climbers approach from the Khovd side.

Eejkhairkhan Uul (2,275m) This stands just north of Gobi A Strictly Protected Area. Since 1992, the mountain has been under special state protection. You will need a permit to climb there (see box, opposite page).

FOLLOW BRADT

For the latest news, special offers and competitions, subscribe to the Bradt newsletter via the website www.bradtguides.com and follow Bradt on:

- www.facebook.com/BradtTravelGuides
- @BradtGuides
- @bradtguides
- pinterest.com/bradtguides

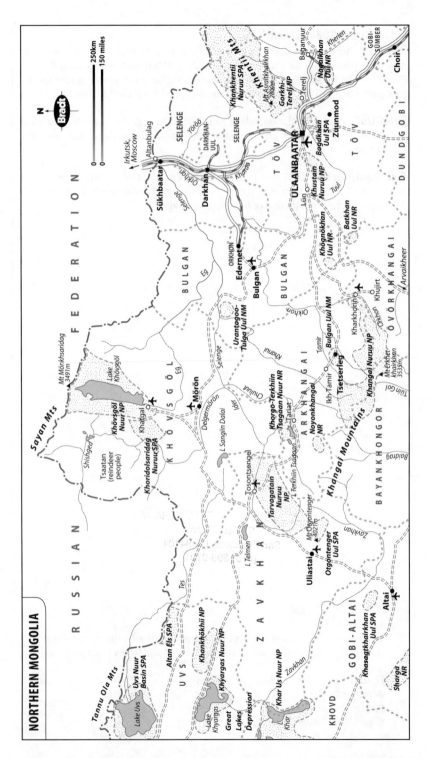

NORTHERN MONGOLIA

RUSSIAN FEDERATION

Bradt

N

0   250km
0   150 miles

Tannu Ola Mts

Sayan Mts

Mt.Mönkhsaridag 3491m

Lake Khövsgöl

Irkutsk, Moscow

Altanbulag

Sükhbaatar

SELENGE

Yöröö

Khankhentii Nuruu SPA

Mt.Asralkhaikhan 2800m

Baganuur

Kherlen

Gorkhi-Terelj NP

Nogoikhan Uul NR

GOBI-SÜMBER

Choir

SELENGE

Selenge

Orkhon

DARKHAN UUL

Kharaa

SELENGE

TÖV

O-Terelj

Khankhentii Mts

Darkhan

ULAANBAATAR

Bogdkhan Uul SPA

Zuunmod

Uvs Nuur Basin SPA

Altan Els SPA

Lake Uvs

UVS

Khankhökhii NP

Khyargas Nuur NP

Lake Khyargas

Great Lakes Depression

Khar Us Nuur NP

Khar

KHOVD

Zavkhan

Tes

Shishged

Tsaatan (reindeer people)

KHÖVSGÖL

Khövsgöl Nuur NP

Khatgal

Khoridolsaridag Nuruu SPA

Mörön

Delgermörön

Eg

Eg

Selenge

L.Sangiin Dalai

Ider

Chuluut

ZAVKHAN

Tosontsengel

L Telmen

L Terkhiin Tsagaan

Khorgo-Terkhiin Tsagaan Nuur NR

Tarvagatain Nuruu NP

Mt.Otgontenger 4021m

Otgontenger Uul SPA

Tariat

Uliastai

Khasagtkhairkhan Uul SPA

GOBI-ALTAI

Altai

Sharga NR

Urantogoo-Tulga Uul NM

Eg

Edernet

Bulgan

ORKHON

BULGAN

BULGAN

Khanui

Orkhon

Tamir

Bulgan Uul NM

Ikh Tamir

Noyonkhangai NR

ARKHANGAI

Tsetserleg

Khangai Mountains

Khangai Nuruu NP

Mt.Erkhetkhairkhan 3533m

Kharkhorin

Orkhon

Khujirt

Arvaikheer

ÖVÖRKHANGAI

Khustain Nuruu NP

Tuul

Tún

Khögnökhan Uul NR

Batkhan Uul NR

Lün

BAYANKHONGOR

Baidrag

Tüin Gol

DUNDGOBI

TÖV

348

9

Northern Region

It surprises many would-be visitors to learn that Mongolia is not one huge desert but a country of lakes, rivers, mountains and heavily forested regions, where hillsides and valley meadows are spangled with alpine flowers. Despite the long cold winters northern Mongolia basks in summer sunshine (with a few showers as opposed to long-lasting, gloomy weather). Opportunities for tourism are endless, and new *ger* camps in well-located sites provide comfortable facilities, good food and hot showers, which make all the difference at the end of a travelling day.

Mongolia's northern aimags are Khövsgöl, Zavkhan, Bulgan, Selenge, Orkhon and Darkhan-Uul.

The northern region's taiga (forest) zone is adjacent to and part of the vast forested region of southern Siberia. In the taiga of northern Khövsgöl you will find coniferous forests of Siberian larch and pine, as well as rocks covered with mosses and lichens of brown, green and amber colours. Animals of the forest are hunted for their hides and skins. To combat this, Mongolia's conservation movement efforts to protect rare species (among them snow leopard and musk deer) have included engaging the help of ex-hunters to train the national parks' staff. They in turn ensure that campers leave their camping sites with no trace of having been there and 'tread lightly', as the green slogan says, in this wonderful, wild part of the world.

The economy of this region is based on timber and agriculture; the country's timber industry is centred in Bulgan Aimag. The northern provinces of Selenge and Bulgan are relatively prosperous and well connected by rail links to the capital, via the Trans-Mongolian railway.

KHÖVSGÖL AIMAG

Khövsgöl Aimag is named after Lake Khövsgöl, one of Mongolia's largest lakes. The lake and its surroundings are spectacular and the area is a natural draw for tourists. Mongolia's northernmost province is situated on the border with the Tuvan and Buryat republics of the Russian Federation. Local minorities include Tannu Uriankhai (Tuvans), Darkhad, Khotgoid and Tsaatan (reindeer people). The western and eastern parts of the aimag are mountainous with an intricate system of wetlands and lakes in the northwest Darkhad Basin, which includes Lake Tsagaan. Rivers such as the Ider and Selenge cross the southern part of the province, joined by the Delgermörön, which flows from the northwest through Mörön, the aimag centre. The Sayan Mountains lie along the northern border with Russia; the highest peak, Mönkh Saridag (3,491m), stands between the northern tip of the lake and the Russian border. Another mountain range, the Khoridolsaridag, extends west from Lake Khövsgöl. The mountain regions are forested throughout and are rich in animal and bird life. The wet meadows and

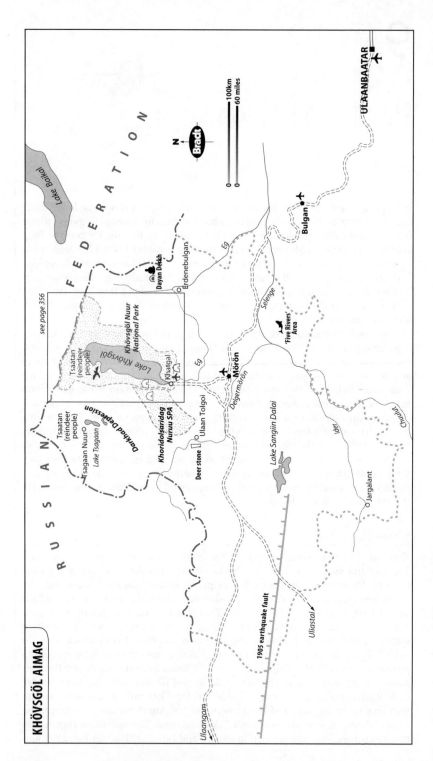

KHÖVSGÖL AIMAG

RUSSIAN FEDERATION

Lake Baikal

see page 356

Tsaatan (reindeer people)

Khövsgöl Nuur National Park

Lake Khövsgöl

Khatgal

Tsaatan (reindeer people)

Tsagaan Nuur

Lake Tsagaan

Darkhad Depression

Khoridolsaridag Nuruu SPA

Ulaan Tolgoi

Deer stone

Dayan Deekh

Erdenebulgan

Eg

Selenge

Eg

Delgermörön

Mörön

'Five Rivers' Area

Bulgan

ULAANBAATAR

Lake Sangiin Dalai

Ider

Chuluut

Jargalant

1905 earthquake fault

Uliastai

Ulaangom

N

Bradt

100km
60 miles

0

0

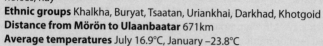
lagoons are important for waterfowl. Tsaatan people, who have domesticated reindeer for generations, live in birch-bark wigwams in the remote, forested areas northwest of Lake Khövsgöl.

The road into Russia is for local traffic only, since no tourist vehicles can enter or exit this way. The main east–west road in the northern regions from Ulaanbaatar is mostly unpaved and crosses the country via Bulgan Aimag, to Mörön and on to the far west. New *ger* camps have sprung up along the lakeshores; their facilities are excellent and in keeping with the natural environment. Lake Khövsgöl and the national park are part of Mongolia's 'Golden Circuit', a popular triangle of the most visited places which includes the Orkhon Valley and South Gobi, and the local economy is being rebuilt around tourism. The lake freezes in winter and there are opportunities for skating and also for cross-country skiing.

MÖRÖN Located 100km south of Lake Khövsgöl, Mörön means 'river' in Mongolian. The Delgermörön River, a great fishing river, passes south of the town. The climate in this mountainous part of Mongolia is cooler. Local people tend to build wooden houses rather than live in tents, so you will see fewer traditional *gers*. Mörön has become a tourist town; foreigners usually arrive at the airport and drive through to Lake Khövsgöl, stopping perhaps at the market to shop on their way. You can buy meat, potatoes, onions, garlic and some other vegetables. The market, the jeep and minibus stand and petrol station are situated 1.5km northwest of the town centre. There are several hotels in town. Daatgal Bank (⏱ *09.00–16.00 Mon–Fri*) is located in a grey building, northeast of the square, and changes US dollar notes.

Getting there from Ulaanbaatar

By air Eznis Airways (*www.eznisairways.com*) and Aero Mongolia (*www.aeromongolia.mn*) have direct flights daily from UB to Mörön during the tourist

Northern Region   **KHÖVSGÖL AIMAG**

9

season (June–September) but not in winter. The cost is around US$185. To book in advance go to www.flightsmongolia.com. The airport is situated 5km from the centre of town; jeeps, taxis or local buses will take you from Mörön airport into town or on to Lake Khövsgöl (and vice versa).

By road Minivans and jeeps travel daily between Ulaanbaatar and Mörön and some continue to Khatgal. The journey by road from Ulaanbaatar to Khövsgöl takes two days. The one-way cost by long-distance bus from UB is T35,500 (US$25). The onward journey from Mörön to Lake Khövsgöl usually involves jeeps, which leave Mörön market daily. It costs US$100 for a jeep and driver, less for a shared jeep or minibus.

Getting around Getting around is best done using private transport. Horses and tents may be hired – ask at the tourist centre (see below).

Tourist information
Å **Khövsgöl Tourist Centre** ✎1382 2206; e dalai37@yahoo.com. The centre's main activity is providing information & organising general sightseeing/adventure tours in the local area.

Owns a 3-star hotel, restaurant, bar & internet café in Mörön town centre & a tourist camp by Lake Khövsgöl.

Where to stay
⌂ **Delgermörön Hotel** One block north of the main square. **$**

⌂ **Edelweiss Hotel** (16 beds, 8 standard rooms) Town centre. Offers laundry services, sauna, tennis & billiards. Book via Khövsgöl Mon Travel (✎11 322878; e info@montravels.mn; www. montravels.com). **$$–$**

⌂ **Government Tourist Hotel** The airport road near the monastery; ✎38 41 3479. **$$–$**

⌂ **50/100 Hotel** m 993 82345; located on the main street. The restaurant serves good food & is a popular place to eat. It gets booked up so ring & book ahead of time. **$**

Where to eat and drink
The above hotels have restaurants. Local dishes include mutton, yoghurt, noodles, meat and onion soup; cost is around T4,500 for a main dish.

✗ **Chinggis Restaurant** ✎1382 2610; ⊕ 10.00–midnight. Chinese meals. *Approx T3,500–5,000.*

✗ **Dul Restaurant and Bar** ⊕ Restaurant 06.30–midnight; bar 18.00 until late. Mongolian & European meals are served. *Average T5,500.*

✗ **Jargalan Restaurant** ✎1382 4409; ⊕ 10.00–19.00. European & Mongolian meals. *Approx T4,500.*

✗ **Marco Polo Restaurant** ✎1282 1134; ⊕ 10.00–19.00. European & Mongolian food. *Approx T4,500.*

Shopping
⛺ **Tes Supermarket** ✎1382 1212; ⊕ 09.00–22.00. Mainly groceries.

⛺ **Market** Located in the town centre by the main road; ⊕ 10.00–19.00. Sells clothes, food, etc.

Other practicalities
▣ **Internet café** Located in the Dul Restaurant; ✎1382 2206; ⊕ 24hrs; T800/hr.

▣ **Post office internet café** ✎503 8000; ⊕ 10.00–18.00; T800/hr.

What to see and do in Mörön
Deer stone complex at Ulaan-Uul 17km west of town. Worth visiting if only for a short while. Taxis cost around T700/km.

Mörön Museum (🕐 *09.00–18.00 Tue–Sun; entrance fee T3,600*) East of the main square, this museum's exhibits include, as the main attractions, artefacts belonging to the minority Tsaatan (reindeer people), an exhibition of local flora and fauna, and an ancient mammoth tusk.

Danzandarjaa Khiid On the airport road west of the town centre is a new monastery building that has replaced an earlier version, Möröngiin Khüree, that a century ago housed up to 2,000 monks. There is now a community of around 30 monks. The monastery's temples contain Buddhist statues and *tanka* paintings (Buddhist scroll paintings). Services are held in the mornings around 10.30–11.00.

SIGHTS IN KHÖVSGÖL AIMAG
Lake Khövsgöl (Khövsgöl Nuur) Created by volcanic activity, it is part of the Baikal rift system, resulting from pressures associated with tectonic plate activity, when the Indian and Asian continents met around 55 million years ago. In an ongoing process the surrounding land was raised and deep rifts were formed, in turn creating lakes such as Lake Baikal and Lake Khövsgöl, which is the younger lake. It is also Mongolia's deepest lake with a maximum depth of 262m; it is 134km long from north to south, and at its greatest width 39km. Some 90 rivers and streams flow into the lake, and only one river, the Egiin Gol, flows from it. Later the Egiin Gol joins the Selenge to flow into Lake Baikal, in southern Siberia. Lake Khövsgöl contains 2% of the world's fresh water: it is crystal clear. The lake is surrounded by

---

LAKE KHÖVSGÖL'S LEGEND: THE MOUNTAIN TOP AND THE PLUG

Years ago an old woman was wandering in the northern regions in a particularly remote part covered by volcanic rocks, surrounded on all sides by mountains. She was surprised to meet a tiny child the size of an elf, who decided to accompany her on her desolate journey. They travelled for three days without food and rest until they came to a large rock, under which was a trickle of water; they stayed in its shade and dug around the spring to make a well. Life became possible and they settled there. The boy grew to normal size, he hunted and sang and the pair looked after each other. Every day they drank spring water from their well at the base of the large boulder, but they were always careful to place a stone over the well to stop it flowing over. One day the boy's singing attracted a beautiful girl who was passing and in time it became clear that they would marry.

All went well and the old woman accepted the girl. Unfortunately, one inauspicious day the young couple forgot to replace the stone on top of the well and a huge quantity of water poured out and flooded the area. A monster arrived to have a drink and the boy, who was now strong and bold, killed it and buried it under a mountaintop. Water was still pouring from the well, so the old lady, seeing the predicament, dived into the lake and placed a stone on the spring to plug it. Sadly, she drowned in the process.

To this day, the small island in the middle of Lake Khövsgöl is known as the plug, and the larger island is said to be the mountaintop under which the monster is buried. If you climb Mount Urandösh (2,793m) to the west of the lake you will notice it has a flat summit. The young couple named the lake 'mother lake' in honour of the old lady.

mountains, thick pine and larch forests and lush, green meadows where yaks and horses graze peacefully.

The western shore offers the best hiking and camping possibilities. You may pitch your tent there if you are on your own, or book into one of the *ger* camps situated near the shore (see pages 355–6). The lake and its rivers offer some wonderful fishing. Among the nine species in the lake are the Baikal *omul*, *lenok*, *umber*,

A GOLDEN JOURNEY: BEIJING TO UB, PART 2 — *Hallie Swanson*

(see Part 1, page 230)

We head north towards Lake Khovsghal, known as 'The Blue Pearl of Mongolia', near the Siberian border. It's a long ride but there are fascinating stops along the way. Kharkhorin, formerly known as Karakorum, was the glittering capital of the 13th-century Mongol Empire. European travellers like Marco Polo were astounded by its sophistication and opulence. In the 16th century, Tibetan Buddhism expanded into Mongolia and the Erdene Zuu Monastery was built. Today lamas worship in the beautiful temples and at dawn you can hear the monks chanting their ancient mantras as the sun rises and illuminates the elegant stupas.

Our journey continues with a stopover at a *ger* camp near Tsagaan Nuur (White Lake). This astonishingly beautiful, crystal-clear lake is renowned for its fish and birdlife. It was formed thousands of years ago by the Khorgo volcano, now extinct. We climb to the top of the crater and are rewarded with panoramic views of the lake and across the alpine meadows dotted with volcanic rocks. Hot and dusty, we head for the lake and a swim in the clear water. My son gets out his fishing rod in the hope of a catch, and we picnic on cold mutton dumplings and warm Mongolian tea, later stretching out for a nap in the sun.

Khövsgöl nuur is one of central Asia's great beauty spots and well worth the effort to get there. The sapphire blue lake is ringed by hills and forests where wild ibex, bear, sable, moose and wolverines roam. We clamber into a rickety motorboat and chug along to our destination, Ar Davkhar Eco Camp. It's on a remote side of the lake and so secluded we have the place to ourselves. Our *gers* have lovely views stretching across a blossom-filled meadow to the lakefront. There's a corral with a handsome herd of horses we later ride, and a few yaks that toss their shaggy heads at us. (We try to ride them as well and one takes off towards the hills with my daughter clinging on for dear life!)

The camp has a wooden sauna where we gather to let the warmth relax our saddle-sore muscles enough for a breathless dash out into the freezing water of the lake. A few bracing shots of Chingghis vodka later we revive and hang out with our hosts, who along with Chinzo have built a blazing bonfire. Songs and stories under a sky full of stars keep us up way past midnight. The owner's daughter tells us that she studied abroad. As she put it, 'I went because I wanted to see the world, but I came back because there is no place else so beautiful, so wild and so free.' As fireflies flitted past and the setting moon gilded the lake in a silvery sheen, we all knew she was right.

Our journey was arranged by Panoramic Journeys UK (www.panoramicjourneys. com).

Siberian roach and a kind of grayling endemic to Khövsgöl. The main attractions of the region are the scenery, hiking, fishing, camping and the lifestyle of the local people, including the reindeer herders. Some of the best views are seen from the hills and mountain summits, so they are well worth the climb, but it is advisable to take a guide. It takes two days to climb Mount Urandösh (near the *ger* camps west of the lake) and some routes are extremely dangerous. People may choose to ride across the mountains over passes to the Darkhad Basin or Depression where there are good birdwatching opportunities.

Khövsgöl Nuur National Park (*Entrance fees T1,500 pp, T3,000 per vehicle*)

Located on the shores of Lake Khövsgöl, the park was established in 1992 to preserve the lake and its watershed. It comprises thousands of square kilometres of mountains, forests, pastures and meadowland, which includes the lake, the basin of the River Üür (to the east of the lake), part of the Sayan mountain range, as well as the villages of **Khankh** and **Khatgal**, towns to the north and south of Lake Khövsgöl.

The taiga surrounding the lake is inhabited by moose, reindeer, *argali*, Siberian ibex, lynx, snow leopard, red deer, Siberian roe deer and wild boar, while birds such as capercaillie and hazel grouse live in the upland regions. Eurasian otter hunt for fish in the rivers and black stork, osprey cranes and waterfowl inhabit the lowlands, lakes and marshes. Wild flowers such as orchids, anemones, saxifrages, rock jasmine and gentians are found on the mountain ridges between the rocks, while meadow flowers include edelweiss and many herbs which are used for medicinal purposes.

Fees are collected at the park gates on the main road several kilometres before Khatgal; if the gate is unattended you can buy your permit at the park's headquarters, or from a ranger.

Ger *camps on the shores of Lake Khövsgöl* There are many camps along the lake, and some excellent ones at Toilogt. Costs vary between US$45 and US$55 per person depending on the area and what is offered. Self-catering camps cost from US$10, while camping near a *ger* camp and using the facilities costs US$3 per person. You can hire a fishing boat to fish or go for a quiet row; from US$10 an hour.

▲ **Boojum Expeditions Ger Camp** (also called Khovsgol Inn or Lodge) m 99115929; contact PO Box 902, Central Post Office, Ulaanbaatar; e info@boojum.com; www.boojumexpeditions. A well-run eco-friendly camp, advance booking over 30 days is required with a deposit of 50%. **$$–$**

▲ **Juulchin's Ger Camp** Contact Juulchin Foreign Tourism Corporation, Genghis Khan Av 58, Ulaanbaatar; \ 11 328428; e juulchin@mongol. net, jlncorp@magicnet.mn; www.mol.mn/juulchin, www.mongoliaonline.mn/juulchin. Located in Toilogt (see map), at a marvellous site near the lakeshore, this is a comfortable, long-established *ger* camp with good facilities. **$$–$**

▲ **Dalai Tour** Contact Mon Travels; \ 11 322878; e info@montravels.com; www.montravels. com. Located southwest of the lake; venue of the Tsaatan Festival (see box, page 362); facilities for

120 persons, 30 gers; wooded houses, restaurant (vegetables & home-grown produce), museum art shop & other facilities. **$**

▲ **Toilogt Ger Camp** Contact Huvsgul Travel Company; PO Box 116, Ulaanbaatar; \ 11 326478; m 991 16227. On the isthmus at Toilogt. It has hot showers, good food & excellent service; unsurprisingly, the camp is often totally booked in the summer months by tour groups. There are 2 Toilogt camps called Northern & Southern Toilogt, with a combined capacity of 100 people. **$**

▲ **Nature's Door Expedition Centre & Ger Camp** m 992 60979/991 10132; www. naturesdoor.mn. Located a half-hour's boat trip from Khatgal, these attractive wooden lodges & traditional *gers* are situated in a lakeside meadow carpeted with edelweiss & wild thyme. Facilities include hot showers & a glass-fronted restaurant

KHÖVSGÖL NUUR NATIONAL PARK

KEY
Strict nature reserve
within the national park
Horse-riding track · · · · ·

overlooking the lake. It serves excellent food & the cost is US$45 (T64,000) pp per day in shared *ger* accommodation (3–4 sharing). It also offers an 'Adventure Lodge Package' which includes luxury lodge accommodation (twin or dbl) with facilities & food, plus all other outdoor activities & excursions from US$120/day. **$$$$–$$$**

➤ **Khantaiga and Khangard *ger* camps** No telephone. 5km north of Khatgal in the Jankhai area, these camps cater for large tour groups. **$**

➤ **Jankhai and Erdene Uul *ger* camps** No telephone. Situated where the road meets the lake in the Jankhai area, these cabins & *gers* charge

reasonable rates – with hot showers & saunas included. Erdene Uul is self-catering. **$$$–$**

➤ **Nomin Sky** m 991 12282; e nominsky@ mongoltour.mn. Located on the eastern shore of the lake, in a place called Alag Tsaram Valley. Has 10 *gers* & 6 wooden houses. **$$–$**

➤ **Galt Hot Spring** Galt sum; 352885/ 353288; e info@nemekh.com. This camp is located near the hot spring & can cater for up to 125 people. **$$–$**

➤ **Khuvsgul Ecotour** Khatgal sum; m 991 49143; e khuvsguleco-tour@yahoo.com. Has 14 *gers* & 5 wooden houses. **$$–$**

Khatgal town Located on the southern tip of Lake Khövsgöl is a collection of log cabins known as Khatgal. Originally founded as a camp for Manchu soldiers (1727), it later became a Russian trading town. In the early 20th century the first steamboat operated on the lake between Khatgal and Khankh, the town on its northern shores closest to Russia. Mongolia's first wool-washing mill was built here in the

1930s. Khatgal became the aimag centre until the airport brought more prosperity to Mörön. Gradually the town declined in importance but, since 1990 and the opening of the national park headquarters, Khatgal has gradually been redeveloped as a centre for tourism with new *ger* camps and shops. The Craft Store is located at the Blue Pearl Hotel on the main street where you can buy locally knitted hand-spun camel-hair socks, gloves and mitts, as well as traditional carvings, games such as *daam* (draughts), and other souvenirs – all of which help to support the local economy and sustain jobs associated with tourism in the area.

Where to stay and eat

🏠 **Blue Pearl Hotel** On Khatgal's main street. Provides comfortable & clean rooms, hot showers, room service; meals can be brought to your room. **$**

🏠 **Khövsgöl Lake Hotel** (also called the **National Park Hotel** as it is run by the national park) On the main street, 100m from the Blue Pearl Hotel. Caters for the park staff but also has some rooms for guests. **$**

🏠 **Garage 24** (hostel & *gers*) Garages (belonging to the former Soviet Union) converted into a friendly, low-budget hostel run by Nature's Door (📞 *9926 0979*). Offers well-designed accommodation in bunk-room dormitories (US$8–10/night) & provides traditional *ger* accommodation, hot showers & a restaurant/bar with a south-facing veranda for morning coffee. Nature's Door also jointly runs an expedition centre & *ger* camp on the lakeshore. **$$$**

ENVIRONMENTALLY CONSCIOUS DEVELOPMENT

Boojum Expeditions – a Californian travel company, founded and run by Kent Madin and Linda Svensden – set up a charitable fund. It invested with Seecon International to develop sustainable sanitation in Khatgal; the model eco toilet they designed is used in Khövsgöl aimag and also *ger* districts in Ulaanbaatar and elsewhere in Mongolia. See www.boojum.com/extras/Ecosan_Toilets_in_Mongolia.pdf.

Nature's Door has invested in two camps in the Khövsgöl area and is helping to develop small businesses in the region, linked to tourism and sustainable development. The company, like others including Boojum Expeditions, believes that tourism should respect the environment and benefit the local community.

At the campsites the aim is to leave no trace. 4th World installed a mobile sawmill at Khatgal, where wood was cut for the camp buildings using timber from outside the national park and old, dry timber from derelict log cabins in Khatgal. Furniture is also made locally, and the company has undertaken a tree-planting programme to replace the trees. Pürevdorj, the owner of another Toilgot *ger* camp, has added an innovative element to the camp's activities by bringing a Swiss cheese maker to Khövsgöl.

Environmental awareness is helping to ensure proper sewage treatment, whereby camps have installed composting toilets, and some (including Nature's Door camps) are powered using solar energy, while special solar-powered water-filtration systems help to ensure that no pollution reaches the lake water. Nature's Door also grow their own vegetables which helps them to be self-sufficient. These practical steps are encouraging others to do likewise and to ensure that the lake remains unpolluted. See also Mongol Ecology Centre (MEC), who are working to conserve this beautiful lake in the long term (*www.mongolec.org*).

Offices
Khövsgöl Nuur National Park Headquarters Based in the centre of Khatgal village, the gateway to Lake Khövsgöl. You will see displays of the park's wildlife and receive information on where to go and what to do. If you want to understand the park in some detail, the chief ranger and his staff give introductory talks on the flora and fauna of the region – well worth attending. Lecture times are posted on a noticeboard; if not, ask when the next talk will take place.

Khövsgöl Guide Association Based at the Blue Pearl Hotel in Khatgal and will help to organise hiking or horse treks with English-speaking guides trained by the national park staff – experts in low-impact camping. Horse trails follow the western shore and some cross to the Darkhad Basin; the eastern lakeshore is not as well visited or as attractive.

Khöridolsaridag Nuruu Strictly Protected Area This borders Lake Khövsgöl National Park on the western side and was designated to protect a unique combination of landscape and wildlife habitat comprising a steep-sided mountain range which combines tundra, taiga, forested steppe and mountains – all at close proximity. Wildlife species such as *argali*, ibex, Siberian moose, snowcock and sable inhabit these areas. It is not an area that is open for visitors.

Other attractions around Lake Khövsgöl
Mineral springs and hot springs Multiple mineral springs rise and flow from the sides of mountain valleys around Lake Khövsgöl; these waters are known throughout Mongolia for their medicinal properties. In Mongolia it is thought that if you eat the fish from the streams, they too are said to have curative properties.

Khar Us (Black Water) Spring Just 65km along the western shore of Lake Khövsgöl, where the trail turns west via the Jigleg Pass (Jiglegiin Davaa) to Tsagaan Nuur, spring water gushes from beneath a large rock and from many smaller springs nearby. Each spring is marked with a sign to say which part of the body they are thought to cure.

Bolnain Rashaan Situated 60km east of the lake from Mörön, these springs flow into pools of varying temperatures where you can bathe. The water is said to have curative properties and it is also a lovely place to relax. Plan a two-day return trip if travelling from one of the western shore *ger* camps. You will thus need to camp overnight or stay with a herding family, and this can be arranged with tour companies and local guides. There are several other springs in the area but this is the most popular one.

Cave at Dayan Derkh This cave lies east of Lake Khövsgöl. Inside there are some cave paintings of interest and it's worth exploring. There is also a small newly constructed monastery at Dayan Derkh on the site of a former monastery which was destroyed. On the way there from Khatgal you will find several deer stones and memorial monuments south of the village of Chandmani-Ondor.

Tsagaan Nuur and the Darkhad Basin Some 50km west of Lake Khövsgöl, this low-lying area has more than 200 lakes, the largest being Tsagaan Nuur (64km²). Tsagaan Nuur village is located near the lake in a district of the same name. It is surrounded by extensive marshland, mountains and forested hills, the natural home of the Tsaatan minority reindeer people. The Tsaatan are difficult to find and usually avoid contact with strangers, though sometimes visitors will come across their camps. Other than the Tsaatan homelands, the main attraction of the area is its waterfowl. There are also great possibilities for fishing and birdwatching, though remember to bring plenty of repellent and mosquito nets. Transport and access to inland, off-road places in the area is difficult but well worth the effort. Birdlife includes Pallas's fish eagle, greater-spotted eagle, lesser kestrel, black stork, osprey, whooper swan, white spoonbill, damoiselle crane and daurian partridge.

There is also a standard visitor fee to the area of T5,000 per person per day; in addition a permit is required when visiting Tsagaan Nuur district (obtainable from the local administration via your guide). Boojum Expeditions (see page 165) arranges tours in the Khövsgöl region, with its own *ger* camps at Renchinlkhümbe (*www.hovsgol.org/camp.html*) and Jigleg (on the pass to Darkhad Basin). For Bulgan Fault see *Zavkhan Aimag* map, page 364.

Archaeology Although there is not a current visitor trail to see these fascinating ancient remains that litter the northern regions in and around the Darkhad Valley and Lake Khövsgöl, I predict that when better visitor information is available archaeology will become a major attraction to the area. Research projects such as the Deer Stone Project have laid the foundations for this. See box, *Deer stones*, below.

ACTIVITIES
Birdwatching The Khövsgöl area offers a variety of birdlife, so don't forget your binoculars. Here you will find birds of the forest such as red-throated thrush, blue

---

DEER STONES IN NORTHERN MONGOLIA

The impressive Deer Stone Project (DSP) was undertaken in northern Mongolia by a joint team of Mongolian and US archaeologists from the Smithsonian National Museum of Natural History. For several years, beginning in 2001, the team studied and recorded many ancient monuments, hitherto virtually unknown to the outside world. The Darkhad Valley northwest of Lake Khövsgöl sets a boundary between the steppe (south) and the Siberian taiga (north) – an ancient north/south crossroads over the millennia. As a result, over time, the landscape is littered with the remains of hundreds of ancient monuments, such as deer stones (ancient monoliths).

In other parts of Mongolia during the 20th century Russian archaeologists completed important Bronze Age work in different locations. In the last ten years, Turkish, French and German archaeologists arrived, or returned, to Mongolia to study ancient Turkic and medieval sites. American archaeologists also worked on sites in central and western Mongolia. In this northern region, DSP concentrated on the Darkhad Valley and surrounding areas. Dr William Fitzhugh led a multidisciplinary team to explore and find evidence of cultural links, covering a large swathe of land from Mongolia to the Pacific northwest through polar regions, looking at inter-connections between regions and material they discovered. Back in the mid-1950s anthropologists theorised that Mongolian Bronze Age art may have influenced Inuit (Eskimo) objects such as death masks and animal motifs on ornamental objects. The Deer Stone Project has recorded, categorised and dated (where possible) a huge number of deer stones. Deer stone findings are mapped and described with meticulous detail. See www.si.edu/mci/english/research/conservation/deer_stones.html and www.mnh.si.edu/arctic/.

9

'MONGOLIA SUNRISE TO SUNSET': ULTRA MARATHON CHALLENGE

David Bernasconi

Mongolia is fast developing as a country for adventure tourism and offers challenges such as 'Sunset to Sunrise', Mongolia's annual ultra-distance marathon, a race internationally recognised for being a well-organised and an environmentally conscious event. It takes place annually in August in one of the most exotic settings in the world, beside Lake Khövsgöl in northern Mongolia.

The 'Mongolia Sunrise to Sunset' allows one to explore Mongolia by taking part in the annual 42km marathon or 100km ultra marathon. Runners, supporters and nature lovers from around the world can join the group in Ulaanbaatar, from where travel is arranged by scheduled flights, and then by car, to the remote lake region of Khövsgöl, situated on the northern borders of Mongolia with Russian Siberia. The lake, flanked by 3,000m mountains, is surrounded by forests of larch and spruce and is a spectacular setting for the race. Altitude at the basecamp is 1,650m, the optimum level for high-altitude training. Here, in the 'middle of nowhere', hot showers, good food and drink are all available, and visitors relish living in the unique ambience of traditional round-framed *gers*.

The race itself offers runners (and walkers) the opportunity to explore the picturesque lakeshore scenery and the mountain ranges above the lake. It begins at first light. The course follows a rough track through the woods and hugs the lakeshore for the first 12km. It then climbs above the treeline to the highest point, a 2,300m pass. There is a downhill stretch to marshy wetlands before the route ascends a second pass, a flower-covered meadow offering an opportunity to circle a ceremonial cairn, or *ovoo*, to honour an ancient religious tradition. From here the course descends back to the lakeshore for a final dash to the midway station to start a loop that takes the runners into new territory along unpaved roads and trails. The final 25km hugs the lakeshore path once more.

Water and first-aid stations mark every 12km of the course and a system is in place for contestants to write messages and relay them should they be in difficulty. Local horsemen gallop alongside ready to transport the messages, as they did in the days of Genghis Khan. Message pads, space blankets, a course map and a number of other items, like a whistle, are issued to each runner in case anyone should go off course.

Ecotourism is part of the race's ethos, an approach which respects this pristine wilderness area. Here the air is clear and sunshine is extremely strong with August temperatures around 18°C. For runners and non-runners alike, the days before the race can be spent soaking in the sun, horseriding, kayaking, mountain biking, hiking and, of course, running.

'Sunrise to Sunset' is a non-profit-making event. Any proceeds, managed by ecoLeap foundation, are used to support projects that keep the park free of litter, aid the sustainable development of Khövsgöl National Park, the park's nomadic communities and the villages that border the park. The race offers runners the opportunity to visit the land of 'Blue Skies' and to run beside one of the most beautiful lakes in the world.

For full information visit 'Mongolia Sunrise to Sunset's website (*www.ms2s. org*) or visit Facebook.

At the end of the 20th century Mongolian reindeer were on the verge of extinction and their numbers had decreased drastically from 2,280 to 616. Life was becoming more difficult as a result for the Tsaatan reindeer herders, whose name literally means 'those who have reindeer' (*tsaa buga*). To try to counteract this, the Mongolian Reindeer Herders' Society and the Mongolian Red Cross Society, together with Italian researchers, helped to deliver food and aid to the herders over the hard winters of 1999–2001. Thanks to their support, and further support from the Itgel Foundation from 2002 reindeer slaughtering and trading was reduced, veterinary care was introduced and the herds have begun to increase once more.

woodpecker, three-toed woodpecker, yellow-crested bunting and pine bunting, while in the meadows there are wagtails, ortolan bunting, demoiselle crane, sandpiper, lapwings and ringed plovers, and in the lagoons birds such as tufted duck, ruddy shelduck, goldeneye, shoveler, teal, Slavonian grebe and whooper swans are all present. Other species of Khövsgöl Aimag include swan goose, osprey and Daurian partridge.

Fishing The Five Rivers area, approximately 50km south of Mörön, on the border with Arkhangai Aimag, is where five rivers (the Ider, Delgermörön, Bügsei, Selenge and Chuluut) converge. The area offers excellent fishing, and specialised companies have set up their own fishing camps here. On pages 216–19 you'll find all the information you need on what to bring, the choice of fish and equipment, the best season to go and so forth, as well as a list of expert international fishing tour companies and UK suppliers of fishing tackle.

For further information contact Borkhüügiin Zorig at the Taimen Tour Travel Agency (\ *11 311643*; e *info@taimentour.com, taimentour_zorig@yahoo.com; www. taimentour.com*), who have their own cabins and organise general tourism and fishing trips; and Andy Parkinson (*www.fishmongolia.com*).

SUGGESTED ITINERARY In the Saddle (see page 166) offers a Mongolian riding holiday including some fishing. The itinerary begins with a flight from Ulaanbaatar to Mörön, Khövsgöl's provincial centre, from where you travel north 140km by jeep to a fishing camp on the River Ider. There you spend a week camping and fishing for *lenok*, *taimen* and grayling, and you should also have time to explore the nearby hills and mountains, pick wild berries, drink plenty of vodka and generally chill out.

ECOTOURISM Successful programmes based around Lake Khövsgöl have involved participants joining with park staff to learn surveying techniques and standard field biology methods to investigate mammals, birds and plants in the area. The results of the research are designed to help future monitoring programmes, with particular attention given to wildlife under threat from (illegal) hunting, notably the snow leopard, *argali*, brown bear and musk deer. It is a great way to get to know the country and the lives of local people; for further details contact Steppes Travel (see page 165).

In addition, Steppes Travel published a booklet called *Lake Khövsgöl National Park: Visitors Guide* which is on sale in Ulaanbaatar at US$7 or available directly from the company. It has a good chapter on nomadic life and also some excellent pictures of flora and fauna (some of which appear in this guide).

THE TSAATAN

The Tsaatan (reindeer people) comprise families of a small but growing population. They are now making efforts to marry Mongolians in a bid to increase their community. They live in the high mountains of northern Khövsgöl Aimag. Originally they are Tannu Uriankhai or Tuvan, related to the Turkic people of the neighbouring Republic of Tuva. In the early 1980s, the government grouped them around Lake Tsagaan in an attempt to settle them, though they would not be 'settled' easily.

Like Mongolia, Tuva was part of the Qing Empire but became separated from Mongolia at the beginning of the 20th century as a result of Russian interference. Tuvans wrote in the old Mongolian classical script until they received the Latin, then the Cyrillic alphabet in the 1930s. Subsequently, when Mongols were forced into collectives by socialist reformers, these shy Tsaatan herders disappeared into the woods and mountains with their reindeer.

Nature is on the side of the Tsaatan and not the tourist, as they inhabit one of the harshest and most inaccessible regions of the world. The northern fringes of Mongolia are on the edge of civilisation. Their encampments are usually found after riding long distances through larch and silver birch forests, and tend to be more easily accessible in spring and summer. (If you are going to undertake such a journey, bring a fishing rod as there are many excellent opportunities to fish in the streams and rivers.) Tsaatan, who possess few ways of communication, travel with the seasons, journeying in summer by canoe on rivers and in winter, when the cold weather comes and the river water freezes, crossing these rivers while riding on their reindeer. They barter goods in exchange for wool hide and furs. In spring, unsettled weather breaks the ice while strong winds and sudden storms buffet the land. In the hot, short summers, marigolds, forget-me-nots, primroses and anemones bloom, as if by magic, and in the skies the winds carry thousands of migratory birds. Forests are predominately made up of larch but there are also pine, birch, poplar and some spruce trees. Pine thrives on the south-facing slopes, while trees like poplar, aspen and birch grow on the less sunny, northern slopes.

Tsaatan construct birch-bark, teepee-style dwellings and hunt using horns made of larch wood to imitate animal calls. They catch fish by spearing them with long poles; reindeer milk is part of their staple food from which they make cheese, butter and yoghurt. Occasionally, they eat reindeer meat but overall they prefer not to kill their deer. They have become a focus of attention for tourists who now flock to see them. One wonders if this is a good thing: having admirably survived the 20th-century political changes, are they now to end up dependent upon handouts from one 'chopper' visit to the next? If so, and should they choose, don't be surprised if they employ their disappearing tactics again.

In the past decade there has been so much interest in the Tsaatan that they now choose to send their children to schools in Khatgal and hold a number of special events such as the Reindeer Festival which takes place annually in July, by Lake Khovsgol, when Tsaatan benefit directly from tourism – see box, *Reindeer festival*, on opposite page and visit www.mongoliatourism.gov.mn/index.php/events/49-tsaatan-festival. The Itgel Foundation was set up in 2002 on their behalf by Morgan Keay and Lilliana Goldman and many tours book through this organisation (see further details on Itgel on opposite page).

The Itgel Foundation (*www.itgel.org*) This is a joint US/Mongolian NGO established by Morgan Keay and Lillian Goldman in 2002 to help preserve local traditions, culture and environment in a variety of different ways – handing over responsibility to local people and communities. The foundation's grass-roots bottom-up approach ensures self-sufficiency is inbuilt into each project and local people take change. Help such as veterinary care and procuring new breeding stock is given, such as reindeer, to strengthen the herd and its numbers. The secondary school was built in Tsagaan Nuur village to help the children there. TCVC – see below – is one of Itgel's programmes.

Tsaatan community and visitors centre (TCVC) (m *9552 3973/9567 9908;* e *visittaiga@gmail.com; http://visittaiga.org/about.html*) Located at Tsaagan Nuur northwest of Khövsgöl Lake by the Tsaatan (or Dukha) community, TCVC was set up through the Itgel Foundation. It is designed to help plan visits to the reindeer herders in their home regions and is managed by the Tsaatan themselves. The TCVC acts as a 'gateway' to control visitor numbers and to minimise exploitative tourism. But this is not working because tour companies (and individual tourists) are bypassing the small percentage charged. The President of Mongolia Ts Elbeadorj visited the reindeer people in December 2012 and in March 2013 the government pledged to do more to support them by reviving reindeer husbandry and enhancing the livelihood of the Tsaatan. UNDP is also running programmes to help. However, on the ground, work needs to happen. Better management of tourist facilities at temporary camps would help much needed sanitation facilities (dug-out loos) to improve hygiene; it is difficult for local reindeer herders to manage sanitation and water needs for people who arrive (mostly unexpectedly) to see them.

ZAVKHAN AIMAG

Zavkhan province has some wonderful and varied scenery, dominated by the high, snow-capped mountains of the Khangai range, with many rivers (Ider, Tes, Zavkhan and Buyant), lakes and springs. In contrast are the low, rolling dunes of Altan Els and Borkhyn Els, which continue into neighbouring Uvs Aimag in the west. While the southern and western parts are dominated by deserts and salt lakes, mountains and rivers dominate the rest – the Zavkhan River sets a natural border to Gobi-Altai Aimag before it enters Lake Airag in Uvs Aimag. Zavkhan shares a boundary with many provinces: Khovd and Uvs (in the west), Gobi-Altai and Bayankhongor (in the south) and Arkhangai (in the southeast). It also borders the

---

REINDEER FESTIVAL

The festival includes displays of reindeer, games and horse and yak riding, canoe and boating sports on the lake and even reindeer polo! A typical year's programme for the festival located at Dalai Tour *ger* camp (see page 355) includes handmade arts and crafts exhibitions, festival events, participation in the sports, and tickets for the closing ceremony – set in natural surroundings, on the shores of Lake Khövsgöl – usually held in July.

The annual Ice Festival at Lake Khövsgöl, held in March, also involves the Tsaatan and their reindeer in events. See Ice Festival tours arranged by Panoramic Journeys (*www.panoramicjoourneys.com*).

ZAVKHAN AIMAG

RUSSIAN FEDERATION

Ulaangom

Möron

1905 earthquake fault

Lake Oigon

L Sangiin Dalai

Lake Kholboo

Lake Telmen

Lake Bayan

Tosontsengel

Lake Khar

Tarvagatain Nuruu National Park

Lake Khar

Borkhyn Els (sand dunes)

Zagastain Pass 2500m

Khömiin Tal

Sand dunes

Solongot Pass 2000m

Uliastai

Tsetserleg

Lake Dögön

Sand dunes

Mt Otgontenger 4021m

Otgontenger Uul Strictly Protected Area

Gants Pass 2000m

N

Bradt

0 ——— 50km
0 ——— 30 miles

Altai

Republic of Tuva (Russian Federation) in the north and shares its northeastern boundary with Khövsgöl Aimag.

As might be expected, Uliastai is a convenient place to stop when travelling around the country, although most people prefer the better southern roads when driving west from Ulaanbaatar.

BRIEF FACTS: ZAVKHAN AIMAG

Area 82,500km^2
Aimag centre Uliastai
Districts 24
Elevation of Zavkhan 1,760m
Livestock and crops Sheep, goats, cattle, horses, potatoes
Ethnic groups Khalkha
Distance from Uliastai to Ulaanbaatar 984km
Average temperatures July 15.4°C, January −23.1°C

HIGHLIGHTS
* Otgontenger Mountain
* Otgontenger Hot Spring
* Bulgan Fault
* Khömiin Tal research site for wild horses (advance permission needed to visit)

Zavkhan's economy is based largely on livestock, particularly sheep. Zavkhan has an important timber business, based at Tosontsengel. Minority people include the Khotgoid and Khoshuud. Views from some mountain passes, like the Zagastain Davaa at 2,500m on the road from Tosontsengel to Uliastai, are alone worth the journey.

ULIASTAI This town is quiet and pleasant, with a central area consisting of hotels, restaurants and markets and an industrial part of town taken up with offices and stockyards for the timber and livestock businesses. A climb to a pavilion on a hill near the town will give you some good views. At the top you will find some pieces of animal sculpture of elk, *argali* and ibex.

Getting there from Ulaanbaatar

By air There are scheduled regular flights from Ulaanbaatar, Khovd and Mörön by Eznis Airways (*www.eznisairways.com*) and Aero Mongolia (*www.aeromongolia.mn/flightschedule*).

By road Private jeep or minibus. The public bus will cost you T35,000, depending on the type of vehicle; Russian jeeps are cheaper.

Where to stay and eat

The **Uliastai Hotel** (**$**) and **Tegsh Hotel** (**$**) both serve food and charge similar rates: single rooms cost US$10 per person, double rooms US$15–20 per person.

The **Chigistei Restaurant** in the centre of town provides Mongolian dishes, charging around T2,500 for a main dish.

What to see and do in Uliastai

History Museum (*10.00–16.00 daily; entrance fee T3,000*) Also known as the Museum of Famous People, this is in the centre of town on the main street south of the square. It exhibits the works of well-known local people such as the writer Yavuukhulan and the first democratically elected president, P Ochirbat.

Dechindarjaa Khiid This is located in a *ger* district 3.5km north of the town (look out for a shiny tin roof). Opened in 1990, the monastery has a friendly community of monks who allow visitors to attend their ceremonies.

Guides Zavkhan Aimag is one of the most unexplored aimags of Mongolia. However there is guide there who is experienced and first rate – in other words a tiptop guide. His name is Tudevvaanchig Battulga (known as Tudevee) (e *tudevee_b@yahoo.com*). He comes from a herding family in Zavakhan, speaks fluent English and has worked throughout Mongolia; his clients are international. He is a freelance guide and has worked with leading tour companies like Fish Mongolia and Panoramic Journeys UK (see pages 167 and 165).

SIGHTS IN ZAVKHAN AIMAG

Otgontenger Uul Standing about 40km east of Uliastai, Otgontenger Mountain (4,021m) is Mongolia's second-highest mountain and remains snow covered throughout the year. The mountain is part of the Otgontenger Strictly Protected Area, which protects many rare species of animals, such as red deer, Siberian, musk deer, and rare plants. As one of the country's most sacred mountains Otgontenger is worshipped by local people. This holy mountain has been put forward for listing as a World Heritage Site.

Otgontenger Hot Springs (*Tourist price T57,000*) Located 20km south of the Otgontenger peak in the Rashaan river valley, this is part of the Baga Mountains, a spur of Otgontenger. There are 30 springs and the water temperature reaches 50°C here. A spa resort has developed around these hot springs at an altitude of 2,500m. The resort is used mainly by Mongolians for specific medical purposes, although tourists are welcome.

Sand dunes You will need your own transport to see these dunes, which are found mainly in the western part of the province at Altan Els, Mongol Els and Borkhyn Els. In the southwest the Mongol Els dunes stretch 330km along the Zavkhan River, a scenic route to Lake Erdene. Borkhyn Els dunes are easily accessible from the road when driving south from Uliastai to Altai, the centre of Gobi-Altai. The main attraction is the changing light on the dunes seen when driving in the area.

Earthquake fault This fault lies near **Lake Oigon**, running from the Khangiltsag River west to **Sangiin Dalai Lake** in Khövsgöl Aimag. The fault, the world's longest active volcanic land fault, was created by an earthquake in 1905, measuring 8.2 on the Richter scale. The quakes opened fissures 60m deep and

KHÖMIIN TAL WILD HORSE SITE

The wild horse site at Khömiin Tal (*www.takh.org*) is located in Zavkhan Aimag near Khar Us Nuur National Park (Khovd Aimag) in an area of Lake Dörgön that borders Khovd and Zavhan aimags. Khömiin Tal was set up between 1998 and 2000. The first consignment of 22 wild horses left from Le Villerat (in the Cévènnes National Park) in the south of France in 2004 and were flown from Nîmes airport to Khovd in western Mongolia; from there they were transported by a smaller cargo plane to a nearby landing strip and then trucked to the release site within at Khömiin Tal. In 2011 the Czech Republic flew four Przewalski's to western Mongolia, a journey of 17 hours from Prague. Currently (2013) there are around 37 *takhi* in an area of 2,500km². The long-term aim is to allow them to leave the fenced release site and roam freely. There is a field and workshop centre at Seer camp in Khömiin Tal where four Mongolians and one French ranger are based full time. They live in *gers* powered by solar panels and monitor the wild horses on site. Visitors are welcome but are asked to give at least one month's advance notice of their arrival. Other *takhi* sites include the one at Takhiin Tal in the remote southwest Gobi-Altai where the wild horses were originally reintroduced in 1991/92. The wild horse site most easily accessible to visitors is at Khustain Nuruu National Park (in Töv Aimag) southwest of Ulaanbaatar. Khömiin Tal and Takhiin Tal sites were designed to have more distance between humans and the horses and are also set up for breeding, behavioural studies, conservation and scientific research purposes. Khömiin Tal and Takhiin Tal are well worth visiting for those prepared and equipped to travel to such remote sites. Alongside the conservation work community schemes have been set up to involve local people in felt-making handicrafts and other projects to enable them to increase their earnings. Summer schools are held for children on environmental education. See maps for location of Khömiin Tal, page 364.

For further information on Takhi, see *Khustain Nuruu National Park*, pages 275–6; *Natural history and conservation*, page 130.

10m wide. The fault line can be traced for 400km by a trail of broken ground and streams, including a land slippage (ie: a ledge) of 11m where the land either fell or was raised along the fault.

Wildlife There are several good areas for birdwatching: around **Otgontenger Mountain** you may see bar-headed goose, lammergeier, Altain snowcock, mallard and Hodgson's bushchat. Wild fauna includes grey wolf, Siberian ibex, *argali* and Siberian marmot. Snow leopard have also been recorded in this area.

At **Khar Lake** notable species are white-headed duck and great bustard and, at **Telman Lake**, swan goose, saker falcon, lesser kestrel and Siberian crane.

SUGGESTED SHORT ITINERARIES From Uliastai drive east to **Otgontenger Spa Resort**, 20km south of the peak. Base yourself in the mountains, take walks and daily hot baths and have a restful time. You can find accommodation at *ger* camps along the Rashaan river valley for around US$45 per day. For transport, to hire a jeep costs US$100 per day, less if touring – negotiable with the driver.

Southern route by jeep (a three–four-day camping journey) From Uliastai drive south (44km) to the Gants Pass in Tsagaankhairkhan district and continue southeast to Otgon district (86km), from where you should turn north along the River Buyant, a mountain/lake area. Return via the sand dunes at **Altan Els** and **Borkhyn Els** (100km) before arriving back in Uliastai. The timing and logistics should be worked out with a Mongolian tour company, and/or local guide/translator.

BULGAN AIMAG

Bulgan Aimag is a mixture of dry grasslands in the south and forests in the north, bordering Siberia. The territory has huge resources of wild fruit, berries and medicinal herbs and grows around 50,000ha of wheat and vegetables. There are coal deposits, and rich gold, copper and molybdenum mines. Orkhon Aimag was created in 1994 around the city of Erdenet where the copper deposits are mined. Other industries are connected with animal products, namely hides and meat, fur and wool. The province has good roads and a railway line connecting Erdenet to the Trans-Mongolian railway. The province is crossed by the Orkhon River in the south and by the Selenge River in the north. Ethnic minorities include the Buryat.

BULGAN The town is centred on a long, narrow park that runs parallel to the Achuut River. The city hall, stadium and Aimag Museum stand together on the main street. The Bulgan Hotel is opposite on the other side of the park near the river; there is a bank on the main street; and the daily market is on a parallel street on the north side of town.

Getting there from Ulaanbaatar
By air Eznis Airways has flights between Ulaanbaatar and Bulgan on Tuesday and Saturday, which take one hour 25 minutes (315 miles); check website for details of flights: www.flightsmongolia.com/domestic_flight/bulgan.html.

By road There are a few direct buses between Ulaanbaatar and Bulgan but it is more common to take a minibus from Ulaanbaatar to Erdenet for around T11,000, or an overnight train for around US$20. On arrival, hire a jeep (cost from T800–1,000 per kilometre).

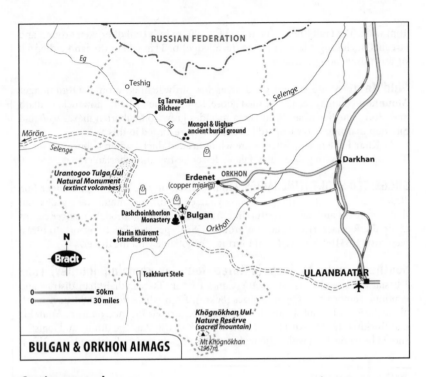

BULGAN & ORKHON AIMAGS

Getting around You'll need to make private arrangements for transport – see pages 237–9 for tour operators.

 Where to stay

🏠 **Artsat Mogoi Hotel** (Snake Hotel) Northeast cnr of the central park. **$**

🏠 **B&TS** ☎305779; e btsets@yahoo.com. This charming small camp is located near historic Khogno Khan Mountain. Offers friendly service & decent traditional food. **$$**

🏠 **Bulgan Hotel** South side of the park in the town centre. De-luxe rooms with bathrooms. **$$–$**

BRIEF FACTS: BULGAN AIMAG

Area 48,700km²
Aimag centre Bulgan
Districts 16
Elevation of Bulgan 1,208m
Livestock and crops Sheep, camels, goats, horses, potatoes, hay, wheat
Ethnic groups Khalkha, Buryat and Russian
Distance from Bulgan to Ulaanbaatar 318km
Average temperatures July 16°C, January –20.5°C

HIGHLIGHTS

- Uran Uul and Togoo Uul extinct volcanoes
- Eg Tarvagtain Bilcheer – scenic area (*bilcheer* means 'pasture')
- Deer stones and Turkic balbal (stone figures)

MONGOL HORSES, HORSEMANSHIP AND TRADITIONS

Danielle Harris

Mongolian horses are very well suited to their environment. Although herdsmen breed for increased size, the harshness of their winters keeps the horses small and very shaggy. They have amazing endurance capacity. It is considered traditional knowledge that a horse can carry a rider 60km in a day and run for 30km without slowing. Mongolian horses are extremely tough and almost fearless. In the winter they cross frozen rivers and eat snow to get water. Horses are kept in free-ranging herds in the countryside where they are counted at least twice a day by the man of the household. One or two of the best riding horses are kept saddled at a tie rack outside the *ger* for daily use. Often a *'nom-hu'* kid's horse is also kept near the *ger* to babysit the toddlers. When another horse is needed, a catchpole (*uurga*) or a soft rope is used to snag it out of the herd. Each herder knows the character of each of his 25–300 horses, ie: which is the fastest (*horton*) or most gentle (*nom-hu*). Although only the stallion of the herd is named, a complex description of colour, age and markings is used to identify each horse. There are different words for every age up to eight, and hundreds of words to describe colour and markings.

Mongolian horsemanship is extremely advanced. The saddles are built in a wooden scoop with high cantle and pommel and two horsehair cinches to keep them snug. These saddles allow a rider to stand in the stirrups and turn completely around to keep hold on a wily horse at the end of the catchpole, or in the glory days, to shoot an arrow at unsuspecting pursuers. The stirrups are also tied together under the belly of the horse to allow the rider to reach all the way to the ground without falling. The structure of this equipment is designed to keep the rider and horse united through an immense range of motion. Generally horses are ridden with one hand on the reins to free the other hand for a catchpole or anything else it may be needed for.

It is considered offensive to strike a horse – especially the face – in a tradition that is widely held to be based on a decree by Genghis Khan himself. Therefore, families employ an 'educate the children not the horse' strategy to avoid getting kicked and bitten. Children are taught to ride at such a young age that the average horseman doesn't need to pay any attention whatsoever to his horse. He instinctively guides it and stays in the seat. Indeed, I have seen a man pass out drunk, upside down with his head bumping against his horse's knee as it walked on, to then awaken, right himself in the saddle and continue riding. The horse continued so stoically, in fact, that I was tempted to try and buy it and may have succeeded but for its owner's inebriated state. Although it is primarily men who are expert horsemen, some women can and do ride with the best of them, especially those who grew up without elder brothers.

⌂ **Hoyor Zagal** Rashaant sum; ☏ 455822; e hoyorzagaljuulchin@hotmail.com. This camp is the biggest camp in the region with 30 *gers*, hot showers & good food. **$$$**

✖ **Where to eat and drink** The Bulgan Hotel (see opposite page) serves Mongolian food, with dishes costing T2,500–4,500. Canteens in town serve hot food and cold drinks at cheaper prices; expect to pay around T2,000 for meat dumplings.

What to see and do in Bulga

Aimag Museum (🕐 *10.00–16.00 daily; entrance fee T1,500*) This museum stands on the main street beside the Ethnographic Museum. Exhibits include displays on local history and culture, as well as one on Mongolia's first astronaut, J Gürragchaa.

Ethnographic Museum (🕐 *10.00–16.00 daily; entrance fee T1,500*) Located on the main street beside the Aimag Museum, this museum exhibits items of rural use such as hide bags for fermented mare's milk and saddles.

Dashchoinkhorlon Khiid Situated 3km west of the city, this is a modern monastery, built in 1992 to replace the older one, which was destroyed in the 1930s. It houses a statue of Tsongkhapa, the great reformer of Tibetan Buddhism and founder of the Gelugpa order, who lived from 1357 to 1419. There is a small community of monks there.

SIGHTS IN BULGAN AIMAG

Uran Uul and other volcanoes Located 60–70km west of Bulgan city, the extinct volcano Uran Uul is part of the 1,600ha Urantogoo Tulga Uul Mountain Natural Reserve. Uran Uul crater is around 600m wide and 50m deep, and at the bottom of it is a small lake 20m in diameter. In the centre of the lake on high ground are some green trees. Other extinct volcanoes are Tulga, Togoo and Jalavch Uul; they stand 12km south of Uran Uul and also enjoy protection in the reserve. Tulga Mountain looks like a brazier, which is the Mongolian meaning of its name.

Eg Tarvagtain Bilcheer Located in Teshig district, this is a scenic area of forests, rivers and mountains, ideal for hiking and camping. Unfortunately, access is not easy owing to the poor road conditions.

Deer stones Around 20km southeast of Bulgan are seven ancient stones, decorated with images of deer and thought to date from the 7th to the 3rd century BC. In the extreme south of the province, approximately 75km south of Bulgan, is the Tsakhiurt stele, an ancient standing stone that is also decorated with a number of deer images. To get there you will need a jeep and driver and travel by off-road routes.

STONE STATUES (ALSO KNOWN AS 'STONE MEN')

Stone men, like deer stones, are thought to commemorate local chieftains, dignitaries and military leaders. The earliest standing stones date from the Bronze Age (Hun period), while others are associated with the Turkic and Uighur periods of the 6th–10th centuries. Turkic funerary stones, known as *balbal*, appear to commemorate military leaders. Some good examples are found in the Shine-ider district.

Typical examples show stone men wearing tunics and holding drinking cups in their hands. Such examples are found in Bulgan Aimag, for example the statue at Züünturuu, north of the village of Bulgan in Bugat district; the anthropomorphic figures in Saikhan district which probably date from the Turkic period; and the famous Enkh-Tolgoi statue in Selenge Aimag (which was 'fed' by local people as may be seen from the state of its mouth!).

DEER STONES

Deer stones are standing stones – cultural monuments dating from the Bronze Age (4th to 3rd century BC). They are usually located at burial sites and erected to mark the grave or commemorate a local person of high rank. Mongolian people are proud of their forebears and regard these ancestral burial stones as sacred. Often small piles of rocks are found beside them. These, too, are considered sacred.

The deer is significant in that it reflects a belief that the Mongol nation sprang from the union of a male and a female, represented by a wolf and a doe. This is the opening passage in *The Secret History of the Mongols* – the 13th-century chronicle of the life and times of Genghis Khan and the birth of the Mongol nation. The deer are very often stylised in form with elongated bodies and large curved antlers. Good examples are found in many provinces, particularly in the western, northern and eastern regions. Deer stones are widespread in western Eurasia and central Asia and are known as the Scytho-Siberian type. Hundreds of deer stones found in the northwestern part of Mongolia belong to the Mongol-Transbaikal type. Fourteen deer stones can be found in the Delgermörön river valley, around the Delgersaikhan River west of Mörön in Khövsgöl Aimag.

For further information, see box *Deer stones in the northern regions*, page 359.

Stone statues Standing stones are found throughout the country and date from different periods. See box, *Stone statues*, on the opposite page, which describes the stones of the Turkic period, such as the ones found 25km north of Bulgan, referred to as *balbal*; some are thought to mark the graves of warriors and chieftains.

ORKHON AIMAG

ERDENET Orkhon Aimag was created in 1994 and is surrounded on all sides by Bulgan Aimag. Erdenet, the centre of Orkhon Aimag, is a very modern city, built in 1974, because of the big copper mine nearby. Some 350km northwest of Ulaanbaatar, Erdenet is Mongolia's third-largest city. It was built with Soviet aid following the Soviet model and has a population of 100,000 (2013). Copper-ore mining is the main industry. Gold is also mined. A new cashmere plant opened in 2013 – the second largest in the country. Erdenet is linked by a spur railway line to Darkhan and the Trans-Mongolian railway.

Getting there from Ulaanbaatar There are two ways to get to Erdenet from UB (via Darkhan): along the 380km-long road and the 12-hour overnight train.

By train Ulaanbaatar to Erdenet via Darkhan takes around 12 hours. The train leaves UB in the evenings and arrives the following morning in Erdenet (times subject to change); currently it departs UB at 19.30. The railway station in Erdenet is located 10km east of the town centre; there are taxis or microbuses that go to and from the station; return tickets may be bought at the bus stop on the east side of Erdenet or at the railway station. There are three classes: hard sleeper costs T6,800; soft (or closed compartment) T20,300; and open compartment of six beds T15,000.

Northern Region ORKHON AIMAG

9

By road Long-distance buses cost T13,000 – a ticket cannot be bought in advance and must be purchased on the day of travel. The bus station is on the road to the train station on the east side of town. Four to five buses leave each day. The first bus departs Ulaanbaatar Dragon Terminal [off map, 232 A4] at 10.00 and the last at 16.00. The trip takes six hours. Minibuses and jeeps are found south of the square beside the market. A microbus costs T14,000 and is a bit faster than the public bus. The driver and passengers wait around until 14 people have committed to travel and then leaves. Microbuses depart for Erdenet from the Dragon Centre in UB and arrive at the East Erdenet station. The standard rate of private travel is is T500–800 per kilometre, depending on the type of vehicle and the deal you strike with the driver. A taxi costs T25,000 per seat and is fastest, leaving, like the micro bus when full (four passengers). Taxis use a parking spot on the north side of the train station in UB as their base. On arrival in Erdenet they go to the east side of town and stop or deliver passengers to their homes or hotels.

Getting around Tourist information is available from tour company guides and local guides found via hotels. During the tourist season local guides may be found at the bus station.

 Where to stay and eat The hotels serve food, usually beefsteak, burgers and Chinese beer. Otherwise try the local market canteens and bars in town.

⌂ **Tamir Tov** South of the sports centre and the football field. Clean & quiet with a restaurant on the 1st floor. **$**

⌂ **Selenge Hotel** Opp the post office on on Sükhbaatar St, west of the park; ☎ 7035 8882. A modern hotel building, with a good standard of rooms with bathrooms. **$**

⌂ **Erdenet Inn** East of Selenge Hotel next to DHL. **$$–$**

⌂ **Molor Erdene** North of the cultural centre; m 9530 7030. Hot Pot restaurant on the 2nd floor. **$$–$**

Shopping

👑 **Erdenet Carpet Factory Shop** 2km west of town; www.carpet.mn/web/en/. Sells a huge array of carpets & felt products.

👑 **Bayan Shopping Centre** Town centre; (⊕ 10.00–20.00 Mon–Sun). Made up of a variety of little shops selling clothes, toys, shoes & food.

👑 **Good Price** On the road leading north of Bayan Shopping Centre; ⊕ 8.00–22.00 Mon–Fri, 9.00–21.00 Sat–Sun. Small supermarket; has local as well as imported food & goods.

What to see and do in Erdenet In the park opposite Selenge Hotel, near the EMC building, a new fountain shows its true colours at night. On Tuesdays, Thursdays and Saturdays (the 'even' days) the fountain is turned into a light show, with the jets moving to music. The best time to come is after dark when the lights are on, although it is still pleasant to come earlier, around 20.00, when the fountain is moving to music without lights, especially to get a seat, as it feels like most of the town comes out to watch! The music does not seem to be exactly the same each night, but the last song is usually the Mongolian national anthem – so learn the words and impress your Mongolians friends! (Josh Wilkie, writer/blogger – see box, *Meteorite watching*, opposite page.)

Aimag Museum (⊕ 09.00–13.00 & 14.00–18.00; *entrance fee T2,000*) Located in the centre of town and exhibits cultural items of the area including some beautiful bronze sculpture and interesting artefacts; traditional combs and bowls.

Cultural Palace On the square off Sükhbaatar Street. Puts on films and song and traditional dance performances as well as pop concerts and classical music recitals.

Mining Museum On the second floor of the Cultural Palace, on the square off Sükhbaatar Street.

Sports Palace South of Sükhbaatar Street, opposite the square, the palace holds wrestling competitions, and ice skating in winter.

SIGHTS IN ORKHON AIMAG
Khögnökhan Uul Nature Reserve Situated in the extreme south of the province. It was designated to protect taiga and steppe plants in an area that comprises several different natural vegetation and climatic zones from mountain forest to grassland steppe. It is a sacred mountain worshipped by local people. The area is visited by tourists although access to the mountain requires a 4x4 vehicle.

Birds At Teshigiin (102° 40.00'E, 49° 54.00'N) you may see swan goose, white-necked crane, common crane and mallard.

Erdenet spring This calcium hydrocarbonate and sulphate spring at Erdenet Mountain remains undeveloped.

SUGGESTED ITINERARIES
Camping and exploring the past Much of Mongolia's charm lies in the fact that you have the freedom to camp and wander at will through some magnificent countryside. You might choose to follow a line of discovery leading through some exciting countryside in quest of ancient burial monuments such as deer stones and *balbal*. Plan your itinerary with a local guide with knowledge of where the stones are – this may involve some riding and hiking. See *Tour operators*, pages 165–9 and 237–9.

METEORITE WATCHING IN MONGOLIA

Josh Wilkie (www.engineerontheroad.com)
I went up to the hill behind Unduur Lug, the Russian/Mongolian communist friendship monument about 200m northwest of Selenge Hotel, in Erdenet, to watch the Perseid meteor shower. The meteors usually radiate from the direction of Perseus and Cassiopeia, but they will appear anywhere in the sky. Mongolia's 250+ days of sunshine and nights of clear skies really add to the spectacle – something I have never been able to see at home in Scotland because of frequently poor weather and living so close to a big city. It was actually the night before the peak of the meteor shower, which is usually on 12 August each year, but I still saw five or six meteorites in just over an hour, some especially bright. It should be twice that number tonight. Apparently, seeing meteorites is quite common in Mongolia, due to the lack of light pollution, good weather and outdoor lifestyle, so you may be lucky enough to see them any time of the year.

I recommend taking a sweater and someone to snuggle up with and finding a reasonable-sized rock to lean back against, and spend a few hours watching these amazing meteor showers.

SELENGE AIMAG

Selenge Aimag borders on Töv (south), Bulgan (west), Khentii (east) and the Russian Federation in the north. If you look for Selenge Aimag on a large-scale map, you'll see that it lies around 250km south of Lake Baikal, a well-known landmark in southern Siberia. There are mountain ranges such as the Bürengiin Nuruu in the west and the Khankhentii Mountains in the east, and two major river valleys bring Mongolia's great rivers, the Selenge and the Orkhon (which enters the province from the southwest), to a point where they converge just south of Sükhbaatar, the aimag centre. The river flows north to enter Lake Baikal. Selenge is a prosperous and interesting province with open-pit gold mining in the north and east regions – including Boroo gold mine, a Canadian-run hard-rock gold mine. Large-scale agriculture produces 40% of the nation's grain and this aimag is known as the breadbasket of Mongolia. The transport system is good; the Trans-Mongolian railway bisects the province in a north–south direction, and express trains pass through between China and Russia, though there are also local services. Altanbulag is Mongolia's northern border town on the main road to Ulan-Ude in Russia. Kyakhta is the Russian border town. The main city of importance within the province is Darkhan, an industrial town, surrounded by its own aimag, Darkhan-Uul, created in 1994 (described at the end of this section). The key cultural site of Selenge Aimag is Amarbayasgalant Monastery.

SÜKHBAATAR Located in the extreme north near the Russian border, this is a quiet agricultural frontier town. The daily market behind the Selenge Hotel is a thriving one. Money can be changed at the bank during normal opening hours or with money-changers who frequent the market when the trains arrive. The station is in the centre of town and plays a dominant role in its life and structure. Sükhbaatar is a long, narrow town that follows the railway track. The market and town square are in the northern part, while the truck station and one of the main hotels, the Orkhon Hotel, are found south of the town, on the road to Ulaanbaatar.

BRIEF FACTS: SELENGE AIMAG

Area 41,200km²
Aimag centre Sükhbaatar
Districts 17
Elevation of Sükhbaataar 626m (the lowest administrative centre in Mongolia)
Livestock and crops Sheep, goats, cattle, horses, potatoes, hay, wheat, fruit
Ethnic groups Khalkha, Buryat, Dörvöd, Ööld, Russian
Distance from Sükhbaatar to Ulaanbaatar 311km
Average temperatures July 19.1°C, January –1.9°C

HIGHLIGHTS
* Amarbayasgalant Khiid
* Selenge Gol
* Yöröö Bayan Golyn Rashaan – spa
* Honeybees

Getting there from Ulaanbaatar

There is no local airport since the train takes most of the passenger traffic and cargo.

By train International trains to and from Beijing and Moscow usually stop late at night or early in the morning at the border crossing for about two hours. There is a local service between Ulaanbaatar and Sükhbaatar. Tickets cost T3,500 for a hard seat and T7,500 for a soft seat. The difference is not in the actual seating but in the number of people per compartment. For long journeys the difference is between two and four berths in soft class and four and six berths in hard class. The extra space offers a degree of greater comfort, especially if travelling long distance. The local (stopping) train journey to Ulaanbaatar takes 9½ hours.

By road Shared taxis travel between Sükhbaatar and Darkhan (92km) and less frequently to Ulaanbaatar (310km) owing to the number of trains. If you want to explore the area and visit Amarbayasgalant Khiid, drivers and jeeps are available outside the station. Standard jeep hire costs apply T500–1,000 per kilometre depending on the type of transport and negotiations with the driver.

Where to stay

🏠 **Hotel Selenge** Near the market in the north, not far from the station. Good standard rooms with bathrooms. **$$**

🏠 **Orkhon Hotel** In the southern section near the truck station. **$$–$**

🏠 **Railway Station Hotel** Beside the railway station. Provides dormitory rooms. **$**

Where to eat and drink
Hotel restaurants charge around T7,000–15,000 for an average meal, or there are the more lively canteens in the market, which offer more choice at half the price.

SIGHTS IN SELENGE AIMAG
Amarbayasgalant Khiid
On the southern slopes of the Bürengiin Nuruu, near Selenge town, this monastery lies in the west (Sant district) of Selenge Aimag, north of the main Darkhan–Erdenet road. Amarbayasgalant is one of the four great monasteries of Mongolia and the most important northern monastery. It is one of the largest monasteries, too, and is also considered architecturally the most beautiful; the proportions of the main temple are exquisite. It is a World Heritage Site; see www.whc.unesco.org.

Built in 1737, the roof-tile work and the enamel ceilings are works of great craftsmanship. Pillars inside the building act as rain ducts. Unfortunately, some buildings were damaged during the religious purges of the 1930s and ten of the 37 temples were destroyed.

Structure and layout The style of the monastery is predominantly Chinese and it has a more unified composition than Erdene Zuu Monastery in the Orkhon river valley. A wall surrounds the temple buildings with the main gate facing south. The symmetric layout can best be seen from a diagram showing the ground plan. Principal buildings are situated along the north–south axis with secondary temples alongside. The main two-storey temple (Tsogchin Dugan) and Labrang (the Bogd Gegeen's living quarters) are central to the whole on the north–south axis. East and west of the entrance are identical temples, the Bell and the Drum temples. Two pavilions stand to the east and west of the main temple, while behind it to the north are temples of guardian figures and other divinities. The tomb of Zanabazar, the 16th-century religious and state leader, is situated among these temples. At the beginning of the 20th century the monastery housed around 8,000 monks, who each had their own special place of worship and lived in *ger* compounds that once flanked the temples on the east and west sides. Restoration work was completed with the help of UNESCO.

SPECIAL TOURS AND ITINERARIE
'Magic Canoe Tour'
It is an adventure to canoe on the great rivers of northern Mongolia. It is possible to do this on your own, but Tseren Tours (*www.tserentours.com*) – founded by Tseren and her Dutch husband Rik – arranges canoeing and fishing trips, with time to stop at Amarbayasgalant Khiid, a beautiful monastery by the River Evin in Selenge Aimag. The valley is famous for its cherry groves.

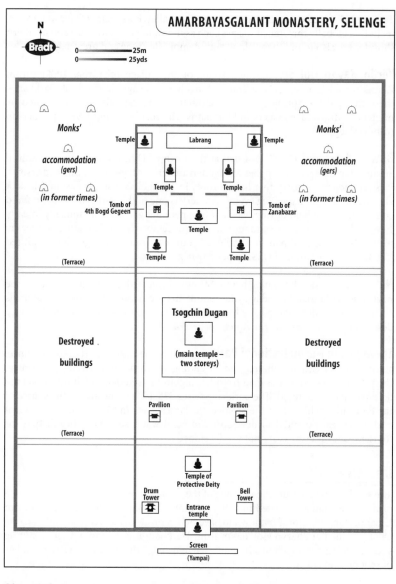

N

Bradt

0 ——— 25m
0 ——— 25yds

Monks'

accommodation
(gers)

(in former times)

Temple

Labrang

Temple

Temple

Temple

Tomb of
4th Bogd Gegeen

Temple

Tomb of
Zanabazar

Temple

Temple

Monks'

accommodation
(gers)

(in former times)

(Terrace)

(Terrace)

Destroyed

buildings

Tsogchin Dugan

(main temple –
two storeys)

Destroyed

buildings

(Terrace)

Pavilion

Pavilion

(Terrace)

Temple of
Protective Deity

Drum
Tower

Bell
Tower

Entrance
temple

Screen

(Yampai)

River Selenge The largest river of Mongolia, the Selenge rises in the Khangai Mountains to flow northeast through southern Khövsgöl, Bulgan and Selenge aimags, before entering Lake Baikal, which is linked to the Arctic Ocean via the Angara and Yenisey rivers. It is 992km long, most of which (593km) flows through Mongolian territory. This river receives 30.6% of the flow of all rivers in Mongolia. It is joined by some of the greatest fishing rivers in the country: the Möröndelger, the Orkhon, the Ider, the Chuluut, the Eg and others.

Birdwatching In the Selenge and Orkhon river valleys you may see Bailhal teal, greylag goose and bean goose; and great bustard and lesser kestrel in the uplands.

Tsaagan Lake, located north of the Selenge river valley, is a special site for waterbirds, including globally threatened species such as the swan goose. Mallard and northern shoveler are also found there, along with damoiselle crane and greylag goose.

Yöröö Bayan Gol Spa Located south of the village of Yöröö, 100km from Züünkharaa – a town on the Trans-Mongolian railway line south of Darkhan – these thermal hot springs are in an attractive mountainous area frequented by hunters, with wooden chalets and hot baths. The cost is around US$15 per person (cabins sleep four).

Bow and arrow factory Located at the town of Dulaankhaan, 60km south of Sükhbaatar, the factory supplies Mongolian archers with modern bows and arrows. It is an ancient industry that has its roots in Mongolia's warrior past and is kept alive by present-day sporting events. Archery is one of the 'three manly sports' and competitions are held during Naadam (the national games, held annually in early July) and throughout the summer months. The factory is worth visiting on the way to Sükhbaatar or Darkhan. You will need your own transport to get there; by hired jeep this will cost around US$100 per day trip.

National parks The Khankhentii Strictly Protected Area cuts through the northwestern aimag boundary. The mountains are densely forested and animals such as wolves, deer and elk are hunted. Birds include owls and woodpeckers (see description of the park in *Töv Aimag*, page 274).

Tarvagatain Nuruu National Park Located in the eastern part of the province, starting 50km east of Uliastai and extending northeast into Arkhangai Aimag, the park is bisected by the road from Ulaangom to Tseterleg which travels via the Solongot Pass (see map). The park comprises 525,440ha. The area is the source of the River Ider, which joins the Selenge, the largest river in Mongolia. This national park has great potential to develop its mineral water springs as health spas for tourism, but these areas are not yet developed.

DARKHAN-UUL AIMAG

The small Darkhan-Uul Aimag is one of the youngest of Mongolia's provinces, one of three new aimags created in 1994. Its centre is Darkhan, located 219km from Ulaanbaatar. This aimag is known to have rich deposits of coal, copper and iron ore. Coal is mined at Sharyn Gol, 63km from Darkhan; in addition new gold mining sites are being developed in adjacent Selenge Aimag. There are also a large number of schools and colleges.

DARKHAN One of the country's larger towns is situated some 100km south of the border with Russia and is connected to Ulaanbaatar by a surfaced road. The town was built almost from scratch out of a small railway settlement in the 1950s as a new industrial town, with local mining of iron ore. The town grew to become important, and has a current population of over 100,000 (2013). It is surrounded by agricultural land and the Trans-Mongolian railway passes through it. Darkhan is divided into four parts: the older town near the railway station with the new town south of it, and two industrial estates to the north and south. Businesses include a large steel plant, the production of building materials, textiles (processing raw hides to produce leather and sheepskin coats), agricultural produce (centred on meat processing for export), fruit and vegetable canning and flour milling. Although not highly geared for tourism the city has good shopping and is a popular stop for tourists on their way to Amarbayasgalant Monastery.

Getting there from Ulaanbaatar

By train There are five trains a day from Ulaanbaatar to Darkhan, a journey of 7½ hours. Trains between Ulaanbaatar and Erdenet stop at Darkhan. The ticket office at Darkhan train station is open 08.00–noon, 16.00–18.00 and 22.00–02.00 daily, and a ticket (one-way) from Ulaanbaatar to Darkhan costs US$10. An international office deals with tickets to Irkutsk and Moscow. Trains also travel from Darkhan to Erdenet.

GLOBAL XCHANGE: VOLUNTEERING IN MONGOLIA   *Faith Trend*

Global Xchange (*c/o VSO, 317 Putney Bridge Rd, London SW15 2PN;* 020 8780 7500/7670; e *enquiry@globalxchange.org.uk; www.vso.org.uk/globalxchange/ index.htm*) is a volunteering organisation, supported by VSO, CSV and the British Council, for young people between the ages of 18 and 25. It organises six-month volunteer programmes – based for three months in the UK and three months in an exchange country. The volunteers are organised into teams of 18: nine young people from the UK and nine from the exchange country. Global Xchange is responsible for all aspects of the volunteers' programmes, including local transport and accommodation, and for the actual programme costs. However, volunteers are asked to raise £600 towards the costs of their trip abroad.

My programme was situated for the first half in Mongolia, and in Luton, Bedfordshire, for the second half. In Mongolia, our host community was based in a town called Sükhbaatar, in the province of Selenge, close to the Russian border. The town has a population of over 20,000. Owing to deforestation the area is surprisingly dry and sandy and the town is full of communist-style buildings, memories of the time when Mongolia was closely linked to the Soviet Union.

With a Mongolian counterpart, I worked in one of the schools in Sükhbaatar. Our main aim was to teach English and organise extra-curricular activities for the children. We also arranged a number of community activities, as a team, based on our research into community needs. We collected toys and clothes for the childcare centre, since two of the volunteers we worked with knew how much the children needed new clothes. Among other projects was a family health day, which was organised to promote healthy eating and lifestyles and, on another occasion, we painted a local kindergarten.

We spent three months living in host homes with our Mongolian counterparts, which helped us to get truly involved in the culture and allowed us to learn about the local Mongolian customs and traditions. It was a fascinating experience to live with this family and despite the obvious language barriers, I felt very close to them by the end of my stay.

The programme taught me a great deal and I have come away much wiser. Living in a different culture was an unforgettable experience and I have gained so many good new friends, especially my counterpart, with whom I am in constant touch by email.

9

Mongolian bees have proved to be hardy and industrious and range over 3km. Ask for honey with your breakfast bun and discover for yourself how delicious the honey these bees produce is! Around 1,500 bee swarms are registered.

Mongolians would like to invest more in this industry, which they believe could be as profitable as cashmere and gold. Apiculture (beekeeping) dates back to the 13th century when the Mongol khans filled their drinking fountains with alcohol, milk and honey. Ancient manuscripts show a picture of the fountain in Karakorum, where mead (a honey drink) poured from one of the branches of a silver tree/fountain. Mongolian folklore and folk songs extol the quality of its honey.

Beekeeping has been developed in several aimags including Selenge. In 1959, 20 swarms were imported to the province from Buryatia and put into hives in Shaamar Research Centre, Shaamar district. Nearly 5,000 swarms were raised in Selenge, in the Bilgüün Sudar beekeeping farm in Darkhan, and elsewhere. Övörkhangai Aimag produces up to 30 tonnes of honey a year. Mongolia's third annual conference on beekeeping, held in 2013, reported growing honey production; eight different honey products are now available at local markets.

For early history of Mongolian bees see www.save-bee.com.

By road There is a good paved road from Ulaanbaatar to Darkhan and the journey takes five-plus hours, depending on the form of transport. Shared taxis and minivans depart frequently to Ulaanbaatar (south), less often to Sükhbaatar (north); they leave from the main square in the new town.

Jeeps for hire (with drivers) are found at the market and at the railway station; the average cost is T800 per kilometre.

🏠 Where to stay

🏠 **Darkhan Hotel** New town, on the east side of the park.**$**

🏠 **The Kiwi Hotel** One of the top hotels outside Ulaanbaatar. Rooms are comfortable & well decorated, the service is excellent & bars & restaurants also are highly rated. **$$$**

🏠 **Nomin Hotel** New town, on the east side of the park. **$**

🏠 **Woods Hotel** New town, just south of the park. **$$**

🗙 Where to eat and drink
The Darkhan and Woods hotel restaurants charge T8,000–18,000 for a main meal. Cafés and bars in the old town serve cheaper food at around T2,000 per dish. You will find beef as well as mutton dishes and more vegetables on the menu than in other parts of the country.

What to see and do in Darkhan

Aimag Museum (🕓 *10.00–17.00 Mon–Sat; entrance fee T2,500*) Located in the new town, southeast of the park near the post office, this museum has exhibits of traditional costumes, religious artefacts and archaeological finds.

Kharaagiin Khiid In the old town of Darkhan, the temple is in an interesting wooden building. There is an active community of monks and religious items are on sale.

SUGGESTED ITINERARIES Travel from Ulaanbaatar by train to Darkhan and stay overnight in the town. Set out by jeep with a guide the following day to visit Amarbayasgalant Monastery, including picnicking in the hills nearby so you can look down on the rooftops and the general layout of this splendid temple complex. Return to Darkhan and have dinner there. Using the same jeep and driver, visit the hot springs at Yöröö Bayan Gol, east of Darkhan, then relax and/or go hiking and enjoy the outdoor life. It is a very out-of-the-way place and roads are not paved so allow five days for the journey. Plan with a tour company, in advance, or a guide/translator and jeep driver on the spot. (See *Tour operators*, pages 165–9 and 237–9.)

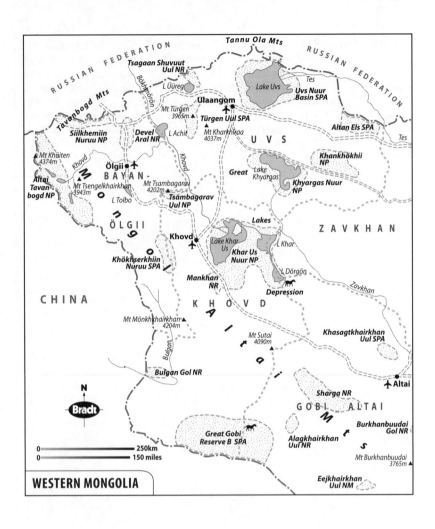

WESTERN MONGOLIA

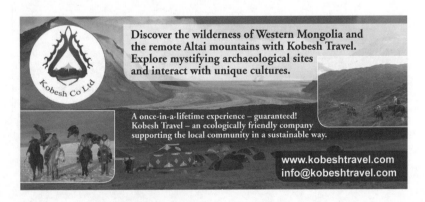

Discover the wilderness of Western Mongolia and the remote Altai mountains with Kobesh Travel. Explore mystifying archaeological sites and interact with unique cultures.

A once-in-a-lifetime experience – guaranteed!
Kobesh Travel – an ecologically friendly company supporting the local community in a sustainable way.

www.kobeshtravel.com
info@kobeshtravel.com

10

Western Region

The western aimags – Khovd, Bayan-Ölgii, Uvs – are very attractive and well worth a visit for the hardier traveller. But they are remote and transport is not easy, with few public bus services. Despite the fact that villages are run-down and there is a small albeit growing tourist infrastructure, those with a pioneering spirit and good stamina will enjoy the region, which is quite unlike other parts of Mongolia. Just bear in mind that the roads are appalling and be prepared to rough it.

Students on their long summer break, hunters and a few tourists venture out west. The overland trip from Ulaanbaatar to Ulaangom (Uvs Aimag) takes a minimum of two days' hard driving. The journey from Ulaanbaatar to Khovd can be achieved in two days, or in a day if you are prepared to drive almost non-stop from 04.00 onwards … the roads, bad as they are, are improving!

KHOVD AIMAG

Khovd is the most visited of the western aimags. The province is divided by the Mongol Altai range. Melting snow from the mountains replenishes the water table every spring, providing Khovd with more than 200 fast-flowing rivers as well as many lakes and streams. The rivers run into the sands and disappear. This

---

BRIEF FACTS: KHOVD AIMAG

Area 76,100km²
Aimag centre Khovd
Districts 17
Elevation of Khovd 1,405m
Livestock and crops Goats, sheep, cattle, horses, camels/potatoes, wheat, melons
Ethnic groups Khalkha, Kazakh, Uriankhai, Zakhchin, Myangad, Torgut, Ööld and Khoton
Distance from Khovd to Ulaanbaatar 1,425km
Average temperatures July 18.9°C, January –25.4°C

HIGHLIGHTS
* Cave paintings at Tsenkheriin Agui
* National parks' mountains and lakes
* Birdwatching, climbing, hiking and riding
* Deer stones and rock carvings

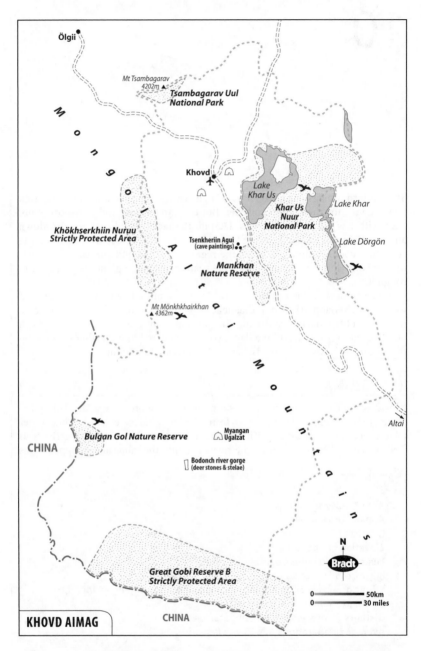

Ölgii

Mt Tsambagarav
4202m ▲

*Tsambagarav Uul
National Park*

Khovd

Lake
Khar Us

*Khar Us
Nuur
National Park*

Lake Khar

Lake Dörgön

*Khökhserkhiin Nuruu
Strictly Protected Area*

Tsenkheriin Agui
(cave paintings)

*Mankhan
Nature Reserve*

Mt Mönkhkhairkhan
▲ 4362m

Altai

Bulgan Gol Nature Reserve

Myangan
Ugalzat

CHINA

Bodonch river gorge
(deer stones & stelae)

N

Bradt

*Great Gobi Reserve B
Strictly Protected Area*

0 — 50km
0 — 30 miles

KHOVD AIMAG

CHINA

subterranean groundwater comes to the surface in springs, creating green oases in the desert, and provides water for livestock, and wild animals in remote places. Semi-desert and saltwater marshes characterise the aimag where the southern and northern sections are barren and dotted with salt lakes. The Great Gobi Strictly Protected Area B extends from Gobi-Altai Aimag in the south into Khovd, along the border with China.

KHOVD The town of Khovd was founded in 1731 as a Manchu outpost. The city is situated on the River Buyant, a tributary of the Khovd River, northern Mongolia's biggest river, after which it is named; at one time it was called Jargalant, which means 'happy'. With its attractive, tree-lined streets – poplars, planted when the Manchus occupied the place – it is a busy, bustling city. From a farming community, producing livestock products (hides and wool), it has emerged as western Mongolia's major city with a population of 35,000 people. The main college in the west is centred here. Of special historical interest is the Manchu fort and the ruins of a walled compound at the northern side of the city, built during the Manchu (Qing) dynasty in the late 1700s; its walls were surrounded by a moat, now filled in. The compound included temples, a Chinese graveyard and the homes of the ruling Chinese families, mostly destroyed when the Manchus were forced to leave the region some 200 years later, in 1912, following a fierce two-day battle after a ten-day siege. There is a thriving market south of the town near the truck station, where you can buy carrots, cabbage, turnips, beetroot, radishes and watermelons – for which the province is famous. Like most markets it is surrounded by a container market selling tinned foods, tea and dumplings at low prices (T1,500).

Getting there from Ulaanbaatar

By air Domestic airlines Aero Mongolia (m *991 640050*) and Eniz (☎ *11 331111*) offer direct flights to Khovd city airport from UB (almost four hours' flight time) and Hunnu Air (formerly Mongolian Airlines) also flies to Khovd and Bulgan airports.

From Khovd to UB by plane (tourist price) costs approximately US$265; return fares (UB–Khovd) work out cheaper at around US$450 (all prices are subject to change). To compare prices and to book in advance visit www.flightsmongolia.com/domestic_flight/hovd.html.

By road Roads are rough, so be forewarned, although new paved roads are under construction. For short distances, riding a horse or a camel is a lot easier and more comfortable. Shared jeeps are the best way to get around if travelling in a small group; to hire a jeep and driver will cost in the region of US$80–100 per day; touring costs less and is negotiable with the driver. A bus from UB (daily) will cost T65,000 and will take two days to get there. Buses also travel to and from Khovd via Arvaikheer, Bayankhongor and Altai; the cost is around T43,000 one-way (a bumpy two–three-day journey).

Car mechanic The Hovd Tour company (*1-1 Magsarjav Street, Jalgalant sum, Khovd (also spelled Hovd)*; m *9904930, 9949919, 9919080*; e *info@hovdtour.mn*; *www.hovdtour.mn*) has an automotive garage, **Khaan Automotive Garage**, if rally drivers experience a breakdown and need car parts or repairs.

Where to stay There are a number of hotels in the city centre that provide rooms with showers, fridge, jug kettle and cable television but there are also excellent opportunities to camp along the Buyant River – that is, until the weather turns cold. In summer many local families choose to move out of the city and enjoy camping along the riverbanks where the water is fresh and cool. To check other *ger* camps see www.mongoliagercamps.net/home/map_of_mongolia.

10

Hotels
Buyant (42 beds) In the north of the town, near the main hospital; ☎ 43 23807. Oldest hotel in town. Service needs improving. Restaurant bar, internet, laundry. **$$–$**

🛏 **Myangat Ugalz** (30 beds) In the north of the town, near the main hospital; ☎43 22086. Laundry, café, cooks for guests. Meals cost T1,500, Mongolian menu. **$**

🛏 **Tsambagarav Hotel** (23 rooms) Located in the centre in front of the main or State Hospital; m 994 32424. Considered the best hotel in the province; newly built B&B with restaurant; serves Mongolian & European dishes. Hotel's souvenir shop sells local handicrafts. *US$45–65 pp per night.*

🛏 **Tüshig** (12 beds) ☎43 22245; e obatzorig@ yahoo.com. B&B, restaurant, sauna. **$**

Guesthouse

🛏 **Orgil Guesthouse** Located near the main square. Bed only. *US$10.*

Ger camps

🔺 **Bayanbulag Camp Resort** (50 beds) m 994 32525; ⊕ during summer. B&B 30km from Khovd town, with sports hall. **$**

🔺 **Buurchiin Gazar** (20 beds) m 994 32118; ⊕ during summer. B&B, 7km from Khovd town, by the Buyant riverside, surrounded by trees, with restaurant, bar, sauna. **$**

🔺 **Grand Ger Camp** 8km from the town; ⊕ during summer. Restaurant, bar. **$$**

🔺 **Mungun Uul** (10 beds) 8km from the town; m 994 32120; ⊕ during summer. B&B, ger camp. **$**

✗ Where to eat and drink

✗ **Bolor Café** Behind the theatre; ⊕ 10.00–22.00 daily. Serves a large variety of food including chicken, fish & stir-fries. Bolor has fast service & is very comfortable for a few people. English & Mongolian menu. *Around US$5.*

✗ **Buyant Restaurant Bar** Next door to the Buyant Hotel; ☎1432 23807; ⊕ 08.00–midnight daily. Offers traditional Mongolian dishes. *US$5–10.*

✗ **Ikh Mongol Restaurant/Bar** Next to the theatre; ⊕ 09.00–23.00 daily. Traditional Mongolian & Asian menu. *Around US$5.*

✗ **Naran Restaurant** Between the light-green HAS & dark-blue HAAN bank buildings; ⊕ 09.00–midnight daily. It is a 2-storey yellow building. The bar is on the 2nd floor. It is famous in Khovd for its variety of food & beverages. English & Mongolian menus. *Around US$5–10.*

✗ **Tsambagarav Restaurant** In the Tsambagarav Hotel; m 994 32424; ⊕ 07.00–22.00 daily. Mongolian, European & Asian menus; meal prices cost from T4,000–7,200.

✗ **Tsomorlig Café** Opposite the police station; ⊕ 10.00–22.00 daily. Mongolian traditional meals, many kinds of salads, beverages & other kinds of meals. *US$5.*

Shopping Local food is to be found at market stalls and in street canteens at the going rate: currently T800–2,500 per dish. You will find many more vegetables here, including root crops like radishes and beetroot; rice is popular and noodles are also served.

🏪 **Central Market of the Western Region** On the left of Ayuush Sq; ⊕ 10.00–18.00. Sells food, clothes, groceries, electronics & car spare parts.

🏪 **Ikh Buyan Market** Next to the Central Market of the Western Region; ⊕ 10.00–18.00. Sells mainly food, groceries & clothes.

🏪 **Souvenir shop** Nr Ayush Sq; ⊕ 09.00–18.00. Sells handmade crafts & paintings by local artists.

Communications

🖥 **Internet** At the post office; ⊕ 08.00–20.00; T500/hr.

🖥 **Internet café** At the Bldg of the Democratic Party; ⊕ 10.00–17.00; T800/hr.

What to see and do in and around Khovd

Aimag Museum (⊕ *09.00–18.00; entrance fee T2,800*) One block north off the main square, next to the post office, the museum features a facsimile of the cave paintings at Tsenkheriin Agui (see page 388). It also exhibits a collection of Khovd national costumes, Buddhist and Kazakh art; wild animal skins like the critically endangered snow leopard; and a collection of ancient deer stones.

Türeemel Amarjuulagai Khiid Just two minutes' walk north of the main square, this monastery replaced the original Shar Süm (Yellow Temple), which was built in the 1770s on the outskirts of the city. It was completely destroyed in the religious purges of 1937.

JOURNEY HOME: FINDING MY ROOTS
Azaa Ulziitogtokh

All my life I grew up hearing about and imagining my grandfather's birthplace, but I never went there until I was old enough and the political situation had changed. This was the case for most people who grew up in cities in Mongolia in the 1970s/80s. Our summer holidays were spent in *dachas* (small, wooden, Russian-style cabins) on the outskirts of Ulaanbaatar. As a child, I remember my granddad told me stories about the province where he came from. He was a very educated and intelligent person and he was also a lama (monk); he studied in a monastery until the revolution of 1921. Later during the anti-religious campaigns to destroy Buddhism my granddad left the monastery. He became an accountant and a part-time herdsman; somehow he managed to look after his four small children after my grandmother died when the youngest was only a year old. How pleased he would have been to see the successful lives of my uncles and aunts today. (The author would like to add: 'Proud of you too Azaa!' – a highly trained accountant for an international organisation).

My grandparents came from Khovd Aimag. They are Uriankhai people – known as the Altai Mongols, an ethnic population in Khovd and Bayan-Ölgii provinces. Uriankhai follow strict customs, which in fact are followed by most Mongols. We were taught as children to respect older people and learn from them. We were taught by example and through traditional sayings. Even as a child, this advice always sounded better than preaching or nagging. For example, if a child was lazy and didn't finish a job, they would say: if you put salt in the food, it should dissolve; meaning if you start a job, finish it. To teach respect, they would say: you have a brother like a coat has a collar. We learned not to be spoiled, but to be tough.

It is the local Uriankhai custom to arrange marriages between young people. There is a ceremony to introduce the bride to each member of the groom's family. It is important for the bride to respect her in-laws, and in turn for them to respect her. It is believed that family blood is cleared after nine generations, therefore it is important to marry 'out of the family'. People say that this is one reason why there are so many talented and intelligent people among the Uriankhai!

Having heard my granddad's tales in my youth I finally got to see the western region and learn more about its hospitality and local customs. People in Khovd region are so friendly, you almost feel uncomfortable to take so much pleasure, and they will insist on providing meals and giving gifts. Most people eat dairy products and meat, especially boiled mutton and steamed dumplings. As half the population grow watermelons, there are always plenty of melons to offer guests. It is an exciting place to visit to experience the lifestyle and customs and see such magnificent landscape.

Magsarjav Theatre (*Tickets from US$10 (tourist price)*) In the centre of town off the main square (east side), the theatre offers traditional local song and dance entertainment.

Yamaat Ulaan Uul ('Red Mountain of Goats') To the northeast of the town, this bright red granite hill rises abruptly and offers a fairly tough day's hike to the summit. Ibex may be spotted on the mountainsides.

Baatarkhairhan Mountain Next to Khovd airport (2km from town centre). This mountain is a historical site with many ancient petroglyphs.

Mineral springs There is one big spring northeast of the city on the road to Buyant and Myangad sums. It is said that it cures poisoned drinks! There is another spring on the mountain directly behind the town, called 'drop spring', about 5km from the city centre. Local people believe it is good for heart conditions.

Buyant River The Buyant River goes through the town and many people enjoy swimming in it.

SIGHTS IN KHOVD AIMAG

Tsenkheriin Agui Some 90km southeast of Khovd city, these caves are famous for their remarkable paintings that date from the Palaeolithic Age (20,000–15,000 years ago). The paintings are an outstanding example of the cave art of Stone Age man, depicting bulls, ibex, wild sheep (*argali*), camels and gazelles and, interestingly, showing mammoths and ostriches that lived in Mongolia at that time. The animals, birds, snakes and trees are painted on a yellow and white background in deep red and brown pigments, but unfortunately they have been defaced by graffiti.

Two caves were excavated in 1967 by a joint Soviet–Mongol team. Research confirms that Stone Age hunters populated the whole of the mountainous region of western Mongolia along the Altai and the Great lakes. The largest cave is 15m high with a floor measurement of 12m by 18m. Bring a good torch, warm clothes and watch out for bird droppings underfoot.

National parks and nature reserves

Bulgan Gol Nature Reserve Located near the southwestern national border over 250km from Khovd, the reserve was originally established to preserve sable and Mongolian beaver. You may see stone marten and the eastern imperial eagle. It is difficult place to reach, with no proper roads.

Great Gobi Strictly Protected Areas A and B On the southern border with China, 300km from Khovd, the protected area is designated in two sections: A and B. The areas protect wild ass, wild camels and rare antelopes and also many small rodent species including rare pikas and jerboas. Rarely visited by tourists; permission is required. For further details on protected areas see pages 140–1.

Khar Us Nuur National Park (*Entrance fee T2,500 & T4,500 per vehicle*) In the northwest part of the province, around 60km east of Khovd town, this national park was set up in the basin of the Great Lakes of western Mongolia to protect water- and marsh-birds. It comprises three large lakes: **Khar Us**, **Khar** and **Dörgön**, home to rare migrant pelicans. The steppe area around them protects the habitat of steppe antelope. Birds of prey like falcons, steppe eagles and buzzards inhabit the region, living on many small rodent kills, as well as larger kills of marmot and desert fox. The bird sanctuary on the western shore of the lake is open to tourists and birds listed there include the endangered white-headed duck and rare relict gull.

Khar Us Nuur (Black Water Lake) Mongolia's second-largest freshwater lake (72km by 27km) is in the eponymous national park. It is relatively shallow with an average depth of 4m. Among the many species of birds are Dalmatian pelican, white-headed duck, swan goose, Pallas's fish eagle, greater spotted eagle, lesser kestrel, white-naped crane, great bustard, white spoonbill and great crested grebe; it is the perfect habitat for waterfowl. The best times to see the birds are in May and late August. Since the lake is huge and access is difficult it is advisable to be accompanied by a guide or park ranger, who can bring you to the best birdwatching spots. The marsh delta where the Khovd River enters the lake is a good place, but watch out for mosquitoes and use insect repellent. You will need a permit to visit the national park; this can be obtained from the Khar Us National Park office in Khovd (43 2334; e kharus@magicnet.mn). Prices are subject to change.

Khar Nuur (Black Lake) On the northeastern aimag boundary with Zavhan, 100km east of Khovd, Khar Nuur receives water from Khar Us and drains into Dörgön Lake. It covers an area of 37km by 24km with a maximum depth of 7m. Birdlife abounds on its low desert shores, and it is also rich in fish.

Between the Khar and Khar Us lakes are the twin peaks of **Jargalant Khairkhan Uul** (3,796m) and **Yargaitin Ekh Uul** (3,464m) – wonderful places to camp, birdwatch and hike to see wildlife. Here you may spot birds such as saker falcon, Hodgson's bushchat, lammergeier, Altai snowcock and Mongolian accentor; look out for Eurasian lynx, Pallas's cat, grey wolf, corsac fox, red fox, Siberian ibex, *argali* and the elusive snow leopard (a snow leopard mother and her three cubs were filmed in summer, autumn and winter 2012/13 by a Japanese television crew). World wildlife Mongolian teams monitor snow leopards in this area.

Dörgön Nuur To the south of Khar Nuur, Dörgön Nuur is 145km southeast of Khovd town, on the boundary with Zavkhan and Gobi-Altai aimags. Although it receives fresh water from Khar Nuur, it is a saltwater lake, covering an area of 305km².

To the east of Dörgön Lake is **Khömiin Tal Wild Horse Site** – see *Zavkhan Aimag*, page 366. This interesting research base and site for *takhi* is most easily accessed via Khovd Aimag overland routes. (See location on map, page 384.)

Khökhserkhiin Nuruu Strictly Protected Area Located on the northwest border with Bayan-Ölgii, 50km west of Khovd, this protected area of 65,920ha is

CAMELS OF THE WEST

Mongolia has the third-largest camel population in the world. Camels of the west have thick, russet or red-brown wool and are very handsome creatures; fine camel hair is one of Mongolia's exotic exports. Camels are the two-humped Bactrian variety, which unlike the single-humped dromedary, can survive exceedingly cold temperatures; milking is a special skill and females have to be coaxed by whistles and songs to let milk down. The milk is rather salty and, like Guinness, is an acquired taste.

designated to protect the habitat of *argali* sheep, ibex and snow leopard. Access is difficult and is a strictly protected area. Birdlife includes yellow breasted bunting, alpine accentor, white-winged snowfinch and white-winged redstart.

Mankhan Nature Reserve (*Entrance fee T1,000 pp & T3,000 per vehicle; limited tourist facilities*) A protected area for endangered species of antelopes, Mankhan is located 95km southeast of Khovd city. The park, also a bird sanctuary (so bring binoculars), is often visited due to its proximity to the cave paintings at Tsenkheriin Agui.

Tsambagarav Uul National Park On the northwestern boundary of Khovd Aimag with Bayan-Ölgii Aimag, 80km north of Khovd, the 110,960ha national park was set up to protect the habitat of rare species like the snow leopard. It offers possibilities for climbing and hiking. Despite its height of 4,202m, Tsambagarav Bogd, Mongolia's fifth-highest mountain, is fairly accessible. Any mountain tour requires good planning and competent, experienced guides. For climbing you will need crampons, an ice axe and ropes, and plenty of experience to reach the summit.

For more casual visitors, there is a jeep route to the mountain base from the main Khovd–Ölgii road, leading through Kazakh villages along the Namarjin Valley to a turquoise lake. Another place to visit is the Bayangol Valley, which has remarkable views of Khar Us Nuur. Driving is difficult due to poor road conditions, so it is best to find a driver who knows the area. If you want to hike and climb there are several tour companies specialising in mountaineering or hiking in the area (see page 166).

 Countryside camps These camps are useful for hiking and nature treks.

▬ **Bishrelt Enerel** (10 beds) Unch sum, 320km from Khovd town; ☼ during summer. **$**

▬ **Bodonch Camp** (10 beds) 270km from Khovd town; ☼ during summer. **$**

▬ **Büregten Öndör** (10 beds) Üyench sum, 300km from Khovd town; ☼ during summer. **$**

▬ **Myangan Ugalzat** (10 beds) Tsetseg som, 280km from Khovd town; ☼ during summer. **$$–$**

▬ **Urtunt Ger Camp** (10 beds) Altai sum, 290km from Khovd town; ☼ during summer. **$**

BAYAN-ÖLGII AIMAG

Bayan-Ölgii Aimag nestles among the towering snow-capped peaks of the Altai range, with steep ravines falling to dry, arid steppe. The province borders on China's Xinjiang Autonomous Region in the southwest and the Altai Republic (part of the Russian Federation) in the northwest. In the far north of Bayan-Ölgii there is a short length of border with the Tuva Republic (also part of the Russian Federation). Mongolia's highest mountain, Mount Khüiten (4,374m) in the Tavan Bogd Mountains, belongs to this area, located in the northwest where the borders of three countries, Mongolia, China and Russia, meet. Mount Khüiten is surrounded by glaciers and permanent snow; its lower reaches are covered by pine and larch forests while willow trees grow by mountain streams. Much of the aimag is treeless and vegetation is sparse. Camels are well adapted to the harsh, arid conditions; wool and milk is taken from them and they are also used as much-needed transport but unfortunately herd sizes are in decline. Hunting and subsistence agriculture are the main occupations. This westernmost aimag of Mongolia is unlike Mongolia's other provinces. The population consists primarily of Turkic Kazakhs – the largest minority in Mongolia. Kazakhs have their own language and customs. Around 90%

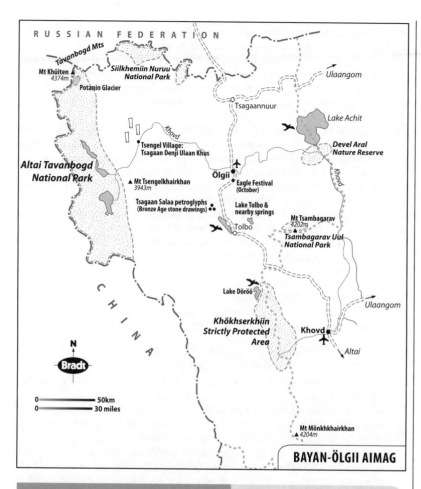

BAYAN-ÖLGII AIMAG

BRIEF FACTS: BAYAN-ÖLGII AIMAG

Area 45.700km²
Aimag centre Ölgii
Districts 14
Elevation of Ölgii 1,710m
Livestock Goats, sheep, cattle
Ethnic groups Kazakh, Khalkha, Dörvöd,
Uriankhai, Tuva
Distance from Ölgii to Ulaanbaatar 1,636km
Average temperatures July 15.5°C, January –17.8°C

HIGHLIGHTS

* Kazakh eagle hunting
* National parks – mountains, lakes and waterfalls
* Archaeology – stone men and petroglyphs
* Adventure tourism – rally driving, climbing, hiking, rafting

10

of the population are Muslims. Many emigrated to Kazakhstan in the 1990s but found that life was no easier there and some have returned.

The alpine lakes and mountains are protected by a number of national parks (see page 399). Besides natural beauty, the aimag offers many archaeological sites including *balbal* (Turkic stone figures), deer stones, *kurgan* (burial mounds) and 10,000 petroglyphs at Tsagaan Salaa (Baga Oigor River).

ÖLGII Located in the valley of the Khovd River, the centre of Bayan-Ölgii means 'cradle' or 'birthplace'. The town square is surrounded by local government buildings, shops and a museum. Four main streets run in parallel pairs from the main square. There is a post office, the bus station, a department store, a cinema and a number of restaurants. The flat-roofed buildings, made from twigs and mud, give the town a Middle Eastern look; other obvious Islamic-style buildings include a mosque and *madrasa* (Muslim place of learning). The earth-oven flat bread is typically Kazakh and is baked in much the same way throughout central Asia. Kazakh can be written in Arabic script, as you will notice on street signs, but mostly they're in Cyrillic. There are 101,526 Kazakhs in Mongolia according to the 2010 census – most live in western Mongolia.

Getting there from Ulaanbaatar

By air There are scheduled four-hour flights from Ulaanbaatar – see Aero Mongolia (*visitor centre, main square;* \ *8808 0025*) and Eznis (*2nd Fl, Cashmere*

MONGOLIAN KAZAKH EAGLE HUNTERS   *Alan Gates*

The aimag (province) of Bayan-Ölgii is in the far northwest of Mongolia with about 1.5 million head of livestock and a human population of roughly 100,000, mainly Kazakhs. They speak their own language and their culture is quite unlike the rest of Mongolia. Whereas most Mongolians are Buddhists the Mongolian Kazakhs are mostly Muslim, and they love to hunt with their eagles.

The Kazakh word for eagle is *berkut* and a hunter who trains and hunts with a berkut is known as a *berkutchi*. They use golden eagles that live and breed in their mountains, and they only use the female of the species, as she is larger than the male. This size difference is typical of all diurnal birds of prey, the larger female *berkut* is used mainly for hunting foxes; the hunting season is in winter, usually between early October and early February.

Hunting is done on horseback as is virtually everything in Mongolia; the *berkut* is carried on the right arm as opposed to Western falconers who carry their hawks on their left. The greater weight of the female *berkut* is supported by a forked support fitted to the saddle called a *baldark*. She is hooded with a specially made hood called a *tomega* to keep her calm. It is removed when scanning vast areas of steppe from a high vantage point to take advantage of those wonderful 'eagle eyes'. An eagle can spot movement, even the slightest twitch, from a great distance – sometimes a mile or more. An experienced *berkutchi* can read his *berkut's* body language and will release her to fly, sometimes from just the feel of her tightening grip on his gloved arm, indicating she has spotted prey. When the *berkut* is in pursuit the Kazakhs show their mastery of horsemanship, and often the high-speed descent of the mountain and subsequent race across the steppe is an exhilarating experience.

The Kazakh tradition of using the *berkut* to hunt foxes, and at one time wolves, goes back centuries. The skill and knowledge has been passed down

Bldg, next to post office; ✆ *7042 7337*) flight schedules are online. It is also possible to fly out of Bayan-Ölgii to Kazakhstan or elsewhere in central Asia, with a tour group.

For booking in advance go to www.flightsmongolia.com/domestic_flight/ulgii_western_mongolia.html.

By road A public bus runs from UB to Ölgii Monday, Wednesday and Friday, leaving Dragon Centre depot at 15.00; cost T85,500 (US$60). A jeep (hired or shared) is the usual means of long-distance transport; from UB to the far west costs around US$600 per jeep and driver.

Tourist information and tour guide operators

ℹ Visitor information centre Southeast cnr of Main Square; shared with the Protected Areas Administrative Office. You may find more abut the area's national parks. The centre will help with tours, transport and travel plans (Aero Mongolia shares the same building).
Agii Maksum Kobesh Travel, Ölgii; m 991 07676/981 67676; www.kobeshtravel.com. One of the most experienced guides in Mongolia & founder of his own travel company. He has arranged tours for many TV companies & has a global set of clients. He also teaches English in a state school, & has trained a generation of young Mongolians. He is currently developing a new hotel in the centre of town.
Doshan Kazakh Tour, PO Box 111, Ölgii; m 994 22006; www.kazakhtour.com. Excellent guide & interpreter.

through the generations: father, son and grandson. It is not unusual to see boys of ten years old and younger handling their father's *berkut*, who can be nearly as big as they are.

To experience some time living with a *berkutchi* family and going out on a horseback hunt with a trained *berkut* is best done through a guide/interpreter.

Winter in Mongolia can be cold, and winter in the highest aimag can be even colder, so it is wise to pick the month to visit with some thought. October is the first month that hunting with the *berkut* really starts, and for most of the month the temperature is not seriously low. October is also when the Altai Eagle Festival is held in Ölgii, a celebration of the Kazakh tradition and their love of the golden eagle. Generally held over two days and attended by up to 70–80 *berkutchi* dressed in their finery, they compete for the best livery of themselves, their horse and their *berkut*. On the second day they compete on the steppe in a number of flying tests to find the overall winner.

If successful hunting is your goal, then a visit in November holds more promise. The temperature has dropped, the *berkuts* are fitter after the lazy days of summer, and if you are lucky there is a dusting of snow. During December, January and February the temperature is getting serious with midday temperatures sometimes not getting above −20°C.

Alan Gates has trained, hunted and bred golden eagles for 40 years, and enjoyed many hunting trips with the Kazakh people in Mongolia, Kyrgyzstan and China. For more information visit his website (www.eaglefalconer.com). Alan recommends guide/interpreter/tour operator Canat Cherazadda of Blue Wolf Travel (see page 394), who is Kazakh and is related to many of the best berkutchi families.

Canat Cherazadda Blue Wolf Travel, PO Box 071, Ölgii; ☎70422772; m 991 10303; e info@bluewolftravel@gmail.com; http://bluewolftravel.com. Recommended by contributors to this guide.

Altai Expeditions Bayan-Ölgii; m 994 27003; e bek@altaiexpeditions.com; discover-bayanolgii.com/altai-expeditions. Offers expedition travel & tours – own *ger* camp facilities. Works with the local NGO, Kazakh Family Development, that involves local people & their handicrafts & other skills.

Kobesh Travel Bayan-Ölgii; m 991 07676, 9816 7676; e maksum_agii@yahoo.com; www.kobeshtravel.com. Specialises in adventure tours around Mongolia, particularly in the western region; Kazakh eagle hunting, fishing & wildlife tours. See ad, page 382.

🏠 Where to stay

🏠 **Bastau Hotel** (15 rooms) m 976 9942 7087 Centre of town next to the main square. Hotel café serves Mongolian dishes. Dormitory rooms with cold showers are available from US$10. **$**

🏠 **Duman Hotel** Town centre. Considered one of the best hotels. Bedrooms have hot showers & Wi-Fi service is provided. **$$–$**

🏠 **Hotel Tavan Bogd** A short distance from the main square (west side). The hotel restaurant serves local spicy dishes for around T3,000–7,000 (US$2–5). It is considered as one of the better hotels in town; rooms can be pricey. **$$–$**

🏠 **Traveller's Guest House** m 994 24505; e nazkana@fastmail.fm. The only guesthouse in town with Wi-Fi & hot showers; provides services such as airport collection & helps arrange tours. **$**

Ger *camps*

🏠 **Altai Expeditions** (11 *gers*) 8km outside town; Altai Expeditions m 994 27003. All facilities including a restaurant.

🏠 **Blue Wolf** 1km south of town on the Khovd road; Blue Wolf Travel m 99110303 or 504 20303; e info@bluewolftravel.com; www.bluewolftravel.com.

🍴 Where to eat and drink
In addition to that served at the Hotel Tavan Bogd, good local food is available at Kazakh teahouses and small café restaurants. Guanzes and Uighur Guanzes (serving the small local Uighur population), located near the market, offer milky tea and *buuz* or khoshuur dishes at T3,000+. The market-bazaar sells kebabs at around T500–1,000.

🍴 **Pamukkale** Turkish Restaurant, located northeast of the Main Square near the police station; m 990 94593/991 99944; ⊕ 10.00–23.00 daily. Known to be the best restaurant in town; opened in 2005. Serves Turkish & Mongolian food, kebabs, soups & chicken dishes along with delicious Turkish coffee & desserts. The atmosphere is great & the food delicious. *Meals cost around T15,000, or T4–9,000 a dish.*

🍴 **Blue Wolf Restaurant** Located south of the Main Square next to the Blue Wolf *ger* camp, 1km south of town centre on the road to Khovd. Serves Kazakh food that caters for local tastes & international travellers. Many eating there have meals included with their accommodation costs. *Meals cost around US$10.*

Shopping
The **market (bazaar)** (*northeast of Central Square, east of the Aimag Museum;* ⊕ *noon–18.00 Tue–Sun; free admission*) sells fruit, vegetables, meat and milk products, Chinese goods and Kazakh handicrafts. Stalls sell a variety of products from embroidery to cashmere. It is a convenient place to stock up on food and other supplies because just at the main entrance is the meeting place for shared jeeps, ready to travel to outlying districts.

What to see and do in Ölgii
Aimag Museum (⊕ *9.00–noon & 13.00–17.00 Mon–Sat (closes for lunch) and 10.00–17.00 Sat; entrance fee T5,000*) Located in the centre of town, the museum

exhibits on three floors, displaying items of local culture, history and natural history, with explanations in text translated into English. Outside a number of standing stones are exhibited. The museum shop sells Kazakh crafts.

Kazakh National Theatre (*Tickets US$5 (tourist price)*) A few minutes' walk south of the main square, the red walled building of the theatre is easily recognised as it is the tallest building in Ölgii. Puts on local cultural performances in the tourist season. Tickets may be bought on the day in the basement of the building.

Bathhouse Southwest of the square on Sagsai and Tsagaannuur Road. Provides hot showers (T1,500), massages (T10,000) and haircuts (T2,000).

Other practicalities The post office in centre town has several ATM machines, an internet café, printing and fax machines; posts packages and postcards worldwide.

SIGHTS IN BAYAN-ÖLGII AIMAG

Hot springs The springs are high above the treeline at 2,480m, 50km west of Delüün district centre and around 100km southwest of Bayan-Ölgii, and to visit them you will need your own transport. It is a beautiful area, undeveloped at present, but has potential for tourism. Other springs in Delüün district are Chikhert warm spring at Chigirt and Gantsmod hot springs.

Lake Tolbo Lake Tolbo (*tolbo* meaning spot or stain) is on the road from Khovd to Ölgii (140km northwest of the former, 70km south of the latter). A high-altitude freshwater lake, Tolbo was the venue of a major battle fought between Bolsheviks and White Russians. The shoreline is treeless and the water clean but it is ice cold and only the bravest swimmers dip in there. Chikhertiin Rashaan (springs) are east of the lake. In this area you may spot red fox, bar-headed geese and saker eagles.

CULTURAL LANDSCAPE

The mountainous landscape of western Mongolia is an exciting discovery both in terms of landscape and culture. Put the two together and you have a really potent combination: cultural landscape. Getting to grips with the ancient past throws up challenges to discover more about the remote mountainous Altai region around Bayan-Ölgii. There are tantalising relics of past civilisations about which we know very little – standing stones and mounds of past times haunt the imagination and demand better explanations. Archaeological work by researchers at the University of Oregon has located and listed many items in this area so that the past is beginning to reveal its legacy to the present. To discover more about what to see and do visit their website: http://mongolianaltai.uoregon.edu/cultural_landscape.php.

UNESCO (http://whc.unesco.org/en/list/) defines 'cultural landscape' as a landscape endowed with powerful, religious, artistic or cultural associations'. Petroglyphic complexes of the Mongolian Altai were registered in 2011 as a World Heritage Site.

The Mongolian government along with UNESCO has protected three major archaeological sites in the Altai area of western Mongolia. These sites include the petroglyphs of Bayan-Ölgii Aimag at Tsagaan Salaa-Baga Oigor in Ulaankhus district; findings at Upper Tsaagan Gol (Shiveet Khairkhan); and findings at Aral Tolgoi in Tsengel district. The development of Mongolian culture from prehistoric times to the present day may be shown and illustrated over a period of 12,000 years by such rock art – ancient drawings that both reflect on and record human culture in this region. The petroglyphs and the rocks themselves are well preserved because they are found far enough away from roads to avoid damage by the urge that people have to draw over them. Herders of the area have become involved in their protection. See *Archaeology*, pages 10–13.

Lake Döröö Located in a remote part of Tolbo district on the main road to Khovd, 45km from Tolbo town and 75km south of Ölgii, this is a superb mountain lake. The area around the lake seems to have been an important burial site as there are many tombs there. It's an ideal place for camping and hiking, though you'll need your own transport.

TEXTILES AND EAGLE HUNTERS IN WESTERN MONGOLIA

Beshlie McKelvie
Fine horses and fierce eagles are the wings of the Kazakhs.

Ancient Kazakh proverb

Mongolia is one of the most wild and remote places on earth, near the Russian and Kazakhstan border, in the high Altai Mountains.

Kazakh nomads have roamed the mountains and valleys of western Mongolia with their herds since the 19th century. Traditionally the Mongolian Kazakhs are Sunni Muslims. The men hunt with eagles. The women of the nomadic eagle hunters will spend up to five months in the freezing winter months hand embroidering *tuskizz* (blankets) for their *gers*.

The hunters who use the golden eagles have lived in equilibrium with them for as long as falconry can be traced in history. I rode side by side with these nomadic hunters astride strong mountain ponies that have lived out on the steppe as far back as man can remember. We rode over 60km to the eagle festival. It was fast at times, taking off at a wild gallop at the sight of a fox, over scraggy rocks with landscapes so vast they take your breath away and touch your heart.

The festival was held beneath a great mountain where some 70 nomadic hunters turned out. They were all dressed in their finest wolf coats and fox hats, wearing hunting pouches made from bright textiles with adorning leather and fur, and mounted proudly on horseback with their loyal partners, the golden eagles. They were here to test their skills before a panel of judges. The high fierce shrieks could be heard as up soared the eagle with the hunter mounted on horseback and so the games began. It was a relationship so extraordinary, so ancient and deeply woven between man and wild bird. The most amazing bond and understanding I have ever encountered between sky and earth.

Birds The lakes of Bayan-Ölgii offer a variety of birdlife such as swan goose, bar-headed goose, Dalmatian pelican, redstarts and snowfinch, while in the mountains areas there are falcons and eagles including golden eagle, Pallas's fish eagle and saker falcon.

Petroglyphs and deer stones There are a great many of these fascinating ancient historic stones found in the aimag – examples can be found at **Tsagaan Salaa**, some 50km south of Ölgii, whereas examples of petroglyphs of the Stone and Bronze ages are located near the Ölgii–Khovd road. A local guide can show you some of the better-known examples. Deer stones are also found near Tsagaan village, around 100km west of Ölgii at **Tsagaan Denj**, and **Ulaan Khus** beside the River Khovd in the northwest part of the province (see map). Your own transport is essential to visit these sites, as is a driver who knows the region.

Festivals
Kazakh Nauryz (New Year) A three-day festival celebrated at the spring equinox is the biggest holiday of the year for Kazakh people. The tradition is to first clean your home, then to visit relatives beginning with the oldest; feast on traditional soup, meat dishes and fermented milk; parade in traditional costumes; and participate in games including Kyz Kuar (the women's chase on horseback). There are also theatrical events and concerts; tugs of war and much else.

At times it was like being in an ancient fairy tale. Sleeping out in *gers* beneath the stars, washing in rivers and cooking on fires. I had to pinch myself at times to know this was real. I was told by a shaman that Mongolia is a place where you are spiritually invited when you are ready. I felt so blessed to be here, with these kind, humble nomadic people, with their shamanic ways and deep understanding of their environment in which they live and survive.

Trade justice for the developing world and for this generation is a truly significant way for the developed countries to show commitment to bringing about an end to global poverty.

Nelson Mandela

I was also in Mongolia to research my next textile project. I have always been fascinated by the rich, intricate textiles that are based on ancient Islamic art arabesque – hand embroidered by the women of this ancient culture.

The Lianong goats owned by every nomadic family have survived for thousands of years in these cold windswept conditions where a valuable underwool is produced. Mongolian cashmere is the finest and softest in the world. Cashmere wool is combed each spring by the nomadic herders with generations of expertise.

And so I plan to return to wild western Mongolia to work with the local women to start a joint project to set up a small women's co-operative where their skills will be harnessed and woven into something beautiful, something magical, something wearable.

I can't wait to return …
See www.beshliemckelvie.com.

Eagle Festival (UNESCO World Cultural Event) The major Golden Eagle Festival (GEF) is held annually in early October near the town of Bugat, 9km south east of Olgii, organised by the Eagle Hunters Association along with local tour companies. It costs US$40 per person for two days. Buses depart from the town centre – the bus laid on by Kazakh Tours costs US$10 for two days – and take you to the festival site and back. Seventy eagle hunters parade on horseback displaying their trained eagles and showing their skills as hunters; there are games, camel races and competitions, like the Kazakh game of *tiyn teru* – picking up a coin from the ground from a galloping horse. Prizes are given to the best-dressed man, woman and child.

The major eagle festival is sponsored by travel companies like Nomadic Expeditions. Several smaller eagle festivals happen during the month of September arranged by local travel companies: eg: Altai Expeditions and Blue Wolf Tours at Sagsai (20km west of Ölgii) on the third weekend of September; a 6km camel race is another highlight. The festival costs US$30. Food and drink are sold on location and transport provided for around US$10.

MINOR PROBLEMS: MORRIS MINOR TO MONGOLIA

Rob Kinder

Twenty-four-year-old law students Rob Kinder and Duncan Ealand took part in the Mongol Rally. In this annual event 200 teams endeavour to drive clapped-out cars with small engines a quarter of the way around the world, raising money for charity at the same time. There is no set route, absolutely no back-up and just a few haphazard plans of how to get to Ulaanbaatar. Not satisfied that this was going to be difficult enough we opted to do the journey in 'Jill', a 1965 Morris Minor bought for £100.

Driving in Mongolia in any vehicle is not for the faint-hearted, and driving in a beaten-up classic car could be considered lunacy. On our first day over the border both sides of our rear suspension snapped and our exhaust fell off. Mongolia does not really 'do' roads but prefers a chaotic muddle of dirt and sand tracks. Most are pot-holed and many cursed with a ridged surface that shakes you to the bone. But don't give up, because tarmac has arrived and is beginning to be laid around the country. Some of this heads west out of UB and it was somewhat frustrating to find it all being resurfaced when we eventually got there.

That we got there at all was a miracle. Twice we found ourselves lost in the Gobi, something advisable only to the most adventurous of travellers. Fortunately you can always rely on GPS. The *Ger* Positioning System is faultless: seek out one of these small white tents, homes to nomadic Mongolians, and find out where on earth you are. 'Jill' required much TLC, some of which was provided by enterprising local mechanics. Perhaps our most desperate but reassuringly 'British' moment was using a rugby ball as a replacement for the broken suspension. We had spares for most parts of the car and nearly all were required. It is essential to have jerrycans for fuel and water, and a good stove for cooking.

Crossing from west to east gave us the chance to see much of what Mongolia has to offer. We rarely encountered more than a few camels and inquisitive goat herders and it was an unforgettable experience to carve through this stunning country. See more about our journey on the website www.minorproblems.co.uk.

National parks Khökhserkhiin Nuruu (mountain range) is a strict area shared with neighbouring Khovd Aimag. It lies roughly 130km so The Khökhserkhiin Mountains extend over 50km southeast to the r the Mongol Altai range. Here you may see snowcock and rare fauna ibex, Siberian deer and *argali* (wild sheep). The park is not frequented by tourists.

Altai Tavanbogd National Park (ATB) (*Entrance fee T3,000 & T4,500 for vehicles*) This park of some 636,161ha is the largest in Mongolia. It lies some 150km west of the aimag centre, Ölgii, and within its boundaries are Mongolia's highest mountain, Mount Khüiten, and some stunning mountain lakes, among them Khoton, Khorgon and Dayan. Rare species of wildlife found here include *argali*, ibex, Asiatic red deer (maral deer) and elk, while Altai snowcock and eagles are among the bird species. Besides natural attractions the area also has archaeological sites including burial mounds near the main road towards the southern end of Khorgon Lake. There is also a wooden mosque in the area, which serves the local Kazakh community. Activities include hiking, fishing and rafting. Accommodation is confined to camping; bring your own gear if travelling independently; alternatively, tour operators provide tents.

There are two ways to approach the park: via the main road from Tsengel, which might require being pulled through a 200m-wide stream by a local truck, or the longer scenic route from Sagsai to Dayan Lake.

Permits You must get your permit sorted before you arrive. Go to the Parks Administration office in the visitor centre on the southeast corner of the main square in Bayan-Ölgii town. You need a permit, particularly to enter Tavanbogd National Park, because it is a border area with the Russian Federation. A shuttle bus will get you to the base camp, run by local tour companies. Tours are either guided or you can go on your own and pay for additional services, like hiring tents. There are five protected areas in this western aimag.

Siilkhemiin Nuruu National Park Designated to protect Mongolia's wild sheep, this park lies along the province's international border with the Russian Federation, and on the aimag's eastern boundary is **Devel Aral Nature Reserve**, home of the ring-necked pheasant, wild boar and beaver. The reserve extends into neighbouring Uvs Aimag. These remote areas are not frequented by tourists and going there involves expedition-type travel, bringing with you all the necessary equipment and supplies.

On the border with Khovd Aimag are two protected areas: Tsambagarav Uul National Park (110,960ha) and Khökhserkhiin Strictly Protected Area (14,080ha). The first was established to protect its glaciers, habitat of snow leopards, while the latter was designated to protect *argali* and ibex.

Permits to enter and information about the parks can be obtained at the Mongol Altai Nuruu Special Protected Area office in Ölgii (✆ *71 2122*). This office can also help with mountaineering queries. A visit to the Tavanbogd National Park requires a special permit from the local office of the Border Guards Department (in Mongolian: Khiliin Tsergiin Gazar). This may involve permission from the local Tagnuulyn Gazar (Office of Intelligence) and would require you to visit the barracks northwest of the town. Altai Tours (✆ *71 2309*), a local travel agency, can help organise permits.

Climbing The massif of Tavanbogd (Five Holy Peaks) Uul comprises five peaks: the highest is Khüiten (4,374m), which means 'cold peak'. It was first climbed in

KAZAKH HUNTERS

Kazakhs have a tradition of hunting on horseback with trained steppe eagles. The trainer wears a heavily padded glove on the right arm on which a hooded eagle perches, until its little leather hood (*tomega*) is removed and it sees its quarry, a fox or squirrel, and within moments it plummets and seizes it. A well-trained eagle flies back to its master's saddle when other horses approach. Following the hunt there is entertainment in Kazakh *gers*, which differ from the usual Mongol *gers* in that they are highly decorated with woven carpets and textiles. Rock-hard camel cheese is served, followed by the boiled head of a sheep and often a local delicacy, which turns out to be horse sausages. Kazakhs drink very strong tea; despite the ban on alcohol, there is plenty of goat's milk, *airag*, which is offered to visitors. Kazakh herders spend the summer and autumn months in *gers* but many spend the winter months in their houses in the mountains or in town. Among the best eagle hunters in the west are Sailou and his sons; Iris and his son Nurhairat; Doutkhan and his sons and grandsons; and Ablaikhan and his sons. For further information contact Agii Maksum of Kobesh Travel (*www.kobeshrtravel.com*).

1955 and was given the name Mount Nairamdal (Friendship Mountain). All the high peaks are snowcapped and the mountains around them contain large glaciers; the largest is the Potanin Glacier at 19km long. The mountain peak marking the

'RUFFLING FEATHERS' OH! 'MARRIED TO AN EAGLE!'

Anthony Pletts

My wife and I arrived in Ölgii full of trepidation. This was to be a journey marking the coming of age of our 14-year-old son, who was oblivious to our concerns. We had employed Blue Wolf Travel (for contact details, see page 394) on the basis they were the only tour operators who replied to our emails, even if these replies were scant and took weeks to materialise. Happily, at ground level, Blue Wolf were amazingly efficient. Our US$75 each day turned out to cover a translator, driver, van, even a cook who proved to be adept, much to my wife's delight, at knocking up delicious vegetarian fare.

We were driven out to a stunningly beautiful valley in the Altai Mountains, where we were told Kazakh hospitality awaited us. Our host was a new contact for Blue Wolf and initially his whole family seemed shy. There appeared to be some embarrassment about the basic conditions of the long-drop toilet and wooden hut (Kazakhs only live in *gers* in the summer; survival during the fierce winter months of the eagle hunting season demands solid walls). After a comedic misconception involving everyone thinking my wife was seven months' pregnant because of the amount of clothes she was wearing, a common vein of humour was established. Soon we were exchanging stories of our respective cultures over temperate measures of vodka and looking forward to saddling up and spending a few days in the wild.

Our host greeted us the next morning fully dressed up in his fur hat, embroidered long coat and thick gloves while supporting a magnificent hooded golden eagle on his right arm. He embodied nomadic splendour, while we looked like something out of a Thelwell cartoon in our brand-new jodhpurs, chaps and meeting point of the Chinese, Russian and Mongolian borders is 4,082m high but is not named.

Mountaineering The mountaineering season runs from June to September. Mongolia has over 100 glaciers and 30–40 permanently snowcapped mountains, located mostly in the western region. To climb any mountain you must have the necessary experience, be fully equipped and hire local guides. You must have permission too: a climbing permit is required before climbing any mountain in a Mongolian national park; permits are available from the Ministry Environment and Green Development in Ulaanbaatar (*Khudaldaany 5, Ulaanbaatar;* ✆ *11 326649;* e *env.pmis@gov.mn*). The Mongol Altai Club (*PO Box 49-23, Ulaanbaatar*) are the undisputed experts in mountain climbing in Mongolia and should be consulted before undertaking any serious climbing activities.

Suggested hiking tours in the western region A recommended tour is Mongolian Altai Trek by **Kazakh Tours** – a two-week trekking adventure in the Altai Tavan Bogd National Park for hikers. This tour will give you an in-depth insight not only into the landscape of the area but also its culture – with music and Kazakh lifestyle. For all information: m 994 22600; www.kazakhtour.com. Doshan will help with all arrangements.

For mountain walking tours and climbing tours to the 'Five Holy Peaks' of the Tavanbogd, and for tailor-made mountain treks in western mountains, contact the following **tour companies**:

riding hats. This was to be our first experience of riding in a straight line, having only taken lessons in a training ring.

Before setting out we were warned that not catching anything was a strong likelihood. My wife was relieved, yet prior to reaching the crest of a nearby mountain our eagle was swooping down on a fox that it then bowled down the cliff face. In hot pursuit the hunter recovered his stunned prey, forced open its mouth and, with brutal ritual, let the eagle rip out its tongue. It was not something I had been prepared for (some travellers choose to remain distant from the kill), though in that instant I was also aware that my son was both turning into an adult before my eyes and utterly absorbed in the intensity of the moment.

While the hunting was unforgettable, it was the eagle that captured our hearts. There is nothing to compare to the feeling of being on top of the world with a golden eagle perched on your arm. To feel her warm appreciation as you stroke her feathers and marvel at the unique bond shared between hunter and eagle. As our host commented, 'My wife says I am married twice, once to her and once to the eagle!'

For a trip that seemed so unfathomable and mysterious in preparation I was surprised to find myself feeling so at home and relaxed during its passing. I was relieved that nothing of the fox was wasted. The meat was fed to the eagle and the pelt sold, assisting our family in living off the land at the very fringes of survival. Making the whole experience complete my son said it was the best thing he had done in his life, and that was before our host presented him with a precious keepsake and told him he was now a part of his extended family. My wife had a tear in her eye, though she has since been making karmic donations to the National Fox Welfare Society!

Great Genghis Expeditions www.
greatgenghis.com. Offers journeys on horseback,
by camel & in jeeps to visit the high mountains &
lakes of Khovd, Bayan-Ölgii & Uvs aimags.

Karakorum Expeditions www.gomongolia.
com. Pioneered mountain tours in this region.
Kobesh Travel m 991 07676/981 67676; www.
kobeshtravel.com

River rafting Don't forget travel insurance, waterproofs, mosquito repellent and
sleeping bag. An itinerary might begin with a flight to Ölgii, from where you drive
to Khoton Lake, a beautiful place with snowcapped mountains and fast-flowing
rivers. Rafting 25km from Khorgan Lake (also called Khurgon Lake) to Mogoit
River on 2–3-class rapids, you continue to Tsengel district and visit Kazakh and
Tuvan families. You then raft through high mountain cliffs areas on 3–4-class
rapids surrounded by towering mountain ranges where you may spot *argali* and
ibex. Overnighting in Ulaan Khus district, you then drive to Ölgii town and on
to Tsagaan Aral (150km). This trip travels through the Gobi. From Tsagaan Aral
you raft to Bayan Lake (1–2-class rapids) through a mixed landscape of desert,
forest and mountains, passing Tsambagarav Mountain (4,202m) on the way. Camp

MOUNTAINEERING

There are many glaciers and permanently snowcapped mountains in
Mongolia's western region, which attract climbers. Mount Khüiten (Cold
Mountain), Mongolia's highest peak (4,374m), was previously known as
Mount Nairandal (Friendship Mountain); part of the Tavanbogd range located
in Bayan-Ölgii Aimag, it lies on the borders of Mongolia, China and Russia.
Other main peaks of the western region are:

- **Otgontenger Uul** (4,021m) in Zavkhan Aimag, also called Peace
  (Enkhtaivan) peak.
- **Türgen Uul** (3,965m) in Uvs Aimag; the highest peak in this range is
  Tsagaandelgi.
- **Kharkhiraa Uul** (4,037m) in Uvs Aimag (highest peak, Tsagaanshuvuut).
- **Sutai Uul** (4,090m) on the border between Gobi-Altai and Khovd aimags.
- **Altan Tavan Uul** (4,150m) in Bayan-Ölgii Aimag; has a 19km glacier.
- **Tsast Uul** (4,204m) on the border between Bayan-Ölgii and Khovd aimags.
- **Tsambagarav Uul** (4,202m) in Khovd Aimag.
- **Mönkhkhairkhan Uul** (4,362m) on the border between Bayan-Ölgii and
  Khovd aimags. The main peak is Sükhbaatar (4,204m) or Tavankhumst
  (the name differs on various maps).
- **Tavanbogd Uul** (4,374m) in Bayan-Ölgii Aimag.

Heights of mountain peaks and ranges tend to differ on Mongolian maps, in
statistical handbooks and encyclopaedias. Those given in this guide are the
most recent.

The best time to climb is from the beginning of July until the end of
August; you will need permits from the Ministry of Nature and Environment
(*Khudaldaany 5, Ulaanbaatar;* ☏ *11 326649;* e *env.pmis.gov.mn*). The sport
requires a high degree of professionalism. For serious mountaineering advice
(not advice on hiking and mountain walks, mainly dealt with by the specialist
tour operators, climbers should write to the Secretary of the Mongol Altai
Club (*PO Box 49-23, Ulaanbaatar*).

Be forewarned if you join a riding and walking tour combination. The pace and travel times often don't match unless carefully planned. Either the riders are happy and the trekkers are not, or vice versa, for all sorts of different reasons – half the party are late or lost, supper is cold or there is no food left; people are wet and exhausted, and tempers become frayed. It takes a good, professional tour guide to sort it all out and come up with solutions.

In fact in the far west, particularly in the mountain/glacier regions, if given the option of walking or riding, and you are not as fit as you might be, riding is better. Certain things are unavoidable; for example, if the terrain becomes very boggy due to rain and rivers becoming torrents because of snowmelt. To avoid potentially difficult inter-personal situations, choose small group sizes of four–five people – like that it is easier to keep together. Make sure not to mix Kazakh/Mongol ethnic groups when using guides, horsemen and drivers, because there can be a total lack of co-operation between the two. No matter what it says on holiday brochures in Mongolia things have a habit of turning out differently – usually better! However, a good guide who takes the initiative and has the ability to adapt the programme to the needs of his or her clients is a must.

and continue rafting from Bayan Lake to Ulaan Tag (2–4-class rapids), surrounded by high, rocky cliffs; then on from Ulaan Tag to Erdenebüren in Khovd Aimag (1–5-class rapids), where you camp overnight and drive by car in the direction of Khovd town (106km). The next night you camp near the beautiful Khar Us Lake, where you can go fishing or hiking, before flying back to Ulaanbaatar.

UVS AIMAG

Uvs Aimag is dominated by the Great Lakes Basin, a chain of lakes, wetlands, sand dunes and marshes sitting beside mountains and forests which stretch across the province from the aimag's southwestern boundary with Bayan-Ölgii and Khovd to its eastern boundary with Zavkhan, around the enormous Uvs Lake. In 2003, Uvs Nuur was nominated by UNESCO as a World Heritage Site (see box, *Uvs Nuur Basin World Heritage Site*, page 407). The avifauna is diverse: geese, swans and rare pink pelicans inhabit the lakes and wetlands, while pheasants are found in the highlands. The economy of the province is dominated by livestock breeding. Recently some light industry has developed. Uvs supplies the western region with fuel from its coal and lignite mines. Ethnically the area is dominated by the Dörvöd (almost 50%), from which the aimag received its original name 'Dörvöd'. Historical monuments include the Oirat Altan Khan's Palace. The main attractions of the province are its natural sites – lakes, mountains and birdlife. Volcanic ruptures and faulting can be seen on the journey between Öndörkhangai and Züünkhangai.

ULAANGOM Located around 25km southwest of Uvs Lake in the Great Lakes Basin area, Ulaangom is a relaxed, tree-lined town with a good range of shops, hotels and a rapidly growing market which sells clothes, household goods and other items including furs and hides. The main square at the town's centre is surrounded by public buildings including the city hall, post office, cinema and the bathhouse;

Western Region   UVS AIMAG

10

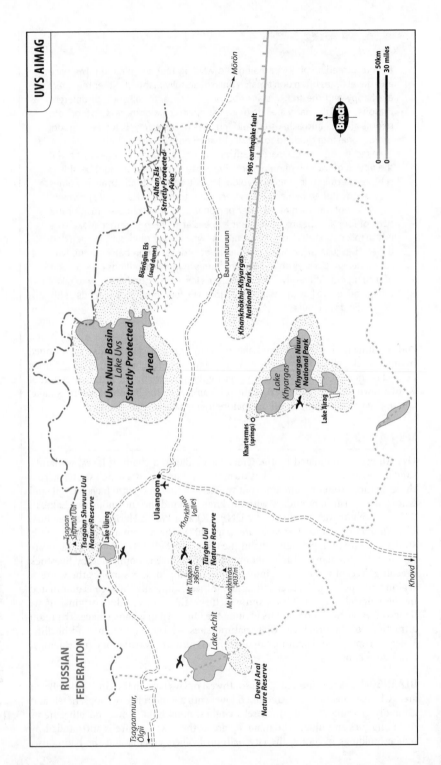

RUSSIAN
FEDERATION

Tsagaannuur,
Ölgii

Tsagaan
Shuvuut Uul
Tsagaan Shuvuut Uul
Nature Reserve

Lake Üüreg

Ulaangom

Kharkhiraa
Valley

Mt Türgen
3965m
Türgen Uul
Nature Reserve

Mt Khakhiraa
4037m

Lake Achit

Devel Aral
Nature Reserve

Khovd

Uvs Nuur Basin
Lake Uvs
Strictly Protected
Area

Böörögiin Els
(sand dunes)

Altan Els
Strictly Protected
Area

Baruunturuun

Khankhökhii-Khyargas
National Park

1905 earthquake fault

Möròn

Khartermes
(springs)

Lake
Khyargas

Khyargas Nuur
National Park

Lake Airag

N
Bradt

0   50km
0   30 miles

Area 69,600km²
Aimag centre Ulaangom
Districts 20
Elevation of Ulaangom 939m
Livestock and crops Sheep, goat, cattle, horse, hay, millet
Ethnic groups Dörvöd, Khalkha, Bayad, Khoton
Distance from Ulaangom to Ulaanbaatar 1,336km
Average temperatures July 19.2°C, January –33.6°C

HIGHLIGHTS
* Adventure tourism, camping
* Natural sites – mountains and lakes
* Uvs Nuur – lake
* Kharkhiraa Valley
* Achit Nuur – lake

Hotel Kharkhiraa, the main hotel, is also on the square. There is a public park to the west side. Uvs Strictly Protected Area office, which provides information on the national parks, is located beside the public park on the main road leading west to Bayan-Ölgii Aimag. The airport is situated on the southeast side, 1km from the town centre on the road to Khovd. The jeep/truck station and market are located northeast of the main square.

Getting there from Ulaanbaatar

By air Scheduled flights by Hunnu Air (formerly Mongolia Airlines) from Ulaanbaatar leave on Wednesdays and Sundays (almost four hours' flight time); Enzis Airways also fly to Ulaangom (see schedules: www.flightsmongolia.com/domestic_flight/ulaangom.html). Costs US$265 (one-way).

By road Expect exciting and bumpy drives over high mountain passes; this is one area where it is well worthwhile hiring a jeep and a driver who knows the country. The area offers an amazing variety of scenery in a single day's journey, from sand dunes to alpine lakes. The bus will cost you around T60,000. Jeeps are available for hire at the jeep station (northeast of the main square of Ulaangom); standard costs range from T500 to T1,000 and up to T1,500 if hiring a top-of-the-range vehicle, which you are more likely to find in UB. People prize their vehicles out west so private hire may involve the owner/driver of the vehicle to minimise possible damage to it by careless driving, or by people not used to driving conditions and Mongolian road surfaces.

Tourist information Tourist information is available from tour guides or from local guides who offer their services. For local guides, ask at the tourist office, the national parks office, or otherwise ask at hotels or the bus station.

☑ National Parks/ Strictly Protected Areas Office On the main road to the west; ☎22184. Offers information on the parks & will issue visitor permits. The office also runs an information *ger* (⊕ May to mid Sep only). This *ger* may relocate to the airport (as planned in future).

⌂ Where to stay

⌂ **Bayalag Od Hotel** (20 rooms) One block south of the main square in the centre of town; ☎ 145 22245. Next to the elementary school, this is considered the best hotel in town; the hotel's restaurant (listed below) serves up to 60 people. **$$–$**

⌂ **Main Hotel** (20 beds) ☎ 145 23982/24286/23409. B&B, restaurant, bar, billiards. **$$$–$$**

⌂ **Kharkhiraa Hotel** In the town centre on the main square. **$**

⌂ **Khetsuu Khad** (10 gers) ☎ 310158; e skhaliun@mongol.net; www.khetsuukhad.mn. The camp is 230km away from the aimag centre near the Great Lakes Basin, & can cater for 30 people at a time. The location is truly magnificent, with the lake a stone's throw away & snowcapped mountains as a backdrop. **$**

⌂ **Tavan Od Hotel** (35 beds) Town centre, next to the Shine Ireedul school; m 994 52555/58555. B&B, restaurant, bar, sauna, billiards, garage. The restaurant serves Mongolian & European dishes. **$$**

✗ Where to eat and drink

✗ **Bayalag Od Restaurant** ☎ 145 22245; ⊕ 07.00–23.00 daily. Mongolian meals. *Around US$5.*

✗ **Chinggis Restaurant** By the main road; ⊕ 09.00–22.00 daily. Mongolian, Chinese & European meals. *From US$5.*

✗ **Ikh Mongol Restaurant** ☎ 145 23093; ⊕ 09.00–22.00 daily. Mongolian, Asian & European meals. *From US$4.*

✗ **Shine Erin Café** Nr the market; ⊕ 10.00–22.00 daily. Traditional Mongolian meals, generous portions compared with other places. *US$4.*

✗ **Tavan Od Restaurant** m 994 52555/58555; ⊕ 07.00–23.00 daily. Mongolian, Chinese & European meals. *US$5–10.*

✗ **Tungalag Tamir Café** Next to Central Market; m 994 52800; ⊕ 10.00–22.00 daily. Mongolian traditional food. *US$4 max.*

✗ **Ulaan Sarnai Café** Town centre; ⊕ 09.00–20.00 daily. Mongolian & Chinese meals. *US$3–5.*

✗ **Uvs Nuur Complex Restaurant** ☎ 145 23982/24282/23409; ⊕ 07.00–23.00 daily. Mongolian, Chinese & European meals. *From US$4*

Shopping

🛒 **Central Market** Town centre; ⊕ 09.00–18.00 Tue–Sun. You can buy anything here.

🛒 **Shine Zuun supermarket** Town centre; ⊕ 10.00–18.00. Food, groceries, clothes.

🛒 **Tavan Od Shop** Tavan Old Hotel; ⊕ 09.00–22.00. Mainly groceries.

🛒 **Uguumur supermarket** Town centre; ⊕ 10.00–18.00. Food & clothes.

Other practicalities

Internet cafés

🖥 **Post office** ⊕ 08.00–17.00; T800/hr.

🖥 **Uran Gan** Left of the Municipal Building; ⊕ 08.00–18.00; T500/hr.

🖥 **Building of Khödölgööön (New Village Movement)** By the Palace of the Democracy; ⊕ 08.00–17.00; T500/hr.

What to see and do in Ulaangom

Aimag Museum (⊕ *10.00–17.00 Mon–Fri (closed for lunch); entrance fee T1,500)* North of the public park on the west side of town, this museum features displays on local wildlife, musical instruments, national costumes and Buddhist art.

Dechinravjaalin Khiid On the airport road southwest of the main square, this temple was founded in 1757. In its prime the monastery had seven temples with a community of 2,000 monks. It was destroyed in 1937. A monastery of the same name was built in the 1990s but it has little of its former importance.

Experienced guides and tour companies Because this aimag is so remote and tourism is only beginning to develop here, it is important to connect with the best (tiptop!) guides and tour operators – specialists who can help arrange your journey. **Professor Khayankhyarvaa Terbish** (known as Terbish) is head of the Ecology Department at the National University of Mongolia, in Ulaanbaatar. He and his wife Shinebayar Urantsetseg founded and run **Great Genghis Expeditions** (*www.greatgenghis.com*), a tour company that specialises in wildlife tours. Birdwatching and wildlife tours are their speciality.

Mongolica (*www.mongolica.org*) is a newly launched company that focuses on professional birdwatching holidays and wildlife photography tours. Visit the website for details.

The **Mongolian Ornithological Society** (*www.mos.mn*) has organised birding tours in Mongolia since 1999, and most members have experience in guiding. See also www.birding.mos.mn.

SIGHTS IN UVS AIMAG
National parks and strictly protected areas
Uvs Nuur (Great Lakes Basin) Located predominately in the northern and northeast section of the province, bordering the national boundary with the Russian Federation, this cluster of reserves covers 712,545ha and is made up of four units:

- Uvs Lake - birdwatching
- Altan Els (dunes)
- Türgen Mountain
- Tsagaan Shuvuut mountainous area

Overall, the major ecosystems include mixed mountain and highland systems covering an extremely diverse landscape from cold desert, desert-steppe, tundra, and alpine mountain zones, to marshes, sand dunes, forests, floodplains, wetlands and salt lakes. It is very unusual to find such ecologically diverse areas so close together; Uvs Great Lakes Basin is matched by few other places in the world. International research carried on in the area concentrates on hoofed animals, rodents and birds, and wetland ecosystems. The area as a whole is listed as one of UNESCO's World Biosphere Reserves.

Uvs Nuur Located in the centre of the aimag's northern region, Mongolia's largest lake looks like an inland sea. It is fed by the River Tes and has no outlet. The lake

UVS NUUR BASIN WORLD HERITAGE SITE

This vast lake area of over one million hectares in western Mongolia was selected in 2003 by UNESCO (*www.unesco.org*) as a World Heritage Site – and was joined in 2004 by the Orkhon river valley, another nominated site of special interest. Uvs Nuur Basin (Uvs meaning 'salty water') was chosen because of the richness and variety of its landscape – the site is made up of 12 protected areas, each representing a different ecosystem. Such great diversity brings with it many species of plants and animals along with a variety of birdlife – migrating birds, waterfowl and seabirds. The closed salt lake system is of particular scientific importance for climate and weather studies. The range of ecosystems include semi-desert, dunes, steppe grasslands, forests and mountains. Snow leopard, *argali* (wild sheep) and ibex roam the hills far from human contact.

10

water is five times saltier than the ocean and there are no fish in the lake, but nonetheless the water and shores attract many thousands of birds – supporting around 20,000 waterfowl each year. Some 359 species have been recorded, including Pallas's fish eagle, relict gull and the endangered swan goose. A quarter of the bird species are resident and the rest are migratory. The lake is visited by numerous seabirds although the sea is some 3,000km away.

Access to the lake's shores is difficult due to marshy ground. Located at an altitude of 759m, it is the lowest point in western Mongolia. Surrounded by sand dunes, the lake is overlooked by snow-crested mountains (mainly in the south). Mountainous wild animals include snow leopard, deer and ibex, foxes and wolves. Owing to the extreme climate (recorded winter temperatures of -57°C and summer temperatures of over 40°C) this area has been chosen for climate-change research by international scientists. The road to the lake from the west crosses the Ulaan Davaa Pass, which has stunning views. Your own transport is essential. The lake is around 40km from Ulaangom and will take you an hour's drive. Wildlife of the area includes rare species like the Mongolian gerbil.

Altan Els Also known as **Böörögiin Els**, these golden sand dunes lie in the northwest corner of the aimag on the national border with the Russian Federation. The road to Ulaangom from Zavkhan Aimag passes south of this area. Altan Els is a massive belt of sands, the most northerly sand dunes in the world, extending from the eastern part of Uvs Lake across many hundreds of kilometres to **Altan Els Strictly Protected Area**. The park offers a place of natural beauty with plenty of wildlife. Plan to be completely self-sufficient as there are few facilities in the region, ie: bring plenty of petrol, food, water and camping gear. The desert areas are home to rare gerbils, gerboas and the marbled polecat

Türgen Uul Nature Reserve Located around 40km southwest of Ulaangom, the way into the reserve is via Kharkhiraa river valley, about 30km from Ulaangom. Türgen Mountain (3,965m) and Kharkhiraa Mountain are both part of the reserve. The mountain areas support red deer, ibex and wild boar. This area is visited by campers and hikers because of its beautiful scenery. Here you may see lammergeier nesting on outcrops on high stoney mountainsides, Altai snowcock and rock ptarmigan.

Kharkhiraa Valley Kharkhiraa river valley is an excellent camping spot and a good base from which to see the surrounding countryside. You'll find it 30km southwest of Ulaangom. This beautiful river valley is surrounded by pine forests and meadows carpeted with wild flowers in early summer. The twin peaks of **Kharkhiraa Uul** (4,037m) and **Türgen Uul** (3,965m) dominate the area. Khoton people, known for their shamanistic practices, inhabit the region.

To get there it is necessary to hire a jeep and driver; make arrangements to be collected if you are staying overnight and bring plenty of food, as you will need to be self-sufficient. Local families are very hospitable and often provide food and lodging in family *gers*; log cabins and huts provide lodging if you are not camping but it is difficult to book them in advance, unless you know a family and have their mobile telephone number.

Tsagaan Shuvuut Uul Located on the northwestern border near Lake Üüreg, Tsagaan Shuvuut rises 3,496m and is easiest to appreciate at a distance for its stunning mountain peaks. There are few visitor facilities and you will need your own transport, camping equipment and supplies.

Achit Nuur On the western border, over 150km from Ulaangom and extending into Bayan-Ölgii Aimag, this is the largest freshwater lake in the province and provides stunning views at sunset when reflections are mirrored in its waters. It's a scenic place to camp; there is fishing and birdlife, but watch out for millions of mosquitoes. Achit Lake is home to around 20 breeding pairs of Dalmatian pelicans, though their number has declined dramatically in recent years due to hunting. It is also home to Pallas's cat and red fox, lesser kestrel and Pallas's fish eagle. Again you will need your own transport to reach here.

Devel Aral Nature Reserve The reserve (extending into Bayan-Ölgii Aimag) is situated in the basin of the Usan Khooloi and Khovd rivers that feed from Achit Lake, between Bayan-Ölgii and Uvs aimags. This protected area, comprising 10,300ha, is home to ring-necked pheasant, wild boar and beaver; the last two species are becoming increasingly rare in Mongolia. It is a main distribution area of sea buckthorn. There are no tourist facilities and again you will need your own transport.

Ölgii Nuur This lake lies in the southwest near a small town of the same name, just off the main road from Ulaangom (100km south) to Khovd (120km north), not far from Khar Us Lake. Access is easy. The lake is fed by the Orlogo River and offers fishing (grayling) but the lake waters are brackish. It is not an area for camping on account of the exposed conditions and lack of shelter from the wind.

Üüreg Nuur This lake lies in the northwest part of Uvs, 95km from Ulaangom above the road from Ulaangom to Ölgii (250km) between two mountain passes, Ulaan Davaa (southwest) and Ogotor Khamar Davaa (southeast). Üüreg Nuur is a saltwater lake containing unidentified minerals. It is surrounded by 3,000m-plus peaks such as Tsagaan Shuvuut Uul (3,496m) and is a great place for swimming, fishing and hiking. You may see Pallas's fish-eagle. A big advantage is its accessibility, just off the main road. The lakeshores offer the best camping ground in this area, though you'll need your own transport and there are no tourist facilities.

Khyargas Nuur National Park (*Entrance fee T2,500 payable to a ranger when you see one; vehicles are charged T6,000*) Nestling in the southern mountains of Uvs aimag, 130km southeast of Ulaangom, this protected area was established as a national park in 2000. It comprises some 332,800ha. The saltwater lake receives less attention than Uvs Nuur and although it is smaller (84km by 32km) and less spectacular, it still has abundant fish. The range of birdlife alone makes it worth a stopover. There are some hot springs at the northwestern side of the lake.

Lake Airag South of Khyargas Nuur (above), this is part of the Khyargas Nuur National Park and is connected to the larger lake by a water channel. Deer stones are found in the vicinity, though little is known about them.

Khankhökhii-Khyargas National Park This national park, established in 2000, lies in the southeastern section of Uvs aimag and covers an area of 220,550ha of forested mountains. The highest peak is Altanduulga Uul (2,928m). Entry costs are as above; there are few visitor facilities here.

SUGGESTED ITINERARIES
Four-lakes tour This tour begins with a four-hour flight from Ulaanbaatar to Ulaangom followed by a 75km drive by jeep to the northwest point of Khyargas

Hiking for eight days with local guides, using pack camels to carry the gear, you cross two mountain passes and trek through some of the most beautiful and remote valleys in the country. The snow-covered peaks of Kharkhiraa and Türgen dominate the horizon; you will enjoy viewing crystal-clear lakes, glaciers and fast-flowing rivers (crossed on horseback), as well as birdwatching and seeing wonderful flora and fauna. Great Genghis Expeditions (*www.greatgenghis.com*) can arrange such a trip.

Even in the summer it can snow up in the mountains, but the landscape is breathtaking in any weather. During the summer months there are nomadic families along the way, sometimes on the move, travelling with large herds of animals and their homes on the back of camels and yaks.

Lake to visit the mineral springs at **Khartermesiin Rashaan**, before heading southwest, following the lakeshores, to birdwatch. Next you drive west to Ölgii Lake (just over 100km by road), camping along the way, and continue a further 100km west to Lake Achit, crossing mountain passes and fording rivers on the way.

As you'd expect, this leg of the itinerary needs an experienced driver and guide as some of it is off-road. Take enough food to be completely self-sufficient, although you may find that you can buy food from the Dörvöd, a minority people who live in this region. From Achit Lake drive 89km via the Khamar Pass to Lake Üüreg, where you can explore the Tsagaan river gorge on the west side of the lake. Keep a look out for ancient rock paintings of animals. You then return to Ulaangom (95km) via the Ulaan Davaa with its magnificent views.

Logistics and timing need to be carefully worked out with a tour operator, using local transport, equipment and guides or go it alone and camp but be well equipped and bring food supplies.

Western mountains and lakes riding tour You begin your tour by flying from Ulaanbaatar to Ulaangom, where you stay overnight, then drive 95km to Üüreg Lake and from there on to Tsagaan Nuur (a small lake not marked on tourist maps). Camp overnight then drive to Khöshööt to meet up with the guides and horses, to begin a six-day ride to Tsengel Uul, south along the Khargant River, enjoying wonderful mountain lake scenery before returning to Buyant settlement (not marked on tourist maps). The total distance is around 160km and is covered over five–six days.

Dune and mountain/desert tour The itinerary begins with a flight to Ulaangom, where the trek begins in the desert-steppe. The first day is spent hiking around the sand dunes of Böörögiin Els looking at desert herbs. The next day you can hike to visit nomadic families, see their horses and yak carts in action and meet up with herders who provide horses which you can hire for the day; alternatively, you may prefer to hike and experience some magnificent mountain views. There are caves to explore in the area. (See *Tour operators*, pages 165–7 and 237–9.)

11

Eastern Region

The eastern region of Mongolia consists of Khentii, Sükhbaatar and Dornod provinces. The main attractions of this region are the grasslands, wild animals and birds; and the fact that Genghis Khan was born here, in Dadal district in northern Khentii and is possibly buried in this region. There is continued speculation as to his final resting place.

Many aimag centres were originally created around monasteries, but Baldan Bereeven Monastery, the monastery of greatest note in eastern Mongolia, located in Khentii Aimag, was never a provincial centre. It was a great centre of Buddhism prior to its destruction in the communist government's anti-religious purges of the 1930s; the temples are currently being restored.

Extensive grasslands, or steppe, stretch across eastern Mongolia from the Khentii Mountains to the eastern borders with China and Russia. There are some areas of mixed landscape, especially in the southeast, which has golden sand dunes, lakes and mineral springs. The grasslands, which predominate, provide important grazing lands for livestock, although most of Mongolia's eastern steppe is uninhabited and

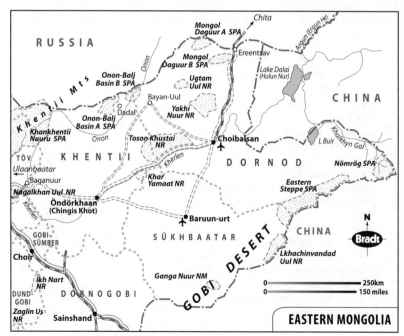

EASTERN MONGOLIA

underdeveloped. This may not last because oil has been discovered in the region and although difficult to drill for and transport this sort of development would mean economic growth. But it would also cause great disturbance to the wildlife. The steppes of eastern Mongolia are the world's last unfragmented natural grasslands; they are considered to be of global importance because they have remained so undisturbed, whereas the grasslands of neighbouring Russia and China have been slowly modified by agriculture and industrial development. As time goes on the same is beginning to happen to Mongolia's eastern grasslands as roads and railways cut through ancient animal migration territories. Traditional herding practices are still used in Mongolia, and livestock densities are relatively low, particularly in the easternmost aimag of Dornod.

Apart from its unique grasslands, eastern Mongolia is home to rare species of cranes and vast herds of migratory gazelles. Gazelles were once widespread in Mongolia and neighbouring areas of Russia and China but are now limited largely to the eastern steppes of Mongolia because of habitat destruction and hunting in China and Russia, and the disruption of their migration routes. Mongolian gazelle population, too, has declined in range and size over the last few decades; its continued survival will be threatened if present trends continue. There are estimated to be over two million gazelles, but migrating species always pose a conservation challenge as they cannot be confined to protected areas and they often cross international borders. Cross-border conservation projects are now in place.

KHENTII AIMAG

The aimag is named after the Khentii Mountains, which dominate the northwestern part of the province. Mountains in the region are under 2,000m and are thickly forested and well watered. The watershed of three huge drainage basins – the Arctic Ocean, the Pacific Ocean and the inland basin of central Asia – come together at Chandmani Mountain (1,854m) in Khentii Aimag. The rivers, more than 70 and including the Onon and the Kherlen, provide lush scenery but at times they make

BRIEF FACTS: KHENTII AIMAG

Area 80,300km²
Aimag centre Öndörkhaan (Chingis Khot)
Districts 19
Elevation of Öndörkhaan 1,027m
Main livestock and crops Sheep, cattle, horses
Ethnic groups Khalkha, Buryat
Distance from Öndörkhaan to Ulaanbaatar 331km
Average temperatures July 18.8°C, January –23.2°C

HIGHLIGHTS
* Dadal district – birthplace of Genghis Khan
* Sacred mountain Burkhan Khalduun – Genghis Khan's resting place?
* Mountains and grasslands
* Galtai Cave
* Horseriding, hiking, camping
* Mineral springs

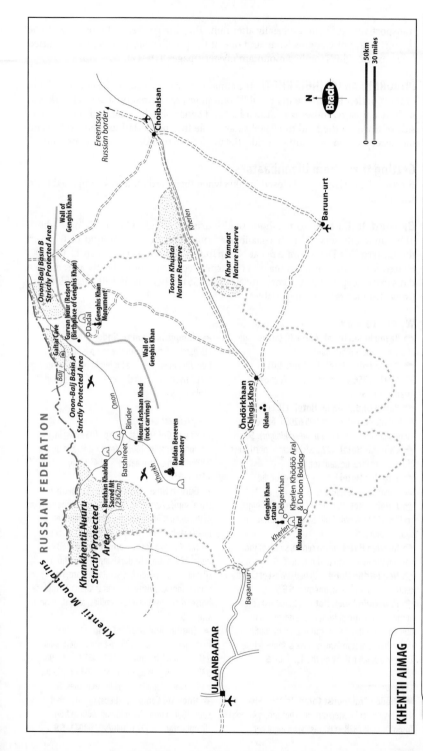

KHENTII AIMAG

transport very difficult, especially after rain. The aimag is generally regarded to be the birthplace of Genghis Khan and one of the possible places where he is buried (see box, Genghis's tomb: a mountain mystery, pages 416–17).

ÖNDÖRKHAAN (CHINGIS KHOT) The aimag centre is located on the northern bank of the Kherlen River. The main public buildings are centred on a central park and include a theatre, museums, a town hall and shops. The bus station is on the west side of town on the road to Ulaanbaatar, while the sports stadium, post office and monastery are on the southeast side; the town is surrounded by flat steppe land.

Getting there from Ulaanbaatar
By air The aimag airport closed in 2008 when the paved road was completed from Ulaanbaatar.

By road It is a four- to five-hour road journey to Öndörkhaan (Chingis Khot). The public bus service from Ulaanbaatar runs daily, leaving around 08.00 from the Eastern Bus Departure Area at NaranTuul (Black Market), and costs T10,000. Shared jeeps and minivans make the journey regularly from Ulaanbaatar; allow a day's drive. Jeep and driver costs are around US$120 per day or T800 per kilometre (long-distance rates are negotiable).

 ## Where to stay

⌂ **Bayan Bulag Hotel** (20 beds) On the edge of town on the airport road. **$**

⌂ **Bayan Erdes Hotel** (30 beds) ☎0156 3007/2416/2256. Restaurant, bar, Mongolian/ Asian menu. **$**

⌂ **Bayan Undur Manal Hotel** (10 beds) Back of the post office; m 995 62099. Tea, coffee, Mongolian menu, bar (☺ *noon–midnight*). **$**

⌂ **Chinggis Hotel** (22 beds) Located northwest of the post office. Restaurant. **$**

⌂ **Jargalan Hotel** (15 beds) Back of the Municipal Bldg. Restaurant. **$**

⌂ **Jonon Hotel** Back of the Municipal Bldg; m 995 62202. Newly built B&B, with restaurant, shop, laundry. **$**

⌂ **Kherlen Hotel** Town centre, south of the park on the main road to the airport. **$**

⌂ **Negdelchin Hotel** (25 beds) West of the city centre. Restaurant, bar, internet. **$$$**

⌂ **Khuvchiin Jonon Hotel** (18 rooms) Located in the town centre in front of the government buildings, right of the hospital. Built in 2006, rooms here are standard, de luxe & semi-deluxe. There is a small bakery on the 1st floor. **$**

Ger *camps*
▲ **Khodoo Aral Tourist Camp** In Delgerkhan sum, near River Kherlen & next to hot spring Avraga Toson; ☎11 457828; e ikhzasag@mongol.net.

▲ **Chinggisiin Toonot Binder Tourist Camp** (15 *gers*) In Binder sum, the camp is about 2km from Binder village. The highlight of the camp is that 3 rivers merge in the area – offering good fishing. **$$** .

Regional *camps*
▲ **Bayan Gol Tourist Camp** (95 beds) In Ömnödelger sum, 160km from Öndörkhaan, 240km from Ulaanbaatar; ☎11 451016; m 919 14408. **$$**

▲ **Gurvan Nuur Tourist Camp** (26 beds) In Dadal sum, 270km from Öndörkhaan, at the junction of the Onon & Balj rivers, the place where Genghis Khan was born; m 991 15000/995 64334. **$**

▲ **Ikh Avarga Toson Tourist Camp** (68 beds) 125km from Öndörkhaan, 240km from Ulaanbaatar; m 880 00990. Restaurant, bar, sauna, snooker, visiting Genghis Khan's birthplace, horseriding, visiting local families, testing mineral water. **$**

▲ **Khuduu Aral Tourist Camp** (110 beds) In Delgerkhaan sum, 125km from Öndörkhaan, 240km from Ulaanbaatar; ☎11 457826; m 966 53813; e ikh_zasag@ mongol.net. Horseriding, visiting local families, trekking activities. **$**

▲ **Onon Yol Camp** (24 beds) In Batshireet sum, 180km from Öndörkhaan, 400km from Ulaanbaatar; m 992 08040/992 08041. **$$**

✖ Where to eat and drink
Eating out is relatively inexpensive; meals cost from around T11,500.

✖ **Alag Bars Centre** ✆ 0156 22253; ⏲ 11.00–22.00 daily. Bar, restaurant, Mongolian, European & Asian menu.

✖ **Alt Margad Restaurant** ⏲ 11.00–22.00. European & Mongolian menu.

✖ **Bayan Erdes Restaurant** ✆ 0156 3007/2416/2256; ⏲ 09.00–midnight daily. Bar, Mongolian & Asian menu. *From T20,000.*

✖ **Bayan Undur Manal Café/bar** Back of the post office; m 995 62099; ⏲ noon–midnight daily. Mongolian menu. *From T20,000.*

✖ **Culinary Café** Vegetarian food & bakery located centre town near the post office; ⏲ daily.

✖ **Huvchiin Chono Restaurant** Jonon Hotel; ✆ 0156 2540/3845; m 995 62222; ⏲ 08.00–midnight daily. Mongolian & European menu.

✖ **Khökh Chandmani** ✆ 0156 23237/22429. Restaurant/bar.

✖ **Modern Café** Nr main road; ⏲ 10.00–22.00 daily. Chinese menu.

✖ **Nature Restaurant/bar** m 990 93701; ⏲ 10.00–midnight daily. Mongolian, European & Asian menu. *From T20,000.*

♀ **Baylag Hurkh Bar** ✆ 0156 22798; ⏲ 18.00–23.00.

Shopping
🏪 **Altanbulag Market** ⏲ 09.00–18.00. Also known as Middle Market. Mainly groceries.

🏪 **Chinggis Plaza** ⏲ 10.00–18.00 Mon–Sat. Also known as East Market. Food, groceries, clothes.

🏪 **Khökh Chandmani Market** ⏲ 08.00–19.00. Also known as West Market on the west of the city. Food, groceries, clothes.

🏪 **Souvenir shop** Next to the Middle Market; ⏲ 10.00–22.00. Handicrafts made by local people, paintings by local artists.

Other practicalities
Internet
🖃 **Post office** ⏲ 24hrs; T800/hr.

What to see and do in/around Öndörkhaan

Ethnographic Museum (*Next to City Hall;* ✆ 22204/2187; ⏲ 09.00–18.00 Tue–Sat; entrance fee T2,500) In the centre of town at the east end of the park, this museum is one of the best of its kind in the country and is certainly worth a look. It contains traditional costumes, Mongolian toys, religious statues, *tankas* (religious scroll paintings) and books that must have been rescued in the late 1930s. The four museum buildings were the 18th-century home of the Tsetsen Khan, a Mongol prince who governed most of eastern Mongolia during the Manchu reign.

City Museum (✆ 11 22204/2187; ⏲ 09.00–18.00 Tue–Sat; entrance fee T2,500) This small museum stands on the north side of the park and was recently renovated. Exhibits include displays on flora and fauna, traditional cultural items and armour of the 13th-century Mongol Empire, modern history of the region, famous people and animals.

Ger Palace of Genghis Khan (⏲ 10.00–16.00 daily; entrance free) In the city centre. With carved furnishings and a statue of Genghis Khan; photos in Mongolian costume can be taken.

Gundgavirlan Khiid (*Southeast of the park*) This monastery was built way back in 1660. Indeed, the first Buddhist School of Philosophy in Mongolia was founded here. The monastery was closed in 1938 and most of the buildings were pulled down in the 1950s, though it reopened in 1992. The principal temple is housed in a *ger*; visitors are welcome.

The Avarga-Toson Steppe Spa (230km southeast of UB, on Lake Toson in Khentii Aimag). A health spa/sanatorium. It opened in the late 1970s, and is based around artesian mineral springs of the area. These ancient mineral waters have curative properties, treating skin conditions and stress. Treatments include mud and sand treatments, the use of medicinal teas and vitamin-enriched milk and milk products, exercise (lake swimming and indoor gym) and massage therapy.

For horseriding tours, stopping for a night at the spa, contact Selena Travel (*www.selenatravel.com/mongoliatour.html*).

GENGHIS'S TOMB: A MOUNTAIN MYSTERY   *John Man*

Where is Genghis Khan buried? This is one of the world's great unanswered mysteries, of peculiar fascination because it is almost universally assumed that the ruler of half Eurasia must have been buried with matching wealth.

The few sources are not much help. The one that should offer the greatest help, *The Secret History of the Mongols,* offers none at all. Genghis, it reveals, died in August 1227 while campaigning in north China, and then 'ascended to Heaven'. Clearly, it intended the burial to remain secret. Chinese sources are little better. Two envoys visited what they thought was the site within ten years of his death, but did not identify the place. Anyway, they say that horses had been driven over it to disguise the spot; and they were not allowed past a line of guards and guard posts set well away from the grave.

Almost certainly, Genghis was brought back to the Mongols' heartland, today's Khentii Aimag – probably for a simple burial, as befitted his nomad roots. Here in the Khentii Massif is a sacred mountain associated with Genghis from his youth: Burkhan Khaldun – Holy Khaldun. Today that mountain is identified as Khan Khentii, the King of the Khentii. Mongols assert that this is where Genghis was buried, in a yet-to-be-discovered grave.

Though only a day's drive (some 200km) from Ulaanbaatar, Khan Khentii is not easy to get to for cars. It's in the Khentii National Park, and visitors need permission. There's a rough 30-mile approach track, several peat bogs, a steep ridge and a river (the upper Kherlen) to negotiate. It all depends on the weather and the state of the bogs. Horsemen, though, go often enough to make a path to the summit.

Buddhist and shamanists have worshipped up here possibly for centuries. At the very top, capping a feature we will get to in a moment, is a well-built *ovoo*, one of those rock shrines with which Mongolians honour high places. This one consists of a circular wall some 5m across, from which rises a pole topped by a silver war helmet and black horse tails – Genghis's war standard. All around are a hundred or so smaller *ovoos* (made over the last century, by the look of them).

Is Genghis really somewhere on the mountain? For those who want the truth, there are problems, the main one being that there is no certainty that Khan Khentii is in fact the Burkhan Khaldun of the historical sources. Names shift with time. Today's mountain does not quite fit with details in *The Secret History*. Perhaps Burkhan Khaldun was a different mountain. Perhaps the name referred to a range

SIGHTS IN KHENTII AIMAG
Genghis Khan's birthplace This is believed to lie at the confluence of the Onon and Balj rivers at Delüün Boldog in Khentii Aimag, 25km south of the national border with Russia. It's a magnificent area of lakes, rivers and forests and days could be spent in the area simply because of its natural beauty. The best way to get there is by road, although allow plenty of travel time as road conditions can be difficult in rainy weather, especially in summer. The nearby Gurvan Nuur ('Three Lakes') Resort provides wooden huts at US$5 per person or you can camp close by. The distance from Öndörkhaan is some 250km.

Genghis Khan monuments There are two Genghis Khan monuments. One is a large rock on a hillside with an inscription in old Mongol script marking his birthplace at Delüün Boldog (although locals say it is in the wrong place). It stands

containing a number of peaks. Perhaps each clan had its own sacred mountain, its own Burkhan Khaldun. No-one knows.

Believers point to so-called evidence. Firstly, on the lower flanks of Khan Khentii are the remains of a temple, possibly the one known to have been built by Genghis's great-great-grandson, Kamala, who was in charge of the burial site. Secondly, a vast mound of stones on the mountain's summit looks like an enormous *ovoo*. One scientific paper calls it 'an ancient tomb … (which) may be the tomb of Genghis Khan'. And thirdly, collections of stones on the upper slopes look like graves, suggesting that this is a cemetery not only for Genghis, but for some of his heirs as well.

Yet all of this 'evidence' is extremely shaky, as I have seen in three expeditions up the mountain. The temple is of later origin (on the evidence of a few scattered tiles). The 'graves' are not graves. I dug up one of them and found nothing but peat. They are geological features – 'stony circles', as geologists call them, made by rain, frost and time acting on streams of stones moving downhill immeasurably slowly.

These stones all come from the top – a dome so regular that it does indeed look artificial. Could it be? It is about 250 by 200 by 30m in size, which gives a weight of about 630,000 tonnes. It could have been built in a few years by 2,000 men working with 900 oxen, supplied by herds, tents, pastures, and horses based in the valley below. But the idea is totally at odds with both tradition and the sources. Mongols did not build mounds for royal graves, and the sources speak only of a *secret* grave. It is hardly conceivable that such a vast project would have left no traces in official histories or the earth or literature or folklore.

The clinching argument is from geology, which suggests a far better explanation. Over the last 50,000 years, the mountain was covered by ice several times, grinding it down. Some 13,000 years ago, the last of the melting ice dropped its rocky detritus to form the vast, neat oval, much as it is today, except that cold, ice and summer rains continued to eat away at the cairn, breaking the rocks and carrying them downhill in slow-motion streams. Men *could* have built it up. But they didn't. Ice broke it down.

It's possible that Genghis is up there; certainly almost everyone believes it, but belief, however strong, is not the same as certainty. The mystery remains.

John Man is the author of Genghis Khan: Life, Death and Resurrection.

11

3km north of Bayan-Ovoo, the centre of Dadal district, in the Delüün Boldog hills some 250km from the aimag centre Öndörkhaan. The better-known Genghis Khan monument is the one unveiled on 31 May 1962 to commemorate the 800th anniversary of his birth. Situated in the middle of Gurvan Nuur area, it's a life-size figure carved in relief on a white stone in the shape of a number of mountain peaks with old Mongol script running down one side of the stone. When the Mongols held their Genghis Khan anniversary celebrations, the Soviets protested and the organiser of the celebrations was sacked from his Politburo job amid a great deal of soul searching. But the monument was not removed. Since 1990 Genghis Khan has been openly celebrated. In 1962, a set of Genghis Khan anniversary postage stamps was published, of interest to stamp collectors and tourists and obtainable from the central post office off Genghis Khan Square in Ulaanbaatar.

Khajuu Bulag mineral spring Located 1km west of the Genghis Khan hillside monument, the spring has excellent-tasting fresh water and many people fill their water bottles here. The spring is not a developed as a tourist site (yet). There are many undeveloped springs in this aimag.

'Wall' of Genghis Khan Situated in the northeast part of Khentii the wall or ancient rampart extends through Dornod province to China and Russia. Most likely, it has nothing to do with Genghis Khan but locals like to think it has and have named it after their hero. The wall itself is mostly in ruins. It can be seen along the main road from Öndörkhaan towards Bayan-Uul town (in Dornod).

Galtai Agui At 80m, Galtai Agui is the deepest cave in Mongolia. It lies 70km northwest of Bayan-Ovoo, Dadal district centre, and practically on the national border with Russia. Since the caves are so near the Russian border you need permission from the local police to visit the area. If you want to go there a local guide/translator will help to arrange the permit; otherwise contact the police directly, which is best done in Öndörkhaan (✆ *39 2109*).

Archaeological sites Many Bronze Age graves and tombstones (though not 'tombstones' as we would know them) are located at different sites on the south bank of the Kherlen River in Jargaltkhaan district. Some sites are listed below. To find them you will definitely need a guide who knows the area well, in addition to your own transport. Many of these ancient tombs were found and identified by archaeologists searching for the tomb of Genghis Khan. In 1993, a media announcement stated that during the search in Delgerkhaan district by a joint Japanese/Mongolian team more than 3,500 tombs were identified dating from the Hun period to the Mongol Middle Ages. In the summer of the same year several large tombs were discovered, thought to be the tombs of high-ranking officials from the court of Genghis Khan, although this has not been confirmed. Mongolian people found the whole idea of disturbing ancestral tombs upsetting but, despite this, archaeological research continues.

Bronze Age graves are also found in Batshireet district at Barkha and at upper Onon; in Ölziit district at Deed Ölziit; in Delgerkhaan district at Doloon Uul and on the south bank of the Kherlen River at Kherlen Bayan-Ulaan; and in Tsenkhermandal district at Melzelei Uul. They are also found in groups (memorial stones/graveyards) in the mid-Kherlen region; in Bayanmönkh district on the north bank of the Kherlen River at Bayan Tsögts; and finally, there's a group of tombstones in Dadal district that include those known as the Onon group at Sügtein Adag.

Stone Age petroglyphs Discoveries of ancient rock drawings and figures sculpted in stone (known locally as Stone Men) were made in 1974 by a joint Soviet/Mongol team in the Binder district and in the northeastern part of the province. Designs on the rocks consist of circles and geometric figures and even prints in the shape of feet (as opposed to the hand prints found at Lascaux Caves in France). Many of the drawings resemble those of the same period found in western Mongolia that depict rhinoceroses, bulls and boars, like those discovered at Tsenkheriin Agui in Khovd Aimag.

Sacred mountain *ovoos* at Arshaan Khad Mesolithic to early Neolithic petroglyphs have been discovered at Mount Arshaan Khad (meaning 'Cliff with Springs'), a sacred site located in the Binder district in the northeastern part of the province. It is worshipped by local people who continue the tradition here by placing a stone or some precious object on a cairn-like pile of rocks, called *ovoos*; offerings placed on them are consecrated to mountain spirits, the most important ones at the mountain's summit. Over the centuries many offerings have been made here, although such worship was frowned upon during the communist period in the 20th century. To get here you'll need your own transport, camping equipment and supplies.

Stone statues It is not clear whether or not these stone figures are grave markers, as there are not always graves nearby. Some carry inscriptions in several languages including Tibetan, Chinese, Mongolian and Arabic. You need time, a good map and a local guide/translator to find the sites, although some are quite easily found, including the stone figure (1.8m high) west of the town of Öndörkhaan, and the five stone statues located in Batshireet district on the northern arm of the river Egiin Gol at the far end of Givkhistei Valley. Furthermore, to the north of the statues in Batshireet district there is a row of Turkic stone men and in front of them is a burial site marked by stones placed in a square.

Turkic inscriptions on stones are found in Burgalt Valley, Tsenkhermandal district, in Binderiin Rashaan and in Batshireet district. This is a short list to work from if you have an experienced guide. Without one it's almost impossible to locate the sites, because there is no signposting and none of the sites is developed for tourism. They simply stand on their own, symbols of an ancient past.

Qidan ruins (947–1125) Ruins of the town of Züünkherem (meaning 'eastern fortress') are associated with the Qidan period, whose Chinese dynasty, the Liao, reigned from the mid 10th to the early 12th century. They lie 25km west of Öndörkhaan in Mörön district, the northern frontier of the Qidan (also spelled Kitan) Empire. Ruins of the fortress of Öglögchiin Kherem are on the slopes of Mount Binder. The remains include parts of the fortress walls (7–12m high by 1.5–3m thick), a double rampart of granite and the ruins of the town of Baruunkherem ('western fortress') with its seven gates (now destroyed).

National parks and protected areas
Khankhentii Nuruu Strictly Protected Area This protected area enters the province in the northwest corner. It is predominantly based in neighbouring Töv Aimag and is described there (page 274). Specially zoned areas admit visitors.

Onon-Balj Basin Strictly Protected Area Divided into two areas (A and B), this park is located on the northern international border with the Russian

Federation. It is designated to protect a unique geographical zone of northern taiga forest surrounded by arid-desert steppe valleys.

Toson Khustai Nature Reserve This area of 469,928ha is located on the eastern border and extends into the neighbouring Dornod Aimag. Toson Khustai Nuur and the Salbar valleys are the main habitats of the white-tailed gazelle. The reserve was designated to extend its habitat from the Kherlen River northwards.

Khar Yamaat Nature Reserve Located on the eastern border of Khentii Aimag and extending into Dornod Aimag, the reserve protects Khar Yamaat and the Turuu Öndör Mountains, a continuation of the Khankhentii mountain range. Natural vegetation includes pine and aspen groves, and many unusual medicinal plants rarely found in steppe areas. It is a relatively unvisited area with few tourist facilities. To visit the reserve you will need your own transport.

Flora and fauna In the regions of the strictly protected areas of the Onon-Balj river valleys you will find Baikhal teal, Siberian crane, white-naped crane and Pallas's fish eagle. These rivers harbour endangered Amur sturgeon, Arctic lamprey eel, Khadray whitefish, river crayfish and water snake; wolves, musk deer and moose inhabit the mountains of these river valleys.

In the valley of the Kurkh River you will find lesser white-fronted goose, Siberian crane, hooded crane, common crane and black stork.

In the mountains of the Khan Khentii you will find greater spotted eagle, eastern imperial eagle, saker falcon, black-billed capercaillie, Ural owl, Eurasian pygmy owl and rufus-tailed robin among many other species. It is also an area of elk, red deer, lynx and brown bear. There are fish, such as the protected taimen in the rivers.

Baldan Bereeven Monastery Baldan Bereeven Monastery (also known as
Palden Drepung) is situated in beautiful countryside in the Khankhentii Mountains, 300km northeast of Ulaanbaatar in Ömnödelger district in Khentii Aimag. It takes nine hours to drive there from UB. It is advisable to check the route in advance, if possible, as muddy conditions may hamper your journey, especially after heavy rain, which can fall in summer.

The monastery's history begins in the late 1700s, when the Öndör Gegeen, Mongolia's 'Living Buddha', sent a group of monks to find an auspicious site on which to build a monastery in the east, as the three other directions (north, south and west) had already established monasteries. The monks chose this eastern site because of its extraordinary geographical position, and the auspicious omens,

each evening and slept out under the stars … guarded by my faithful dog. Occasionally I heard wolves howling in the distance but they kept away.'

Lucy travelled with food for two weeks: rations were limited to a hunk of yak meat, rice, potatoes and the delicacy of muesli. The cooker she bought proved useless. She recommends a small Russian-made pump-up paraffin stove for cooking; otherwise she made fires, something the Mongolians are wary of encouraging, since steppe fires devastate the countryside each year.

Eventually, it was the cold – the perishing September evenings – that forced Lucy to turn back.

'Although I wore thousands of layers, it still wasn't enough to keep out the biting chill. My toes were frostbitten and there was little I could do about it. I spent most of my time walking alongside Trigger to warm up.'

Back in Ulaanbaatar Lucy renewed her visa for a further month. At a *ger* hostel on the outskirts of town, she was introduced to the delights of a Mongolian foot-pump shower and was further surprised by technology to find that the music in local discos was more up to date than in the UK.

'People wore the latest gear and I had to pinch myself to realise where I was.' She also said a sad farewell to Wolfie.

'I never had to say goodbye, I just brought him to the part of town where I found him and ducked away as a crowd of dogs chased him in the other direction. I felt bad but there was little else I could do … I was moving on.'

11

such as rocks shaped in the form of animals and birds by the searing power of wind and extreme weather. In their search the monks discovered a landscape that included the shapes of a lion, a tiger, a Garuda bird and a serpent. They also noticed at the time an old couple boiling tea. This was interpreted as a welcoming sign to build on that particular site. Three Tibetan-style temples and a number of other smaller buildings were constructed and the building was completed in the 1780s. *Gers* surrounded the monastery to house several thousand monks, and a nunnery was built on the far side of the mountain valley. Unfortunately, the main temples and many of the adjacent buildings were destroyed in 1937, in accordance with the communist government's anti-religious policy. This kind of destruction was systematic and countrywide. In 1991, restoration work began when one of the side twin-temples was rebuilt by the local community. Since then further restoration has been completed with the help of foreign volunteers.

Statues of several Buddhas, regarded as living spirits, continue to be worshipped there, including deities such as Maitreya Buddha, who symbolises the continuity of the Buddhist teachings, and Tsongkhapa, a master of 14th-century Buddhist teaching and founder of Gelugpa Tibetan Buddhism. In the grounds, all that remains of the past is a circular path of stone that was used for meditation walks, two old stoves and a cave, Eej or Mother Cave. It is believed that when you enter and then emerge from this cave you will be regarded as a newly created being, having left the 'mother's' womb. The only surviving painting in the monastery is of a *soyombo*, the Mongolian state symbol, painted by an anonymous Buddhist artist. The artist predicted that it would survive through periods of great difficulty, which

RIDING EXPERIENCE: MONGOLIA ON HORSEBACK   *Antonia Tozer*

In late summer 1992, I rode with a Mongolian companion for eight weeks through the Khentii Mountains to experience the grass roots of the country and its people. My main purpose was to reach Burkhan Khaldun, a mountain where Genghis Khan was reputedly buried. I soon discovered that since the departure of the Russians in 1990, practically all Mongolians had entered a period of 'Genghis Khan' mania and were clearly rejoicing in their heritage.

My visa extended, Tüvshin and I set off from the capital Ulaanbaatar to the one-street town of Batsümber. Tüvshin was a 22-year-old country boy who had taken part with me in an Operation Raleigh expedition and whom I felt I could trust to handle horses well. The first task was to buy our horses. By dusk, plied with plenty of *airag*, I succeeded in purchasing three pint-sized ponies for the princely sum of US$95. The prices vary enormously, depending on whether or not the horses you buy are bred for racing.

I chose strong reliable ponies aged around nine years, all with relatively docile temperaments. Mongolian ponies are often unused to being handled and are ridden when only half broken-in. A peculiar trait (mainly due to a lack of training) is their dislike of being approached from their offside (right) – always approach from the left side or, in horsey language, the near side. This makes loading a pack animal difficult, although not impossible. Riding style is reminiscent of single-handed, cowboy neck-reining, or polo style. Certainly one is unwise to attempt to pick up any hoof without testing the water carefully!

Within 36 hours we had set out in a northeasterly direction along a wide track that led us through meadow after meadow of flowers, including entire fields of edelweiss. In eight weeks we travelled 1,000km, averaging 20km a day. Our routine was to rise has proved true as it was shot through by three bullets during the anti-religious campaigns of the 1930s, but was not destroyed.

Although local people believe that Baldan Bereeven is the holiest place in the world, two harmful spirits are said to live there, causing the monks to become distracted from their studies. The most harmful is a giant devil. In order to subdue it, a small statue stands on its head (in the side temple which has been restored) with a large stone on its toe so it will never stand upright again; the other malevolent spirit, Mara, is said to live on the northern side of the monastery in a mountain gap. In order to subdue it and to restore harmony, a Buddha statue is placed there among the rocks.

SÜKHBAATAR AIMAG

Sükhbaatar Aimag is situated at the eastern edge of the Gobi and consists of the open steppes of eastern Mongolia – a landscape of endless grasslands stretching as far as the eye can see – broken only by a few hills surrounded by colourful wild flowers. There are many small lakes and some extinct volcanoes. The province is sparsely populated by Khalkha and two minorities, Dariganga and Üzemchin, who live mostly in the south. Sükhbaatar, after whom the province is named, was one of the leaders of the revolution of 1921; his father came from the region. The southeastern Dariganga region and the mountains of Shiliin Bogd Uul are of interest for the local culture and natural landscape but they are remote and transport must be arranged privately. You also need a permit since it is close to the border with China.

early and journey during the cooler part of the day. After breakfast, we packed and loaded the ponies, which took around two hours. We rarely stopped for lunch and snacked instead in the saddle. By early afternoon we would look for a campsite where the grazing was good (most important), then hobble and turn the horses loose for a while, later tethering them to stop them from straying too far at night.

Despite their beauty, the cedar and larch forests of the Khentii are inhospitable. Fast-flowing rivers and tributaries cut between densely forested hills, which frequently made our way treacherous. We would find ourselves waist high in bog (hard to know whether to dismount or not) only to find the horses completely stuck and unable to move! River crossings were problematic – once I watched helplessly while our pack pony was swept half a mile downstream. Happily, in true Mongolian style, he recovered and seemed totally unaffected by his mishap! During less stressful moments, Tüvshin would draw on his vast repertoire of Mongolian folk songs to lift our spirits as we rode along.

When we neared the holy mountain we passed through a small settlement where I was required to register with the *somon* head (Mongolia's equivalent of a local mayor). I was charged a tiny fee (US$0.15) for having a camera, then given a tourist souvenir depicting Genghis Khan and told that women were barred from climbing to the summit. I was mortified! I ended by sending my horses and my camera to the top with Tüvshin.

I spent the rest of the autumn with a local family who adopted me. Eventually I sold my horses to them at no profit but was happy they would be in good hands. After emotional farewells between me and my horses (which the Mongolians found hilarious!) and my hosts, I returned to UB aboard a passing jeep.

BARUUN-URT Located in the centre of Sükhbaatar Aimag, the town is mainly populated by workers employed at the nearby zinc and coal mines. The levels of sulphur in the area mean that it is better to drink bottled water only. This is an undeveloped area and few tourists come here. There are several hotels and the Aimag Museum is worth visiting.

Getting there from Ulaanbaatar

By road You have the option of daily long-distance buses (T21,500) from the capital, departing from Naran Tuul (Black Market), or private jeeps and minibuses (hire in UB or locally). For a jeep and driver from UB, touring costs are negotiable and local jeep-hire rates are lower than in UB; the standard rate is around T800 per kilometre.

Where to stay All of the following are comfortable, with good service.

Ganga Hotel A short walk from the centre of town in the northeast suburbs. **$**

Hotel Delger East of the main square in the centre of town. **$**

Sharga Hotel West of the main square in the centre of town. **$**

Where to eat You could try the restaurants at the hotels (above), or there are a number of bars and restaurants in town serving Mongolian and Chinese food. Simple noodles and meat dishes cost T750.

What to see and do in Baruun-Urt

Aimag Museum (⊕ *10.00–16.00 daily; entrance fee T2,500 (locals pay less)*) In the centre of town, this museum exhibits costumes representing the region's three ethnic groups. The silversmiths and blacksmiths of Dariganga were once famous.

Erdenemandal Khiid The original monastery, 20km outside Baruun-Urt, was destroyed in the 1930s. It is gradually emerging as a new site just west of the town square. Statues of Gombo and Sendem, Buddhist deities, hidden during the communist years of the 20th century when Buddhism was persecuted, are now on display in this new temple. Visitors are welcome.

BRIEF FACTS: SÜKHBAATAR AIMAG

Area 82,300km²
Aimag centre Baruun-Urt
Districts 13
Elevation of Baruun-Urt 981m
Livestock and crops Sheep, goats, cattle
Ethnic groups Khalkha, Dariganga, Üzemchin
Distance from Baruun-Urt to Ulaanbaatar 560km
Average temperatures July 19.9°C, January –23.3°C

HIGHLIGHTS
* Shiliin Bogd Uul – holy mountain
* Taliin Agui – cave
* Altan Ovoo – volcano
* Archaeological sites

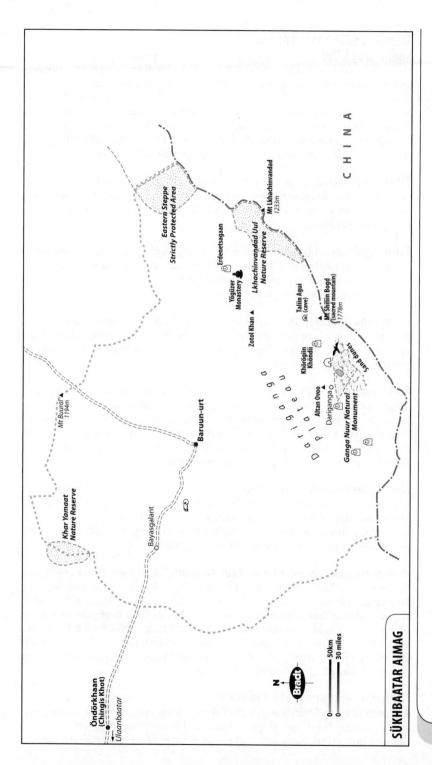

SÜKHBAATAR AIMAG

Öndörkhaan
(Chingis Khot)
Ulaanbaatar

N

Bradt

0   50km
0   30 miles

Khar Yamaat
Nature Reserve

Mt Buural ▲
1194m

Bayasgalant

Baruun-urt ●

Eastern Steppe
Strictly Protected Area

Erdenetsagaan

Yogüzer
Monastery

Lkhachinvandad Uul
Nature Reserve

Mt Lkhachinvandad
1233m

Zotol Khan ▲

Taliin Agui
(cave)

Mt Shiliin Bogd
(sacred mountain)
1778m

Dariganga plateau

Khörögiin
Khöndii

Altan Ovoo ▲
Dariganga ○

Sand dunes

Ganga Nuur Natural
Monument

C H I N A

SIGHTS IN SÜKHBAATAR AIMAG

Shiliin Bogd Uul Located 60km southeast of Dariganga district centre, this is the highest peak in Sükhbaatar at 1,778m. The mountain is sacred to Mongols and is surrounded by stories that tell of renewed strength for those who climb it. Shiliin Uul is one of around 180 extinct volcanoes in the area. Its crater is 2km wide and over 300m deep. From the crater rim there are excellent views across Inner Mongolia to the south; sunrise and sunset are the best times to be there. Because it is in a border area, a permit is required to visit Shiliin Bogd, obtainable at the police station (↘ 51 751) in Baruun-Urt, which is on the west side of town.

Altan Ovoo Standing in Dariganga district, 60km northeast of Shiliin Bogd (above), this is a sacred extinct volcano worshipped by the local people and offers wonderful views and a good half-day's hiking, though you'll need your own transport to get there.

Taliin Agui Some 14km northwest of Shiliin Bogd Uul, Taliin Agui is a 200m-long basalt cave with stalagmites. The cave walls are naturally multi-coloured and very beautiful. You'll need to bring a torch and beware of the slippery ground; you'll need your own transport to get here too.

Dariganga Plateau The Dariganga Plateau lies in the southern part of the province and is where the sand dunes of the Gobi and the grassy plains of the northern steppe converge to create what looks like thousands of hectares of perfectly natural golf courses.

Archaeological sites Stone men found in Khentii aimag differ from those of other provinces by the cut of the stone and other small details. Four stone men statues measuring more than 1m tall are located in Dariganga district. The figures are shown in a kneeling position with their left hand resting on one knee. Three of them, carved in marble, are found at Altan Ovoo. As usual, you'll need your own transport and a good local guide to find these sites.

Khörögiin Khöndii stone men Located 35km north of Shiliin Bogd Uul in Khörögiin Khöndii, Khörög Valley, there's a famous statue of a seated figure wearing boots and a conical hat with a drinking bowl in his right hand, his left hand resting on one knee. There are more than 50 such statues in the region, which is well worth exploring if you have your own transport and guide.

Erdenetsagaan stone men and tombstones There are several stone figures in this area, located in Naran. Some have beards and others earrings and they may be seen as individual characters. Numerous interesting stone figures are found in the same district several kilometres east of Naran. One has a large nose, an earring in one ear and holds a drinking bowl in his right hand, while his left hand rests on his belt. Another stone statue close to him is easily recognised by its pot belly. Bronze Age graves are found at Zunkhovd in Erdenetsagaan district as well as at Zalaa and Shar Khad in Mönkhkhaan district.

National parks and protected areas
Eastern Steppe Strictly Protected Area Partly located on the southeastern border, it extends east into Dornod Aimag and is described there (see page 434). The area protects the natural steppe and is not designed for tourist development.

Lkhachinvandad Uul Nature Reserve Located 200km southeast of Baruun-Urt near the border with China, the purpose of the reserve is to preserve and protect the elk habitat in the mountain steppe. This area is gradually opening up for ecotourism, though there are few tourist facilities at present. To reach it you'll need your own transport. Juulchin's *ger* camp at Ganga Nuur provides accommodation (US$65 pp inc meals).

Ganga Nuur Natural Monument This lake lies some 200km due south of Baruun-Urt, close to the border with China. The area surrounding the lake grew as a result of a sand block formed by wind movement. It is a beautiful freshwater lake located between the mountain steppe and Gobi with its own special micro-climate. Here you may see the rare swan goose and white-naped crane.

'ON THE ROAD' FROM EAST TO WEST   Hazel Adamson

My love of travel began aged seven on an expedition to Europe and has since taken me to over 50 countries, but a journey undertaken in Mongolia is quite different from anything I have ever experienced elsewhere in the world.

We left dusty Ulaanbaatar in a Russian jeep driven by a local, who spoke no English but often broke into traditional 'long songs' on the ride to the far west of the country. Although maps of the country depict roads, in reality there were just wide open spaces, with a hint of a track. It never ceased to amaze how the driver managed to find his way based on instinct alone, borne out of years of bouncing around in his father's truck.

In any other country, a road trip where you really are on the road for many hours day after day could easily become tedious – not in Mongolia. There is always something to keep your attention through the amazing array of wildlife, ever-changing scenery and people-watching. We spotted vultures, yaks, goats, sheep, gazelles, cows and hundreds of marmots scurrying in and out of their burrows. And horses galore. Mongolia could be awarded the prize for being the most fanatical horseriding nation in the world – children learn riding as they take their first steps. In desert and in snow land, there were camels with one hump, with two humps and even white ones.

The landscape was stunningly spectacular and almost untouched by modern development except for the occasional satellite dish attached to an obscurely remote *ger*. Every corner of the country led to another geographical wonder, from vast steppe grassland to gorges and 3km-wide valleys. The further west we got, snowcapped peaks dominated, with countless lakes, streams and rivers dotted throughout the mountain range, while I clung on to my seat as we went over endless pot-holes.

At night, under the clear skies, we could see more stars than we believed existed, amid the clouds of our own breath, as it was rather chilly in sub-zero winter temperatures. Fortunately, evenings were lively affairs spent pitching our tent and singing songs around the fire, or joining a family in their *ger*.

Inside the nomad's home, sat on the floor, gathered around a low table, we were treated to a feast of *makh*: boiled bones, fat and body parts all served together as soup, making traditional loud slurping noises as we sucked out the bone marrow. A round of *airag*, fermented horse milk, which was definitely an acquired taste, would quickly follow. But good humour is all part of nomadic life.

The Mongolian tour company Juulchin provides a new *ger* camp 10km east of the lake (US$40 pp inc meals). You'll need your own transport if you're not on an organised tour. Permits will be checked if travelling independently and you'll need to arrange this in advance; Baruun-Urt police station (✆ *51 751*), on the west side of town, provides permits.

SUGGESTED ITINERARY Juulchin Foreign Tourism Corporation arrange this tour which begins by flying from Ulaanbaatar to Baruun-Urt, from where you can drive 190km south over the grasslands to visit the dunes at Ganga Nuur. Staying at the *ger* camp near the lake for several days, you can explore the sacred volcanic mountains at Altan Ovoo and Shiliin Bogd (a permit is required to visit this border area and visit the cave at Taliin Agui). You can also explore the local archaeological sites and Lkhachinvandad Uul Nature Reserve, where you may see elk in the mountains, though you will be more likely to see antelopes on the surrounding steppe.

DORNOD AIMAG

Dornod Aimag is the easternmost aimag of Mongolia, a land of remote grassy steppes where Mongolia meets both of its big neighbours, sharing the border with China to the southeast and Russia to the northeast. Far from Ulaanbaatar, the province is probably the least visited in Mongolia. The territory is made up of the Great Dornod steppe and the well-known Menengiin Tal plain, famous for the huge population of white-tailed gazelles that graze there and the rare crane species that breed in this area. The River Kherlen cuts through the province. Choibalsan, the aimag centre, was named after Choibalsan, Mongolia's prime minister from 1939–52 (see box, page 430). There are several national parks and new cross-border programmes are now operating to help to preserve the natural habitats and breeding grounds of rare wild species. The battle fought in 1939 by Mongolian and Soviet forces against the Japanese (see box, page 32) took place on Khalkhyn Gol, on the eastern border with China. There are several ethnic groups, including Buryats

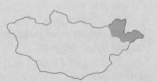

BRIEF FACTS: DORNOD AIMAG

Area 123,600km²
Aimag centre Choibalsan
Districts 14
Elevation of Choibalsan 747m
Livestock and crops Sheep, cattle, goats, horses, hay
Ethnic groups Khalkha, Buryat, Barga, Üzemchin
Distance from Choibalsan to Ulaanbaatar 655km
Average temperatures July 19.9°C, January –21.3°C

HIGHLIGHTS
- National parks and protected areas
- Birdwatching
- Menengiin Tal – grassland plain
- Buir Nuur and Khökh Nuur
- Kherlen Bars Khot – ruins of the Qidan period

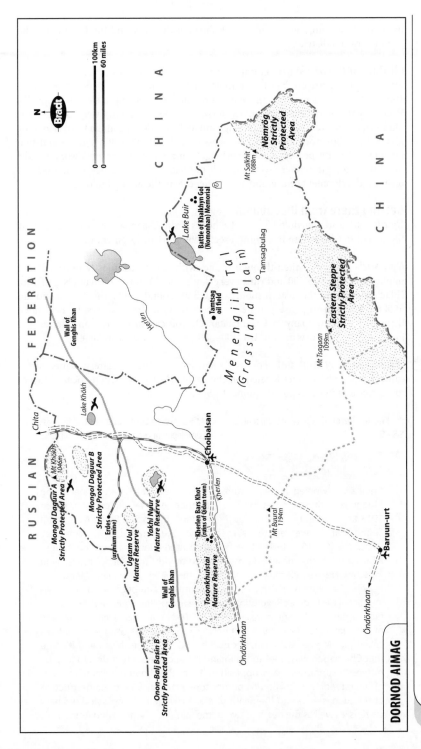

DORNOD AIMAG

living in Bayandun, Bayan-Uul and Dashbalbar districts, and the Üzemchin who live in Sergelen district.

CHOIBALSAN Located in a central position on the Kherlen River, centuries ago this was a trading centre on the caravan route. As Bayantümen, it became a town in the 19th century and is now the centre of economic development in eastern Mongolia. Following the departure of the Soviet Russians in 1990, buildings were looted in the old town on the west side. The buildings still look run-down and the town is looking forward to a burst of economic activity associated with oil drilling. The population includes minority people, Khalkha Mongols and Chinese residents/workers. The new buildings in the eastern sector include the National Parks Office, the market, the business development centre, and an internet café in the library building.

Getting there from Ulaanbaatar
By air There are scheduled flights (1½ hours) from Ulaanbaatar – with Eznis daily flights UB to Choibalsan in summer; see: www.touristinfocenter.mn.

By road There is limited through traffic, with few roads, mostly unpaved. The public bus costs T25,500 and runs every day except Tuesday – leaving Naran Tuul (Black Market) in the eastern suburbs of UB at around 08.00. The drive is around 565km. You can organise private transport to visit the countryside, best done through a tour company in Ulaanbaatar. Or you can hire a jeep and driver; the journey from UB costs around US$400–500 (touring rates negotiable).

 Where to stay and eat For food, you can try the hotel restaurants, street canteens, and the market located on the east side of town, where local dishes of meat, rice and noodles go for around T1,500.

🏠 **Kherlen Hotel** New hotel in town centre. **$$–$**

🏠 **Scorpion Corporation Hotel** Business Development Centre of Eastern Mongolia. **$**.

What to see and do in Choibalsan

Natural History Museum (⊕ *09.00–17.00 Mon–Fri; entrance fee T2,500*) In the old town on the square, this museum has exhibits on the flora and fauna of the steppe region.

Town Museum (⊕ *09.00–17.00 Mon–Fri; entrance fee T2,5000*) Housed in the former Government House in the old town, this museum has memorabilia from the socialist period.

SIGHTS IN DORNOD AIMAG

Menengiin Tal This dry, unspoiled steppe land was declared a strictly protected area in 1992. Herds of up to 40,000 Mongolian gazelle migrate across the plain, reminiscent of the East African migrations of wildebeest. It is an example of the last large undisturbed steppe ecosystem in the world. Within it, Sangiin Dalai Nuur is a salt lake covering 7.5km². It's rarely visited and you'll need your own transport.

Buir Nuur Located on the eastern border with China, this is the largest freshwater lake in eastern Mongolia, covering 615km². Part of the lake (the northwest shore) belongs to China. It is a beautiful area in terms of wildlife, and the lake itself has many different species of fish including mirror carp, golden carp, silver carp, grayling, amur catfish, burbot and whitefish. But unfortunately this leads to poaching and fishing disputes with fishermen from Inner Mongolia (part of China). The lake is a good site for birdwatching. Look out for Oriental stork, Siberian crane, white-naped crane and swan goose. There are few facilities so you will need to bring tents. You'll also need your own transport to get here.

Khökh Nuur The 'Blue Lake' is a shallow salt lake in an area where the elevation of the land is just 552m – the lowest point in Mongolia. It lies in the northeast corner of the province, 180km from Choibalsan off the main road to the Russian border, 50km south of the border town of **Ereentsav**. The lake covers an area of 95km². It is possible to visit the lake on the way to the Mongol Daguur Strictly Protected Area, which is situated along the border with Russia, 50km northwest of the lake. You'll need to bring your own transport, camping equipment and supplies. It is a freshwater lake, rich in fish. A small island in the lake is a good habitat for gulls. The herring gull, also known as the Mongolian gull, is found here in huge numbers.

Qidan Ruins of Kherlen Bars Khot In the Kherlen river valley on the north side of the road, 90km west of Choibalsan in Tsagaan-ovoo district, are the ruins of **three fortress towns**, settlements of the Qidan period (947–1125). They have been grouped under the general name Bars Khot. They were built by the Qidan (also called Kitan) and used into the Mongol Empire period. In the area there are some Turkic *balbals* (stone figures) and a rock known as Genghis Khan's bed, as he was supposed to have stayed there.

Within the **first town** are the remains of four temples with tiled roofs, the pedestals of three statues and, not far from the ruined temples, some stupas and, nearby, two crumbling towers.

The **second town** lies 1km from the first settlement and is known as Baruun Düüregiin Kherem. Some relics of the ancient period of the Xiongnu have been found, suggesting a settlement that pre-dates these ruins.

Some 15km north of the first town, the fortified **third town** is thought to be the encampment of a Yuan dynasty khan called Togoon Tömör who reigned from

1333–70. In defeat he may have fled to this area from China although records say he died in Inner Mongolia.

Tombstones and stone statues Tombstones can be found in Gurvanzagal district west of Choibalsan. The tombs, dating from the end of the Bronze Age, are surrounded by large stones placed in the ground to form a square wall. There's a large square tomb at a place called Gotsogiin Bulag in the same area. West of it are some inscribed stone figures. Stone men statues are located at Gotsogiin Bulag. You will need local help to find these sites, and your own transport.

Battle of Khalkhyn Gol (Nomonhan) Memorial On the battle ground on the eastern border with China; for background information on the battle see box, page 32.

NATIONAL PARKS
Nömrög Strictly Protected Area Located in the easternmost part of Mongolia, over 350km east of Choibalsan and surrounded on three sides by Inner Mongolia (China), this protected area of 311,000ha includes the foothill region of the Hingan Mountains. Originally it was a deciduous forest area, which over time has become a region of predominantly herbaceous meadow steppe. Numerous small streams rise in the mountains and are thickly lined with willow, aspen and birch. The climate of the Hingan mountain area is moist, in contrast to the surrounding dry steppe land to the west. Adjacent arid plains are characterised by small freshwater lakes, thin pine forests and poplar trees.

The park's flora and fauna are influenced by neighbouring Manchuria. As a result, many of the plant and animal species living here cannot be found elsewhere in Mongolia, such as the Ussuri moose. Eurasian otter can be found here, European elk and brown bear, also grey wolf and red fox. The area is important because it protects a naturally structured transition zone from the Manchurian mountains to the eastern Mongolian steppe lands. In contrast to much of Mongolia, Nömrög is virtually unpopulated and untouched with less than 1% of the land used for agriculture. Such isolation and remoteness has protected the area so far. The government is working with the WWF and other organisations to expand this protected area to the west in order to secure the future of this exceptional natural ecosystem. For further details visit www.panda.org/resources.

THE DECLINE OF THE MONGOLIAN GAZELLE

Following the construction of the Trans-Mongolian railway, gazelle numbers declined drastically and their range became almost entirely restricted to eastern Mongolia. Continued livestock grazing, hunting and poaching have also taken their toll. The eastern steppe has particular importance as a feeding ground and as a rest site for the remaining herds of Mongolian gazelle before they migrate. It is still possible to see more than 20,000 gazelles gather in one herd for the autumn migration; as many as 50,000 antelopes have been observed in one day within the protected area.

The Mongolian government plans to expand the territory to the northwest in the form of a migration corridor, with particular emphasis on the antelopes' calving grounds. Hunting is prohibited, but moderate livestock grazing should still be possible.

CRANES OF MONGOLIA *Dr George Archibald*

Six of the world's 15 species of cranes are found in Mongolia, although two species, the Siberian and the red-crowned, are observed only occasionally in a few areas of the far east. Of the remaining species, the demoiselle crane is abundant and widespread throughout much of the country while the Eurasian, hooded and white-naped are found only in the northeast. Although hooded cranes do not breed in Mongolia, Eurasian cranes breed here occasionally and white-naped cranes are regular breeding residents on wetlands of the northeast.

The demoiselle crane is the smallest of cranes. Unlike most other cranes that build platform nests in shallow wetlands, demoiselle cranes often nest in grasslands and agricultural fields. Two dark speckled eggs are laid on dry ground. Mongolian people admire and protect demoiselles. Sometimes the cranes are found near *gers* and they appear to benefit from the herds of domestic animals maintained by Mongolian nomads. The name of the demoiselle in Mongolian means 'lovely bird'.

In autumn the demoiselle cranes migrate across the Gobi, the Tibetan Plateau and the Himalayas before reaching their wintering grounds on the plains of India. The Eurasian cranes that summer in Mongolia migrate either to India or to southeast China. Hooded cranes migrate to Japan and southern China.

The Daurian steppe of eastern Mongolia and adjacent Russia has the world's largest number of breeding white-naped cranes. In autumn, they gather in large numbers on open land. They fly across northeast China to the mouth of the Yellow River and from there, southwest to the middle regions of the Yangtze River.

The Siberian crane is the most threatened of crane species. There are fewer than 2,000 birds alive and their survival is based on vast expanses of shallow wetlands. Unfortunately, many critical wetlands where these cranes spend the winter in China are being heavily impacted by the activities of humans. Occasionally sub-adult Siberian cranes spend the summer in northeast Mongolia.

The red-crowned crane is the second rarest of the crane species. Numbering just over 2,000 birds, about 700 cranes are non-migratory residents of Japan's most northerly island, Hokkaido. The remaining birds are migratory and breed in northern China and southeastern Siberia and winter on the Korean Peninsula and coastal China just north of the mouth of the Yangtze River. A few pairs are sometimes reported on wetlands in summer in eastern Mongolia.

During the past decade, considerable research has been done on white-naped cranes in northeast Mongolia. Over 100,000ha of wetlands and grasslands along the Ulz River and adjacent areas have been protected as the Mongol Daguur Nature Reserve.

Russia, China and Mongolia have signed an agreement to protect important crane habitat on the Daurian steppe, by joining separately managed nature reserves in the three countries into a single international protected area. These rolling steppes, with many lakes and wetlands, are among Asia's most important and most beautiful regions for breeding cranes, ducks and other waterbirds

For more information about cranes and other waterbirds, please contact the **International Crane Foundation** *(PO Box 447, Baraboo, WI 53913-0047, USA;* ☎+1 608 356 9462; e cranes@savingcranes.org; www.savingcranes.org).

11

Flora and fauna At least 47 mammal and 255 bird species have been documented in this area of mountain steppe grasses with willow and birch woodland, including numerous rare and endangered species, among them swan goose, saker falcon, great bustard and white-naped crane and also blue rock thrush, yellow-bellied flycatcher and great black water snake. Chinese parrotbill is known to nest on two small steppe lakes near the Hingan Mountains.

Eastern Steppe Strictly Protected Area
Located in southeast Mongolia on the border with Inner Mongolia (China), some 250km from Choibalsan and extending west into Sükhbaatar Aimag, this is eastern Mongolia's largest protected area (570,374ha). It was established in 1992 to protect the country's last intact steppe from overpopulation and overgrazing. The territory extends in a wide strip for 200km along the Chinese–Mongolian border and belongs to the highest category of protected area. No visitors, unless with special permission for research purposes, are allowed in the area.

Flora and fauna The dominant feature of the land is the feather grass steppe consisting of various *Stipa* species. In the western section of the region, this becomes sandy desert steppe covered with *Caragana* bush. Trees, such as willow and poplar, grow near springs and marshes. Twenty-five species of mammals and 154 species of bird (including 88 breeding species), two amphibians and five reptile species have been recorded living within the park boundaries. Mongolian gazelle, a species of antelope which a few decades ago was found in the steppe regions throughout the country, is now limited to the eastern steppes, as well as neighbouring regions in Russia and China.

Mongol Daguur Strictly Protected Areas
This area lies on the northern boundary with the Russian Federation, over 200km from Choibalsan. Founded in 1992, the protected area consists of around 103,000ha and is divided into two distinct zones: area A consists of hilly steppes south of the Tari Lakes Basin (in Russia), while area B, 30km away, is a 20km corridor of wetland on the River Ulz. The Daurian Mountain steppes and system of wetlands and forested hills have some important natural features. Visitors may see Siberian plants and animals as well as desert/steppe species in this region.

Mongol Daguur is an important breeding and resting site for countless numbers of endangered bird species. These include six species of crane, including the rare Siberian crane, Manchurian crane and hooded crane, unique to central Asia. Three of these

SPECIES CONSERVATION

White-naped crane (*Grus vipio*) Mongolian and German scientists have worked side by side to study the conservation of this threatened crane species. Local Mongolian rangers were trained by German ornithologists, camping by the lakes and rivers of Mongol Daguur in eastern Mongolia. The project was done in co-operation with the Eastern Steppe Biodiversity Project (ESBP) to give the Mongolian rangers a greater responsibility by identifying the birds and assessing the importance of their breeding and feeding areas. The team found that livestock, agriculture and steppe fires had destroyed large parts of the crane's breeding grounds. It is an example of ongoing conservation work in the area.

crane species, the white-naped crane, common crane and demoiselle crane, breed in the protected area. Some of the 260 documented bird species in the region are listed as globally endangered including the relict gull, the Manchurian duck and the great bustard. These may be seen in the Ulz river valley of the Mongol Daguur area. Lake Tari, a large lake located on the Mongolian–Russian border, northeast of the park, is a breeding ground for the rare relict gull. You may see little curlew, Madagascar curlew, white spoonbill and species like the Caspian tern, in huge colonies.

Flora and fauna Over 300 plant species have been found here including several endemic to the region. Over 100 medicinally important plant species are, as yet, unstudied. There are 29 mammal species inhabiting the Daurian steppe of this area, including the Daurian hedgehog, which occurs exclusively in northeastern Mongolia, and Pallas's cat, which reaches its northernmost range here.

In 1995, the government of Mongolia, with support from WWF, founded Mongolia's first cross-boundary protected area. The establishment of the International Daurian Protected Area, in the boundary region between Russia, China and Mongolia, is a milestone in conservation history. This initiative is largely because of the work of Dr George Archibald, who kindly wrote the specialist box, *Cranes of Mongolia*, page 433.

Yakhi Nuur Nature Reserve
Located in the northwest part of the province around 70km northwest of Choibalsan, this reserve was established in 1998. It is an area of 251,388ha and protects the lake and its surroundings. Sometimes the lake dries up in summer but it is still a good area to see birdlife, which includes steppe eagles, golden eagles, buzzards and other birds along the Galyn River that flows into the Yakhi Nuur. Mongolian gazelles may be seen on surrounding plains.

Ugtam Uul Nature Reserve
This area of 46,160ha on the River Ulz, 175km northwest of Choibalsan, protects two holy mountains, Mount Ugtam and Mount Khairkhan, as well as the ruins of a Buddhist monastery. The area is the frontier between the forest steppe and the steppe zones. To visit you will need your own transport, camping equipment and supplies.

SUGGESTED ITINERARIES Contact Tseren and Ric at Tseren Tours (see page 239) and Nyama at Selena Travel (see page 239).

Appendix 1

LANGUAGE

The following is just a brief introduction to the Mongolian language. If you'd like to learn Mongolian, there is a self-study course for beginners, *Colloquial Mongolian* by Alan J K Sanders and Jantsangiin Bat-Ireedüi, published by Routledge in 1999 and reprinted in 2002, ISBN 0-415-16714-0, price £16.99, or as a pack with two one-hour audio cassettes £32.00.

PRONUNCIATION

Consonants Mongolian consonants generally are pronounced pretty much as in English, as are pairs like ch, sh and ts, but there are a few points to note:

j is like the j in 'jam'
kh is like the ch in 'loch'
z is like the dz in 'adze'
final n is nasalised as 'ng'

The consonants f, k and p are found only in loanwords, and f and p are pronounced rather similarly. The Cyrillic letter 'shch' is found only in Russian words.

Vowels Back vowels (from the back of the mouth) and front vowels (from the front) do not appear in the same word, but neutral vowels (i and ii) may appear with either. Vowels may be short, long and glided:

Back vowels

short: a as a in cat
long: aa as a in bath
o as in hot
oo as au in haunt
u as u in Yorkshire us
uu as oo in ooze
i as short i in ill

y as long i
short: ya as yu in yumyum
long: yaa as ya in yarn
yo as ya in yacht
yoo as in yore
yu as you in you
yuu as long you

Front vowels

short: e as e in den
long: ee as a in Dane
ö as in earn
öö as long ea in earn

ü as u in put
üü as long ü
short: ye as ye in yes
long: yüü as in Yusuf

Neutral vowels

short: i as i in tin

long: ii as ea in team

Diphthongs The diphthongs in Mongolian include ai (as in 'eye'), ei (as in 'pay'), oi (as in 'boy') and üi (as in 'Louis')

Stress In words with short (single) vowels, the stress falls on the first short vowel. In words containing a long (double) vowel or diphthong, the stress falls on the long vowel or diphthong. In words with more than one long vowel the stress falls on the penultimate long vowel.

Useful words and expressions (Note that punctuation style as used in English is not used in Mongolian language.)

Greetings and basic communication

hello (good morning, etc)	*sainbaimuu*	bad	*muu*
goodbye	*bayartai*	good	*sain*
yes	*tiim*	how far?	*ali khir kholve*
no	*ügüi*	how long?	*khir udaanve*
please give me	*ögönüü*	how much?	*yamar ünteive*
please tell me	*khelenüü*	when?	*khezee*
thank you	*bayarlaa*	where?	*khaan*
less	*bag khemjee*	excuse me!	*uuchlaarai*
more	*dakhiad*	help me, please	*tuslaarai*
enough	*khangalttai*	go away!	*yav yav!*
now	*odoo*	it doesn't matter	*khamaagüi*
later	*daraa*	don't mention it	*zügeer*

Common sentences

I do not understand	*bi oilgokhgüi baina*
Speak more slowly, please	*ta jaal udaan yarinuu*
Repeat that, please	*ta dakhiad neg khelj ögönüü*
Write it down for me, please	*ta nadad bichij ögööch*
I want (need)	*nadad kheregtei*
I do not want (need)	*nadad khereggüi*
Please wait for me!	*namaig khüleej üzeerei*

Travelling

passport	*pasport*	hand luggage	*gar teesh*
valid	*khüchintei*	customs	*gaali*
entry/exit visa	*orokh/garakh viz*	customs duty	*gaaliin tatvar*
transit visa	*dairan öngörökh viz*	bus stop	*avtobusny zogsool*
travel on official business	*alban ajlaar yavakh*	railway station	*galt teregnii buuda*
travel on a tourist trip	*juulchilakh*	street	*gudamj*
		square	*talbai*
airport	*nisekh ongotsny buudal*	policeman	*tsagdaa*
ticket	*tasalbar*	northwards	*khoid züg rüü*
boarding pass	*ongotsond suukh tasalbar*	southwards	*ömön züg rüü*
baggage	*achaa*	to the east/left	*züün tiish*
excess baggage	*ilüü achaa*	to the west/right	*baruun tiish*
		straight ahead	*chigeeree*

Some useful sentences relating to travel

I have lost my luggage	*bi achaagaa geechikhlee*

I have lost my way		*bi törchikhlöö*	
How do I get to the town centre?		*khotyn töv khürtel yaaj yavakhve*	
Call a taxi, please		*taksi duudaarai*	

Accommodation

hotel	*zochid buudal*	WC (lavatory)	*jorlong, biye zasakh gazar*
vacant room	*sul öröö*		
single room	*neg khünii öröö*	toilet paper	*jorlongiin tsaas*
double room	*khoyor khünii öröö*	hot water	*khaluun us*
with bath/shower	*vaantai/shürshüürtei*	cold water	*khüiten us*
there isn't (any)	*baikhgüi*		

Useful sentences relating to accommodation

| Can I have this clothing cleaned? | *en khuvtsasyg tseverlüülj bolokhuu* |
| Can I have this clothing laundered? | *en khuvtsasyg ugaalgaj bolokhuu* |

Health

doctor	*emch*	arm/hand	*gar*
pharmacy	*emiin sang*	leg/foot	*khöl*
hospital	*emneleg*	heart	*zürkh*
blood	*tsus*	stomach	*gedes*
chest	*tseej*	throat	*khooloi*
ear	*chikh*	tooth	*shüd*
eye	*nüd*		

Some useful sentences relating to health

I'm not feeling well	*minii biye muu bain*
It hurts here	*end övdöj bain*
Send for a doctor!	*emchid khüng duudaarai*
Call an ambulance!	*türgen tuslamj duudaarai*

Money

bank	*bank*	traveller's cheque	*zamyn chek*
money exchange desk	*möngö solikh gazar*	commission	*khuuramj*
		money order	*möngönii guivuulag*
currency exchange rate	*valyutyn khansh*	credit card	*zeeliin/kredit kart*

Shopping

shop	*delgüür*	gold	*alt*
department store	*ikh delgüür*	silver	*möngö*
grocer's	*khünsnii delgüür*	jewellery	*alt möngön edlel*
market	*zakh*	musical instruments	*khögjmiin zemseg*
books	*nom*	paintings	*uran zurag*
carpets	*khivs*	souvenirs	*beleg dursgal*
embroidery	*khatgamal*		
Please show me that	*ta üüniig nadad üzüülenüü*		
I'd like to buy	*bi avmaar bain*		
How much does it cost?	*en yamar ünteive*		
Can you do it cheaper?	*ta ün buulgakhuu*		
I'll give you (insert appropriate number)	*bi tand … tögrög ögyi … togrogs*		

Restaurants and meals
Drink

beer	*shar airag*	vodka	*arkhi*
milk	*süü*	red wine	*ulaan dars*
coffee	*kofe*	white wine	*tsagaan dars*
drinking water	*uukh us*	koumiss	*airag*
juice	*shüüs*	tea (black)	*khar tsai*
tea-based milky drink	*süütei tsai*		
mineral water	*rashaan us* (or *gaztai us* - from Russian 'gas' = 'sparkling')		

Food

meat	*makh*	potatoes	*tömös*
beef	*ükhriin makh*	green salad	*nogoon zuush*
pork	*gakhain makh*	vegetables	*nogoo*
mutton	*khoniny makh*	cabbage	*baitsaa*
chicken	*takhia*	bread	*talkh*
fish	*zagas*	salt	*davs*
boiled	*chanasan*	sugar	*chikher*
fried	*sharsan*	soup	*shöl*
baked	*khuursan*	vegetarian (person)	*nogoon khoolton*
rice	*tsagaan budaa*		

Numbers

1	*neg*	40	*döch*
2	*khoyor*	41	*döchin neg*
3	*gurav*	50	*tavi*
4	*döröv*	51	*tavin neg*
5	*tav*	60	*jar*
6	*zurgaa*	61	*jaran neg*
7	*doloo*	70	*dal*
8	*naim*	71	*dalan neg*
9	*yös*	80	*naya*
10	*arav*	81	*nayan neg*
11	*arvan neg*	90	*yör*
12	*arvan khoyor*	91	*yören neg*
20	*khori*	100	*zuu*
21	*khorin neg*	101	*zuun neg*
30	*guch*	200	*khoyor zuun*
31	*guchin neg*	1,000	*myang*

Note that the numerals adopt an '-n' form when objects are counted – eg: 40 is *döch* but 41 is *döchin neg*. Similarly 'three' is *gurav* but 'three books' is *gurvan nom* (literally 'three book'). The plural suffix of nouns is not used when the number of objects is specified: *olon nom* = 'many books'.

When used, the plural suffixes include uu/üü, eg: *nomuud* 'books'; or s is added, eg: *ügs* from *üg* 'word', etc.

Time

day	*ödör*	today	*önöödör*
night	*shön*	tomorrow	*margaash*

yesterday	*öchigdör*	What time is it?	*kheden tsag bolj bain*
this week	*en doloo khonog*	At what time?	*kheden tsagt*
this month/year	*en sar/jil*	At half past four.	*döröv khagast*
this morning/ evening	*önöö öglöö/üdesh*		

Days

Monday	*davaa* or *negdekh ödör*
Tuesday	*myagmar* or *khoyordokh ödör*
Wednesday	*lkhavag* or *guravdakh ödör*
Thursday	*pürev* or *dövövdekh ödör*
Friday	*baasan* or *tardakgh ödör*
Saturday	*byamb* or *khagas sain ödör*
Sunday	*nyam* or *büten sain ödör*

THE MONGOL CYRILLIC ALPHABET

Mongol Cyrillic	Transliteration	Mongol Cyrillic	Transliteration
Аа	Aa	Рр	Rr
Бб	Bb	Сс	Ss
Вв	Vv	Тт	Tt
Гг	Gg	Уу	Uu
Дд	Dd	Үү	Üü
Ее	Yö/yö	Фф	Ff
Ёё	Yo/yo	Хх	Kh/kh
Жж	Jj	Цц	Ts/ts
Зз	Zz	Чч	Ch/ch
Ии/Йй	Ii	Шш	Sh/sh
Кк	Kk	Щщ	Shch/shch
Лл	Ll	Ъ	(nil)
Мм	Mm	э	y
Нн	Nn	ь	i
Оо	Oo	ЭЭ	Ee
Өө	Öö	Юю	Yu/yu or Yü/yü
Пп	Pp	Яя	ya

Note: The Cyrillic letters Ъ, э and ь do not appear as the first letter in Mongolian words. The hard sign Ъ is not transcribed. The letter Ю is transcribed as yu at the beginning of back-vowel words and yü at the beginning of front-vowel words.

Appendix 2

BUS SCHEDULES

EASTERN AND WESTERN PROVINCES The table below is the short travel company version of the main bus schedules for buses leaving Ulaanbaatar. It includes a booking cost – so if cross-checking you will find different prices to those quoted online. A travel company (if asked) can procure tickets, which will save you a lot of trouble and possibly many hours waiting around.

Province and centre	Days operating	Price in T
Zavkhan Aimag, Uliastai sum	Mon, Wed, Thu, Sun	48,000
Orkhon Aimag, Erdenet city	Every day	11,000
Övoörkhangai Aimag, Arvaikheer sum	Every day	20,000
Ömnögobi Aimag, Arvaikheer sum	Every day	27,500
Sükhbaatar Aimag, Baruun-urt sum	Every day	25,600
Selenge Aimag, Suükhbaatar sum	Every day	Bus 14,000, train 18,900
Khovd Aimag, Khovd sum	Every day	65,000
Bayan-Ulgii Aimag, Ulgii sum	Tue, Thu, Sat	75,000
Bayankhongor sum	Every day	27,000
Bulgan Aimag, Bulgan sum	Mon, Wed, Fri	16,500
Gobi-Altai Aimag, Altai sum	Tue, Wed, Fri, Sun	46,000
Gobi-Sümber Aimag, Choir sum	Mon, Wed, Thu, Fri, Sat, Sun	8,000
Drakhan-Uul Aimag, Darkhan hot	Every day	10,000
Dornogobi Aimag, Saikhan sum	Every day	Train 21,500
Dornod Aimag, Choibalsan sum	Every day	31,000
Dundgobi Aimag, Mandalgobi sum	Every day	13,000
Khövsgöl Aimag, Mörön sum	Every day	32,000
Khentii Aimag, Öndörkhaan sum	Every day	13,000
Töv Aimag, Zuunmod sum	Every day	2,000
Uvs Aimag, Ulaangom sum	Mon, Wed, Thu, Fri, Sat, Sun	65,000

Appendix 3

FURTHER INFORMATION

BOOKS
Travel

Allen, Benedict *Edge of Blue Heaven* BBC Publications, 2000. Exciting adventure travel by horse and camel.

Becker, J *The Lost Country: Mongolia Revealed* Hodder & Stoughton, London & Sydney, 1992. Mixture of Mongolian fact and fiction.

Burgess Watson, Claire *Silk Route Adventure: On Horseback in the Heart of Asia* Robert Hale, 2007. A journey from Mongolia through central Asia on horseback.

Carr, Alistair *The Singing Bowl* Can be ordered directly from www.classictravelbooks.com or from www.thesingingbowl.co.uk. An account of the author's travels in Mongolia and China; tales of travelling with the Reindeer people.

Hare, J *The Lost Camels of Tartary* Little, Brown, 1998. A courageous journey to search for wild camels and ways to ensure their survival.

Hare, John *Mysteries of the Gobi* I B Taurus, 2009. Modern-day exploration following the story of the wild camel in the Gobi regions of Mongolia and China.

Isaacson, Rupert *Horse Boy* Little, Brown, 2009.

Kemp, H *Step by Step* Interserve, 2000. The indigenous Christian church in Mongolia.

Man, J *Gobi: Tracking the Desert* Weidenfeld & Nicolson, 1997. An interesting and sensitive account of the life of Gobi people.

McGregor, Ewan and Boorman, Charley *Long Way Round* Sphere, 2005. World travels by two friends on motorbikes – a journey that takes them through Mongolia from far west to Ulaanbaatar and on into Russia.

Middleton, N *The Last Disco in Outer Mongolia* Sinclair-Stevenson, 1992. Upbeat view of the first impact of democracy on young Mongolians.

Treanor, David *Mission Mongolia* Summerdale, 2010.

Stewart, S *In the Empire of Genghis Khan: A Journey among Nomads* HarperCollins, 2000. An epic journey by horseback across Mongolia.

Waugh, Louisa *Hearing Birds Fly* Little, Brown, 2003. An account of nomadic life dominated by the seasons.

Golden oldies

Andrews, R *Across Mongolian Plains* Appleton, New York and London, 1921 (reprint Lightning Source, 2001). The famous naturalist's account of his first visit in 1919.

Andrews, R *The New Conquest of Central Asia* American Museum of Natural History, 1932. Reports on the expeditions of 1921–30.

Carruthers, D *Unknown Mongolia* Hutchinson, 1913 (reprint Asian Education Services, New Delhi, 1994). Travels in Tuva and Mongolia in 1910–11; a great book on early exploration and travel in Mongolia.

Grubov, V I *Plants of Central Asia: Plant Collections from China and Mongolia* Science Publishers, 2003. Authoritative work on plants; costly.

Haslund-Christensen, H *Men and Gods in Mongolia* Dutton, 1935 (reprint Adventures Unlimited, USA, 1992). Travels among the Torgut Mongols, translated from Swedish.

Lattimore, Owen and Eleanor *The Desert Road to Turkestan* Kodansha America, 1995. Travels in Mongolia in the 1930s.

Natural history, environment

Batsaikhan et al, N *A Field Guide to Mammals of Mongolia* Zoological Society of London, 2010. English–Mongolian edition. Covers a wide range of habitats, diverse animals and plants.

Braunlich, Axel and Gombobaatar, Sundev *Birds of Mongolia* Helm Field Guides, 2010. The first comprehensive guide to describe and illustrate Mongolia's birdlife.

Khayankhyarvaa, Terbish and Boldgiv, B (eds) *A Guide to the Amphibians and Reptiles of Mongolia* Admon Print, Mongolia, 2013. Covers interesting species like the Gobi racerunner lizard *(Eremias przewalski)* and the sand toad or Raddle's toad *(Buffo raddei)*

Yamarmura et al, N *The Mongolian Ecosystem Network* Springer, 2013.

History

Bawden, C R *The Modern History of Mongolia* Kegan Paul, 2002. Insight into Mongolian life from the 17th century to the 1960s.

Bulgaa Altangerel, et al (ed) *Transcontinental Neighbours – 50 years of Mongolia-UK Diplomatic Relations 1963–2013 Vol 1* Mongolia and Inner Asia Studies Unit, Cambridge, 2013

Endicott, Elizabeth *A History of Land Use in Mongolia: The Thirteenth Century to the Present Day* Palgrave Macmillan, 2012.

Man, J *Genghis Khan* Bantham Press, 2004. A gripping account of Genghis Khan's rise and conquests.

Man, J *The Mongol Empire, Genghis Khan, his heirs and the founding of modern China*, Bantham Press, 2014

Morgan, D *The Mongols* Blackwell, 1990. Popular account, with a touch of humour, of the birth and growth of the Mongol Empire.

Onon, U *The Secret History of the Mongols* Curzon Press, 2001. A modern translation of the oldest known Mongolian account of the life and times of Genghis Khan.

Rossabi, Morris *Modern Mongolia: From Khans to Commissars to Capitalists* University of California Press, 2005. On political and economic life and gives a chronological account of political and economic development 1990–2004.

General

Jacobson-Tepfer, Ester and Meacham, James *Archaeology and Landscape in the Mongolian Altai: An Atlas* Esri Press, 2010.

Lawless J *Wild East: The New Mongolia* Summersdale, 2002. A portrait of Mongolia; an account of social change.

MPR Academy of Sciences *Information Mongolia* Pergamon, Oxford, 1990. Sound articles and good illustrations compensate for the communist politics of this encyclopaedia.

Nordby, J *Mongolia* World Bibliographical Series, vol 156, Clio Press, 1993. Invaluable guide to English-language books about Mongolia.

Sanders, A *Historical Dictionary of Mongolia* Scarecrow Press, Lanham and London, 2003. Alphabetical listing of people and places mostly from the modern period, with bibliography and appendices.

Taylor Weidman and Nina Wegner *Mongolia's Nomad's: Life on the Steppes* Independent Photobook, 2012.

Trumpington, Jean *Coming up Trumps: a Memoir* Macmillan, 2014. An extraordinary life story dedicated to education and furthering human relations.

Turnauer, Christine *Presence* Hatje Cantz, 2014. Portraits, a photography book.

Music

Pegg, Carole *Mongolian Music, Dance and Oral Narrative: Performing Diverse Identities* Washington University Press, 2001. A book on the power of music and dance with traditional stories recorded on accompanying CD.

Religion

Croner, Don *Guide to Locales Connected with the Life of Zanabazar* digital ebook.

Rinpoche, Arjia *Surviving the Dragon* Rodale Books, 2009. A Tibetan lama's account of 40 years under Chinese rule, his life in the USA with an account of his recent visits and social work in Mongolia.

Language

Bawden, C *Mongolian–English Dictionary* Kegan Paul International, 1997. The best and most up-to-date dictionary, based on modern Mongolian usage.

Sanders, A and Bat-Ireedui, J *Colloquial Mongolian* Routledge, 1999. Up-to-date self-study grammar with cultural insights (cassettes).

Specialist bookshops

Daunt Books 83 Marylebone High Street, London W1U 4QW; ℡ 020 7224 2295; www.dauntbooks.co.uk.

John Sandoe (Books) Ltd 10 Blacklands Terrace, Chelsea, London SW3 2SR; ℡ 020 7589 9473; www.johnsandoe.com.

MAPS

The Mongolia Road Atlas (1:1,000,000). Published by Gazryn Zurag Co Ltd.

The Mongolia Geographic Map With trilingual place names in English, Russian and Mongolian.

'Reise Know How' Mongolia Digital Road Maps Useful if your satellite connections and systems work. It can be bought online.

WEBSITES
General

www.infomongol.com
www.mongolnet.com
www.mongolmedia.com
www.mgl-uk.com
www.un-mongolia.mn

Government

www.mef.pmis.gov.mn Ministry of Education, Culture and Science
www.mof.pmis.gov.mn Ministry of Finance and Economy

Business and services

www.mol.mn/mbda Mongolian Business Development Agency (MBDA)
www.mol.mn/mcci Mongolian Chamber of Commerce and Industry (MCCI)
www.mongoliabritishcc.org.uk British Mongolian Chamber of Commerce
www.mongolialondonbusinessforum.co.uk Mongolia London Business Forum

In Mongolia

www.bizmongolia.mn
www.mongoliamarket.mn
www.ulaanbaatar.net/businesses/hotels
www.mongoliatourism.gov.mn Mongolian National Tourist Office
www.travelmongolia.org Mongolian Tourism Association
www.aeromongolia.com Aero Mongolia
www.airtrans.mn Air Trans ticketing agency
www.blueskyaviation.mn Blue Sky Aviation (private)
www.enizairways.com Enzis Airways
www.hunnuair.com/en Hunnu Air
www.miat.com Mongolian Airlines (MIAT)

Carbon offsetting

www.carbon-offsets.com
www.cdmgoldstandard.org.
www.ebico.co.uk
www.global-cool.com
www.puretrust.org.uk

List of web addresses of the state universities of Mongolia

www.num.edu.mn National University of Mongolia
www.must.edu.mn Mongolian University of Science
www.msua.edu.mn Mongolian State University of Agriculture
www.hsum-ac.mn Health Sciences University of Mongolia
www.humanities.mn University of the Humanities

Appendix 3 FURTHER INFORMATION

A3

Index

Page numbers in **bold** indicate main entries; those in *italic* indicate maps